Principles
of Information Systems
for Management

Principles
of Information Systems
for Management

Fourth Edition

Niv Ahituv
Claremont Graduate School/ Tel-Aviv University

Seev Neumann
Claremont Graduate School/ Tel-Aviv University

H. Norton Riley
California Polytechnic University at Pomona

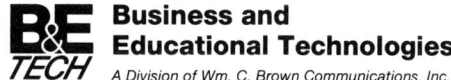

B&E TECH **Business and Educational Technologies**
A Division of Wm. C. Brown Communications, Inc.

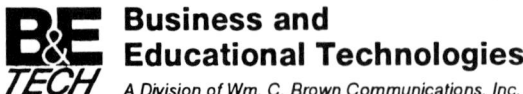

Business and Educational Technologies

A Division of Wm. C. Brown Communications, Inc.

Vice President and Publisher *Susan A. Simon*
Acquisitions Editor *Paul Ducham*
Managing Developmental Editor *Linda Meehan Avenarius*
Advertising/Marketing Coordinator *Jennifer Wherry*
Product Development Assistant *Sandy Ludovissy*
Designer *Anna Manhart*
Visual Processor *Miriam Hoffman*

Wm. C. Brown Communications, Inc.

Chief Executive Officer *G. Franklin Lewis*
Corporate Senior Vice President and Chief Financial Officer *Robert Chesterman*
Corporate Senior Vice President and President of Manufacturing *Roger Meyer*
Executive Vice President/General Manager, Brown & Benchmark Publishers *Tom Doran*
Executive Vice President/General Manager, Wm. C. Brown Publishers *Beverly Kolz*

To our parents

Contents

Preface

Information systems refer to computer-based information processing systems that are designed to support the operations, management, and decision functions of an organization. Information systems in organizations provide information support for decision makers at various management and decision levels. They thus encompass transaction processing systems, management information systems, decision support systems, and strategic information systems. While each one of these systems merits a specialized book in itself, this book attempts to take a more generic approach to the subject of information systems and to provide a comprehensive conceptual foundation for the study of such systems.

The field of information systems is interdisciplinary in nature. All concepts, approaches, and contributions of various disciplines that were deemed necessary are therefore included in the book. We have tried to build a solid conceptual framework having a validity and relevance to the field of information systems that will be independent of the fast rate of technological development characteristic of the field.

The book is divided into three parts. Part I provides the background for the parts II and III by defining and explaining basic technical, behavioral, economical, and organizational concepts relevant to information, decision making, and systems. Part II discusses the methodology and practice of developing a computerized information system, beginning with the formulation of a comprehensive master plan and going through the successive stages of the information system life cycle. It also delineates various types of information systems. Part III deals with the organization, management, and control of the information system and with the social impact of information technologies.

The text is intended for a one-semester course or could be used by managers who are specializing in or interested in learning more about information systems. Individual chapters or sections of the book may be used in a minicourse or a seminar on one or more of the topics covered in the book.

The three previous editions of the book have been well accepted and widely adopted. Students using the book have varied in background, preparation, and goals: undergraduate and graduate students; information systems majors, business majors, and majors in other areas (e.g., computer science, engineering, library science, social sciences); system analysts and software developers; practicing managers at different levels and with different functions. These readers have come from backgrounds ranging from extensive previous course work and practice in computers and information systems to no previous exposure at all.

This fourth edition has been updated to reflect the rapid changes that continue to occur in the information systems field. Reviewers, colleagues, and students have suggested additional topics, areas for expanded coverage, and other improvements. These suggestions have been incorporated in this edition.

The features of this revision are the following:

Updating the material in all chapters and bringing it to the state of the art in information systems in 1993

Additional emphasis throughout on the increasing impact of personal computers and workstations, and on the changing role of the user in system definition and development

More coverage of the growing use of computer networks of all kinds and the influences of those networks on the nature of information systems in use

Expanded recognition of the contribution of software engineering methodologies in improving the information system development and maintenance process

New material dealing with the implications of current trends and issues such as downsizing, outsourcing, client-server architectures, CASE tools, global information systems, computer viruses, and artificially intelligent computers

The book can be used in an introductory course for information systems majors and nonmajors alike. For managers, decision makers, and users of information systems, it provides the terminology, and the basis to ask intelligent questions. For majors in information systems, it also provides a solid base from which to embark later to subjects such as systems analysis and design, database technology, management of information systems, and models of information in organizations.

No fundamental background in a functional field or any specific discipline is necessary to understand the material in the book. We assume that the reader has been exposed to those rudimentary concepts of computers and data processing that are covered in any introductory computer course or textbook. Appendix A of the book serves as an optional section for readers without prior exposure to computers or as a review for those who have. In addition, we have attempted to explain each concept in the body of the book. A set of updated references at the end of each chapter provides for supplementary reading, if desired.

The book is based on the recent literature of the field and recent empirical findings. It also draws on the experience of the authors as managers, system analysts, consultants, and users of various information systems on the one hand, and as students and teachers of an information systems course who had to struggle through without a suitable textbook on the other hand.

We wish to thank James (Dimitrios) P. Plagianis (MBA, University of British Columbia), who helped compile the case study. We acknowledge the contribution, small or large, of students, colleagues, and practicing information system professionals, whose comments on the first three editions and class lectures helped us to improve the text. We are also indebted to the reviewers of this edition: Roberta M. Roth of University of Northern Iowa; George M. Kasper of College of Business Administration, Texas Tech University; Donald Blouin of Madonna University, School of Business; David Wrend of St. Joseph's University; Eugene T. Dolan of University of the District of Columbia; William L. Harrison of College of Business, Oregon State University; Richard B. Huntoon of Mount Mercy College; Albert L. Harris of Appalachian State University; and Ellen D. Hoadley of Loyola College in Maryland.

Finally, we want to recognize the support of our wives (three), children (twelve), grandchildren (three, so far), who, after reading the section on telecommuting, made a wish that our future offices would be at our networked homes.

Niv Ahituv
Seev Neumann
Tel-Aviv, Israel

Norton Riley
La Verne, California

Part I

Background

Chapter 1 Introduction

Information systems are vital to the operation and management of every modern organization. This book is concerned with the design and use of computer-based information systems in organizations.

In this introductory chapter, we discuss the basic concepts and role of information systems, list the fields and disciplines contributing to information systems, note the factors that contribute to success of information systems, and present a synopsis of the chapters that follow.

Information is a resource, produced by information systems, that is vital to the operation and management of organizations. There are other resources that organizations utilize, such as energy, personnel, capital, materials, machinery, and the like, but increasingly, large shares of these resources are being devoted to information systems. Information is not a natural resource, such as oil and coal, that is subject to great expense or to political constraints; nor is it a resource that must be mostly acquired from the environment external to the organization, such as personnel or raw materials. If properly developed, managed, and used, information systems can provide the most cost-effective resource for the organization.

The subject of this book is organizational information systems. We attempt to study the conceptual foundations of information systems, and the development, operation, management, uses, parties, control, structure, and impact of these systems. Three basic concepts are woven into the fabric of this book: information, system, and organization.

Information is data that has been processed and is meaningful to a user. A system is a set of components that operate together to achieve a common purpose. With these two basic definitions, we can easily proceed to a definition of organizational information systems. Since information is data that has been processed, it follows that some data has to be collected and transmitted, then processed and stored. To be meaningful to users, the information must be retrieved and distributed to them. The users belong to a system called "organization." One of the components (or subsystems) of an organization is the "information system." The components of this system are people, hardware, software, data, and procedures. The organizational information system thus collects, transmits, processes, and stores data, and retrieves and distributes information to various users in an organization. To reiterate, information systems produce information that supports the operation and management functions of an organization.

We are primarily concerned with computer-based information systems in this book, though much of the discussion is pertinent to all types of information systems: manual, mechanical, electromechanical, or electronic. We exclude the informal information systems that exist in all organizations, such as the ''grapevine.'' We also exclude some formal specialized (or single-purpose) information systems that may exist in organizations, e.g., a process-control system supervising a chemical process, or publications distributed to the organization's consumers (such as catalogs) or to its personnel (such as the company's house organ). By using simple definitions, we hope to avoid the kind of controversy over definitions discussed elsewhere [8, ch. 1].

The ensuing chapters deal with the major types of formal, computer-based information systems that exist in an organization. We discuss in chapter 5 systems classified by types of decision or by user (e.g., transaction processing system, decision support system, management information system); in appendix A, we talk about systems classified by mode of operation (e.g., online systems, batch systems). We describe in chapter 11 different structures of information systems (e.g., centralized, decentralized, distributed).

Machiavelli, in 1513, made the following observation about systems in general:

> There is nothing more difficult to plan, more doubtful of success, nor more dangerous to manage than the creation of a new system. For the initiator has the enmity of all who would profit by the preservation of the old system and merely lukewarm defenders in those who would gain by the new one [3, p. 1].

Indeed, the development, operation, management, and use of information systems in organizations, in particular, is an involved activity. It is becoming more and more so because these systems are installed in organizations that are becoming ever larger and more complex in their processes, and more diverse in their operations. That is why computer and related information technologies are vital features of modern information systems. These technologies can become the villain of an information system, rather than a benefactor, if improperly designed into the system and controlled thereafter. This book is, therefore, an attempt to show how these information technologies must blend with other components (users, managers, procedures) to make an efficient and effective information system.

We wish to make clear that we will refer to organizational information systems, and not to one comprehensive information system. Chapter 5 demonstrates that there exists in an organization a federation of information systems that facilitates the operation of the organization and provides information for management control. The various information systems may be loosely or tightly connected; they may share common resources or have independent resources. What unifies all these systems is the overall planning and control exerted by top management, which is derived from the organization's objectives, strategy, and structure. We stress this duality: the design and use of information systems in an organization on the one hand, and the management of the information system resources within the organization on the other.

Figure 1.1 Foundations of the field of information systems

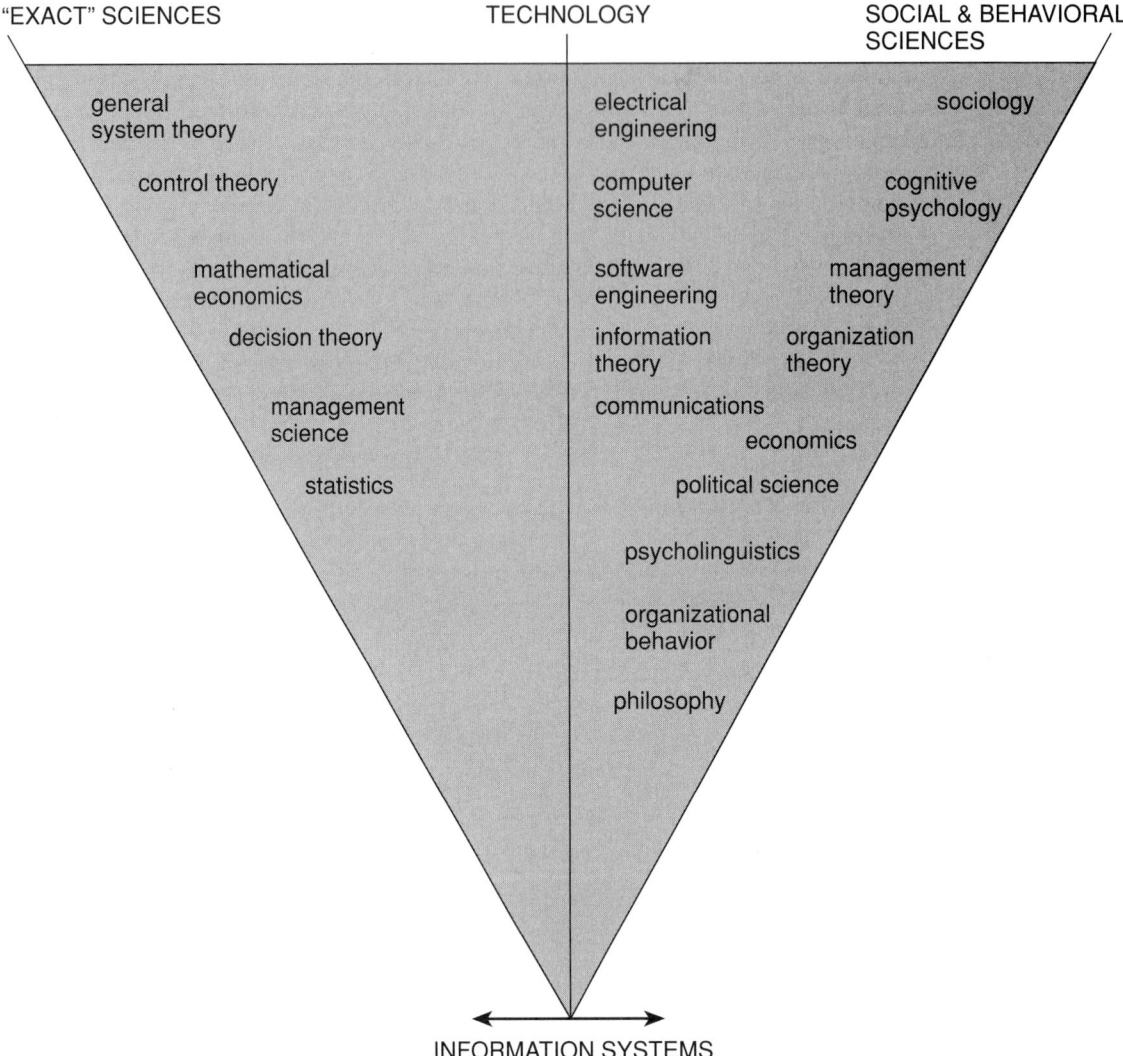

"EXACT" SCIENCES   TECHNOLOGY   SOCIAL & BEHAVIORAL SCIENCES

general system theory

control theory

mathematical economics

decision theory

management science

statistics

electrical engineering

computer science

software engineering

information theory

communications

economics

political science

psycholinguistics

organizational behavior

philosophy

sociology

cognitive psychology

management theory

organization theory

INFORMATION SYSTEMS

Fields Contributing to the Study of Information Systems

The field of information systems is by nature interdisciplinary. In fact, several disciplines have made significant contributions to information systems. Figure 1.1 places the field of information systems at the intersection of three main disciplines: exact sciences, technology, and social and behavioral sciences.

We can also view information systems as a rich depository of theoretical foundations and empirical findings from the fields depicted in the figure. McLean and Swanson offer a similar list of contributing fields with examples of works that have made contributions to information systems [19].

Several of the fields listed are closely related to each other, e.g., computer science and management science. Others overlap in their treatment of phenomena related to information systems. Some, such as system theory, attempt to make interdisciplinary connections among several fields. There is no universally accepted theory of information systems. As the chapters of this book illustrate, the information systems field is eclectic, drawing from various disciplines.

The collective opinion nowadays is that an information expert, as well as a manager, or a user, has to master some knowledge in the following foundations: organizational aspects of information systems, managing information systems, systems approach, cognitive process, economics of computers and information, and contemporary information technology. Appropriate development and use of information systems stem from the concurrent application of these foundations. This book attempts to blend the necessary components. Part I (chapters 1–4) lays the foundation. Part II (chapters 5–11) gradually leads the reader from theory to implementation; while chapter 5 is still theoretical, the next chapters discuss planning, design, and implementation. The third part (chapters 12–15) integrates the treatment of information systems by introducing managerial, user-oriented, and social aspects. Appendix A provides a review of current information technologies.

The interdisciplinary nature of information systems emanates from the process of information flow within the organization. The process begins with events, continues with their conversion into a language (code) that describes them, goes on to the processing of the coded events, and pauses with their perception by a human being. The human being processes the information, and his or her outputs (responses, directives, actions) generate new events. This is a feedback process that begins and ends with events. The value of the information can be assessed by the adequacy of the human being's reactions to the events. This entire process is shown in figure 1.2.

Different disciplines and fields pertain to the various components of the process. Some components are mechanical while some are human. The part pertaining to the coding and transmission of events is the subject of *communication* (or *information*) *theory*. The logic and methods of converting data into required and usable information belong to the field of *systems analysis;* the data processing technology is treated by *computer science* and *software engineering;* while the economic evaluation of the system is analyzed by *computer economics* and *information economics.* The latter two fields rely heavily on *decision theory, statistics,* and *microeconomics.* The human parts of the process, including perception, memory, and response, pertain to *cognitive psychology.* The simulation of human processes by automatic machines is the subject of *artificial intelligence.* The last part of the process, where decisions and reactions are generated, is treated by cognitive psychology with a descriptive approach and by decision theory and information theory with a normative approach. Language is a means for data transmission and display of decisions; it is the subject of *psycholinguistics.*

Figure 1.2 The process of information flow in organizations

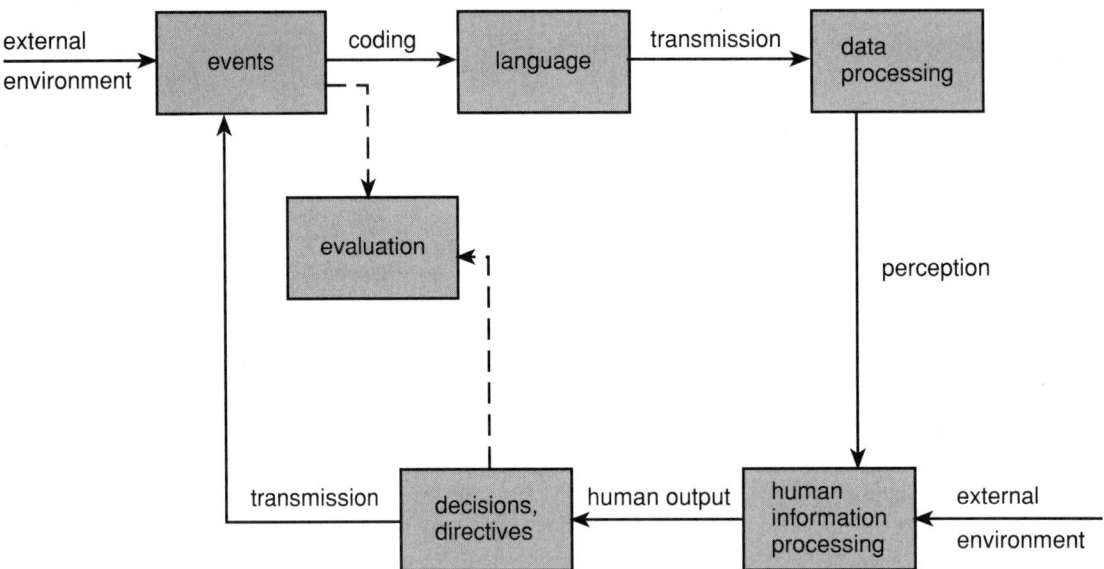

The continuous feedback inherent to the process is researched by *control theory* and *cybernetics*. Other aspects of the process of information flow are treated by *management science* models, *management theory,* and *organizational theory.* The synthesis of these interdisciplinary components into a system with goals and constraints is supported by *general system theory.*

It is beyond the scope of this book to present the principles and content of these fields and disciplines. Many of them are discussed in the context of the chapters that follow. Major representative works pertaining to contributing disciplines are referenced here for your convenience: general system theory [28]; cognitive psychology [14, 23]; philosophy [6]; linguistics [5]; organization theory [2, 10, 20]; information (communications) theory [25]; artificial intelligence [9, 30]; economics of computers [26, 12]; management science [1]; organizational behavior [13]; cybernetics [29]; computer science [27, 15]; software engineering [24]; information economics [21, 22, 12]; psycholinguistics [4]; accounting [7]; decision theory [17, 18, 11].

Factors Contributing to Success of Information Systems in Organizations

Surveys of organizations using computerized information systems show that the systems can be classified as successful or unsuccessful with quite clear distinction. Several criteria are offered for evaluating the success of a system. These criteria relate to both the professional information system staff and to management and users of the information system. Measuring how well the criteria are realized is often difficult since subjective feelings of the system's users are involved.

For a system to be deemed successful, it must be *profitable;* its benefits to the host organization must outweigh its costs. The system must improve the *performance* of its users. An information system must be *applied to major problems* of the organization; surveys show that attacking major issues is an important characteristic of successful information systems. *User satisfaction* is also evidence that the system is successful. Only if the system meets at least some of these criteria will users *use* it intensively. We can summarize that a successful information system is "profitably applied to an area of major concern to the organization, is widely used by one or more satisfied managers, and improves the quality of their performance" [8, p. 21].

Information system literature and research report on many attempts to specify the critical variables that, properly handled, promise information system success [see, for instance, 16]. Such variables include user involvement, user attitudes and cognitive style, top-management support, budgets, user education and training, psychological climate in the organization, organizational maturity, resource availability, and organization size. All these variables, and many more, are important. Any single variable may lead to failure of a system, but no variable alone determines success. The outcome is usually the result of complex interplay among the variables that determine the starting point, the development process, and the resulting system. A unique combination of variables is peculiar to each organization. We emphasize this point repeatedly in the following chapters. An information system cannot be bought off the shelf. It must be tailored to the organization—to its management, the users and implementors of the information system, the resources, and the technology available.

We stress repeatedly that the development of an information system is not merely a technological project, for it also has managerial, organizational, and behavioral implications. Each system must be adapted to the relevant environmental, organizational, and personal situations. Many information systems have failed because of concentration on the technical aspects while organizational behavioral problems were overlooked [16, pp. 2–6].

That is why we conclude each chapter with a list of practical, technical, organizational, and behavioral implications for the multiple parties involved in the design and use of information systems. These parties include management, users, and the information system staff, who must all work together to develop and operate successful systems. You will note in the following synopsis that the book deals with all the factors contributing to the success of information systems: technology; human behavior; organizational issues; and the interrelations of management, users, and information system staff.

Plan of the Book

Figure 1.3 illustrates the logical sequence of the chapters in this book. It shows which chapters are prerequisites to other chapters, as well as alternative logical paths if a reader wishes to focus on some topics and postpone others (for future reading, we hope). Each numbered box in the figure represents a chapter.

Human reaction to information depends on how the information penetrates a person's cognitive mechanism. Important data may be overlooked or misunderstood because it fails to attract attention; it must compete with an almost infinite number of

Figure 1.3 Schematic diagram of contents of the book

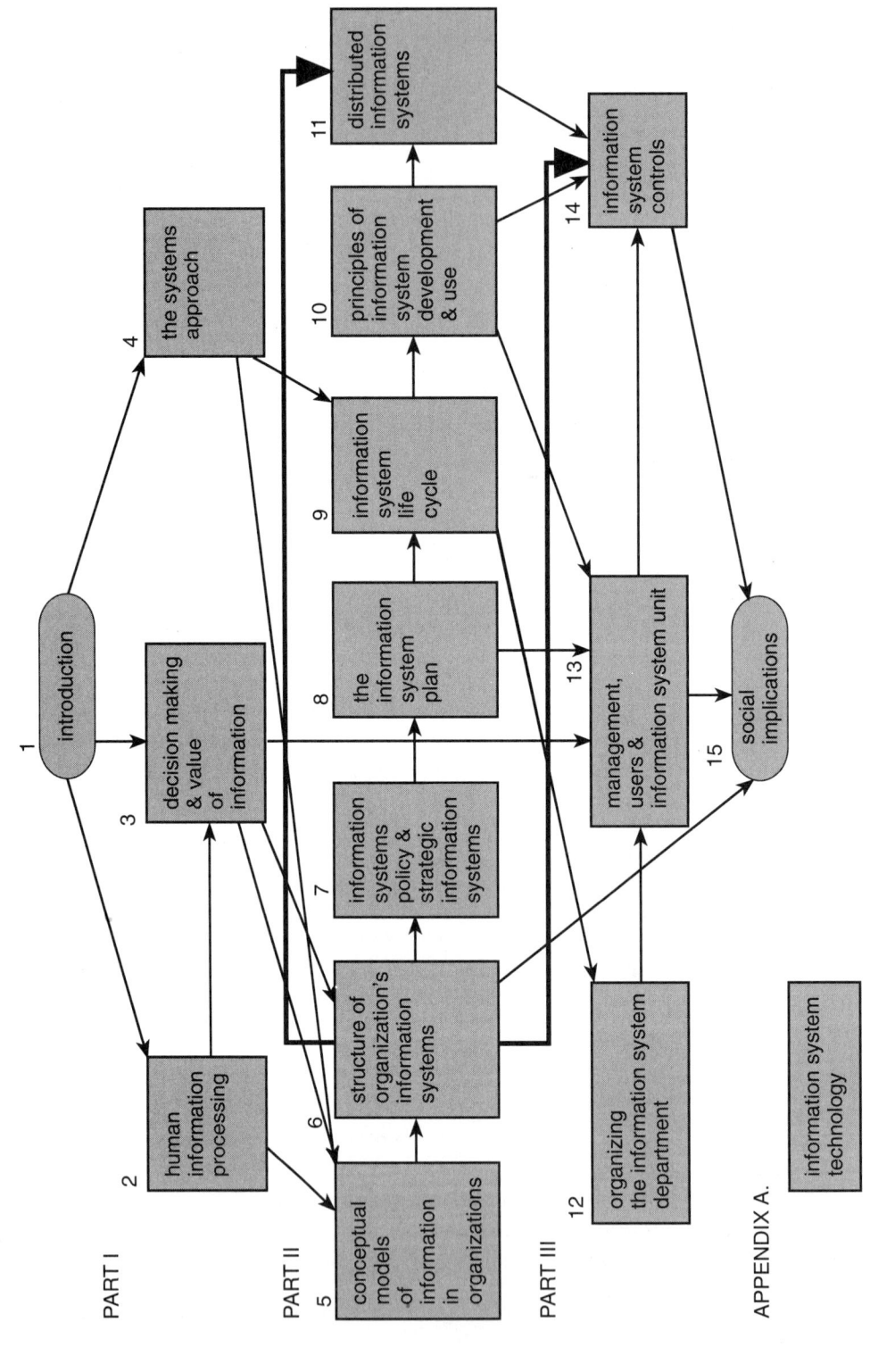

other external stimuli. An information system in an organization may fail because it is implemented in an environment with an unresponsive psychological climate. Therefore, it is essential for information system users, managers, implementors, and operators to be familiar with some psychological and behavioral aspects related to information systems. These aspects are reviewed in chapter 2.

Life consists of a continuing series of decisions. The importance of the decisions varies, depending upon the time at which they are made, the situation, and the person(s) making them. However, all decisions are based on our best knowledge at the time they are made. This knowledge is continuously revised by information. Therefore, information must be evaluated in accordance with the decisions it supports. Chapter 3 describes the decision-making process and relates it to the value of information.

We live, work, and function in various systems. These systems may be large, complex supersystems, such as big organizations, or small, simple subsystems, such as departmental units or families. To study the behavior of systems, the systems approach must be adopted. Chapter 4 describes the systems approach and its use in the process of problem solving. The chapter illustrates the concept of a system, its scope and structure, the different roles of components and individuals in the system, and their interrelations. It then discusses various classes of systems, with emphasis on a control system.

An information system is the arterial system of an organization. It provides decision makers with facts and forecasts, and it conveys policies and instructions to operating organizational levels. Any attempt to understand the role and structure of information systems must involve a comprehensive model incorporating interrelated organizational and informational concepts. Chapter 5 introduces some prevalent models of organization, incorporates information concepts into them, and comes up with a comprehensive model. The model then serves to classify various types of organizational information systems.

Information systems are not a mere collection of hardware, software, and people. They are designed to fit an organization's strategy and structure. They have to provide for the information needs of the operations level as well as for the various management levels of the organization. Chapter 6 outlines the characteristics and components of different computer-based information system structures. It precedes the chapters that deal with the development of information systems since the methodology of development depends to a large extent on the type of system (e.g., a mainframe-based transaction processing system versus a microcomputer-based decision support system).

All information systems activities within an organization and the structure of the information system unit emanate from relevant strategies and policies adopted by general management. Information systems is an organization within an organization. Chapter 7 describes the role and importance of overall information system policy and then the use of information systems as a strategic weapon to pursue organizational goals.

For the information system function to assume a more central role within organizations, proper planning is vital to ensure that the role played by information systems will be congruent with the objectives of the host organization. Chapter 8 describes the planning methodology that should be used to make information systems responsive to organizational objectives. It shows the advantages of a strategic approach over more traditional planning approaches.

Once the organization has established its information system policy and the priorities for developing its various individual information systems, it has a framework within which these individual applications can be developed. Chapter 9 delineates the various phases and activities of an information system life cycle. It explains why information systems are periodically replaced by new versions; it outlines the various activities and emphasizes the different roles of developers, users, and management; and it indicates the milestones along the life cycle of different types of systems.

Development of an information system is more a skill than an art. An information system developer must comply with well-structured procedures established to facilitate the development of systems. While the system developer is encouraged to incorporate intelligence, experience, and intuition into development, these human qualities add to rather than substitute for standard practices. A manager/user should actively participate in the development of information systems that support his or her activities. Chapter 10 concentrates on those steps of system development in which the roles of managers and users are paramount.

Information system activities can be centralized, decentralized, or distributed. With contemporary telecommunication facilities, this has become an important policy issue for management. Chapter 11 focuses on the possible distribution profiles of information systems and ties each into the organization's strategy and structure.

Information is a vital resource for every modern organization. Information is not generated to be simply stored; it has to be provided to users accurately and on time. A considerable portion of an organization's budget is invested in this resource, and it must be utilized effectively and efficiently. The organization has to carefully plan and allocate resources to manage information. The way these resources are organized, controlled, and motivated is the main issue of chapter 12.

Chapter 13 focuses on the interrelations and roles of general management and users of information systems. Management should foresee the organizational needs, guide the information system function, and control its progress. Users should understand pertinent systems, participate in development processes, and exert control on ongoing operations.

Information systems are, by nature, open systems interacting with a dynamic environment. They are usually complex, with many different kinds of components—people, machines, programs, etc. Being open and complex, they are highly vulnerable to inadvertent or deliberate adverse intrusion. Since we cannot safeguard every single transaction along the processing cycle, we have to devise control features to guarantee information reliability. Possible information system controls are the main concern of chapter 14.

Since the introduction of the first computer, information technologies have progressed at an astounding rate. Today's computers are not just faster, they are smaller, more reliable, and cheaper than earlier ones. Consequently, computers are found in almost every facet of daily life, in both organizations and at home. Perhaps no other human invention has so rapidly had such a profound and pervasive effect on society.

The concluding chapter of the book, 15, reviews current and projected developments in various technologies of our information age and traces their organizational and social implications.

To make a theory applicable, technology has to provide tools for its implementation. Information systems, particularly for management, are realizable only due to the rapid progress of information processing technology. In fact, technology advances so rapidly in this area that we sometimes wonder which comes first: theoretical foundations or technological achievements. Appendix A briefly reviews information processing technology. It delineates the data processing cycle and highlights its major components: data capture, input, processing, output, and storage activities. The second part of the appendix focuses on the contemporary technologies of database management systems, terminal networks, computer networks, and microcomputers. Emphasis is on the usefulness of the various hardware/software features, rather than on their technical specifications. This appendix can be used as a reference for concepts appearing in various chapters of the book; a reader who lacks computer technology literacy is well advised to read appendix A before reading chapter 6.

Key Concepts

artificial intelligence	information economics
cognitive psychology	information system
communication theory	management science
(information theory)	management theory
computer economics	microeconomics
computer science	organizational theory
control theory	psycholinguistics
cybernetics	software engineering
decision theory	statistics
general system theory	systems analysis

References

1. Anderson, D. R. *An Introduction to Management Science: Quantitative Approaches to Decision Making.* 6th ed. St. Paul, MN: West Publishing Co, 1991.
2. Anthony, R. N. *Planning and Control Systems: A Framework for Analysis.* Boston: Harvard University Press, 1965.
3. Biggs, C. L., E. G. Birks, and W. Atkins. *Managing the System Development Process.* Englewood Cliffs, NJ: Prentice-Hall, 1980.
4. Cherry, C. *On Human Communication.* Cambridge, MA: MIT Press, 1957.
5. Chomsky, N. *Aspects of the Theory of Syntax.* Cambridge, MA: MIT Press, 1965.
6. Churchman, C. W. *Design of Inquiring Systems.* New York: Basic Books, 1971.
7. Demsky, J. S. *Information Analysis.* Reading, MA: Addison-Wesley, 1972.
8. Ein-Dor, P., and E. Segev. *Managing Management Information Systems.* Lexington, MA: Lexington Books, D. C. Heath and Company, 1978.

9. Feigenbaum, E. A., and J. Feldman, eds. *Computers and Thought.* New York: McGraw-Hill, 1963.

10. Galbraith, J. R. *Organizational Design: An Information Processing View.* Reading, MA: Addison-Wesley, 1973.

11. Gregory, G. *Decision Analysis.* New York: Plenum Press, 1988.

12. Kleijnen, J. P. C. *Computers and Profits: Quantifying Financial Benefits of Information.* Reading, MA: Addison-Wesley, 1980.

13. Likert, R. *The Human Organization: Its Management and Value.* New York: McGraw-Hill, 1967.

14. Lindsay, P. H., and D. A. Norman. *Human Information Processing.* 2d ed. New York: Academic Press, 1977.

15. Lorin, H. *Introduction to Computer Architecture and Organization.* New York: John Wiley & Sons, 1989.

16. Lucas, H. C. *Why Information Systems Fail.* New York: Columbia University Press, 1975.

17. Luce, R. D., and H. Raiffa. *Games and Decisions.* New York: John Wiley & Sons, 1957.

18. McGuire, C. B., and R. Radner, eds. *Decision and Organization.* 2d ed. Minneapolis, MN: University of Minnesota Press, 1986.

19. McLean, E. R., and F. B. Swanson. ''Management Information Systems: An Academic Perspective.'' Graduate School of Management, UCLA: Information Systems Working Paper no. 5–80, 1980.

20. March, J. G., and H. A. Simon. *Organizations.* New York: John Wiley & Sons, 1958.

21. Marschak, J. ''Economics of Information Systems.'' *Journal of the American Statistical Association* 66 (1971): 192–219.

22. Marschak, J., and R. Radner. *Economic Theory of Teams.* New Haven, CT: Yale University Press, 1972.

23. Newell, A., and H. A. Simon. *Human Problem Solving.* Englewood Cliffs, NJ: Prentice-Hall, 1972.

24. Pressman, R. S. *Software Engineering: A Practitioner's Approach.* 3d ed. New York: McGraw-Hill, 1992.

25. Shannon, C. E., and W. Weaver. *The Mathematical Theory of Communications.* Urbana, IL: University of Illinois Press, 1949.

26. Sharpe, W. F. *The Economics of Computers.* New York: Columbia University Press, 1969.

27. Tremblay, J. P., and R. B. Bunt. *An Introduction to Computer Science: An Algorithmic Approach.* 2d ed. New York: McGraw-Hill, 1989.

28. von Bertalanffy, L. *General System Theory: Foundation, Development, Applications.* New York: George Braziller, 1968.

29. Wiener, N. *Cybernetics.* Cambridge, MA: MIT Press, 1948.

30. Winston, P. H. *Artificial Intelligence.* 3d ed. Reading, MA: Addison-Wesley, 1992.

Chapter 2   *Psychological and Behavioral Aspects of Information Systems*

Human reaction to information is highly affected by the way the information penetrates the human's cognitive mechanism. We may overlook or misunderstand important data because it fails to attract our attention. It has to compete with almost an infinite number of other external stimuli surrounding us.

In organizations, management information systems (MIS) might fail because they have been implemented in an environment with an unresponsive psychological climate. Therefore, it is essential for information system users, managers, implementors, designers, and operators to be familiar with some psychological and behavioral aspects related to information systems. These aspects are reviewed here.

Introduction

Understanding human behavior is a prerequisite to the successful design and implementation of all information systems. Human behavior plays an important role in three different levels of human/information relationships.

1. *The macro level of information system environment*—Information systems are not installed in a vacuum. They are implanted into a living body, i.e., an organization or a department, which possesses internal relationships, politics, habits, authority, and labor climates. Any attempt to disregard the prevailing forces and to impose a revolution (rather than a gradual evolution) is doomed to fail. Hence, psychological factors related to group behavior are relevant to our discussion.

2. *The individual level of data digestion*—Human beings are continuously exposed to enormous numbers of stimuli. Since cognition of all the stimuli is impossible, most are eliminated by a complex cognitive process. Even those that are finally perceived may be subject to biases. Thus, a better understanding of human information processing enhances the usefulness of information systems.

3. *The micro level of programmed decisions*—Decisions that were made in the past by people at the bottom level of an organizational hierarchy are often made nowadays by computer programs. Genuine replication of human decisions requires understanding of human information processing and decision making.

This chapter concentrates on the cognitive process, perception biases, and group behavior, while the decision-making process is discussed in chapter 3.

Human Information Processing

Information systems in organizations support human decisions by providing decision makers with relevant information. Hence, the human decision maker is the prime target of any information that is processed and displayed by computerized or manual facilities. Human information processing is achieved through a complex and not completely understood mechanism called the *cognitive process.*

There are two different approaches to investigating the cognitive process. Physiological research concentrates on biochemical and biophysical phenomena observed in the brain, nervous system, and sensory system while exposed to various stimuli. Psychological research regards the human body as a black box and investigates the nature of the cognitive process by relating reactions (outputs) to stimuli (inputs). The results of such experiments and observations make it possible to accept or reject various conjectures about the cognitive process.

The Cognitive Process

A prerequisite to any human perception is paying *attention.* Being attentive enables us to detect and identify a stimulus so that we can transfer its message for further processing. The location of further processing is the *short-term memory* (STM), in which the information is held no more than a few seconds. The major analysis of the information is performed in the *long-term memory* (LTM), where it is classified, stored, and analyzed, perhaps triggering a decision to react (see fig. 2.1). (For a detailed and lively description of this cognitive process, see Lindsay and Norman [13].)

Attention
A person can read the newspaper and listen to music at the same time, or watch TV and simultaneously hug a child. We all have several channels through which we receive external signals. These channels are our senses. However, the way these channels are activated and the intensity of their effort is a question for research.

The old theory that only a single channel is active at any one time has been proved inaccurate. We all know, for example, that listening to somebody does not prevent us from paying attention to a newly lit fire, or even to the sound of an airplane passing by.

Modern theories [4, 14] contend that all channels are active all the time, but the intensity of their activation fluctuates. For example, while conversing, our sense of hearing is highly activated, yet our eyes are open for significant stimuli. Actually, our

Figure 2.1 The cognitive process

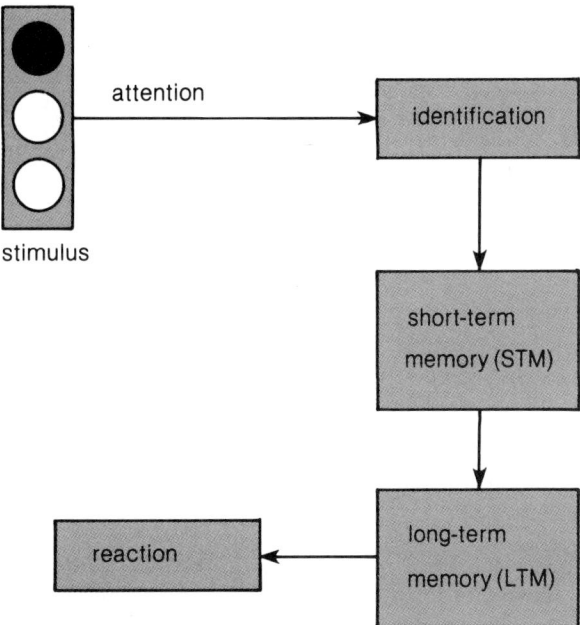

eyes and the cognitive mechanism behind them continuously filter surrounding signals. When we become aware of an important signal, our attention switches over from hearing to vision. A similar event may happen when you are standing at a crowded, noisy party. You select a conversation you wish to listen to, but also receive stimuli from another conversation if it attracts your attention.

We can conclude that we are spending a given amount of energy on attention. The energy is not equally distributed among the different attention channels. This enables us to be selective. However, all the low-active channels are standing by to encounter important signals. We increase the degree of activation whenever we seem to have a need to do so.

Current theory also incorporates biological cycles into the attention model, claiming that the total amount of attention energy is not necessarily constant, but may vary a long time, depending upon the time of the day and other factors. In fact, we all recognize that some of us are less attentive in the mornings whereas others of us are less attentive in the evenings. If you know your attention cycle, you may even get an edge on your partners by scheduling competitive events at hours when you are fully attentive.

Identification

Whenever a signal manages to attract attention, it is transferred to the next cognitive stage, which tries to identify the stimulus. This stage is called *identification* or *recognition*.

Figure 2.2 Faces at the window

There is no consensus of theory on identification. Psychologists have developed different schools of thought in their attempt to understand recognition processes. The two extremes of theory are the *holistic approach* and the *template theory*.

The holistic approach is highly affected by *Gestalt psychology*, which holds that we first perceive a stimulus as a whole, trying to guess what it is. We then verify or reject our guess by examining more and more evidence collected from the stimulus fragments. In other words, this is a top-down approach, according to which the decomposition of a signal into its components is subsequent to an initial recognition based on preconceptions.

The template theory *(pattern recognition)* suggests that identification is performed in exactly the opposite way. We first decompose the signal to the most elementary units; we compare each element to patterns already stored in our mind (templates) through learning and experience, trying to find a matching scheme; we identify an element only after finding a match; and finally we recompose the elements to get the whole pattern. For example, the letter A is decomposed to three bars. The bars are then matched according to their angle, length, proportion, and location to various templates that we possess until recognition is obtained. A major question arising here is how we identify new stimuli on the first occasion they are encountered.

The current prevailing theory, developed by Selfridge [22], synthesizes ideas taken from both extremes. Its main philosophy is based on the idea that we, in fact, incorporate two mechanisms to aid us in identifying stimuli. The first mechanism is *data driven,* namely, it reflects the structure of the arriving data. The second mechanism is *conceptually driven,* namely, we utilize preconceptions to interpret the data, particularly when they are not perfectly clear. For example, we may perceive figure 2.2 as faces looking through a window even though some details are missing.

Selfridge gave his theory a pictorial name: *pandemonium theory*. He believes that recognition is performed sequentially by four types of "demons." The first group captures the signal and memorizes it for a while. The members of this group are called the *image demons*. For example, when we see an object and close our eyes, we maintain the image of the object for a split second. The second group analyzes the signal by locating its major components. Each demon in this group is responsible for operating a specific matching feature, and when it makes a match, it "yells." These demons are called the *feature demons;* they analyze the signal by fragmentation. The third group synthesizes the outcome of the previous group's work and attempts to reconstruct a complete, recognized picture. These are the *cognitive demons*. Finally, there are the *decision demons*. They make the conclusive evaluation and decide whether recognition has been attained. If they are not satisfied, the process is repeated.

We can easily detect a combination of data driven and conceptually driven elements along the pandemonium path (fig. 2.3). For example, suppose you are faced with the signal 13OY. Your image demons memorize it and your feature demons easily identify its components. Your cognitive demons state that we have here a number, 130, and a letter, Y. However, your decision demon, more conceptually driven, fails to understand the meaning of this signal (unless you are sitting in a math class). It urges the feature and cognitive demons to reconsider their analysis/synthesis, which might now end up with the word BOY. Now the decision demon is pleased and transfers the signal to the next station, short-term memory.

Short-term Memory (STM)

The image demons capture and hold signals for a split second, until their peers have completed the recognition. Their memory is called *sensory information storage* (SIS) and has nothing to do with STM. The STM holds the information for a short time—perhaps a few seconds.

Experiments reveal the following basic characteristics of STM:

1. *Transitoriness*—The information stored in STM is there only a short time. Experiments indicate that data consisting of three words are successfully recalled after three seconds 80 percent of the time (tests); after nine seconds, only 30 percent of the time. In other words, STM is transitory; it cannot memorize information.

2. *Limited capacity*—The capacity of STM is limited to about seven units of information plus or minus two [16]. Hence, larger volumes of data are split into smaller groups of that limiting size. In fact, all of us have experienced tests where we were asked to repeat a series of numbers or words. We normally quit in the middle of the series if it is too long.

3. *Chunking*—The term "unit of information" varies according to the material being perceived and the person involved. When a person masters a language, individual symbols are grouped into chunks and each chunk may become an information unit by itself. For example, the group of symbols 354 is

Figure 2.3 The pandemonium process

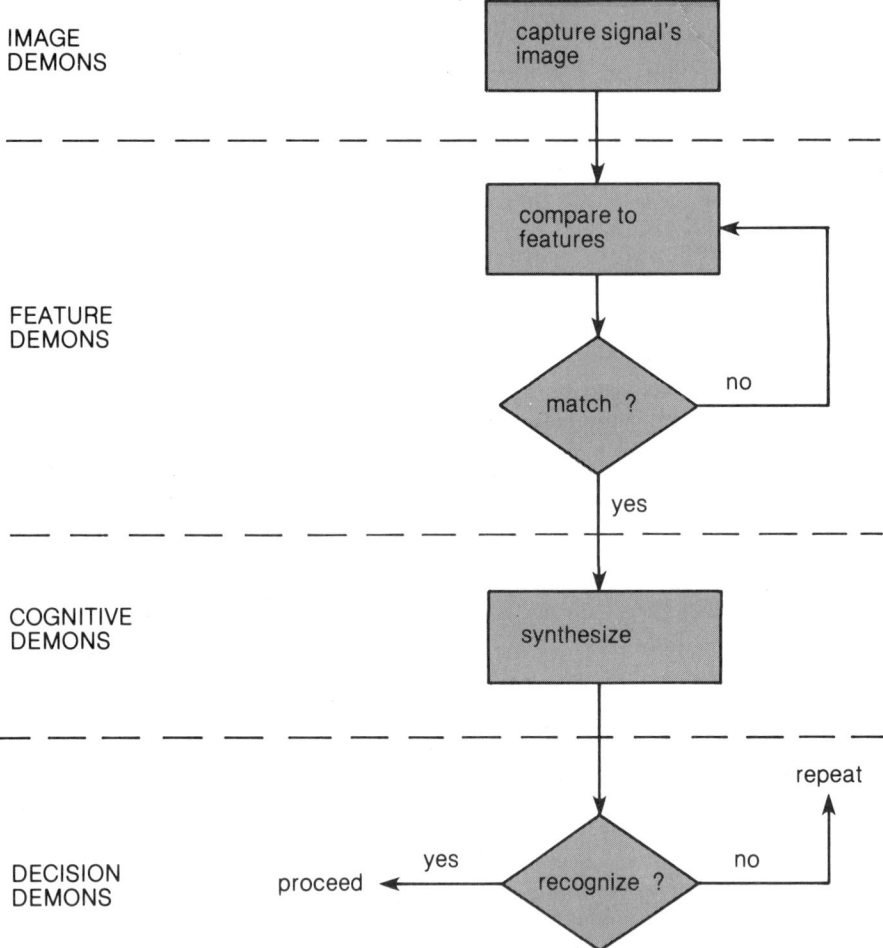

perceived as a single chunk—the number three hundred and fifty-four—because we are familiar with the decimal convention. However, the series 101100100 would normally be perceived as a group of nine units, although it is the same number, written in binary digits. It is probable that if we had a fluent command of binary arithmetic, this series would have become a single chunk, one of 7 ± 2 similar chunks that could be simultaneously stored in STM.

The implications of these characteristics for information system design will be discussed later.

Long-term Memory (LTM)

Three conditions must be met for data to be absorbed by the LTM:

1. The data has been stored in STM for more than a second.
2. There is attention.
3. There is a learning process.

The first two conditions are self-explanatory. The third condition refers to a process of rehearsal—several repetitions of the data. You have probably noticed a tendency to forget a telephone number you have dialed only once or twice. But if you called the same number several times over a relatively short period, sooner or later you stopped looking in the telephone directory. You memorized the number—committed it to LTM—due to sufficient rehearsal. One may say that while STM has relatively fast read (recall) and write (commit to memory) times, LTM has relatively fast read time but slow write time.

Our LTM is much more complex than a mere storage device. It encompasses cataloging mechanisms, retrieval methods, shortcut routes, and search networks. For example, while reading this text, you are, we hope, storing its concepts among concepts and abstractions relating to your education and studies, and not among instances relating to your love affairs. This would create new entries in your catalog of stored data. Suppose you are asked to detail your activities of Tuesday night, three weeks ago. It might take a while until you respond. Meanwhile, you activate some sort of search mechanism by which you reconstruct your recent activities until you narrow the domain of your search and then focus on and retrieve the requested information. Another time you find yourself applying a shortcut. For example, if asked about the home phone number of Jane Fonda, you would immediately reply that you had no idea. You did not have to scan all your memory in order to give this answer. Hence, we sometimes use shortcuts, particularly when we know that we do not have the requested information.

Many scientists believe that LTM capacity is infinite, that it keeps forever every piece of information that has ever entered there, and that we are unable to recall everything because the retrieval mechanism is not perfect. This conjecture is based on hypnosis experiments in which people related events that they had never been able to recall consciously. As a matter of fact, it often happens that many of us are sure we know something but cannot recall it, such as, the name of a movie star featured in a film we saw five years ago. ("I have his name on the tip of my tongue. I even remember his face, but I can't recall the name.")

Many experiments on LTM have been conducted and many theories have been developed. The major problem in this area is that we cannot see what is going on inside the human memory, nor can we exactly relate psychological observation to physiological phenomena. Hence, human memory remains more or less a black box, studied not from its inside but from outside observations by associating reactions (outputs) to certain stimuli (inputs). The prevailing supposition [18], however, classifies the memory content into *events* and *concepts*. The term *events* represents all the recorded history of our life. Concepts are items of knowledge obtained along our life, and are characterized by the following:

1. *Superordinates*—The class to which the concept belongs. For example, a table is a piece of furniture.
2. *Properties*—The characteristics of the concept. For example, a table has four legs.
3. *Instances*—Occurrences related to the concept. For example, there is a green table in the dining room.

The last category interfaces between concepts and events. There are links (associations) within and between groups of events and concepts. The links construct a network that enables efficient search and retrieval.

An immediate implication is that data presented in familiar format and within nonalien context facilitates human reaction.

Biases in the Cognitive Process

It is widely agreed that human beings try to process information in the most efficient way. In other words, since we are continuously bombarded by an infinite number of external stimuli, we prefer to complete the perception of data as quickly as possible, in order to clear the way for the next signal. This is basically a positive quality, although it may lead to some errors. In particular, when we try to speed up cognition by complementing a data-driven process with a conceptually driven support, we might end up with wrong perception. Let us examine now some of the common biases in the cognitive process [see 13, 5, ch. 8].

1. *Confusion*—In the earlier states of recognition, we tend to confuse symbols that are visually similar (that is, when we face visual material), such as F and E, C and O, etc. In a later stage, when STM is involved, we tend to confuse data that are acoustically similar, such as F and X, M and N, C and T, etc. The reason for the second type of confusion stems from our habit of repeating the sounds of the symbol in our mind—some sort of an inner speech. This can be done only after data has passed through the recognition phase and entered STM.

2. *Ambiguity*—We tend to interpret data within a wide context and not in a discrete fashion. This is why we sometimes think we have understood a phrase, and therefore do not initiate an in-depth inquiry, only to find out later that we were misled by ambiguities. Take, for example, the following sentence: "The child finished drinking the coke and gave the straw to the cows." Which straw is it?

3. *Information overload*—The limited capacity of the STM is 7±2 chunks. Therefore, a long series of data without breaks or rehearsals will vanish on its way to the LTM. Moreover, the sensory system and the LTM might also deteriorate under constant and long exposure and consequently stop performing well, particularly when we are under stress or are tired.

4. *Filtering*—Since we are not capable of absorbing all the stimuli surrounding us, we filter only the signals that we preconceive to be valuable. There is a catch here; how can we tell which signals are irrelevant if we have not perceived them? In practice, we use some intuitive techniques. First, we use a *limited problem space.* We will not examine infinite domains of data and feasible solutions, but rather confine ourselves to familiar territory determined by past experience and learning. For example, if you are looking for a dictionary, you will probably not begin the search in the garage.

An extension of the limited problem space phenomenon is *anchoring.* We tend to start *human information processing* by examining well-known data and comparing the newly arrived information to the initial anchor.

Finally, we prefer concrete data that does not require further manipulation. Only when we feel there is no other choice do we process the data in our mind. This property is called *concreteness.*

5. *Biased intuitive statistics*—Our preconceptions or personal preferences often cause us to unintentionally falsify statistical data. For example, we assign higher probabilities than are justified to possible outcomes that are subjectively preferred. Generally speaking, we tend to confuse probabilities and outcomes, and the emergent bias is normally in favor of an optimistic view (see Kahneman and Tversky [9] for a comprehensive discussion of such phenomena). For instance, most people assign a higher probability of accident to flying than to driving. Another statistical bias is described by the law of *just noticeable differences* (*Weber's law*). It stipulates that people recognize a change in a certain value only if the ratio between the change and the initial value is greater than a given minimum constant. For example, if we examine several sequential accounting statements, we might overlook some trends if the changes in the absolute figures are below a just noticeable difference.

6. *Self-confidence symptoms*—Scientific research proves that presentation of compressed data—aggregated, summarized, and appropriately selected—does not degrade decision making, provided that significant data is not missing. Indeed, it can even improve decision making. Nevertheless, decision makers are reluctant to rely solely on summarized data because it impairs their confidence (probably because they do not have an anchor—the original raw data). In this sense people trade off efficiency with self-confidence.

Another factor contributing to self-confidence is *feedback.* We always prefer to have feedback to our reactions. When we perceive data and consequently react, we would like to get feedback to reinforce our previous cognition. That is why online information system terminals display a confirmation signal upon completion of the keying of an input record.

Finally, in chapter 3, you will learn that unused data, or data that does not modify our view of certain events, does not theoretically have any economic value. Psychological research, however, indicates that human beings tend to retain unused data, and that they also like affirmative information even when it does not reveal anything new. This means that they

Figure 2.4 Newell and Simon's model of human information processing
SOURCE: Newell, A., and Simon, H. A., *Human Problem Solving,* New Jersey: Prentice-Hall, 1972.

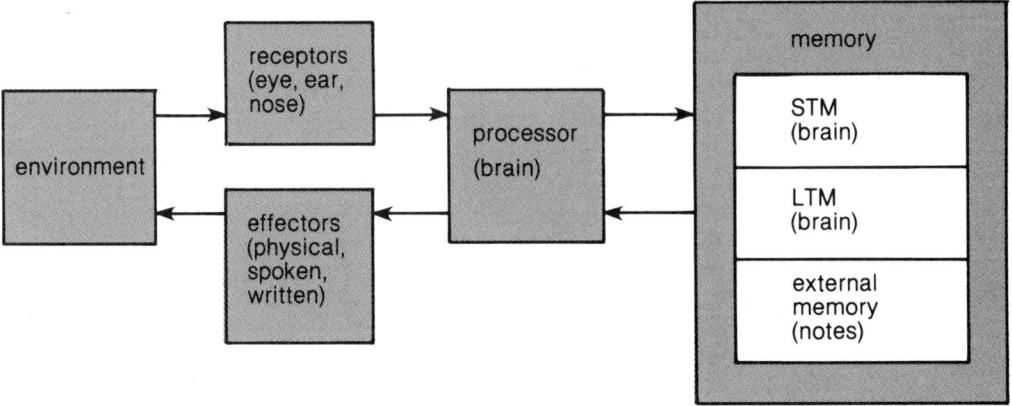

value such data, which we very often regard as obsolete. Take for example the desire to learn about the weather forecast. Many people watch the weatherperson on television and then switch to another channel for reconfirmation, although they know that both channels draw the weather information from the same source. For more about confidence in decision making, see Levin, Chapman, and Johnson [12].

In the next section we will delve into the implications of the cognitive process and biases for information systems development and use.

The Cognitive Process and Information Systems

The journey through the cognitive process is intended to establish an appropriate background for understanding the impact of the process on the design and use of information systems. Many information systems are discarded, not because of technical inadequacy, but because they fail to account for behavioral factors of their users, particularly when these factors conflicted with MIS experts' preconceptions of efficiency. Hence, a widely used, yet not optimally efficient system, is more effective than an elegant, yet unused one.

We will first review the cognitive process through a compact synthetic model, and then discuss its implications for information systems.

The Cognitive Process Revisited

Newell and Simon [17] developed a formal model of human information processing for use in research on artificial intelligence. The model is conceptual and does not pretend to exactly depict human organic processes. Yet, it compresses our previous discussion into a brief description. Its analogy to the structure of a computer system is clearly seen in figure 2.4.

According to the model, the initial interaction between an individual and the *environment* is triggered by stimuli attracting the human senses. These senses, termed *receptors,* transfer the information to the *processor* (brain), which employs various types of *memory,* depending upon its needs. In many cases the processor, being reluctant to count solely on human memory, would prefer to record the data on *external memory* (notes or magnetic media) for further use. Decisions made by the processors are conveyed to the environment via *effectors,* which could be mouth (speech), fist (beating), leg (kicking), or hand (writing). If we substitute some of these terms with some others, we immediately get a description of a computer system: data enter into the system via *input devices* (receptors); are processed by *CPU* (central processing unit); are stored in *registers* (STM), *internal storage* (LTM), and *external storage devices* (external memory); and are displayed via *output devices* (effectors).

Information systems play four roles in connection with this model. As part of the environment, they provide the receptors with data. They may also transmit data from the effectors to other locations. They serve as external memories to expand the capacity of stored information. And they may substitute for some human decisions (see ch. 3) and support many others. It is very important, therefore, to properly combine human and computerized information processing.

Cognitive Aspects in Information Systems Design

Chapter 10 will elaborate on various aspects of information systems design. However, it is now time to present some direct conclusions stemming from the discussion of the cognitive process. Most of the conclusions focus on the methods of displaying information rather than keying in or processing data.

As a primary rule, we have to be aware of the fact that the reported information is going to compete with an enormous number of other stimuli. It has to penetrate a filtering mechanism. Therefore, it has to be displayed so that the user's attention is attracted, particularly when it conveys significant exceptions or important trends. This could be achieved by background coloring (on preprinted forms or screens), asterisks or underlines (on printouts), blinks and reverse video (on screens), or sounds (on terminals). These make certain that users do not overlook important information.

We have to remember that information is not stored in the LTM unless there are several rehearsals of it. Hence, redundancy of major data is not bad, so long as it does not go beyond the point where it becomes a nuisance.

We have to take into account that the cognitive process is conceptually driven as well as data driven. Therefore, it is much easier to absorb data when it is presented in a familiar rather than an unfamiliar context and format. Familiar context refers to the use of prevailing terms and jargon, common practices of writing and presentation, natural degree of precision (don't present national budgets in pennies), etc. The presentation should be user-oriented rather than computer- or system-designer-oriented. For example, accounting records are completely symmetric in the sense that assets and credits could be written on the right instead of the left side, and liabilities and debits could be written on the left instead of the right side, without causing any harm. However, could you imagine the reaction of an accountant should you provide him or her with a statement in which debit and credit sides have been switched?

We have to remember that information overload is harmful. Therefore, we have to split the flow of data into reasonable quantities. If possible, we can extract and summarize data. On the other hand, summarized data might disrupt users' confidence. A compromise could be to present summaries but maintain accessibility to raw data, so that the user can refer to it whenever he or she feels like doing so.

Many people are lazy; they do not want to execute further manual processing on data presented to them. The system designer should inquire about possible analyses frequently performed by users and try to build these routines into the information system, preferably as optional procedures that can be called up upon request.

Note that contemporary software tools allow users to significantly reduce many of these problems. For instance, interactive programs provide menus so that users can run various routines upon request. This, in fact, equips users with a variety of options that accommodate individual tastes and time constraints. A user who is in a hurry can request both rough and final figures, while another user (or the same user at another time) can exercise a lengthy sensitivity analysis. Splitting the terminal screen into windows enables users to observe raw data on one part of the screen and final results on another part, at the same time. Such tools are labeled *friendly software* and are very useful in alleviating cognitive problems.

The biased statistics phenomenon implies that indicators that seem very clear to a systems designer might be misinterpreted or overlooked by users because implicit figures fail to become explicit. Therefore, any ratio, difference, or percentage that might have significance should be explicitly calculated and displayed.

A feedback mechanism is vital for smooth interactions between people and machines. People are conditioned to get feedback on their actions; otherwise they lose confidence. There is a well-known case [24] of an online information system that was carefully designed to handle a predefined capacity of transactions. However, immediately after its installation, the system failed to cope with the planned volume of data. An investigation indicated that the design had not included response to the input clerks upon completion of their record keying, so the clerks could not tell whether the operation was successful. They tricked the system by issuing a query immediately after keying a new record, and the system's response was viewed by them as confirmation that the record had been captured. Consequently, the volume of data traffic that was passing through the terminals, communication lines, and main computer was doubled, and the system almost collapsed. The system was revived after a simple feedback signal confirming capture was built into it.

Last, but not least, decisions to scrap or ignore some data should be made with extreme care. In fact, we have to carefully consider not only the data to be included in a system, but also the data to be eliminated from the system. Individuals value unused or old data much more than we imagine, and we have to take this into account (remember the old journals and the yellowed letters that used to occupy grandpa's basement?).

The preceding suggestions usually decrease the efficiency of information systems. However, our main objective is effectiveness [10, ch. 1]. This is measured by the use of a system. Efficiency is a good criterion so long as it does not decrease users' satisfaction.

Cognitive Style

The previous discussion has reviewed the prevailing paradigm of the cognitive process. Although some of the details are still debatable, the discussion characterizes the cognitive process as performed by human beings. However, psychological research indicates that people differ in how they gather and process data—they have different styles of approaching data and solving problems.

Cognitive Styles

Differences in cognitive style are revealed in two phases of human information processing: data gathering and information evaluation. The first phase involves data collection and review, or preparation of the information for decision making. The second phase refers to data analysis and problem solving.

When gathering data, individuals tend to be either *preceptive* or *receptive*. Preceptive individuals wish to grasp the whole picture (Gestalt) and refrain from going into details. They look for certain cues—deviations from or conformities to their expectations and standards—that they hope will lead to a satisfying degree of knowledge of the current relevant status. Consequently, they prefer filtered, summarized, and selected information rather than the whole batch of raw data. In short, they try to match clues with preconceptions. Receptive individuals, on the other hand, are attentive to details. They look at complete raw data before making any decision and are reluctant to rely on summarized, transformed data.

The second realm in which cognitive style varies is problem solving. Individuals tend to be either *analytic (systematic)* or *intuitive (heuristic)*. Analytic persons look for a method to achieve the best solution. This implies that they prefer rigorous optimization models and quantitative reports. Intuitive individuals, on the other hand, do not commit themselves to any dogma or method. They are determined to solve a problem but not to utilize a particular technique. They might try various approaches and proceed in a trial-and-error fashion. They are pleased when they reach a satisfying, acceptable solution.

A person's cognitive style, then, can be characterized as preceptive-analytic, preceptive-intuitive, receptive-analytic, or receptive-intuitive. We will now discuss the implications of cognitive style for information systems. The reader can refer to Benbasat and Taylor's article [3] for further elaboration (see also Ein-Dor and Segev, [6, ch. 7]).

Cognitive Style and Information Systems

A preliminary question that can be asked is, Why should we bother with cognitive style? After all, information systems may last longer than the individuals holding certain positions. Sooner or later a particular person is replaced, and so is his or her cognitive style. Wouldn't it be ridiculous to redesign the information system whenever someone is leaving or coming? This is true. We are not going to recustomize information systems whenever there are personnel changes. However, we can take cognitive style into account at two levels: individual and group.

At the level of the individual, we do not advocate the design of different systems for various individuals. But we do recommend that systems maintain enough flexibility to satisfy individuals with different cognitive styles. This implies that systems should include many optional features that could be activated upon request. For example, you may design a set of well-formatted summary reports or exclusive exception reports. But if, at the same time, you do not block the access to raw data, and you provide users with appropriate query tools, you actually customize the system for users who have different cognitive styles. Similarly, if you do not restrict the system to only a limited number of quantitative models, but rather attach to the system a variety of techniques and intuitive methods, the system will likely be useful to many more users. In fact, providing the user with a repertoire of options is a major principle in building decision support systems (DSS) (see [10] and the discussion in ch. 6).

A concrete application of such an approach is seen in some software products called electronic spreadsheets. The electronic spreadsheet (Lotus 1-2-3®, Excel®, and others) allows the user to easily perform all sorts of calculations on the screen. Depending on personal choice, users can then display the results in different modes, such as tables, graphs, or pie charts. Some electronic spreadsheet programs contain all sorts of display and graphic options and the user has only to select those that are desired.

At the group level, there are indications that various skills and professions possess certain cognitive style patterns [15]. For example, auditors are more compatible to the receptive-systematic style; architects and securities salesmen to receptive-intuitive; marketing managers and psychologists to preceptive-intuitive; and production and logistic managers, statisticians, and financial analysts with preceptive-systematic. These, of course, are statistical findings, rather than rules of nature. Still we may recall them whenever we have to design an information system for a particular group of users.

Research in cognitive style has not yet developed a normative approach to information system design. Findings in this area may help to provide ideas on how systems should interact with users and how data should be displayed under various circumstances. However, operational guidelines to MIS design based on cognitive style theory are still unavailable and the contribution of the area to MIS is still debatable. For further discussion on this debate, see Huber [8] and Robey [20].

The Psychological Climate

Information systems are not installed in a vacuum. They are inserted into living organizations that maintain common practices, habits, and attitudes. Newly arrived systems might shake delicate equilibriums among various parties. They might encourage or interfere with personal or group ambitions. Consequently, they may be fostered or opposed because of a *psychological climate,* not because of their ''objective'' technical quality.

The psychological climate affects information systems at all stages of the life cycle (see ch. 9). It may trigger initiative to develop a new system, but it may also extinguish new ideas. It influences the level of user cooperation while systems are developed. It generates receptiveness or opposition during implementation. It regulates the frequency of use, and hence the success, of systems after they have been installed. Understanding and proper treatment of psychological climates are vital, therefore, if information systems are to be useful.

The Evolution of a Psychological Climate

Psychological climates develop out of continuous interactions among parties involved in the information systems progression (or regression) in an organization. The three major parties involved are users, management, and information systems (IS) professionals. Other important parties are customers and data processing (DP) vendors [6, ch. 8].

Users, defined here as those who use a system as part of normal activities, evaluate a system according to the direct benefits gained from it. If they feel that the system contributes to their competence in task performance, they will intensify its use, and consequently become more receptive to new ideas and further development. On the other hand, if they find the system awkward to use and have to wrestle with it, they will be reluctant to accept any further development of computerized systems within their territory. More than that, users are exposed to customers' reactions. They are the first to hear complaints or commendations from customers. Customers' attitudes, particularly when negative, are quickly disseminated among various circles in the organization, so we can see how the psychological climate is created by users.

Management has preconceptions about information systems. As a result, management develops expectations of systems. These expectations may be above or below system capabilities. In other words, management may regard a proposed system as an ultimate solution for its problems, when, in fact, the system only relaxes problems and supports managers. In such a case, disappointment is inevitable. On the other hand, management might underestimate system potential and, therefore, confine IS professionals to simplistic applications. Dissatisfaction among professionals, in this case, is a direct consequence.

IS professionals also contribute to the evolution of a psychological climate. Sometimes, in order to increase their esteem, they overpraise their products (i.e., information systems), which later turn out to be mediocre, and certainly not outstanding. The resulting frustration created among other parties might be irreparable. Conversely, IS experts may lack the vision and the imagination required to develop advanced MIS; in this case, they would finally be treated as no more than programming clerks. In many situations the IS experts are newcomers who have not grown up in the organization and who are unaware of political power plays and unwritten rules. They start pursuing their task by stepping on so many toes (even nondeliberately) that the psychological climate they create cannot recover.

Customers very often get used to certain procedures, forms, and practices and find it difficult to adjust to new systems. They protest either by shifting to competitors or with vocal complaints. Both result in a foul climate.

Finally, DP vendors are sometimes very eager to pursue sales and may blur possible inadequacies of the system they propose. In different circumstances they might oversell systems that are much above needs. In both cases, the psychological climate is polluted.

We have to remember that it is difficult to maintain a favorable climate. The psychological climate can easily be destroyed and once it is ruined, a lot of effort is required to recover lost ground.

Resistance to Change

Resistance to change is a dominant factor in nearly all information system implementation. Moderate resistance is revealed in reluctance to cooperate, concealing key information, and maintaining private, parallel (manual) systems. Extreme resistance may evoke an outright rejection of a system or even sabotage. Resistance to change is a typical phenomenon not only in information systems; it is detected whenever an innovative process is introduced to a group of individuals. However, the fast advancement of computerized systems has increased the intensity of this problem.

Note that resistance to change is not only a user "disease." It is detected among information system professionals as well. Very often they object to the introduction of new technology (the use of fourth generation software instead of traditional programming—see ch. 10); they attempt to block the acquisition of equipment by end users (microcomputers); or they resist the formation of new organizational units (information centers—see ch. 12). Common to all of these situations is the professionals' feeling that their status as "supreme wisdom" in data processing is in jeopardy.

Causes for Resistance to Change

Imagine being employed for twenty-five years in the accounts receivable department of an organization. You have been recently awarded a gold watch by management in recognition of your dedication. Suddenly, some young consultants start to snoop around your desk, proposing the installation of a computer that will virtually replace a major portion of your duties. Naturally you and your colleagues become suspicious and sooner or later develop resistance. You are afraid of losing your job. Even if your position is secure, you will have to adjust to new procedures and forms and learn to operate computer terminals. You are going to lose your manual files and notes because they will all be electronically recorded. You were the departmental maven; you knew the status of every customer; your help was requested to locate every lost document. Now you are going to report to a machine.

Your boss is also unhappy. He has mastered a significant volume of information that is vital to the business. Now, since the information is in the computer, everybody has access to it. In particular, his superiors will not call his office anymore for urgent queries on certain customer balances. Your boss is worried also because some of the positions he supervises might be eliminated, which means budgetary cuts and a reduction in power.

One of your friends, working in another company, has experienced a conversion to a computerized system and tells you some horror stories about program errors, hardware malfunctions, customers' anger, etc. Naturally, you and your peers are reluctant to cooperate with the IS experts. In fact, you are overjoyed to hear rumors about a probable postponement of the project.

In short, the introduction of new systems annoys individuals and groups for the following reasons:

1. It replaces current functions and, hence, causes the elimination of some positions.
2. It stimulates changes in organizational structures and, hence, in power and authority.
3. It modifies current procedures and, hence, generates confusion and uncertainty.
4. It requires the establishment of more structured activities and, hence, reduces the prestige of the "old stars" of the manual systems. Moreover, while disclosing current decision procedures, it may bring discredit to employees whose practices were not always strictly regulated.

Management of Change

Sociological research indicates that the process of change in individuals, as well as in groups, consists of the following stages [see 10, pp. 199–205, and 21]:

1. *Unfreezing*—Disturbing the current stable equilibrium and, consequently, introducing the need for change.
2. *Moving*—Presenting new directions and conducting a learning process until the material is thoroughly digested.
3. *Refreezing*—Integrating the change with existing behavioral frameworks to recreate a whole, natural entity.

Resistance to change reflects an incomplete or unsuccessful unfreezing. It means that either the subjects are not motivated enough or they fear change more than they value probable benefits. Hence, resistance to change can be softened. *Change management* involves one or more of the following tactics:

1. Explanation of the deficiencies currently observed.
2. Explanation of how bad the outcomes are going to be should the proposed changes not be adopted.
3. Elaboration on the concreteness of the benefits (for individuals as well as for the group as a whole) of the proposed changes.
4. Encouragement of users to submit their own ideas of how the new system should look. Incorporation of those ideas into the newly designed system so that the users feel that they have contributed to the success of the new system.
5. Frequent consultation with the users, asking them to reflect on your ideas, and seriously considering their comments.

There are several arguments that can soften resistance to change. In the case of the accounts receivable department example, one of the following reasons could convince reluctant employees of the need for change.

1. The current state is really bad and may lead to restaffing in the department, so that jobs are not as secure as they seem to be.
2. The current state is nearly catastrophic and may lead to bankruptcy and, consequently, to the firing of employees.
3. A computerized system will release clerks from monotonous tasks and leave them with more sophisticated functions such as credit analysis and customer follow-ups.
4. Gaining experience with a computerized system is very important nowadays and expands job opportunities and prospects for promotion.
5. Computerized systems have almost never displaced existing personnel, so firing is out of question. Rather, these systems increase the capacity for handling future growth—departmental performance will improve and so will its prestige.

In addition to these, intense user involvement during system design, together with appropriate education and training, will probably assist in change management.

The likelihood of confronting resistance to change is particularly high during system implementation. Chapter 10 discusses implementation aspects and provides some concrete tools to cope with resistance to change.

Practical Conclusions for Information System Design and Use

The following twenty items are listed here as guidelines for information systems design and use.

1. During information system development, the developers should consider behavioral aspects of individuals—such as perception limitations—and of groups—such as resistance to change.

2. Displayed information cannot penetrate human minds unless it attracts attention. Therefore, important data should be emphasized by special symbols, colors, blinks, sounds, or redundancy.

3. Information recognition is driven by external stimuli as well as by previous concepts. The more familiar the context of the information, the better recognition is facilitated. Therefore, use common jargon and prevailing conventions when designing information display methods.

4. Part of information identification is performed by pattern recognition. Strict presentation of data improves recognition.

5. STM has a limited capacity (7 ± 2 units). Do not overload it with data because the data may vanish.

6. Chunking enables human beings to condense elementary information units into larger units. Therefore, if information is displayed in a familiar fashion, a faster perception can be expected.

7. Information cannot be memorized without rehearsals. Therefore, if you want users to capture important information, repeat the display several times (redundancy).

8. Human memory is not organized sequentially. Human information retrieval is supported by a complex system of associations. Hence, if data is displayed in a familiar mode that matches previously absorbed information, a person is more likely to find an appropriate link between past and new data, and consequently to achieve a more comprehensive analysis.

9. People tend to confuse similar signals, particularly during the recognition stage. Such confusion can be avoided if various messages are appropriately differentiated.

10. Even people who have mastered statistics tend to perform biased intuitive statistical analysis. They may confuse probabilities with preferences. Therefore, when presenting figures, make sure that the statistical meaning is fully elaborated and clearly expressed. Emphasize differences and trends.

11. People are more confident when they have access to raw data so that they can double-check results. Therefore, every summary reporting system must contain features enabling suspicious users to refer to the original data.

12. An interactive system must have a built-in feedback mechanism to confirm the receipt of new data. Otherwise, users lack confidence.

13. When you design a system, consult with users before ignoring some data items. What you believe to be irrelevant or not useful might still be valued by users. Unused data is sometimes valuable just because users feel more secure knowing that the data exists.

14. Beware of scrapping files until you have proof that they have no value.

15. People do not like to perform manual analysis of already processed data. Therefore, any involved computation that can be done by the computer is preferred (subject to a certain degree of economic rationality).

16. Information systems serve a variety of users having different cognitive styles. Systems should be designed to comply with these various styles. The best way to do this is to enrich the system with a broad repertoire of reporting and query features, thus allowing users to utilize various models and reporting formats according to preference. A menu-driven system is appropriate for this purpose.

17. When a system is designed to serve a homogeneous group of users who are likely to have the same cognitive style, the design should fit that type of perception.

18. Information systems are installed in environments that have developed a long tradition of habits, rules, and practices. It is, therefore, a preliminary task of the system developers to learn these traditions. Should the planned system comply with existing tradition, it will be implemented more smoothly. Should it not comply, at least the developers have knowledge of future hurdles and risks.

19. The best way to deal with resistance to change is to avert it rather than to fight it after it has arisen. Careful management of change (the carrot-and-stick technique, user involvement, training) may help.

20. Remember, above all, the term "friendly software." This software uses prevailing terms, does not require the key-in of obscure characters in a rigid sequence, allows the user to select routines by means of a menu, contains help options, and provides for many sorts of output. Such a package is most likely to be easily accepted by the users.

Summary

This chapter has outlined some psychological and behavioral aspects of individuals and groups in relation to information systems.

At the level of the individual, we first traced the cognitive process and human information processing. People process data only if they are attentive to signals. Their attention is attracted by stimuli that stand out from all the other stimuli. The several attention channels (vision, hearing, etc.), are each operating at low volume so long as they are idle. When a channel detects a potentially interesting signal, its attention increases, at the expense of other channels, and it triggers the cognitive process.

The next step in the process is identification or recognition. Whether people grasp the whole picture first and then separate it into parts (Gestalt theory) or they perceive details first and then induce the whole (pattern recognition or template theory) is still debatable. The most widely accepted theory nowadays combines both schools. It claims that recognition is data driven—stimulated by external signals—as well as concept driven—supported by preconceptions. The model emerging from this approach is called pandemonium. It claims that recognition is obtained through four possibly iterative stages (pictorially, by four groups of demons): image demons capture the signal for a split second (also known as sensory information storage); feature demons fragment the signal and analyze it; cognitive demons synthesize the results of the analysis; and a decision demon either decides on the identification or, if in doubt, iterates the process.

Recognized information is transferred to the short-term memory (STM), which has a limited storage capacity (7±2 units) and cannot hold the information for more than a few seconds. It has the property of chunking, when familiar data are condensed into larger information units.

Data approaches the long-term memory (LTM) only after staying and being rehearsed in STM. In the LTM, information is stored almost forever. Retrieval is aided by catalogs and search networks (associations). Data on events and on concepts is treated differently, although some links have been established.

The cognitive process is not perfect; it contains some inherent biases. Some of the common biases are confusion between visually or vocally similar signals; ambiguity due to various preconceptions; loss of information because of overload; loss of information because of filtering; wrong deduction due to improper intuitive statistics; and lack of confidence due to inaccessible raw data, lack of feedback, and overevaluation of obsolete, unused data.

Newell and Simon's model describes the cognitive process as analogous to a computer system. People receive data through receptors (input devices); process data in a processor (CPU); store data for the short run in the STM (registers); store data for the long range in the LTM (memory) and external memory (external storage devices); and transmit their decisions through effectors (output devices).

Some important conclusions pertinent to information systems and human information processing are: (1) important data should be emphasized, (2) some redundancy is useful for successful perception, (3) familiar context facilitates perception, (4) too much information will not be absorbed, (5) accessibility to raw data increases users' confidence, (6) people are reluctant to process data manually and therefore any process that can be performed by the computer should be, (7) statistical results should be explicitly displayed and not left to intuition, (8) feedback is vital, and (9) old data should be handled cautiously.

Individuals may have different cognitive styles. When gathering data, some people are preceptive—they look for the whole picture—whereas others are receptive—they wish to get all the details. When analyzing data, some people are intuitive—they look for cues and seek a satisfying solution. Others are analytic—they systematically search for an optimal solution.

Information systems should be designed to serve individuals with various cognitive styles. The systems should include summary reporting as well as accessibility to raw data; they should provide analytic tools as well as heuristic approaches. They could be tailored to a particular cognitive style only if it is known that they are intended to serve a homogeneous group of users. In short, information systems should be friendly to their users.

Psychological climate is a term for the atmosphere created in organizations by information systems development and use. It is continuously influenced by the degree of conformity between the experience with and the expectations from information systems. The major forces affecting the psychological climate are users, management, and information systems professionals. Customers and data processing vendors may also influence this climate.

A major factor in the psychological climate is resistance to change. Humans are reluctant to proposed changes because changes threaten stability. Individuals are afraid of losing jobs, authority, or prestige and therefore form coalitions and power groups to oppose changes.

Change should be managed with care. First, people have to perceive that preserving the status quo is not beneficial; the unfreezing stage. Second, they have to move to a revised state; the moving stage. Finally, the change has to be integrated with existing systems; the refreezing stage. User involvement in the process of change is essential to the success of a new system.

Key Concepts

ambiguity
anchoring
attention
biased intuitive statistics
change management
chunking
cognitive process
cognitive style: analytic, heuristic, intuitive, preceptive, receptive, systematic
concepts
conceptually driven
concreteness
confusion
data compression
data driven
demons: cognitive, decision, feature, image
detection
effectors
environment
events
external memory
feedback
filtering
friendly software

Gestalt psychology
holistic approach
human information processing
identification
information overload
just noticeable differences (Weber's law)
limited problem space
long-term memory (LTM)
memory
moving stage
pandemonium theory
pattern recognition (template theory)
preceptive
processor
psychological climate
receptive
receptors
recognition
refreezing stage
resistance to change
self-confidence symptoms
sensory information storage (SIS)
short-term memory (STM)
template theory (pattern recognition)
unfreezing stage

References

1. Ackerman, P. L. "Determinants of Individual Differences During Skill Acquisition: A Theory of Cognitive Abilities and Information Processing." *Journal of Experimental Psychology: General* 117 (1988): 299–329.

2. Anderson, J. R. *Cognitive Psychology and Its Implications.* 3d ed. New York: Freeman, 1990.

3. Benbasat, I., and R. N. Taylor. "The Impact of Cognitive Styles on Information System Design." *MIS Quarterly* 2 (June 1978): 43–54.

4. Broadbend, D. E. "Communication Models for Memory." In *The Pathology of Memory,* edited by G. A. Talland and N. Waugh. New York: Academic Press, 1969.

5. Davis, G. B., and M. H. Olson. *Management Information Systems: Conceptual Foundations, Structure and Development,* 2nd ed. New York: McGraw-Hill, 1985.

6. Ein-Dor, P., and E. Segev. *Managing Management Information Systems.* Lexington, MA: D. C. Heath, 1978.

7. Gerlach, J. H., and F. Kuo. "Understanding Human-Computer Interaction for Information System Design." *MIS Quarterly* 15, no. 4 (1991): 527–49.

8. Huber, G. P. "Cognitive Style As a Basis for MIS and DSS Designs: Much Ado about Nothing?" *Management Science* 29, no. 5 (May 1983): 567–79.

9. Kahneman, D., and A. Tversky. "Prospect Theory: An Analysis of Decision Under Risk." *Econometrica* 47, no. 2 (March 1979): 263–91.

10. Keen, P. G. W., and M. S. Scott Morton. *Decision Support Systems.* Reading, MA: Addison-Wesley, 1978.

11. Keren, G. "Cognitive Aids and Debiasing Methods: Can Cognitive Pills Cure Cognitive Ills?" In *Cognitive Biases,* edited by J. P. Caremi, J. M. Fabre, and M. Gonzales. Amsterdam, Holland: Elsevier, 1990.

12. Levin, I. P., D. P. Chapman, and R. D. Johnson. "Confidence in Judgements Based on Incomplete Information: An Investigation Using Both Hypothetical and Real Gambles." *Journal of Behavioral Decision Making* 1 (1988): 29–41.

13. Lindsay, P. H., and D. A. Norman. *Human Information Processing.* 2d ed. New York: Academic Press, 1977.

14. Mackay, D. "Aspects of the Theory of Comprehension, Memory and Attention." *Quarterly Journal of Experimental Psychology* 25, no. 1 (1973).

15. McKenney, J. L., and P. G. W. Keen. "How Managers' Minds Work?" *Harvard Business Review* 52, no. 3 (1974): 79–90.

16. Miller, G. A. "The Magical Number Seven, Plus or Minus Two: Some Limits on Our Capacity for Processing Information." *The Psychological Review* 63, no. 2 (March 1956): 81–97.

17. Newell, A., and H. A. Simon. *Human Problem Solving.* Englewood Cliffs, NJ: Prentice-Hall, 1972.

18. Norman, D. A., ed. *Models of Human Memory.* New York: Academic Press, 1970.

19. Quinlan, P. *Connectionism and Psychology.* Chicago, IL: The University of Chicago Press, 1991.

20. Robey, D. "Cognitive Style and DSS Design: A Comment on Huber's Paper." *Management Science* 29, no. 5 (May 1983): 580–82.

21. Schein, E. H. *Brainwashing.* Cambridge, MA: Center for International Studies, MIT, 1961.
22. Selfridge, O. "Pandemonium: A Paradigm for Learning." In *Symposium on the Mechanization of Thought Processes.* London: HM Stationary Office, 1959.
23. Tversky, A., and D. Kahneman. "The Framing of Decisions and the Psychology of Choice." *Science* 211 (1981): 453–58.
24. Warner, C. D. "System Performance and Evaluation - Past, Present, and Future." In *Proceedings of the Fall Joint Computer Conference.* 1979.

Questions

1. Describe how a stimulus results in a reaction.
2. How do information systems relate to the model of the cognitive process?
3. What are the characteristics of the four possible cognitive systems?
4. Who are the parties involved in an organization's information system and how does each affect the psychological climate?
5. How might biases in the cognitive process affect perception?
6. How can efficient management of change overcome natural resistance to change?

Problems

1. Discuss how knowledge of the cognitive process might be applied to the display of information. How might this knowledge also impact design of data entry systems?
2. Applying many of the suggestions for making the information system more human-oriented also decreases the efficiency of the system. Explain why this is so and why, in spite of this, the suggestions should be implemented.

Chapter 3   Decision Making and the Value of Information

Life consists of a continuous series of decisions. Which route is the best to drive home? Which bonds and shares should we purchase for our portfolio? Which brand of toothpaste should we use? The importance of the decisions varies, depending upon the time, the situation, and the person(s) making them. However, all our decisions are based on our best knowledge at the time of making them, and our knowledge is continuously revised by information. Therefore, information must be evaluated in accordance with the decisions it supports. We now turn to a review of the decision-making process and relate it to the value of information.

A Descriptive Model of Decision Making

In the previous chapter we described the cognitive process, starting with an external stimulus and proceeding to its being perceived and stored. The next cognitive step is our reaction to the stimulus. For example, when we witness an accident on the highway, we might stop, we might proceed, or we might not even notice it. When we react to a stimulus, it is presumed that prior to our reaction we made a decision whether and how to react.

The *decision-making process* is intensively investigated by various scientific disciplines, particularly psychology and artificial intelligence. Psychologists are interested in learning how human beings make decisions. This is a part of their study of human mind and cognition. Scientists who study artificial intelligence are more interested in imitating human behavior using computer programs. They attempt to create machines that will simulate human reaction to various stimuli, such as chess playing, medical diagnosis, or portfolio selection. In both sciences the modeling of human decision making is of great importance. Since information systems are primarily made to support decisions, it is very important to review what is known about human decision-making processes.

Figure 3.1 Human decision-making process

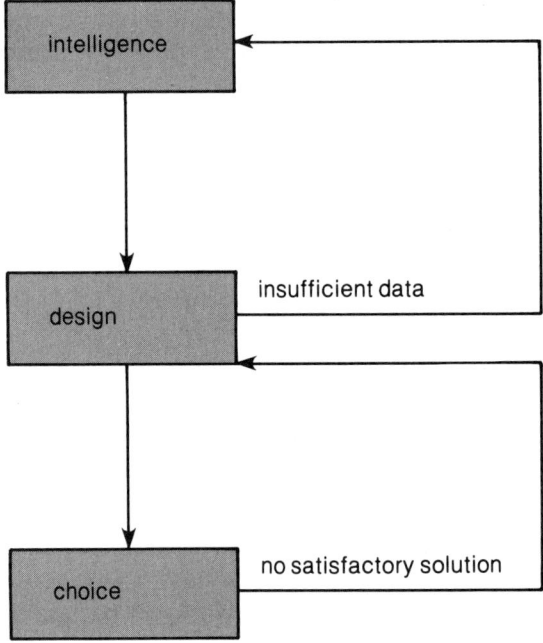

Simon's Model

H. A. Simon is considered a pioneer in the development of human decision-making models. His individual work [33] and his joint research with A. Newell [27] established the foundations for human decision-making models. His basic model depicts human decision making as a three-stage process (fig. 3.1). These stages are

1. *Intelligence*—Problem identification and data collection
2. *Design*—Planning for alternative solutions
3. *Choice*—Selecting a solution and monitoring its application

Intelligence

Prior to any decision making, the decision maker has to be aware of the need to make a decision. Generally speaking, two types of reasons might trigger a decision-making process: *problem detection* or *opportunity seeking.*

Problem detection refers to the detection of anything that is deviant—something that does not match a predetermined plan, a norm, or a standard. For example, the manager of a manufacturing firm identifies an unexpected decrease in sales. This requires a reexamination of production and marketing policies.

Opportunity seeking is finding some promising circumstances that seem to offer the decision maker a chance to better his or her wealth. For example, the manager of a manufacturing firm believes that indicated changes in consumer behavior or weaknesses detected among competitors offer solid ground for introducing a new product. Again, this requires a reexamination of production and marketing policies. This might result in the same decision as in the previous case, although the stimulus is totally different.

Whatever the stimulus that starts the decision-making process, the intelligence stage encompasses collection, classification, processing, and presentation of the data necessary to prepare the informational ground for the later stages of the decision-making process.

Design

During the *design stage* the decision maker and assisting staff outline alternative solutions, each of which involves a set of actions to be taken. They frequently use quantitative techniques and design tools such as are common in management sciences and systems analysis. The data gathered in the previous stage is now used by statistical and other models to forecast possible *outcomes* for each alternative.

Each alternative solution is examined under certain criteria. Is it technologically and economically feasible? Does it conform to regulations and common practices? Does it comply with budget and time constraints? What are its outcomes? Is the organizational unit affected by the alternative ready to adopt and execute it?

Solutions are then evaluated in order to provide the decision maker with the pros and cons for each. For example, in the case where sales are dropping, one possible solution is to intensify marketing efforts, such as by increasing advertising, hiring additional salespersons, and increasing salespersons' commission and bonus (each of which can be subdivided into different variants). An alternative is to develop a new brand or product. In the latter case, technological and time factors play an important role.

If the available data is found insufficient, the decision maker may choose to go back to the intelligence stage before making any further move. Hence, the decision-making process is an *iterative process* rather than a sequential process.

In any case, neither a final decision nor any consequent action is taken during the design stage. The decision maker then proceeds to the next stage, choice.

Choice

In the *choice stage* the decision maker is faced with various alternatives. One alternative must be selected, which becomes the formal decision and consequently generates actions to be taken. This may seem deceptively easy, but in reality there are many difficulties that usually make choice a complex stage. Let us examine them.

1. *Multipreference*—In most cases, the outcome is not measured by a single variable (unidimensional), but by several variables, not all of which are comparable. It is actually like the problem of spouse selection. Would you prefer that your spouse be wealthy and homely, or poor and beautiful? (We

will assume that the combination of wealth and beauty are unobtainable and that the combination of poor and homely calls for iterating the intelligence stage.) In businesslike decisions, we may have to determine trade-offs among various attributes of outcomes, such as customer satisfaction vis-à-vis cost of quality control. The trade-offs are not always measurable in monetary values.

2. *Uncertainty*—In many cases, outcomes are uncertain, and we have to assign probabilities to various results (see the discussion on deterministic and probabilistic systems in ch. 4). Sometimes even probability assignment is not an easy task and we have to exercise subjective judgment. Should we choose an alternative with a high chance of gaining a mediocre, yet satisfying, outcome, or an alternative with a low chance of gaining a very appealing outcome?

3. *Conflicting interests*—Organizations are composed of individuals and groups, each of which maintains a different set of preferences, ambitions, and expectations. It is likely that any decision will comply with only part of these preferences. For example, a decision to introduce a new product might hurt some of the sales personnel, at least for the short range until the new product has gained some public recognition. However, such a decision could boost the activity and morale of the production department and profit the organization in the long range. The decision maker has to assess these implications prior to making any choice.

4. *Control*—A major factor in choice among alternatives is the manageability of a policy once it has been determined. The decision maker has to assess the following: Is there enough information to enable follow-up and supervision of the new plan? (See the discussion on control in ch. 4.) Are there enough reserve resources to cope with failures? Are there fallback alternatives? Is the decision reversible?

5. *Team decision making*—In organizations many decisions are made by teams rather than by individuals. Naturally, selection of a solution that satisfies all the members of a team is much more complex.

These points demonstrate that the choice stage is not trivial. Actually, it might happen that managers table all the suggested solutions and send their staff back to the drawing board or even to collect additional data. This indicates again that the decision-making process is iterative rather than sequential.

Information Systems and the Decision-Making Process

Simon's model can be used to describe quick and short-range decisions, such as selecting the route to drive to work, as well as long-range strategic decisions, such as developing a new product. The only difference is the depth and duration of each stage. However, since our concern is with management information systems, particularly for business environments, we assume that each stage may take a relatively long period, measured in hours, days, or even months, rather than minutes.

It is obvious that each stage in the decision-making process requires a different type of information and is therefore supported by information systems with different characteristics. The information systems associated with each stage are discussed below.

MIS for the Intelligence Stage

The basic purpose of the *intelligence stage* is to acquire knowledge of what is going on internally or in the environment. Such knowledge might detect problems or raise opportunities. MIS for this stage should provide the decision maker with integrated, well-analyzed, and well-formatted data. However, it is not expected to perform sophisticated forecasts nor to utilize advanced quantitative models. It should scan data and indicate situations calling for attention. It should also provide communication channels for problems to be transferred to appropriate organizational levels.

Basically, the MIS for this stage consists of two tools: (1) predefined routine (periodic) reports and (2) features to service ad hoc queries. The routine reports delineate the current status of the organization, trace trends, and display exceptions. Nobody is capable of predicting all the information that will be required for every situation. Therefore, we equip the system with query features to provide the decision maker with a means to retrieve data (for ad hoc purposes) if the routine reports fail to match his or her needs.

For example, an information system for marketing management produces periodic reports on sales distributed according to regions or product type. These reports indicate the current status. The system also describes the history of sales during the last months for trend analysis. It might display exceptional increases or drops in sales in certain regions or for certain customers, in order to attract the decision maker's attention to these particular cases. However, should the manager wish to obtain the accounts receivable balances of all customers whose amount of purchase of product X is greater than 75 percent of their total purchase during the last quarter, it is likely that this information is not included in one of the predefined reports. Appropriate software and an online inquiry system, together with a handy terminal or a PC, may be necessary to respond to such a query.

Information for the intelligence stage is classified into two categories: *external information* generated outside of the organization; and *internal information* captured in the organization and reflecting its activities. External information is normally harder to obtain, since it is not always captured on a magnetic medium. However, recent developments of public databases (e.g., Dow-Jones, Compuserve) have made such information conveniently accessible.

It should be noted that in most cases, the internal information for the intelligence stage is a by-product of the normal data processing in organizations. If transaction processing systems (see ch. 6) are cleverly designed, then obtaining intelligence information does not require huge additional effort.

MIS for the Design Stage

In the design stage it is assumed that all the relevant and accessible data is already available for further analyses. Consequently, the information system for this stage should incorporate planning and forecasting models. Cooperative effort of management science experts and information systems professionals can provide a set of programmed models and analytic tools that could be used to sketch various future scenarios and predict and assess possible outcomes. A typical MIS for the design stage includes operations research models such as linear programming and networks and statistical models such as regression and analysis of variance. For example, in marketing management, the decision maker may wish to use network models to design product distribution, and econometric models to predict future demand.

The development of interactive software communicating with computerized data bases has facilitated data retrieval. When such tools are incorporated with software programs specially devised for planning aid (e.g., PERT [Program Evaluation and Review Technique], spreadsheet programs), it becomes quite convenient to provide decision makers with sufficient analysis of decision alternatives. The proliferation of microcomputers, particularly their software, is boosting the use of computerized systems for the design stage. (For more details see appendix A, on information system technology.)

It is important to note that design-aid systems *never* replace human decision making. They are capable only of supporting decision-making processes. At this level of management there are always additional factors that cannot be computerized, such as morale and ethics. Therefore, we often call them *decision support systems (DSS)*. An elaborate discussion of DSS is found in Keen and Morton's text [14]; see also chapter 6.

MIS for the Choice Stage

Upon reaching the stage of choice, the decision maker expects the MIS to provide three types of information: (1) highlights of the various suggested solutions; (2) possible scenarios and outcomes that might be developed as a result of taking various courses of action; and (3) feedback data for monitoring the implementation of the chosen decision.

The first type of information is merely a set of well-formatted reports summarizing the main assumptions, analyses, and results for each alternative. Managers, especially when they have confidence in their staff, are not interested in the bits and bytes of each model, nor in the internals of the programs used. It is highly important to extract only the most meaningful information for presentation.

The second type of information is vague and unstructured. Ideally, the decision maker would like to have some sort of oracle that gives answers to ''what if'' questions. ''What is going to be our profit if we introduce a new product?'' ''What is going to be our cost if we increase salespersons' salaries by 5 percent across the board?'' Apparently no computerized information system in the world is capable of providing answers to all the questions of this type. However, partial answers are attainable if we adapt simulation tools in our MIS and interface them to users by flexible query instruments (i.e., terminals and interactive software). This area in MIS, which is also considered part of DSS, is rapidly developing; many basic tools already exist (e.g., software packages for financial planning and spreadsheet programs).

The third type of information that is required for monitoring and controlling implemented decisions brings us back to solid ground. Feedback and control are achieved by collecting detailed data, processing and aggregating it, and screening it to provide significant information to management. We have to determine which data is important and when, and then adapt reliable channels to convey the information to decision makers on time. For example, if the marketing manager decides to introduce a new product, the information system department should establish a channel to update the manager on the progress in the production department. This channel might not be maintained in a normal situation. Furthermore, after the new product has been distributed, the manager would like to have more refined and frequent sales reports than usual, at least for the beginning period. Note that some office automation systems include programs that are devised to record, monitor, and follow up decisions.

Summary

We have seen that the characteristics of an information system vary in accordance with the role it plays along the decision-making process. In certain stages the required information is very well defined and structured, whereas in other parts of the process it is vague and poorly structured. Figure 3.2 summarizes the informational aspects of decision-making processes.

In the next section we will notice that information requirements vary according to decision types.

Structured and Unstructured Decisions

In his early work, Simon [33] distinguished between two types of decisions: *programmed* and *nonprogrammed*. The first term refers to human decisions that could be simulated by a computer program. The second term refers to human decisions that cannot be consistently replicated by a machine. In later literature these concepts were broadened to include a continuous spectrum of decisions ranging from programmed to nonprogrammed, and the prevailing terms are now *structured* and *unstructured* decisions.

To demonstrate this idea, examine this situation. Suppose a secretary in an office follows a standing procedure each morning. He or she has to measure the quantity of typing paper on the shelf, and if the amount is less than fifty sheets, a new order for one thousand sheets should be issued. By installing an appropriate detector attached to a computer, the secretary's task could be replaced by a computer program that would automatically issue an order upon receiving a certain signal from the detector. Hence, the decision to order (or not) is highly structured and can be programmed. However, the initial instruction specifying the quantities of fifty and one thousand sheets and the

Figure 3.2 Information required for decision-making process

decision stage   information required

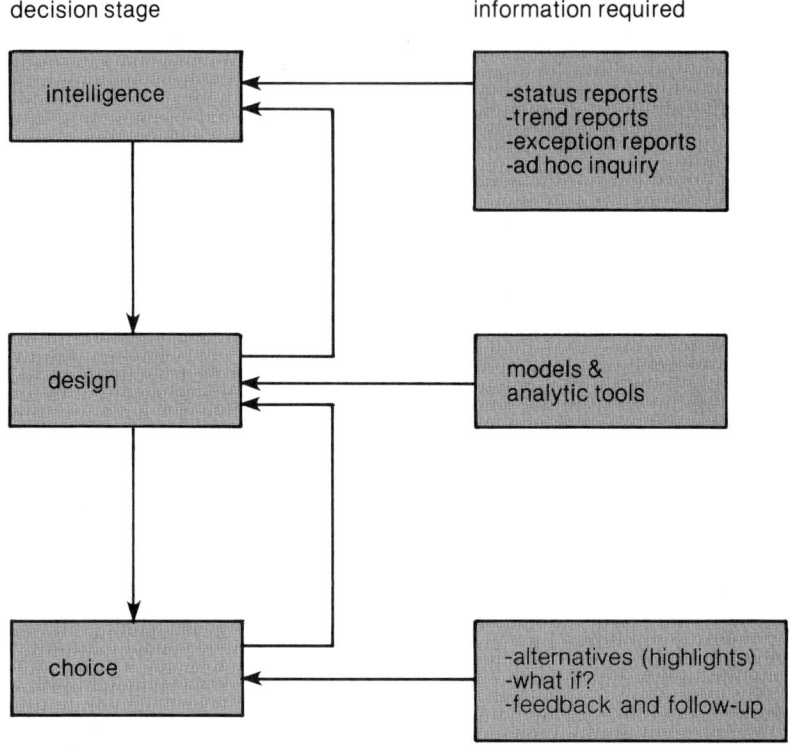

frequency of the routine check is not that structured. Still, it could be based on an inventory control model in operations research, and therefore it is partly structured. Suppose an inventory control model is applied to this case. Then, presumably, one has to select the most adequate model. The selection of the model is a nonstructured decision.

Structured decisions are based on clear logic; they are usually quantitative; the factors and the outcomes are well defined; their time horizon is short; usually they are routine and repetitive; and they are programmable. Structured decisions are normally made at the low levels of the organization (see ch. 5).

Unstructured decisions involve heuristics, trial-and-error approach, intuition, and common sense in addition to logic; the relevant factors and outcomes are somewhat vague and tend to be more qualitative than quantitative; decisions are ad hoc and seldom replicate previous decisions; their time horizon is long; they are not programmable. Unstructured decisions are normally made at the middle and top levels of the organization (see ch. 5).

Decisions under Various Degrees of Uncertainty

We have defined a spectrum of decision types ranging from structured to unstructured. Along this range, decisions may be characterized according to the degree of *uncertainty* of the problem involved. Three categories are detected in this respect:

1. *Deterministic*—Decisions that are made under certainty. For example, if we know all the grades that a student has achieved in his or her studies, we can decide whether the student is entitled to graduate. *Deterministic* decisions can often be made by a programmed *algorithm;* a sequence of operations that, through a clear route and a definite termination rule, derives the final decision. Hence, such decisions are frequently called *algorithmic* decisions and are likely to be structured.

2. *Probabilistic*—Unstructured decisions that abide by rules of statistics and probability and hence can become algorithmic (or programmed). Normally this would be a decision made under risk; there is no certainty, yet the probabilities of the relevant events are known. For example, an insurance company has to calculate the premium for a life insurance policy applicant. The premium depends mainly on the applicant's date of death, which is a random event. However, the company uses a mortality table that is based on the mortality experience of a large population of past insureds. The insurance company uses the death probability relevant to the applicant's age to determine the premium. In fact, in many insurance companies, ready-made computer programs read in the applicant's age and the face value of the policy; locate the death probability in the mortality table; add factors of interest rate, expenses, and profit; and finally print out a policy with premium notice. Such programs illustrate how *probabilistic* decisions can be transformed to algorithmic decisions.

3. *Random*—Unstructured decisions that are made under complete uncertainty; probabilities of events are not known, and sometimes even the events are not well defined. For example, how should a city council react to a major earthquake hitting the city? Random decisions are *heuristic.* They are based on experience and common sense. They cannot be programmed, though they may be supported by computerized systems. In such a situation the decision maker would be pleased upon reaching a feasible solution rather than an optimal solution.

We will now examine information requirements for the different categories of decisions.

Decision Types and Information Systems

It is obvious that information requirements vary according to the type of decisions to be supported by an information system. Structured decisions require well-defined and clearly designed information, such as exception reporting and account balances. It is relatively easy to design such systems. In many cases the computer program actually substitutes for human decisions. We are all familiar with computer warnings for not paying the electricity bill or credit card accounts. The decision to send this warning is fully programmed.

Computer programs cannot substitute for unstructured decisions. They can only support such decisions by providing the decision maker with more data, by screening alternative scenarios, and by reducing the degree of uncertainty. Information system failures occur when people misunderstand this fact of life and attempt to impose highly formal information systems on situations where they are not suitable.

Types of Decision-Maker Objectives

A controversial matter in economics and in decision theory is what kind of objectives motivate a decision maker to make a decision. The traditional economic approach claims that human beings are *optimizers,* namely, they always attempt to reach an optimal solution. This school of thought believes in rational behavior, which implies that a nonoptimal solution is not accepted by individuals. The "classical" utility theory is based on a set of axioms reflecting rational behavior (for a summary of various sets of axioms, see Luce and Raiffa [18, ch. 13]).

A different view on human objectives, *satisficing,* was developed by Simon [32]. According to the satisficing approach, human beings are limited in their computing power and in their information collection and digestion capacity. Therefore it is not likely that they can reach an optimal solution. Instead, they pose an "aspiration level" they wish to accomplish, and they stop looking for a better solution when they reach one that complies with the aspiration level criteria. (See Ahituv and Wand [6] for a quantitative model demonstrating this approach.)

Experimental findings published by Kahneman and Tversky [12] support the arguments that the human decision-making process does not abide by axioms of rational behavior. These researchers proposed another theory for human decision making, called the *prospect theory.* The main premise of the theory is that prior to reaching a decision, humans perform some editing on the data they have. In particular, they narrow down the domain of possible alternatives and they impose subjective weights that reflect their preference on the probabilities of the outcomes. (See also [28] for an example of information evaluation using prospect theory assumptions.)

Recent research in Utility Theory has attempted to incorporate some empirical findings on human behavior into the traditional axiomatic economic approach, in order to derive rigorous models and mathematical functions that realistically delineate human preferences and decision-making behavior. For details, see Machina [20], and Karni and Safra [13]. In any event, it is safe to conclude that scientists have not reached a consensus on how humans make decisions and rank-order alternatives.

The implication of this debate on information system design is somewhat indirect but certainly does exist. In a situation where it is believed that an optimal decision can be obtained (e.g., an inventory control problem), the information system should be equipped with analytic, quantitative tools (inventory control models or mathematical programming) that allow for an optimal solution. Under circumstances where an optimal solution is farfetched (e.g., takeover of a firm or R&D problems), the information system should include interactive, heuristic tools ('what if' routines, electronic spreadsheet programs, or PERT) that orderly assist the user in advancing to an acceptable solution, but one in which optimality is not guaranteed. These types of tools are very common in decision support systems (see ch. 6).

The Value of Information

The previous section outlined the decision-making process. We can conclude that information has a great impact on decision making. Therefore, any attempt to assess the value of information should be closely tied to the decision supported by the information. In other words, information does not have an absolute universal value. Its value is related to *who* uses it, *when* it is used, and in *what* situation it is used.

In this sense information is similar to any other commodity. If we wish to assign an economic value to water, for example, we first have to determine the circumstances in which the value is assessed. Obviously the worth of a glass of water is different for someone who has lost his way on the Arctic glaciers than it is to a wanderer in the Sahara Desert. Similarly, the value of knowing the results of a horse race depends on the person (whether he or she is a potential gambler), the time (before or after the race), and the situation (whether the bookmaker is accessible).

The problem becomes even more complicated, as we shall soon see, because the information value itself is not uniquely defined, and the quantity of information, or how many "units" of information we have, is rarely measurable. We will elaborate now on the problems of value and quantity of information. (See also [1] and [3] for comprehensive discussions on the value of information.)

Types of Information Value

There are alternate definitions of the value of information, as is demonstrated in this example. Suppose you intend to gamble on a horse race, and someone you fully trust offers you the exact results of a forthcoming race. Let us assume that the information is accurate and is offered solely to you. No one else will have the information prior to the commencement of the race, so certainly you are going to have a significant edge, if you acquire it. How much are you willing to pay for the information?

If you ask various scientists, you will get at least two different answers. A scholar of decision sciences, who has probably mastered statistics and probability theory, will immediately calculate your expected net income with the new information, subtract from it your expected net income without the new information, and tell you that you should not pay more than the resulting difference. If the requested price is less, you certainly have a good bargain. This difference is called the *normative* value of information. It is based on the assumption that you always reach an optimal decision.

An experimentally oriented scientist will say, "Hey, this is only in theory. In practice, we cannot always optimize. Let's do some experiments and measure the *payoffs* gained after using the new information. Let's subtract the payoffs gained when we do not utilize the information; the result will give us the *realistic* (revealed) value of the information." In other words, the value of information should be measured empirically by its impact on our performance.

Now suppose you cannot ask for the advice of these distinguished scholars, nor can you spend too much time on sophisticated calculations. You make an intuitive guess and quote a price for the offered information. In this case you have set a *subjective* value on the information. There is nothing wrong with that, and certainly you should not be ashamed. We often perform subjective evaluation in reality.

Let us pose again the preliminary question. What is the value of information? We still do not know. However, no matter how the value is defined, we already have an important observation. It is always a *relative* value, based on comparisons between payoffs gained under different sets of information. There is no absolute value of information. Bearing this important conclusion in mind, we can now discuss the various alternate values of information (see also [1] and [3]).

The Normative Value of Information

The concept of the normative value of information has been developed mostly by economists and statisticians and is derived from decision theory. Major contributions to this area are found in Marschak's work [21] and in McGuire and Radner's text [19]. It is often called the normative theory of individual decision or, more generally, information economics.

The basic premise of the theory is that we always have some preliminary knowledge about the occurrence of events (states of nature) that are relevant to our decisions. This knowledge is reflected by an a priori probability of occurrence that we assign to each event. The probability might be objective, as in the case of tossing a coin, or subjective, as in the case of predicting the winner in the Superbowl. Additional information—the coin is biased or the quarterback is injured—might modify our view of the occurrence probabilities and consequently change our decision and expected payoff. The value of the additional information is, hence, the difference in expected payoff obtained by probability modifications.

Let us examine another example. Suppose our knowledge and experience of a certain region indicate that one out of ten oil drills is successful (the figures are imaginary). It costs $1 million to drill. If the well produces, our payoff will be $100 million; otherwise, we gain nothing. Our optimal decision can be derived from table 3.1, a decision table.

The rows entitled "net payoff" indicate the payoffs gained in various combinations of decisions and events. If we decide to drill and the well produces, then the net payoff is $99 million ($100 million − $1 million). The rows entitled "expected net payoff" are derived by the multiplication of each net payoff by the probability of the event associated with it: $9,900,000 = $99,000,000 × 0.1. The right-hand column designates the totals of the expected net payoffs.

Obviously, under these circumstances, we will decide to drill in this region, having an expected net payoff of $9 million, which is better than gaining zero, should we decide not to drill.

Table 3.1   Decision Table for Oil Drilling

Event:		Success	Failure	Total Expected Net Payoff
A Priori Probability:		.1	.9	
To Drill	Net payoff	$ 99,000,000	$ −1,000,000	$
	Expected net payoff	9,900,000	−900,000	9,000,000
Not to Drill	Net payoff	0	0	
	Expected net payoff	0	0	0

Table 3.2   Probability Table of the Seismic Test

	Signal	
"Real" Event	Possible "success"	Possible "failure"
Success	.9	.1
Failure	.2	.8

Now suppose a geologist offers to conduct a thorough seismic test of the proposed drilling site. However, this test is not fully proven. When oil really does exist, the test detects it 90 percent of the time and fails to detect it 10 percent of the time. Moreover, when there is no oil, the test may mislead and indicate that there is oil 20 percent of the time. The cost is $1 million per test. The proposed test can be described by a probability table (table 3.2).

The probability table is a common presentation of an information system in the normative theory. It is often called an *information structure*. Note that each row totals 1.0.

If we acquire the geologist's services, how does it affect our decision and expected payoff?

If we buy the services and always decide not to drill, then we certainly lose $1 million (the cost of the test). If we always decide to drill, then our initial expected net income of $9 million is reduced by the test cost, leaving us with a net expected payoff of only $8 million. These two strategies are initially inferior to not performing the test, and therefore we rule them out.

Let us examine the expected net payoff in the case where we drill on a "success" signal from the test and refrain from drilling on a "failure" signal.

Using *Bayes theorem,* the probability of success, given a "success" signal—Pr(success/ "success")—is as follows:

$$\frac{\text{Pr("success"/success)} \cdot \text{Pr(success)}}{\text{Pr("success"/success)} \cdot \text{Pr(success)} + \text{Pr("success"/failure)} \cdot \text{Pr(failure)}}$$

Substituting our values from tables 3.1 and 3.2, we get

$$\frac{.9 \times .1}{.9 \times .1 + .2 \times .9} = .33 \text{ (rounded).}$$

Similarly, we get the probability of failure, given a "success" signal—Pr (failure/ "success")—as follows:

$$\frac{.2 \times .9}{.9 \times .1 + .2 \times .9} = .67 \text{ (rounded).}$$

The total probability of obtaining the "success" signal—Pr("success")—is calculated as follows:

Pr("success"/success) $\cdot$ Pr(success) + Pr("success"/failure) $\cdot$ Pr(failure); which is

$$.9 \times .1 + .2 \times .9 = .27$$

and therefore the complementary probability of getting a "failure" signal is .73.

Hence, in 73 percent of the cases we spend $1 million on the test and do not proceed, so we lose $1 million. In 27 percent of the cases we drill. In that case our expected net income would be

$$.33 \times 98,000,000 + .67 \times (-2,000,000) = \$31,000,000. \tag{3.1}$$

All together, our expected net payoff is

$$.27 \times 31,000,000 + .73 \times (-1,000,000) = \$7,640,000. \tag{3.2}$$

The emerging result clearly indicates that it is not worthwhile to buy the information (the test) for $1 million, since without it we might do better ($9 million on the average). Actually, we can calculate the maximum price that we would be willing to pay for the proposed test. Suppose it were offered free. Then expression (3.1) becomes

$$.33 \times 99,000,000 + .67 \times (-1,000,000) = \$32,000,000$$

and expression (3.2) becomes

$$.27 \times 32,000,000 + .73 \times 0 = \$8,640,000.$$

Table 3.3   Information Structure of Another Seismic Test

"Real" Event	Signal	
	Possible "success"	Possible "failure"
Success	.95	.05
Failure	.0	1.0

Table 3.4   A Complete and Perfect Information Structure

"Real" Event	Signal	
	Possible "success"	Possible "failure"
Success	1	0
Failure	0	1

Surprisingly, we should not use the information even if we get it free because it actually scrambles our knowledge (the expected net payoff without it is $9 million and with it is $8,640,000!). The information structure presented in table 3.2 is called a "noisy" one since it does not display deterministic signals. You should not, however, deduce from this that a noisy system is never worthwhile. Examine for a moment the structure in table 3.3, which reflects another test.

The new test indicates a successful well in 95 percent of the cases where oil exists, even though it never fails (100 percent accuracy) to indicate a dry drilling. Despite its utility, the structure is still noisy.

In this case, when we observe a "success" signal and we drill, we certainly succeed, so our net payoff is $99 million (excluding the test cost). However, we drill only after getting a "success" signal. The probability of getting it—Pr("success")—is as follows:

Pr("success"/success) · Pr(success) + Pr("success"/failure) · Pr(failure), which is

Pr("success") = .95 × .1 + 0 × .9 = .095.

Hence, in 9.5 percent of the cases we drill and find oil and in 90.5 percent we do nothing. Our expected net payoff (excluding the test cost) is:

.095 × 99,000,000 + .905 × 0 = $9,405,000.

You can now figure out the value of the information provided by the second test. It is exactly $405,000 ($9,405,000 − $9,000,000), so it is worthwhile to acquire the test for any price that is less than $405,000.

Finally, suppose we are offered a perfect test that always predicts the right event. This is called a *complete and perfect* information structure, and its probability structure is described in table 3.4.

In this case, if the test is carried out, we drill when we observe a "success" signal; otherwise, we do nothing. We will get a "success" signal in 10 percent of the tests. Hence, our expected net payoff is

$.1 \times 99,000,000 + .9 \times 0 = \$9,900,000.$

Consequently, even for a perfect test we would be unwilling to pay more than $900,000, and probably even less.

The preceding example depicts a quantitative calculation of the value of information. The main advantages of the normative value are first, it compels the evaluator to execute a systematic and well-structured assessment, which is not frequently performed in MIS, and second, it enables an *ex ante* evaluation; the comparison of alternative systems and their possible payoffs is done prior to the installation of a concrete system.

However, this approach is rarely applicable since it requires exact measurability of all the factors—the a priori probabilities, the conditional probabilities of signals, and the payoffs. In reality we are not always capable of even estimating these figures, especially the probabilities of events. Furthermore, in reality we do not always express payoffs in monetary values, and therefore cost and payoffs become incomparable by rigorous mathematical computation. The normative approach assumes also that, given the signal, the decision maker is perfect and never errs. In reality, it is sometimes difficult to distinguish between "bad" systems and "bad" decisions, not to mention possible wrong perceptions of signals (see ch. 2 and [2]).

To demonstrate, let us consider another example. Suppose we wish to install a communication network among fire stations throughout a city. Consider the following alternatives:

1. A communication network among the fire stations—In this case we maintain control only over stationary servers. Once a fire engine is dispatched, no contact is made until after it returns to its home station.

2. A communication apparatus in every fire engine—In this case, the dispatcher may opt to reroute a moving server, should it be necessary.

Mathematically, the problem is solvable by management sciences and information economics tools (see [4] ch. 8). However, in order to apply the solution, we have to learn all the probabilities of calls and signals, arrival and service distributions, etc. Even if these are attainable, comparing the communication (information) networks will result in expected response time for calls, which certainly affects the number of casualties and injuries, and amount of property loss. How can we measure on the same scale the saving of lives, the misery of human beings, the loss of property, and the cost of the communication system? Probably we cannot. That is the main reason why these models are rarely applied, and if they are, it is mostly for a very structured problem, such as inventory control.

A last, but not least, hurdle is that the models are individual oriented. When we come to organizational reality, we have to face many individuals with different decisions and preferences. A system that is suitable for one is inappropriate for the other or simply does not serve his or her needs. An extension of the normative theory, called team theory [22], attempts to evaluate information systems for groups of people who satisfy some initial constraints. Again, team theory is not widely applicable.

The Realistic Value of Information

We already recognize that information supports decisions, decisions trigger actions, and actions affect the achievements of the information user (individual or organization). It is thus a logical deduction that by measuring differences in achievement, we can trace the impact of information, provided that the measurement is carefully performed, the relations among variables are well defined, and possible effects of irrelevant factors are isolated. The common term for achievement is *performance,* and the measured difference in performance due to informational factors is called the realistic or *revealed* value of information.

The use of performance as a surrogate for information value offers a significant advantage. We are no longer required to study the bits and bytes of the system, to formulate mathematical models, or to inquire about probabilities and strategies. We consider information processing/decision making as a black box. We feed the black box with various controlled inputs and we measure the outputs.

Another advantage is the measurability of the variables, particularly the output. In a business environment, performance can be measured by profit, response time, accuracy of reaction, etc. Still, we might have problems in relating change in performance to changes in the information and in isolating uncontrolled variables. But these problems may be overcome.

An experiment of this type was conducted by Mock [23]. He measured the effects of providing the decision maker with up-to-date or delayed prices of raw materials for production decisions and found the value of information with respect to its recency (timeliness). The experiment was conducted in a laboratory environment, where the experimentees had to respond to information displayed on terminals attached to a computer, which simulated a businesslike situation. Mock was also able to calculate the normative value of information, since the decision problem was highly structured. A comparison between the normative and the realistic values showed significant differences. Two other experiments were conducted by Hedberg [11] and Edstrom [9]. Both measured the impact of an online vis-à-vis batch information system (see also [8] for a summary of other experiments in this field).

There is no doubt that the realistic value is a good measure because it takes into account human factors related to perception and preferences as well as the technical characteristics of the information system. As a matter of fact, the normative approach is sometimes criticized because of its fundamental premise that human beings are fully rational and wish to optimize. The realistic value adheres to the satisficing idea because it reflects the performance that is actually attained rather than the one that should be attained.

Recall our introductory story about horse-race gambling. If the gambler makes an additional $200 due to the additional information, then $200 is the value of the information, notwithstanding that he could have made $700 had he been rational and in full command of statistics and probability theory.

However, we have a major obstacle in applying the realistic value approach. It is an *ex post* measure; namely, it stems from an existing system(s), so it requires an installed system(s) prior to its assessment. This could be handled so long as we remain on experimental ground. In laboratories we can install several alternative systems, control external factors, and measure the performance of human guinea pigs. But, could you imagine a company installing several alternative systems simultaneously, measuring the performance achieved by each system, and then eliminating the inferior systems? It is a totally unrealistic scenario.

The problem of experimenting with an information system before it is fully constructed has been partly resolved by recent technology. The availability of fourth generation software packages called *application generators* allows system developers to develop and test *prototypes* of an information system during the development stage (see chs. 9 and 10 for more details on system development). In some cases, prototyping may help in measuring the realistic value of information before a full-scale system is installed. However, the contribution of prototyping is better realized in measuring the subjective value of information (see next section).

To sum up, we can use the realistic value approach if we are able to set up an experiment, provided that it is not too expensive and its similarity to reality is assured. Never mislead yourself and others by magnified deductions, such as if a half-pound frog is capable of long jumping eight feet, then a two-hundred-pound frog will long jump 3,200 feet.

The Subjective Value of Information

Most information systems, in particular those supporting middle and top management, support decisions in which events are not strictly defined, probabilities are unobtainable, the decision-making process is obscure, and the outcomes are scaled by multiple and incomparable dimensions. In such cases we may either attempt to perform a multiattribute analysis, as presented later in this chapter, or derive an overall subjective value.

The subjective value reflects people's comprehensive impression of information. In several studies, individuals were confronted with alternative outputs (reports) and asked for opinions on each. Usually they were requested to rank order the alternatives, to designate their satisfaction on a scale (from 1 to 10 or from 1 to 7), or to estimate how much they were willing to pay for each report.

A typical example of this type of research is presented in Munro and Davis [25]. They used a scale from 1 to 7 to determine the subjective value of information. The variables investigated were decision type (structured or unstructured) and decision area (administrative or academic).

Ronen and Falk [29] conducted an experiment whose participants had to buy different degrees of detailed (disaggregated) data in order to make some financial decisions. They used the amount of money offered as an estimate for the subjective value.

You could conduct a hypothetical experiment yourself. For example, if the price of a newspaper is hiked, at which point would you stop buying it? This breakeven point is probably your maximum subjective value of the newspaper information.

Several problems stem from the subjective value approach. How objective is the subjective value? In other words, can we rely on the subjective assessment when we evaluate and select an information system, or is it so tied to individuals that the entire evaluation might change upon the substitution of some key personnel?

The second problem involves monetary comparison. In many cases, the subjective value is an ordinal number, say between 1 and 7, which does not enable any monetary interpretation. Suppose, for example, that system A is graded 4 and system B is graded 4.5. System A costs $20,000 and system B costs $25,000. It is hard to tell which system should be installed.

The last, but not least, problem is one with which we are already familiar. The subjective value is again an ex post variable. It can be measured after the information is available. We can prepare some artificial reports and perform an experiment, distribute a questionnaire, or conduct interviews; but would they represent reality? A partial solution can be obtained by devising prototypes, as explained earlier during the discussion of realistic value.

An expansion of the subjective scaling method can be performed by using the Analytic Hierarchy Process (AHP) developed by Saaty [30]. An application of AHP to the evaluation of an accounting information system is reported by Arbel and Seidmann [7].

Some Concluding Remarks

We have thus qualified (actually, disqualified) the practicality of three approaches to measuring the value of information. We suspect that your a priori expectations were that, upon reading this section, you would have a definite and decisive method of measuring the value of information. However, we cannot point out the ultimate value of information, nor can anybody else. All we can do is convey some thoughts and ideas and classify them. It is your task to decide which method to utilize, when, where, and how.

We have yet another problem, and that is how to measure the quantity of information. We will discuss that now.

The Quantity of Information

The previous discussion on the value of information could be regarded as a detour. We managed to treat the information value without assigning any quantity measure to the information. In other words, we did not start our discussion by raising the question of how many information units we have, but skipped directly to the question of how much the information is worth.

This is not the normal way to treat economic commodities and services. Normally we begin with the definition of the entity (shirts, tomatoes, crude oil, transportation services, milk, storage, medical services, etc.). Then we assign an appropriate measure for the entity (units of shirts, weight of tomatoes, barrels of oil, length of roads, volume of milk, capacity of warehouse, hours of work). Having the measure, we then quantify the amount of the entity to arrive at its monetary value.

Let us assume that our basic entity is data. Let us even narrow the discussion to only written and printed data, represented by letters and digits. We can certainly quantify data by counting the number of characters (letters and digits), the number of words, or the number of sentences. In data processing we can count the record length and the number of records. Suppose we are faced with the number 535253500. It contains nine digits. What is its worth? We still cannot tell because we do not know the *meaning* of the number. It could be the winning number in a lottery; a portion of a telephone number; or if we write it 535–25–3500, it could be a Social Security number. We must identify the user, the time, and the situation in which the data is used before we can perform any type of evaluation.

Although characters, words, and sentences are legitimate measures for the quantity of data, there is a more sophisticated technique for measuring: the entropy function.

The Entropy Function

The entropy function is a prevailing concept in physics, particularly in thermodynamics. It serves as a measure for the degree of disorder (randomness) or diversification in certain states of nature. Shannon and Weaver [31] suggested that this function be adopted for use in communication and information theory. We can demonstrate their ideas using a simple example.

Suppose you toss a coin and examine the results. "The probability of getting heads or tails is the same: one half." Denote these two possibilities p_h and p_t, respectively, and calculate the following expression:

$$H = -(p_h \log_2 p_h + p_t \log_2 p_t)$$

where $\log_2$ is the logarithmic function on the base of 2.

Put the value of one-half into this expression and you will obtain

$$H = -(\tfrac{1}{2} \times \log_2 \tfrac{1}{2} + \tfrac{1}{2} \times \log_2 \tfrac{1}{2}) = -[2 \times \tfrac{1}{2} \times (-1)] = 1.$$

The term denoted by H is called the entropy function. In this case its value equals 1, and it indicates complete uncertainty about the outcome of a toss.

In order to clarify the nature of the function, let us examine another case. Suppose we know that the coin is unbalanced so that the head appears more often—say, in 60 percent of the tosses. The entropy function in this case is

$$H(unbalanced) = -(0.6 \times \log_2 0.6 + 0.4 \times \log_2 0.4) =$$
$$-[0.6 \times (-0.74) + 0.4 \times (-1.32)] = 0.972.$$

Notice that the entropy value has decreased. Intuitively we may say that the degree of disorder was reduced because one of the events (heads) appears more frequently—the game is less uncertain. Following the same logic, we would expect the entropy to further decrease as the probability of one of the events increases. In the extreme case, suppose the coin always falls so that the head side faces upward. The p_h value equals 1 and p_t equals 0.

$$H(certainty) = -(1 \times \log_2 1 + 0 \times \log_2 0).$$

The second term is not instantaneously defined. For the sake of our discussion we assume that $0 \times \log_2 0$ equals zero. Hence,

H(certainty) $= -(0 + 0) = 0$.

We note that under certainty the entropy value has been reduced to zero. Actually you can easily notice that in the case of only two possible events, the entropy function reaches its maximum value when the probabilities are both equal to one-half and its minimum value is obtained under certainty. The greater the uncertainty, the more information is required to clarify the situation. The values of the entropy function then reflect the amount of transferred information necessary to reduce uncertainty to various levels.

The general formula of entropy for numerous events, say n, whose probabilities of occurrence are $p_1, \ldots, p_n$, is

$$H = - \sum_{i=1}^{n} p_i \log p_i.$$

The use of the number 2 for the logarithmic base is not a must, but it is usually convenient. The entropy reaches its maximum when every event has the same probability of occurrence, namely, $p_i = 1/n$ for all i. In this case we get

$$H = - \sum_{i=1}^{n} (1/n) \times \log (1/n) =$$
$$-n \times (1/n) \times \log (1/n) = \log n.$$

And, indeed, for the toss of a balanced coin, $H = \log_2 2 = 1$.

Note that if the number of events, n, increases, but still all of them have equal probabilities, $1/n$, then the value of H will also increase. This makes sense because the degree of uncertainty increases, since we have more possible events to consider.

Under certainty, one of the events (say, p_1) always occurs where all others never occur. Hence,

$$H = - (1 \times \log 1 + \sum_{i=2}^{n} 0 \times \log 0) = 0.$$

This is consistent with our concept of the quantity of information. In other words, you do not have to transfer information if everyone knows what is happening. For example, we all know that the sun rises in the east. The value of this information is zero.

We may conclude that the function of information is to reduce uncertainty by reducing the variety of choice (fewer events) or decreasing the randomness of events. In both cases, the entropy function reflects the quantity of information that is required to reduce uncertainty.

Entropy and Coding

The entropy function and some later extensions of the concept are widely used to develop efficient codes and to measure the capacity of communication channels. Examine this example. Suppose the characters available to you are only the binary digits

Table 3.5   A Binary Code for Class Grades

Grade	Code
A	00
B	01
C	10
D	11

Table 3.6   Nonuniform Grade Distribution and Its Entropy

Grade	Probability (p_i)	$\log_2 p_i$	$p_i \log_2 p_i$
A	.25	−2	− .5
B	.50	−1	− .5
C	.15	−2.74	− .411
D	.10	−3.32	− .332
			−1.743

Table 3.7   A Revised Grade Code

Grade	Code
A	01
B	1
C	001
D	000

(bits)—0 and 1—and you wish to code the final grades A, B, C, and D in a class (no Fs in our class). You may set an arbitrary code as in table 3.5.

Note that only a two-bit-long code is required to convey all the information. If we assume that the probability of each grade is equally likely—0.25—then the entropy function becomes

$$H = - \sum_{i=1}^{4} 0.25 \times \log_2 0.25 = -4 \times 0.25 \times \log_2 0.25 = 2.$$

We see that the entropy value is equivalent to the number of bits required to communicate each event (message length). Generally the entropy value serves as an estimate for the average message length in a communication network. Based on this we can define the quantity of information as the average code size (number of bits) necessary to identify a message from the set of messages to which it belongs.

Now suppose the distribution of grades is not uniform as in the preceding example. It is, rather, presented by the probabilities in table 3.6.

The entropy value equals 1.743 bits. If we maintain the preceding code, we will have an average (constant) message length of two bits. However, the entropy value implies that a shorter average message length is possible. Let us check the code in table 3.7.

The new proposed code is based on the frequency of the messages. In 25 percent of the messages (grade A), we will transmit two bits; in 50 percent (grade B), one bit; in 25 percent (grades C and D), three bits. The expected (average) message length would then be

$$.25 \times 2 + .5 \times 1 + .25 \times 3 = 1.75 \text{ bits.}$$

On the average, we save 0.25 bits per message if we switch over to the new code. Moreover, the entropy value (1.743) implies that we could not do much better even if we look for another code because we would never get below an average of 1.743 bits. In fact, we may develop a ratio that indicates the efficiency of a code.

I_n—information capacity needed (the entropy of the events)

I_c—information capacity of the code (the entropy of the code),

and define

$$R = 1 - I_n/I_c.$$

This ratio reflects the percentage of "wasted" code, or, how far the code is from maximum efficiency. If we had used the code in table 3.5 for the nonuniform distribution of grades (table 3.6), we would have gotten

$$R = 1 - \frac{1.743}{2} = 0.1285.$$

This means that we are 12.85 percent above the most efficient code size.

The ratio derived from the code given in table 3.7 is

$$R = 1 - \frac{1.743}{1.75} = 0.004,$$

which means that we are very close to optimum. This ratio is called *redundancy* since it reflects the amount of "redundant" bits that could have been saved. It should be noted that when it comes to communication lines and channel capacity, redundancy might hamper efficiency. However, information systems in general are not always hurt by redundancy. On the contrary, redundancy may sometimes be required to simplify code structure; some redundancy helps in solving backup problems; and redundancy certainly improves the perception of data (see ch. 2).

Note that if the code does not provide a unique deciphering procedure it is not acceptable. In the first example, every two bits constitute a message. In the second example, the deciphering rule is the following: A message is completed when you encounter a 1 bit or after three consecutive zeros. If we could not establish this rule, we would have to reject the code in spite of its efficiency.

Entropy and Value of Information

The entropy function is widely used in communication networks and in coding for the assessment of *channel capacity* and code efficiency. However, for economic evaluation of information, its use is limited. It is deficient in relating *meaning* to messages. In other words, it does not convey any significance to the bits and probabilities. Thus, while reflecting a technical aspect, the entropy function lacks the semantic aspect of information.

For example, if you toss a balanced coin and wish to transmit the results, you get an entropy value of one. If your physician tells you that you require major surgery and have a fifty-fifty chance of surviving, you still get an entropy of one. Obviously, the value of the information that would give you better prior knowledge of the outcome is different in these two cases. The difference cannot be expressed by entropy values. The results of experimental research conducted by Ronen and Falk [29] also discourage the use of entropy as a measure for the value of information. Similar results were derived analytically in [19, ch 6].

Therefore, we confine ourselves to utilizing the entropy function for technical specification of codes and communication channels, and we refrain from using it in an economic evaluation of information.

Information System Evaluation

The previous discussion focused on problems of information measurement. Our main concern was information value and quantity. We could not arrive at clear-cut conclusions, definitions, terms, and practices. However, rapid advancements in information processing technology compel us to establish evaluation practices, even though the theoretical foundations are somewhat impractical.* In other words, when you have to design or select a new information system, you have to perform evaluations and comparisons of alternatives and come up with a clear decision, whether your conclusions stem from a well-formulated theory or from some rule of thumb. Furthermore, most information systems are too large and complex, making it impossible to isolate rigorous probabilities, identify discrete events and signals, write down explicit payoffs, and develop rigid decision rules. Apparently we ought to find practical methods for evaluation of information systems (which is wider than evaluation of information).

In general, our search for evaluative methods is concentrated in two areas: the information system's attributes (characteristics) and its benefits. In the first case, we attempt to identify the major characteristics of the systems, such as the timeliness, accuracy, or data formatting. In the second case, we try to indicate the anticipated benefits after the system has been installed—reduction of inventory levels, faster service, shorter credit periods, and the like.

---

*Some parts of this section are cited from ''A Systematic Approach Towards Assessing the Value of an Information System'' by N. Ahituv in *MIS Quarterly* 4, no. 4 (December 1980). Copyright 1980 by The Society for Management Information Systems Research Center. Reprinted by permission of the publisher.

Let us illustrate these methods. Suppose you consider the purchase of a new car and compare various brands. You can base your comparison on the manufacturers' specifications: fuel consumption; maximum speed; mean time and mileage between routine servicing; engine displacement; acceleration rate; etc. In this case you fragment the whole system (car) into some major properties and hope to get a clue as to the best buy.

On the other hand, you could compare the benefits provided by each brand: the amount of money that you save on gas; the time it takes you to drive home; the number of times you visit a service station during a year; your safety; etc.

Of course, it would be ideal if we could relate characteristics to benefits and come up with an explicit formula by which we can measure the impact of attributes on benefits. However, more often we analyze only one of the areas and assume that the other one is implied.

Information System Attributes

The basic premise here is that the quality of an information system is affected by its major characteristics (*attributes*). Hence, should we wish to distinguish between systems, we would do better to refer to sets of representative attributes than to a system as a whole. In a similar way we distinguish between persons by referring to attributes such as height, weight, color, sex, etc.

The principal categories of information system attributes are the following (see also Kleijnen [16, ch. 7]):

1. Timeliness
2. Content
3. Format
4. Cost

Timeliness

Timeliness is not a single attribute, but a class of attributes all related to the time factor in information update and retrieval. Figure 3.3 diagrams some of these attributes.

Suppose a relevant event occurs at time t_0. It takes a while to record (to code), to keytype, and to process the data, so the related file(s) is updated at time t_1. It might also take a while until the user (decision maker) gets the report detailing this event—say, at time t_2. Eventually the *currency* (age) of the data presented to the user is measured by the difference $t_2 - t_0$. The currency of the file is $t_1 - t_0$ and the *response time* of the reporting subsystem is $t_2 - t_1$. Normally the user is interested in the currency of the data presented to him or her—namely, the difference $t_2 - t_0$. When this amount of time is very short, we describe the system as a *real-time* system. Real-time systems are feasible only if an online technology is adopted (as opposed to batch processing). Of course, the total currency is implied by the file currency ($t_1 - t_0$) and response time ($t_2 - t_1$). However, you may require a system in which the response time is instantaneous yet the update is performed only once a day. In this case you will face the same data all day long, but you will get it immediately upon request.

Figure 3.3 Data flow along time

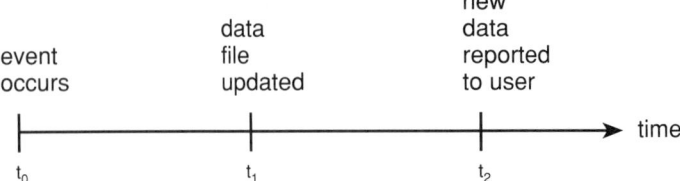

Let us examine a case of personal bank accounts. A relevant event could be the cashing of a check. Keying and computer processing update the customer account. A balance report conveys the information to the teller at the branch. If the entire operation is performed in batch-processing mode on a daily basis, then the currency of data the teller uses is one day. Now, suppose the check's data is immediately keytyped into the computer, yet printed reports are distributed once a day; or suppose data is entered into the computer in batches daily, yet the teller possesses a terminal for queries. In both cases the data currency is still one day, yet file currency and response time are different. Only when the input and output are instantaneous can we refer to a system as a real-time information system. We have here three time-related attributes, of which the total currency seems to be the most important.

In addition to currency, you may sometime consider the *frequency* of reports. For example, if you own a credit card, you probably receive a monthly statement of your daily transactions. For most purposes a monthly frequency is sufficient (note that the currency of data in this case ranges from approximately two months to a few days). If you manage a portfolio of bonds and shares (yet you are not a professional broker or speculator), you will probably be satisfied with daily rate information from the stock exchanges. Moreover, you probably would not like yesterday's information at the end of today's business hours, nor would you insist on waking up at 3:00 A.M. to have yesterday's rates. Morning delivery of the data is quite reasonable. Hence, we have here a typical cyclical value depending upon the frequency and timing of reports.

To conclude, currency and frequency are common attributes related to timeliness. The former is highly emphasized in most systems; the latter is particularly important in periodic information systems.

Content

Content attributes relate to the meaning of information to decision makers. Meaning is difficult to measure. Nevertheless, we have to take it into account. Generally speaking, for top- and middle-level management, information content is more crucial than timeliness. Neumann and Segev [26] even found a spillover effect of content on other attributes of information.

Accuracy   The importance of accurate data varies with the type of decisions supported by the data. Long-range strategic decisions involve data that is normally less accurate than the data required for low-level prompt decisions (see ch. 5 for further discussion).

Theoretically, we measure accuracy by comparing the actual data to the "true" events. Practically, it is not always applicable; first because we do not often know the "true" events; second because this is an ex post evaluation, and we prefer an ex ante assessment. We overcome these problems either by taking samples of data and performing statistical estimates or by investigating the quality of the keying and editing functions in our information system. Normally we can expect more accurate data whenever a more comprehensive validation check is involved (e.g., online keying to computer vis-à-vis offline data capture).

Relevance   Information is relevant if it leads or might lead to a different decision. It might also be relevant if it reaffirms a previous decision. If it does not have anything to do with your problem, it is irrelevant. For example, information about the weather conditions in Hawaii in January is relevant if you are considering a trip to Hawaii in January or if you have already booked the trip and need reinforcement (in the latter case the value is more psychologically essential than statistically computable). Otherwise the information is useless.

Again, measurement of relevance is a severe problem. A mathematical treatment of relevance is discussed in Feltham's monograph [10]. Even there the author admits [pp. 83–84] that relevance measurement usually provides an ex post value. In practice we try to design relevant reports after performing a qualitative information requirement analysis [24] and imposing the requirements on the reporting design. The use of prototyping techniques is certainly a great help.

Exhaustiveness   Sometimes information is relevant yet incomplete. In this case we say that the data is inexhaustive. For example, if you plan to tour Hawaii and get the average temperatures in January, but not the amount of precipitation for that month, your information is relevant but not exhaustive. We would expect a better decision when the exhaustiveness is greater.

Once more we are faced with a problem of ex post measurement since it is hard to criticize information exhaustiveness prior to making a decision and examining the results. As was mentioned in the discussion on relevance, information requirement analysis and prototyping may help, though these are not the ultimate solutions.

Redundancy   Is redundant information good or bad? There is no clear-cut rule about it. For example, if your mother keeps telling you how nice the neighbor's daughter or son is, and you should really try to marry this person, you might develop adverse feelings due to information redundancy (and some other factors). However, when the sheriff posts signs to warn against swimming in a beach infested with sharks, redundancy might help. Generally redundancy is not bad when we wish to shed or to stress some data. It becomes boring and may cause negative reaction if we exaggerate. The possible merits of redundancy can be measured by experiments.

Table 3.8   Entropy of Accounting Statements

Item	Amount	Amount/Total (p)	$-p \log_2 p$
A	1000	0.25	0.5
B	1000	0.25	0.5
C	500	0.125	0.375
D	500	0.125	0.375
E	1000	0.25	0.5
Total	4000		2.25

(a) Entropy equals 2.25

Item	Amount	Amount/Total (p)	$-p \log_2 p$
A&B	2000	0.5	1.0
C&D	1000	0.25	0.5
E	1000	0.25	0.5
Total	4000		2.0

(b) With additional aggregation, entropy is reduced to 2.0

Level of detail (aggregation level)   The traditional attitude toward data aggregation was that information was lost, yet this was necessary because of time and space limitations. This attitude has been changed in statistics as well as in MIS (see [8]). We now understand that too-detailed data might confuse, mislead, and prevent the user from acquiring comprehensive knowledge of a problem area. It is likely that for each decision problem there is an optimal level of detail (not too much and not too little). For example, the required level of detail of a firm's accounting statements varies among different information users. Auditors require a detailed statement, shareholders would probably be satisfied with a more condensed statement, and the Bureau of Statistics would like it even shorter.

Theoretically the optimal level of detail is defined as the level under which any more detailed information would not improve our decision and above which any further aggregation would worsen the decision. In practice it is difficult to identify this optimal level. Lev [17] suggested adopting the entropy function for aggregation measurement, particularly in accounting statements. The idea is fairly simple. Take each item in the statement and divide it by the total. Assuming all items are nonnegative figures, we get ratios ranging from zero to one. These ratios may be treated, then, in the same way as probabilities. Thus, different aggregations provide different values of entropy. Table 3.8 illustrates this idea.

Part (a) of table 3.8 displays an accounting statement in which entropy equals 2.25. In part (b), some of the items (A and B, C and D) have been combined, giving an entropy of 2.0. Hence entropy has been reduced by 0.25 due to additional aggregation.

Although it is clear from a mathematical viewpoint, we still lack any interpretation related to the meaning of the various items. We could have obtained the same result had we combined items A and E instead of A and B. Therefore this tool is useful, but in only a limited number of applications [see also 29]. In practice we are mostly limited to qualitative analysis of aggregation requirements.

Format

The format of reported information has many possible attributes. Some of these are listed here.

1. *Medium*—The instrument by which the report is provided, such as printed, visual display, plotter (graphs), microfilm, etc.

2. *Ordering*—The way the data is arranged in the report, such as the order of the columns (horizontal ordering), the sequencing of details and totals (vertical ordering), etc.

3. *Graphic design*—The setting of the report, such as colors, letter sets, font, use of graphs, etc.

The main problem regarding evaluation of format-related attributes is that quantitative variables cannot be obtained, hence the use of an analytical approach is almost impossible. Two methods can be used to incorporate these attributes for the assessment of the information system. First, since in reality the number of alternatives here is very small, the user may be asked to rank order his or her preference explicitly. Second, some of those attributes, which are no more than technological characteristics, can be used as constraints for the other categories of attributes. For example, use of a line printer imposes a constraint on response time. As usual, the most recommended approach to evaluate format alternatives is prototyping.

Comprehensive Evaluation Incorporating Information Attributes and Cost

The previous discussion presented a somewhat arbitrary list of attributes related to the assessment of the value of an information system. Its main purpose was to demonstrate an approach, rather than to set an ultimate attribute list. In addition to the value attributes, we also have to incorporate the cost of each alternative system. We may treat the cost as an additional attribute.

Suppose we have an exhaustive and representative list of information attributes and have managed to assess their values. How do we proceed to a comprehensive evaluation of the information system?

In an ideal situation, from the evaluator point of view, every relevant attribute would be known and measurable; the user benefit (utility) function related to each individual attribute would be clearly defined; and the trade-offs among the various attributes would be available and would provide a clear mathematical formulation of the (joint) user utility function relating to all the attributes. In this case, an adequate optimization technique would lead to an optimal solution. However, such cases rarely occur.

Suppose that constructing a joint utility function is not feasible. Moreover, even the marginal utility function for each individual attribute is not available. The user can only rank order the possible values of attributes (provided that they are measurable) according to his or her preferences. In that case, one of the following evaluation methods is recommended:

1. *Lexicographical ordering* [15, pp. 77–79]—This approach is useful if the value of attributes can be rank ordered according to their importance and if trade-offs are not accepted among them (the user is not willing to trade a possible decrease in a certain attribute for an increase in another). For example, suppose the response time, t, is the most important attribute. Hence, if $t_1 > t_2$ (t_1 and t_2 being estimates of response time for systems 1 and 2), then system 2 is selected regardless of the value of any other attribute (if the user prefers a shorter response time). If $t_1 = t_2$, then the next attribute is examined, and so on.

   This method should be used if one attribute is clearly dominant. It can be refined by bounding attributes between some given constraints. However, cases in which such *dominance* exists are quite rare.

2. The *efficient frontier* [15, pp. 69–77]—Let $y' = (y'_1, \ldots, y'_n)$ and $y'' = (y''_1, \ldots, y''_n)$ be two sets of information attributes. We say that y' dominates y'' whenever $y'_i \geq y''_i$ for all i, and $y'_i > y''_i$ for some i. (The relations $>$ and $\geq$ reflect the preference of the user and not necessarily the numerical values of the attributes.)

   In our case, system j dominates system k if at least one value of its attributes is better than the corresponding value of k and if the other values of j are not worse than the corresponding values of k.

   The set of all the systems that are not dominated by any other system (cost is considered as an attribute) will be called the ''efficient frontier.'' Each proposed system that does not belong to the efficient frontier can be eliminated. However, the problem remaining is how to select *a system* out of all members of the efficient frontier. Keeney and Raiffa [15] suggest some heuristic ways, such as setting constraints to all the attributes less one and selecting the best system with regard to the remaining attribute, so long as the constraints are satisfied. (In the next section we present a case in which the efficient frontier approach has been applied.) A further refinement suggested by them would be to weigh each attribute and select the system with the best ''weighted average.''

3. *Statistical analysis*—If you can afford to produce some representative reports and conduct a survey among users, you may come up with enough data to perform some statistical analysis. A typical analysis would provide you with a rank order of some alternatives, based on users' assessment of various attributes. Munro and Davis [25] and Neumann and Segev [26] present approaches of this type.

Table 3.9 Rank Ordering of Proposals' Attributes

	Proposal					
Attribute	A	B	C	D	E	F
Hardware	S	S	A	A	A	I
Upgrading ceiling	S	S	A	A	S	I
Modularity of upgrading	S	S	I	A	A	I
Software	A	S	S	A	I	I
Similar experience of manufacturer	A	S	S	S	I	I
Backup	I	I	A	I	S	S

(S = superior; A = average; I = inferior)

Evaluation of Information System Attributes—A Case

We will now present a real case in which information system attributes have been analyzed in order to select a minicomputer [5]. The analysis incorporates some of the aforementioned techniques. Note that although the attributes are different, the approach is similar to our previous discussion.

A regional distributor (franchise) of an international company that produces cameras, films, X-ray machines, developing chemicals, etc., had some severe problems in the management and control of the film developing laboratory. Too many customer orders were lost, delayed, mishandled, or mistakenly mailed. Sudden shortages in developing chemicals caused delays in lab operations. The management had a vague feeling that computerized data processing would improve its operations and its planning.

A feasibility study was completed. It recommended the installation of a minicomputer to handle the lab data processing and the bookkeeping of the entire firm.

The feasibility report, with a cover letter, was sent to various minicomputer manufacturers. A mandatory requirement was that a turnkey system be proposed, including hardware, software, operating procedures, and assistance in implementation. The possibility of smooth future upgrading was highly stressed.

Six proposals were received. Each attribute in each proposal was ranked relative to the corresponding attributes in other proposals. The results are exhibited in table 3.9.

It is important to note that there was no attempt to assign absolute "grades" to the proposals' attributes. The entire evaluation was based on relative comparisons among the various proposals.

In the next step, the number of "S," "A," and "I" appearances was counted for each proposal, resulting in table 3.10.

The weighting approach was then used to rank order the various proposals: three points were allowed for "S," two points for "A," and one point for "I" (see the "total score" column in table 3.10). Another rank ordering was performed for the purchase price. Both orderings are graphically illustrated in figure 3.4.

The price ordering from low to high was D, F, E, B, A, C. The quality ordering from the bottom up was F, D and E, C, A, B. It is clear that proposals B and D are not dominated by any other proposal, whereas all the others are dominated (if you take C,

Table 3.10   Rank-ordering Summary

Manufacturer	No. of "S"	No. of "A"	No. of "I"	Total Score
A	3	2	1	14
B	5	0	1	16
C	2	3	1	13
D	1	4	1	12
E	2	2	2	12
F	2	0	4	10

Figure 3.4   Efficient frontier

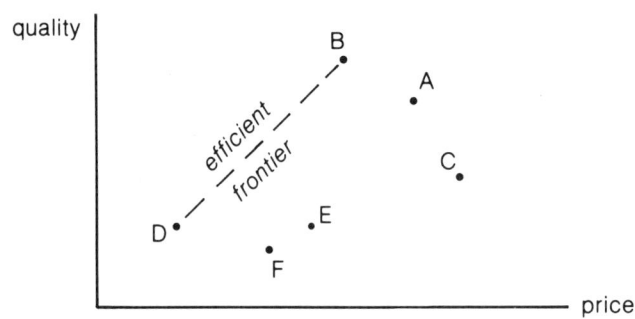

for example, then B is better in quality and lower in price than C). Thus it was recommended that proposals D and B be investigated further. At this point some members of management and user departments (i.e., lab and bookkeeping) viewed live demonstrations of systems B and D and then began negotiations with manufacturers B and D. The price difference between B and D was around $20,000 ($25,000 versus $45,000), and what was actually being investigated was whether system B was worth the difference. Eventually proposal B was accepted, and the system is now in operation.

This case may provide hints for evaluating information systems. Evaluation is not purely a mathematical analysis; neither is it the fruit of only intuition. It requires a lot of user and management involvement in addition to expert skill and analytical tools. However, the most fundamental requirement of evaluation is that it be systematic and consistent.

Information System Benefits

In many cases we prefer to assess the impact of information systems rather than, or in addition to, making an analysis of the attributes. If we can measure benefits and relate them to cost, we will be in a position to decide whether the development of a new system is worthwhile or not. If we can differentiate between benefits of various proposed systems, we might be able to select the most economically justified system. The main premise is that various sets of system attributes imply different sets of benefits.

Therefore, if we focus on benefits (and cost), we may skip, or at least shorten, the attribute analysis, which from time to time might be tiring and obscure. After all, our major interest is in the outcomes, or benefits, and not in the system characteristics. The way we treat benefits depends on a basic property: tangibility. We will now elaborate on the distinction between tangible and intangible benefits.

Tangible Benefits

Our prime target in system evaluation is to determine the *tangible benefits* anticipated as the result of installation of a system. Tangible benefits are those that can be quantitatively assessed. The best measurement of tangible benefits would obviously be in *monetary* values or values that can be transformed to monetary equivalents. We list here some examples of common tangible benefits:

1. Reduction in inventory levels—A common measure for evaluating inventory control systems. This benefit is easily transformed to money by estimating the monetary value of the reduction and the amount of money saved on interest payment. Sometimes space saving is also taken into account.

2. Reduction of credit line—A useful measure to justify accounts receivable, cash flow, or billing systems. Calculation of the monetary value of better liquidity is instantaneous.

3. Reduction in work hours—A common measure to evaluate benefits of personnel allocation, maintenance control, and production scheduling systems. The monetary equivalent of work hours saved can easily be obtained.

4. Increase in sales—A measure used to assess profitability of distribution, marketing, finished-goods inventory control, and customer order systems. Estimates of sales increases are not always immediately available. However, if they are assessable, they provide a useful tangible benefit.

5. Decrease in maintenance costs—A monetary measure for evaluating maintenance control and spare-parts inventory control systems.

When we do have tangible benefits, we can compare them to the development and operation costs of the various proposed information systems as predicted along the anticipated system life cycle (see ch. 9) and conduct a (relatively) rigorous cost/benefit analysis.

Sometimes we can identify tangible benefits, but find it difficult to express them in monetary terms. Here are some examples.

1. Shorter response time—A measure used to justify the installation of computerized dispatching systems for emergency services such as police, ambulance, or fire fighting. In these cases the shortening of response time results in a saving of lives. Economists as well as politicians are reluctant to determine trade-offs between lives and cost. Even if we consider a dispatching system for business services, such as appliance maintenance, couriers, or supply services, we might not have the appropriate techniques and data to calculate explicit monetary benefits (for further discussion, see [4] ch. 8).

2. Reduction of the number of negative responses to customers—A measure used to evaluate finished-goods inventory control and distribution systems. Reduction of negative responses implies sales increases and goodwill improvement. The latter is hard to estimate monetarily.

The best way to handle tangible nonmonetary benefits is to present them to the decision makers (management, politicians) and let them use subjective judgment to decide whether the benefits merit the required cost.

Intangible Benefits

Tangible benefits are more prevalent in information systems for low-level management decisions, such as inventory control, customer orders, or accounts receivable. As we go up the organizational hierarchy, we find it more and more unlikely that MIS justification is based on a rigorous quantitative analysis. The benefits of information systems for middle- and top-level management (see discussion in ch. 5) are seldom tangible. More often we are involved with arguments such as the following: improving decision-making processes; broadening planning horizons; widening information bases for decision making; facilitating data integration. The obscure definition of the benefits is not mainly due to ill-defined information systems, but to the unstructured nature of the decisions supposed to be supported by the information. If you provide the president of a company with an earlier and more accurate accounting statement, it is unlikely that anybody could quantify the marginal benefit gained by the company. Still, we all feel that the new statement has additional merits.

A frequent example is the conversion of traditionally organized files (sequential, index sequential, etc.) to a modern data-base-management-system (DBMS—see appendix A on information system technology). The proposed DBMS would probably have many applications. Furthermore, it would establish the foundations for MIS based on integrated data. It would smooth updating and therefore improve data currency and accuracy. Yet, most of these are *intangible benefits*. It is even hard to explain them to a layperson.

Frequently we find that proposed systems offer tangible and intangible benefits. In these cases, we first consider the tangible benefits and then use the intangible benefits for supplementary argumentation.

Chapter 13 outlines some pragmatic tools for information system evaluation. These tools emerge from the more abstract discussion in this section.

Practical Conclusions for Information System Design and Use

Consider the following list of twelve practical conclusions for information system design and use.

1. Decision making is a three-stage process. Each stage requires a different type of information. Therefore, information requirement analysis should begin with an explicit definition of the decision stage to be supported by the information.

2. The data provided to decision makers for problem solving should emphasize exceptions and discrepancies. Data provided for opportunity seeking should emphasize unused resources or better (previously overlooked) alternatives.

3. The information system for policy design should attempt to incorporate (quantitative) models and forecasting techniques.

4. An adequate information system should provide the means to monitor policy implementation after the policy has been selected.

5. It is easier to design information systems for structured decisions than for unstructured decisions. In the former case, the system may partly replace human decision making; in the latter, information only supports and assists human decision making.

6. The value of information should be calculated ex ante, or prior to the development and implementation of an information system. If it cannot be derived by rigorous analysis, experiments should be performed and estimates (even subjective) made. Information system prototypes can be of great help.

7. The value of normative information is likely to be computable only (if at all) for information supporting low-level (structured) management decisions; middle- and top-level management will probably use subjective evaluation or measure the realistic information value through experiments, sampling, and prototyping.

8. Entropy is useful mostly for communication and coding problems. It is rarely applicable to MIS.

9. In information system evaluation, try to identify the system characteristics that have the most influence on information quality (its usefulness for decision making). Then try to define a quantitative measure (attribute) for each characteristic. Measure the attributes in each specific system and compare the results. Try to assess the trade-offs among attributes.

10. Attribute analysis is useful whenever system technology and major properties are known or attainable.

11. Cost/benefit analysis requires that benefits and costs be comparable—benefits should be transformable to monetary figures. If they cannot be so expressed, the users should weigh the benefits vis-à-vis the costs.

12. Tangible benefits are much more convincing than intangible benefits. Intangible benefits should be used only as supportive arguments to tangibles, unless there is no choice.

Summary

This chapter has described the decision-making process and tied it to information evaluation.

Decision making is a three-stage process. The first stage, intelligence, deals mainly with collection and preparation of data, either for problem detection or for opportunity seeking. The second stage, design, deals with the development and evaluation of alternative ways to cope with the problem or to pursue the opportunity. The third stage, choice, involves selection of a preferred solution and monitoring of its implementation. The choice is not always straightforward: we might have multiple objectives; we usually operate under uncertainty; there might be conflicting interests; and control of the implementation is not always feasible.

Information requirements vary throughout the decision-making process. The intelligence stage requires a solid information base to provide comprehensive data that indicates exceptions and trends. The design stage involves use of models and statistical tools. The choice stage requires more heuristic processing such as "what if" programs. An additional requisite for this stage is the availability of control and feedback systems.

Decisions are classified as structured or unstructured. The former term refers to short-range, low-level, narrow-horizon, programmed decisions. The latter term characterizes mainly strategic decisions. Structured decisions require well-defined information and may sometimes be performed by computer programs. Unstructured decisions might be supported by information, but the human mind is irreplaceable here.

Consequently, the value of information depends on the type of decisions supported by the information. It is always a relative number, based on comparisons of outcomes under different information sets.

The normative value of information is calculated for highly structured situations where all the factors are known and quantifiable, and the decision can be modeled and analyzed.

The realistic value of information is derived from measuring actual performance achieved under different information sets.

The subjective value of information emerges from individual subjective assessment of various information alternatives.

A recommended approach to evaluate proposed information systems is to build system prototypes. Contemporary software technology (e.g., application generators) has paved the way for this approach. Prototypes may help in measuring realistic and subjective values of information.

The quantity of information is sometimes measured by the entropy function, which is based on probabilities of relevant events. The situation must be highly structured if the entropy function is to be used. Its use is limited to assessing communication channel capacity and code efficiency. It cannot contribute to an evaluation of information semantics.

Information systems evaluation is more complex than information evaluation because it involves technological and behavioral aspects of the system. A possible approach to evaluating a system is to determine the characteristics (attributes) of the system (including costs) and compare the series of attributes of various systems.

A different approach to evaluating information systems is to trace their possible benefits. Tangible benefits, particularly if expressed in monetary figures, are preferred. Intangible benefits are used for supplementary argumentation or whenever tangible benefits are not obtainable.

This chapter discussed the attributes and value of information and the nature of decisions supported by various types of information. The next chapter attends to system concepts, to the systems approach to problem solving, and to information systems development.

Key Concepts

accuracy
aggregation level
algorithm
application generators
Bayes theorem
benefits: intangible, monetary, tangible
channel capacity
choice stage
coding
content
currency
data base management systems (DBMS)
decision: algorithmic, deterministic, heuristic, nonprogrammed, probabilistic, programmed, random, structured, unstructured
decision-making process
decision support systems (DSS)
design stage
dominance
efficient frontier
entropy
ex ante
exhaustiveness
ex post
external information
format
frequency

graphic design
information structure
information system: attribute, evaluation
intelligence stage
internal information
iterative process
level of detail
lexicographical ordering
opportunity seeking
optimizers
ordering
outcomes
payoff
performance
problem detection
prospect theory
prototypes
real time
redundancy
relevance
response time
satisficing
timeliness
uncertainty
value of information: normative, realistic, relative, revealed, subjective

References

1. Ahituv, N. "A Systematic Approach Towards Assessing the Value of an Information System." *MIS Quarterly* 4, no. 4 (December 1980): 61–75.
2. Ahituv, N. "A Comparison of Information Structures for a Rigid Decision Rule Case." *Decision Sciences* 12, no. 3 (July 1981): 399–416.
3. Ahituv, N. "Assessing the Value of Information: Problems and Approaches." *Proceedings of the 10th Annual International Conference on Information Systems.* Boston, MA (December 1989): 315–25.
4. Ahituv, N., and O. Berman. *Operations Management of Distributed Service Networks: A Practical Quantitative Approach.* New York: Plenum Press, 1988.
5. Ahituv, N. and M. C. Munro. "Controlling the Acquisition of a Small Business Computer." *Cost and Management* 57, no. 2 (March-April 1983): 6–15.
6. Ahituv, N., and Y. Wand. "Comparative Evaluation of Information under Two Business Objectives." *Decision Sciences* 15, no. 1 (Winter 1984): 31–51.
7. Arbel, A., and A. Seidmann. "Designing a Multi-Micro Distributed Accounting Information System." *Human Systems Management* 5, no. 4 (1985): 283–91.
8. Dickson, G. W., J. A. Senn, and N. L. Charvany. "Research in Management Information Systems: The Minnesota Experiments." *Management Science* 23, no. 9 (1977): 913–23.
9. Edstrom, O. *Man-Computer Decision Making.* Göteborg, Sweden: Gothenburg Studies in Business Administration, 1973.
10. Feltham, G. A. *Information Evaluation.* Sarasota, FL: American Accounting Association, 1972.
11. Hedberg, B. *On Man-Computer Interaction in Organizational Decision Making: A Behavioral Approach.* 2d ed. Göteborg, Sweden: Gothenburg Studies in Business Administration, 1973.
12. Kahneman, D., and A. Tverskey. "Prospect Theory: An Analysis of Decision under Risk." *Econometrica* 47, no. 2 (March 1979): 263–91.
13. Karni, E., and Z. Safra. "Preference Reversal and the Observability of Preferences by Experimental Methods." *Econometrica* 55, no. 3 (May 1987): 675–85.
14. Keen, P. G. W., and M. S. Scott Morton. *Decision Support Systems.* Reading, MA: Addison-Wesley, 1978.
15. Keeney, R. L., and H. Raiffa. *Decisions with Multiple Objectives: Preferences and Value Tradeoffs.* New York: John Wiley & Sons, 1976.
16. Kleijnen, J. P.C. *Computers and Profits: Quantifying Financial Benefits of Information.* Reading, MA: Addison-Wesley, 1980.
17. Lev, B. *Accounting and Information Theory.* Sarasota, FL: American Accounting Association, 1971.
18. Luce, R. D., and H. Raiffa. *Games and Decisions.* New York: John Wiley & Sons, 1957.
19. McGuire, C. B., and R. Radner, eds. *Decision and Organization.* 2d ed. Minneapolis: University of Minnesota Press, 1986.
20. Machina, M. J. " 'Expected Utility' Analysis Without the Independence Axiom." *Econometrica* 50 (1982): 277–323.

21. Marschak, J. "Economics of Information Systems." *Journal of the American Statistical Association* 66 (1971): 192–219.
22. Marschak, J., and R. Radner. *Economic Theory of Teams.* New Haven, CT: Yale University Press, 1972.
23. Mock, T. J. "The Evaluation of Alternative Information Structures." Ph.D. diss., University of California, Berkeley, 1969.
24. Munro, M. C. "Determining the Manager's Information Needs." *Journal of Systems Management* 29, no. 6 (June 1978): 34–39.
25. Munro, M. C., and G. B. Davis. "Determining Management Information Needs: A Comparison of Methods." *MIS Quarterly* 1 (1977): 55–67.
26. Neumann, S, and E. Segev. "A Case Study of User Evaluation of Information Characteristics for System Improvement." *Information and Management* 2 (1979): 271–78.
27. Newell, A., and H. A. Simon. *Human Problem Solving.* Englewood Cliffs, NJ: Prentice-Hall, 1972.
28. Newman, D. P. "Prospect Theory: Implications for Information Evaluation." *Accounting, Organization and Society* 5, no. 2 (1980): 217–30.
29. Ronen, J., and G. Falk. "Accounting Aggregation and the Entropy Measure: An Experimental Approach." *The Accounting Review* 28 (October 1973): 696–717.
30. Saaty, T. L. *The Analytic Hierarchy Process.* New York: McGraw-Hill, 1981.
31. Shannon, C. E., and W. Weaver. *The Mathematical Theory of Communication.* Urbana, IL: University of Illinois Press, 1949.
32. Simon, H. A. *Models of Man.* New York: John Wiley & Sons, 1957.
33. ————. *The New Science of Management Decisions.* New York: Harper & Row, 1960.

Questions

1. Simon suggests three stages in human decision making: intelligence, design, and choice. Describe these stages and explain how they relate to each other.
2. Explain by example how an MIS might meet the dual needs of the intelligence stage.
3. What is meant by a decision support system (DSS)?
4. What is the role of feedback in an MIS?
5. Describe the types of decisions that are easily programmed as well as those types that are not.
6. Differentiate among the three types of information value.
7. Why is it said that the normative value approach can rarely be applied to an MIS?
8. Relate the subjective value of information to measuring the benefits of an information system.
9. What does the entropy function measure? Explain how this relates to information system design.
10. List the class of attributes that comprise "timeliness" and describe how they contribute to the quality of an information system.

Problems

1. Show how cognitive style might impact the use of information systems for structured and unstructured decision making.

2. Suggest possible measures of MIS performance in a retail environment (such as a department store or supermarket). Which of the attributes of an information system apply to these performance measures? What are the tangible or intangible benefits associated with improved performance?

3. "Theoretically the optimum level of detail is defined as the level under which any more detailed information would not improve our decision and above which any further aggregation would worsen this decision." Describe how this statement might impact decisions regarding

   a. the data to be acquired and stored.

   b. the presentation of the data on a terminal.

   c. the format of printed output.

4. A library intending to automate the circulation process was trying to decide whether to purchase a microcomputer or to use the university's computer via a remote terminal. What attributes must be analyzed in order to compare the two possibilities? How could this evaluation be accomplished?

Chapter 4   The Systems Approach

We all live, work, and function in various systems. These systems may be large, complex supersystems, such as big organizations, or small, simple subsystems, such as departmental units or families. To study the behavior of systems we must adopt the systems approach.

This chapter describes in specific terms the systems approach and discusses how to use it in the process of problem solving. The concept of a system and its scope and structure are illustrated. It is important to understand the different roles of components and individuals in the system and their interrelations. Finally, various classes of systems are discussed, with emphasis on a control system.

Background

A system is a set of interdependent components (subentities) that create a whole entity. The components are dynamically linked. That is to say, each one affects and is affected by other components. The system concept is a broad one. It encompasses every facet of our lives—the solar system, educational systems, transportation systems, information systems, organizations, an automobile, the family, and the human body. Some systems, such as organizations, are supposed to have a common purpose (or purposes); others, such as the solar system, need not (unless we wish to get into theology). Linkages make an entity a system. The way we look at it, that is, the purpose(s) we ascribe to it, sets a boundary around the linked components that differentiates the system from its environment.

The systems approach is concerned with a holistic entity, but does not neglect the components of the entity. It recognizes the activities of the components while simultaneously considering the activity of the whole system that contains them. For example, the application of the systems approach to the issue of busing in a city would necessarily mean that in addition to consideration of the student population, the teacher population, the location of schools, the attitudes of parents, and the availability of buses, the matter of distances and travel time from residences to schools is not neglected. The omission of only one factor could lead, in this case, to a system that is not optimal even though some of its components are optimal. For example, the routes of the school buses could be arranged in a way that would minimize average daily travel time but would achieve a low degree of integration. Alternatively, a high degree of student integration could be achieved, but only with excessive average travel times.

This phenomenon, called *suboptimization,* indicates that the system under consideration was not studied under the systems approach. We can avoid suboptimization if we understand the systems approach. Many systems designed prior to the 1970s were suboptimal because independent systems were designed for interdependent activities.

The *systems approach* is primarily a philosophy of structure that coordinates in an efficient and optimum manner the activities and operations within any system. In addition, it is an approach that enables analysis of complex problems and situations. The actual problems and conditions we face and deal with are, after all, complex and dynamic. With the systems approach we are concerned with individual components, but we emphasize their role in the system rather than their role as individual entities.

Every organization is composed of *subsystems,* one of which is the information system. The subsystems interact and contribute to the common purposes of the organization. The effectiveness of these subsystems considered collectively as a system may be greater than the sum of the effectiveness of each subsystem considered separately. This phenomenon is labeled *synergism.* The synergistic effect is described by Aristotle's statement, ''The whole is greater than the sum of its parts.''

One of the attributes of modern organizations is their increasing complexity and the specialization of their subsystems. Each organizational unit has its own objectives and can thus lose sight of how their activities and goals interrelate with those of the organization as a whole. Implementation of the systems approach cuts across traditional functional lines of the organization to gain optimization for the entire organization and to reduce conflict between different units.

In a university, for example, the vice-president for academic affairs wants to have a large inventory of courses in order to satisfy students' preferences. The vice-president for administration, on the other hand, wants to schedule courses with large enrollments in order to minimize investment in classrooms and academic personnel. The systems approach is the manner in which the administration of the university should view the interrelationships of the various subsystems of the university system.

Reasons for Adopting the Systems Approach

What are the reasons for our concern with the systems approach? Why is our era considered to be the systems era? The answer is twofold.

On the one hand, we are confronted with accelerating diversity and complexity in modern organizations and in society as a whole. On the other hand, we have at our disposal theories and tools to deal with diversity and complexity. Complexity is attributed to all the following factors: the technological revolution; expanding markets; the effect of research and development; the constant rise in the standard of living; constant product changes; interdependency within the international economic and political systems; and increasing interdependency of the private and nonprivate sectors of the economy.

Concurrently there are new theories and techniques that make possible the application of the systems approach to management. We will list and briefly describe them. Some are more extensively explained in other chapters of this book; others are covered in detail in the references at the end of this chapter.

General Systems Theory

The notion of *general systems theory* was first formulated by von Bertalanffy, orally in the 1930s and in various publications after World War II. Von Bertalanffy postulated [8] that there exist models, principles, and laws that apply to generalized systems or their components irrespective of the particular discipline (be it a physical or a biological system), the nature of the components, and the interrelationships between them. The task of general systems theory is the formulation and derivation of these principles that are applicable to systems in general. It introduces "system" as a new scientific philosophy of nature in contrast to the analytic and mechanistic philosophy of nature of classical science. Classical science in its various disciplines, such as the social sciences, tried to isolate the elements of the relevant observed universe (freely competing individuals in this case) in the expectation that by putting them together again, conceptually or experimentally, the whole or system (society) would result and would be intelligible. General systems theory advocates that, for an understanding, not only the elements but their interrelations as well are required (the structure and dynamics in social systems, in this case), and that parallel systems in other disciplines may offer many insights to the system under study.

General systems theory gave impetus to mathematical systems theory, which has become an extensive and rapidly growing field. A variety of approaches have developed, differing in emphasis, focus of interest, and mathematical techniques. These attempt to describe aspects, properties, and principles of what is included under the term "system," and thus serve different theoretical or practical purposes. Theoretical approaches include cybernetics, control theory, information theory, network theory, game and decision theory, computerization, simulation, and so forth. Some of these approaches have significant implications for the development and use of information systems in organizations, the subject matter of this book. Concepts and methods of analysis based on them are used in various chapters.

For example, the theory of information-feedback systems explains how the output of the system leads to a decision resulting in some type of action that corrects the output, which in turn leads to another decision. Or, concepts drawn from decision theory and cognitive psychology contribute to a better understanding of the way users of information systems perceive stimuli (e.g., exception reports), interpret them, and go through a decision-making process.

Systems Technology

Modern technology and society have become so complex that the traditional branches of technology are no longer sufficient to describe and explain the complexity. New techniques and tools based on the theoretical concepts of general systems theory make possible the application of the systems approach to management. Models that originated in specified fields of technology have been recognized to have much broader significance and to be independent of their special realizations. The spectrum of these tools ranges from highly sophisticated mathematical models to computer simulation to more-or-less informal discussion of systems problems. For example, several operations research techniques, developed for military purposes during World War II, are now applied to complex organizational problems, such as producing optimal lot sizes, minimizing inventory costs, and the like.

The Electronic Computer

All organizational systems generate data that reflects their activities and operations. This data is collected and processed by information systems. The manual, mechanical, or electromechanical information systems that existed in organizations prior to the electronic computer were relatively slow and inaccurate in processing data and producing information that combined all facets of the organization. In addition, such systems lacked the computing power and speed needed to implement the new *systems technologies*. Traditionally, therefore, organizations developed and used discrete information systems patterned along functional lines (e.g., marketing information systems, accounting information systems). The emergence of the computer and computerized information systems provided the potential for application of the systems approach to the analysis and design of information systems.

It is only natural that with the increasing expansion of systems thinking and studies and technologies, awareness of the "systems" concept has penetrated our lives. It is used by scientists, managers at all levels, and the general public. Any cursory analysis of textbook and newspaper content, and the media at large will reveal how widespread is the use of the concept. We are now resigned to being part of the systems era and receptive to the systems approach for solving problems, although we must evaluate the costs and benefits of its implementation.

Using the Systems Approach for Problem Solving and for Information System Design

The decision-making process as described in chapter 3 reflects the systems approach to problem solving. The process incorporates the steps of intelligence, design, and choice. The systems approach is also the cornerstone of the phases involved in the process of developing an information system, as described in chapter 9. The two processes demonstrate the two major stages of the systems approach.

1. The *expanding stage*—A system is first partitioned (expanded) into its components (or subsystems) in order to reduce the level of complexity and interactions among the components. In this way the components and their interrelationships can be analyzed. This is the stage of analysis.

2. The *contracting stage*—The components are organized and integrated into a new system. This is the stage of synthesis (or design). At this stage, old components and interrelations may be deleted or changed and new components and interrelations may be added.

Table 4.1 illustrates the major activities performed in these two processes. The three steps involved in the process of developing an information system parallel the six steps of applying the systems approach to problem solving.

Table 4.1   The Systems Approach to Information System Development and Problem Solving

Information System Development	Problem Solving
1. Information system analysis	1. Defining the problem 2. Gathering data relevant to the problem
2. Information system design	3. Identifying alternative solutions 4. Evaluating the cost and effectiveness of the alternatives 5. Selecting the best alternative
3. Information system implementation	6. Implementing and monitoring the selected alternative

1. *Defining the problem*—There is an inherent bias toward confusing real problems (or opportunities) with symptoms. A reduction in sales may be a symptom of product obsolescence or of the elimination of quantity discounts. The scope and structure of the problem or system can be determined only by careful examination. This is done by defining the objectives and the relevant environment of the system and by tracking down the inputs to the system, the components that process (transform) the inputs into outputs, and the attributes of the outputs. The components of the system (or problem) may be subsystems of the system under analysis; the system under analysis may be a subsystem of a larger system. Hence, precise definition of the problem or system is crucial; otherwise the problem solver would be restricted to a solution or a system that is suboptimal or that encompasses more than is needed.

2. *Gathering data*—The steps of problem definition and data gathering constitute the stage of problem understanding. A problem or system is understood and studied by collecting data about its goals, inputs, outputs, environment, transformation processes, and constraints. There are various techniques of data collection: observation, questionnaires, interviews, sampling, or simulation. Each has its advantages and disadvantages (benefits and costs), and their use must be tailored to the specific problem at hand. More about these techniques will be said in chapters 9 and 10.

3. *Identifying alternative solutions*—Once the problem has been understood, we can attend to the stage of problem solution, which comprises the last four steps of the problem-solving process. Ideally, we should attempt to have more than one alternative solution, but we should also narrow down many alternatives to a few. Having too many alternatives tends to obscure the problem-solving process, to increase its costs, and to make it unmanageable. On the other hand, in most nontrivial business problems, the problem-solving process is jointly applied by several decision makers. Having only one alternative solution detracts from the opportunity to present and debate the advantages and disadvantages of various solutions, to provide management with more options, or to formulate a solution that is a combination of various alternatives.

4. *Evaluating alternative solutions*—Each alternative has associated with it both advantages (benefits) that contribute to solving the problem at hand and disadvantages (costs). These must be evaluated and attached to the proposed alternative. In many business problems the costs and benefits are partly intangible (immeasurable). The problem solver in such a case must attempt to come up with measurable costs and benefits (usually in monetary terms) by resorting to approximations, using surrogate measures, and probabilities. This is the essence of solving a nonstructured problem.

   For example, assume that a firm is faced with declining sales due to product obsolescence. One alternative is to invest in internal research and development for a new product. A second alternative is to acquire the rights to a new product from an outside source. In terms of measurable values, the second alternative may involve less time and less cost. In terms of immeasurable values, the first alternative may lead to the creation of a sound research and development (R&D) department and to the generation of additional future products.

5. *Selecting the best alternative*— At this stage the problem solver is faced with more than one alternative, each having its costs and benefits, with benefits outweighing costs. The problem solver applies a decision rule, or a yardstick, to summarize and rank the alternatives. Such a decision rule may be, for example, the rate of return associated with each solution, the fastest time to implement a solution, and so forth. Sometimes all alternatives may be rejected; then we return to the third step in the process—identifying alternative solutions. We then either define new alternatives, or an alternative of ''doing nothing,'' and proceed to the next step in the problem-solving process. Another possibility is to conduct a more detailed analysis of the alternatives that were rejected.

   ''Doing nothing'' about a problem is a legitimate alternative that must be evaluated in terms of its costs and benefits. Using the previous example of an obsolete product, if we decide not to invest in R&D and not to acquire the rights to a new product, but decide to continue production of the current product, we must evaluate the consequences of declining sales and a reduced market share together with the benefits of retaining the money needed for R&D or for acquisition of rights.

6. *Implementing and monitoring the selected alternative*—Once the best solution (or system) has been selected, it must be implemented and followed up. At this step it is the responsibility of the problem solver(s) to present a program that implements the solution and solves the problem. A solution that cannot be achieved is not a complete solution. It is not enough to understand the problem and to recommend a solution. In addition, you must describe how to implement it.

   As an example, if management decides to invest in developing an in-house R&D department, the problem-solving team should explain how the firm can go about the task and how the task can be controlled. This would entail specifications of needed capital, personnel, space, machinery, and a timetable.

Sometimes the solution cannot be implemented, or it incurs costs that were underestimated in the previous steps of the problem-solving process. In such a case, the problem solver can go back and select the next best alternative (and this is an additional reason for identifying more than one alternative) or go back to one of the earlier steps in the process (redefine the problem, gather more data, identify more alternatives, or reevaluate the alternatives).

To recapitulate:

The systems approach can be applied to the processes of information systems development and to problem solving.

The two processes are sequential and iterative. Each step logically follows the previous step, but it is possible and sometimes necessary to halt progress to the next step and to go back and resume the process at one of the preceding steps.

In most nontrivial business problems more than one person is involved in these processes. In problem solving, a manager may recognize a problem or an opportunity; various technicians may develop and evaluate the alternatives with the manager; then the same or another manager or a committee may select the best alternative; and other technicians may implement it. In information systems development, a manager may recognize information needs; an information analyst may define it with the manager and develop alternative systems that satisfy those needs; and a systems designer may then design the best system, which will then be implemented by programmers, operators, and the like.

A Systems Approach Example

The coach of the Automatics basketball team is preparing for a crucial home game against the Manuals team. The two teams are unbeaten in the College Northwest Conference, and the winner will advance to the national play-offs. If the coach thinks in systems terms, he views his team as a system whose environment is the other teams in the conference, the referees, and the home crowd. The system he studies is divided into subsystems (players and coaching staff). The subsystems comprise components (centers, forwards, guards, assistant coaches). All of these components have some bearing on the result of the game. The coach decides to take the systems approach in order to determine the game plan.

1. *Defining the problem*—The objective of the Automatics is to win the game and advance to the play-offs. This objective can be achieved by the system's outputs, in this case the performance of the Automatics relative to the performance of the Manuals. This means that the past performance of the two teams has to be studied. At this stage the coach recognizes that the problem (or opportunity) he faces is his team losing (or winning) the game. The coach decides to go to the next step of his analysis and learn more about his problem.

2. *Collecting data*—The Automatics have two assistant coaches, a trainer, and a student manager who provide scouting reports on the Manuals and a report on the physical condition of the players. Game films and newspaper reports are also reviewed. The coach contacts several other coaches in the conference and learns their opinions of the way the referees assigned to the game tend to interpret the rules of the game. The coaching staff then processes the data and comes up with the following significant facts.

Both teams are known for their aggressive, high-scoring, and quick style of play. The Manuals usually employ a zone defense, which is more suited to their very tall center.

The starting center and one of the forwards of the Automatics, who have been recently injured in practice, could play only in spots. This would give the Manuals a significant height advantage. The information about the injuries, however, is unknown to outsiders.

Since it is a home game, the home crowd advantage is estimated to be worth at least ten points. The local fans are used to the quick play of their team and in the past have booed when the team tried to slow down the game.

The lowest winning margins of the Manuals were in games in which the opposing teams applied slow-down tactics.

The referees for the game are veterans and tend not to be intimidated by the local crowd. At this stage the coach recognizes that a possible cause for his problem (a loss) is the doubtful contribution of his injured center and forward and the subsequent height advantage of the Manuals.

The problem has now been understood, and the coach proceeds to take the steps necessary to solve it.

3. *Identifying alternatives*—The Automatics can (a) employ a full-court press defense and rely on outside shooting, or (b) employ a zone defense and slow-down tactics on offense from the start and take only high-percentage shots.

4. *Evaluating alternatives*—(a) The local fans and sportswriters like a quick, aggressive play, even if the Automatics lose (although the coach could later refer to the good excuse of having two injured players). If the guards have a good day, the Automatics would take away the rebounding edge of the Manuals. Such style of play may cause many turnovers by the Manuals. However, if this game plan fails in the early minutes of the game, the Manuals might build a significant margin and the Automatics would not be able to switch to the alternative game plan and catch up with them. (b) A slow-down game assures a win, or a loss by a small margin. It takes away the height advantage of the Manuals. If well executed, the Automatics would have gained an additional weapon if they win and advance to the play-offs. The coach could use fewer substitutes and rely on his best players. However, the local crowd may tend to vocally express its distaste for such a game style, even if the Automatics eventually win. If the Automatics lose, the coach will be highly criticized by the fans, the sportswriters, and the college administration.

5. *Selecting the best alternative*—The coach decides to select the second alternative that best meets the objective of winning the game: the Automatics will start with a slow-down style of play. They will change to a quick style (the first alternative) only if the Manuals build up a margin of ten points, or in the last five minutes of the game if the Automatics then lead by at least fifteen points.

6. *Implementing and monitoring*—The coaching staff prepares appropriate practice sessions in which the emphasis is on a slow-down offense and on a quick switch to a fast offense. Extra care is taken not to leak the information about the injured players (in fact, they will suit up for the game and participate in pregame warm-ups). The coach emphasizes in his weekly meeting with the local sports writers, in his press releases, and in his interview with the student daily paper the importance of using all the means within the rules to reach the national play-offs for the first time in the history of the college and that nice guys do not necessarily finish first. The assistant coaches are assigned responsibilities for monitoring individual players during the game and for collecting statistics.

Determining the Scope and Structure of a System

The Scope of a System

Studying, defining, and measuring the characteristics of a system are the first stages in the process of system analysis. A system has eight basic characteristics (fig. 4.1).

Goals and Purposes
Any organizational system has a short-term goal(s) and a long-term purpose(s) that can be explicit or implicit. The purpose of a profit-making firm may be to maximize its profits; the purposes of a university may be to advance research and knowledge. The purpose of the system directs the formation of the system's goals and objectives.

Two classes of measures—an effectiveness measure and an efficiency measure—are used to reveal to what extent the purpose or goal was achieved by the system and how well it was doing it. While an *effectiveness* measure answers the question, Are we doing the right thing?, an *efficiency* measure is a response to the question, Are we doing things the right way?

The purpose of a state highway patrol department may be to maintain highways in an accident-free condition. A possible measure of effectiveness is the number of accidents per mile of highway. The smaller the measure, the more effective the department is in achieving its purpose. However, since the department has limited resources at its disposal (budget, cars, personnel), we are interested in measuring its efficiency in utilizing these resources. Possible measures of efficiency are the number of accidents per mile per work hour, or per dollar of budget. The higher these measures, the less efficient was the department in achieving its purpose.

Figure 4.1 Characteristics of a system

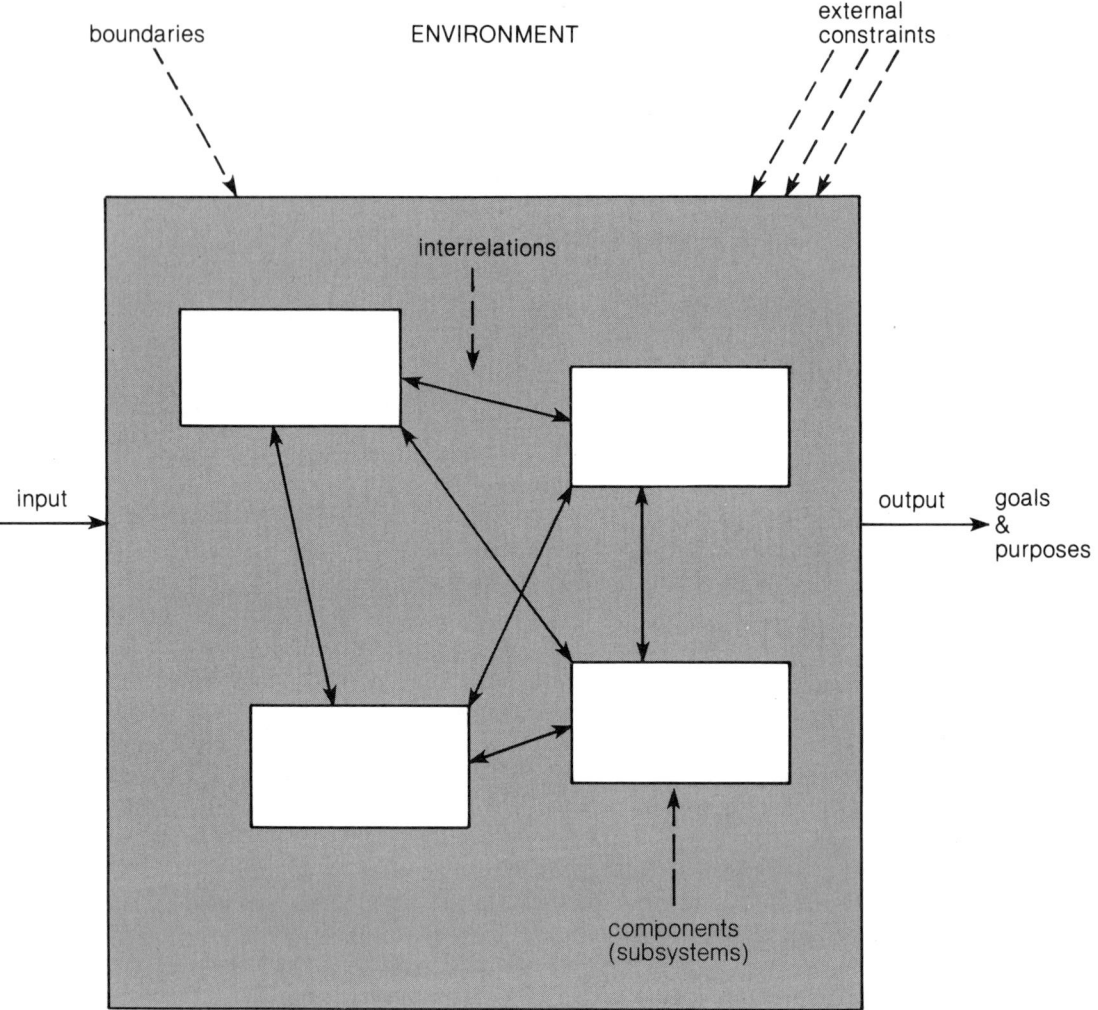

Inputs

A system accepts input resources. Typically, the input resources of an organization are capital, personnel, information, energy, materials, inventories, machinery, and the like. The system's components process these inputs and transform them into outputs.

Outputs

A system produces outputs that are used to achieve its purpose. A manufacturing firm produces goods and services; a theater produces shows; a transportation system produces passenger-miles and freight-miles.

Boundaries and Environment

The features that define and delineate a system form its *boundaries*. The system is inside the boundaries; the *environment* is outside the boundaries. Determining the boundaries of a system is, in many cases, not simple. Often the boundaries of a system are arbitrarily determined by the person studying the system. There are two guiding principles in determining what is a system and what is not: (1) Do the boundaries constitute a self-contained entity? and (2) Is the entity controllable by the system within the boundaries?

Figure 4.2 illustrates an arbitrary determination of boundaries. Figure 4.2a describes an entire plant as a system and applies to a plantwide problem. In figure 4.2b only the production department constitutes the system; other departments become a part of the environment. This figure applies to an examination of a local production problem.

The interactions between a system and its environment are termed *interfaces*. These occur at the boundaries and take the form of inputs and outputs. An interface between the production department and the personnel department in an organization may take the form of a standard weekly request for additional employees. In this example, the organizational system may be broken down to these two subsystems in order to study them separately. The accounting department of the organization is then part of the environment of these two subsystems. If the organization as a whole is studied, then an interface between it and its environment may take the form of the channel that transfers raw materials from its suppliers.

Components and Interrelations

The system's components perform the processing (transforming) of inputs into outputs. A process is an activity, or procedure, in which components consume input resources to produce some output. For example, in a baking process, the baker (a component) uses flour, butter, chocolate, (input resources) and an oven (a component) to make a cake (output). The transformation process is done within the boundaries of the system (the bakery).

The distinction between a *component* and a *subsystem* is arbitrary and is determined by the nature of the system under study and the person(s) studying the system. For example, the bakery section in a big restaurant may constitute a subsystem that can be broken down to several components (bakers). Alternatively, a system study may consider the bakery section as a basic component of the restaurant that does not require further breakdown. For practical matters, we will consider components to be the basic elements of a subsystem (a machine or a person). While a subsystem is studied as a system, a component is not.

The subsystems and their interrelations constitute the *system structure*. The breakdown of a system to its subsystems is often an arbitrary process, since a subsystem can be broken down further to its subsystems. This is actually the essence of the process of systems analysis, which begins by breaking down a system under study to its subsystems, then analyzing their behavior and the nature of the interrelations among them. One of the main objectives of adopting this method is to reduce the complexity of the system under study. This process of analysis, decomposition, or decoupling of a system

Figure 4.2 Boundaries and environment of a system: (a) the plant A system; (b) the production department subsystem

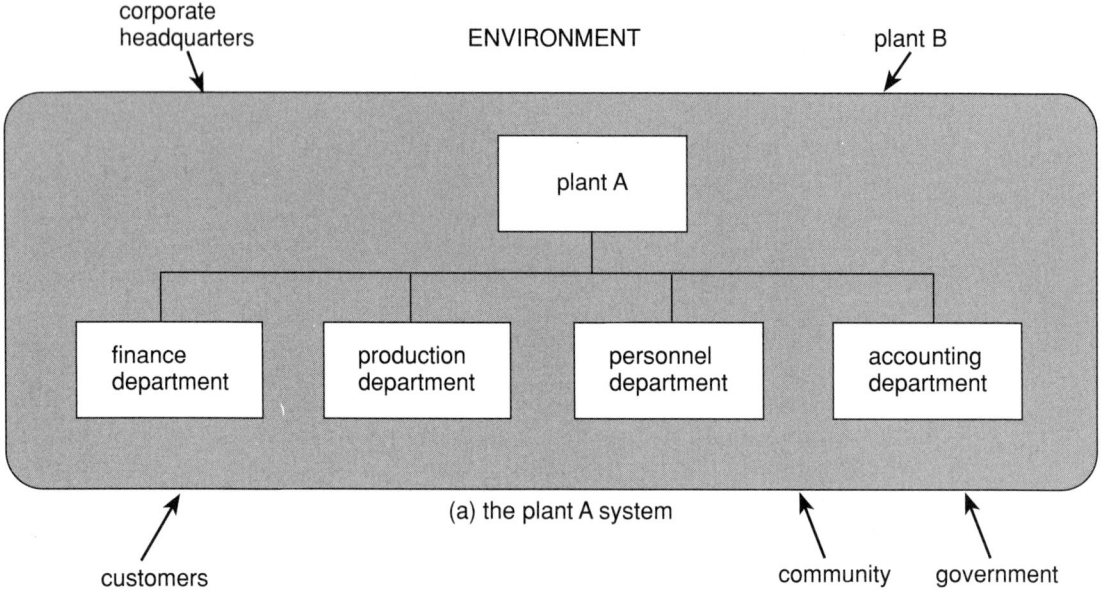

(a) the plant A system

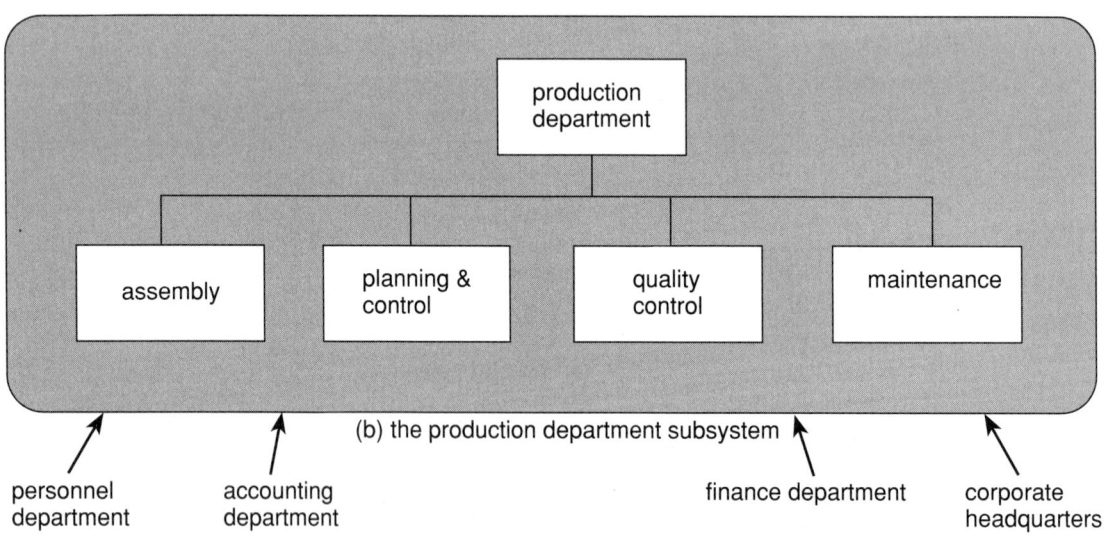

(b) the production department subsystem

stops at the level of a subsystem whose inputs and outputs are defined but the transformation process that goes on within it is not. This system is termed a *black box*. It is quite common that a subsystem is regarded as a black box at the early stages of analysis, the intention at that point being to study its internal structure at a later stage of the analysis.

For example, if we conduct a system analysis of a firm, we may decide to study its production subsystem, then its marketing subsystem, and so on. We will define the boundaries of each functional subsystem, focus on the production department, and track down its components, while temporarily treating the other functional departments as black boxes.

Constraints

A system is affected by external *constraints* that are imposed by its environment. Business organizations, for instance, have to cope with rules and regulations established by various federal agencies, such as the Federal Reserve Board, the Federal Trade Commission, and the Securities and Exchange Commission. The personnel department in a company may prevent the production department from firing an unproductive employee. The "accident-free" purpose of the highway patrol department can be achieved by closing down all the highways. However, this would not comply with constraints imposed by the system's environment.

The constraints relevant to the system under study have to be identified and their implications must be analyzed. The constraints affect the structure of the desired system. Neglecting to consider them may lead to a design of a system that is not optimal. A case in point is the time constraint of top-level managers. Many information systems produce very detailed reports that are not read by managers. This could have been prevented had the reports been produced on an exception basis.

The Structure of a System

The systems approach requires that the system analysts and designers consider the system as a whole. The system may be too complex or too large for detailed analysis. Therefore, the system is factored into subsystems. This process of *factoring* and defining more narrow boundaries is continued until the subsystems are of manageable size. At this point some subsystems are considered black boxes with no known internal structure. The factoring process, which comprises a careful study of the emerging boundaries and interfaces of the subsystems, determines the structure of the entire system that will result. The factoring process generally leads to hierarchical structures (fig. 4.3).

The hierarchical structure reflects how the purpose and goals of the whole system have been partitioned to subgoals. Each subsystem has a specialized function that contributes to the goals of the system above it in the hierarchy. The assembly unit contributes to the target production of the production department, which contributes thus to the profit target of plant A, which contributes to the profits of corporation XYZ.

Figure 4.3 Hierarchical structure of an organization

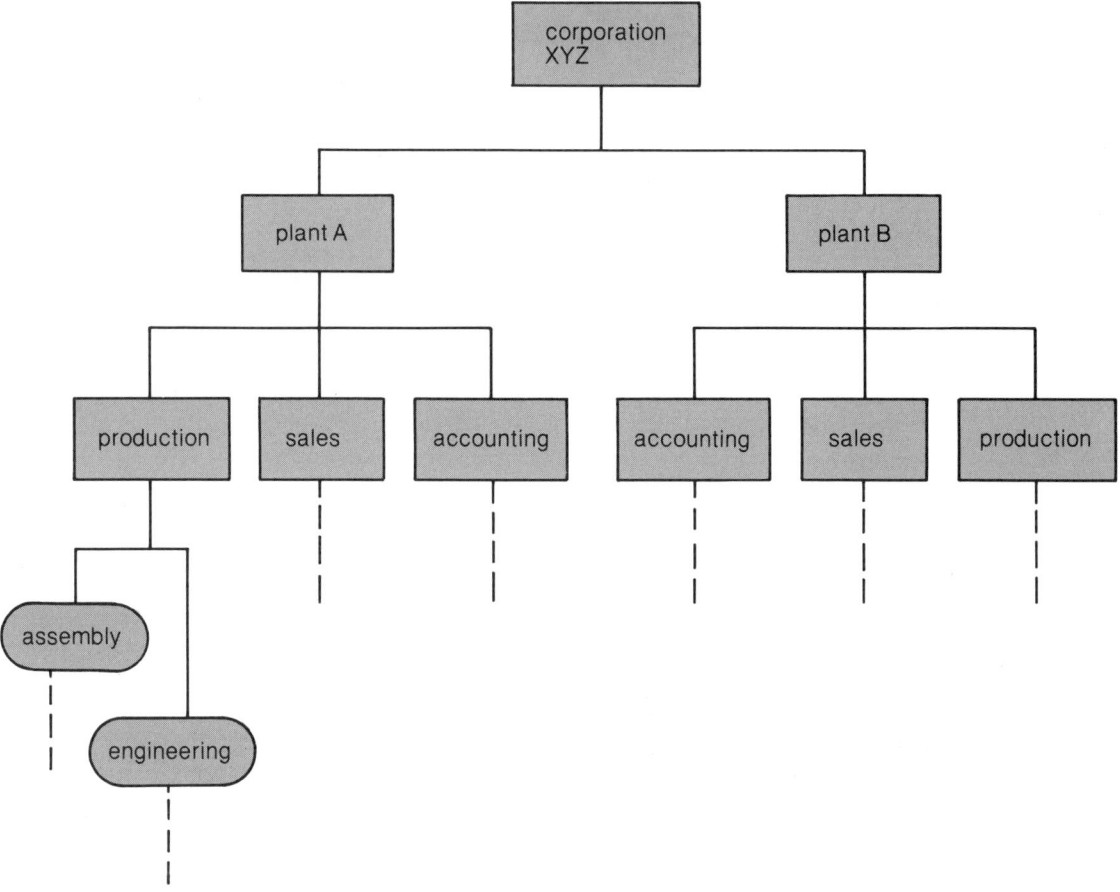

There is no known way of determining an optimum structure. That is why there is a variety of organizational structures (by function, by product, by region, by projects, etc.). A system designed in two different ways (namely, partitioned to subsystems differently) will lead to two different systems. Another danger inherent to the factoring process is by now the familiar risk of suboptimization, which increases as boundaries are made more narrow.

Interactions among Subsystems

Since each partitioned subsystem is defined as to inputs, outputs, and interfaces with other subsystems, the system study is complicated by the emergence of many *interactions* that have to be analyzed. The number of interactions can rise quickly as the number of subsystems increases. The more interactions in a system, the more complicated is the analysis of the system.

There are three sources of interactions:

1. Internal *coupling* of inputs and outputs, in which an output of one subsystem serves as an input to another subsystem (fig. 4.4a).

2. Internal coupling due to common resources used by more than one subsystem (fig. 4.4b). The degree of coupling (and interaction) is increased when the allocation of a common resource to one subsystem reduces the allocation to another subsystem.

3. Coupling due to a common environment. For example, a company is decentralized geographically, with branches serving regional customers. A loss of goodwill in one region will affect the other branches. In this example the customers constitute the common environment (fig. 4.4c).

Coping with Interactions

There are various methods for either reducing the number of interactions among subsystems or controlling them through better coordination and communications among the subsystems. These include the following:

1. Selecting a system structure that groups together closely interacting activities—For example, if an organization is structured by product (passenger car division, truck division), it may have fewer interactions than if it were organized by function (production, accounting, finance, personnel, marketing). The benefits of reduced interactions must be weighed against the costs of fewer opportunities for specialization of the function in a structure by product.

2. Using the exception principle to reduce interactions—So long as a subsystem acts within a preestablished range, it is treated as a temporarily independent component. When the subsystem exceeds the range, an interaction is established with another subsystem that has to deal with or know about the event.

3. Reducing interactions by establishing *clusters of subsystems* (fig. 4.5)—In each cluster there are closely interacting subsystems with a single interface between the clusters.

4. Reducing interactions by decoupling tightly linked subsystems—*Decoupling* means loosening the connection so that the subsystems can operate in the short run with some measure of independence. For example, a firm fulfills every sale order by immediately producing it, which requires great coordination between the sales and the production subsystems. The following are some methods of decoupling that apply to this example (fig. 4.6).
   a. Buffers (fig. 4.6a)—Establishing a finished-goods inventory allows the two subsystems to operate more independently.
   b. Flexible resources (fig. 4.6b)—With some slack production capacity, the production subsystems can cope with a randomly increased stream of sale orders.

Figure 4.4 Sources of interaction: (a) internal coupling of inputs and outputs; (b) internal coupling due to common resources; (c) coupling due to common environment

(a) internal coupling of inputs and outputs

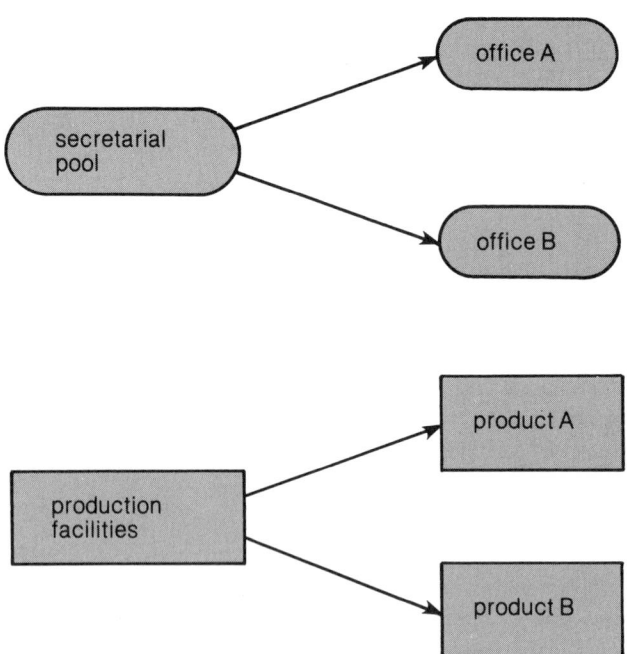

(b) internal coupling due to common resources

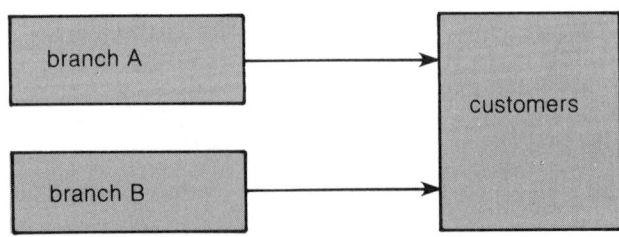

(c) coupling due to common environment

Figure 4.5 Clustering of subsystems: (a) all subsystems interacting; (b) the functions cluster interacting with the files cluster through DBMS interface

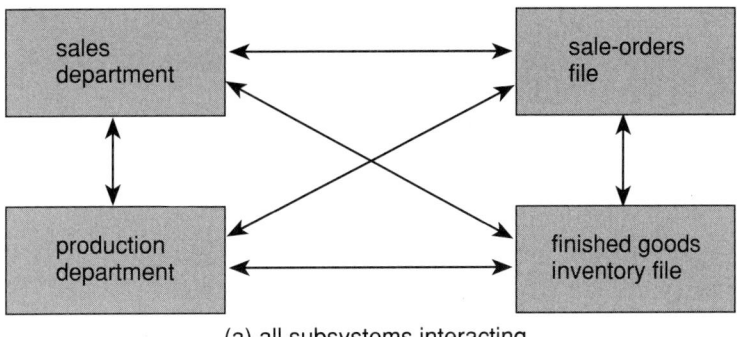

(a) all subsystems interacting

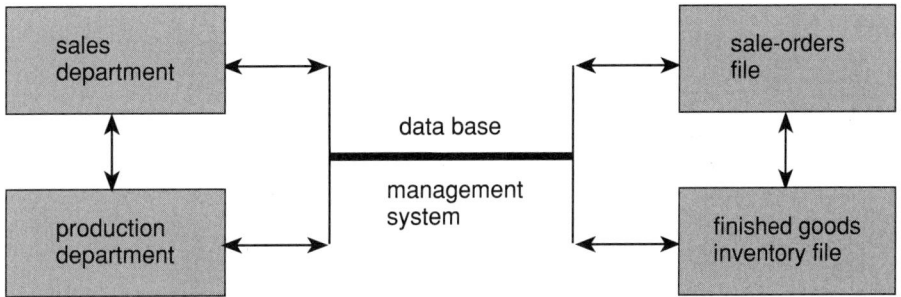

(b) the cluster of functions interacting with the
cluster of files through the DBMS interface

    c. Standardization (fig. 4.6c)—Standard specifications of products and quantities to be produced allow the production subsystem to reduce its interactions with the sales subsystem.

    As stated before, the factoring process and the methods for dealing with the ensuing interactions can generate alternative system structures, ranging from a loosely to a tightly coupled system. There is a trade-off among these structures in terms of their costs (such as costs of maintaining inventories and slack resources, or the problem of suboptimization) and benefits (reduced complexity, manageable subsystems, better coordination). The systems designer should rely on his or her experience and know-how in order to select a structure that best suits the system under study. The structure is determined after taking into account the system's boundaries, components, constraints, goals, interactions among the components, interactions with the environment, and the inputs and outputs of the system and its components.

Figure 4.6 Methods of decoupling: (a) buffers; (b) flexible resources; (c) standardization

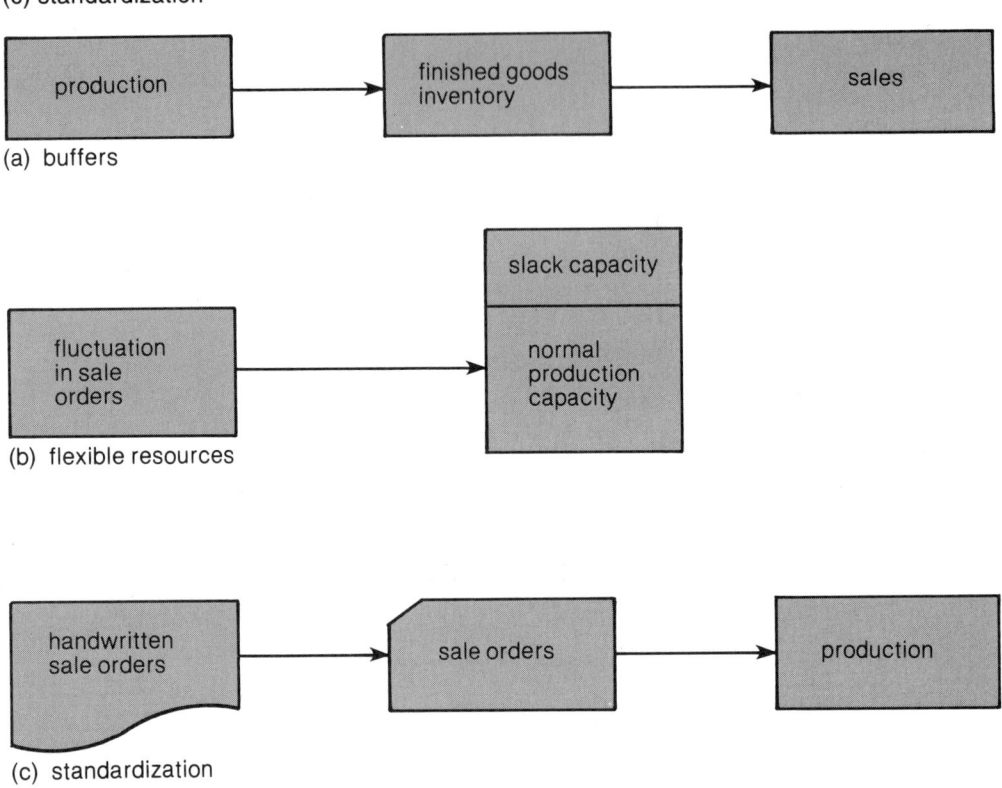

(a) buffers

(b) flexible resources

(c) standardization

The Necessary Conditions for an Entity to Be Conceived as a System

In *The Design of Inquiring Systems* [4], Churchman defines nine conditions that must be met in order for an entity to be conceived as a "system." Churchman refers to human-designed systems, not any and all systems. His definitions shed more light on the previous discussion of characteristics of systems and clarify implications for the designer and the users of the system. The conditions are stated from the point of view of the designer who is studying a given entity. These conditions are reviewed and illustrated by using a management information system as an example. [For a discussion of these conditions and their implications for organizations, see 5.]

1. "S is *teleological*"—This means that a system has a purpose. The purpose of a management information system is to provide information to all levels of management in the relevant organization. If the purpose of a management information system is inaccurately defined as processing transactions and

updating operational files (a transactions processing system), then the resulting system will fail to efficiently meet the information requirements of top-level management.

2. "S has a *measure of performance*"—The purpose of the entity is the primary criterion for the relevance of such measure and serves as the basis for constructing a measure of performance. As previously stated, the measures of performance should reflect the effectiveness of the entity in achieving its purpose and the efficiency of the inputs (resources) of the entity in achieving its purpose. The first class of measures expresses a relation between the purpose and the entity's outputs. The second class of measures expresses a relation among the entity's purpose, outputs, and inputs. A possible effectiveness measure of performance for a management information system is the number of decisions at various organizational levels that were supported by the system's outputs (either routine reports or responses to ad hoc queries). Possible efficiency measures of performance are the number of supported decisions per work hour of system's staff or per dollar of system's expenditures, or the throughput of the system (number of jobs per unit of time). Without such measures of performance, the user of the system cannot monitor the effectiveness and efficiency of the system.

3. "There exists a *client* whose interests (values) are served by S in such a manner that the higher the measure of performance, the better the interests are served and, more generally, the client is the standard of the measure of performance"—The managers of the organization are the clients of the management information system. But should the system serve the top-level managers, the middle-level managers, the low-level managers, or a combination of these? The answer identifies the client(s) of the system. The client's preferences (value system) should be inherent in the system's measure of performance. If a manager prefers exception reporting, this implies one measure of performance. If he or she prefers to receive detailed routine reports, that implies another.

4. "S has teleological components which coproduce the measure of performance of S"—A system is comprised of purposeful (teleological) subsystems. Each of these subsystems attempts to achieve its own purposes and has measures of performance for them. The performance measure for a system as a whole must be related to the performance measures for each of its subsystems. When a system's designer changes a subsystem (component), he or she changes its measure of performance somewhat, which in turn produces a change in the performance measure of the whole system.

A management information system includes the programming subsystem, which in turn comprises various programmers, each being a purposeful component pursuing his or her personal goals. The manager of the system may promote a junior programmer to a senior programmer, thereby improving the programmer's personal measure of performance. The programmer, as a result, becomes more productive, thereby improving the performance measure of the management information system.

5. "S has an environment (defined either teleologically or ateleologically) which also coproduces the measure of performance of S"—The environment of a system consists of things outside the system that cannot be changed by the system's activities. However, the nature of the system's measure of performance depends on its environment and varies if the environment changes over time, or if the environment imposes new constraints on the system.

   Information requirements of managers in an organization tend to change over time. The management information system must adapt itself to these changes in order not to sustain reductions in the system's measure of performance.

6. "There exists a *decision maker* who—via his or her resources—can produce changes in the measures of performance of S's components, and hence changes in the measure of performance of S"—In organizations the managers are the decision makers. Resources are acquired and allocated under their control. A change in the allocation of resources among the subsystems of an organization can affect their measures of performance and hence change the organization's performance measure.

   The manager of the management information system can transfer money appropriated for purchased software to in-house software development, thereby affecting the measure of performance of the system.

7. "There exists a *designer* who conceptualizes the nature of S in such a manner that the designer's concepts potentially produce actions in the decision maker, and hence changes in the measures of performance of S's components, and hence changes in the measure of performance of S"—The designer of a system is that individual (engineer, management consultant, architect, planner) who specifies the components of the system and their interrelations, thus determining the structure of the system. This specification must be based on a concept of the system as a whole, on its purpose, and on the measurement of its performance. The decision makers of the system must be convinced by the designer that his or her concepts can affect the system's measure of performance in order to allocate resources to the implementation of the designed system. In a management information system, the designer corresponds to the information analyst who may be in charge of developing a new computerized application. The designer must present a system plan that will motivate the managers of the system to support the development and implementation of the application.

8. "The designer's intention is to change S so as to maximize S's value to the client"—The system should be designed by a person whose interests are identical to those of the user of the system. The designer is successful to the extent that he or she can accurately measure the client's real needs of the system.

Many management information systems fail because their designers developed a system that was challenging and sophisticated but did not really meet the information requirement of the less technologically sophisticated users. An estimate of the user's intentions can be based on the measure of performance of the system.

9. "S is 'stable' with respect to the designer in the sense that there is a built-in guarantee that the designer's intention is ultimately realizable"—This means that it is verifiable that the designer's intentions are credible, legitimate, and trustworthy, and that his or her activities will improve the system for the client.

A management information system may employ its own internal auditors, outside consultants, or a steering committee to oversee the design process of a new application. These bodies serve as guarantors of the system, and the system designer should include them in the definition of his or her system.

The System's Trinity: Designer, Decision Maker, and User

In his nine conditions reviewed in the preceding section, Churchman distinguishes three purposive individuals who are prerequisite for a system to be successful in achieving its desired objectives: the client (user), the decision maker, and the designer. According to the conditions, if an entity is to be considered a system:

a. It has a user who is interested in the performance of the entity
b. It has a decision maker who affects the performance of the entity by controlling its resources
c. It has a designer whose preferences conform with the user's preferences and who designs the system so that it can be operated by the decision maker
d. The designer wishes to maximize the benefits to the user and
e. The system is capable of executing the designer's plans

Figure 4.7 illustrates this system's trinity.

The different personalities, perceptions, preferences (value systems), motivations, and purposes of the individuals involved in developing an information system were discussed in chapter 2 in accordance with the tenets and concepts of cognitive psychology. Churchman offers insights into the intricate interrelationships among such people from a systems theory point of view. For clarity's sake, assume that the designer, decision maker, and client are represented, respectively, by the information systems analyst, the programming unit, and a manager for whom an application is being developed.

In an extreme case all three roles may reside in one person. There are many situations where the systems analyst designed, programmed, and implemented a small application. It is not unheard of that a manager would analyze a problem and program a solution for his or her own use. In fact, we speculate that with the future developments in software and hardware technologies, such situations of end-user computing would proliferate. However, in most situations the client, decision maker, and designer are highly complex entities made up of interacting individuals. Each entity has its own purpose, and so has each individual within these entities.

Figure 4.7 The system's designer, decision maker, and client

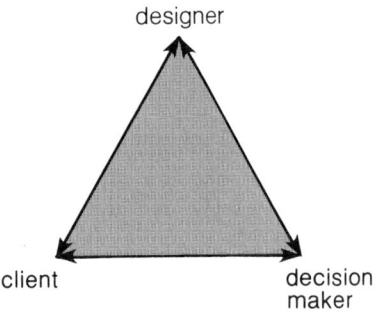

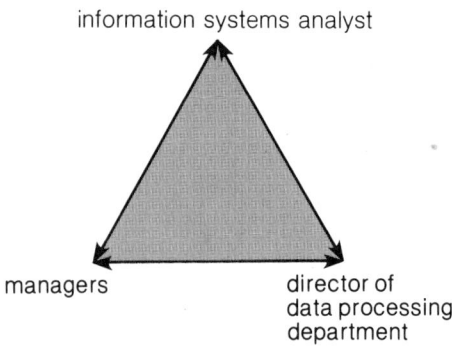

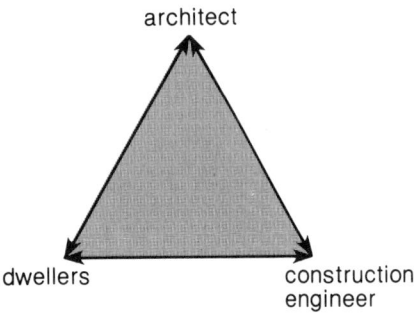

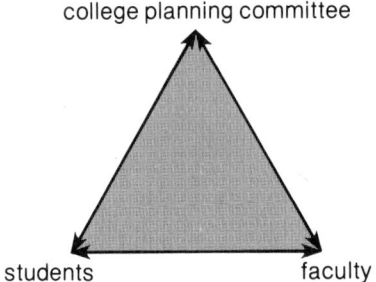

Each entity (system) can produce alternatives that lead with varying degrees of success to its desired objectives. For the client there is a set of possible futures and, based on a personal value system, he or she has a real preference for one future (state of nature) over others. Since resources are limited, the client cannot achieve his or her ideal future but instead must create a future that is as close to the ideal as the resources allow. The client thus applies a ''trade-off'' principle. The designer is successful to the extent that he or she can accurately measure the client's real preferences and estimate the underlying principle behind the client's trade-offs. This is a rather complicated task, particularly if the client is a group of persons.

Imagine the executive committee of a firm requesting the quick development of a real-time, online inquiry system with a response time to queries of not more than ten seconds. The designer of the system evaluates various design alternatives and realizes that the stipulated response time would impinge upon the performance of other applications being processed by the firm's computer. The designer's choice is further complicated by the problem of identifying the client. Is the client the committee as a whole or the chief executive officer? We can somewhat relax the complication by assuming that the designer's value structure is identical to the client's. But the third element of the system's trinity, the decision maker, is the one who controls the resources of the system and hence creates the real future of the client. The decision maker also has a value structure—a trade-off policy for alternative futures—that need not be identical to the client's and designer's value structures.

The programming unit in our example is at the time busy developing a computer-aided graphic design system and will be reluctant to turn away from this highly challenging task. The designer's role in this case will be to try to change the decision maker—to change its value structure—or try to select a more responsive decision maker. Churchman [4, p. 52] offers this piece of common sense:

> Since the client's interests are the same as the designer's, the designer should choose as the decision maker that complex of wills (potential producers) which the designer's conceptualizations can influence to produce the maximum gain in S's measure of performance relative to the client. Hence the designer should always conceptualize how his recommendations can be implemented in order to select the optimal decision maker.

To recapitulate, the designer, the decision maker, and the client are all important and have a role in the task of developing a system. They need to understand their roles as well as to have a theory about the system. They must try to understand how they can learn about the system, what influence they can have on the system's development and implementation, and where and why they should exert influence or compromise for the good of the system's purpose.

Classification of Systems

In order to use the systems approach as a method for analyzing complex systems, such systems must be classified and characterized. Classification is the first step in developing a theory. It provides for the relation of a system being studied to a certain class that has defined characteristics and a known method of treatment. The classification is qualitative in nature, and the boundaries among different classes of systems are not always sharp. Therefore, there is sometimes an element of arbitrariness and presumptuousness in assigning a given system to one class or another [for a discussion of some classes of systems, see 1].

Natural and Human-Made Systems

Natural systems are part of nature, while human-made systems are created by humans. We are concerned with human-made systems. Note that natural systems are not teleological.

Abstract and Concrete Systems

An *abstract* system is an orderly arrangement of components all of which are concepts. For example, languages and number systems are abstract. In an abstract system, components are created by defining, and the interrelations between them are created by assumptions.

There are two main classes of abstract systems:

1. A *procedural* system, which is an orderly arrangement of procedures, regulations, and laws, whose purpose is the solution of problems or the accomplishment of tasks. For example, a legal system and an organizational structure are procedural.

2. A *conceptual* system, which is essentially a symbolic construct. Einstein's theory of relativity is conceptual. A subclass of conceptual systems is *abstracted* systems—that is, conceptual systems corresponding with and explaining a certain aspect of reality.

A *concrete* system is one in which at least two components are objects. We are concerned in this book only with such systems. There are two main classes of concrete systems:

1. A *physical* system, which is a set of physical components that operate together to accomplish an objective—i.e., a computer system and an irrigation system.

2. A *social* system, which is an organized and coordinated group of people who operate together to achieve common purposes—i.e., organizations.

Closed and Open Systems

A *closed* system is one that has no environment. It has no interaction with any element not contained within it; it is completely self-contained. For example, a system of signal lights whose operation is not affected by traffic or human operators is a closed system.

An *open* system is one that has an environment and interacts with elements in the environment. It exchanges resources (inputs and outputs) with its environment. For example, organizations and information systems are open.

A relatively closed system is one that exchanges with the environment only controlled and well-defined inputs and outputs. An example is a computer program. An open system, on the other hand, may be subject to random and undefined inputs and disturbances from the environment.

Deterministic, Probabilistic, and Random Systems

These classes pertain to the degree of randomness inherent in the behavior of a system.

A *deterministic* system operates in a perfectly predictable manner. Since the processing by its components is known with certainty, knowledge about its inputs enables prediction of its outputs—a computer program, for example.

A *probabilistic* system operates in a probable manner. There is some degree of risk in predicting its outputs, since each output has a unique probability of appearance. A quality control system is one such example.

A *random* system operates in a completely unpredictable manner since there is uncertainty about its rules of behavior and the interrelations among its components. The stock exchange is a random system.

Human, Machine, and Human/Machine Systems

A machine system is an automatic physical system that operates without human intervention. It is a relatively closed and deterministic system and always performs exactly as it is supposed to perform. Its behavior is predictable and easy to control—a computer, for example.

A human system is basically comprised of human elements. It is an open and probabilistic system whose behavior is relatively unpredictable, such as is the strategic planning systems in organizations.

A *human/machine* system is a combination of human and machine subsystems. An example of a human/machine system that emphasizes the human elements is a transaction-processing system. An example of a human/machine system that emphasizes the machine elements is a process-controlled chemical plant. A human/machine system is an attempt to use the best characteristics of both.

Purposeful Systems

A *purposeful* system is one that can produce the same output in different ways in the same state and can produce different outputs in the same way and in different states. In other words, it has the characteristic of equifinality—the ability to achieve the same final end by different means and from different states. Human beings are the most familiar example of such systems. A computerized information system is another example (provided that its human elements are considered). The reports it produces can be printed, or they can be displayed on a cathode ray tube (CRT) with the system in a state of all output devices being active. If the state of the system changes—e.g., its devices are down—the system can still produce the same reports by manually processing its data. The system can change its course of action only if directed by the operators to do so.

Adaptive and Nonadaptive Systems

An *adaptive* system is one that can modify itself or its environment when either has changed to the system's disadvantage. In this manner the system attempts to regain some of the efficiency lost as a result of the change. An example is the organization.

A *nonadaptive* system is one that does not react or respond when there is a change in its environment or its state. An example is a pressurization system in a passenger airplane.

Simple and Complex Systems

These classes are characterized by the level of complexity of the systems being classified. A *simple system* (simplex) is one with a few components and a small number of interrelations among them. An example is a small barber shop. A *complex system* is one with (relatively) many components and many interrelations that can be fully described. An example is a computer hardware system. And an exceedingly complex system is a complex system whose components and interrelations cannot be fully described. An example is a large organization.

Open-Loop and Closed-Loop Systems

An *open-loop* (open-end) system is one that has no component performing a system-control function (the concept of control is defined next)—there is no comparison between its input and output. An example is an atom bomb. Such systems are rare and are usually found as natural entities.

A *closed-loop* (closed-end) system is one that contains at least one component that performs a system-control function. All organizations are closed-loop systems with some form of an information system constituting the subsystem providing for the system's control.

In this book we are mainly interested in two systems: the organization and the information system. Both can be classified as systems that are open, purposeful, adaptive, closed-loop, human-made, human/machine, concrete, complex, social, and probabilistic. This is not to say that some subsystems of the organization and its information system cannot display characteristics that would classify them differently. For example, a computer is a machine system, relatively closed and deterministic.

The Process and Elements of Control

In a closed-loop system at least one subsystem has a system-control function.

> This subset (or subsystem) compares achieved outcomes with desired outcomes and makes adjustments in the behavior of the system which are directed toward reducing the observed deficiencies. It also determines what the desired outcomes are. The control function is normally exercised by an executive body which operates on a feedback principle [1, p. 670].

The essence of *control* is sensing the system's outputs, comparing them to the objectives (standards), and generating a corrective action if necessary. The corrective action taken by the control subsystem usually takes the form of a change in the inputs to the controlled system, but it may also lead to a change in the structure of the controlled system or to changed objectives (standards). For example, the goal of a firm is to capture a market share of at least 25 percent. The quarterly sales report indicates that the firm has only 18 percent of the market. The firm's president compares the target to the outcome and can decide that (a) the target is attainable if the advertising budget is increased, or (b) the target is unrealistic and should be adjusted downward, or (c) new products should be developed.

A closed-loop system contains two components that are linked together by a feedback loop (fig. 4.8). These are the controlled subsystem and the control subsystem. The feedback channels communicate the sensing signals to the control subsystem and the *corrective signals* to the controlled subsystem.

The process of control is thus based on information feedback. Feedback is essential to an adaptive system. Feedback that reduces fluctuations around the standard is termed *negative feedback*. In a system with a negative feedback control process, the corrective signals reverse the direction in which the controlled subsystem is moving. Negative feedback hence reduces the entropy of a system. All control mechanisms in

Figure 4.8 A closed-loop system

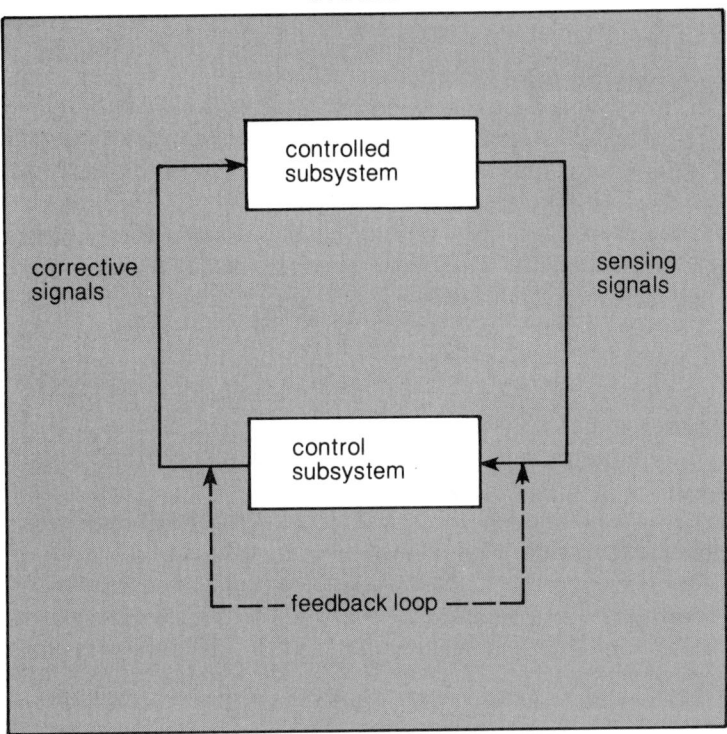

organizations are based on a principle of negative feedback. For example, if labor costs significantly overshoot the budgeted costs, employees may be terminated, or overtime work may be curtailed. *Positive feedback,* on the other hand, amplifies the fluctuations around the standard. In this case the corrective signals reinforce the direction the controlled system is moving in and tend to increase its entropy—for example, applying the brakes when you are traveling uphill on a straight and clear road to meet your beloved.

The negative feedback control system comprises five elements:

1. Determination of the conditions to be controlled, the outputs used to measure them, the measuring units, and the measuring frequency. These conditions represent the state of the controlled system relative to its goals.

2. A *sensor* for measuring the conditions and sending the sensing signals to the control unit.

3. A *standard* for the conditions being measured.

4. A *control unit* (a comparing device) that compares the measurements with the standards.

5. An *action generator* (activating unit) that generates a corrective signal to the controlled subsystem.

Figure 4.9 illustrates the control process and uses an organization as an example. One of the characteristics of the control process is that it is distinct from the transformation process. A typical organization transforms inputs (resources) into goods and services to achieve some goals. In the process of transformation, source documents (hard-copy or electronic) are created that describe the physical goods and services and the consumption of resources (other source documents collected may be external, describing environmental events). These source documents are the sensors of the control unit. In an organization the information system serves as the control unit. It collects raw data in the form of source documents (sales vouchers, quantities produced, ledger entries, daily employee-hours, etc.), processes them, and compares them to preestablished standards and norms (budgets, productivity ratios, etc.). It produces information that the managers at all levels use to make decisions. The decisions are transmitted back to the transformation process in the form of written and oral instructions and regulations.

A prerequisite for the control mechanism is information about the system's activities and about the standards. The information generated by the information system is either used for current control or is stored and periodically used for deciding whether to change or replace existing standards. Control is thus triggered by information.

There are additional notions inherent in the system control process:

1. *The reaction of the controlled system to the corrective signal*—The reaction is a function of the system's structure and the nature of the corrective signal. In other words, the ability of a system to be controlled is affected by (a) the quality of the corrective signal (unambiguous, timely, reliable); (b) the adaptive and learning characteristics of the controlled system and its components; and (c) the nature of the inputs to the controlled system (sometimes, for example, new employees cannot be hired).

2. *Delays*—Each stage in the control process is associated with delays and time lags that contribute to a built-in delay of the process as a whole. It takes time to collect data, process it, compare it to standards, reach a decision, and transmit a corrective signal. The implication for information system design is that the structure of the control system must be adapted to the behavior of the controlled system, so that the control process will function at the proper pace.

3. *The law of requisite variety*—The law states that in order to control each possible state of the elements of a controlled system, the control system must have a corresponding variety of possible response states (a "response" to every "question"). Since the control process senses the output of each system component and transmits corrective signals back to the components, implementation of the law would require substantial information processing and transmission capacities. A firm wishing to control a fleet of 1,000 cars

Figure 4.9 The transformation process and the negative feedback control process of a system

SYSTEM (organization)

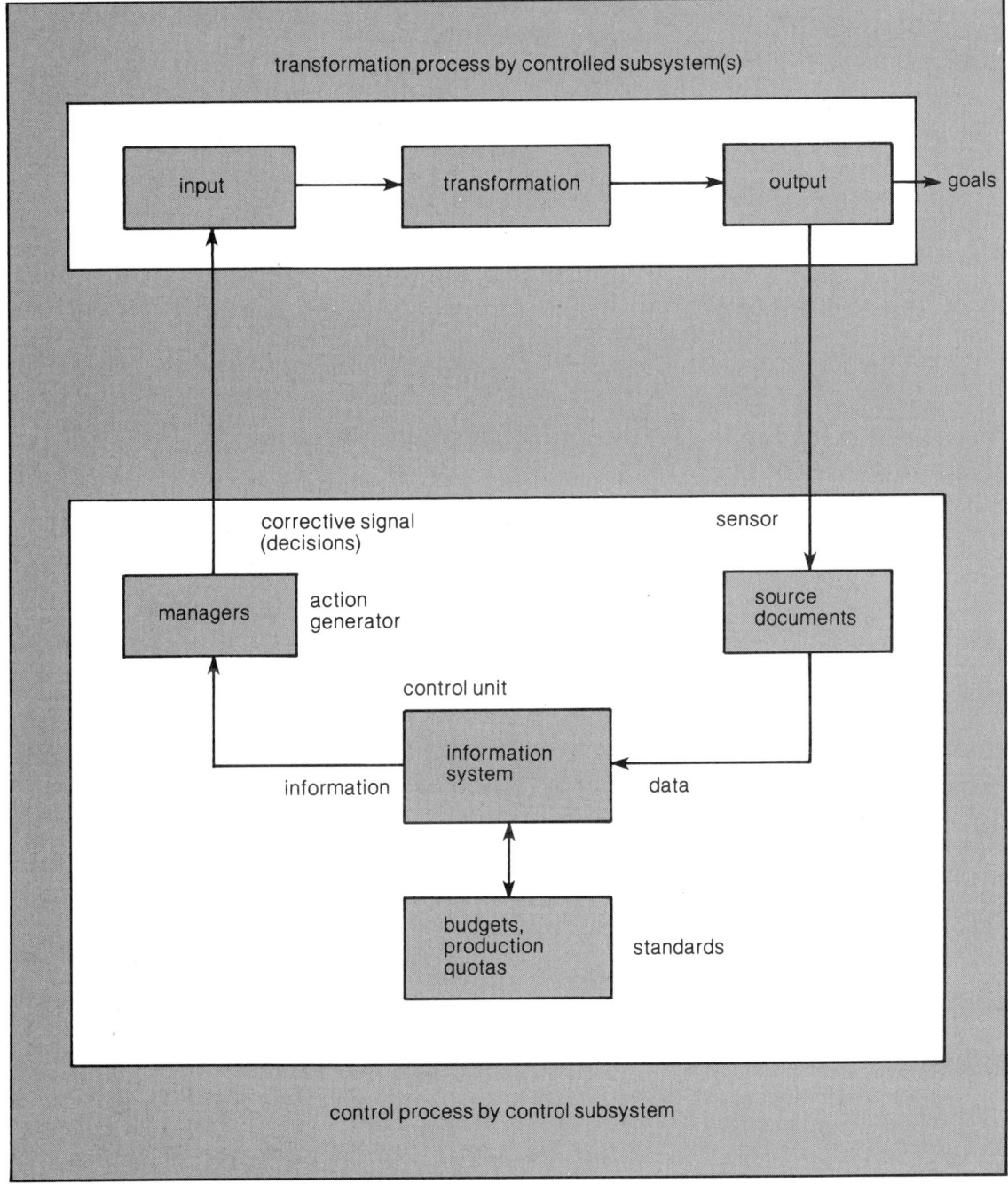

would have to receive data on each car and generate a corrective action for each possible variation in the state of each car. This obviously cannot be done by one individual. The various solutions to the problem reflected by the law of requisite variety have implications for the process of information system design. Here are some:

a. The variety of possible states of elements of the controlled system that are reported and need some response can be reduced by establishing a range of states that are considered to be "normal." Only states outside the range are considered to be out of control (analogous to exception reporting).

b. The variety of states can be subdivided and delegated among several controllers. This implies that the capacities of the control elements (either manual or automatic) can be increased.

c. The control subsystem can be designed as a human/machine system in which the computer generates programmed control responses to expected and well-defined states, and the human generates nonprogrammed responses to unexpected and ill-defined states.

Practical Conclusions for Information System Design and Use

The following list is included here to guide the user in information system design and use.

1. Most systems are subsystems of larger systems. The objective of subsystems should conform to the objective of the system in order to avoid suboptimization.

2. When studying a component of a system, its role in the system should be analyzed rather than its role as an individual entity.

3. The information system is one of the subsystems of the organization.

4. Current computer hardware and software enable the development of information systems that cut across organizational boundaries and provide integrated information for management decisions.

5. The systems approach to problem solving is essential to information systems development. It comprises the stages of information systems analysis, information systems design, and information systems implementation.

6. Real problems in organizations are often confused with mere symptoms of problems.

7. Exact definition of a problem, of an information requirement, or of a system is a prerequisite for a solution or design of a system.

8. Data collection methods should be evaluated in terms of their costs and benefits before being adopted for use in the processes of problem solving and information system development.

9. The number of system design alternatives considered by the systems designer should be more than one, but should be narrowed down to a manageable number.

10. "Doing nothing" about a problem is a legitimate alternative whose costs and benefits must be evaluated.

11. The processes of problem solving and information system design are sequential and iterative.

12. Components of a system being analyzed can be regarded as black boxes. The interfaces of these black boxes with other subsystems are studied, while their internal structure is deferred for a later study.

13. A system that is too complex or large to be analyzed as a whole should be factored into subsystems. The process of factoring should continue until the subsystems are of manageable size.

14. Interactions among subsystems can be either reduced or controlled through better coordination or communications among the subsystems.

15. In designing information systems, the system designer should consider having buffers, slack resources, and standards in the system. These will allow for decoupling of subsystems—fewer interactions. The costs of these decoupling methods should also be considered.

16. The designer should build into the system measures of performance that reflect the efficiency and effectiveness of the system in achieving its goals and purposes.

17. The design team should include representatives of three parties—the designer, the user of the systems, and the decision maker of the system (the party that controls the resources of the system).

18. The performance measures for a system must be related to the performance measures of its subsystems.

19. The designer is successful to the extent that he or she can accurately measure the client's real needs of the system.

20. The designer should include in the designed system tools and methods that serve to audit the designed system.

21. The designer should attempt to design a human/machine system that best characterizes both of the individual systems.

22. Since the environment of an information system in an organization constantly changes, the designer should provide adaptive capabilities in the system.

23. In designing a control system, the designer should consider having the system provide an automatic response to usual situations and a human response to unusual situations. This is implied by the law of requisite variety.

Summary

This chapter has described the systems approach to the processes of problem solving and information system development.

A system is a set of interdependent components. The systems approach is a philosophy of structure that coordinates the activities of subsystems within a system. It enables analysis of complex problems and systems. Implementation of the systems approach cuts across traditional functional lines of the organization and prevents suboptimization. The justification for using the systems approach stems from the accelerated diversity, complexity, and size of a modern organization on the one hand, and from modern theories and tools to deal with them on the other.

A system is determined by defining its goals, environment, boundaries, and constraints and then tracking down its inputs, outputs, components, and their interrelations.

Systems are factored into subsystems in order to simplify the study of components and their interactions. There are various mechanisms to cope with the complexity introduced by the interactions.

Several conditions are necessary for an entity to be called a ''system.'' These include identification of the system's purpose, its measures of performance, and the different roles of the system's designer, decision maker, and client.

Various classes of systems are introduced to show that organizations and information systems are open, purposeful, adaptive, closed-loop, human-made, human/machine, concrete, complex, social, and probabilistic systems.

The process of control in systems is based on information feedback. The control system is comprised of a sensor, a standard, a control unit, and a corrective action generator. The feedback loop links together these elements and transmits the sensing signals and the corrective signals between a controlled system and a control system.

The chapter ends by listing the implications of system concepts for the design and use of information systems.

Readers who are interested in learning more on General Systems Theory and the Systems Approach may refer to references [2], [3], [6], and [7].

This chapter concludes Part I of the book, which presented and described concepts of systems, information, and human information processing. These concepts and their implications are required for the discussion in the next chapter of the various models of information in organizations.

Key Concepts

action generator
black box
boundaries
clusters of subsystems
components
constraints
control
control unit
corrective signals
coupling
decoupling
effectiveness
efficiency
environment
factoring
feedback (negative, positive)
general systems theory
information system development process
interactions
interfaces
law of requisite variety

measure of performance
problem-solving process
sensor
standard
system structure
systems: abstract, abstracted, adaptive,
   closed, closed-loop, complex,
   concrete, conceptual, deterministic,
   human/machine, natural, nonadaptive,
   open, open-loop, physical,
   probabilistic, procedural, purposeful,
   random, simple, social
systems approach
system's client, designer, decision
   maker
systems technologies
suboptimization
subsystem
synergism
teleological systems

References

1. Ackoff, R. L. "Towards a System of System Concepts." *Management Science* (July 1971): 661–71.
2. Boulding, K. "General Systems Theory—The Skeleton of Science." *Management Science* (April 1956): 197–208.
3. Churchman, C. W. *The Systems Approach.* New York: Dell Books, 1968.
4. ———. *The Design of Inquiring Systems: Basic Concepts of Systems and Organization.* New York: Basic Books, 1971.
5. Mason, R. O., and E. B. Swanson. "Measurement for Management Decision: A Perspective." *California Management Review* (Spring 1979): 70–81.
6. von Bertalanffy, L. "General System Theory." *General Systems.* Yearbook of the Society for Advancement of General System Theory (1956): 1–10.
7. ———. *General System Theory: Foundations, Development, Applications.* New York: George Braziller, 1968.
8. ———. "The History and Status of General Systems Theory." In *Trends in General Systems Theory,* edited by G. J. Klir, 21–38. New York: John Wiley & Sons, 1972.

Questions

1. What is meant by the system approach?
2. Explain how Aristotle's statement "The whole is greater than the sum of its parts" relates to the analysis of systems.
3. Differentiate between effectiveness and efficiency.
4. Explain what is meant by factoring and why it is necessary.
5. What are the three sources of interactions among subsystems and how can they be reduced?
6. Give an example of an ateleological system.
7. How do the client, the decision maker, and the designer interact in system design?
8. What is the role of performance in the conception of a system?
9. Can we have an open, abstract system? Explain the rationale for your answer.
10. What is the function of system control?
11. How can a system designer reduce the variety of possible response states without decreasing the effectiveness of the system?
12. Distinguish between the control process and the transformation process.

Problems

1. A large airplane manufacturer has set up a computer consulting firm as a subsidiary. The firm uses the manufacturer's computer and acts as a consultant to both the manufacturer and to external organizations. The firm is establishing an information system to control project management. Describe the scope and a possible structure for such a system.
2. The consulting firm mentioned in problem one employs subject specialists in the various areas in which the firm does consulting (aerospace, steel manufacture, car manufacture), computer specialists, and management specialists. Using your knowledge of the structure of a system, how should the firm be organized? How would this affect the project management information system (if at all) that the firm plans to use in order to control its consulting projects?
3. "Information requirements of managers in an organization tend to change over time. The management information system must adapt itself to these changes in order not to sustain reductions in the system's measure of performance." Suggest ways in which an MIS could be designed to be adaptable. Discuss control measures and types of feedback necessary.
4. Describe possible outcomes for a system in which the designer
   a. inaccurately defined the problem; and
   b. incorrectly identified the client.
5. Relate the classification of information systems (deterministic, probabilistic, or random) to the types of information value which they might contain (i.e., normative, realistic, subjective).

Computerized Retax Bus System (CRBS)

The Government of Ontario Transit (GOT) was established in 1967 as an interregional transport system funded by the Ontario Provincial Government in Canada. Since Ontario province's satellite cities and their populations are widely spread, GOT needed a new system which could provide efficient and quality services within a low traffic volume area. The public was suffering from inconsistent bus service hours and inadequate stopping locations. Thus, GOT appointed a team of industrial engineers to develop some innovative ideas for solving transit problems in the Ontario area.

As a result of this study, in 1986 GOT requested Advanced Transport Systems (ATS), a world renowned consulting company, to develop the Retax demand responsive bus system. The main services provided were to be advanced transport planning, project analysis, vehicle control and monitoring systems for on-demand and/ or scheduled bus services. ATS accepted GOT's request to develop a prototype with a computerized demand responsive system to serve a selected small city.

As a result, the Computerized Retax Bus System (CRBS) is serving an area of 125 square kilometers with a population of about 40,000 at Scarborough (near Toronto) under a large-scale trial operation.

Eighteen buses serve 118 stops, 36 of which are equipped with call posts. These buses operate on demand, serving stops as required, in no fixed order and at no fixed times. They travel on fixed routes, from an origin to a terminal point, serving basic stops regardless of demand and arriving at stops in a set order according to a timetable or at set intervals.

Travel requests are reported via call posts or private or public telephones. Bus movements are followed continuously, and the control computer automatically allocates the travel requests to the buses in service, overlapping to ensure good passenger loads and good service. The operating mode is chosen to suit the time of day and transport requirements. During the morning and evening peak hours, traffic volume is handled largely by scheduled bus services, while demand-responsive buses are used chiefly to provide service in the residential areas off the fixed routes.

At first, commuters resisted. CRBS caused quite a resistance among commuters due to a lack of confidence in a system that didn't use human drivers. However, its popularity rose steadily because of its flexibility and the quality of services. Demand almost doubled within six months.

Questions

Regarding the Computerized Retax Bus System (CRBS) as a system, describe the following:

1. the environment and boundary of the system

2. inputs, processes, and outputs

3. the people who constitute the system trinity in CRBS

Part II

Information Systems—
From Theory to Practice

Chapter 5 Conceptual Models of Information in Organizations

The role of information in organizations is analogous to the role of blood in living organisms. Blood provides organic tissues with food and oxygen; information provides decision makers with facts and forecasts and conveys policies and instructions to operating organizational levels. An information system is thus the arterial system of organization. The systems approach requires that any attempt to understand the role and structure of information systems shall involve a comprehensive model incorporating organizational as well as informational concepts.

This chapter introduces some prevalent models of organizations, incorporates information concepts into them, and comes up with a comprehensive model. The model will then serve to classify various organizational information systems.

Models of Organization

Introduction

The main purpose of this book is to facilitate the understanding of the role and structure of information systems in organizations. Knowledge of the way organizations are built and act is an important cornerstone to understanding the role of information in organizations.

First we will review some of the theoretical and empirical approaches to understanding organizations. Whenever you have to learn something, be it a phenomenon or an abstract concept, you probably select one or more of the following methods:

1. Examine the whole population of the objects in your inquiry (if feasible).
2. Examine a selected sample of objects.
3. Create a model of the real objects and examine the model.
4. Deduce your suppositions from examination of surrogate yet similar objects.
5. Deduce your suppositions from pure logic.

Each of these methods might suit a different set of circumstances. For example, if you want to learn about dinosaurs, you cannot take samples, nor can you examine a whole object. You will probably locate some fossil bones, use some logic, and develop a model of a dinosaur skeleton. If you want to learn the public's attitude to a certain candidate for the presidency, neither logic nor models and surrogates will help, and since you cannot investigate the entire population, you will poll a sample.

Organizations, our concern here, are too many for us to examine them all. They are too "human" and not rigorous enough for us to use pure logic. They are too complex to be replaced by surrogates. We are left with sampling and modeling—we may examine a few of the organizations and then attempt to generalize by constructing models based on our findings.

Models are sometimes risky in the sense that they might be too simplistic. They may ignore parts of the phenomena they ought to describe. On the other hand, their usefulness in understanding phenomena and concepts is so great that we tend to take that risk. It is, however, a good practice always to bear in mind the deficiencies of models (shortcuts, relaxing assumptions, compromises)—even while we derive substantial benefits from their use.

Modeling an Organization

Have you ever thought of an appropriate way to describe an organization? You may, if you wish, take photographs of all the offices and persons involved and prepare an album. But would it help to understand the organization? If you were given an album of photographs of all the offices and individuals employed by General Motors, would it facilitate your understanding of the company?

You may, if you wish, obtain a financial statement of an organization, which is, in a way, a model of the firm. But would it reveal anything beyond the financial status of the organization? Would it depict hierarchical levels, decision-making processes, and communication channels?

Or you may draw an *organizational chart* (fig. 5.1), which would certainly reflect hierarchical levels and partly reflect formal communication channels. Would it satisfy your requirements?

The answer depends on the purpose of describing the organization. Certainly both the financial statement and the organizational chart are models describing an organization, but each of them is used for different purposes. The former might help in financial analysis, while the latter might help in designing promotion routes.

Chapter 3 led us to relate information to decision making; chapter 4 directed us toward the systems approach. Naturally, if we want to incorporate information in models of organization, we have to search for models that are holistic (describe the organization as a system), and that focus on decision making within the organizational system. The models we have chosen were developed by Anthony [2] and Forrester [7]. We combine these with the concepts of Simon [10], which were already presented in chapter 3.

Figure 5.1 An organizational chart

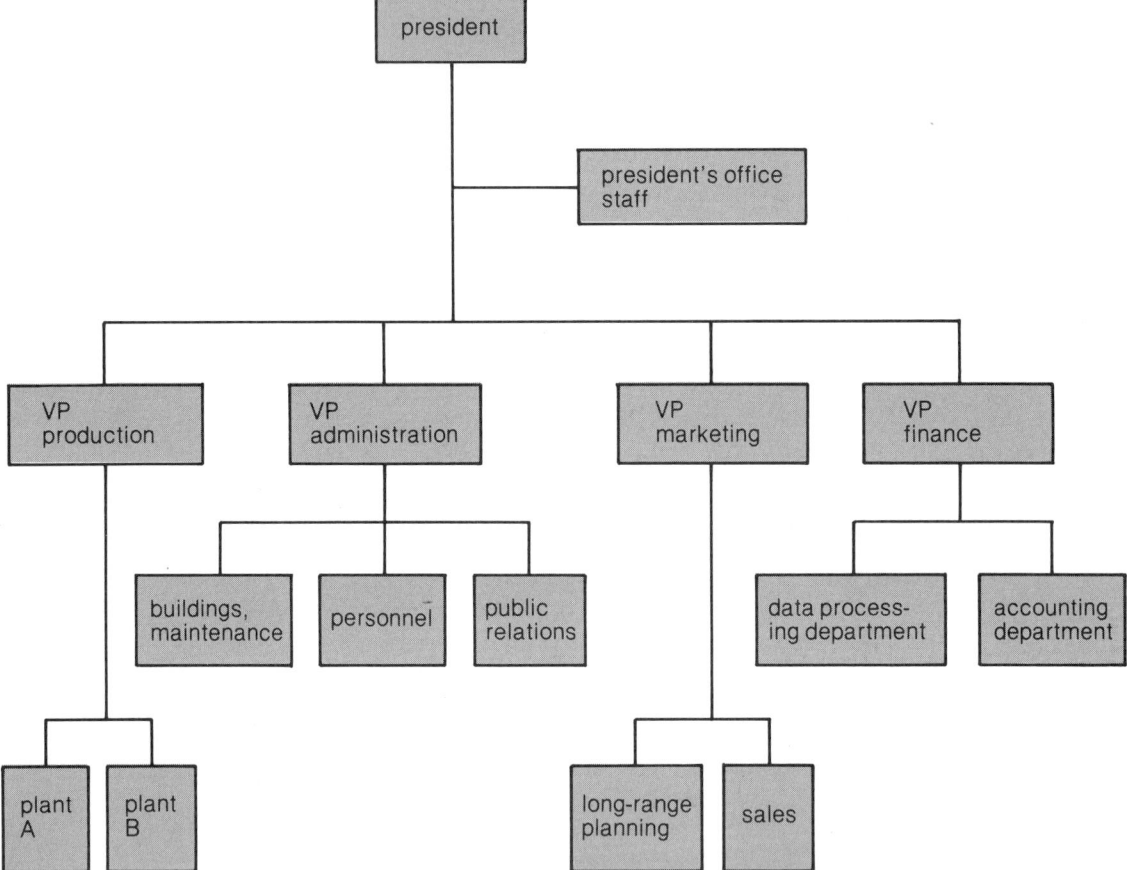

Anthony's Model

A reasonable way to view an organization is through its hierarchy of decision making. Anthony [2], who focused on the managerial portion of the organization, classified the management process into three levels.

1. *Strategic planning (SP)*—"Deciding on objectives of the organization, on changes in these objectives, on the resources used to attain these objectives, and on the policies that are to govern the acquisition, use, and disposition of these resources."

2. *Management control (MC)*—Assuring "that resources are obtained and used effectively and efficiently in the accomplishment of the organization's objectives."

Figure 5.2 Management levels in organizations

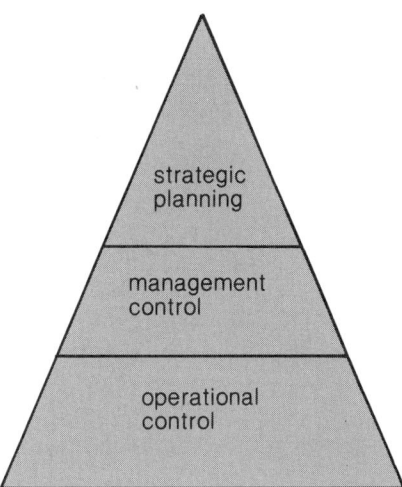

3. *Operational control (OC)*—''Assuring that specific tasks are carried out effectively and efficiently.''

Figure 5.2 illustrates Anthony's idea of management levels as a three-level pyramid. The SP level of managers controls the long-term activities and decisions of the organization; the MC level controls the medium-term activities; the OC level controls the short-term activities of the organization.

Let us examine two examples of this *hierarchical model of organization.* Suppose we want to classify decisions made in the production division of a manufacturing firm. Decisions on annual production volume and annual budget certainly lie in the SP level. Decisions on monthly production scheduling, which imply machine and personnel allocation, are part of the MC level. Daily control of working shifts and individual shops are examples of the OC level of decision making.

The second example deals with the registration of students in a university. The total number of students to be admitted and allocated among schools would be decided at the SP level. Registration procedures and eligibility criteria would be set up at the MC level. The decision whether to accept or reject an individual applicant (excluding very special exceptions) would be made at the OC level.

Management Functions

Early in this century a Frenchman, Henry Fayol [6], classified five functions that are normally handled by managers. His definitions still hold today. According to Fayol, all managers perform the following functions:

1. *Planning* what is to be done.
2. *Organizing* the appropriate structure to accomplish the plan.
3. *Staffing* the organization with appropriate personnel and coordinating their activities.

Table 5.1   Management Functions at the Various Managerial Levels

Management Function	Managerial Levels		
	Strategic Planning	*Management Control*	*Operational Control*
Planning	Long-range	Medium-range	Short-range
Organizing	General framework	Departmental level	Small unit level
Staffing	Key persons	Medium-level personnel	Operational personnel
Directing	General and long-range directives	Tactics and procedures	Daily and routine activities
Controlling	Aggregate level	Periodic control and exceptions	Regular and continuous supervision

4. *Directing* (commanding) the staff toward the accomplishment of the plans.

5. *Controlling* the activities so that the objectives can be met.

When we incorporate these management functions into Anthony's model, it turns out that each function is performed at each managerial level. However, there are variations concerning the scope of each function in the various levels. These variations are presented in table 5.1.

Draw an analogy from the military: while the top-level managers are involved with wars (strategy), the middle-level managers are engaged in battles (tactics), and the low-level managers are controlling the organizational skirmishes, patrols, raids, ambushes, recruiting, and training.

In summary, the scope of each function narrows as we move downward in the organizational hierarchy. At the bottom, managers deal with more detailed data referring to shorter periods. They have a shorter planning horizon and a smaller span of control. The effects of their decisions are detected earlier and more easily. The implication is that control in these levels is more concrete. In other words, adopting Simon's terms (see ch. 3), we may say that decisions at the upper level are completely unstructured, whereas at the bottom they are fairly close to being structured.

The tight relationship between types of decision (Simon) and management level (Anthony) is a very important point and will be referred to throughout this chapter.

Anthony's Model—An Expansion

The three levels of the organizational pyramid (fig. 5.2) concentrate on the managerial levels in organizations. In fact, organizations also employ people who do some work besides managing others. Naturally we can expand the hierarchical model to include the *operations* (OP) of the organization as well. This is illustrated in figure 5.3 (a similar expansion is presented in Davis and Olson [4] and Ein-Dor and Segev [5]).

Figure 5.3 Hierarchical model of organizations

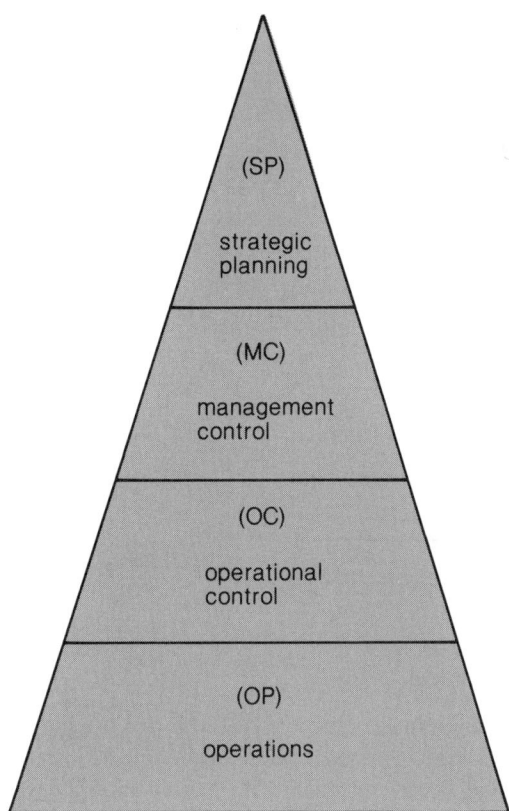

At the level of operations, inputs are physically transformed by the organizational resources (personnel, capital, machinery, information, etc.) into outputs (goods and services). This is the level of the bank teller, the secretary, the lathe operator, or the truck driver.

Following our previous examples, the operations level of the production division would be the entire personnel working in production—the production line, mainte- nance, and quality control workers. The operations level of the student registration system would include all the clerks employed at the registrar's office.

Obviously decisions at this level are structured (at least partly) and their scope is very narrow. They require accurate data up to the last detail. The control of the deci- sions should be instantly attainable, at least in theory (in practice, control is not main- tained permanently, and might have some snags). Note that most of the management functions, particularly planning, organizing, staffing, and directing, are not applicable for this level.

Figure 5.4 Flows and stocks in a distribution system

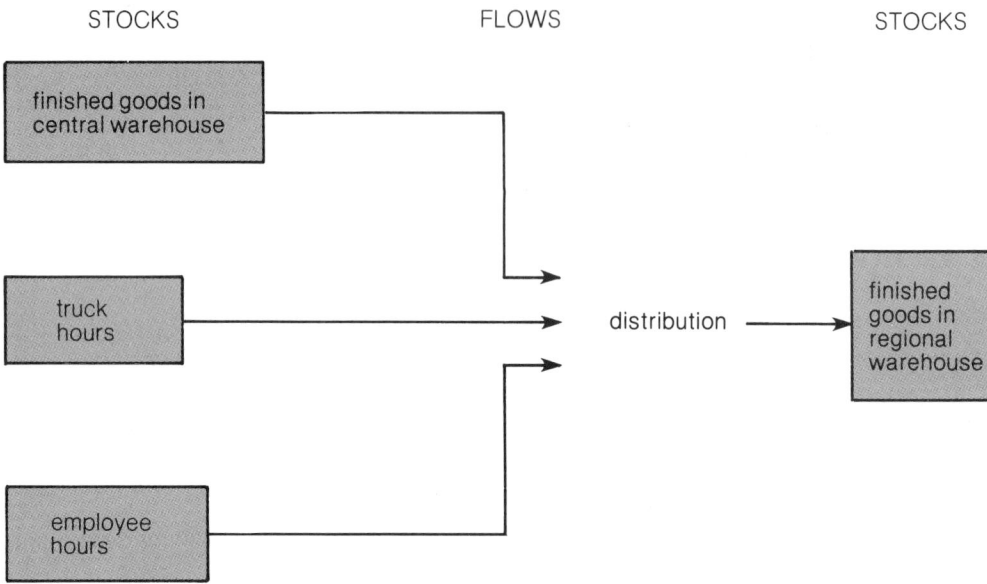

Industrial Dynamics Model

The preceding model has described the organization from a hierarchical viewpoint—it has distinguished various authority levels and reflected the different types of decisions made at each level. It has not dealt with flows and processes within and across organizational levels.

A different approach is to follow processes performed in an organization. In other words, we can observe various activities, combine them into processes, and then classify the processes. This approach is common in *industrial dynamics,* originally developed by Forrester [7]. The model that emerges is called the industrial dynamic model, or Forrester's model. We will now briefly review Forrester's model.

Basic Terms

An organization, according to Forrester, is a collection of *levels (stocks)* and *flows* (to avoid confusion with Anthony's "levels," we will use "stocks" for the discussion on Forrester). A stock is a buffer of any type of entity—raw materials inventory, cash, personnel, etc. A flow is a sequence of activities that transfers entities from one stock to another—production line, recruiting function, purchase of equipment, etc. It is possible, of course, for certain flows to interlace. Figure 5.4 exhibits these notions.

In figure 5.4 there are three different source stocks: materials (finished goods), equipment (trucks), and personnel. All three contribute to the generation of a flow of finished goods from a central to a regional warehouse, which is the subsequent stock in this case. Obviously there are flows and stocks preceding and proceeding to the

Figure 5.5 Physical and information flows in a distribution system

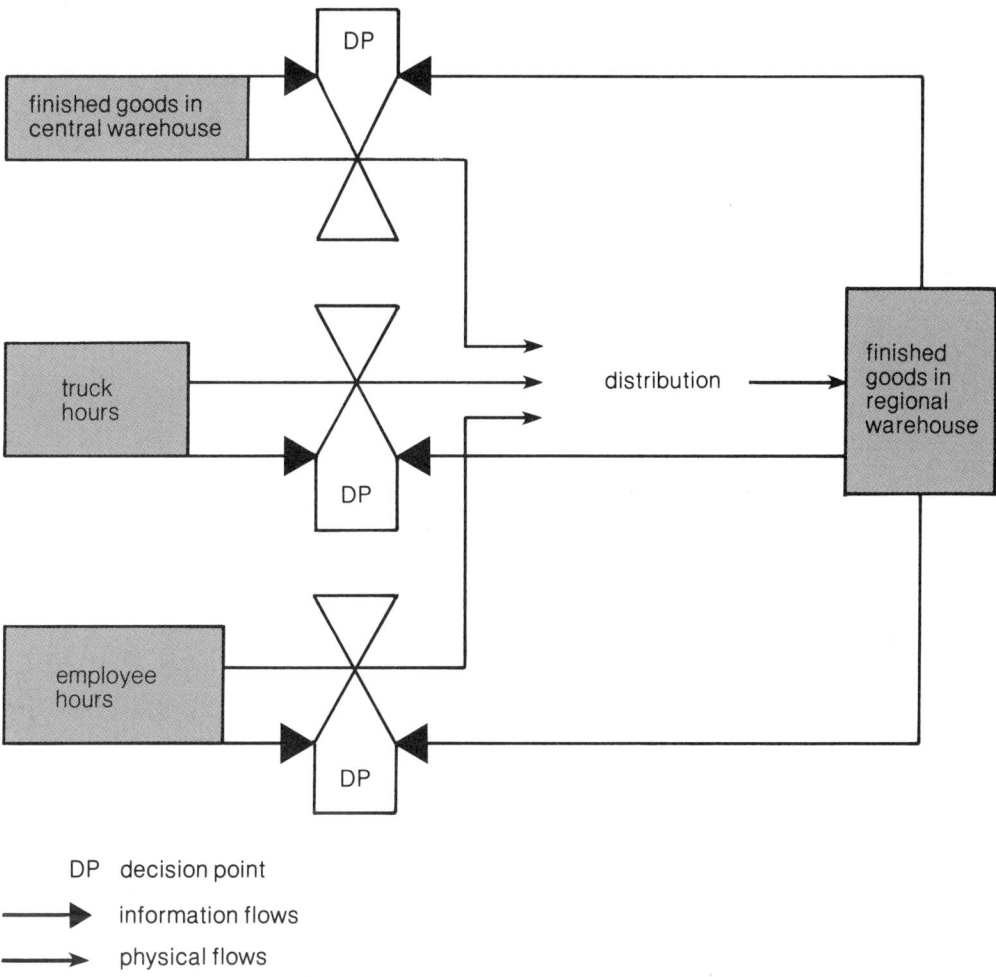

DP   decision point

⟶   information flows

⟶   physical flows

segment described in figure 5.4—production of goods, purchase of trucks, recruiting personnel, and regional distribution. Indeed, the entire organization can be described in that manner, although the description might be fairly complex.

The flows between stocks are regulated by *decision points,* which adjust the *flow rates* in accordance with information received about stocks. Hence we can superimpose on the stock-flow diagram an additional chart delineating information flows and decision-making points that affect physical flow rates. Figure 5.5, which augments figure 5.4, illustrates the role of information and decision making in Forrester's model.

A manager (decision maker) in this model is a function whose input is information about stocks and whose output is decision affecting physical flow rates. For example, the stocks of finished goods at the central and regional warehouses are reported to a decision maker who will consequently decide on the size and composition of shipments. In fact, figure 5.5 is somewhat simplistic since decisions about shipments, trucks, and employees are interdependent, and therefore the information lines should have connected almost all the stocks with all the decision points. However, we believe that the basic concepts of the model are now clear, even with the oversimplified diagram.

Basic Functional Systems

Figure 5.5 has exhibited three physical flows, each of a different type: finished goods are materials; trucks are equipment; and employees are human resources (personnel). Generally Forrester distinguished between five physical functional systems, each of which is composed of stocks and flows.

1. *Materials*—The system that transforms raw materials to finished goods.
2. *Customer orders*—The system that captures and processes the orders, that, in fact, trigger all the other activities in a business organization.
3. *Capital*—The system that provides and monitors the funds for the organizational activities.
4. *Personnel*—The system that handles human resources.
5. *Equipment*—The system that provides physical (nonhuman) resources.

The supervision of these systems is possible due to the existence of the sixth system, the information system. The information system contains stocks (data files) and flows (programs), too. The activities of the organization are pursued through the cooperative efforts of all six systems.

We will illustrate the model with the following example: Suppose there is an increase in customer orders in a certain region. It turns out that inventory stocks at the regional warehouse cannot meet the demand. Consequently an urgent shipment has to be delivered from the central to the regional warehouse. This requires the arrangement of additional trucks and drivers and also the commitment of more money to pay for salaries and other expenditures. In fact, we see here that a stimulus at the customer order system activates flows between stocks related to all the functional systems. Certainly most of these movements would not have been possible if each system had not been tied together through the information system.

Some Concluding Remarks

We have reviewed two models of organization, incorporated with some concepts taken from Fayol and Simon's works. None of the models is a complete description of the organization, and none explicitly sheds light on information systems within the organization. Their benefits and deficiencies should be assessed in accordance with the circumstances in which they are used.

The hierarchical model clearly distinguishes between management levels and, when incorporated with Simon and Fayol's ideas, characterizes various types of decisions made at each level. However, it is not dynamic in the sense that it does not trace flows and processes within and across levels.

The industrial dynamics model has exactly the opposite characteristics. It clearly follows the processes involved in an organization and explains the cooperative relationships among its various systems. However, it does not make a distinction between managerial levels. For example, in figure 5.5, we have stock labeled "trucks," which is part of the equipment system. The trucks stock might be affected by any of the following decisions:

1. To purchase new trucks
2. To service each truck after every 10,000 miles of travel
3. To dispatch a particular truck to carry a certain load

It is most likely that each of these decisions would be made and carried out by a different organizational level. Yet the model does not reflect this distinction, although from the information systems viewpoint the distinction is essential.

The merits of these organizational models, besides their contribution to the understanding of organizations, lie in the attempt to merge them, thereby benefitting from the advantages of both models, as well as specifically noting the informational aspects of the comprehensive result. This will be done in the next section (for another relevant discussion of information processing and organizations, see [8]).

Information in Organization

An extensive and pioneering effort to synthesize the ideas of Anthony, Forrester, and Simon into a comprehensive model was undertaken by Blumenthal [3]. A similar yet more compact approach is also presented in Ein-Dor and Segev's text [5, ch. 1]. We will follow Blumenthal's line here.

Building the Model

The model presented here is very formulated. Reality obviously cannot be as neat as the model. Nevertheless, the model is a great help when we have to understand and classify phenomena observed in reality. That is why this model is essential to the field of MIS.

The direction of building the model is bottom-up. We will begin with blocks constructing the bottom level of the organization and conclude with components at the top.

Functional Unit (FU)

The most basic activities of an organization are handled by *functional units* (FUs). A functional unit receives information about stocks, makes some elementary decisions, and regulates physical flow rates. Figure 5.6 depicts the structure of a functional unit.

At the bottom of figure 5.6 we can see the normal physical flow moving from one stock to the next. Information about a stock, combined with information from other functional units, is transferred to a *decision center* (DC) which, accordingly, instructs an *activity center* (AC) of actions to be carried out. The actions regulate the rate of the physical flow. Note that the information is also available to the activity center, which may undertake some actions under its discretion whenever such actions are highly structured (almost fully programmed). The decision center is also guided by management directives determining goals, policies, and procedures. It may also convey

Figure 5.6 A functional unit (FU)

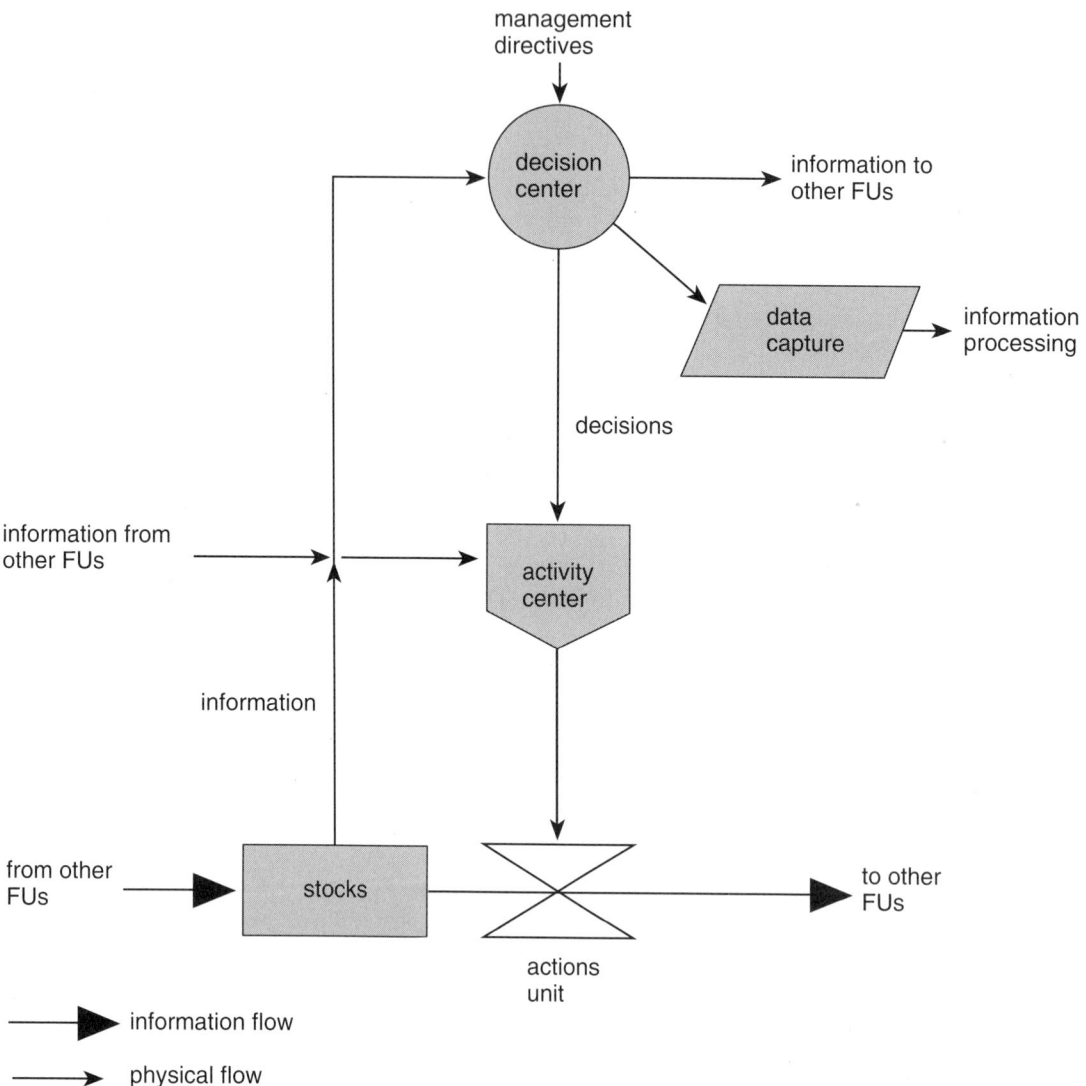

relevant information to other FUs directly or via an information processing system (data capture). A functional unit thus comprises a decision center, an activity center, and an actions unit.

In order to clarify these concepts, let us return now to the example of a distribution system illustrated in figures 5.4 and 5.5. The functional unit associated with the central warehouse of finished goods is illustrated in figure 5.7.

Figure 5.7 The functional unit of a central warehouse

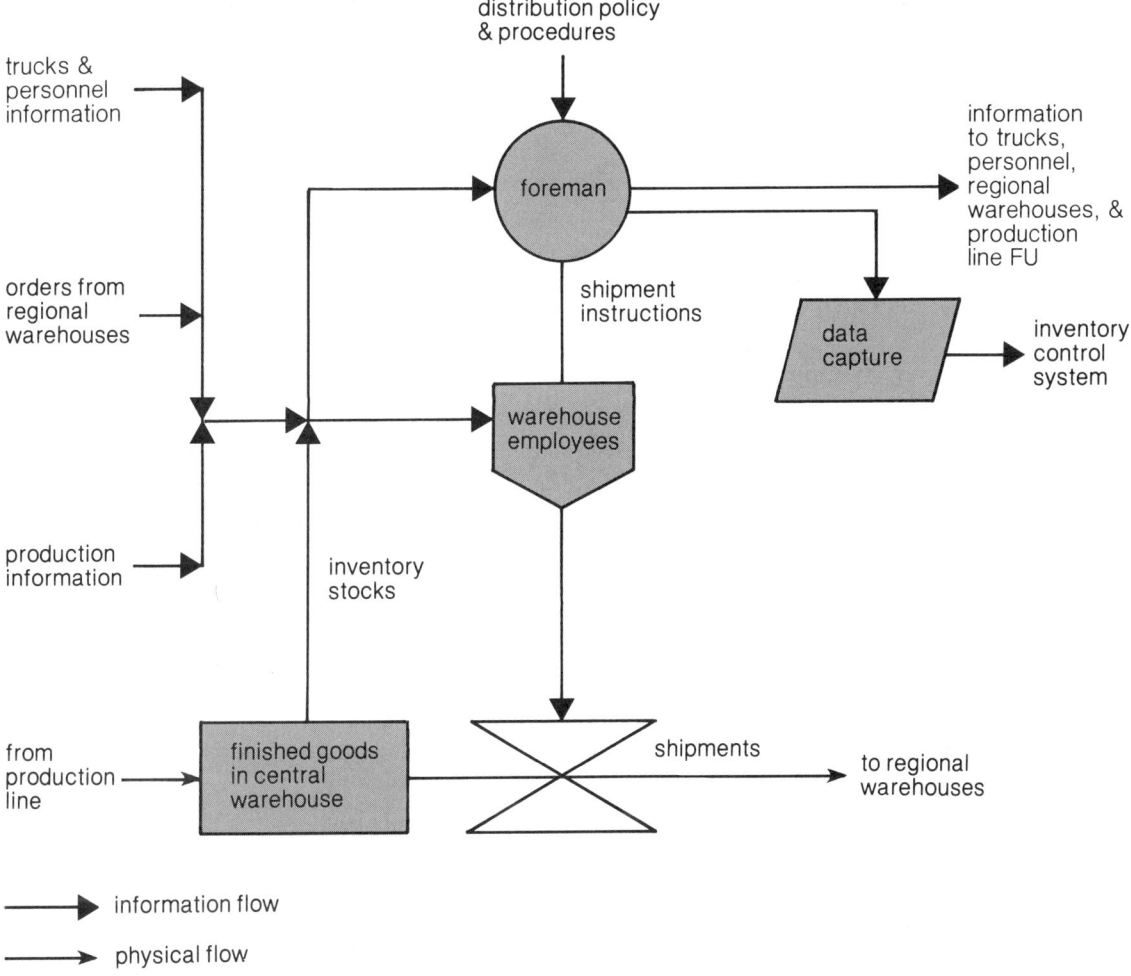

The functional unit at the central warehouse is informed of inventory stocks and regional orders. If trucks and drivers are available and standing rules and procedures permit (which possibly take into account inventory safety levels, minimal volumes of lading, truck routing, production forecasts, etc.), the central warehouse initiates shipments. In many cases shipments are carried out almost automatically, sometimes as a result of the instructions of a computerized system. However, sometimes supervisor intervention is required, probably in cases of urgency or noncompliance with standard procedures. The central warehouse also generates data as a result of its actions. This data is captured and processed and may be used by other functional units.

Figure 5.8 Schematic representation of management and operations

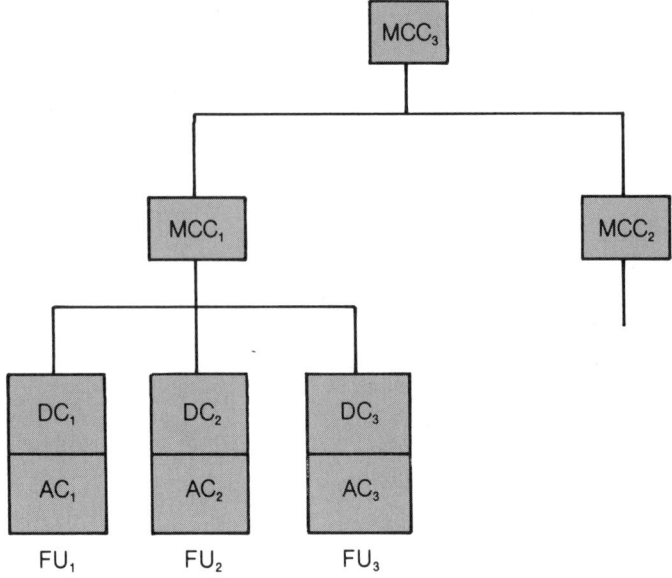

MCC   management control center

DC   decision center

AC   activity center

FU   functional unit

Management Control Center (MCC)

Functional units are the basic blocks composing the operations level of the hierarchical model (see fig. 5.3). They are directed by managerial functions composing the operational control level. A managerial function is termed a *management control center* (MCC). "A management control center is one or more management people together with his or their supporting staff, which acts as a decision center for a group of functional units, or for a group of subordinate management control centers" [3, p. 31]. In other words, the distinction between a decision center at a functional unit and an MCC is that the former always supervises an activity center, while the latter always supervises other decision centers, either of FUs or of other MCCs. Figure 5.8 illustrates the position of MCCs in the model.

Figure 5.9 MCCs and FUs in a distribution system

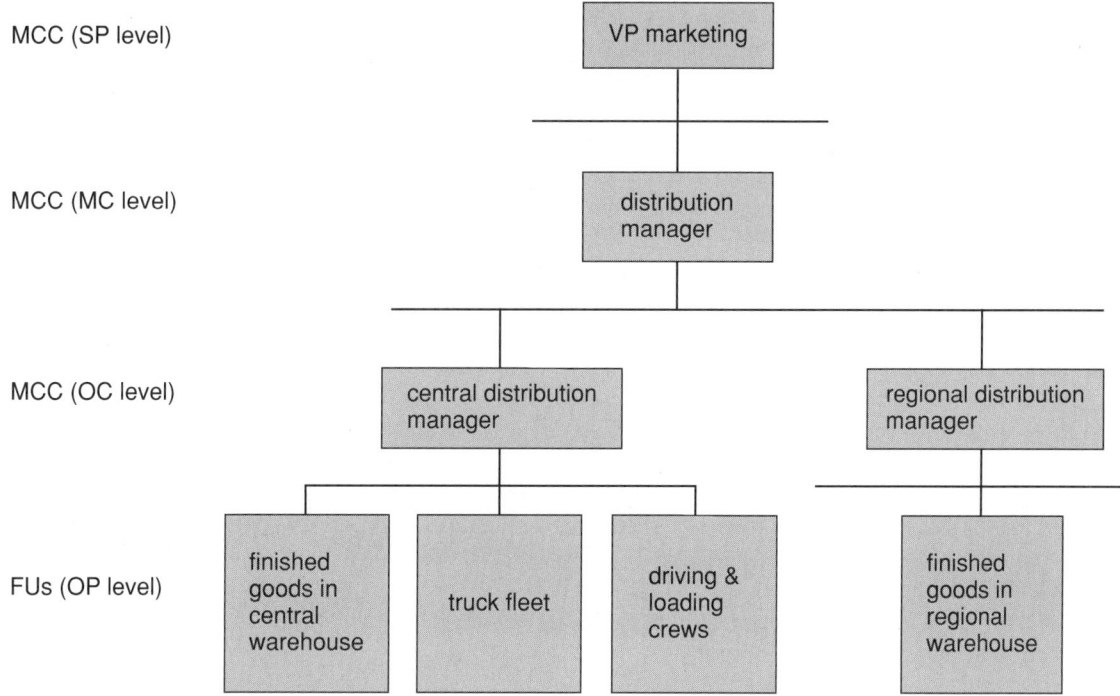

Note that the term *MCC* refers to any managerial function regardless of its location in the organizational hierarchy. Certainly we may refine the classification of MCCs, associating each of them with a particular level in Anthony's model.

Figure 5.9 applies the MCC concept to the example of the distributing system that we previously developed.

Incorporating Information into the Model

So far we have completed building an organizational model that combines the hierarchical approach (Anthony) and the dynamic approach (Forrester). The former approach is represented by the various levels of MCC; the latter is expressed in the detailed description of functional units. Information was just briefly mentioned in the definition of FU. We now complement the model by introducing information into it.

In figure 5.6 we stipulated that activities performed in functional units generate data. We may generalize by saying that most of the internal data (as opposed to data arriving from the environment) is, indeed, generated in the lowest level of the organization and reflects activities and events occurring there. This data is captured and processed to provide supportive information to both the operational and managerial levels. Hence we may identify two modules composing the information system: the *operational control module* (OCM), which supports the functional units; and the *management control module* (MCM), which supports the management control centers.

The OCM mainly encompasses processing of daily transactions, capturing data, and maintaining files for further (and more sophisticated) processing. This module would normally perform data entry and validation, file updates, and routine calculations. It would display information related to individual items or small groups of items. In the example of the distribution system, the OCM captures inventory transactions, updates inventory master files, records trucks' and drivers' working hours, issues shipment orders, prints out bills of lading, etc. It maintains all the files that might also be used by the MCM.

The MCM rarely captures and processes raw data. It mainly aggregates and manipulates data already captured by the OCM in order to trace trends, provide forecasts, deal with exceptions, etc. In chapter 3, while describing the decision-making process, we discussed how information can support decision making. That discussion exactly applies to the MCM. In fact, the MCM can be divided into submodules, each of which is associated with a different level in Anthony's pyramid. The submodule for the OC level would mainly deal with exceptions and daily supervision and control. The submodule for the MC level would facilitate short-range planning, resource scheduling, budget control, etc. The submodule for the SP level would be more involved in trend analysis, forecasts, and budgeting.

Referring now to the distribution system example, we may designate the following information as part of the MCM output.

1. For the OC level—Truck status report; shortage of particular items in the inventory; notification of exceptional orders; returns report.

2. For the MC level—Time and money spent on truck maintenance and repair; overtime payments report; dormant items in the inventory; distribution planning and scheduling for the coming quarter.

3. For the SP level—Implications of the change in interest rate for the cost of holding various inventory levels; seasonality of the demand for various groups of items; forecast of warehouse space requirements for the next five years; itemized distribution costs (cost of inventory, personnel, transportation, space, etc.).

Note that none of these applications generates data. They are all based on existing data, mostly captured through operations. However, when it comes to the SP level, the existing internal data cannot satisfy the information requirements and should, therefore, be augmented by external data, such as interest rates, or figures taken from forecasts of the national economy. Various sources of external data are now conveniently accessible to managers in the form of online public data bases. These will be discussed in chapter 6.

An Overview of the Comprehensive Model

The model that we have built draws its concepts from various sources. The hierarchical classification of managerial control levels is based on Anthony's model. It results in the division of information systems into operational and managerial modules. The dynamic approach of Forrester is reflected in the structure of the functional units. It clarifies the process of data creation and capture. Simon's idea of decision classification helps to determine the exact role of each managerial level. Consequently, it determines the information requirements for the various levels. The overall result is a comprehensive model, illustrated in figure 5.10.

On the left side of figure 5.10 we see the hierarchical model of an organization. The bottom level in the hierarchy corresponds to functional units and flows, depicted at the middle of figure 5.10. Functional units report to managerial levels such as management control centers (MCC). On the right side we see the information modules associated with the organizational levels.

Blumenthal's model is not the only method to define an information system. There are a few other attempts to establish theoretical frameworks for information system definition. For example, in [1], Ahituv takes a totally different approach: an information system is formulated in a mathematically rigorous manner by way of a sequence of axioms, definitions, and theorems. The mathematical technicalities in [1] are beyond the scope of this book; readers who are interested in such an approach (particularly members of the academic community) are advised to refer to [1].

The Concepts of Data Base and Model Base

It is important to note once again that almost the same raw data serves both the operation and management modules. The difference between the modules is revealed in the programs and not in the raw data. Conceptually, we therefore distinguish between the *data base* and the *model base* of an information system. The data base is the collection of all the data items. The model base is a collection of application programs using the data base. In this sense we may say that the OCM and MCM are, in effect, different model bases sharing the same data base. The abstract concepts of model base and data base have found their way to concrete realization in modern information-processing technology. This is discussed in appendix A.

Information Attributes and the Comprehensive Model

In chapter 3 we mentioned various attributes characterizing information. The attributes have been grouped into four major categories: timeliness, content, format, and cost. These and associated attributes are certainly affected by the information requirements of each organizational level; the requirements are derived from the vertical location of each level in the organizational hierarchy. Therefore, it is logical to relate information attributes to organizational levels. This is exhibited in table 5.2, which represents the value of information attributes in terms of a continuum from the operations level to the strategic planning level.

In summary, we may say that lower levels are characterized by information that is rigorous and well defined. Upper levels create more problems for information systems designers because their requirements and benefits are ill defined.

Figure 5.10 Comprehensive model of information in organization

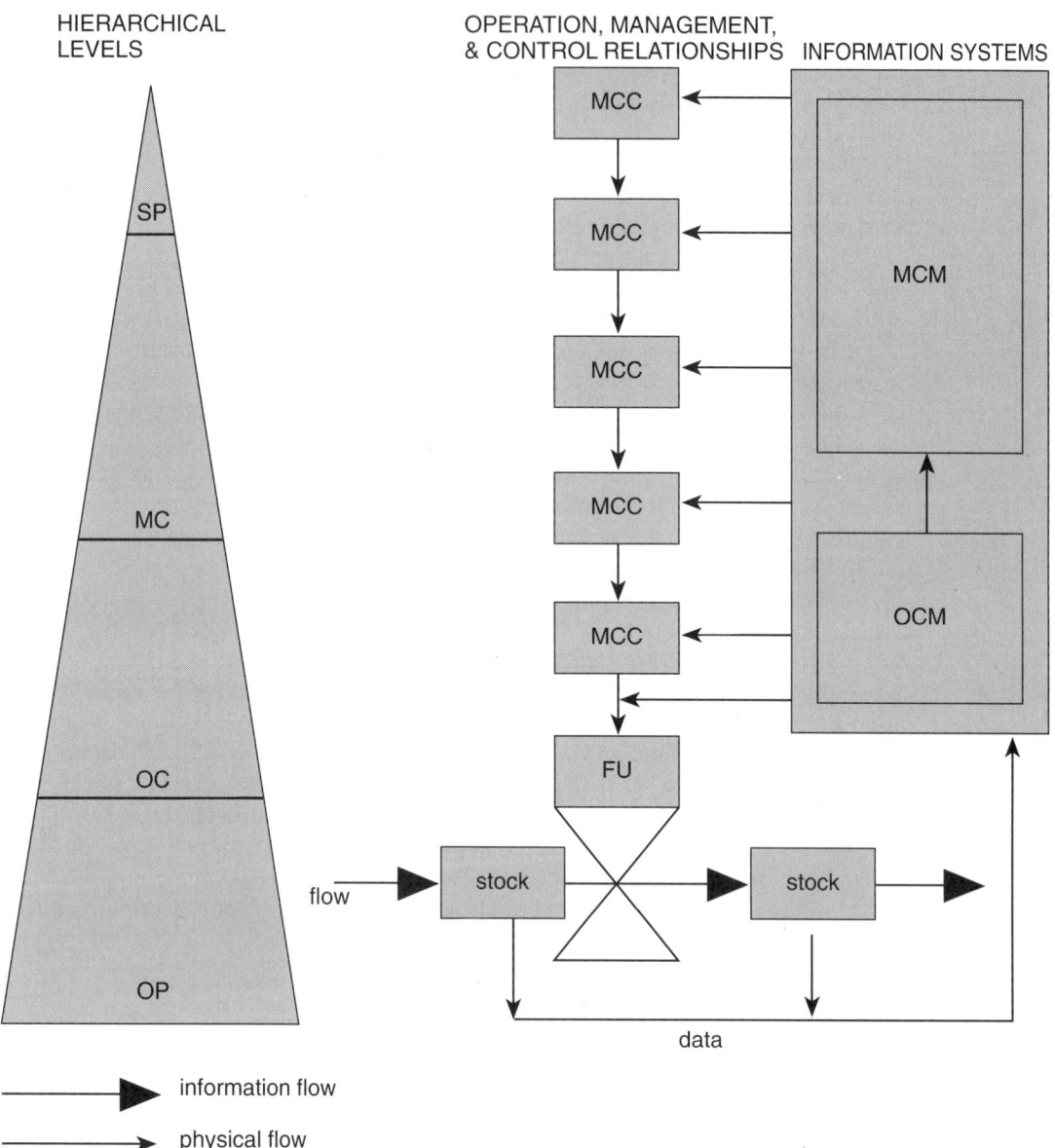

HIERARCHICAL
LEVELS

OPERATION, MANAGEMENT,
& CONTROL RELATIONSHIPS INFORMATION SYSTEMS

Table 5.2   Information Attributes and Organizational Levels

Attribute	Organizational Level			
	OP	*OC* *MC*		*SP*
Timeliness				
Currency	Up-to-date ⟵――――――――――⟶ Relatively old			
Response time	Instant ⟵――――――――――⟶ Slow			
Frequency	Constant ⟵――――――――――⟶ Varies			
Content				
Accuracy	High ⟵――――――――――⟶ Relatively low			
Relevance		No difference		
Exhaustiveness		No difference		
Redundancy		No difference		
Aggregation level	Very detailed ⟵――――――――――⟶ Very aggregated			
Format				
Medium	Mostly online ⟵――――――――――⟶ Mixed printouts and terminals			
Ordering	Fixed ⟵――――――――――⟶ Flexible			
Graphic design	Fixed ⟵――――――――――⟶ Flexible			
Cost				
Cost	Easily assessed ⟵――――――――――⟶ Hard to assess			
Benefit	Tangible ⟵――――――――――⟶ Intangible			

Classification of Organizational Information Systems

The comprehensive model developed in the previous section is somewhat abstract and too neat. However, it provides a framework for creating terms of reference for classifying and discussing various types of information systems. Unfortunately there are almost as many definitions of management information systems as there are people writing on the subject (for a sample of definitions see [5, ch. 1]). In this section we will define and classify some of the common terms in the area and attempt to relate the prevailing jargon to the foundations laid in the previous sections.

Management Information and Operational Information

Organizations use information in their current operations and in management decision making. We must therefore distinguish between *operational information* and *management information.*

Operational information is used daily and routinely and allows the organization to carry on its daily tasks. It serves the operations level (OP) or functional unit in the comprehensive model (fig. 5.10) and is produced by the operational control module (OCM). Operational information includes, for instance:

Updated balances of checking accounts in a bank

Calculated payrolls

Telephone bills

Schedules of routine machine maintenance

Table 5.3 Characteristics of Management Information and Operational Information

Operational Information

1. Standard and routine
2. Maximum efficiency has to be derived from the computer
3. Reliability of information as to exactness and objectivity is a dominant factor
4. Relative lack of flexibility due to the complexity and comprehensiveness of the module producing the information
5. Based on internal data

Management Information

1. Individualized, customized, nonstandard
2. Efficient utilization of the computer is not a dominant factor
3. Evaluations, projections, samples, and subjective information may be used
4. Module producing information must be flexible
5. Based on internal and external data

Unlike operational information, management information is used by managers as the need to make decisions arises. It supports the process of decision making, a process inherent in all levels of management and all managerial functions. Management information serves the operational control (OC), management control (MC), and strategic planning (SP) levels in the organization (fig. 5.10) and is produced by the management control module (MCM) of the information system. Management information includes, for instance:

Comparative analysis of billing systems

Costs of alternative truck routes

Aging distribution of loans to customers

A time series of sales

Response to a query about the balance of a preferred bank customer

Information systems simultaneously produce operational and management information. Nowadays, such information systems operate with the aid of a computer. The production of operational information is, in fact, no more than a takeover of manual tasks by a machine. However, management information derived from computer-based information systems constitutes a new element in the field of management. Table 5.3 compares management information and operational information.

The module of a computerized information system that supports operations provides standard, routine, and current reports. It collects the source documents and the keyed-in data that reflect the transactions at the operations level, processes them, updates the various files of the organization, and generates reports. Relatively high volumes of inputs and outputs are processed by the computer programs used by this module. The users of the output cannot usually request ad hoc nonstandard queries or initiate special supplements of nonroutine information. The content of the output generated must exactly reflect the real physical transactions taking place. For example, checking account balances in a bank must reflect all deposits and withdrawals and cannot be based on a sample of such transactions. The operational module must actually operate as an efficient "paper factory." Even a small change in the content of a record or in the layout of a screen or an input form may require considerable investment in software and hardware components of the system.

The module of a computerized information system that produces management information provides data that is customized to the needs of managers. The higher the level of the manager, the more important (financially) are the implications of the decisions made by the managers using the information and the less important are the costs of producing the information. Hence the efficiency of the computerized system is not a paramount factor: a programmer may stop a computer that is running a program to update customer balances in order to compile and test a computer simulation program; the simulation will then be used to explore various market shares in order to decide whether to market a new product. The data used by such a program may reflect samples collected by the marketing research department. In addition, the system must be flexible enough to accommodate a new graphic display terminal that will be used by the manager(s) making the relevant decision. While operational information results from the processing of internal data (transactions), the management information in our example results from the processing of both internal data (availability of personnel, machinery, capital, etc.) and external data (consumer demand, competition in the market, etc.). Chapter 6 discusses how data can be retrieved from external data bases.

A Framework for Information Systems in Organizations

The framework and terminology of the following discussion is based on Simon's classification of decisions into *structured, unstructured,* and *partially structured* (semistructured) and on his conceptualization of the decision-making process (see ch. 3 and Simon [10]). It is worthwhile to briefly review these concepts (the review is based on Neumann and Hadass [9]).*

Classes of Decisions and the Decision-Making Process

A distinction can be made between completely structured decisions and unstructured ones, although in reality there is a continuum with completely structured decisions at one extreme and completely unstructured ones at the other. The process of making a completely structured decision is algorithmic; the process of making an unstructured decision is heuristic.

1. A *structured decision* is one in which all the steps in the decision-making process are structured.
2. An *unstructured decision* is one in which all the steps in the decision-making process are unstructured.
3. A *semistructured decision* is one in which some of the steps in the decision-making process are structured and some are unstructured.

---

*This section is partly cited from the paper "DSS and Strategic Decisions" by S. Neumann and M. Hadass. Copyright 1980 by the Regents of the University of California. Reprinted from *California Management Review* 22, no. 2, pp. 77–84. By permission of the Regents.

Table 5.4 Role of MIS and Classes of Decision

	MIS Role	
Decision Classes	*Decision Making*	*Providing Supporting Information*
Structured decision	Active	—
Semistructured decision	Active	Active
Unstructured decision	—	Active

Decision making is not an activity performed at a specific point in time; it is a stepwise process. According to Simon, this process comprises three main phases: (1) intelligence, (2) analysis and design, and (3) selection or choice. These concepts are useful in defining the classes of decisions.

The module of the organizational information system that provides management information for decision makers will be termed *management information system (MIS)*. It can be defined in terms of its application to the different classes of decisions.

1. It is an information system that makes structured decisions. For example, a computer program can process inventory transactions and automatically reorder optimal replenishments.

2. It supports the process of making unstructured or semistructured decisions by performing some of the phases of the decision-making process and providing supporting information for other phases. For example, computer programs can report production cost overruns, thus performing the intelligence phase. They can calculate the impact of various alternatives of solving the problems for the design phase, leaving a manager to complete the design phase and make the choice of the best alternative.

Table 5.4 describes the contribution of MIS activities to the various classes of decisions.

Two types of logical components of the MIS are distinguished.

1. *Structured decisions system* (SDS), which makes the structured decision.
2. *Decision support system* (DSS), which supports unstructured and semistructured decisions.

The Physical Structure of Information Systems in Organizations

The two logical components of the MIS (SDS and DSS) do not necessarily correspond to the conventional physical structure of information systems in organizations. The physical structure usually consists of two information subsystems, the decision support system (DSS) and what may be termed the *administrative data processing systems* (ADPS). The latter subdivide into a *transactions processing system* (TPS) and a structured decision system (SDS). The TPS processes the source documents (that reflect the current transactions) and produces reports and messages (that help the organization keep track of its activities and resources).

Figure 5.11 A physical structure of information systems in organizations
SOURCE: Neumann, S. and Hadass, M., "DSS and Strategic Decisions," *California Management Review* 22, no. 2, p. 80.

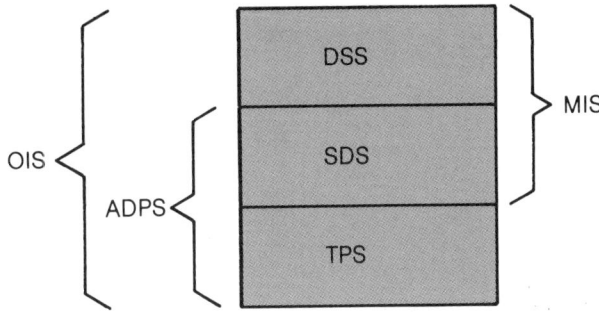

These information subsystems will be described more fully in chapter 6. Each one is not necessarily a single or distinct physical information system. There can be a confederation of information systems in an organization. This confederation of information systems can be termed *organizational information system* (OIS). The term "confederation" is used to stress the fact that interrelationships among the various information systems do exist but are not so tight as to impede independent development of each system at an appropriate time. The adoption of a master plan for information systems (discussed in ch. 8) will provide for efficient development of the various systems under the right priorities, but will keep sight of their vital interrelationships. The physical structure of the OIS is diagramed in figure 5.11, using these terms.

Various scholars and practitioners use a number of names and terms when describing the components of the organizational information system. Whatever terminology you may prefer, you should relate the information subsystems defined here to the various organizational levels of the comprehensive model described in a previous section of this chapter.

The transactions processing system (TPS)—Supports the activities of the operations level (OP)

The structured decision system (SDS)—Supports decisions of the operational (OC) and management control (MC) levels

The decision support system (DSS)—Supports decisions of the management control (MC) and strategic planning (SP) level.

In the real world we do not have this clear-cut classification free of overlapping. The SDS can support decisions at all managerial levels, although it is mainly used by the OC level, used less by the MC level, and infrequently used by the SP level. The DSS can also support decisions at all managerial levels, although it is mainly used by the SP level, less used by the MC level, and infrequently used by the OC level. The TPS, on the other hand, almost exclusively supports the OP level.

Table 5.5   Characteristics of SDS and DSS

Attribute	SDS	DSS
A. The User/Decision Maker		
1. Decision maker's environment (internal & external)	Constant, steady, relatively simple	Changing, dynamic, complex
2. Decision maker's level	Operational control	Strategic planning
3. System development initiative	Pushed to decision maker	Comes from decision maker
4. Decision maker's involvement in system development and use	Passive	Active
5. Decision-making style	Predetermined, universal, impersonal	Individual, personal, subjective
B. The Decisions Supported by the System		
1. Structuredness	Structured	Semistructured
2. Time-horizon orientation	Historical, past-oriented	Future-oriented
3. Routineness of use	Routine	Ad hoc, unique
4. Decision-making process	Well defined, algorithmic	Heuristic, iterative, exploratory
5. Importance to the organization	Local, operational	Strategic, organization-wide
6. Decision process phase supported	All phases	Some phases
C. The Information System		
1. Data sources	Largely internal	Largely external
2. Design predetermination	Structured	Unstructured
3. Data base	Well defined, narrow, detailed, specific	Data redundancy, broad, integrated, aggregated
4. Model base	Predetermined models, quantitative, universal, explicit	Tailor-made, model building blocks, qualitative, heuristic, implicit, exploratory
5. System design orientation	Data-oriented	Decision-model oriented
6. Operating mode	Batch and interactive	Interactive
7. System success criteria	Robustness, operational efficiency	Flexibility, adaptability
8. Frequency of use	Predetermined	Undefined frequency

Characteristics of Decision Support Systems and Structured Decision Systems
Decision support systems and structured decision systems, two logical components of the MIS, have characteristics that substantially differ and so merit a short discussion of some important implications for the designers, executors, and users of the information subsystems. Table 5.5 presents various characteristics of both subsystems.

The characteristics are associated with three classes of attributes: (1) those related to decision makers (users) using the information subsystems, (2) those related to the decisions supported by the subsystems, and (3) those reflecting the nature of the design and operation of each subsystem. The relevant characteristics of each attribute are exhibited as extremes in a continuum running from SDS to DSS.

It is clear that the characteristics of the DSS are diametrically opposed to those of SDS and thereby mandate different design and implementation strategies. The chronological development of information systems in organizations usually went from TPS to SDS and only then to DSS. This may be a result of failure to recognize the different nature of the subsystems, the unavailability in the past of modern technologies (in software, hardware, and communications), and the fairly recent attempts to study the interactions among decisions, attributes of information, and organizational levels (summarized by our comprehensive model in figure 5.10). A detailed discussion of the different modules of the information system will be left for chapter 6, but two remarks are pertinent at this point.

1. All modules rely on the existence of a common data base collected and updated by the transaction processing module.

2. The organization is a living entity with changing environment, goals, activities, and, therefore, decisions. The scope of the information modules also changes in the course of time; unstructured decisions may become structured or semistructured, and new, unstructured decisions may emerge.

Characteristics of Management Information Systems

Organizational information systems, like information systems in general, collect data and store, process, and retrieve information. They simultaneously produce operational information and management information. While the subject matter of this book is all information systems, particular emphasis is devoted to management information systems. The term MIS has been given many different meanings, including the following:

The total organizational information systems—the OP, OC, MC, and SP levels

The decision-making modules of the information system—the MC and SP levels

Any existing data processing system in the organization

In this book, the term MIS is applied to those information systems that provide management information. It thus excludes the transactions processing systems (see figure 5.11), although these closely interact with the MIS. A management information system is defined here as an information system that makes some managerial decisions and provides managers at all levels of an organization with the information needed for making other decisions.

Many MISs are based on transactions processing systems (data processing systems) and evolve from them. At some point the data stored in the TPS can be processed further to provide information for management decision making, provided that additional capabilities are added. We can thus summarize the characteristics that give MISs their special qualities.

1. A modern MIS will always rely to some extent on computer technology (although the computer is not a prerequisite). MIS existed before the invention of the computer, but due to the quantity and complexity of data in modern organizations, it is inconceivable that, without computers, information for decision makers could be generated within a reasonable time.

2. A well-designed MIS relies heavily on human decision-making processes. The decision makers in the organization receive various degrees of support from the MIS, ranging from relatively simple aggregation of data to utilization of the computer as a problem solver.

3. An MIS is heavily dependent on a data base. The concept of a data base applies when the computerized files of an organization are integrated in a way that facilitates easy access to all information items by all users, regardless of physical or functional residence of both data and users.

4. An MIS relies heavily on a model base. The model base contains the programs with which the data is organized and processed. The programs generate programmed decisions and programmed models that simulate or take part in human decision-making processes. While the data base and model base may be developed independently, they are basically complementary: the data base provides the model base designers with input needed for their models; the model base indicates the type of data that should be incorporated in the data base. The data base and model base make the MIS, in a sense, a model of the real organization.

5. A well-designed MIS relies on a communications network that provides interactive, fast access by managers to the information stored in the data base and to the models in the model base.

Practical Conclusions for Information System Design and Use

The following conclusions are listed here to assist the user in information system design and use.

1. The use of models in understanding organizational processes is very helpful. However, models tend to be simplistic because of some initial relaxing assumptions. Therefore, we have to examine models carefully before we apply them to a realistic environment.

2. Analysis of an organization might require the use of several models simultaneously—an organizational chart depicts managerial responsibilities and lines of command; financial statements reveal the requirements of accounting information; process flowcharts clarify the relationships between various activities. Selection of the appropriate model(s) depends on the main concerns of the analysis.

3. Classification of managerial functions into hierarchical levels is prerequisite to an analysis of information requirements—strategic planning requires information of different characteristics than tactical planning (management control).

4. The industrial dynamic model, or any other process-oriented model, is particularly useful to design an information system for a process rather than for an organizational unit (department or section). A process might flow

across intraorganizational borders; if confined to the organizational structure, we might overlook some important interfaces and later get into trouble when trying to integrate several "discrete" systems.

5. The comprehensive model of information in an organization is too neat to be real. Reality is much more obscure and ill defined. However, careful observation will probably reveal an operations level and a few managerial levels in every organization; each level requires different information. This may help you to design useful information systems.

6. In reality, managerial functions are characterized not only by their location in the pyramid, but also by managerial and cognitive style (see ch. 2), by the maturity of the organization and its data processing systems, and by many other factors. This does not necessarily mean that the comprehensive model presented here is useless; it only indicates that you have to carefully examine and modify the model before and while you make use of it.

7. Designers of information systems must distinguish between the data base—the collection of data—and the model base—the processing requirements. This is essential not just for conceptual reasons, but mainly because current technology provides different tools to handle these entities, and often the data base and model base are managed by different units in the organization.

8. There is a clear distinction between management information and operational information. The first supports decisions of managers at all levels or makes managerial decisions. The latter supports the daily running of an organization.

9. Organizational information systems are composed of different modules (subsystems). Each module, as a member of a confederation, should be designed to serve the information needs of managers at a given organizational level, but with due regard to the fact that they are interrelated.

10. Design of any information system starts by establishing the decisions and activities to be supported by the information and the derived information requirements (see also ch. 10).

11. The transaction processing system is the infrastructure of organizational information systems. Without it no data can be collected to build, expand, and update the data base of the organization.

12. Different design and implementation strategies should be adopted for designing and implementing the structured decision systems and the decision support systems.

13. Design and operation of organizational information systems are on-going processes: new environmental constraints and opportunities, new technologies, and new goals lead to new or changed decisions, which in turn lead to new or changed information requirements.

14. The data base and the model base of the organizational information system are complementary entities. A rational strategy for information systems development is to design these bases in a parallel manner since each contributes to and draws from the other.

15. The system designer should not delude himself or herself into thinking that the systems he or she designs will supply all managers with all the information they need. Some decisions, particularly at the strategic planning level, are too unstructured and random to permit complete analysis. Such decisions—which (regrettably or not) include the most important ones—must be left in human hands, with relatively little aid from the information systems.

Summary

The role and structure of information systems in organizations cannot be understood without understanding the way organizations behave. The real-life behavior of an organization can be approximated by a model that describes the organization (after all, a model is an abstracted reflection of some real-life entity or phenomenon). The models presented in this chapter describe the organization as a system and focus on decision making within the organizational system.

Anthony's hierarchical model focuses on three different managerial control activities in organizations:

1. The strategic planning level (top-level managers) controls the long-term activities and decisions of the organization.
2. The management control level (tactical, middle-level managers) controls the medium-term activities and decisions.
3. The operational control level (low-level managers) controls the short-term activities and decisions of the organization.

Managers at all levels plan, organize, staff, direct, and control. However, the scope of each of these managerial functions narrows as we descend along the organizational hierarchy. Most of these functions are not performed at the bottom level of Anthony's model. At this level, real activities transform physical inputs into goods and services.

Forrester's industrial dynamics model views the organization as a network of physical flows that connect stocks of resources (capital, employees, inventories, etc.). A flow is a sequence of activities that transfers entities from one stock to another. The flows are regulated by decision points (managers) that adjust the flow rates in accordance with information received about stocks and goals. An information network thus is superimposed on the physical network of stocks and flows.

The hierarchical model, when combined with Simon's distinction between structured and unstructured decisions, characterizes various types of decisions made at each managerial level. However, it is not dynamic; it ignores flows and processes within and across levels. The industrial dynamics model, on the other hand, does trace the processes involved in an organization and explains the relationships among its various systems, including the information system (which is also composed of stocks and flows).

Blumenthal's comprehensive model—synthesizing the ideas of Anthony, Forrester, and Simon—provides the informational implications of these models of the organization. According to the model, the building blocks of an organization are the functional units, composed of a decision center, an activity center, and actions. These units are found at the operations level and are connected by a physical and informational network. They are also connected by an informational network to decision centers that comprise the strategic planning, management control, and operational control levels. The managerial functions performed at these levels are termed "management control centers."

Activities performed in functional units generate data that is captured and processed by the operational control module of the information system. Information supporting the management control centers is generated by the management control module of the information system. The latter module can be divided into submodules, each providing information to a different managerial level.

The comprehensive model enables us to classify various types of organizational information systems. Operational control modules of information systems are termed "transactions processing systems." They capture and validate raw data, provide operational information, and update the data base of the organization. Management information is provided by management information systems, which rarely capture raw source data, and only process data already stored in the data base. Management information systems are comprised of two submodules: (1) the structured decisions system (SDS), which makes structured decisions, thus replacing the human decision maker; (2) decision support system (DSS), which provides information for unstructured and semistructured decisions. All these modules comprise a confederation of information systems termed "organizational information systems."

The term MIS is applied to those information systems that provide management information. MIS is defined as an information system that makes some managerial decisions and provides managers at all levels of an organization with the information needed for making other decisions. A well-designed and modern MIS relies on the following qualities:

Computer technology

Human decision-making processes

Data base

Model base

Communications network

The physical information systems, which are implicit in the logical comprehensive model, are the subject matter of the following chapter. Each module of the organizational information system has different characteristics. While the modules can be developed in parallel or in sequence, each implies a different strategy of design, implementation, and use. Some kind of organizational master plan must be devised to coordinate the development of these modules. This will be the subject matter of chapter 8.

Key Concepts

activity center (AC)
administrative data processing
  system (ADPS)
data base
decision center (DC)
decision point
decision support system (DSS)
flow
flow rate
functional unit (FU)
hierarchical model of organization
industrial dynamics
level
management control (MC)
management control center (MCC)
management control module (MCM)

management information
management information
  system (MIS)
model base
operational control (OC)
operational control module (OCM)
operational information
operations (OP)
organizational chart
organizational information
  system (OIS)
stock
strategic planning (SP)
structured decision system (SDS)
transactions processing system (TPS)

References

1. Ahituv, N. "A Metamodel of Information Flow: A Tool to Support Information Systems Theory." *Communications of the ACM* 30, no. 9 (September 1987): 781–91.
2. Anthony, R. A. *Planning and Control Systems: A Framework for Analysis.* Boston: Division of Research, Graduate School of Business Administration, Harvard University, 1965.
3. Blumenthal, S. C. *Management Information Systems: A Framework for Planning and Development.* Englewood Cliffs, N.J.: Prentice-Hall, 1969.
4. Davis, G. B., and M. H. Olson. *Management Information Systems: Conceptual Foundations, Structure, and Development.* New York: McGraw-Hill, 2d ed., 1985.
5. Ein-Dor, P., and E. Segev. *Managing Management Information Systems.* Lexington, MA: D. C. Heath, 1978.
6. Fayol, H. *General and Industrial Management.* Translated by C. Storrs. London: Sir Isaac Pitman & Sons, 1949.
7. Forrester, J. W. *Industrial Dynamics.* Cambridge, MA: M. I. T. Press, 1961.
8. Galbraith, J. R. "Organizational Design: An Information Processing View." *Interfaces* 4, no. 3 (May 1974): 28–36.
9. Neumann, S., and M. Hadass. "DSS and Strategic Decisions." *California Management Review* 22, no. 2 (Spring 1980): 77–84.
10. Simon, H. A. *The New Science of Management Decisions.* New York: Harper & Row, 1960.

Questions

1. Are Anthony and Forrester's models holistic? Are they comprehensive?
2. Differentiate among strategic planning, management control, and operational control.
3. By way of example, describe the management functions that could be performed by a middle-level manager in an insurance company.
4. What is the role of the manager in Forrester's model?
5. Describe the inputs to and outputs from a functional unit.
6. Does the management control center do strategic planning, make management decisions, or make operational decisions? Explain your answer.
7. How is a model base different from a data base?
8. What are the characteristics differentiating management information from operational information?
9. Why has the transactions processing system not been considered as part of an MIS?
10. Characterize a modern MIS.

Problems

1. Using a branch of a bank as an example for the following:
   a. draw a flowchart of a functional unit.
   b. describe schematically the MCC at the SP, MC, and OC levels and the functional units.
2. For a modern, computerized hospital, who would need operational information and who would need management information? Describe the attributes of the information needed by both groups.
3. Characterize a decision support system and a structured decision system in a manufacturing firm.

Arms 'R' Us Incorporated

Arms 'R' Us Inc. (ARMS) is an American company which provides weapons systems for the United States government. ARMS also provides major weapon systems to North Atlantic Treaty Organization (NATO) countries.

ARMS currently is formed of four divisions: Space, Missile, Ship, and Electronics. These division heads report to the Chief Executive Officer who reports to the Board of Directors.

Each division has five departments which consist of the following: Marketing, Manufacturing, Finance/Payroll, Quality Assurance, and Inventory. Each department is headed by a Director who reports to the respective division's Vice-President.

The work force within each department consists of Supervisors who report to their respective department Directors. Supervisors are responsible for accomplishing the work assigned in their areas of expertise. Workers assigned to each Supervisor set out to accomplish the everyday business of ARMS.

To maintain a competitive edge within the industry, Marketing gathers information related to competitive forces within the defense industry. Each contract awarded to a specific contractor is awarded on the basis of lowest bid received. Marketing information must be received in a timely, cost-effective manner so as to accomplish proper pricing, given industry standards.

Manufacturing produces the products bid on by the corporation. This is the heart of the operation. Products must be produced in a timely and cost-conscious manner to avoid contract loss or interruption due to overruns and schedule delays.

Quality Assurance inspects and tests products that have been manufactured, making sure that quality arms are being produced.

Finance/Payroll ensures that all contracts are managed effectively and efficiently, that all time worked on a contract is documented correctly against that contract, and that all personnel are paid for their services. Worker mischarging must be avoided.

Inventory manages parts associated with the production of a particular weapon system. The inventory area must ensure that all parts related to the production of a system are in the company stores. Stores must be replenished in a timely manner, and Inventory has the responsibility to coordinate with the production line to accomplish this task.

Questions

1. Draw an organization chart.

2. Given ARMS organization chart, build a hierarchical model of the organization and describe briefly what functions are performed by managers at these levels. Include the scope of each function at each level.

3. Describe one division within ARMS in terms of Blumenthal's model.

4. Based on the case study, give a brief description of which areas of the organization process structured, unstructured, and semistructured decisions.

Waveboard, Inc.

The childhood dream of Amy Wave was finally a reality: she was president of her own company—Waveboards, Inc. (WI). It was an aspiration of hers ever since she learned to surf while growing up in the Los Angeles area.

WI manufactures surfboards and sells them, along with beachwear and accessories, in retail shops located along the coastline of Southern California. Waveboards are made using computerized technology to produce a high-quality, streamlined board that follows a patented "keel" design developed by Amy. This unique, high-tech design makes Waveboards popular with surfers of all ages and abilities.

Although operations began in a small, cramped garage behind the Wave family home, for the past two years the administrative offices and modern manufacturing plant have been located in a new industrial park in Torrance, California. WI is arranged in a functional manner, with four departments reporting to Amy. An organization chart for the company is shown in figure 5.12.

The Production Department is concerned with the manufacturing process at the Torrance plant. There are ten employees working in various phases of surfboard production, and two supervisors reporting to the production manager. Raw materials are stored in the warehouse pending orders from the Sales Department. Upon receipt of an order, the appropriate amount of material is moved into the manufacturing area, going through four stages of production before the boards are packaged: cutting, sanding and polishing, painting, and finishing.

In the cutting area, the material is cut and shaped using a computer-generated laser that is very accurate and eliminates waste. The next stage is sanding and polishing, where the boards are manually sanded and given a smooth, glossy finish by a mechanical polisher. The third phase is the painting area, where creative talent is used to give the boards a look that will express the owner's personality. Splashes of bright fluorescent paint and pin-striping are used to create one-of-a-kind designs. In the last stage, finishers apply the company logo and perform a quality check before the boards are packaged for shipping.

Retail Operations oversees five retail shops located in Southern California. In addition to stocking Waveboards, these shops carry surfing goods, beachwear, and accessories that the company purchases from other wholesalers.

The Marketing Department consists of Sales and Advertising/Public Relations. A sales staff of three obtains customer orders from surf shops and sporting goods stores and develops new business, while the Advertising/PR department staff of two purchases advertising spots on billboards, radio, and in magazines. PR also handles customer complaints and acts as a spokesperson for the company.

Administration employs a staff of 12 and consists of accounting, personnel, finance, and MIS, who perform traditional tasks. The company utilizes personal computers for word processing, billing, and electronic mail.

Figure 5.12 WAVEBOARDS, INC. organizational chart

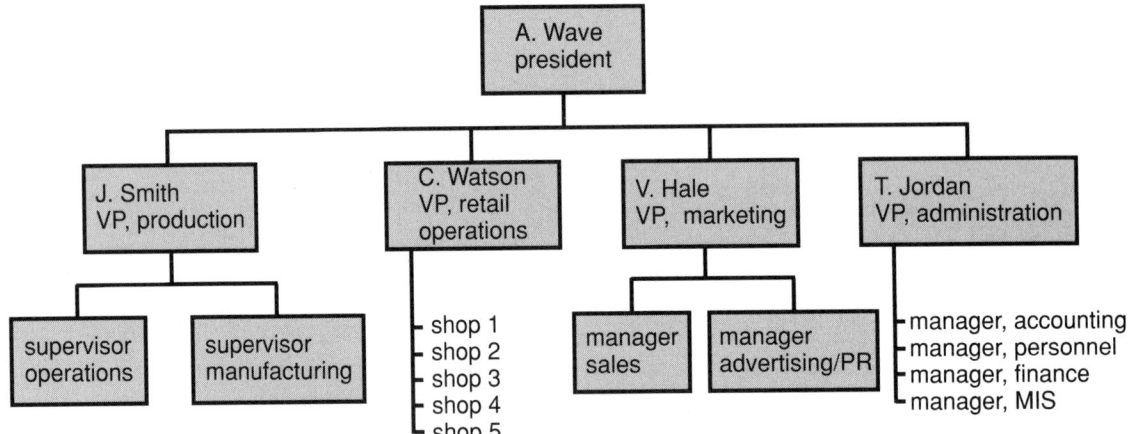

WAVEBOARDS, INC
Organizational Chart

Amy has been considering the feasibility of acquiring a nearby beachwear manufacturer whose production facilities are up for sale. She wonders whether WI's financial success would continue if the business were diversified.

Questions

1. Describe the structure of Waveboards, Inc. according to the Blumenthal model. Identify information provided by the operational control module (OCM) and the management control module (MCM) submodule levels.

2. How can Waveboards, Inc. utilize structured decision systems (SDS) and/or decision support systems (DSS)?

Chapter 6 *Structure of Organizational Information Systems*

Information systems are not a mere collection of hardware, software, and people. They should be structured to fit the organization's strategy and structure. They have to provide for the information needs of the operational level and the various management levels of the organization.

In this chapter we outline the characteristics and components of different structures of computerized information systems.

Note: If you feel that you need an introduction or a review of concepts and tools of information technologies, read appendix A before you read this chapter. Otherwise, this chapter logically follows the previous one.

Introduction

Chapter 5 outlined a comprehensive conceptual model of information in an organization. We used the model to logically classify various types of organizational information systems. You may recall that the model incorporated the different levels of management controls (see fig. 5.3) and the spectrum of decisions made by these levels, varying from completely structured decisions to completely unstructured ones. We will briefly review the main concepts developed in chapter 5 before we describe the physical information systems implicit in the model, and that are, in effect, found in most organizations.

The building blocks of an organization are the functional units, composed of a decision center, an activity center, and actions. These units are found at the operations level and are connected by physical and informational networks. Activities performed in functional units generate data. This data is captured and processed to provide supportive information to both operational and managerial levels. Hence, we may identify two types (modules) of information systems that compose the overall organizational information system.

The *operational control systems* (modules) support the functional units and operational managers. They capture and process data that reflects daily transactions, maintain files for further and more sophisticated processing, and generate "operational" information normally related to individual items or small groups of items. This type of system is called a *transaction processing system* (TPS).

The *management control systems* (modules) support the management control levels in the organization by providing "management" information. They rarely capture and process raw data. They mainly aggregate and manipulate data already captured and stored in files in order to trace trends, provide forecasts, deal with exceptions, and respond to ad hoc inquiries. These systems include *structured decision systems* (SDSs), which make structured decisions, thus replacing the human decision maker, and *decision support systems* (DSSs), which provide information for unstructured and semistructured decisions.

The next section describes computerized transaction processing systems. Note that a TPS processes transactions but does not make any decisions. Since a computerized SDS does make automatic decisions, it is logically a different entity. However, we can incorporate such automatic decisions into the computerized processing of transactions and thus combine the two logical systems (TPS and SDS) into the physical TPS.

We then outline the structure of the typical decision support system. A DSS is not only logically different from a TPS and an SDS, but it also implies human-machine interaction and specific software and hardware elements that are not necessarily part of the conventional TPS. The distinction between the three types of systems—TPS, SDS, and DSS—is illustrated in the following examples of a partial inventory management system.

The lower part of figure 6.1 represents the physical system of supplies entering the warehouse. This system fulfills customers' orders. The upper part of the figure illustrates how a customer's order is processed. In this process the computer does not make a decision. After an ordered item is issued from the warehouse, the relevant files are updated and, if necessary, a stock status report can be generated. In processing such transactions the computer performs only clerical operations.

Continuing with the same example, we now let the computer make a programmed decision on whether to issue the ordered items. The process illustrated in figure 6.2 includes both the processing of the transaction (customer's order), and the making of an automatic decision by the computer. The automatic decision can be more complex and use models that access information from various files. For example, a decision to purchase stock additions can be made as illustrated in figure 6.3. The decision-making process in this case may be complex; it uses a programmed model and accesses two files. Yet, the process can be completely structured, and thus produce an automatic decision. Again, the SDS involved can be incorporated into the routine processing of the purchasing transaction, or it can be a distinct, independent processing step to be followed later by a transaction processing step.

Figure 6.1 A partial inventory TPS and the physical system

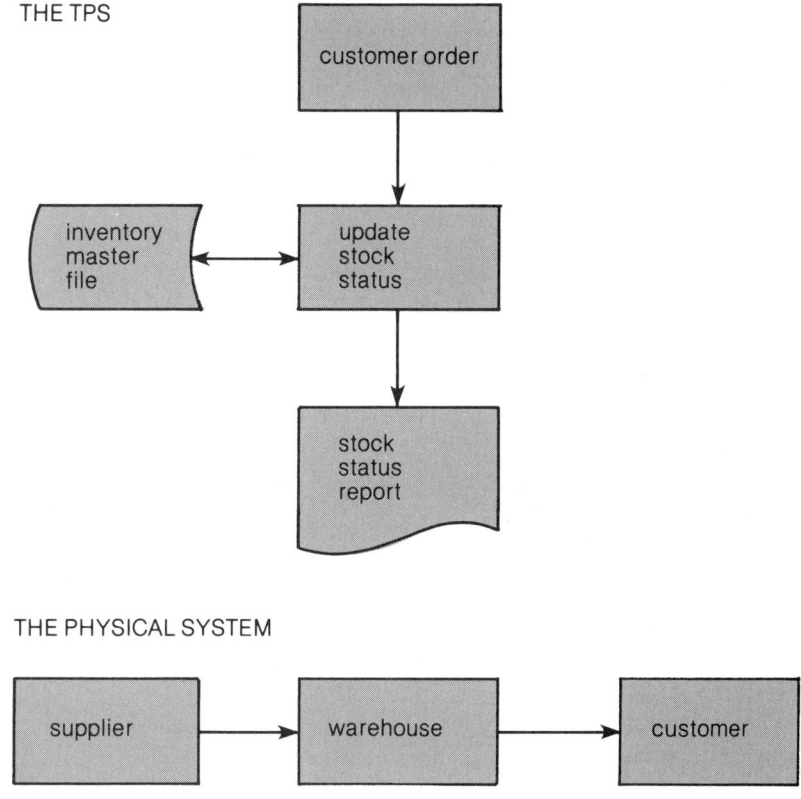

THE TPS

customer order

inventory
master
file

update
stock
status

stock
status
report

THE PHYSICAL SYSTEM

supplier

warehouse

customer

Figure 6.4 depicts a DSS providing information to a human decision maker who is considering the same purchasing problem. This time the manager is making the decision; the system supports him or her by providing data and by quickly calculating the results of various alternatives considered by the manager. The purchasing decisions supported by the DSS may have to do with inventory items that are extremely expensive.

Note that the manager uses programmed models and accesses various files while considering the available alternatives. Eventually the manager makes a decision: either not to decide, or to purchase. He or she can then authorize the issuance of a purchase order, which subsequently will enter the inventory TPS (the manager can, of course, issue the order and immediately have it captured by the TPS).

Figure 6.2 A partial inventory TPS and SDS

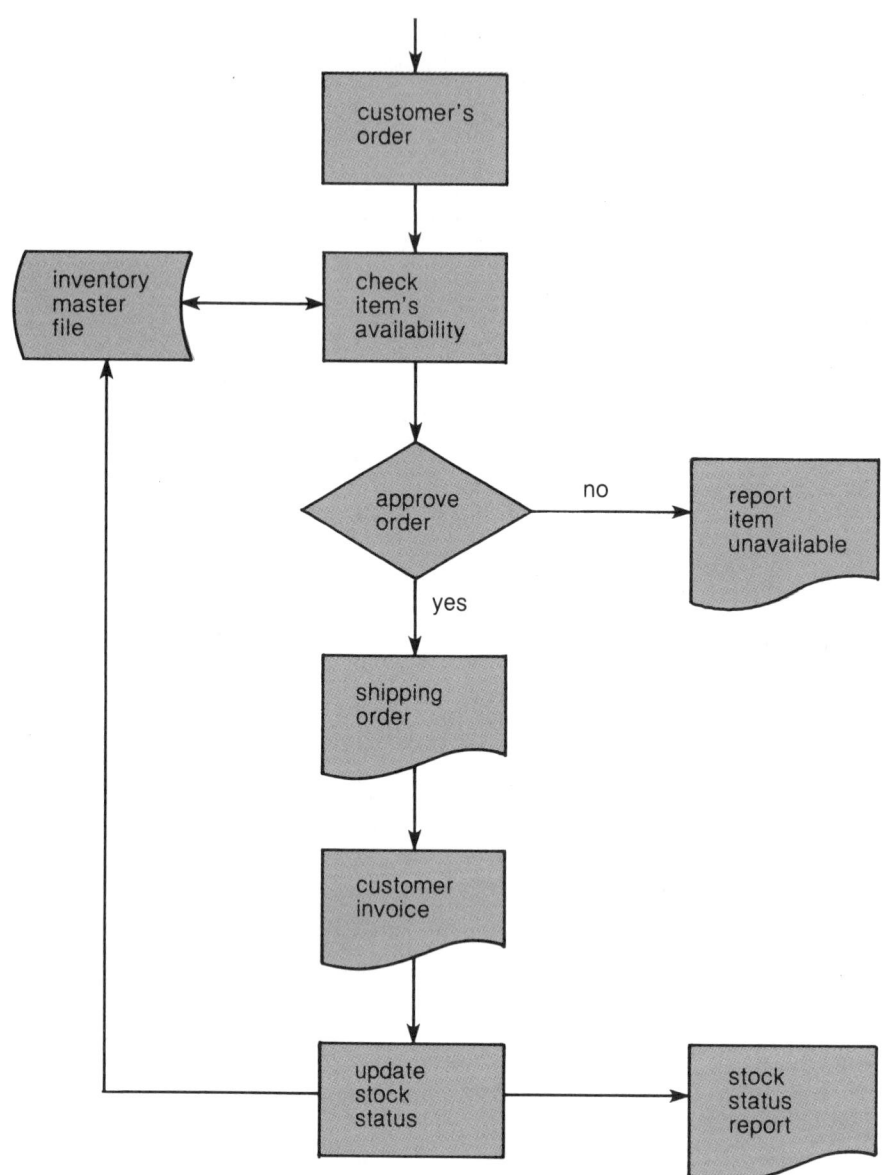

Figure 6.3 Automatic decision and transaction processing in a partial inventory system

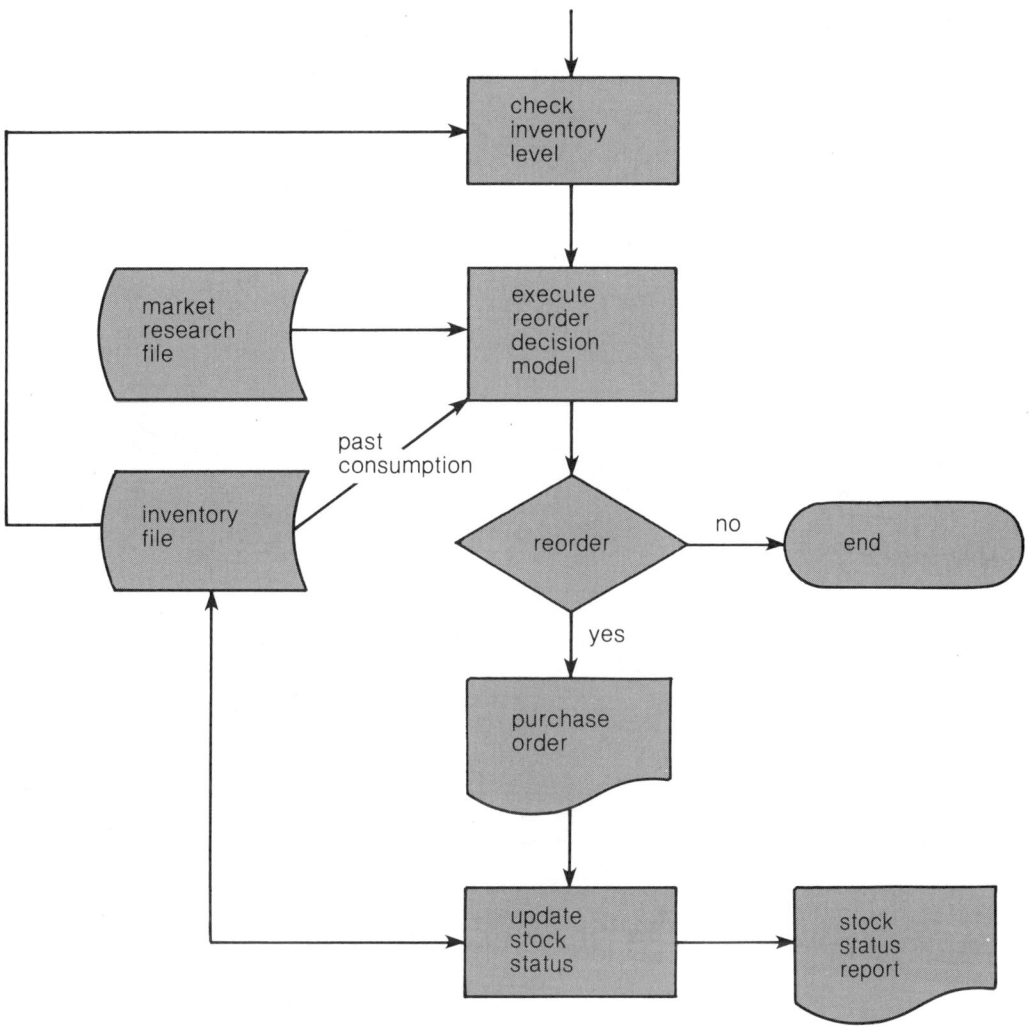

Figure 6.4 A decision support system for purchasing very expensive items

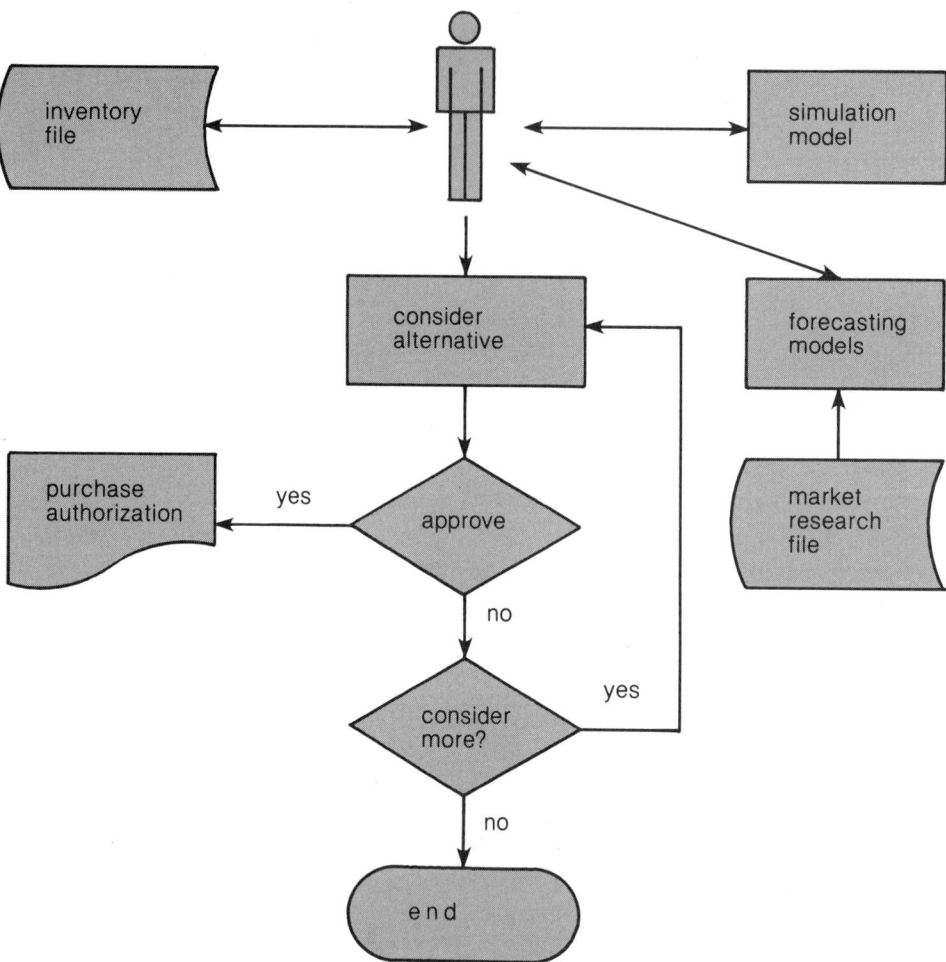

Transaction Processing Systems

Each day hundreds or thousands of activities (events) occur within an organization. Each activity triggers one or more transactions. For instance, a customer's order may initiate an order entry transaction, a billing transaction, and an accounts receivable transaction. Each transaction is made into a record (source document) describing some important facts—what happened, when it happened, who was involved, how much money was involved, how many items were involved, etc. The transactions may be recorded manually (handwritten), mechanically (typewritten, clocked), magnetically (e.g., ATM), or electronically (using a keyboard and a screen). The recorded transactions are called *data.* This raw data can be analyzed in various ways to meet the unique information needs of the organization. Virtually any type of information can be produced from the data. The data, however, represents thousands of facts, which, presented separately, would only confuse the user. The data must be processed to convert it into *information*. This is the task of a transaction processing system. The TPS handles the major part of the work load of an information system. It records and stores most data needed by the information system, and it also generates most reports and documents needed by operational users.

Every organization, small or large, simply cannot survive without a TPS. The TPS can be manual and process a small volume of transactions; or it can be computerized (we will concentrate on these) and process very large volumes of transactions. In most cases, an organization would have several TPSs, each one covering a unique application (e.g., accounts receivable, order processing, or accounts payable). Some of these TPSs are interconnected, either by shared master files or by the output of one TPS serving as the input to another. This interconnection of transaction processing reflects the interconnection between the physical flows within an organization. For instance, a customer request for stock leads to shipment of stock to the customer and issuance of a customer's invoice, and later on to a cash receipt; shipping depletes the inventory, which eventually leads to a purchase order going to a vendor and generating stock addition.

The interdependence between several TPSs is illustrated in figure 6.5 (see [9]). The figure describes four interconnected computerized processing cycles of a wholesale operation. Each cycle consists of several computer applications (a *computer application* is a series of logically related computer programs). For a description of most common computerized business applications, see Eliason [10].

The first cycle, customer order processing (boxes I_1, I_2, I_3, I_4), begins with the receipt of a customer order (I_1). The order is processed, leading to a request to draw from stock the quantity ordered (I_2); a packing slip together with the merchandise is prepared (I_3) and sent to shipping; a bill of lading is prepared (I_4) and sent to the customer with the merchandise.

The second cycle, accounts receivable processing (boxes II_1, II_2, II_3, II_4), begins with the receipt of a document recording the shipment. The document is processed (II_1), leading to invoice copies being sent to the customer and to accounts receivable (II_4). The customer (II_2) processes the invoice and mails cash (this application, of course, is external to the wholesale business). The accounts receivable application (II_4) processes the invoice. The cash receipt is processed by the cash receipts application (II_3), then updated by the accounts receivable application (II_4).

The third cycle, inventory processing (boxes III_1, III_2, III_3, III_4), begins with the preparation of a purchase requisition (III_1) as stock reaches a reorder level. The requisition is processed (III_2), leading to a purchase order being sent to a vendor. The vendor processes the order (III_3) and ships it, together with a packing slip and a bill of lading. These documents are processed by the receiving application (III_4) and the stock is added to inventory (III_1). Note that the vendor's order processing (III_3) is external to the wholesale business.

Figure 6.5 Typical interconnected transaction processing systems

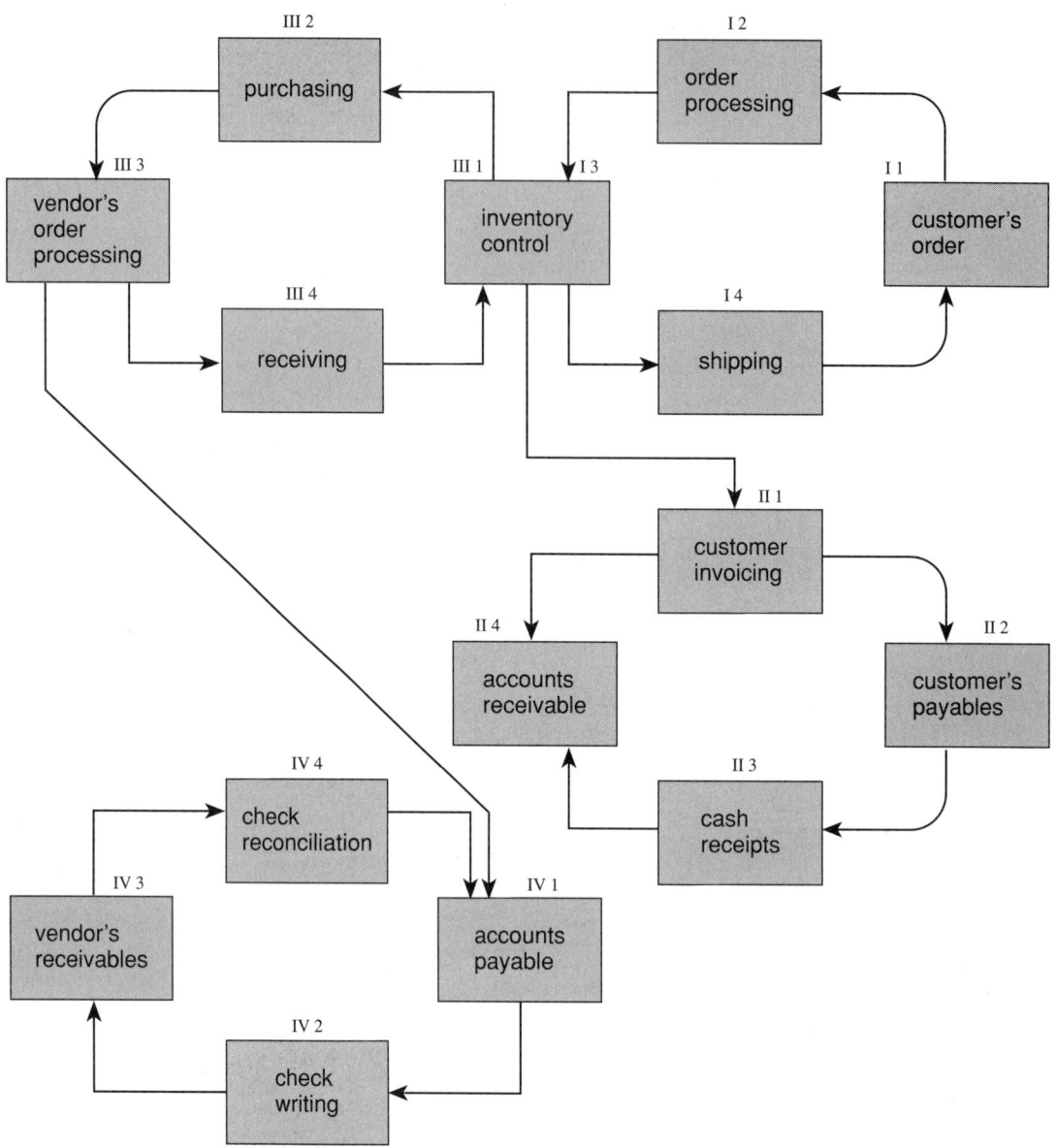

The fourth cycle, accounts payable processing (boxes IV$_1$, IV$_2$, IV$_3$, IV$_4$), begins with the receipt of the vendor's invoice. The invoice is processed (IV$_1$) and a check is printed (IV$_2$). The vendor cashes the check (IV$_3$); the cancelled check is processed by the reconciliation application (IV$_4$), and then recorded by the accounts payable application (IV$_1$). Note, again, that the vendor's receivables application (IV$_3$) is external to the wholesale business.

You can observe that the four cycles are integrated both by output of one serving as input to another and by some shared master files. A customer master file integrates customer order processing with accounts receivable processing; a product master file integrates customer order processing with inventory processing; a vendor master file integrates inventory processing with accounts payable processing.

We will now describe the typical transaction processing cycle. We rely here on several concepts reviewed in appendix A, such as online-processing modes of operations; the various control features of the transaction-processing cycle are surveyed in chapter 14. We first introduce batch transaction processing, then proceed to online transaction processing.

The Transaction Processing Cycle

Many organizational activities occur periodically rather than continually. Employees are paid weekly, or monthly; students' grades are turned in at the end of each term. The source documents recording these activities are gathered into a batch; this group of documents is then processed in a batch, and files (e.g., personnel file, student file) are updated in one large batch on a scheduled date. Batch is usually the most economical way to provide periodic processing, when it is not necessary for files to reflect all transactions up to the latest minute. The *transaction processing cycle* consists of five stages: (1) *recording* and data collection; (2) *conversion* and *verification;* (3) *data validation;* (4) *file updating* and processing; and (5) *reporting.* (See also ch. 14 and [29] for a description of the various TPS control techniques.)

Recording and Data Collection
An organization's performance of a transaction (e.g., sale, purchase) is generally recorded on a document or a form. The form may direct a transaction to take place (e.g., customer's purchase order), or record its performance (e.g., packing slip), or confirm its performance (e.g., invoice). The capture of data is a necessary first step in processing a transaction. The initial recording of the transaction is critical. The design of the recording procedure has a substantial impact on speed and accuracy of recording and on subsequent efforts to detect and correct errors. (See also the sections "Handling of Source Data" and "What Makes a Good Form" in ch. 14.)

Accuracy, completeness, and authenticity of the input transaction data affect all subsequent processing and therefore warrant particular consideration. Furthermore, the volume of data collected can reach staggering proportions. The cost of data collection is often one of the largest single components of operating an information system. It follows, then, that the choice of data collection devices is one of the most important design characteristics of an information system. There is a large variety of data collection devices (see appendix A). These differ in means of recording and sensing information, degree of automation, speed, portability, cost, accuracy, and the like. The form on which each transaction is recorded can be filled in manually or electronically; or it can be typewritten or partially preprinted. Some coding may take place, such as assigning a standard and compressed representation of data recorded in the source document; for example, sex may be assigned a one-letter code (male = M, female = F). *Preprinted forms* and coding reduce the probability of erroneous recording.

Data Conversion and Verification

Data conversion is the process of transforming data from a human-readable medium (such as a handwritten form) to a computer-readable medium (such as a diskette). Recorded transactions go through a data entry process that converts the data into a computer input medium, such as a diskette or magnetic disk (see appendix A for more details). The converted records then become the transaction file.

A typical system may use different types of devices to meet a variety of requirements and data sources. In many cases, the data from the source document is entered through the keyboard of a small computer or an online terminal. The computer-readable result is then usually on a disk or a diskette. If some of the data on the source document is known in advance, then there is incentive to preprint that data in optical or magnetic ink characters that are machine readable. Then additional data can be keyed through a device that will place it back on the source document in that same type font. Subsequently, the entire document can be read through a special reader. Again, the data will eventually end up on a computer-readable disk or diskette.

Remote terminals are now extensively used for direct entry of transaction data into a computer system. In such cases actual source documents are not prepared, and the stages of recording and data conversion are thus integrated; the original recording is computer readable. Examples are automatic tellers in banks and point of sale (POS) terminals in retail businesses. You have to watch, though, that controls are properly devised in such systems, because the absence of a source document (hard copy) may cause control problems (see ch. 14).

The data conversion activities may introduce errors. It is therefore necessary to check the conversion into computer-readable form. The process of ensuring that the data recorded on a source document has been accurately transcribed to a computer-readable form is called *verification*. Verification can be performed by either rekeying the source document or by sight proofreading. In order to save money, not all the data in a record is usually verified. Where complete accuracy of data fields is necessary, 100 percent verification is usually the only answer. With conversion through a terminal or a small computer, verification can be handled by a program in the computer's memory that detects errors, displays them on the computer or terminal screen, and initiates rekeying of the necessary data from the source document.

Data Validation

The boundary separating data verification and data validation was quite clear in the old days of offline keying. With current data entry devices, the boundary is fuzzy (see appendix A). In many cases the stages of recording, data conversion and verification, and validation are merged into one stage of online data entry and validation. However, we can still make the following logical distinction. Verification refers to the accuracy, completeness, and authenticity of converted source documents. It can be handled manually or by a computer program, and it does not require a comparison against master file records. Validation, on the other hand (or computer input editing, as it is often called), is always a computerized process. It involves a transaction file having records already verified and a check of relations between transaction records and master file records.

Data validation is thus the process of screening transaction records against a set of validation criteria designed to detect certain types of inaccuracy, unreasonableness, or incompleteness. Validation checks are usually applied to individual characters and fields and/or to combinations of several fields from the transaction record, either alone or in conjunction with the content of one or more master files. (The section "Data Conversion and Validation" in ch. 14 elaborates on the extent of validity checking.)

Data validation tests should normally be made at the earliest possible point in the transaction processing cycle in order to reject, suspend, and correct invalid records. Figure 6.6 outlines the data validation process in a batch-processing mode.

A computer program, usually labeled *edit program,* reads in the transaction records and tests for all detectable errors. The edit program may, for instance, determine that each customer number in the transaction record matches a currently active customer. The edit program produces a new *transaction file* containing only valid records. It also produces a list of records rejected for errors. The rejected records are then corrected and reentered through the edit program. This process is continued until the input transactions are free of error.

The rejected records represent potentially valid transactions. It is essential to ensure that they are either correctly reentered into the system or discarded as erroneously prepared transactions. A sound control technique is to write the rejected transactions onto a separate "suspense file" together with a code of the edit criteria that led to the rejection. By holding rejected records in suspense, the edit program ensures that they will be corrected and not lost or unduly delayed (see complementary discussion in ch. 14).

To recapitulate, the stages of data verification and validation are intended to correct erroneous transactions before they reach the processing stage of the transaction processing cycle. At this stage computer programs perform file update, computation, and retrieval. Errors can result from an erroneous recording of a transaction or from a faulty conversion of the data to a computer-readable form. In most batch information systems, the verification and validity checks take place prior to the processing stage for the following two reasons:

1. The update and retrieval programs are usually too complex to contain the extra validity checks.
2. The processing programs are normally executed in fixed time intervals (in other than online real-time systems) in one or several computer sites. Input preparation, on the other hand, is a continuous process throughout a certain time period and is distributed in many locations. Error corrections will be more efficient if done close in time and distance to the transaction occurrence.

Figure 6.6 Data entry, validation and correction based on batch processing

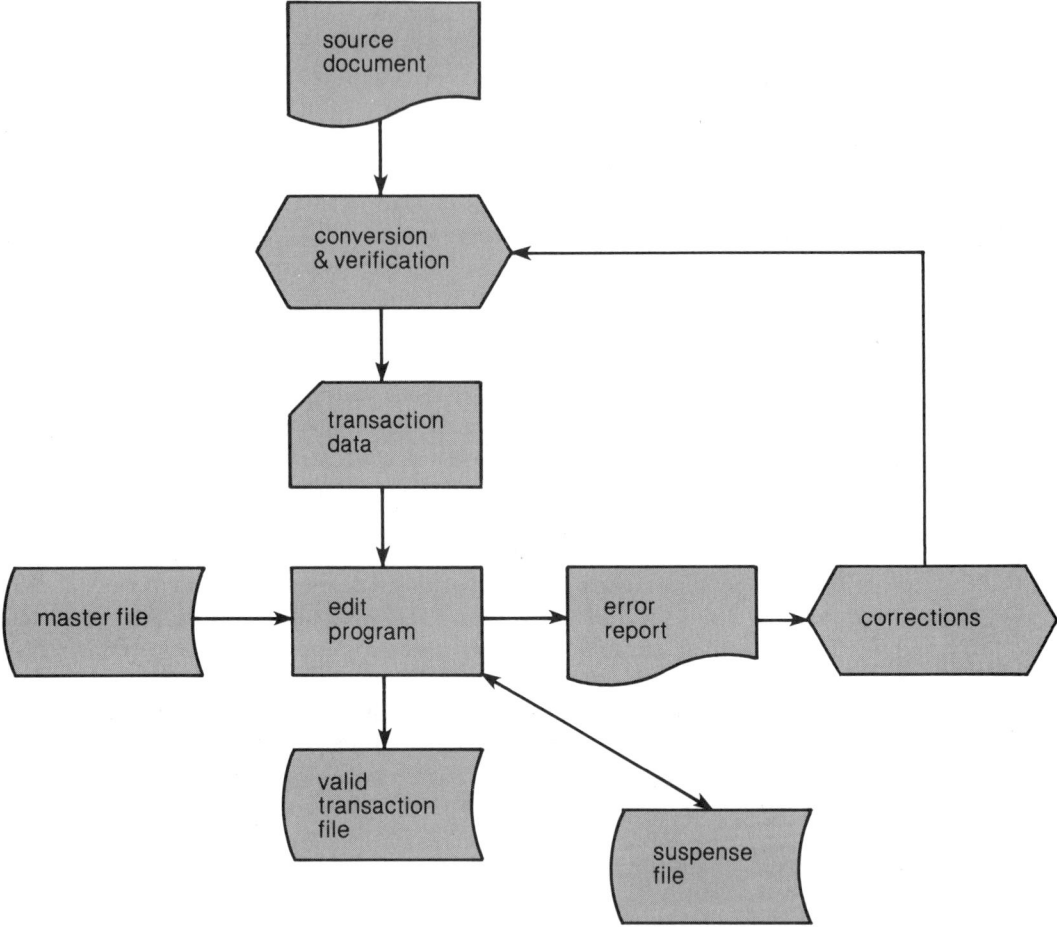

Modern technology makes it possible for the recording, data verification, and data validation stages to be integrated by direct recording of data into a microcomputer or an online terminal. The separation between the stages is determined by the technological and economic alternatives available to a specific organization (see appendix A on selection of input medium). Generally speaking, the more sophisticated the data entry devices are, the more integrated the stages can be.

File Processing and Updating
When the input transaction file has been edited, corrected, and cleared for use, *file processing* occurs. Processing the transaction file may take various forms and involve this file alone or this file in conjunction with one or more master files.

Figure 6.7 File organization and processing methods

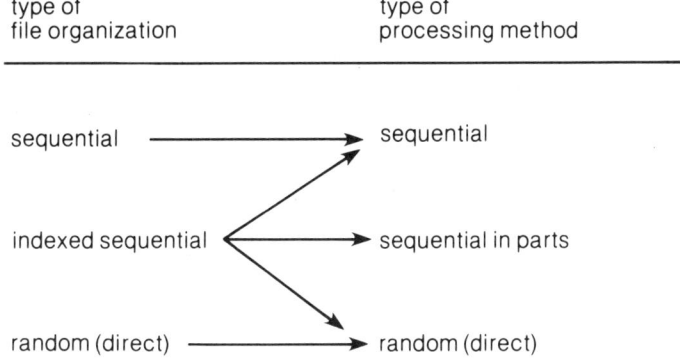

type of
file organization

type of
processing method

sequential ——————→ sequential

indexed sequential ←————→ sequential in parts

random (direct) ——————→ random (direct)

Sorting is a common example of processing the transaction file alone. Sorting is the arrangement of records into some predetermined order, using a field (or fields) in the record as a sorting key. There are many ways to sort records, depending on the file media and equipment used. Sorting is an important data processing activity, requiring a significant part of the information processing effort. If it is performed prior to *input editing,* the purpose is to detect duplicate transactions. If it is performed subsequent to input editing, the purpose is to have the transaction file in the same order as the master file to which it applies. (This is a prerequisite for updating a master file organized sequentially.) Sorting may also be performed prior to printing output in order to have the data in a form that is convenient for distribution—for example, arranging a customer bills output file by zip codes before printing it.

Processing the transaction file may involve other master files, from which data is retrieved only. One example is the processing of sale transactions for billing. Such transactions may contain a customer's number only; the customer's name and address are then obtained from the customer name-and-address file. Another example is the processing of a batch of inquiry transactions, such as requests to print various student records. For each transaction of this type, the student master file is accessed and a record retrieved for printing.

Updating is an example of processing the transaction file in conjunction with one or more master files. The *master files* are the permanent files of the organization and are maintained on a regular basis. Examples are the personnel file, the accounts payable file, and the general ledger file. The format of fields in master file records usually remains constant even though the field contents may change frequently. Master files must be kept accurate by updating fields in the records, by adding new records, and by deleting old ones. For example, students are deleted from a student file once they graduate, and incoming students are added to the file periodically.

The procedure for updating the master file depends on the type of file organization and the type of processing methods. These are described in appendix A and are summarized in figure 6.7.

Figure 6.8 Salespeople update and analysis application

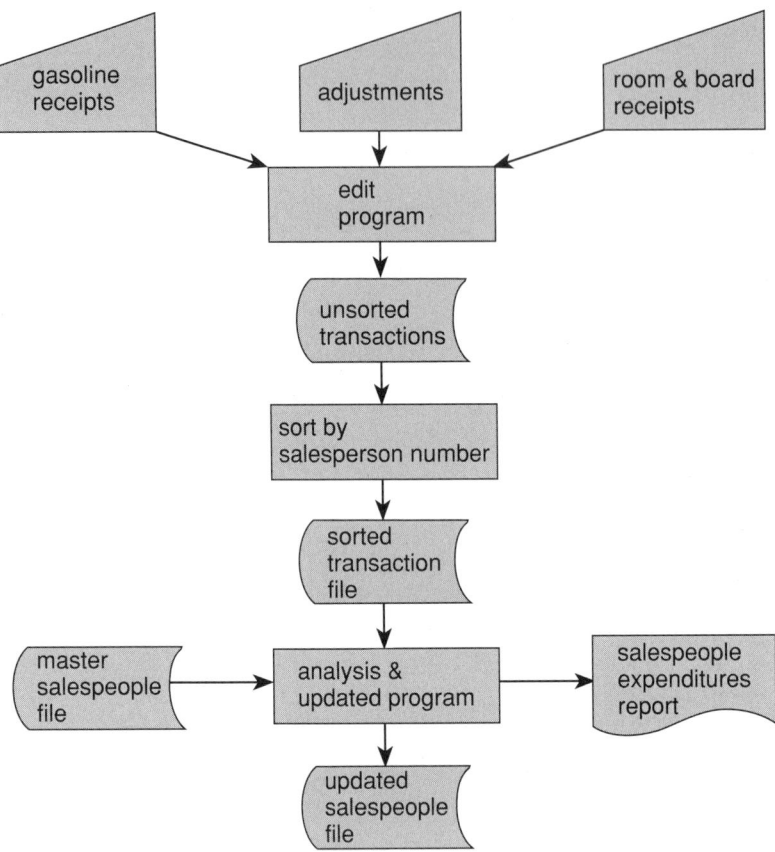

In general, the record in the master file to be updated is read, updated, and then written onto an updated file. In a sequential processing system, we usually assume that the files are sequentially organized by the key fields of the records, and are therefore processed sequentially. Updating a file essentially involves reading each master file record. If there is no transaction that applies to the record, the record is rewritten without change. If there is a transaction that applies to the record, the record is updated with changes; transactions reflecting new entities are used to add records to the file. If there is a transaction that indicates that the relevant record should be deleted, then the record is simply not rewritten onto the updated file. In essence, the current master file is rewritten to produce a new, updated file. Figure 6.8 illustrates this approach of sequential batch processing of a salesperson master file.

Inputs to the monthly salespeople update and analysis computer application consist of keyed receipts of gasoline and room and board expenditures incurred by the salespeople, as well as adjustments. The keyed receipts represent transaction records that update or add to variable fields in salespeople's records. They do not alter fundamental (static) information stored in master files. For instance, they alter the year-to-date expenditure field in the salespeople's record, but not the address field. The keyed adjustments represent change or addition records, which are used either to alter data fields considered constant in the master file (such as salespeople's names and addresses), or to add a new salesperson. This type of record adds to file contents, alters contents, and/or adjusts for errors.

After keyed data is edited, the transactions are sorted by salespeople's numbers and processed by the analysis and update program. This processing entails totaling and posting expenditures to master file records, adding and deleting salespeople records, and printing a report. The previous salespeople master file was produced as output from the last monthly process. The salespeople master file output from this month's process will, in turn, become the input to next month's process. Batch processes normally produce other output files, which can be used in other applications. For instance, the salespeople update program can produce a check file that will be used by a check program to print checks for reimbursing the salespeople.

The sequential process may seem cumbersome and somewhat archaic. You are right; however, in many organizational applications that do not require online update and retrieval of data, this process is still the backbone of data processing.

Note that batch processing is also applicable when direct access storage devices are in use. In such cases some sorting and rewriting operations can be skipped, provided that the master files are not sequentially organized (see appendix A). However, the basic principle of operating in batches is not changed so long as the orientation of the TPS as a whole is not online.

Reporting

The *reporting* stage provides the interface between the TPS and the users of its output. Effective reporting that aids the user in his or her perception of relevant information can substantially contribute to the usefulness of the system. Not all outputs (results) from the system are reported (or displayed). A large proportion of the results may be stored in the data base without being reported in detailed form. Other outputs may be stored for further processing. A payroll TPS, for example, can produce several outputs, including files (new payroll master file, check file), printed reports (tax reports, summary reports, check register), and documents (paychecks).

The TPS produces three major types of output: preplanned reports, preplanned responses to inquiries, and transaction documents (see [4]). *Preplanned reports* are predetermined as to content and format (e.g., balance sheets). They cover a predetermined time period and report either a status at a point in time (e.g., stock on hand) or a flow during the period (e.g., monthly sales). Preplanned responses to inquiries are generally associated with limited output, usually with respect to part of the records in a master file (e.g., exception reporting—a report of all students whose grade point average is below D).

A *transaction document* (or action document) is an item such as an invoice, paycheck, bill, or purchase order. Transaction documents can initiate some action, such as a purchase order, and they can be used to report a confirmation of a completed action (e.g., a list of cashed paychecks). A document designed for return and use in processing the completion of a transaction is known as a *turnaround document*. Examples are optically readable forms sent with customer billings with the request that they be returned with the payment. Transaction documents can also provide background information to the recipient and be used for reference purposes. For example, copies of students' grade cards do not initiate action by the teacher; they are both a confirmation that grades were assigned and reference documents, should inquiries arise.

The various reporting techniques and reporting media (see appendix A) are each associated with costs and benefits. Some of these are

Preprinted paper forms

Computer generated paper forms

Optically readable forms

Terminal output (printer)

Terminal output (visual display)

The form of displayed output can vary. An alphanumeric display uses only a limited number of characters (the alphabet, numerals, special characters). Alphanumeric output is almost always a *tabular display* (i.e., columns labeled with a heading); only rarely does it appear in narrative form. *Graphic display* presents information by means of graphs and patterns (e.g., trend curves, probability distributions). Compared to tabular reports, graphic reports are not used very widely by transaction processing systems.

Local and Remote Input/Output

The various stages of the transaction processing cycle can take place in physically adjacent locations or in locations far apart. Also, the transactions and the computer can be physically separate. Similarly, there are various means of moving the transaction inputs to be processed and moving the output back to the users. Local processing is the term used when the transactions and the processing are physically adjacent; remote processing is the term when they are physically separate.

Remote processing may rely on mail, couriers, and transportation facilities to move inputs and outputs. In most cases, however, it relies on data communication facilities and on remote data entry devices to send transaction records in batches and to receive reports and documents. So long as processing and updating of files (including validation of transactions against the master file) are not involved, this remote job processing should be classified as part of a batch transaction processing system. It does not merit any special discussion, since conceptually it was covered in the preceding sections. In other words, the only change that we now introduce into the transaction processing cycle is that data and information moving from one stage to another, or from one location to another, are transmitted electrically and not physically.

Facilities that are dependent on a distant data processing system linked by communication lines are thus equipped to perform part of the transaction processing cycle. Typically, they have data entry equipment that enables them to convert *source documents* into computer-readable input transactions, and they may also have printing equipment that can produce reports and documents (see appendix A).

In other cases, such equipment may include a microcomputer. This approach allows the remote facility to handle data verification. Transaction input is then verified and corrected at the point of entry—before it is communicated to the data processing center for processing. When data collection has an immediate effect on existing master files, the discussion applies to online transaction processing systems, to which we now turn.

Online Transaction Processing Systems

In contrast to the delay inherent in periodic batch processing, online transaction processing can provide immediate data validation, or immediate updating and processing, or immediate reporting, or all these stages combined. In an online environment, the user is actually provided with direct access to files and computer programs via remote terminals and communication lines. The user can enjoy an immediate, real-time response.

One of the main characteristics of an online processing system is that the sequence in which transactions are received is random, and each terminal may be treated as a separate transaction input source. Transactions are processed continuously rather than periodically. Files are online and available to the system at all times for data validation and file updating. Errors in transactions may be detected immediately and corrected by the person making the data entry, rather than left for periodic processing, where erroneous transactions are returned to the source individual. The master files are continuously up to date and, thus, almost immediately reflect the occurrence of all events (provided that the transactions are immediately entered).

These advantages of online transaction processing are not gained without substantial costs. Extra computer time is required for processing and for the use of terminals; the application software and the system software are more complex than for batch processing; and a relatively heavy investment in acquisition and operation of terminals, communication lines and devices, direct access storage devices, mainframe computers, and additional control features is necessary (see ch. 14, appendix A, and [29]).

Often online processing entails only part of the transaction processing cycle. This has to do mainly with the stages of data collection and data conversion and verification: transactions may be entered directly through terminals, immediately verified for correctness, then batched and processed at a subsequent time (as with batch processing). The advantages of this mode of delayed batch processing over conventional batch processing are the immediate capture of transactions in a computer-readable form and the immediate feedback for error correction.

Imagine a central warehouse connected online to a computer. The warehouse receives stocks from suppliers and issues stock items to manufacturing units. These transactions have to be entered and the inventory master file has to be updated immediately to constantly reflect quantities on hand. Figure 6.9 summarizes the online processing of these transactions.

Figure 6.9 Online transaction processing of inventory issues and receipts

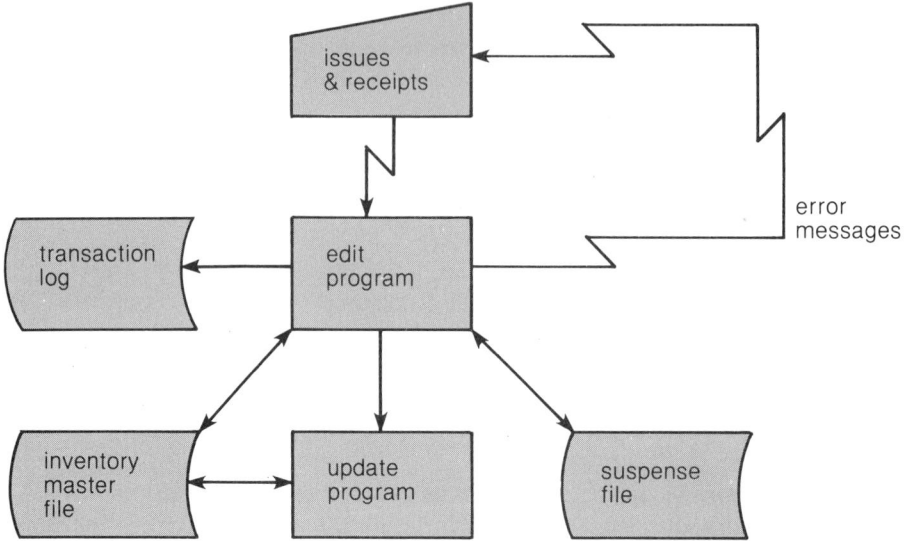

A warehouse clerk, equipped with a computer terminal, enters each transaction into the system as it occurs. At the end of the data transmission, the system sends an acknowledgment to the terminal. This technique assures the clerk that the computer correctly received the transaction.

As soon as the transaction is received at the computer, the following tasks are performed:

1. The transaction (including date and time) is recorded onto a file called the *transaction log*. The transaction log is used for recovery from an error or a malfunction.

2. The transaction is verified and validated (including comparison against a master file record) to make certain it is acceptable. This task is under the control of an edit program that can directly access the master inventory file.

3. If the transaction is erroneous, the system rejects it, displaying the reason for rejection on the screen with an error message (e.g., "item number incorrect"). The erroneous transaction is entered as an error record into a *suspense file* stored on a direct access device. The error record includes a code that indicates the error type, date and time, transaction type (issue or receipt), and the content of the transaction. The error record is maintained until the corrected transaction is entered from the terminal.

4. An *update program* makes the master file record current. There are four types of transactions in our warehouse example, each requiring its own unique handling. Each type is identified by a transaction code:

ADD—Add a new master record for a new stock item

DEL—Delete an existing master record for an item that will not be stocked any more

ISS—Quantity of an item issued

REC—Quantity of an item received

At the end of each working day the following batch system functions are performed:

1. The transaction log is terminated, dumped on a tape or removable disk, removed from the computer, and stored in a safe place.

2. The inventory file and the suspense file are copied onto tapes or disks, and the copies are stored in a safe place for backup and recovery purposes.

3. The system sends and prints on the terminal a list of all stock items that have reached predetermined safety levels. This is done under the control of a print program.

Sometimes a failure destroys the current inventory and suspense files or makes them inaccessible to the system. When this occurs, it is impossible to proceed until the master files have been restored to their prefailure status. Therefore, the warehouse clerk is not allowed to access the system until it is operating with correct information. The restoration of service is accomplished by executing a computer program that recovers all the necessary information. The copies of the master files and the transaction log as of the beginning of the day are inputs to the recovery program. This recovery program repeats all the transaction processing up to the point of failure. The output of the recovery program is the reconstructed master files, which allow the system to be restarted at the point of failure. Once again, the warehouse clerk can access the system.

Structured Decision Systems

The files maintained by the various transaction processing systems (TPSs) serve both the operations and management modules of the information system. The difference between the modules is revealed in the various computer programs, not in the data files. We therefore distinguish between the data base and the model base of an information system. The *model base* is the collection of application programs using the *data base* (see also ch. 5).

The term *structured decision system* (SDS) refers to information systems that make structured (i.e., programmed) decisions. While the TPS supports the activities of the operations level, the SDS makes decisions that are within the realm of operational and management control levels (see ch. 5). The various SDSs cannot develop before the applicable TPSs are developed, since the automatic decisions made by an SDS are the result of processing data maintained by a TPS. For example, an SDS that determines stock reorder quantities cannot function without an inventory TPS, which collects inventory transactions and updates an inventory master file. Such an SDS can operate as an independent application, triggered by manual intervention (e.g., the warehouse manager), or as an application that is part of the processing stage of the inventory transaction processing cycle.

Any SDS incorporates programs (one or more) that instruct the computer to process some relevant data by employing one or more decision models. A decision model represents (summarizes, abstracts) a human decision-making process that is completely structured, and hence, programmable. The SDSs can be developed by one of two complementary approaches. First, as more and more transactions are collected and stored in the data base by TPSs, attempts are made to develop or adopt models that can use this data. Second, the organization can adopt known models or develop custom-made models, then use them to process either currently stored data or new data that was not collected before due to the lack of models.

Suppose a wholesale business has an inventory TPS that updates an inventory master file. The business uses a model (embodied in a computer program) to determine the quantity of each item to order from vendors. The model expresses the quantity to order as

Quantity to order = (quantity to be sold + safety stock + customer back order) − (balance on hand + quantity on order).

This model is admittedly simplistic. It assumes that material will be ordered without regard for purchase order costs and inventory costs, that the order frequency is known, and that the safety stock of each item is predetermined (for more elaborate reorder models see Eliason [10]).

Figure 6.10 illustrates a simple batch-mode SDS that determines reorder quantities based on this model. This SDS is activated at predetermined time intervals. Its input is a customer orders file that is one of the outputs of the customer orders TPS. This file is first sorted by stock item number to facilitate more efficient processing. The records in this file contain the quantities of each item to be sold. The reorder program (incorporating the logic of the model) accesses the updated inventory master file. Each item record in this file contains the safety stock, customers' back orders for the item, balance on hand, and quantity on order. For each item that has customer orders, the reorder program uses the relevant fields in both files and computes the new quantity to order. It then updates the inventory item master record with the new quantity on order and prints a line for each item that needs reordering.

What does this contrived SDS do? It makes reorder decisions that were once made by the firm's buyer, and it makes them in a faster and more accurate way. It uses data that was captured and processed by the customer orders TPS and by the inventory TPS. We may add that the safety stock for each stock item was predetermined by another SDS that employed the following model:

Safety stock = (maximum less normal demand for item) × (vendor lead time + order frequency).

Figure 6.10 A structured decision system for stock reorder quantities

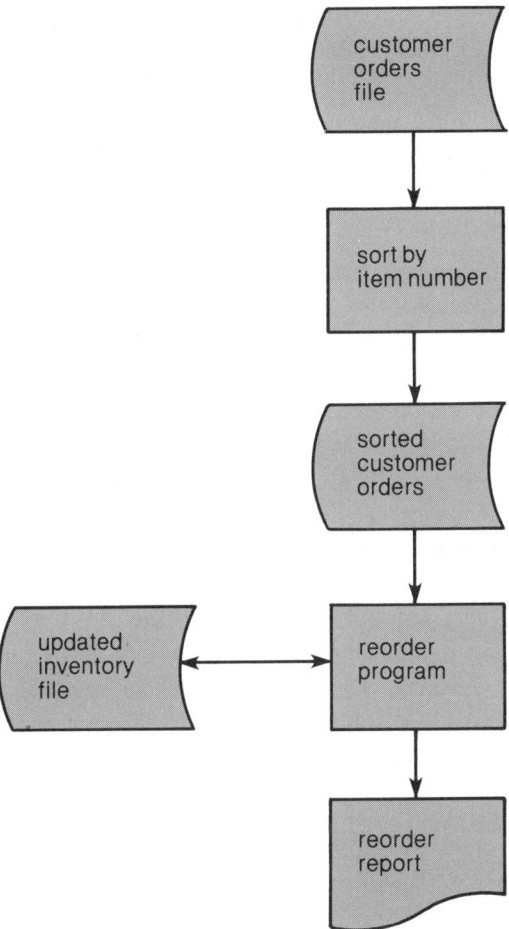

Decision Support Systems

This safety stock model accepts as inputs the data about demand for inventory items, the vendor lead times, and the order frequencies. It processes this data and produces an automatic decision. What happens if the demand is subject to extreme fluctuations and depends on many variables, not all of which can be easily quantified (for instance, consumer tastes, the business cycle, competitive firms, or political considerations)? The demand forecasting then becomes an unstructured decision that cannot be converted to a computer program. It requires assumptions and risk taking by the senior management of the firm. It therefore becomes the concern of the sales manager (rather than the firm's buyer), who uses the reorder reports generated by the SDS described in the preceding section.

The sales manager will then make some assumptions, allow a sales forecasting model to process the assumed figures, change the assumptions, review the resulting forecast, change some more, and so on. He or she will finally select one of the forecasts and establish it as the figure used by the safety stock model. There are several implications in this short example, including the following:

1. Many decisions at the senior management level are unstructured or semistructured.

2. The decision makers at this level must resort to assumptions, intuition, and experience when making such decisions.

3. The decision-making process is an interactive human-machine process. The machine (computer system) supports the decision maker by evaluating various alternative solutions, and the decision maker selects one alternative and, thus, culminates the decision-making process.

4. The computer system provides supporting information to the decision maker by accessing the data base and using one or more models from the model base.

5. The interactive process takes place in a relatively short time. The senior manager cannot wait hours for the results of his or her processed assumptions. Therefore, the process normally requires an online mode of system operation.

6. The internal data base may have to be augmented by external data, such as those relating to business cycles. This data is not routinely captured by the TPS.

7. A prerequisite for the success of the interactive decision-making process is a convenient interface between the decision maker and the model base and between the decision maker and the data base.

These implications indicate, in effect, the necessary components and tools of a decision support system (DSS). Unlike TPSs and SDSs, DSSs are used to help solve the semistructured problems typical of the senior manager's world. They rely on the decision maker's insights and judgment at all stages of problem solving—from problem formulation, to choosing relevant data, to selecting the alternative solutions and evaluating those solutions.

Definition and Attributes of a DSS

The term *decision support system* (also referred to as "management decision system," "management support system," or "strategic planning system") has been subject to a wide range of definitions. At one end is the narrow, specific definition of the DSS as "an interactive, computer-based system which supports managers in making unstructured decisions" [34]. At the other end is the more global assessment that a DSS is an aid in decision making and implementation; succinctly put, the DSS serves as an "executive mind-support system" [23]. It is one of the many tools a manager can choose

Figure 6.11 Conceptual components of a DSS

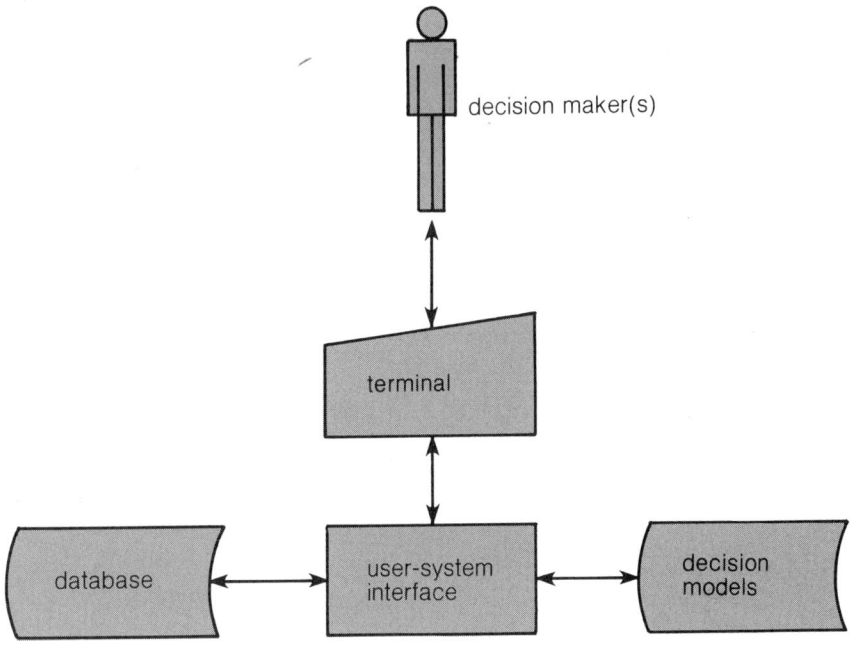

to aid in daily decision-making activities. The decision support system is not an ''automated manager,'' but rather a ''right-hand person,'' standing ready to support, not replace the manager. The hallmark of a good decision support system is not its sophistication or efficiency, but its ability to increase the effectiveness of the manager who employs it.

Another definition, which clearly distinguishes a DSS from an SDS, asserts that ''a DSS is a computer-based information system used to support decision-making activities in situations where it is not possible or not desirable to have an automated system perform the entire decision process'' [13].

Regardless of how a decision support system is defined, conceptually it must possess four essential components: (1) data; (2) decision models; (3) a user-system interface; and (4) decision maker(s). These are illustrated in figure 6.11.

Before describing these components, we should refer to the discussion in chapter 3 on the three stages of the decision-making process: intelligence, design, and choice. Also, in chapter 5 we specified a completely unstructured decision as one where all stages of the decision-making process are unstructured; a semistructured decision as one where one or more of the stages are unstructured.

A DSS supports a semistructured decision; it is designed to support a decision maker in any (but not every) stage of the decision-making process. The decision maker can choose those functions of the DSS that support some stage while not using other functions. For instance, a decision maker may require the use of data but not models. The key to successful human-machine cooperation is this principle of specified DSS support.

Early DSS literature defined DSS-appropriate problems as those that are semi-structured. The degree of problem structure is, indeed, central to DSS. At one extreme, if a decision problem can be completely structured (no human judgment is required), then an SDS can replace the human decision maker. At the other extreme, if no structure can be imposed on the problem, decision support is impossible. It is only between these extremes that DSS is relevant.

Ginzberg and Stohr [13] stated that a problem is semistructured when it is possible to impose some structure on the problem, such as when a decision maker is willing to accept a certain data set or certain models (decision rules) as relevant to the problem situation. Thus, DSS can be defined as systems applicable to problems that can be at least partially, but not completely, structured.

It does not matter to which stage of the decision-making process the structure is applied. Indeed, DSS literature has examples of support for all phases—intelligence, design of alternative solutions, evaluation of and choice among alternatives, as well as monitoring the implementation of the chosen solution. Of course, the type of support will vary from stage to stage since the nature of the activities varies. For instance, relatively few DSSs support the design stage, which typically requires the system to have more problem domain knowledge than is the case for other stages.

Components of a DSS

Before delineating the typical components of a DSS, we wish to remind you of the fundamental premise of the systems approach (ch. 4). Systems, regardless of their specific contexts, share a common set of elements. A DSS, being a system, has a specific *environment,* mainly the users (decision makers) and their decision situations; the system impacts the user by providing some *outputs* (functions); the system consumes some *resources* (inputs); and, the system has some *internal structure,* comprising *components* and their *interrelationship* (linkages, arrangements). (For a systemic treatment of a DSS and its elements, see [2]. Sprague and Carlson [33] elaborate on the internal structure of a DSS.)

The purpose of a DSS is to support a decision-making process. DSS can support decision makers in many ways, including the following:

Retrieving single items of information (i.e., a view)

Providing a mechanism for ad hoc data analysis (e.g., statistical models)

Providing prespecified aggregations of data (e.g., accounting models)

Estimating the consequences of proposed decisions (i.e., sensitivity analysis, causal models)

Proposing solutions

Figure 6.12 Generic components of a DSS

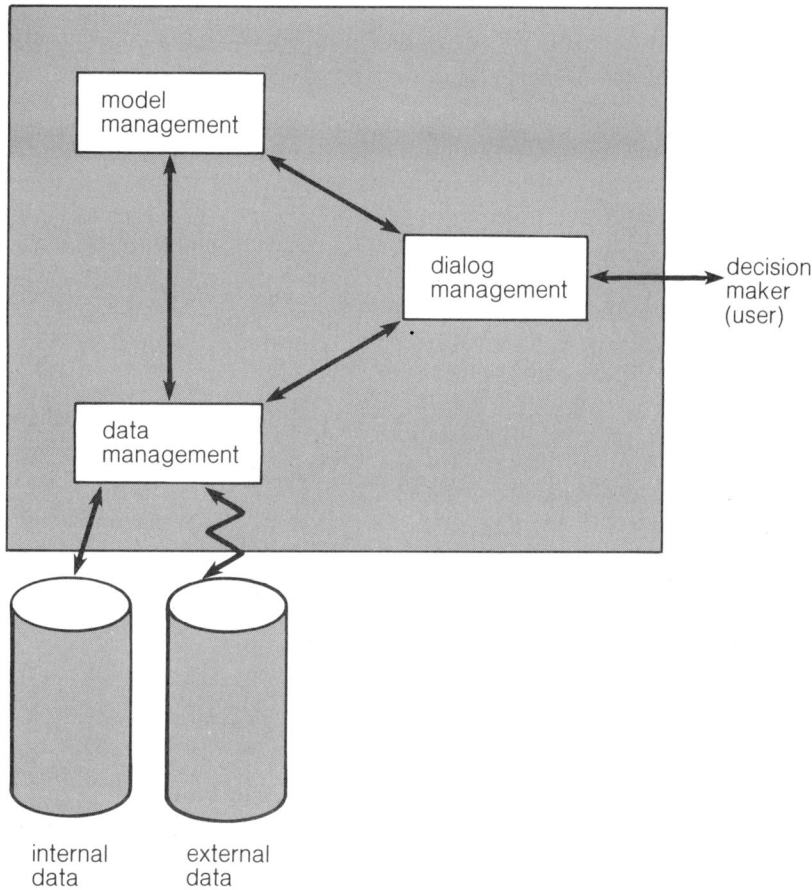

Providing each of these types of support is likely to require different DSS capabilities. This, in turn, will lead to different components and arrangements. DSS literature seems to agree about three generic components (subsystems) of a DSS (see fig. 6.12). These hardware/software components correspond to the conceptual components specified in figure 6.11.

The Dialog Management Subsystem
The dialog management subsystem provides and manages the framework in which outputs are presented to the user and in which inputs are specified by the user. The dialog between the user and the system is two way: output representations (menus, reports, charts) define the context for and prompt subsequent user inputs. An ideal dialog management subsystem has three elements.

1. *User interface*—Concerned with the syntactic aspects of the interaction, the interfacing with specific input and output devices (keyboard, screen, plotter), and issues relating to the style of interaction (is the dialog menu-driven?). The specific design of the user interface element depends on the proficiency of users and the frequency of use.

2. *Request constructor*—Provides the two-way transformations between users' requests and the specific modeling and data access repertoire. In one direction, it translates users' requests for data to valid data base *queries,* and users' model references to corresponding model-invoking commands. In the opposite direction, it translates requests issued by the model base subsystem (see page 174) for the incorporation of user-supplied parameters in a specific model. The specific design of this element reflects the vocabulary of the control element (see 3, following), and the constraints imposed by the data base and model base subsystems of the DSS.

3. *Control element*—Guarantees the smooth operation of the dialog management subsystem; determines the mode of system's use, which can vary between "system-prompted" mode and completely "user-driven" mode. This reflects the structure level of the supported decision situation (system-prompted mode for highly structured situations; user-driven mode where no predefined sequence of activities can be provided by the system).

The Data Management Subsystem

The intelligence phase of the decision-making process involves scanning the environment in search of problems or opportunities. These problems or opportunities are recognized by accessing relevant data. In the case of a marketing decision, for instance, data must be accessed on each of the company's products as a first step in determining which products are to be phased out. This data might include such items as dollar sales, physical volume, total unit cost, and price per unit. Data such as this will normally be systematically collected from the internal environment as part of a routine TPS. However, a DSS, as distinguished from a TPS, will often require collection of data concerning other environments. This may include data concerning competitors' actions, general societal trends, customer demand, or legal and/or governmental constraints. This type of data may be collected routinely or on an ad hoc basis. The relevant data is collected and stored in a data base (computerized or manual) to await the scanning stage.

A manager armed with the objectives of the firm begins the ongoing search for problems or opportunities. This search can take one of three forms, depending upon the type of decision to be made and the level of the decision maker. A structured continuous search is usually performed in order to make decisions that are well defined and regular. The user may extract isolated data in order to perform such functions as monitoring the work flow and scheduling operations of a production department, or he or she may receive prespecified standard reports that act as input to the design stage of the decision-making process.

Data may also be retrieved by a structured, but ad hoc, search in order to make infrequent decisions. Plant location is such a decision since it will normally occur infrequently. Yet the necessary intelligence gathering activities can be clearly structured. The output from such a search usually suggests the process to be used to analyze the situation, but it can also indicate the need for human intervention before the process can begin.

Finally, there are problems and opportunities for which the search must be done heuristically through examination of data by the manager. This type of decision is usually made by senior management. The intelligence phase primarily provides the managers with easy access to the data base. The data retrieval capabilities of the DSS must therefore be rapid. This, of course, has many implications for the design of a DSS. The output from such a search generally identifies the situation but leaves the rest of the decision process to the manager. Sometimes the manager employs some programmed models to manipulate the relevant data and come up with alternative solutions.

The management of data—the ability to store, retrieve, and manipulate—is thus fundamental to a DSS. These activities are performed by the *data management subsystem,* which contains four generic elements. These four elements are

1. The *data base management system (DBMS)*—Provides an access mechanism to data in the data base (the subject of DBMS is covered in appendix A). The DBMS provides such services as data sharing and integration, data definitions (views of items available in the data base), data manipulation (such as handling of queries), and data integrity (e.g., protection, recovery, lack of redundancy, consistency). The DBMS also shields the other subsystems of the DSS from physical aspects of access to the data base.

2. The *query facility*—Serves as the front-end element of the data management subsystem and as the subsystem's interface to the model management and dialog management subsystems. It accepts requests for data from these subsystems, determines how these requests can be filled, translates the requests to DBMS-specific commands, and finally returns the requested data to the issuing subsystem.

3. The *data directory*—Provides the basis for answering preliminary questions submitted by the query facility concerning availability and source of data, or their exact meaning. This element contains *meta-data* (data on the data in the data base). It is much needed in *ad hoc DSSs* (see the following) and DSSs that support the intelligence phase of the decision-making process where data exploration is a dominant need. In more *institutional DSSs* (see the following), the directory's function is internal to the DBMS element and might then disappear as an independent element.

4. The *staging* element—Provides access to sources of data that are external to the DSS. It is an interface between the DBMS element and its DSS-specific data base and other organizational data bases (e.g., those maintained by the TPS) or remote data bases. Its structure reflects the nature of external data

sources from which data is extracted. For instance, if remote data bases are to be accessed, some data communications facility is included in the staging element. (An important new industry, *online services,* has developed to provide data for microcomputer-based DSSs—see the section on external online data bases in this chapter.)

The Model Management Subsystem

Once the data gathering and scanning activities of the intelligence phase are completed, the alternatives to the problems or opportunities must be analyzed and understood. This phase involves the second conceptual component of the DSS, the *decision models.* The model base will usually consist of a wide range of models, depending on the type of decision to be made and the organizational level at which it is applied. The model building blocks and subroutines may include such standard applications as linear programming, capital budgeting, time series analysis, analysis of variance, and multiple regression. A series of operational, tactical, or strategic models can be constructed with these building blocks. The output from these models can perform one of three functions in the decision-making process. It can (1) make the decision; (2) propose the decision; or (3) estimate the consequences of proposed decisions.

There is an equally wide range of modeling techniques to support decisions. The decision model assumes the role of decision maker when the decision is programmed and the process is routine. Conventional transaction processing deals primarily with this type of decision, but many decision support systems are built upon this very foundation. Many nonprogrammed decisions are based on data that enters the system through transaction processing. The models used to make decisions usually involve relatively simple computational or statistical techniques such as simple and multiple correlation, sample selection, factor analysis, or other standard calculations. An example of the decision-making capabilities of a decision model is an insurance renewal rate system in which the computer calculates a renewal rate based on standard statistical and actuarial assumptions. The method differs from that of an SDS only in that the judgment of the underwriters is used to decide whether the standard calculations apply to a particular policy. The underwriter works with the DSS to arrive at the appropriate decision.

Another important type of model used for this type of decision making is the analytical decision model. It arrives at the optimum decision by representing the real-world situation in mathematical form. Probably the most widely used of these optimizing techniques is linear programming. This technique can be employed at both the operational and the tactical levels. It is useful at the operational level when specific values for the parameters are known. At the tactical level these values may not be known and probabilistic estimates may have to be substituted. Probability distributions often serve this function.

The DSS is usually used at the tactical level for decisions that are only partially programmed. Such models are normally employed in the allocation and control of a firm's resources. They would typically be used to perform such management control activities as financial planning, personnel requirement planning, and routine capital budgeting—applications that require much subjective data because of the element of uncertainty involved. Because of this uncertainty and the interaction of several variables, the output from this type of decision model can only propose decisions.

The decision models used for strategic level decision making are normally broad in scope and employed to estimate long-term consequences of the decisions proposed by senior management. They function as a sort of "crystal ball" to enable managers to see the future scenarios that would result from their present decisions.

The types of decisions made at this management level involve an even larger amount of uncertainty and, therefore, are nonprogrammable. Often the only way to approach such a decision is to employ a heuristic procedure. This will not lead to an optimal solution but will provide a decision that is generally superior to many alternative approaches. The best use of models in this situation is an interactive human-machine process. The manager proposes the alternatives and the model supplies the predicted consequences. The simulation model is most commonly used for prediction purposes. It attempts to duplicate the real world under varying states of nature for a given set of parameters. Since a state of nature represents a random event, it is often necessary to generate a random variable for use in the simulation model. The random variable may represent, for example, varying levels of demand relevant to a marketing decision.

Simulation models are well suited to the complexity of strategic level decision making. They are able to deal with problems that cannot be handled by other methods. They are also very versatile, enabling the manager to perform sensitivity analysis on various parameters. This sensitivity analysis capability aids the manager in interpreting the results of the model. From these results the manager can gauge the risk inherent in his or her decisions and modify them accordingly.

Any support beyond direct access to raw data invokes the application of a model. In fact, the management of models and modeling activities is what distinguishes DSS from TPS and SDS. The ability to invoke, run, change, combine, and inspect models is a core service of a DSS. The *model management subsystem* has the following generic elements:

1. The *model base management system (MBMS)*—Resembles, conceptually, the services of the DBMS with regard to data. It provides storage and retrieval facilities for programmed models. It supports the generation of models, perusal of models (i.e., reporting about those available), updating of model parameters, and restructuring of models. An integral part of the MBMS is a *model directory,* which provides information about models in response to users' inquiries, or in support of the model executor's (see 3, following) efforts to integrate several models into a supermodel. Another part of the MBMS can be a staging element that extracts models from remote, online computerized model bases (see section on external online data bases in this chapter).

2. The *modeling command processor*—The interface between the model and dialog management subsystems. It accepts and interprets modeling instructions from the query facility element of the dialog subsystem.

Interpreted instructions are then routed to the corresponding elements: inquiries about models are forwarded to the MBMS; model-building instructions are sent to the model executor.

3. The *model executor*—The heart of the modeling subsystem. It controls the actual running of models by linking together attachable models retrieved from the model base. It also interacts with the *request constructor* element of the dialog subsystem to obtain from the user the parameters and data that are needed by the models being run.

4. The *data base interface*—Connects the model and data management subsystems. It allows running models to retrieve data from the data base and to store outputs on the data base. It translates model requests for data into valid data query formats, and query outputs to the internal data structure of the model.

Note that the preceding description of the three subsystems of a DSS represents a full-blown generic schema. Its full implementation depends on the type of architecture that links the subsystems. The architecture, in turn, depends on the type of decision situations that are supported, on the users, and on the resources of the DSS (for different architectures, see [33, ch. 10]). In practice, DSSs may not exhibit all the elements of the three subsystems as distinct entities (for instance, if the DSS accesses its own dedicated data base only, the staging element will be redundant).

Users of a DSS

The most important conceptual component of a DSS is the user. A decision support system cannot be considered advantageous unless the user employs it to increase his or her effectiveness. The DSS and the user work in tandem to arrive at the best solution.

Once the intelligence and design phases have been completed, a choice must be made from among the alternatives. The DSS can rank the alternatives and provide information to support a choice, but it cannot make the final decision. This requires the intervention of the human decision maker. The decision maker may employ many different methods to arrive at a decision. He or she may prefer a very structured approach in which the output from decision models can be employed to directly determine the decision. More often than not, the decision-making process of the user will be very unstructured and informal, involving a great deal of intuition and business common sense. As observed by the developers of one DSS, "Managers don't really know how they make decisions, and, on top of that, they don't want to reveal the details of decision making of which they are aware, as these tend to be important specifics" [23, p. 119]. This is particularly true in the case of ill-structured problems.

Whatever the method employed by the decision maker, it is important for the technical specialist to be aware of individual orientations when designing a specific decision support system. The DSS should take into account the user's tasks, abilities, cognitive preferences, and ways of arriving at decisions. Because the decision maker makes the policy decisions and, in effect, becomes the model formulator, he or she works with an analyst in translating informal decision models into formal, computerized models. This enables the decision maker to take an active, creative part in the development of the decision support system.

This DSS user-orientation has several implications. The traditional orientation toward technical characteristics, with applications developed from the perspective of operations researchers and management scientists, was myopic. It failed to anticipate how useful such systems could be to all levels of management. The user-orientation allows the full potential of such systems and of the decision maker to be realized.

A decision support system can extend the decision maker's capabilities in several ways. It can improve interpersonal communication by providing the user with tools for persuasion. By establishing a common conceptual basis for decision making, it can provide the decision maker with a vocabulary and discipline that facilitate negotiations and increase organizational control. A DSS also helps the decision maker expand his or her experience by providing a means to explore alternatives.

When we refer to the "user" of a DSS, we actually refer to a range that varies from one person to many. Individual users may be: the ultimate decision maker; an interested party (to a given decision); a "chauffeur" who supports the ultimate decision maker (e.g., a staff assistant); or a "feeder" (someone who provides the system with data). This range implies a great variety of DSS configurations.

The labels of *institutional* and *ad hoc,* which are applied to the DSS, relate to the number and type of users [7]. An institutional DSS is utilized for repetitive decision-making tasks. The classic example of this is the very early DSS developed by Gerrity [22]. This portfolio management system (PMS) involved a computer-based information system used by several portfolio managers within a bank, each addressing the portfolio management problem in a different manner. In contrast, an ad hoc DSS is developed and utilized for problems that are nonrepetitive. It is used for support of decision making in infrequent situations, particularly those with a one-shot, high-payoff nature. An example of this is a corporate merger decision.

Some of the DSS literature has implied that DSS must be used by managers, or perhaps even upper-level managers. However, while many DSSs are used by managers, many others are used by non-managers. In fact, many students have developed micro-computer based DSSs using software such as Lotus 1-2-3 for support in solving problems in marketing or finance courses. The users of PMS were not managers in the traditional sense, but rather investment decision makers. Decision support systems have become commonplace in aiding people in all kinds of pursuits where choices must be made among alternative actions. Because the decision processes of upper-level managers do tend to take on a somewhat different cast, a more specialized form of DSS for executives has come to be referred to as executive information systems (EIS). See [28] for a thorough examination of this topic.

DSSs are used in organizational settings and do not only support lone decision makers. DSSs are often used to coordinate decision-making activities among the multiple, interdependent participants in a decision. Two types of decision support, personal support and organizational support, are distinct and so warrant discussion. Personal support involves a DSS designed for direct and individual use by a decision maker. For example, personal support of departmental budgeting should provide the departmental manager with easy ways to enter, manipulate, and display forecasted values. Decisions requiring organizational support involve large, interdependent organizational units. Any DSS support for such decisions will be as much a vehicle for communications and coordination as for calculations. For example, organizational support for budgeting should provide storage facilities for disaggregated, detailed budgets at the departmental level, and the integration of these by division and for the company as a whole. As these examples illustrate, the same task (budgeting) may require both personal support (the individual manager) and organizational support.

The distinction between personal and organizational support has implications for the DSS hardware and software resources. A personal DSS can be run on a mainframe from a terminal, or on a personal computer or workstation. *Organizational DSS* may utilize a mainframe, or personal computers, or a network of computers. The implication of these organizational systems is, as described above, that they must combine the decisions or information provided by successive levels of the organization. Therefore, the system must provide for linking the individuals involved; this may result from their using the same mainframe, or from having their personal computers networked. In any case, the organizational DSS becomes a multi-tiered structure, at least as far as the software is concerned. For more about the structuring of organizational DSS, see [12].

DSS Resources

There is some discussion akin to the old chicken-egg controversy over which came first: the capability or the need—the software and hardware innovations from which new managerial uses of computers were developed (such as DSS), or the growing need for decision support systems from which stemmed the needed software and hardware. Regardless of the sequence of events, it is evident that the unique characteristics of a decision support system dictate specific hardware and software resources.

A DSS must have certain general capabilities in order to be beneficial to a user. Since the DSS will support users at several different levels of the organization, for both structured and nonstructured decisions, its primary strengths should be flexibility, ease of use, and adaptability. Flexibility implies that it can reflect the decision processes of different users and can adapt to their changing needs. These capabilities generate specific design criteria for both hardware and software. The software used for system development should allow for rapid creation and modification. The system design should allow for quick and easy extensions. The human interface between user and computer should occur through a dialog, with a vocabulary readily comprehensible to the user. The hardware employed should provide display devices that can be used to communicate with the user. Thus, the resources available for DSS fall into five major categories: people, hardware, software, data, and design methodologies (see [2] and [33, ch. 11]). The design methodologies used to construct a DSS are diverse. Two of these will be reviewed in chapter 9: the adaptive design approach and the decision-oriented approach. The other DSS resources are discussed here.

People

People are the resources for DSS design and operation skills. Many roles are involved in developing and operating a DSS. These roles can either be played by humans or by other resources, depending on the availability and cost of human and nonhuman resources. For example, the staging element (in the data management subsystem) can be either a hardware-software mechanism or a human (feeder); data extraction from external data bases will then be either computerized or manual, respectively.

Data

DSS data can be internal, operational, and maintained by the TPS; or it can be external, in either a manual or a computerized form (on online external data bases). Again, these resources can be substituted: an organization can elect to subscribe to an *online service* (see a later section) in lieu of collecting the relevant data itself.

Hardware

The hardware resources include processors (mainframes, personal computers, workstations), terminals, storage (disk or diskette drives), and communication networks. None of these resources is unique to DSS; all are applicable to a TPS or SDS. However, the DSS may impose its own requirements above and beyond what is required for the TPS. What is required depends on the nature of the decision situation and on who will participate.

Certain characteristics of the DSS dictate specific hardware requirements. Decisions made using a DSS need timely data. Often a model must be run several times, with a slight modification each time, before the decision maker is prepared to reach a decision. Any delay in receipt of the results would impair the effectiveness of the results. This implies a fast response, either through an online terminal or by use of a personal computer, so that the user can perform many iterations of the decision-supporting process.

A personal DSS can be run on a standalone PC. The required data can be input through the keyboard or read from a diskette. A problem with this is in ensuring that such data is timely and accurate. A communication link to the source of the data can help with both aspects of that problem. An organizational DSS almost dictates that some kind of communication network provide for linking the participants.

Other requirements of the DSS will affect the hardware configuration requirements. The size of the data base and model base may dictate the amount and type of storage requirements, and whether that is consistent with a microcomputer or needs a mainframe. The makeup of the model base may dictate the kind of processor required, either because of computational load or because of compatibility with the software used by the models (as described in the next section).

The DSS may or may not weigh heavily (compared to the other parts of the total information system) in determining the type and placement of computers, storage, and communication facilities. Either way, it must be considered that it is likely to alter the requirements for hardware, and those costs must be considered.

Software

The greatest number of advances directly related to decision support systems have occurred in the area of software. The myriad user needs have dictated the creation of a broad range of software tailored to individual user needs.

Software for decision support systems can be provided by a vendor, developed by an in-house staff of specialists, or formulated by the users themselves. Software developed in-house can use either a high-level, general-purpose language such as FOR-TRAN or C, or a special-purpose language (e.g., simulation languages or statistical packages such as SAS).

Software is needed to manage the data base and the model base. The large amount and varied composition of the data collected for decision support systems necessitate a sophisticated data management system. This is provided by a well-organized data base manipulated through a data base management system (DBMS).

The software that probably best addresses the complexity of the data base, as well as the differing needs of the users, is that of a relational DBMS (see appendix A). The relational DBMS assumes the onerous task of structuring the data so it can be easily manipulated by the computer. All the manager has to do is tell the system, in a non-technical language, what information is wanted and in what format. This type of DBMS is particularly well suited to top management level decision makers because it is easy to use, provides for quick and easy inclusion of new data, and allows incorporation of data from the external environment. The complete orientation toward the user makes this type of DBMS of particular value to the decision maker. However, the cost implications of increased overhead time, greater storage, and redundancy of data may offset these relational DBMS advantages.

The model base represents the core of the decision-making process. It supports a wide variety of managerial decisions by reflecting the way the manager thinks and by assisting the manager in reviewing alternative solutions. Its basic purpose can be simply stated as aiding in the planning process. The complex manipulation of large amounts of data through several iterations necessitates a development language that is flexible and user-oriented. As in the case of the DBMS, software for model base development and management can either be purchased ready-made from software vendors or computer manufacturers, or it can be developed from scratch using a nontechnical programming language.

Packaged models give the user great flexibility. They can be used separately or as building blocks to construct more complex models. The user can define subroutines in a language such as BASIC and incorporate them into the packaged model. Once the model is constructed, it can just as easily be modified. Sensitivity analysis can be performed through the use of a ''what if'' command, which allows changes in certain parameters to be quickly assessed. There may also be a ''goal seeking'' or ''reverse what if'' command to determine what change is required in one variable to produce specific changes in another variable.

A number of functions beyond the standard algebraic and trigonometric functions are also provided by modeling software. Software for curve-fitting and extrapolation of data, as well as standard business routines such as computing net present value and depreciation, can be specially useful to managers at all levels. Many packages allow for probabilistic specification of variables.

The model base is most effective when the various models used are integrated. This requires the use of a model base management system (MBMS) very similar in concept to the data base management system (DBMS).

Arrays of data in the form of output of the various models are normally stored separately. The MBMS allows, by means of simple commands, for the consolidation of the content of the arrays, as in the case of financial analyses of several companies in a certain industry. These commands also enable the user to specify the exact format of the output report. The formats can be either prespecified or created as needed. The MBMS can perform the following tasks: (1) periodic run of well-established models; (2) special results of an ad hoc model; (3) data analysis models; (4) interactive rerun of a model or set of models; (5) sequential run of a set of interrelated models according to a predefined procedure (see [34]). Most importantly, the MBMS allows for flexibility in both input and output.

The greatest range of resources developed specifically for DSS is in the software area. We will describe four major classes of software resources for DSS.

1. *Specific DSSs (SDSSs)*—Systems tailored to a specific decision situation or particular set of users. Most such systems are custom built by or for the organization concerned. Few SDSSs have become commercially available, since such specificity is usually not compatible with a widely marketable product. Such a DSS might be written in a general purpose programming language, but more likely it will be constructed using DSS tools or generators.

2. *DSS tools*—Software (other than simply a programming language) that can be used to construct a DSS. Each tool can address only a part of the DSS, not all three subsystems. For example, there are numerous DBMS packages available for use with a PC (e.g., dBASE IV) or a mainframe (e.g., DB2) or both (e.g., Oracle). Most available products are relational DBMS and most provide structured query language (SQL) for inquiry purposes. Simple models can be constructed in SQL, more complex ones by embedding SQL in a program written in COBOL or C, for example. Model management must be handled separately. A book by Inmon [19] discusses building DSS with Oracle.

   Combining the tools is facilitated by the use of a *windowing environment* (e.g. OS/2 Presentation Manager, Windows, XWindows) that provides for selecting programs to run and for movement of data from one program to another. Thus the data management, model management, and dialog management can be brought together, although some procedural knowledge on the part of the user is still required.

3. *DSS generators*—Collections of DSS tools in one package. These can be used to construct an SDSS tailored to support specific decision situations. All software in this category provides, to some extent, for management of all three subsystems. Included in this category are a wide range of software products, differing in approach and in capabilities.

   One group of what we have called generators has grown out of the original PC spreadsheet software. Products such as Lotus 1-2-3 manage data in spreadsheet form and provide for modeling through formulas supplied by the user, or through those built into the package. The spreadsheet packages themselves have become more powerful, plus separate *add-in* packages (see [26]) can be used to extend their modeling capabilities. While this type of software began on PCs, mainframe versions of some packages are now available.

The spreadsheet paradigm is limited since it began as a simple tool for personal use on personal computers. More powerful generators are available where more extensive and more complicated calculations are required (see [14]). An example is IFPS Plus, a modeling package that has been in use on mainframes for a number of years. Beginning on a mainframe, it has migrated to personal computers in the form of IFPS Personal.

For even more general use, there are a number of software development platforms or *integrated packages*. These products combine a spreadsheet program with a data base manager, word processor, and communications program. Some of these have already been supplanted by the windowing packages or operating systems. Some other, more powerful packages provide additional capabilities. For example, Guru (see [17]) provides a rule base processor, a natural language interface, numerous utilities (e.g., for constructing menus) and its own procedural (programming) language. Packages such as this are very powerful and extremely flexible—but also more difficult to use.

Yet another category is the software identified with EIS. An example is the Pilot Command Center. Because these products are associated with decision making at a higher level, less emphasis is placed on computation and modeling, and more on information gathering and presentation. See [3] for a report of a particular use of this package.

4. *Generalized DSSs*—Software packages that provide support for a large class of problems, typically usable by individuals within any organization who face decision problems in that general class. Unlike SDSSs, generalized DSSs are not tailored to specific problems, but rather to a type of problem. They differ from DSS generators in that their capabilities can be directly applied to the decision situation, rather than being used to develop an SDSS that can then be applied to the problem. The modeling facilities of these software resources rely heavily on some standard approach, such as statistical analysis functions or generally accepted accounting procedures. Two powerful examples of this are SDSS and Business Wits. Both were developed for mainframe use, but have since been made available on personal computers (see [31]).

Group Decision Support Systems

In large organizations, organizational decision making inevitably involves groups of people (executives). This has given rise to requirements for new decision support systems that can accommodate a multi-user environment. With the advancement in computer technology, particularly in the area of distributed electronic workstations, the concept of DSS has been applied to support organizational decision making. As a result, the concept of a *group decision support system (GDSS)* has been proposed by several management information systems researchers (e.g., [5, 6, 18]). Empirical findings suggest that the technology of GDSS significantly influences idea generation in group decision-making processes [27].

Figure 6.13   Communication channels in a group decision-making process

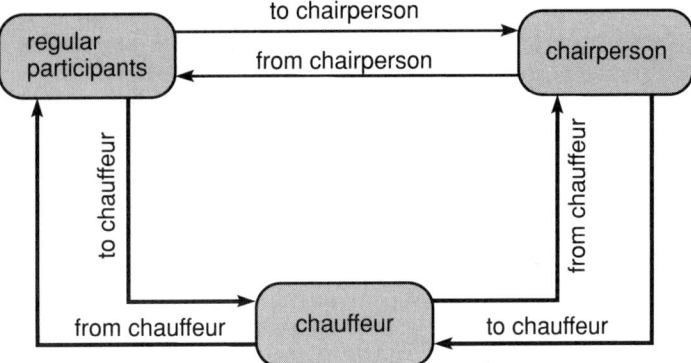

A group decision support system can be defined as a computer-based system that is used to support collective problem solving. A collective decision-making process can be viewed as a problem-solving situation in which

1. there are two or more persons, each characterized by his/her own perceptions, attitudes, motivations, and personalities;
2. participants recognize the existence of common problems and goals; and
3. participants attempt to reach a collective decision.

Decisions may take many forms: rendering an opinion, finding a solution for a problem, making a specific recommendation, defining alternative courses of action, handing down a verdict, or stating a general policy. Two aspects are present in any decision making. One is the *content,* which has to be valid and meaningful. The other is *how* the decision is made (see ch. 3).

A decision that disregards these two aspects frequently leads to unenthusiastic participation of those who must implement it. Calling for a vote when the issue has not been well-discussed gives a bare majority decision, which can result in hostile feelings among those who have been defeated. Because of too little regard for the *how* side of making decisions, they frequently have to be remade [15, 16].

As mentioned above, communication is a very important factor in group decision-making process [27]. Moreover, it has emerged as the core issue in designing and implementing an effective group decision support system.

Three types of participants use a GDSS while in session (see fig. 6.13). The first type is the meeting *chairperson,* the person who presides over the discussion. However, the chairperson does not necessarily have to possess strong computer competence. Therefore, he or she is aided by a *chauffeur:* a technical expert who is proficient in operating the hardware and software features of the GDSS. Typical activities of a chauffeur include: transferring data from an individual's screen to the public screen, data retrieval from a corporate data base, activating a certain software package, producing hard copies of reports, and the like. The chauffeur does not have to be a participant in the meeting but may act as a "shadow operator" that facilitates the process.

The third type is a regular participant who may come to the meeting with some ideas and preparatory work already recorded on a diskette. He or she may wish to operate a microcomputer and periodically impart some of the data to the public screen. Here again, the chauffeur may be of help.

As the ease of use of end-user workstations (microcomputers) improves and the availability of local and wide area networks increases (see appendix A), the extension of DSS to GDSS becomes more common. It is likely that many board meeting rooms of large organizations will be equipped with microcomputer networks in the near future.

Because of the broad range of activities that fall under the category of group decision processes, and because of the general nature of many of the tools that have been developed, some other terms have come to be applied. Within the general theme of supporting group work, the term *groupware* has been used in reference to support systems for business teams that are involved in a variety of activities (see [20] and [21]). These computerized activities are referred to as *computer supported cooperative work* (CSCW). The term *electronic meeting system* (EMS) has also been used to address the fact that it is useful to provide this kind of support for meetings, whether or not the meeting purpose is explicitly focused on decision making (see [26]). These group support systems can also be classified according to the kinds of support provided ([6], [32]).

Much of the attention drawn to GDSS has centered around face to face meetings. Commercial software products (such as OmniQuest Software's VisionQuest and IBM's TeamFocus) run on a local area network and provide a number of tools for setting and controlling the agenda, generating and developing ideas, and ranking and voting on proposed actions. The assumption is that the entire group is present in the meeting room.

Yet as has been frequently pointed out (e.g., [21], [1]), group work may take place within a group that does not necessarily act at the same time or in the same place; groupware includes tools that allow for separation of participants in either time, space, or both. Group support also encompasses tools such as electronic mail, voice mail, and videoconferencing, which are discussed in the next section.

Numerous other taxonomies have been applied to the field of decision support systems, based on the goals of the user or users, the kinds of support to be provided, and the organizational, temporal, and spatial relationships among participants. The field is also evolving to include knowledge bases as another component of DSS leading to the use of expert systems as a part of the decision-making process. More about the latter will be found in chapter 15.

Office Information Systems

Office information systems (OIS) are the combination of hardware, software, and peopleware (persons) in information systems that process office transactions and support office activities at all levels of the organization. The most unproductive workers in many organizations have been office employees and executives. It is basically the lack of office information technologies in the past that made the office one of the least efficient segments of organizations, and white-collar efficiency grew at a fraction of the rate of growth of blue-collar efficiency. By 1980, it was estimated that one-fourth of the national work force was employed in office work, with the number projected to continue to grow significantly; yet the amount of capital investment in support of office workers was typically a fraction of the investment in support of other workers. This began to change in the 1970s, principally with respect to two office activities.

One activity was that of *word processing,* utilizing mini-computers with terminals to substitute for typewriters in the preparation of correspondence and documents. This initially viewed word processing as a separate, standalone application worthy of automation in the way other business activity had been. The other function, *electronic mail,* evolved more as a by-product of the extensive use of terminal networks for other applications. Those who had terminals could communicate with each other through the central computer, thus eliminating some paper flow.

The arrival of the personal computer in the 1980s changed the nature of office automation just as it changed so many other areas of individual and organizational activity. A special, dedicated computer was no longer needed to do word processing: any personal computer would do. Documents could be readily stored on magnetic disks and exchanged between computers by means of diskettes. The personal computers, acquired for whatever reason, could be networked together to provide their users with electronic communication.

What was once termed the office of the future (or automated office, electronic office—sometimes even paperless office) is now viewed as an *office information system.* This recognizes the fact that this is not a separate concern, but a part of the overall information system planning and implementation. Much of the technology is the same as for other parts of the IS, some is separate, and some is still lacking in terms of fully integrating all of the office activity.

The changing nature of the work that people do has made more and more workers involved in what might be called office work. The growing number of what Drucker has termed "information workers" (see [8]) has heightened the necessity for integrating the traditional office work into the other work that people do. We must point out, also, that office activity is no longer constrained to an "office" (see the section on telecommuting in chapter 15). Thus the OIS is a collection of functions performed by workers, whoever and wherever they may be. We will review what these activities are, and discuss relevant technological issues.

Classification of Office Activities and Information

The office activities can be classified into two main categories. These are

1. Activities performed by clerical personnel (clerks, secretaries, typists, messengers)
2. Activities performed by executives and professional personnel (managers, staff assistants, engineers, economists, and researchers)

Obviously there is some activity overflow between the two categories. The dividing line continues to grow more dim as the technology makes things easier. For example, an engineer using a workstation may find it more expedient to create his or her own memo than to have it done by a secretary. Therefore, the characteristic activities discussed here are not necessarily exclusive to one category.

The following is a list of activities typical to clerical personnel:

Typing

Filing and recording documents

Mailing

Message taking and switching

Scheduling meetings and conferences

Calendar keeping

Retrieving documents and preparing materials for meetings and discussions

The following is a list of activities typical to the executive and professional personnel:

Conferencing

Producing information (in the form of messages, memos, reports, etc.)

Controlling performance

The information produced in the office, or that which transfers through it, can be classified into the following types:

Text that is mainly literal

Numeric data (from a TPS or DSS)

Graphical information (graphs, charts, histograms, pictures, drawings, etc.)

Documents

Images of documents

Voice

We can safely say that all of these activities and information types can be automated, i.e., can be computer supported. Doing this in such a way that the result is an office information system can only be achieved if IS management exercises strong control.

We will now examine some of the components of OIS.

Word Processing
Word processing can be done by any personal computer or workstation that has the necessary printing capability, software, and storage. Documents that are typed on its keyboard are stored magnetically and consequently can be easily retrieved, changed,

This desktop publishing system is sold as an integrated unit, ready to produce documents, reports, and other output. Courtesy of Apple Computer, Inc.

 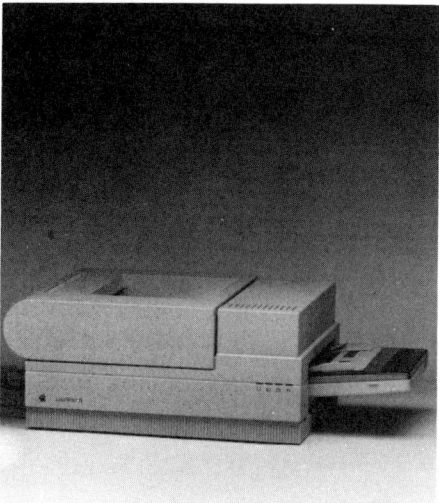

copied, printed, or transferred to another computer. As a standalone device, it is at least a very powerful typewriter. As part of a system, it can be integrated with other activities, such as the *electronic filing* discussed in the next section.

However, there are potentially more significant possibilities. For example, if the word processing computer is the same as the TPS computer, or is networked with the TPS computer, or has diskette drives that are compatible with the TPS computer, then data from the TPS (or from a related DSS) is available to the word processing program. Thus data about sales volumes can easily be incorporated into a memo about production facilities; data about inventory levels can be moved into a pricing proposal. In other words, the opportunity exists to greatly reduce the need for typing, or retyping, of data (text or numeric or otherwise). This not only reduces time and labor costs, but significantly enhances the accuracy of what is being processed.

Where the term word processing is usually associated with the creation of letters, memos, and other documents that are principally text, a somewhat more extensive capability is termed *desktop publishing*. This involves software that provides for the easy incorporation of drawings or pictures, a wide selection of type fonts, and extensive format controls. Such software, especially when used with a computer equipped with a laser printer, provides the ability to produce very high quality (visually, at least) documents with illustrations, headlines, etc. While a principal goal of OIS has always been to reduce the amount of paper that flows in an organization, desktop publishing has probably had the opposite effect. It must be noted that control of word processing is a greater challenge than ever for management because it has become so distributed within the organization.

An E-mail screen. Courtesy of CompuServe Incorporated.

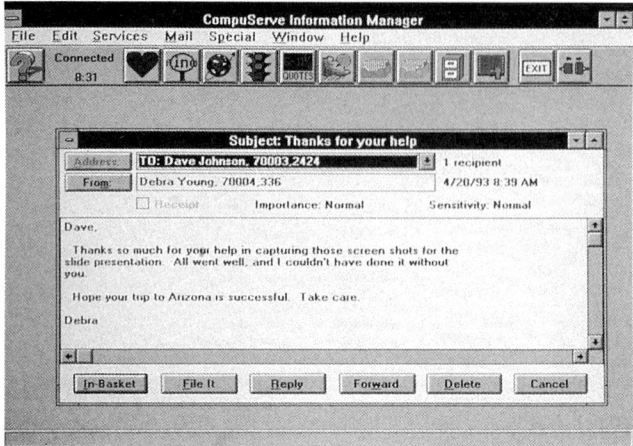

Electronic Filing

A computer with word processing capability provides for the *electronic filing* of documents (outgoing mail, for example) as an almost immediate consequence. The implementation of this function relies on appropriate cataloging and retrieval programs. Of course these controls should apply not just to an individual computer, but to all computers encompassed by the OIS. Most of the work involved concerns conventional office and procedures analysis, not technological issues.

It should be emphasized that this immediate electronic filing pertains to outgoing mail and other documents generated by the word processing system, such as contracts and manuals. The electronic filing of incoming conventional mail and documents requires some different technology and methods.

Electronic Mail

Electronic mail (E-mail) involves the transfer of letters and documents through a terminal or computer network, rather than by means of physical delivery systems. It speeds up these mail deliveries and is less costly and time consuming than mailing paper documents.

Each person on the network has an identifying name or "address" by which mail can be directed to that individual only. The recipient is notified by a message on his or her screen that mail has arrived. The mail can be read, filed, printed, or discarded as required. The program will also provide for replying to the mail or forwarding the mail to another person. Documents to be mailed can be typed directly to the E-mail program, prepared separately by a word processor, or transferred to the storage disk from another source. Distribution lists permit mailing the same document to a number of recipients simultaneously (*broadcasting*).

E-mail may be handled by an independent program, but often is supplied as a utility service by the operating system that controls the network.

Calendar Keeping and Scheduling

Scheduling of meetings and conferences can be facilitated with *electronic calendars.* When a group of people are all equipped with terminals, or their personal computers are linked in a network, their individual appointment calendars can be stored on magnetic disk. Each person maintains his or her own calendar, but all calendars can be accessed by a scheduling program. A person who wants to schedule a meeting can use the program to find a meeting date and time that is convenient for all participants. The program will accept such parameters as the duration of the meeting, the subject, and a range of dates for scheduling the meeting. The program will review the various calendars, come up with a tentative meeting date, and display the date to the participants (on their screens). If the participants approve, the program will finalize the date, enter the date on the affected calendars, then announce the meeting date to the participants. If all do not approve, the program will come up with another tentative date and will again poll the participants.

Image Processing

Images are the digitized form of documents, pictures, or drawings. Once input to the computer by means of an optical scanner or video camera, they can be stored, retrieved, and displayed in much the same way as files of text. This provides for the electronic filing of documents that were not originated on the computer. Bills, checks, receipts, or tickets can all be scanned and processed electronically. Actually, any document bearing on a TPS could be electronically filed in this way, eliminating much of the need for resorting to physical files for answering inquiries, correcting errors, collecting additional data, etc.

The ability to store images adds a dimension to the kind of data that can be placed in a data base for subsequent use. Pictures of people, products, or other entities can accompany the numeric and textual data about them. These can be displayed in response to inquiries, and can also be incorporated into documents or electronically mailed to other locations. This technology is somewhat more expensive than what is required for the activities described earlier (e.g., word processing). It must be established that the benefits justify the costs (see [30]).

Facsimile transmission (FAX) is commonly made from one FAX machine to another. The sending machine scans the document, it is sent over ordinary telephone lines (as sound), and printed by the receiving unit. It is also possible for a computer to be either the sender or receiver.

Voice Processing

Telephone communications may also be processed by computer. Known as *voice mail,* it provides for capturing (in digital form), voice messages on disk. As with E-mail, these messages can be retrieved, replied to, or forwarded. Also, broadcast messages can be sent to predetermined lists of recipients.

The major advantage is clearly that voice communication can take place without establishing a physical connection between the parties, as is necessary with conventional telephone calls. Within an organization, the service is available to anyone on the internal telephone network. In addition, it is possible to capture incoming calls from any telephone anywhere.

A FAX machine sends or receives document facsimiles over ordinary telephone lines.
© John W. Banagan/The Image Bank.

Currently, this service is generally provided by a special dedicated computer. Future technological developments (see chapter 15) will also see this service become an integrated part of OIS.

Videoconferencing

Videoconferencing relies on some form of two-way audio and video transmission among participating sites. Sometimes it is necessary, or at least desirable, for all participants in a conversation to take part at the same time. E-mail, voice mail, and the conventional telephone conference call have their advantages, but each lacks the group dynamics associated with the participants actually seeing each other. Videoconferencing is perhaps the next best thing to a face to face meeting in a single location. The technology for this is available, but it is still quite expensive; also, it is still very much a separate technology—a great deal remains to be done for this to be integrated into other OIS activities.

DSS and OIS

We want to impress upon you our conviction that the various MIS, DSS, and OIS systems and technologies must converge to form an integrated organizational information system. These systems should not be treated as disjointed entities, but as subsets of the comprehensive information system plan of an organization. This plan should develop from an overall corporate information system strategy, and be implemented by adherence to policies that are derived from the strategy. The policies relate to the various systems; thus an organization may have a DSS policy and an OIS policy among other policies. (Information system planning, strategy, and policies are the subject of the next two chapters.)

Video conferencing can substitute for face to face meetings. Courtesy of GPT Video Systems; Norcross, Georgia.

The automation of various office activities has been made easy by the availability of the PC and its inexpensive software. The PC has had a similar effect on DSS, providing individuals with easy access to spreadsheet programs and other tools. In both cases, the PC has had the desired result of putting computing power into the hands of the end users (see more about end users in ch. 12). In the case of office work, automation has also had the effect of diffusing the workload throughout the organization. At the same time, it has made possible the automation of activities without necessarily systematizing them. Clearly, planning and policy making are critical to incorporating individual terminals, personal computers, or workstations into the information system. For a discussion of some of the organizational impact of OIS, see [24]. For an assessment of the value of strategic planning for OIS, see [11].

External Online Data Bases and CD-ROM

Suppose you are managing the investment portfolio for a trust department of a bank. You are looking for a solid stock with some short-term growth possibilities, and you hear a rumor that the XYZ Corporation is planning to announce a merger. It sounds interesting and you want to analyze the financial statements of XYZ for the last ten years. You have a personal computer and a financial DSS based on a spreadsheet package. You are using this for sensitivity analysis of financial data retrieved from the local data base of your bank. The local data base does not have data on XYZ, but you know that this data is stored in the Disclosure data base. Recently you saw an ad in the Wall Street Journal for a company calling itself an *online service*. Subscribers to this service can access the Disclosure data base from a PC with communications capability.

This is just one example of accessing a growing number of remote (external, public) *online data bases* maintained by information services providers. By now you already know that managers in higher echelons of organizations rely considerably on external data in the decision-making process. A DSS, which is intended to support such decision makers, is improved if external data can be downloaded into the DSS data base and manipulated by DSS models.

Access to external data bases is handled by the staging element of the DSS data management component. This element connects the DSS with multiple data sources and extracts subsets of data out of large external data bases for immediate and direct DSS use. Obviously, some data communications facility is part of the staging element if data is to be accessed online. (Basically, it requires a modem and communications software—see appendix A). There are a number of different service providers offering varying types of information. Some provide a narrow range of information, others have a wider selection.

For example, TRW Business Credit Profiles offers a data base of credit information that would tell you about that aspect of XYZ Corporation. That data base is also available through DIALOG Information Services as one of hundreds of data bases that they provide access to. One advantage to this broader type of service is that you can inquire about XYZ Corporation and retrieve not only its credit data (payment of debts and taxes, bankruptcy) but many other kinds of data as well, including stock prices, filings with the Securities and Exchange Commission (SEC), or news and magazine articles about the company. In addition to DIALOG, there are other similar broad-based services with access to many data bases, for example, Dow Jones News/Retrieval and Mead Data Central's LEXIS-NEXIS service. CompuServe is another service that provides many of the same kinds of information data bases, in addition to electronic mail and bulletin board services (see section on *videotex* in chapter 15).

The various services provide different kinds of support in accessing the information they have available. The extraction of data depends on the ability to search the data base or data bases, and that search can be done in different ways, depending on the service used. Pricing is generally based on use (i.e., number of searches carried out), so the user does not pay a premium just for having the data available. Still, it is necessary to determine what kind of service best suits the needs of your particular DSS. The data bases available, the services provided, and pricing are all changing rapidly, so interested management should refer to periodicals such as *Database, Database Searcher,* or *Online* for current information.

As the investment portfolio manager, you may have frequent occasion to want information about companies you have invested in or might invest in. In this case, it may be advantageous to have access to data without using an online service. For example, the SEC filings data referred to above is available in the Disclosure data base. In addition to being accessible through various online services, the data base is available on *CD-ROM*. CD-ROM disks (formerly referred to as *laser disks*) are capable of storing up to 300,000 pages of typed information on a single disk. Some very large data bases can be placed on one, or a very few, small disks. Many of the data bases available online are available on CD-ROM, and the number is growing.

The use of a CD-ROM disk has some drawbacks. It requires a special CD-ROM disk drive (reader), and the data bases are generally fairly expensive. On the other hand, the CD-ROM data base provides unlimited usage at a fixed cost for those users

The CD-ROM disk makes large quantities of data readily accessible to a PC or workstation. © Steve Fuller.

who have a need for a very high number of references to the data. Another difficulty with CD-ROM has been the lack of standards. This means that not all data bases are compatible with all CD-ROM drives.

The CD-ROM technology is changing, and the availability and pricing of products is also changing. At present, it offers an alternative to online services or the use of paper documents; however, it requires careful analysis to determine its applicability to a particular organization's OIS requirements. In addition to the periodicals mentioned above (which cover CD-ROM as well as online services), publications such as CD-ROM Professional specialize in this field.

The use of an online service or of CD-ROM provides a means for obtaining external data for use in a DSS. It remains for IS management to integrate this into the office information system. The staging element of the DSS referred to above may involve substantial software and/or operational procedures to perform the data base search and extract the data in a form usable by the DSS.

Practical Conclusions for Information System Design and Use

The following are some practical conclusions for information system design and use.

1. A decision support system requires special software and hardware elements that are not necessarily part of the conventional transaction processing system.

2. A system designer should take into account that most transaction processing systems are interrelated by shared files or by the output of one serving as input for another.

3. The design of the transaction recording procedures has a substantial impact on speed and accuracy of recording and on subsequent efforts to detect and correct errors.

4. The choice of data collection devices is among the most important design characteristics of an information system.

5. Improper design of a recording form may introduce unwarranted costs in subsequent stages of the transaction processing cycle.

6. Online transaction processing requires more substantial investment in control features than is the case for batch transaction processing.

7. Effective reporting can substantially contribute to the usefulness of the information system.

8. Decision support systems do not replace the human decision maker. They support the manager in one or more stages of the decision-making process.

9. It is very difficult to measure the benefits of a decision support system.

10. A prerequisite for the success of a DSS is a convenient interface between the user and the system—either a human interface (e.g., a staff specialist) or a software/hardware interface (e.g., menus, graphic display terminal).

11. A DSS must be flexible and adaptable to the cognitive and problem-solving styles of its users.

12. A DSS, unlike a TPS, has no justifiable existence beyond the user's ability and desire to use it.

13. Information systems managers should recognize the value of integrating external data bases into their existing information system.

14. Because they offer a whole new dimension of retrieval, storage, reference, and communication outside one's own computer, online services can significantly enhance the computing potential of an organization.

15. A DSS can be a vehicle for communication and coordination among decision makers in an organization.

16. A DSS can provide personal and organizational support (i.e., a group of users).

17. The choice of DSS software and hardware depends foremost on the DSS environment (decision situation and users).

18. It is necessary to plan and to set priorities for computerizing office activities.

Summary

Many activities occur each day within an organization. Each activity triggers one or more transactions. A record (source document) is made of each transaction. The recorded transactions constitute raw data that can be analyzed in various ways to meet the unique information needs of various control levels of the organization.

Transaction processing systems (TPSs) handle the major part of the work load of an information system. They record and store most data needed by the information system and generate most reports and documents needed by operational users. An organization has several TPSs, each one covering a unique application. Some of the TPSs are interconnected, either by shared master files or by the output of one TPS serving as the input to another.

The transaction processing cycle consists of five stages:

1. *Recording and data collection*—A transaction is generally recorded on a document or a form. Accuracy, completeness, and authenticity of recorded transactions affect all subsequent processing and therefore warrant particular consideration. There is a large variety of data collection devices, each with attached costs and benefits.
2. *Data conversion and verification*—Data conversion is the process of transforming data from a human-readable to a computer-readable medium. The converted transactions become the transaction file. The conversion process may introduce errors. Verification is the process of assuring that the data recorded on a source document has been accurately transcribed to a computer-readable form.
3. *Data validation*—Validation is the process of screening transaction records against a set of criteria designed to detect certain types of inaccuracy, unreasonableness, or incompleteness. The process (invariably called *input editing*) is handled by a computer "edit" program, which produces a list of rejected records in addition to a transaction file containing only valid records. The rejected records are corrected and reentered through the edit program. In online systems, some recording, conversion, and validation functions can be performed together.
4. *File updating and processing*—Processing the transaction file may take various forms and involve the file alone or the file in conjunction with other files. Sorting is a frequent example of file processing. This is the arrangement of records in a predetermined order using a field in the record as a sorting key. File updating is an example of processing the transaction file in conjunction with one or more master files. Master files are kept accurate by updating the contents of existing records, by adding new records, and by deleting obsolete ones. The updating process depends on the type of storage device, the type of file organization, and the processing methods.
5. *Reporting*—The reporting stage provides the interface between the TPS and the users of its outputs. Not all outputs are reported; some are stored for future processing. The TPS produces three major types of outputs: preplanned reports, preplanned responses to inquiries, and transaction documents. Each of the various reporting techniques and media is associated with costs and benefits. Displayed output can be alphanumeric (tabular or narrative) or graphic.

The various stages of the transaction processing cycle can take place in physically adjacent or physically separated locations—known, respectively, as local and remote processing. Remote processing may rely on data communication facilities and on remote data entry devices. An intelligent data entry device can also handle data verification.

Online transaction processing may provide immediate data validation, immediate updating, immediate reporting, or all these stages combined. In an online environment, the user is provided with direct access to files and computer programs via remote terminals and communication lines. One form is online data entry and validation of transactions combined with delayed batch processing of these transactions.

Structured decision systems (SDSs) are information systems that make structured (programmed) decisions. They access data bases maintained by the TPS and incorporate one or more decision models that are coded into a computer program. A decision model represents a human decision-making process that is completely programmable.

Unlike a TPS or an SDS, a decision support system (DSS) is used to help solve semistructured problems typical of the senior manager's world. It supports rather than replaces the manager, and thus increases the effectiveness of the user. A DSS supports a semistructured decision in that it is designed to support a decision maker in any stage of the decision-making process. The three generic hardware/software components of a DSS are the dialog management, the data management, and the model management subsystems.

The dialog management subsystem provides and manages the framework in which outputs are presented to the user and in which inputs are specified by the user; it is the interface between the user and the data and model components. The data management subsystem performs the activities of data storage, retrieval, manipulation, updating, and security; it maintains the DSS data base and is also in charge of extracting external data, either from remote, public data bases, or from local organizational data bases. Any support beyond direct access to raw data invokes the application of a model. The management of models and modeling activities is what distinguishes a DSS from a TPS and an SDS. The ability to invoke, run, change, combine, and inspect models is the function of the model management subsystem.

The unique characteristics of a DSS require specific resources that provide flexibility, ease of use, and adaptability to different user styles, as well as easy access to the data base and the model base. The major resource categories are people, hardware, software, data, and design methodologies (i.e., approaches to the development of a DSS). There are many applications of DSS in organizations. They range from microcomputer-based DSSs to mainframe-based DSSs. It is difficult to evaluate their success on a cost/benefit basis. The key to the success of a DSS is the judicious interaction between the user and decision models, and between the models and the data base. Recently, DSSs have been adapted to group decision-making processes. Such systems are labeled GDSS. They are based on a number of workstations linked via a local area network and connected also to the corporate data base. They enable a group of executives to use individual workstations, and impart some ideas to a public screen viewed by all the participants in the session.

Office information systems process office transactions and support office activities at all levels of the organization. They involve a number of technologies that are introduced into the office to improve office productivity and to facilitate organizational communications. These technologies include personal computers and workstations, computer networks, and image and voice processing.

The personal computer has been very influential in the development of OIS, providing an inexpensive word processing and electronic filing capability. At the same time, it allows those who may have personal computers for other activities to perform some of the office work themselves. Integrating these activities usually requires a network that connects the computers; this enables the users to communicate by means of electronic mail, and to computerize calendar keeping and meeting scheduling. Optical scanners provide for electronic processing and storage of documents. Video networks provide for videoconferencing as a substitute for direct face to face meetings.

Telecommunications is the underlying technology in advanced office information systems. This includes communication networks that transmit data, voice, and images. These services are expanding, improving, and becoming less expensive (see appendix A). Communications capability also provides access to online services that make a vast amount of data available to the decision maker.

Key Concepts

ad hoc DSS	executive information system (EIS)
batch processing	facsimile (FAX)
broadcasting	file processing
CD-ROM	file updating
chauffeur	generalized DSS
computer application	graphic display
computer supported cooperative work (CSCW)	group decision support system (GDSS)
	groupware
control element	image processing
conversion	information technology (IT)
data base	input editing
data base management system (DBMS)	institutional DSS
data conversion	integrated packages
data entry	master file
data management subsystem	model base
data validation	model base management system (MBMS)
decision model	
decision support system (DSS)	model directory
desktop publishing	model management subsystem
dialog management component	office information system (OIS)
DSS generator	online service
edit program	organizational DSS
electronic calendars	preprinted form
electronic filing	preplanned report
electronic mail (E-mail)	queries
electronic meeting system (EMS)	recording

remote (external, public) data base	transaction log
remote input/output	transaction processing cycle
reporting	transaction processing system (TPS)
request constructor	turnaround document
sorting	update program
source document	user interface
specific DSS (SDSS)	windowing environment
structured decision system (SDS)	word processing (WP)
suspense file	workstation
tabular display	validation
teleconferencing	verification
transaction document	videoconferencing
transaction file	voice processing

References

1. Alavi, M. "Group Decision Support Systems." *Journal of Information Systems Management* 6, no. 3 (Summer 1991): 36–41.
2. Ariav, G., and M. Ginzberg. "Understanding DSS—A Systemic View of Decision Support." *Communications of the ACM* 28, no. 10 (Oct. 1985): 1045–52.
3. Armstrong, D. "The People Factor in EIS Success." *Datamation* 36, no. 7 (Apr. 1, 1990): 73–80.
4. Davis, G. B., and M. H. Olson. *Management Information Systems: Conceptual Foundations, Structure, and Development.* 2d ed. New York: McGraw-Hill, 1985.
5. DeSanctis, G., and R. B. Gallupe. "Group Decision Support Systems: A New Frontier." *Data Base* 16 (Winter 1985): 3–10.
6. DeSanctis, G., and R. B. Gallupe. "A Foundation for the Study of Group Decision Support Systems." *Management Science* 33, no. 5 (May 1987): 589–609.
7. Donovan, J. J., and S. E. Madnick. "Institutional and Ad Hoc Decision Support Systems and Their Effective Use." *Data Base* 8, no. 3 (Winter 1977): 79–88.
8. Drucker, P. F. "The Coming of the New Organization." *Harvard Business Review* 66, no. 1 (Jan.–Feb. 1988): 45–53.
9. Eliason, A. L. "Administrative Processing Cycles and the Design of MIS." In *Proceedings of the Ninth Annual Meeting of the American Institute of Decision Sciences,* edited by J. D. Stolen and J. J. Conway, 647–49. Atlanta: American Institute of Decision Sciences, 1977.
10. ———. *Online Business Computer Applications.* 3d ed. New York: Macmillan, 1991.
11. Ferguson, C. S., H. J. Watson, and R. Gatewood. "Strategic Planning for Office Automation." *Information and Management* 21, no. 4 (1991): 201–15.
12. George, J. F. "The Conceptualization and Development of Organizational Decision Support Systems." *Journal of Management Information Systems* 8, no. 3 (Winter 1991–92): 109–25.
13. Ginzberg, M. J., and E. A. Stohr. "Decision Support Systems: Issues and Perspectives." In *Decision Support Systems,* edited by M. J. Ginzberg, W. R. Reitman, and E. A. Stohr, 9–32. Amsterdam: North-Holland, 1982.
14. Graham, C., and M. Freely. "When Spreadsheets Aren't Enough." *Datamation* 37, no. 1 (Jan. 1, 1991): 77–79.

15. Gray, P. "The SMU Decision Room Project." *Transactions of the First International Conference on Decision Support Systems,* Atlanta, GA: June 1981.
16. Gray, P. "Initial Observations from the Decision Room Project." *Transactions of the Third International Conference on Decision Support Systems,* Boston, MA: June 1983.
17. Holsapple, C. W., and A. B. Whinston. *Manager's Guide to Expert Systems Using GURU.* Homewood, IL: Dow-Jones Irwin, 1986.
18. Huber, G. P. "Issues in the Design of Group Decision Support Systems." *MIS Quarterly* 8, no. 3 (Sept. 1984): 195–204.
19. Inmon, William H. *Using ORACLE to Build Decision Support Systems.* Wellesley, MA: QED Information Sciences, 1990.
20. Johansen, R., D. Sibbet, S. Benson, A. Martin, R. Mittman, and P. Saffo. *Leading Business Teams: How Teams Can Use Technology and Group Process Tools.* Reading, MA: Addison-Wesley, 1991.
21. Johansen, R. R. *Groupware: Computer Systems for Business Teams.* New York: Free Press, 1988.
22. Keen, P. G. W., and M. S. Scott Morton. *Decision Support Systems: An Organizational Perspective.* Reading, MA: Addison-Wesley, 1978.
23. Keen, P. G. W., and G. R. Wagner. "DSS: An Executive Mind-Support System." *Datamation* 25, no. 11 (Nov. 1979): 117–22.
24. Lee, S. "The Impact of Office Information Systems on Potential Power and Influence." *Journal of Management Information Systems* 8, no. 2 (Fall 1991): 135–51.
25. McGrath, J. "Forecasting Add-ins: Garbage In, Gospel Out." *PC Magazine* 10, no. 7 (Apr. 16, 1991): 119–24.
26. Martz, W. B., D. R. Vogel, and J. F. Nunamaker, Jr. "Electronic Meeting Systems: Results from the Field." *Decision Support Systems* 8, no. 2 (May 1992): 141–58.
27. Nunamaker, J. F., L. M. Applegate, and B. R. Konsynski. "Facilitating Group Creativity: Experience with a Group Decision Support System." *Journal of Management Information Systems* 3, no. 4 (Spring 1987): 5–19.
28. Paller, A., and R. Laska. *The EIS Book: Information Systems for Top Managers.* Homewood, IL: Dow Jones-Irwin, 1990.
29. Porter, W. T., and W. E. Perry. *EDP: Controls and Auditing.* 5th ed. Boston: PWS-Kent, 1987.
30. Rainer, R. K., Jr., H. H. Carr, C. A. Snyder, and G. Deneen. "Image Processing Systems." *Information Systems Management* 9, no. 3 (Summer 1992): 30–37.
31. Rash, W., Jr. "Moving Down to Micros." *Byte* 15, no. 9 (Sept. 1990): 93–97.
32. Sage, A. P. "An Overview of Group and Organizational Decision Support Systems." *IEEE Control Systems* 11, no. 5 (Aug. 1991): 29–33.
33. Sprague, R. H., and E. D. Carlson. *Building Effective Decision Support Systems.* Englewood Cliffs, NJ: Prentice-Hall, 1982.
34. Sprague, R. H. and M. J. Watson. "Bit by Bit: Toward Decision Support Systems." *California Management Review* 22, no. 1 (Fall 1974): 60–67.

Questions

1. Differentiate among (a) a transactions processing system (TPS); (b) a structured decision system (SDS); and (c) a decision support system (DSS).
2. What is an integrated transactions processing system?
3. Describe the transactions processing cycle.
4. What parameters should be considered in evaluating data collection devices?
5. Explain what is meant by data entry and validation.
6. Why and how are files sorted?
7. What happens to a master file during update?
8. What type of output is typical of a TPS?
9. Compare batch processing to online transaction processing.
10. Describe the essential components and capabilities of a DSS.
11. What types of software are most useful for a DSS?
12. How does an MBMS differ from a DBMS?

Problems

1. A mail-order firm receives orders by telephone and by mail in response to its quarterly catalog and magazine advertising. Draw a flowchart showing the automated transaction processing of orders along with automated decision as to (a) what items should be placed on sale in the coming catalog, and (b) which of the four warehouses in the country should ship the goods.
2. Describe how an automated teller machine (ATM) works. Assume that each site contains a standalone microcomputer that periodically communicates with the central bank computer.
3. Create a simple model that could be used as part of a structured decision system in which the computer decides when a journal has enough articles to complete an issue. (Hint: Parameters to be included are journal size, words per page, etc.)
4. What type of model would be needed to support the decision maker of an oil company who must determine where to drill, to what depth to drill, and for how long to drill?

Quarter Moon Bay Public Library

The Quarter Moon Bay Public Library (QBPL) is a library system of five library branches run by the City of Quarter Moon Bay which is located on the coast of California, approximately one hour north of San Francisco. Quarter Moon Bay is a medium size city of 45,000 residents spread over a 75-square-mile area. It was at one time a thriving lumber town, but now it contains a very diverse population who moved there from all over the country because of the natural beauty of the area. During the summer, it also does a fairly large tourist business of coastal travelers.

Joe Friendly, the new mayor of Quarter Moon, is quite a reading buff and wants to share the gift of reading with not only his fellow city residents but with anyone who visits the city as well. He feels that the city needs to modernize its current library of over 150,000 items including books, audio- and videotapes, records, framed art, and many other miscellaneous items. Mayor Joe has informed his head librarian, Beth Fine, that he would like to bring their library into the twentieth century by fully computerizing it. (It is now fully manual using a bookcard/patroncard system for circulation.) He is so enchanted with this idea that he got the city council to approve $200,000 for this conversion.

Mayor Joe is a little concerned about the new computerization because of the physical layout of their current library branches. Quarter Moon Bay is fairly spread out as coastal communities go. The library consists of five branches spread throughout all corners of the community. He is aware of the wide diversity of the library's users,

and, since the library will be on computer, he would like to have the computer collect as much information as possible to aid Beth and her associates in their quest to satisfy the library needs of all of their patrons.

Mayor Joe just happens to have a grandson, Joe III, who is a second-year computer programmer. He has hired his grandson to do all of the software from scratch to the specifications of the library's steering committee (headed by the mayor). Joe III agreed to take this project on with the assistance of your system's consulting firm to review and recommend the best systems design for the library.

The QBPL system currently circulates an average of 1,650 items, of all types, per day. At each monthly city council meeting, Beth has to personally present a detailed report on each major aspect of the branches' operations (purchasing, circulation, staffing, and overhead) broken down by the three major departments within each branch (adult area, children's area, and audio-visual areas).

One of Beth's major concerns is that she has been under considerable criticism for buying items (books, recordings, etc.) that do not seem to be circulating very well. She fears that if the new computer system does not help her with this, she will be demoted to a branch librarian, or worse, lose her job!

Another major concern of both Beth and Mayor Joe is that the overall library's personnel costs seem to be escalating too fast, but they are not sure where this can and cannot be justified, and therefore should be cut back or transferred to another branch. They both hope that the new computer system will help correct these concerns.

Questions

1. Discuss each of the following aspects of the transaction processing systems (TPS) that you recommend to the QBPL:
   a. batch or online system
   b. main inputs to be captured
   c. data validation (if any)
   d. main data files required (include content summary of each file)
   e. transaction reports (indicate periodicity and contents of each report)

2. Discuss the major characteristics of a decision support system (DSS) for the head librarian Beth to aid her in allocation/reallocation of library personnel between branches based on the information gathered by the TPS that you proposed in question 1. Provide an example summary report that Beth might find useful.

3. Make specific suggestions for other possible DSS applications that the library decision makers may find useful.

Printania Score

Printania Score is a small company in the retail business in the West African country of Massina. Printania is involved in the sale of a large range of consumer goods.

Massina occupies 1,240,000 sq. kilometers, and its population is about 16 million people. Massina is divided into five administrative provinces and one district. Although the urban population is growing rapidly, it presently represents only about 35 percent of the total population mostly located in the seven largest cities of the country.

Unlike its neighboring states, Massina benefits from particularly favorable climatic conditions that put the country outside the dramatic cycle of drought and starvation, thus enabling Massina to export food and other agricultural products in important quantities. Also, the political stability of the country contributes to attracting and retaining foreign investments. As a result, the exploitation of many natural resources such as oil, gold, and diamond has been possible. The overall economy has been consistently booming since the 1980s, and the living standards in the urban areas are relatively high.

Printania Score is a partnership formed in 1989 by two entrepreneurs in the retail business. Since then, Printania has established nine stores throughout the country: two each in Bamako (where the headquarters are located) and Segou, and one in each of the five other largest cities (Sikasso, Mopti, Kayes, Gao, and Tombouctou). Each of the nine stores is a profit center headed by a general manager who is responsible for the overall performance.

The purpose of Printania Score is to increase: (1) market share, and (2) profitability.

One of the strategies adopted by management is to establish Printania Score's presence in all major urban centers of the country. With the economic growth of the country and the rapid urbanization of the population during the last 15 years, Printania Score has grown significantly both in terms of geographic presence and market share. Meanwhile, management faces a number of problems:

1. Inventory management is not efficient. Shortage in some products and too high inventory levels in other products are common.

2. Debts collection is not satisfactory. Credit sales represent a sizable part of net sales. In the meantime, uncollectible debts expense is increasing, and collection is not timely in many cases.

3. Cash management is poor. Payments of cash to creditors is not made on time irrespective of cash availability, resulting in the loss of discounts or in unnecessary finance charges.

Printania Score's management feels that these serious problems may be aggravated by the growth of the company. Because of this situation, management made the decision to invest the necessary resources to acquire for the first time a computerized information system.

Questions

1. Identify and describe concisely: (a) a transaction processing system (TPS); and (b) a structured decision system (SDS) relevant to addressing the problems that management is concerned with. Justify the choice of these systems and specify: (a) the major inputs and outputs; (b) the main files; (c) the main programs; and (d) the hardware requirements.

2. Identify a decision support system (DSS) commensurate with management's concerns. Using this case, describe briefly and illustrate the characteristics of a management information system (MIS) as it relates to TPS and SDS. Contrast MIS with TPS and SDS.

Chapter 7 Information Systems Policy and Strategic Information Systems

All information systems activities within an organization and the structure of the information system unit emanate from relevant strategies and policies adopted by general management. Information systems is an organization within an organization.

This chapter describes the role and importance of overall information system policy and the use of information systems as a strategic weapon.

Introduction

A 1986 study of chief IS (information systems) executives and corporate general management [1] indicated the most critical IS management issues and prioritized their importance. Improving strategic planning was ranked first in importance. Effective strategic planning requires the discipline and vision to foresee problems and opportunities within a turbulent and complex environment. It requires the ability to develop strategies and policies based on rapidly changing information technologies (IT).

Using IS for competitive advantage was ranked second in importance. IS is now considered to be a major strategic weapon by many corporations. Competitive advantage results from recognition of opportunities followed by rapid and effective implementation of information technologies to take advantage of these opportunities.

Within most corporations, there are three levels at which strategy must be defined. At the highest level, *corporate strategy* specifies the definition or view of the line of business in which the company will participate and the allocation of key corporate resources to each of these lines. In a turbulent economy, the identity of a company and its allocation of resources may change over time. For example, over the last decade, several major banks have shifted their corporate identity from a bank to an information company that provides diverse financial information and investment services.

The second level of strategy is associated with the *strategic business unit* (SBU), which can be a subsidiary, division, or product line in the company. As the corporate strategy of a company evolves, the resources allocated to existing or new SBUs may change.

Finally, the third level of strategy is that of *functional strategy.* Once a business unit has defined its strategy, each functional area within it must develop courses of action to support that strategy. While different functional strategies (e.g., sales strategy, R & D strategy, manufacturing strategy) may exist for various business units, the appearance of a functional strategy for exploiting information resources and technologies to support the SBU and the other functional strategies is occurring with increasing frequency.

IS Vision, Mission, Strategies, and Policies

Strategies are based on a *vision,* or a set of beliefs (in your needs and capabilities, in future developments). Vision represents an image of future direction. It articulates a view of a future that is different; it is the link between dreams and actions. It must be broad, flexible, and simple enough for everyone to remember and follow. For instance, Pat Riley, the coach of the 1987 world champion L.A. Lakers, provided his team with a vision—to repeat their victory in 1988 and become the first back-to-back basketball champions since 1969.

One of the most celebrated IS visions was that of C. A. Smith, past CEO of American Airlines: the idea of a passenger name record (PNR) for every reserved seat on American Airlines. This vision drove the development of the first computerized airline reservation system (AA's SABRE) in 1968, and it inspired subsequent practical implications, such as seat selection, boarding passes, frequent flier programs, and personal marketing.

A vision leads to a mission. A *mission* statement for IS describes what IS intends to be and what distinguishes it from other functions.

For example:

> The IS department of ABC Inc. intends to be a *leading edge,* high quality provider of *information services,* fully responsive to a *dynamic organization,* while assuring that the *basic infrastructure* is *widely available* to all users.

Focus on the underlined key words:

Leading edge—we (IS) will be there first, not just when it is convenient for us.

Information services—we do not offer plain data processing service; we will offer much more than that.

A dynamic organization—we will not sit still but intend to be aggressive and quick.

Basic infrastructure widely available—we are committed to preserving universal service.

It is the obligation of top management to define the mission (or *charter*) and announce it throughout the organization. If top management fails to define an information system charter, it is the duty of the head of information systems to act as a catalyst. He or she must prepare a draft charter and propose it to top management in order to arrive at a formal charter.

After setting the broad mission of information systems in the organization, the environment and constraints imposed on information systems must be considered. This includes: the objectives, strategies, and policies of the host organization; the user groups within the organization and their information processing needs; and the present and future information processing technologies.

Strategy is an essentially military concept. It is derived from the Greek and can be roughly translated as "the planning of the conquest of enemies through the deployment of resources." Strategy is a conditional sequence of internally consistent resource allocations that defines an organization's relationships with its environment over time. IS strategies thus define the IS function's relationships with users, general management, and entities external to the organizations. They are primarily concerned with developing IS configurations—their organization and management systems—in a manner conducive to the achievement of desired objectives.

Strategies translate into *policies* (covered in the following section). While IS policies must be approved by general management, issuing policies and monitoring the adherence to those policies is the responsibility of the director of the IS function (CIO-*Chief Information Officer*). The policies are necessarily custom-tailored to the specific organizational environment.

The manner of controlling IS policy issuance varies between organizations according to organizational style. The initiation and issuance of policies is only the first step. The second step is the monitoring of policy compliance. It can be limited to a simple determination that a process is in effect to implement policy, that specific individuals are charged with the responsibility of overseeing it within each applicable area, or that routine internal audits are conducted from time to time.

By default, lacking guiding policies, IS managers may be unable to separate information resource delivery decisions (e.g., which user's application should be developed next; who should get the 20 available PCs) from strategic business decisions which are not in their jurisdiction (e.g., without portable PCs, our sales agents would lose to a competitor's agents). This confusion has traditionally been the major source of tension between IS and functional users. Such tension can be reduced by establishing clear policies to distinguish the user domain, the IS domain, and the role of general management.

To summarize this section, IS vision, mission, strategies, and policies are building blocks of a coherent statement about where information systems are going, why they are going there, and how they are going to get there.

Information Systems Policies

We believe it is worthwhile to expand our discussion of policies and to emphasize their importance to information system activities. We will first review the distinctions between objectives, strategies, and policies. Objectives are the desired results to be achieved by the information system function in the organization. They spell out what that function should accomplish. Strategies are broad actions describing how objectives can be achieved. A strategy is a collection of tactical decisions in a number of related areas. For example, an information system objective may be to develop information systems for management that utilize proven and up-to-date technology. A hardware strategy must be formulated to achieve this objective. This strategy refers to hardware capabilities, the selection process, the form of procurement and financing of hardware, and the deployment of hardware within the organization.

Policies are the guidelines or procedures used to carry out strategy. For example, an organization may establish a policy that all vendors proposing hardware submit to a benchmark test of their equipment. The following list suggests different information system policies, grouped by major subject areas. The list is by no means exhaustive and is intended to be illustrative only. It is beyond the scope of this book to describe and discuss the content and merits of each policy. Some are discussed in other chapters (e.g., outsourcing, distributed information systems policy, the organizational structure of the information system unit, information system controls, charge-out systems, application development). Others are the topics of various books, chapters in books, or articles (e.g., computer selection, documentation practices, DSS policy).

1. *Hardware Policies*
   Determination of computer capabilities
   Computer system selection
   Financing of equipment (rent, purchase, lease)
   Use of outside service sources
   Equipment deployment (integrated or distributed processing, downsizing)
   Standardization of equipment
2. *Software Policies*
   Software selection
   Financing of acquired software (rent, purchase)
   Acquisition of software packages
   Software standards and languages
   Employment of external contractors
   Centralization or decentralization of software development
3. *Personnel Policies*
   Training and education
   Recruitment and displacement of employees
   Career development practices
   Centralization or decentralization of human resources
4. *Organizational Policies*
   Committees (information system, steering, audit)
   Location of the information system unit in the organization
   Organizational structure of the information system unit
   Security practices
   Information system unit responsibilities
   Interface between information system unit and users
   Auditing the information system function
5. *Application Development Policies*
   Employment of consultants, software houses, computer manufacturers, and other outside sources
   Development approach (top-down, bottom-up, etc.)

Initiation, approval, and release of applications
Documentation standards
6. *Planning Policies*
Information system planning responsibilities
The planning process
Scope of plans
Monitoring, reviewing, and updating plans
Priority schemes
7. *Financial and Accounting Policies*
Selling services to outside organizations
Overall funding levels for information systems
Information system unit: profit or cost center
Charge-out system for information services

Formulating a Microcomputer Policy—An Example

One policy that is gaining importance in many organizations involves the deployment of microcomputers and their associated technologies (hardware, software, communications, graphics—see appendix A). The reasons for this increasing importance are the proliferation of business uses of microcomputers, the emergence of many microcomputer-based DSSs (see the sections on DSS in chs. 6 and 9), and the establishment of microcomputer-based information centers in organizations (see ch. 12). It is for this reason that we single out *microcomputer policy* for a more extensive discussion.

As with other policies, the final responsibility for formulating a microcomputer policy rests with the top management of the organization. Obviously, the assumption in microcomputer policy prediction is that microcomputers are part of an overall strategy for information processing. It should be pointed out that the major cost of microcomputers is not the initial outlay for hardware and some software, but the continuing costs of data collection and entry, and of programming, if nonpurchased software has to be developed in-house.

The key issues typically covered by a microcomputer policy include the following:

What are the appropriate and inappropriate uses of microcomputers?

Who in the organization approves the acquisition and deployment of microcomputer hardware and software?

What are the roles of users?

What are the roles of information system professionals and the information systems unit in maintaining and supporting users' microcomputer-based systems?

Microcomputers can be appropriately used as the basis for stand-alone systems (for word processing, for graphic display, or for computation), as dumb terminals linked to mainframe computers, or as adjuncts to mainframes through downloading of data for subsequent use by microcomputer software.

The policy must point out what constitutes inappropriate use, particularly for a big organization. Examples of inappropriate use of microcomputers include their use to construct large data bases, programming by nonsystem professionals in high-level languages, and transactions processing without the participation of systems professionals.

Organizations have approached the issue of approval for microcomputer acquisition and deployment differently. The responsibility can be delegated to the information system unit, to the information center (if such exists), to the information system committee (or to a special subordinated committee), or to different functional managers (finance, accounting, marketing, etc.). The issue is important, since big organizations can acquire thousands of microcomputers. When the relatively low cost of these microcomputers is multiplied by the number of units, and when software costs and employee time resources are taken into account, the total dollar amount can be considerable, even for a big corporation.

End users should define their information problems and propose solutions that involve the microcomputer. They should be able to query their data bases and analyze retrieved data without continual assistance from information systems professionals. A microcomputer policy should also establish who gets a microcomputer. For instance, an end user receives a computer if he or she can specify what is being attempted; how this objective is currently being met, if at all; why a microcomputer, rather than an alternative, is desired; how he or she proposes to get the requisite data from wherever it exists; what software will be used, and who will provide professional help when required.

There is a natural tendency of the information system unit to control all activities and resources pertinent to the use of microcomputers in an organization. A lack of policy that explicitly states the responsibility of that unit and its personnel in regard to microcomputers can easily lead to conflicts and clashes between the unit and functional user departments. For instance, a microcomputer policy can involve the following responsibilities of information systems professionals: set procedures for the use of microcomputers; select hardware and software for users; train and assist in using microcomputers; maintain the data bases that are microcomputer accessible; or point out areas in which users may be misled by vendors (through omission or commission).

Keen and Woodman [5] cite a microcomputer policy statement of a large insurance company that clarifies who does what and defines active roles for both information systems and users. The statement (in table 7.1) can be broken down into three parts: the mission, the objectives, and the strategies.

Strategic Impact of IS Activities—A Conceptual Framework

Several conceptual frameworks are helpful to both general management and IS management in considering IS policies. Such frameworks are critical for understanding, considering, and comparing phenomena being observed and studied.

One such framework is Nolan's "stages of growth" model described in chapter 15 of this book. The major contribution of that framework is the concept that information technologies require different management approaches as they evolve through the stages of information systems growth in organizations. Chapter 11 introduces another framework, intended to aid in establishing a policy for distributed information system.

Table 7.1   Microcomputer Policy Statement

Mission	The company clearly recognizes the vast potential of microcomputers for improving productivity, reducing costs, and increasing its competitive edge. To avoid duplication, waste, and inefficiency, and to get maximum benefit from this powerful new tool, the information systems steering committee set the following objectives.
Objectives	1. To promote and coordinate the cost-effective application of microcomputers for improving operational and business procedures and client services. 2. To apply microcomputer technology to opportunities that provide high payback and quick return. 3. To foster cooperation and eliminate potential competition between microcomputers and the existing data processing environment by using the most appropriate tool on an application-by-application basis. 4. To encourage self-sufficiency among end users for recognizing business opportunities that may be exploited through microcomputers and implementing cost-effective, timely solutions.
	To achieve these objectives, the company will:
Strategies	1. Establish a coordination role within information systems to support but not control the use of personal computers. 2. Establish a code of good practice for selecting hardware and software and for development. 3. Establish clear responsibilities for ensuring report and data integrity.

A framework highly pertinent to the issues discussed in this chapter is the Strategic Impact of IS Activities scheme suggested by McFarlan and McKenney [6] and graphically summarized in figure 7.1.

The *strategic grid* framework is based on the notion that senior management must determine the current and future importance of information technologies (IT) to the organization before the right IS strategies can be chosen. Organizations in which both current and future IS applications are significantly dependent upon IT are in the class labeled *strategic;* IT has a strategic impact upon these organizations (banks would typically belong to this class).

Organizations in the class labeled *turnaround* are not totally dependent upon currently installed IT, but the organization has many new IT developments which are expected to give it significant competitive advantage in the future (many retailing companies are currently in this class).

Organization in the *factory* class are very dependent upon IT for their day-to-day operations, but will not gain significant competitive advantage from new IT developments (railroads are typically in this class).

Organizations in the *support* class are neither highly dependent upon IT, nor do they gain significant competitive advantage with new IT developments (many firms in simple manufacturing currently use IT as a support technology and have few strategic IT developments underway).

Each of the four classes represents very different organizational needs for information systems and technologies. Once the current and future IT impact is classified,

Figure 7.1 Information systems strategic grid

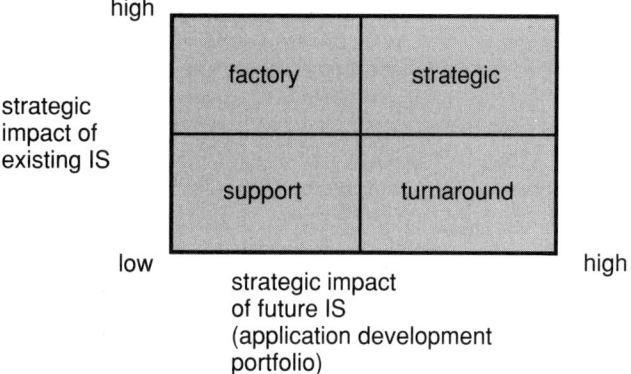

senior management must make a decision on the IS mission (or role) for the organization—support, factory, turnaround, or strategic. A single corporation may be composed of many businesses which have very different classes of IT needs, some being strategic, some support, and so on. Therefore, each *strategic business unit* (SBU) should identify the class of IT impact and adopt the IS strategies that fit it.

IT activity's strategic impact varies between industries and organizations and, over time, within an individual organization. What works in one corporate environment and culture may fail in another one. This is why the *contingency approach* is mandatory when considering IS strategies and policies for a given SBU or organization—the policies adopted must depend on such characterstics as the organizational climate, culture, industry, philosophy of management, organizational structure, or environment.

Both IS management and senior management must share the same perception of the impact of IT. For instance, if senior management sees IT as a support resource, whereas IS management sees it as strategic, there is a mismatch. If senior management is correct, the CIO is going to become frustrated. If the CIO is correct, senior management education is needed. Either way, the misperception must be corrected.

The strategic impact strongly influences the appropriate selection of IS policies and approaches. The sample issues in table 7.2 demonstrate why the strategic grid framework is a springboard for IS policy decisions.

With time, more and more organizations will find themselves in the strategic class, where the use of IT as a strategic weapon is of paramount importance. We now turn to discuss such strategic information systems.

Strategic Information System

A *strategic information system* (SIS) is any information system that supports the competitive strategy of the organization. A SIS can use information technologies (IT) to improve customer links, facilitate product design improvement, develop supplier links,

Table 7.2   Strategic Impact of IT: Strategic vs. Support Role

IS Issues	Support	Strategic
CIO Reports to	Functional Manager	CEO
General Management Involvement	Middle Management	Senior Management
IS Planning	Technical	Strategic
IS Mission	Control	Technological Innovations
Investment in IT	Conservative	Aggressive
Skills of CIO	Technical	Business Management
Focus of IT	Efficiency (Productivity)	Effectiveness (Competitive Advantage)
Organizational Location of IS	Low	High
IS Management Style	Control	Influence
User Involvement	Low	High

generate new sales opportunities, and improve staff productivity. It is important to emphasize that IT can be a significant factor in leveraging an asset base that a firm must have as a prerequisite, e.g., capital, personnel, goodwill, products.

Interest in employing IT as a competitive weapon has grown steadily in recent years. Several of the major accounting firms offer SIS consulting to their clients. Ernst & Whinney has a national SIS service; Arthur Andersen & Co. employed 250 SIS consultants worldwide in the late 1980s. Reports from the IS press indicate that senior managers have become convinced that their competitive advantage must be aided by IT, and that CEOs are taking over information strategy from IS directors, promoting IS out of its support role, and using it to attack the competition.

It is worthwhile to briefly review here the historical development of the main thrust of IS in organizations. Chapter 6 described the typical shift in organizations from transaction processing systems (TPS) to management information systems (MIS), to decision support systems (DSS). The emphasis is now shifting to strategic information systems (SIS). The differences can be illustrated by using an inventory processing system as an example:

TPS—the system records inventory transactions and updates an inventory master file

MIS—the system manages and controls inventory

DSS—the system supports managers in determining inventory policy

SIS—the system processes customers' inventories and links them to the firm's order-entry system

TPSs and MISs used IT to attack the cost side of the firm. IT will continue to do that, but IT will also be used by SISs to invent new information services and products designed to attack the revenue side of the firm. This will move IS units from being cost centers to being profit centers. Another distinctive feature is that TPSs, MISs, and DSSs are internally-oriented (within the boundaries of the firm), while SISs are externally-oriented, impacting the firm's relationships with its environment.

In a 1985 cover story [4], *Business Week* cited ten ways to get ahead with IS: telemarketing, customer service, personnel training, sales, better financial management, product development, market intelligence, locking-in customers, new businesses, and selling extra processing power. Synnott [11] suggests sixty-three information weapon strategies that can be utilized in the process of SIS planning (e.g., using existing information resources to offer new customer services, or selling proprietary information to customers). Wiseman [14] presents over fifty cases of SIS used by American companies.

Strategic Impact of Information Technologies

There are three levels of IT impact on a business organization [7]: the industry level, the firm level, and the strategy level. At the industry level, IT impacts the nature of the industry's products, services, and markets, or the industry's economics of production and distribution. With IT, new services can be developed (e.g., home banking); the life cycle of a product, from the R&D phase to its marketing, can be shortened (e.g., by using CAD/CAM); distribution can be speeded up (e.g., by computerized cataloging); or the market can be expanded (e.g., reaching remote customers by telecommunications).

The following examples highlight several industries that have undergone changes induced by IT:

Publishing—desktop publishing, electronic book ordering

Newspapers—electronic typesetting, computer-to-computer communication of news items and reports

Banking—Automatic Teller Machine (ATM) networks, cash management services

Distribution chains—electronic catalogs, computerized warehouses

Manufacturing—just-in-time inventories, computer-integrated manufacturing (CIM)

Airline companies—booking flights from home or office, computerized reservation systems

Education—computer-literate students, computerized examinations, curricula changes

At the firm level, the impact of IT is determined by the specific *competitive forces* facing the firm. These forces shape the industry structure and the competitive arena for each firm in the industry. Obviously, if IT is expected to significantly impact the entire industry, it will impact a specific firm competing within that industry. This firm-level impact of IT is considered in the following section.

At the strategy level, IT can change the firm's execution of a *generic corporate strategy* by supporting the implementation of one or more generic strategies. Such strategies are used by successful firms to position themselves relative to industry forces in the competitive arena. The strategy-level impact of IT will be discussed following the next section.

Figure 7.2 Forces (targets) in the competitive arena

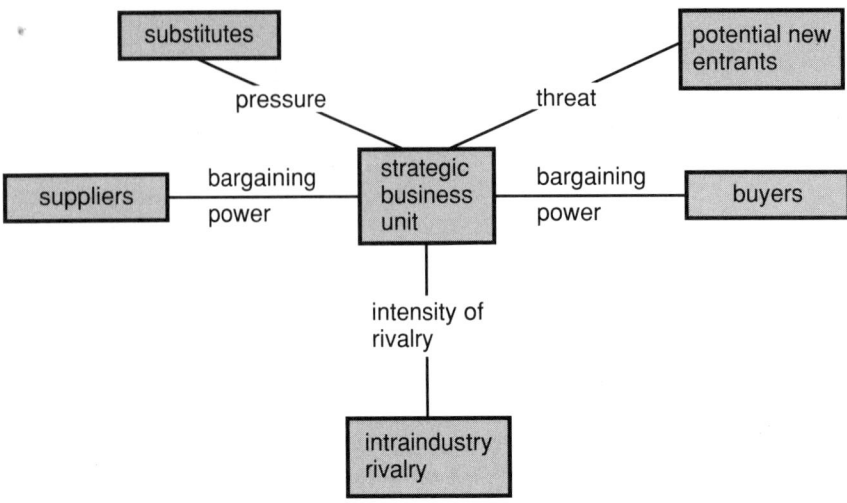

Information Technologies Impact on the Competitive Arena

According to Porter [8], the state of competition in an industry depends on five forces. Figure 7.2 illustrates the interrelationships of a firm or a firm's SBU (either could be the focus of the analysis), with five forces. The five forces are: (1) bargaining power of suppliers, (2) bargaining power of buyers, (3) threat of new entrants into the industry, (4) threat of substitute products or services, and (5) positioning of intraindustry rivals. IT can change the relationships between these forces and the firm.

The manifestation of each force for a specific industry will influence the profitability of a firm and will shape the strategies that the firm adopts (see next section). These forces are, in essence, the targets against which the firm deploys its competitive strategies. Such competitive strategies involve taking offensive or defensive actions in order to create a defendable position in an industry and to cope successfully with the competitive forces, thereby increasing the firm's profitability.

The following examples suggest how IT can affect each competitive force:

1. *Suppliers*
   Increase the number and mix of suppliers (e.g., by accessing commercial data bases that provide information on suppliers)
   Reduce the bargaining power of suppliers by insisting on IT-based linkages (e.g., just-in-time inventories)
2. *Buyers*
   Reduce the bargaining power of buyers by increasing the costs of switching to other suppliers (e.g., by installing terminals at the buyer's site)
   Increase the number of buyers (e.g., by using electronic bulletin boards)

3. *New Entrants*
   Create barriers to entry (e.g., mandatory heavy investments in hardware and software)
   Be the first to offer a new product or service
   Control or own vital data bases
4. *Substitutes*
   Enrich your product with information-based services
   Speed up the life cycle of products (e.g., by using CAD/CAM technology)
5. *Intraindustry Rivals*
   Join forces with rivals (e.g., ATM networks)
   Introduce new information-intensive products

These examples show that if there is a significant impact on a firm through the five competitive forces, IT can be employed as a vital element in the firm's strategy. IT can be used offensively, to increase a competitive edge, or defensively to reduce opportunities of rivals to gain an edge. Each of the competitive forces can be manipulated to some degree, and in some industries, IT provides an effective tool for that purpose.

Information Technologies and Generic Business Strategies

IT can impact the ability of firms to execute a particular business strategy. As noted by Porter [8], a firm's strategy is its general framework for dealing with competition. The achievement of one or more of these strategies gives the firm an advantageous position relative to the industry forces and leads to higher profitability. Porter suggests three generic competitive strategies:

Overall cost leadership on an industry-wide basis—achieve competitive advantage by reducing your firm's costs, suppliers' costs, or customers' costs, or by raising the costs of your rivals (be relatively cheap)

Differentiation of products/services on an industry-wide basis—achieve advantage by distinguishing your firm's products or services from competitors, or by reducing the differentiation advantage of rivals (be perceived as unique)

Focus—achieve differentiation advantage or a low cost advantage in a narrow segment (niche) of the industry

The literature dealing with business strategy and policy suggests many other competitive strategies. In addition to Porter's strategies, we add three more business strategies suggested by Wiseman [13]:

Innovation—achieve advantage by introducing a product or process change that results in a fundamental transformation in the way business is conducted in the industry

Growth—achieve advantage by volume or geographical expansion, backward or forward integration, product-line or entry diversification

Alliance—achieve advantage by forging marketing agreements, forming joint ventures, or making acquisitions or spin-offs related to the strategies or cost leadership, differentiation, innovation, focus, or growth (for a discussion of SIS alliances, see [2])

These competitive strategies can occur in combination (e.g., growth and cost leadership). As noted in the previous section, all can be deployed offensively (e.g., reduce costs of suppliers, preempt innovation by rivals), or defensively (e.g., reduce costs to buyers, imitate innovation by rivals, reduce opportunity of rivals to expand).

IT influences the ability of firms to execute a particular generic strategy, as shown through the following examples:

Cost leadership—focusing applications portfolios on cost reduction (a computerized inventory management system to reduce inventory safety levels)

Differentiation—providing for quick addition of new unique features to a given product by using a CAD/CAM system

Focus—discovering market niches by detailed analysis of private or public data bases

Innovation—American Airlines' SABRE computerized reservation system (CRS) led to a fundamental change of the airline industry and to an enhanced position of AA in the market

Growth—expanding the customer base by selling through a country-wide telecommunications network

Alliance—creating interorganizational *SIS alliances,* such as an ATM network (e.g., Cirrus), in which IT supports this strategy of alliance members

IT can contribute to a generic strategy in a variety of ways; in contrast to other technologies, IT may impact every function of a firm—from R&D to engineering, marketing research, or recordkeeping. A framework for analyzing these impacts is the *value chain* concept.

The Value Chain and Information Technologies

The value chain is an analytical framework to disaggregate a firm into the different interdependent activities that add value to its raw materials and bring the firm's product or service to the customer. It was developed by Porter [9] and later considered by Porter and Millar within an IS context [10].

The value chain is comprised of primary and support activities. Primary activities are those involved in the physical creation of the product, its marketing and delivery to buyers, and its support and servicing after sale:

Inbound logistics—expediting materials to the point of manufacture

Operations—transforming inputs into finished products

Outbound logistics—storing and distributing finished products

Figure 7.3 Where can we add value with IT?

THE VALUE CHAIN

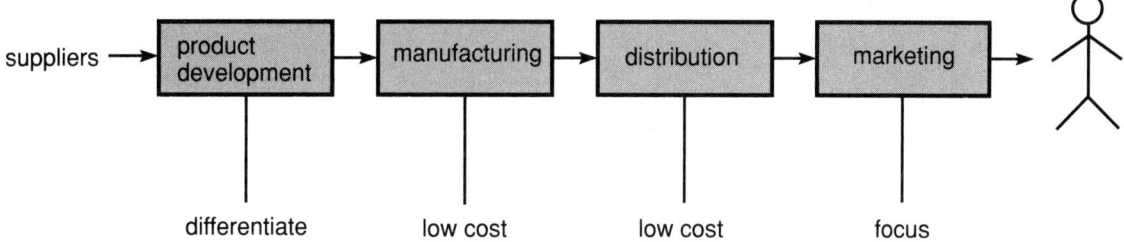

Marketing and sales—promoting and selling

Service—maintaining or enhancing product value through post-sale service

Support activities provide the inputs and infrastructure that allow the primary activities to take place:

Corporate infrastructure—supporting an entire value chain, such as general
management, legal services, finance, public relations

Human resources management—recruiting, hiring, training, development

Technology development—improving product and manufacturing process (R&D)

Procurement—purchasing inputs

Each activity (primary or support) adds value. There is a cost of adding a value in every level of the chain. If the total cost of added values is less than what the customer pays, there is profit. The value chain enables a company to analyze where and how it can add value to products or services and where it can reduce costs. It can thus help identify strategic opportunities.

The concept of value chain is a useful framework for identifying IT opportunities. It is a structural way of looking at how, with IT, a firm can improve its profitability. Figure 7.3 and the ensuing discussion illustrate how IT and generic corporate strategies can be used in conjunction with the value chain framework to analyze strategic opportunities.

IT can be employed in all levels of the chain:

Product development—shorten product life cycle, develop unique product features

Manufacturing—reduce manufacturing costs, improve quality control

Distribution—move information instead of product, reduce cost of delivery

Marketing—supply ordering terminals to customers, identify market niches

Figure 7.4 The value system

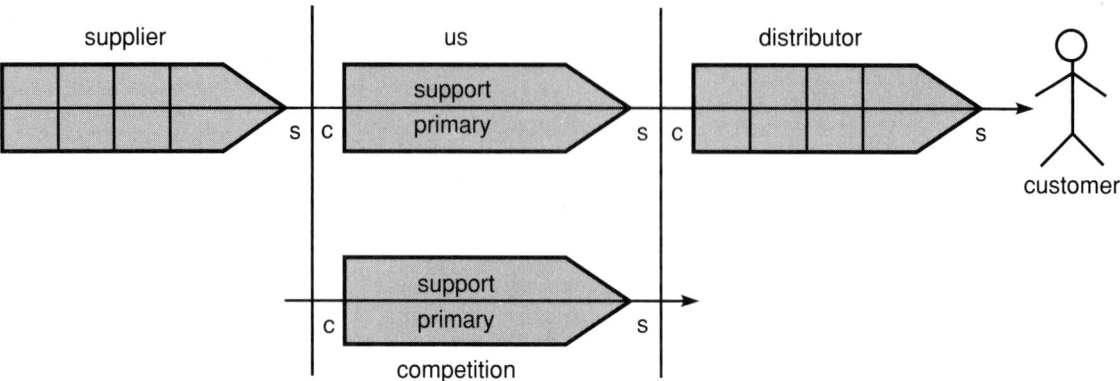

s = supplier
c = customer

Since the value chain is a series of interdependent activities, IT can be used not only at each level of the chain, but also between levels. For example, IT can be used to lower transfer costs between players at two or more levels. Or, information resources that exist at one level can be used to improve performance at other levels (e.g., use information from consumer complaints at the service level to fine-tune marketing, manufacturing, or product development).

Companies need to understand their own value chains, as well as those of key customers and suppliers, in order to uncover potential opportunities. Similarly, understanding competitors' value chains provides insight on the likely sources of competitive attack and defense. These value chains comprise a *value system,* illustrated in figure 7.4.

The value system is the collection of the firm's value chain and individual value chains of suppliers, buyers, and competitors for each product or service. A company can analyze the value system to discover ways of lowering costs or enhancing values of products and services with IT. One way of doing this is to use the critical success factors method (CSF, see ch. 10) to determine the critical activities in the value system for each product or service, and then to explore what IT can do for those CSFs.

Risks of Strategic Information Systems

Any IS development project carries with it *operational* (technical) *risks* that the project will be a failure when implemented. The implementation risks have to do with budget overruns, time slippages, and/or the system not adequately meeting users' information requirements. IS project characteristics that lead to such risks are usually associated with project size, degree of inherent structuredness, and degree of absolute or relative newness of information technology used by the system.

The larger the project size (in terms of person/years or dollars), the more difficult it is to meet preestablished deadlines and cost estimates. Inherent structuredness has to do with how well-defined the project's outputs are and how close they are to the information requirements as defined by users at the outset of the project (e.g., a payroll processing system is relatively well-structured). The lower the degree of structuredness, the higher the project risks.

An IT may be new to a given organization (e.g., online processing is new to an organization that has only batch-processing systems); or, an IT may be absolutely new to all firms in an industry (e.g., when expert systems were used for medical diagnosis for the first time). The newer an IT is, the higher the project risks.

SIS projects are likely to be large, reflecting the growing complexity of the business environment. They will often be the first in an application area, with little previous structure to draw on. Many of these systems will be based on an IT which is absolutely new, or new to the firm. This suggests that high operational risk will accompany information systems that are designed to provide competitive advantages. Methods of dealing with such risks are discussed in chapters 9, 10, and 14 (i.e., ISDLC methodology, IS control practices) and are pertinent to SIS projects.

However, a SIS may technically "succeed," thereby creating potential negative strategic impact to the company implementing it. We refer here not to the SIS project failing, but to the risks of strategic (competitive) disadvantages arising from unanticipated effects of the SIS on industry structure and the competitive position of the firm. Vitale [12] discusses such *strategic IS risks* and proposes a way of assessing them.

1. Once SISs are implemented, their use may require continued investment for sustainability. Organizations with limited resources may be incapable of staying in the race with competitors who have larger resources. Thus, an initial SIS success may turn into a competitive failure.
2. By making IS the major vehicle for producing or delivering its product, a company may risk opening its primary line of business to competitors who have underutilized IS resources (thus waking a sleeping giant).
3. SIS may trigger monopoly litigation. SISs can achieve their initial objectives and then grow in size and effectiveness, eventually giving rise to claims of unfair competition and to government regulation (e.g., claims by airline companies against United Airlines' and American Airlines' computerized reservation systems).
4. Investments in SIS may simply not pay off competitively.
5. Companies developing and implementing SIS may give their customers or suppliers the IT know-how to get along without them in the long run.
6. By increasing the strategic importance of IT, companies may increase the relative strength of suppliers of hardware and software, thus establishing a very powerful supplier.
7. Companies may divert resources and management attention away from their main line of business.
8. The SIS may fail to meet real customer's needs (conceptualization failure).

9. Information about a new SIS is prematurely leaked to a competitor (this may be the reason why the same few successful SISs are reported time and again in the trade papers and in IS conferences).
10. The SIS may be too easy, or require low investment by a competitor, to replicate (inadequate entrenching). Historically, successful innovations are always copied.
11. Sometimes a SIS may be pushed too fast, before the requisite organizational changes are made (refer to the discussion of organizational feasibility in ch. 10).
12. The SIS may lower entry barriers of potential new entrants to the industry (e.g., it educates customers to other alternatives of doing business).
13. A firm may join an inadequate SIS alliance that dissolves after a short life.

A company considering the use of a SIS must understand that a SIS can help its competitive position only if it already has a strong market position that can be leveraged by the proposed SIS (American Airlines was a leader in the airline industry before it developed its SABRE reservation system). SIS is worthless as a discipline in itself, unless it is integrated with the company's business skills. The SIS risks described above can be managed by understanding and assessing them, then taking appropriate action to prevent, reduce, or control them. The following guidelines may be of help:

1. Evaluate the impact of SIS at the firm and industry level before a decision is made to proceed. The future importance of IS should be considered under a scenario in which the proposed SIS is technically successful, and in which it is not attempted (the strategic impact grid could be used here to assess IS importance). Estimate the impact of the SIS on the industry and on the five competitive forces, existing rivals, and new (potentially dominant) rivals.
2. Reduce the risk of being bypassed by continually adopting and adding features to meet additional or changing customers' needs (let the competitors play catch-up).
3. Carefully consider the resources and capabilities of current and potential competitors.
4. Create and promote policies to assure conformity of SIS developed by end users (and not by central IS) with corporate strategy.
5. Promote technical partnership between general management, user management, and skilled IS professionals in SIS projects.
6. Verify commitment and support of top management (all SIS success stories are driven by involved senior managers). SIS changes the way you do business and this is why senior managers must be involved. Their involvement can assure that internal politics for resource allocation does not squeeze out SIS opportunities.
7. Reduce risks of being a follower rather than a leader of a new SIS.
8. Verify that the organization's culture provides for willingness to experiment, to entertain innovative ideas, and to learn from mistakes and misses.
9. Build on internal IT knowledge and IS capabilities and systems (TPSs and MISs), and only then extend this platform externally with SISs.
10. Do not try to win over the well-fed (IS-wise) customers.

Identifying Competitive Applications of Information Technologies

The search for competitive applications of IT will be fruitful in an environment characterized by information-intensive processes or products. There are several unique industry factors which influence the likelihood of strategic IT potential:

The presence of significant information content in key relationships with buyers or suppliers

The presence of competitive pressures within the industry (e.g., due to deregulation, technological innovations, or foreign competition)

The industry's product/service life is limited: perishable products or services (e.g., in the airline industry—flight seats that are not sold; in the hotel industry—rooms that stay vacant)

If the firm's objective is to identify strategic applications of IT, active involvement from functional and general management is necessary. There must be a desire to use IT for competitive advantage and a vision of how this will be done. Delegating this responsibility to IS management will rarely achieve effective results. General managers and IS managers have to share the concern about the strategic opportunities of IT.

Figure 7.5 illustrates a methodology for identifying SIS opportunities. The SIS opportunity process incorporates all concepts and frameworks used in this chapter (i.e., generic corporate strategies, competitive forces, value chain, and SIS risks).

A preliminary stage to the process is the review of the firm's value system. During this stage, the organizational body responsible for carrying out the process (e.g., an ad hoc committee, a dedicated SIS section of IS, a consultant) analyzes all the critical areas in the primary and support activities (and the linkages between them) of the firm's value chain, buyers' value chains, suppliers' value chains, and competitors' value chains. The analysis can pertain to a strategic business unit of the firm (e.g., a major product or service) and not to the firm as a whole. The results of this analysis provide inputs, ideas, and insights for stages 1 and 2.

Stages 1 and 2 are conducted simultaneously, with feedback between them. They focus on a range of strategic targets and the corporate strategies supported by IT that can be used to impact the targets. The targets include buyers, suppliers, possible new entrants, existing rivals, and substitute products and services.

The process should generate the largest possible list of strategic targets. It is from this list that the firm can select those that are deemed suitable for attack (or defense) by strategies supported or shaped by IT. These strategies comprise cost leadership, differentiation, focus, growth, alliances, innovation, and the like. A corporate strategy and its associated SIS can be used to attack multiple targets. A target can be impacted by more than one strategic SIS.

Once a given strategy aimed at a given target is selected, stage 3 deals with the SIS posture. It can be used defensively, to reduce a competitive edge held by a target, or offensively, to increase an edge. The SIS selected can, for instance, create high switching costs for the firm's buyers to defend against a new entrant; alternatively, the firm can join an SIS alliance in order to expand the firm's market.

Figure 7.5 SIS opportunity identification process

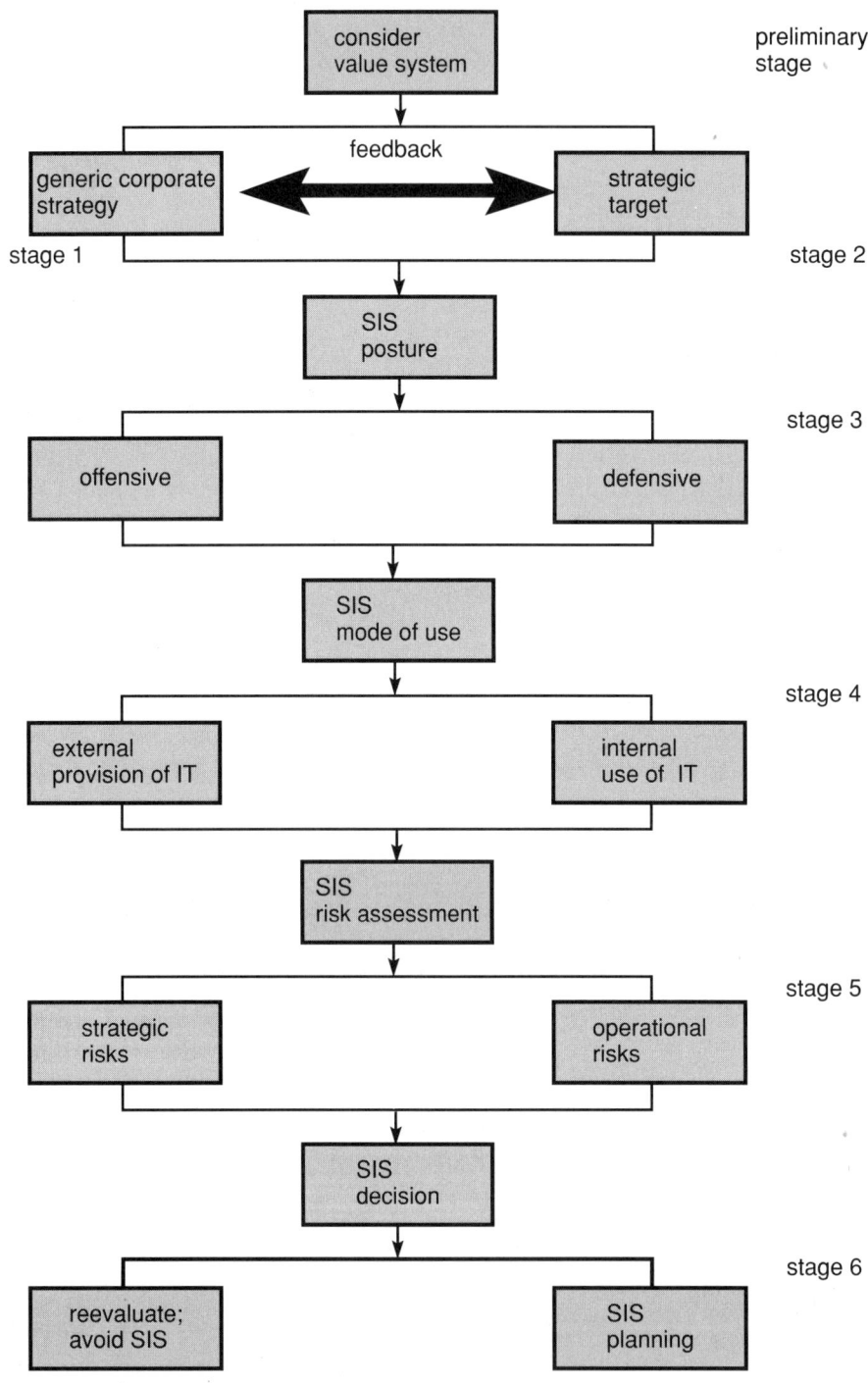

In stage 4, the firm has to consider whether the offensive or defensive SIS is to employ an IT to be used internally or externally, by providing it to the target. For example, for a buyers' target, with a niche (focus) strategy and an offensive posture, the direction of the SIS is external if terminals and an inventory management system are provided to the buyers in order to lock them in. For a cost leadership strategy with a defensive posture, aimed at buyers, the SIS selected may use CAD/CAM technology internally, to reduce costs of product development and manufacturing.

Stage 5 deals with the assessment of operational and strategic risks. The operational risks are evaluated by focusing on the size of the selected SIS, on its degree of structuredness, and on the firm's familiarity with the relevant IT. Based on this evaluation, the firm can select tools to deal with such risks (e.g., formal planning and control techniques, use of external consultants, a steering committee). In addition, assuming that the SIS is successfully implemented, the strategic implications of an initial success must be evaluated.

Finally, a decision has to be made whether to endorse the SIS being considered. The firm can decide to completely avoid the project or to modify it and then reemploy the SIS opportunity identification process to evaluate the modified SIS. A positive decision requires incorporation of the selected SIS into the master plan for IS and the ensuing annual IS plan. These plans are the subject of the next chapter.

The process described above raises important organizational implications for general management and IS management: Who should be responsible for SIS identification and development? Should IS create a dedicated SIS group? Should new SIS skills be created internally or hired? Should there be an ongoing SIS planning process? Some organizations, for example, have established a special unit within IS to monitor the environment and to identify ITs that may lead to competitive advantage (one large company named this unit the "emerging technologies section").

Practical Conclusions for Information System Design and Use

The following list contains practical conclusions for information system design and use.

1. It is the obligation of senior management to define an IS mission; it is the duty of the CIO to act as a catalyst.
2. Issuing and monitoring IS policies is the responsibility of the CIO.
3. IS policies must be custom-tailored to the specific organizational environment.
4. IS resource allocation decisions should be separated from strategic business decisions. The first are the domain of the CIO; the latter are the domain of general management.
5. Senior management must determine the current and future importance of IT to the organization before considering strategic IS issues.
6. IT can support or shape the firm's generic corporate strategy.
7. SISs that are implemented successfully may induce unanticipated negative effects on the firm's competitive position.

8. IS used as a competitive weapon can only leverage assets that the firm already possesses.
9. Sound internal information systems are a required platform for launching SIS projects.
10. General management, functional management, and IS management must be involved in the process of identifying SIS opportunities.

Summary

No information system planning and operation can soundly exist without an IS mission, objectives, strategies, and policies that are approved by senior management. An IS mission (charter) is a declaration of what IS intends to be and what distinguishes it from other functions.

IS strategies are broad courses of action conducted to achieve IS objectives. They define an organization's relationship with users, general management, and entities external to the organization.

IS policies are the procedures used to carry out IS strategies. They are determined during the planning process, and they guide the various planning processes. They can be grouped into hardware, software, and personnel policies, organizational policies, application development policies, planning policies, and financial and accounting policies.

Several conceptual frameworks are helpful to general management and IS management in considering IS policies. Nolan's "stages of growth" model prescribes adopting different management approaches as information technologies evolve through the stages of IS growth in organizations.

The strategic impact of IS activities scheme suggests that senior management must determine the current and future importance of IT to the organization before considering any IS policy issue. Both IS management and senior management must share the same perception of the impact of IT. The IS policies that are adopted are contingent on IS importance and on the specific organization's environment.

A strategic information system (SIS) is any information system that supports the competitive strategy of the organization. TPSs and MISs use information technologies to attack the cost side of the firm. ITs are used by SISs to invent new information services and products designed to attack the revenue side of the firm and to impact the firm's relationships with its environment.

At the industry level, IT impacts the nature of the industry's products, services, and markets, or the industry's economics of production and distribution. At the firm level, the impact of IT is determined by the specific competitive forces facing the firm. These forces shape the competitive arena for each firm in the industry. The five forces are: suppliers, buyers, potential new entrants into the industry, substitute products or services, and intraindustry rivals. IT can change the relationships between these forces and the firm. They are targets against which the firm deploys its competitive strategies.

At the strategy level, IT can impact the ability of firms to execute a particular business strategy. There is a variety of generic strategies, such as cost leadership, differentiation, focus, growth, alliance, and innovation. All can be deployed offensively or defensively.

The value chain is a framework for analyzing possible impacts of IT. The value chain disaggregates a firm into the different interdependent activities that add value to its raw materials and bring the firm's product to the customer. Primary activities are involved in the physical creation of the product and its delivery to buyers. Support activities provide the inputs and infrastructure for the primary activities. IT and generic corporate strategies can be used in conjunction with the value chain framework to analyze opportunities for SISs. The value system is the collection of the firm's value chain and individual value chains of its buyers, suppliers, and competitors.

Any IS development project is associated with operational risks that the project will fail to meet, time and budget constraints, and users' information requirements. The risks are affected by the size of a project, its degree of structuredness, and the familiarity of the firm with the underlying IT. A SIS may operationally succeed but create potential negative strategic impact to the company implementing it. These are the risks of competitive disadvantages, arising from unanticipated effects of the SIS on the industry structure and on the competitive position of the firm. Such SIS risks can be managed by understanding and assessing their impact and then taking appropriate actions to prevent, reduce, or control them.

Active involvement from functional and general management is necessary when identifying strategic applications of IT. The SIS opportunity identification process is a framework to identify and evaluate SIS opportunities. IT starts with an examination of the firm's value system, reviews its generic corporate strategies and the targets in its competitive arena, considers the offensive or defensive posture of a new SIS, and explores whether the underlying IT is to be used internally by the firm or externally by other entities. The process culminates with the evaluation of the operational and strategic risks of the SIS opportunity. The plan for the selected SIS must be incorporated into the planning process for IS. This process is the subject of the next chapter.

Key Concepts

chief information officer (CIO)
classes: factory, support, strategic, turnaround
competitive forces
contingency approach
functional strategy
generic corporate strategy
information technology (IT)
IS mission (charter)
IS operational risks
microcomputer policy

objectives
policies
SIS alliances
strategic business unit (SBU)
strategic information system (SIS)
strategic IS impact grid
strategic IS risks
strategies
value chain
value system
vision

References

1. Brancheau, J. C., and J. C. Wetherbe. "Key Issues in Information Systems Management." *MIS Quarterly* 11, no. 1 (March 1987): 23–44.
2. Cash, J. I., and B. R. Konsynski. "IS Redraws Competitive Boundaries." *Harvard Business Review*, 63, no. 2 (March-April 1985): 134–42.
3. Cash, J. I., F. W. McFarlan, J. L. McKenney, and L. M. Applegate. *Corporate Information Systems Management: Text and Cases.* 3d ed. Homewood, IL: Richard D. Irwin, 1992.
4. "Information Power." *Business Week*, October 14, 1985: 48–57.
5. Keen, P. G. W., and L. A. Woodman. "What to Do with All Those Micros." *Harvard Business Review* 62, no. 5 (September-October 1984): 142–50.
6. McFarlan, F. W., and J. L. McKenney. *Corporate Information Systems Management.* Homewood, IL: Richard D. Irwin, 1983.
7. Parsons, G. L. "Information Technology: A New Competitive Weapon." *Sloan Management Review* 25 (Fall 1983): 3–14.
8. Porter, M. E. *Competitive Strategy: Techniques for Analyzing Industries and Competitors.* New York: Free Press, 1980.
9. Porter, M. E. *Competitive Advantage.* New York: Free Press, 1985.
10. Porter, M. E., and V. E. Millar. "How Information Gives You Competitive Advantage." *Harvard Business Review* 63, no. 4 (July–August 1985): 149–60.
11. Synnott, W. R. *The Information Weapon.* New York: Wiley & Sons, 1987.
12. Vitale, M. R. "The Growing Risks of Information System Success." *MIS Quarterly* 10, no. 4 (December 1986): 327–34.
13. Wiseman, C. *Strategy and Computers.* Homewood, IL: Dow Jones-Irwin, 1985.
14. Wiseman, C. *Strategic Information Systems.* Homewood, IL: Richard D. Irwin, 1988.

Questions

1. Compare objectives to strategies.
2. Define the term "IS vision" and provide an example.
3. Compare TPS, MIS, DSS, and SIS.
4. Discuss the levels of IT impact on a business organization.
5. What are the five forces operating in a competitive industry? Provide examples.
6. Why is it essential to distinguish between operational and strategic SIS risks?
7. Provide examples of ITs used to support five different generic corporate strategies.
8. Describe three sources of operational IS risks.

Problems

1. Use the SIS opportunity identification process to consider the potential use of office automation for a firm in an industry of your choice.
2. Do the same for data-base technology.
3. Do the same for PC hardware and software technologies.

Bank of America Trust Accounting System

The following passages are exactly cited from three newspapers and trade journals.

$80-MILLION FAILURE: B OF A'S PLANS FOR COMPUTER DON'T ADD UP
By Douglas Frants
TIMES STAFF WRITER
(Los Angeles Times, February 7, 1988)

San Francisco—In May, 1986, Bank of America was so confident about the impending success of its pioneering new computer system for trust accounts that dozens of the bank's most important corporate clients were invited to a lavish two-day demonstration at the Santa Barbara Biltmore Hotel.

Holes were cut in the hotel roof to ventilate the rooms full of computers, and color monitors were in place to show off the bells and whistles of what B of A officials touted as the industry's most sophisticated technology for handling trust accounts.

The party's $75,000 tab was minor to officials anticipating the lucrative new business that the system seemed sure to generate when it went on-line within the next few weeks.

End of Good Times

"There never has been a meeting that went as well as this from a point of view of inspiring the customers," said Clyde R. Claus, a 30-year veteran of banking who organized the session as the executive in charge of B of A's trust department. "People were trembling with excitement."

The bash at the Biltmore was the last thing that went right.

Last month, Bank of America acknowledged that it was abandoning the $20-million computer system after wasting another $60 million trying to make it work. The bank will no longer handle processing for its trust division, and the biggest accounts were given to a Boston bank. Top executives, including Claus, have lost their jobs already, and an undisclosed number of layoffs are in the works.

If the episode involved only a handful of ruined careers and the millions lost in pursuit of a too-fancy computer system, it would merit an embarrassing but forgettable footnote in Bank of America's legendary history.

But the story is more important than a simple footnote because it opens a rare window on what author Martin Mayer has dubbed "a decade of decline" at the San Francisco bank, an unprecedented span in which its fortunes plunged from a $643-million profit in 1980 to a $955-million loss in 1987, and the bank fell from largest in the world to No. 29.

Deeper Questions

Further, the total abandonment of a computer system after five years of development and nearly a year of false starts raised questions about the bank's ability to overcome its technological inadequacy in an era when money is often nothing more than a blip on a computer screen.

A spokesman said last week that Bank of America officials would not respond to questions from The Times about the episode.

"Since last year, we have acknowledged that operational problems existed in our institutional trust business and our energies have been directed toward resolving them as quickly as possible," the spokesman said in a prepared statement. "We are not interested in fixing blame . . . We do not believe that it is productive to rehash the situation."

The widely publicized difficulties surrounding the trust computer problems obscure the fact that the Bank of America was once a technological leader, developing the first big commercial computer in the 1950s and inventing the magnetic ink that allows machines to read the codes on checks.

By the late 1970s, however, under the leadership of A. W. Clausen, the bank was skimping on the spending required to keep up with technological advances. Instead, the money went into greater profits. By the time Clausen relinquished the helm of the parent company, BankAmerica, to Samuel H. Armacost in 1981, the bank had fallen far behind in the computer race.

Armacost launched a $4-billion spending program to push B of A back to the technological forefront. The phrase he liked was "leapfrogging into the 1990s," and one area that he chose to emphasize was the trust department.

Financial Role

Trust departments serve as custodians and managers of investments for individuals, corporations, unions, and government agencies. Investments can be real estate, cash, stocks, and bonds. Accounts run from a few thousand to billions of dollars for big pension funds. Banks collect fees for their services and the amounts can be substantial.

In return, trust departments must provide customers with extensive records and statements to explain their actions and balance the accounts. The reporting is similar to balancing a checkbook for thousands of customers with enormously varied demands.

For instance, a $300-million pension fund might cover six affiliates within the company. The affiliates would share the services of an investment manager, whose trading would be reported to the bank as trustee. The bank must allocate each purchase or sale to the proper affiliate account, keep track of dividends, and provide the customer with an ongoing accounting and monthly statements.

Throw in the management of an office building or two, and a picture emerges of the complexity of trust accounting.

Developing a computer system that puts all of this information on the computer screens of customers in a microsecond is enormously complex, and it is vital to be competitive.

Traditionally, the field has been dominated by a handful of big Eastern banks, such as Bankers Trust in New York and State Street Bank & Trust in Boston. Although it was the largest trust bank on the West Coast, B of A in the late 1970s was small by comparison, and it was mired in a 1960s-vintage accounting and reporting system. An effort to update the system ended in a $6-million failure in 1981 after the company's computer engineers worked for more than a year without developing a usable system. So Armacost turned to Claus, who had spent 20 years with New York's Marine Midland Bank before arriving at B of A in 1977.

Gets Ultimatum

Soon after Claus was named executive vice president in charge of the trust department in 1982, Armacost called him to his office on the fortieth floor of the bank's granite tower in downtown San Francisco to discuss the trust department's problems.

"Fix it or close it," Armacost ordered Claus.

Claus soon found that abandoning the business would damage client relationships. Many customers who relied on the bank for trust business as a convenience maintained far larger corporate accounts there. He was equally reluctant to return to the in-house technicians who had produced the stillborn system a year before.

So Claus and two key executives in data processing, Nicholas Caputo and Thomas Anderson, embarked on a search to find an outside vendor to help develop the new system.

In true Bank of America style, the plan was grand: Create a system to surpass Bankers Trust and State Street, and turn B of A into a national power in trust business.

In the fall of 1982, the trust industry held its annual convention in Atlanta. Caputo and Anderson attended, and so did Steven M. Katz, a pioneer in creating software for bank trust departments.

Katz, the computer expert, and Alfred P. West Jr., a marketing specialist, had formed a company called SEI Corp. outside Philadelphia in Wayne, PA. They had parlayed concepts in Katz's MBA thesis into a software system used by about 300 small banks in the 1970s.

Katz left in a dispute, and, in June, 1980, he founded a rival company, Premier Systems, across the street from SEI in Wayne. Insiders referred to the pavement between the companies as "the DMZ."

Katz was in Atlanta trying to drum up business. Caputo knew Katz and invited him to meet with the B of A officials at the Hyatt Regency Hotel. By the accounts of people who were there, it was a stormy beginning.

Basis of System

Bank of America's existing system was based on IBM computers, and the bank officials wanted to stick with the familiar hardware. Katz insisted on using Prime Computer, an IBM rival with which he had a long relationship.

There was also a clash on delivery time. According to one participant, Katz boasted that he could put together a system by 1983, and Anderson argued that the promise was ridiculously optimistic. The argument ended the meeting—but did not doom the partnership.

During the next six months, Bank of America and Katz brought together a consortium of banks that agreed to advance premier money to develop a new, cutting-edge system for trust reporting and accounting.

The other banks, all smaller than B of A, were Seattle-First National Bank (which would later be purchased by BankAmerica), United Virginia Bank (now Crestar), and Philadelphia National Bank. The three smaller banks were using SEI's system.

Nearly a year was spent on additional research before Claus took the proposal to the bank's management committee and got the go-ahead to fund the project in March, 1984.

A contract was signed with Premier to provide a system called MasterNet. While the trust business was by far the biggest task, the contract also called for the bank's technicians to develop eight smaller systems to augment it under the MasterNet umbrella.

While it was not a deadline, the goal was to have the new system, called TrustPlus, in operation by December 31, 1984.

What followed was a textbook structure for designing a computer system.

A committee was formed of representatives from each B of A department that would use the system, and they met monthly to discuss their requirements. Data processing experts from the four banks gathered for a week each month in Pennsylvania to review progress and discuss their needs with the Premier designers.

"The bank seemed to be doing it right," a B of A executive involved in the project said. "The risks were shared with other banks. A proven vendor was hired. And all areas of the bank were involved." Some of the bank data-processing experts found Katz difficult to deal with occasionally, particularly when they offered views on technical aspects of the project. "Don't give us the solutions. Just tell us the problems," Katz often said.

Katz declined to answer questions for this article, saying: "It's our policy not to talk about individual customer relationships."

When the ambitious December 31, 1984, goal passed without a system, no one was concerned. There was progress, and those involved were excited about the unfolding system and undaunted by the size of the task.

The immense size of what they confronted is contained in two minor statistics: B of A devoted 20 man-years to testing the software system and its 3.5 million lines of code; 13,000 hours of training, including rigorous testing, were provided to the staff that would run the system.

After 1985 passed without a working system, some team members detected subtle pressures from corporate brass to come up with a return on the bank's investment, which was approaching $20 million. Customers who had been promised the best system in the world were also concerned.

"Major clients were anxious to get the system and we were real late," one executive who was involved said. "Some of these people were threatening to leave the bank."

Claus, the only person connected with the program who would speak for attribution, denied that he had been pressured over costs or timing. He said Thomas A. Cooper, then the president of B of A, told him in 1986,

"You're not getting any pressure from me to do it unless you're ready."

That spring, Claus decided the system was about ready. Some smaller parts of MasterNet were already working smoothly in other parts of the bank. Test runs for the trust system had not been perfect, but the technicians thought most bugs could be worked out soon. A demonstration run in Wayne had been successful.

Divergent Opinions

So invitations were mailed for the bash at the Biltmore. Although Claus genuinely thought that the system was about ready, others viewed the party as a means of appeasing anxious customers by giving them a taste.

The taste was good.

"It was a very well-staged function, and it really did show the capabilities of a system that had great appeal to us and others attending," said Derek Rowlett, administrator of the $350-million pension fund of the Directors Guild of America.

The plan was to first bring in the institutional trust customers. Although their accounts were larger, totaling assets of $38 billion, there were only 800 of them. The consumer division, with 8,000 smaller accounts, would be converted later.

But the promise that the bank would soon convert the institutional customers to MasterNet was unfulfilled. Technical bugs kept popping up, and the system would not work efficiently enough to handle the conversion.

"There were all kinds of problems," a former bank official said. "You could be sitting at a terminal and it would take too long to get a response, too long for the screen to pop up. Other times, the whole system crashed."

The delays put additional pressure on bank employees, many of whom were also operating the old system and working double shifts and weekends to try to get the new system operating, too.

"It was an especially heavy burden on the people involved," one executive who worked on the conversion said.

Late in 1986, Claus received an anonymous letter from someone familiar with the system who warned against a "rush to convert" and told Claus, who was not a computer expert, that people had "pulled the wool" over his eyes.

Memo to Staff

Claus responded with a memo to the staff assuring them that there would be no conversion before it was time.

The three chief components of the system—trust department, systems engineering, and the bank's securities clearance operation—had reported to Claus at the start of the project, which gave him the authority to ensure full cooperation.

By 1986, his authority had been restricted. The systems group and the securities staff had been given their own bosses who did not report directly to Claus. It made obtaining cooperation, particularly from the securities group in Los Angeles, difficult as the pressure to perform increased in 1986.

These pressures, whether spoken or not, were felt by many involved in the project. The bank had reported severe losses in 1986, and efforts were being made throughout the giant company to cut back. Some of the bank's most profitable businesses were sold, and 9,600 jobs were cut. One who lost his job was Armacost, and with him went his vision of 1990s technology. Clausen was brought back from retirement to run the bank again, and his perception of computers was not enhanced when he reviewed the trust troubles.

The economic cutbacks and Clausen's reaction made it difficult to justify the continued expense of staffing two trust systems when one was mired in costly troubles.

For several months in late 1986 and early 1987, however, tests of TrustPlus had been running with only a few bugs. "There were still bugs, but the users felt they could run with it and work out the bugs as we went along," one former executive said.

A conversion date was set: March 2, 1987.

Just as the data-processing staff was rushing to complete work for the conversion, half of the sixteen-member contingent was pulled off the assignment.

Trust Business Sale

In its push to raise money to offset its losses, B of A had sold its consumer trust business to Wells Fargo for $100 million. B of A was rushing to close the deal by March 31, 1987, so the proceeds could be booked in the first quarter. So, half the data-processing staff was switched to help transfer the accounts to the Wells Fargo system, which was based on SEI software.

On Saturday, Feb. 28, and Sunday, March 1, the remaining staff worked almost nonstop to complete the switch of the institutional trust accounts, which had begun a week before. They pulled it off on that Monday—and it lasted until Saturday, March 7.

That was the day the first of the twenty-four disk-drive units on the Prime computers blew up, causing the loss of a portion of the data base and signaling the beginning of the end. Workers spent a discouraging weekend retrieving data from a backup unit. It was past midnight each night before they left the offices.

Over the next month, at least fourteen more of the disk drives blew up. None had malfunctioned in the previous months of tests.

It turned out that the units were part of a faulty batch manufactured by Control Data Corp., a Minneapolis computer firm. But by the time the cause was discovered, delays had mounted, and other difficulties had arisen. Taken individually, none would have caused the ensuing disaster. Together, they doomed the system.

"When the stuff hit the fan in the springtime, there was a series of really statistically impossible little disasters that became one big one," Claus said.

At the precise time the technical team was struggling with these setbacks in April, the bank decided to move the staff from San Francisco to its data-processing headquarters across the bay in Concord, 30 miles away, in another money saving effort.

For many who had been working under great stress for months, the move became the focus for their frustrations. Several key people quit and morale sank as many who remained grumbled.

The difficulties were not restricted to San Francisco. The securities clearing operation of the eighteenth floor of the Bank America building in Los Angeles was thrown into disarray by the computer woes and its own unrelated problems.

Securities clearing is critical to a trust operation. It involves reconciling thousands of stock and bond trades daily. At the end of the day, the accounts must balance—each purchase and sale recorded in the proper account and matched to the records from the brokers who actually execute the trades. Stocks, or their equivalent, must be delivered and money accepted.

One of the intended functions of TrustPlus was to both reconcile this activity and ensure that transactions were credited to the proper accounts. When it did not work, the securities group had to rely on records from the outside brokers to settle transactions. The practice, called "blind settling," is abhorrent to any well-run operation.

The computer problems confirmed the suspicions of the securities people in Los Angeles, many of whom had never thought that TrustPlus would work. But its defenders maintain that the securities operation had unrelated problems that contributed to its difficulties.

The securities people had become reluctant to participate in the design process. When the problems erupted in the spring, Claus no longer had authority over the division, and many thought he was unable to force its cooperation. An outside consultant later told bank employees that some securities work was destroyed and some was simply stuck away in drawers during the critical weeks after the ill-fated conversion.

And some in Los Angeles were less inclined to put up with the demands of the collapsing computer system because, in March, the bank had announced plans to move the operation to San Francisco, which meant many Los Angeles workers would lose their jobs. Reaction was so strong against the move that the bank put it on hold three months later, but nearly forty people had left by then.

Whatever the complex causes, dozens of highly paid "temporary" workers were brought into the securities group in Los Angeles to straighten out the reconciliation mess at an enormous cost.

In the ensuing months, there were conflicts between the bank staff and the "temps" from Ernst & Whinney and Touche Ross, and there were turf battles among the consulting firms as they jockeyed for the millions of dollars that B of A was paying in an attempt to fix the problem.

The bank's first public acknowledgement of the problems came in a one-line notice in the earnings report it issued in July, 1987. It said $25 million was being placed in a reserve to cover anticipated losses from problems with MasterNet.

Bank officials assured reporters and clients that the problems would be resolved. But within weeks the bank was quietly seeking a buyer for the entire institutional trust department. The effort was unsuccessful because, an official at a rival bank said, there was not much to buy.

Clausen also ordered an in-house investigation of the debacle, which many staff members viewed as little more than a witch hunt. The result was a "one-copy" report that went only to Clausen. In October, Claus and Louis Mertes, the executive in charge of systems engineering, resigned.

Claus acknowledged that he was leaving over the MasterNet problems and took responsibility for them. Mertes, who had been at the bank only two years, has not spoken publicly about his departure.

Another surprise came in January when the bank announced that an additional $35 million would be reserved to "correct problems" with the system, bringing the total spent on fixing the $20-million system to $60 million.

Period of Decline

By then, the institutional customers were leaving. The number of accounts had dropped from about 800 to around 700, and assets under management had declined to $34 billion from $38 billion.

What the bank did not say was that the decision had been made to abandon the system. But over the next few days, it was disclosed that the bank was shifting 95 percent of its trust business to Seattle-First National Bank, now a BankAmerica affiliate, which uses an IBM-based system from SEI.

The remaining accounts, deemed too complex for the Seattle bank, were given to State Street Bank in Boston, one of the industry leaders that Bank of America had set out to overtake nearly six years and $80 million ago.

Even the decision to drop the embarrassing program is not immune to criticism, which was summarized by Claus last week.

"A lot of people lay down on the floor and spilled blood over this system, and why they abandoned it now I cannot understand," he said. "A guy called me this morning out of the blue and said that 95 percent of it was working very well."

80M MIS DISASTER
By David A. Ludlum
CW STAFF
(Computerworld,
February 1, 1988)

SAN FRANCISCO—Bank America Corp. is scuttling efforts to use its trouble-prone MasterNet institutional trust accounting system, which has been five years in the making and cost an estimated $80 million. The banking company recently disclosed that it will shift the processing for 95 percent of its institutional trust accounts—believed to represent about 75 percent of total transactions—to its Seafirst Corp. subsidiary in

Seattle. The transfer will take place in mid-April, according to a letter BankAmerica sent to its clients.

The development appears to bring to a climax an ambitious but ultimately disastrous attempt to deploy a leading-edge information system whose cost was initially pegged at $20 million, according to interviews with industry sources and former BankAmerica employees. On January 21, BankAmerica revealed that, during last year's fourth quarter, it had set aside $35 million to cover expenses arising from MasterNet, following a second-quarter reserve of $25 million. The reserves cover costs such as delayed interest payments, waived fees, additional manpower, and hardware.

Last October, BankAmerica's system chief, Louis Mertes, and its top trust executive, Clyde Claus, resigned in moves attributed to MasterNet's failure to generate timely statements and other data. That failure has led some institutional trust clients to take their business elsewhere. BankAmerica reports serving as trustee or agent for assets of $34 billion held by about 700 institutions, down from $38 billion for 800 institutions reported last summer.

Layoffs Imminent

A BankAmerica spokesman suggested that layoffs may result from the scuttling of MasterNet. "Clearly, there will be reductions over time in our trust operations and systems," he said. "We do expect there will be increased efficiencies."

BankAmerica had hoped MasterNet would enable it to offer trust data-processing services to small and mid-sized banks. Of the MasterNet accounts not going to Seafirst, BankAmerica said late Friday that twenty-nine "more complex" accounts will be processed by State Street Bank & Trust Co. in Boston, although actual management will remain with BankAmerica.

Trust Accounts

Seafirst processes institutional trust accounts remotely on SEI Corp.'s Trust-Aid 3000 system at SEI's headquarters in Wayne, PA, according to an SEI spokesman. The system was designed 15 years ago but was upgraded last summer to run on an IBM 3090 Model 400.

For at least five years, BankAmerica has been building its MasterNet system around the Trust-Plus system developed by Premier Systems, Inc., also in Wayne, which runs on Prime Computer, Inc. processors. Premier was founded in 1979 by former SEI employees with financing from BankAmerica, Seafirst, Philadelphia National Bank, and Crestar Bank of Virginia. It was founded in an effort to improve on the institutional trust system that SEI then offered, according to a source familiar with the project. BankAmerica is the only firm that has attempted to go online with TrustPlus, the source said.

A spokesman for Philadelphia National Bank said his bank is not using TrustPlus but would not elaborate. Crestar officials could not be reached for comment.

In serving as trustees for institutional trusts such as corporate, union, and government pension funds, banks track the performance of the independent money managers that make investments for the trusts, settle their trades, collect income from the investments and make payments to beneficiaries.

BankAmerica brought MasterNet online March 1, 1987, replacing a 20-year-old proprietary batch-processing system. In addition to generating monthly statements, MasterNet was supposed to provide online up-dating and querying.

However, MasterNet failed to maintain current data and fell months behind in generating statements. These difficulties were caused by slow run and response times, communications problems, and leaky disk drives, according to a former BankAmerica employee.

Apathy Problem

MasterNet also suffered a major blow from poor morale at a securities processing unit in Los Angeles that was involved with its development, the source said: In the midst of the conversion, BankAmerica disclosed that it would move the unit from Los Angeles to San Francisco, leading workers there to slack off.

"They did not work hard. They went home early," he said. The bank later decided to keep the unit in Los Angeles.

One BankAmerica trust client looking elsewhere for trustee services is the $370 million Southern California Rapid Transit District, whose pension funds could generate about $300,000 a year for BankAmerica.

"We have an obligation as fiduciaries to keep everything on an even keel. We haven't lost any money, but it's a great inconvenience not having information," said Edward Paull, pension and benefits manager for the fund.

BankAmerica has appointed Richard V. Fulp, an executive vice president and head of the trust group at Seafirst, to run its trust department while continuing to head Seafirst's trust unit. Mertes has not been replaced.

A spokesman for the U.S. Comptroller of the Currency declined to comment on a published report that the agency is investigating BankAmerica regarding alleged banking law violations said to be caused by problems with MasterNet. In 1984, BankAmerica consented to censure by the agency for its failure to inform customers that it was unable to keep current records of securities transactions as the result of a system conversion.

JUST SAY NO TO STRATEGIC INFORMATION SYSTEMS
(PC Week, February 1988)

Because of its failed MasterNet automation project, BankAmerica Corp. has lost a reported $60 million, two of its senior executives, and the confidence of many of its largest customers.

Now, adding possible prosecution to injury, the San Francisco-based bank faces the close scrutiny of a federal agency, according to an article in the *Wall Street Journal.*

The U.S. Comptroller of the Currency has conducted a preliminary review into the possibility that the bank's botched information system, by virtue of its dismal implementation, has violated banking laws, according to the Journal report.

This comes months after news that the head of the BankAmerica's information-systems subsidiary and the executive in charge of its trust division left the company at the same time—just when the MasterNet trust-fund accounting system's failure became public.

However, beset by technical problems, the network never got off the ground.

As strategic-systems mentor Michael Hammer explained at his 1987 forum: ''The only strategic systems worth trying are the ones that scare the hell out of you,'' and most strategic systems ''are only strategic in retrospect.''

Unfortunately, MasterNet is one that, in retrospect, still scared the hell out of you.

Questions

1. Analyze the Bank of America Case in the following order:
   a. salient facts
   b. symptoms and problems
   c. alternative solutions as they were before the final decision to abandon the system
   d. recommendation

2. Assuming that MasterNet was a strategic system, was it treated appropriately? Explain.
3. How risky was the project? Were the risks appropriately treated?

Chapter 8 *The Information System Plan*

For the information system function to assume a more central role within organizations, proper planning is vital. This will ensure that the role played by information systems will be congruent with the objectives of the overall organization.

This chapter describes the planning methodology that should be used to make information systems responsive to organizational objectives, and the advantages of a strategic approach over more traditional planning approaches.

Introduction

A key to the success of the information system function in an organization is a comprehensive, effective planning system. Good planning is one of the basics of good management. You may recall from chapter 5 Anthony's classification of managers into three levels: strategic planning, management control, and operational control [1]. Managers at these levels are, respectively, involved in long-range, medium-range, and short-range planning. The information system function is similar to other organizational functions (e.g., finance, marketing, personnel, production, accounting) in that it is made up of managers at various levels who must plan for the effective and efficient utilization of the resources under their command. The managers in the information system function vary—from the head of information systems to the managers of programming, system design, and operations units, down to project manager, chief programmers, and chief operators. (See the discussion of organizational structure in ch. 12.)

A variety of critical pressures that force one to plan ahead exist in the information systems field. The more important include [2]:

1. Rapid changes in technology—offer different approaches to applications development. As technology changes, planning becomes increasingly important to ensure that the organization does not unwittingly invest in incompatible systems.

2. The scarcity of experienced information system professionals (information analysts, programmers, system designers, project leaders, etc.)—a major force restraining information system planning.

3. Scarcity of other organizational resources (e.g., financial resources)—information systems have to compete against other investment opportunities.

4. Organizational dependence on information systems support—in many organizations, implementation of new strategies (e.g., new products, new billing policy) depends heavily on information systems and hence requires coordinated planning.

The information system planning process has to be an integral part of overall organizational planning. The information system function must constantly cope with changing requirements for its resources. Just as the host organization has to devote resources to planning so that it can adapt itself to the changing conditions of its environment, so must information systems invest resources in planning so that they can respond to changes in their environment. Although the scope and perspective of the two planning efforts may be different, it is imperative that the information system plans interrelate with the organizational planning system. The plans must be tailored to the unique characteristics of each organization. Information system planning must be matched with the circumstances existing in each organization and must alter with changing conditions.

Information system planning begins with the establishment of a strategic plan that provides a framework within which subsequent plans are to be developed. Each stage of the planning process is an elaboration of preceding stages, culminating in the planning of operational applications. (The development process of individual applications is discussed in ch. 9.)

McLean and Soden [9, pp. 23–26] synthesize various views of information system planning and propose a classification of the hierarchy of plans into strategic, long range, medium range, and short range. *Strategic* information system planning is the process of deciding on objectives for the information system function, on the resources required to obtain these objectives, and on the policies that are to govern the acquisition, use, and disposition of the resources (see ch. 7).

Long-range information system planning deals with meeting the future information needs of the overall organization and with the information system organization of the future. It can have a horizon of five to ten years and is largely conceptual. *Medium-range* information system planning deals with meeting the present information needs of the overall organization, projected two to five years into the future. This is a *master plan* for information systems development. The focus of the master plan is managerial. *Short-range* information system planning is equivalent to the information system annual plan. It is relatively operational. It involves individual computer application development schedules, budget preparation, personnel scheduling, timetables, and establishment of performance targets.

The Hierarchy of Information System Plans

Strategic Information System Planning

McLean and Soden [9, p. 83] present the following sequence of steps involved in strategic planning:

1. A setting of the mission or charter of the MIS organization.
2. A formal environmental assessment to identify the MIS opportunities, threats, and risks of concern to the enterprise.
3. The establishment of MIS objectives that define the desired results to be achieved by the function, related as much as possible to the strategic objectives of the overall enterprise.
4. The development of MIS strategies, which are broad courses of action describing how the previously set objectives are to be achieved.
5. The definition of MIS policies as guidelines to be used in carrying out the strategy, giving particular importance to policies relating to the organization of the MIS effort, the allocation of scarce resources, and the setting of expenditure levels for the function.
6. The translation of these objectives, strategies, and policies into long-, medium-, or short-range plans.
7. The implementation of the plans, the measurement of progress against them, and the recycling of the appropriate planning effort over time.

The first and foremost planning task is to define the charter of the information system unit in the organization. This must be done within the purpose of the host organization. It is the obligation of top management to define the charter and announce it throughout the organization. If top management fails to define an *information system charter,* it is the duty of the head of information systems to act as a catalyst. He or she must prepare a draft charter and propose it to top management in order to arrive at a formal charter.

After setting the broad mission of information systems in the organization, the environment and constraints imposed on information systems must be considered. This includes the objectives, strategies, and policies of the host organization, the user groups within the organization and their information processing needs, and the present and future information processing technology.

After establishing the information system mission and appraising the environment, the objectives of the information system function have to be defined, and the strategies or broad courses of action to achieve the objectives have to be developed. The guidelines used in carrying out the strategies are the information system policies. These are specific statements covering the allocation and use of resources (expenditures, personnel, software, hardware) and the organization and monitoring of the information system unit in the organization. (More about information system policies was presented in the previous chapter.)

With the framework concluded, the strategic planning process can embark on implementation—translating the broad, organizationwide objectives and strategies into *long-range conceptual planning, medium-range managerial planning,* and *short-range operational planning.* Note that implementation planning means increasingly more detailed, concrete, and specific plans.

It is sometimes difficult to draw the line between strategic and long-range planning. There are many instances of confusion between the two, with the information system staff setting the objectives and strategies for development of the information system function as part of the long-range plan of the function itself. We make a clear distinction: the strategic information system plan should be developed by the chief executive or top management; long-range and medium-range plans are all derived from the strategic plan; the strategic objectives are constraints imposed on all other information system plans. We thus have a hierarchy of constraints: the long-range objectives constrain the medium-range objectives, which constrain the short-range objectives, which in turn constrain the objectives of individual projects. At each level of planning, more resources are committed to the information system function. By focusing on strategy first, we reduce the risk of inefficient allocation of resources along the way.

Before concluding the discussion of strategic objectives, we think it worthwhile to provide you with the set of information system objectives established by the California state legislature [9, pp. 321–22].

1. That the goal of consolidation and optimum utilization of electronic data processing equipment be pursued whenever possible.
2. That there be maximum practical integration of electronic data processing systems.
3. That service centers be established, as required, to provide data processing services to units of state government not included in consolidation plans.
4. That the goal of any consolidation be to create functional information systems that are designed to process and provide information related to broad areas of subject matter.
5. That the ultimate goal of the state's information systems be to provide the most effective means of data storage, retrieval, and exchange between units and agencies of state and local governments.
6. That such goals as one-time collection of data, minimum duplication of records, and maximum availability of information at lowest overall cost will not jeopardize or comprise the confidentiality of information as provided by statute or the protection of the right of individual privacy as established by law.
7. That there be adherence to proper standards to ensure appropriate compatibility of systems and interchange of data and information.
8. That proper management controls be instituted to ensure the most efficient, effective, and economical use of the state's resources.

Long-Range Information System Planning

The long-range information system plan does not deal with specific projects, or even groups of projects, but with types of user needs and services that might be useful in addressing these needs. This is a major distinction between the long-range plan and the medium-range plan. With a time horizon of five to ten years, long-range conceptual planning is concerned with portraying the general courses of action and broad types of resources to carry out strategies. The planning horizon chosen depends on the need of the specific organization and its information system function. These needs are mainly determined by how much of the future is affected by present decisions. The extent of planning should be such that future events and activities can be seen in their proper perspective and problems anticipated while they are still potential problems [8].

No schedules or priorities of project development are assigned in the long-range plan. Only rough estimates of resource requirements exist. The plan should be updated annually, within the constraints imposed by the strategic plan. It should be generally assumed that the needs and resources can and will change in subsequent annual updates of the plan. Although no specific applications are discussed, the plan should deal with the main characteristics of applications to be developed and installed, based on the long-range priorities of the organization and general trends in the information processing area. While the time and effort invested in preparing the long-range plan are greater than those invested in preparing the strategic plan, they are relatively small compared to those invested in preparing the medium-range plan. The plan should be prepared by senior executives and the information system committee of the organization (see ch. 9) and approved by top management.

The methodology recommended for developing the long-range plan consists of three steps [7, pp. 32–38]. These three steps are

1. Collecting background information—organization strategic objectives for information systems; characteristics of future hardware and software technology; characteristics of future use of human resources (as affected by computer technology and socioeconomic changes); potential external pressures for change (e.g., legislation, regulation); portfolio of information services foreseen by users for the next five to ten years; major current problem areas from the information system management point of view and from the user management point of view.

2. Analyzing overall needs—given the background information and the portfolio of information services, the overall demand for resources in the long run can be established in terms of type (people, hardware, software), capability, quantity, and timing—at least conceptually. This overall demand can then be compared with the currently available resources in order to determine whether these resources together will be capable of meeting demand. The most likely result is that at least some changes will be needed in all types of resources. For example, due to the expected expansion of organizational activities in the international market, more transborder data transfer facilities may be needed in six years.

3. Developing the long-range plan document—outlining the results of the previous steps and their implications for the information system function and the host organization. The document should specify the objectives, the projection of future trends, resource plans, organizational effects, the scope and structure of the information system unit, and potential risks and opportunities.

Items to be included in the information system long-range plan document are listed here [9, p. 463].

a. Statement of objectives
b. Projection of possible future information system environment
c. Projection of possible future user environment
d. Projection of possible future industry environment
e. Alternate information system strategy definition/evaluation
f. System development plan
g. Personnel plan
h. Facilities plan
i. Expenditure plan
j. Organization plan
k. Education plan
l. Hardware plan
m. Recommended implementation plan
n. Evaluation of past performance versus plan by the information system unit
o. Summary of strengths and weaknesses of the information system staff

As you will observe in the next section, the outline presented here does not differ considerably from that for the medium-range plan. Indeed, many organizations either confuse the two or have only long-range and short-range information system plans (see, for example, [10] or [11]).The difference lies in the content and time horizons of the two types of plans. The long-range plan items cover less concrete and less detailed needs, resources, schedules, objectives, and timetables.

The Master Plan: Medium-Range Information System Planning

The product of the medium-range planning process is the master plan for developing the information systems that are necessary to meet the present information needs of the organization. It contains a portfolio of projects to be implemented according to priority, planning for hardware and software procurement, and planning for the budgeting and staffing of multiyear projects and development activities. The planning focus is managerial; it considers the medium-range information system objectives that can be achieved by specific projects and actions.

Every organization involved in developing computer-based information systems must prepare a master plan. The master plan serves to

Cover the development plan for the medium and short range and prepare the resources that will be required for its implementation.

Determine the optimal sequence of development.

Develop systems in a way that will facilitate, where necessary, integration of these systems.

Prevent a wild development of information systems that are unrelated to a comprehensive plan based on the objectives and needs of the host organization.

The planning process resulting in the master plan starts with the objectives, needs, and constraints established by the long-range plan. These are conceptual and broad and are translated into operational and detailed counterparts. The following activities are part of the process: developing a portfolio of projects; ranking and assigning priorities to projects; defining resources and action plans for the selected projects; and preparing a master-plan document.

Developing a Portfolio of Projects

The *project portfolio* identifies information systems projects of merit. These may consist of user applications or internal information system projects (e.g., developing a utility sort program; enhancing the current operating system). This is the list of all applications that users and information system management foresee for the medium-range time horizon, regardless of the current status. We can identify several categories of projects including the following:

Applications currently being developed.

Backlog of applications approved for development but not yet started.

Projects generated by the long-range plan (which contains a portfolio of proposed user applications).

User requests (requests by users for immediate service).

Major revisions to existing applications.

New opportunities—projects that are undertaken due to new information or external factors (e.g., new information technology, new business strategy).

This slate of projects can be derived from various sources. It normally implies that there is an ongoing scanning process in the organization to collect candidates for new projects. The sources can be top management, user management, the information system personnel, and external sources (competitors, software houses, consultants, trade magazines).

Ranking and Assigning Priorities to Projects

Every organization has a large number of potential information system projects. The limited resources of the organization make it impossible to develop and implement all projects simultaneously, and, therefore, force choices among projects. The ranking process may be a difficult task. There are organizationwide projects (e.g., basic transaction processing applications), functional projects (e.g., a computerized credit-rating application), and projects requested by the information system unit (e.g., development of a data base). They compete not only among themselves, but also against ongoing projects, backlog projects, enhancement projects, and major revisions. Here is where organizational objectives and policies are important: there should be resource allocation policies that can serve as criteria for ranking the project portfolio.

The product of these criteria is a *priority scheme* that determines the sequence of project implementation. For example, top priority may be assigned to a computerized reservation system in a new airline because reservation is the central application in this industry. But before the criteria can be applied to the projects, the feasibility of the projects has to be assessed. A delicate issue is how to minimize resource allocation for the *feasibility studies,* yet conduct studies that provide reliable results. The compromise is normally not to enter into a detailed project feasibility study. When a project is subsequently approved and begun, the document summarizing the preliminary feasibility study can serve as one of the inputs to the detailed feasibility assessment. (That is why we defer an elaborate discussion of feasibility studies to chs. 9 and 10.)

It is useful to think of assigning priorities as a two-stage process [4, pp. 55–61]: first, all infeasible projects are eliminated; second, priorities are assigned to those projects that are feasible. The same criteria may play a part in determining both feasibility and priority. Thus, a pay-back period of seven years may be considered the maximum for a project to become feasible, and priorities are assigned to other projects according to the same pay-back criterion.

Of the criteria used to assess priorities in organizations, some are quantifiable, but most are qualitative and so difficult to measure. Establishing priorities is not simple. In a hospital, for example, which application has a higher priority: the inventory re-ordering application that directly affects profitability, or the computer-aided diagnosis project that directly impacts a key task, but only indirectly affects profitability? The following is a sample list of criteria:

Some applications are prerequisites to others: what is the logical sequence of application development?

Can the organization absorb and use the application (this is termed in subsequent chapters ''organizational feasibility'')?

What is the time schedule?

What are the resource requirements in terms of people and equipment?

Does the application solve a major problem or address a key task?

What is the direct and indirect impact on profitability (this is later termed ''economical feasibility'')?

Is the technology required by the application available (this is later termed ''technological feasibility'')?

Is the application compatible with general organizational objectives and strategy?

What is the relationship to other applications in use, under development, or planned?

How does the application compare with applications developed and used in similar organizations?

What is the promotional value of the application? Will the application increase the confidence of users and management in the services offered by the information system unit?

The list reflects the fact that most criteria are intangible. It is therefore extremely important that priorities be determined jointly by user management, top management, and information system management. All are represented on the information system committee of the organization (see ch. 9). It is vital that the priorities be set forth in a document that specifies the reasons for establishing the scheme. The document can stand on its own or be a part of the master-plan document. Like any other part of the master plan, it should be reviewed and updated periodically.

Developing Project Plans

The third step in the medium-range planning process is the development of a detailed project plan for each member of the project portfolio. Such plans specify the resources and activity schedules that pertain to each project. The schedules are quite precise for the near term and more general for future years. Each project should be broken down into major phases of development and operation, and the most likely schedule for each phase decided. The next step is to determine the hardware and software technology and the facilities and personnel needed to support the various applications. The resources needed to perform the supporting activities must then be quantified and scheduled. The analysis performed at this stage may reveal a whole new set of tasks, activities, and even projects that must be undertaken.

The Information System Master-Plan Document

The medium-range planning process culminates with the preparation of the master plan document, which provides a framework for the short-range planning process and all detailed information system planning. The master plan is, in fact, a multiyear work plan that prevents the characteristically disguised unemployment of personnel and equipment between terminations and starts of individual projects. It also prevents the postponement of new project development because of unplanned excessive work loads for personnel involved in maintenance work.

The plan should be a formal document with appropriate summaries and supporting detail. The document is based on the information contained in the system development plan section of the long-range document, and on the activities performed during the medium-range planning process.

The master-plan document consists of three parts: the first part describes and analyzes the current information systems situation and derives problems and needs; the second part lists the application portfolio, sets priorities, and distinguishes between centralized and distributed applications; the third part discusses the implications of the second part on the organization in terms of the organizational structure of information systems related entities, human resource allocation, training, budgeting, and the like. The following list is a typical table of contents for a master plan document:

1. Introduction and executive summary: this chapter states the purposes of the report, describes the methodology and the resources invested in the master plan project, and summarizes the major findings and recommendations.
2. Current information systems situation: a factual description of hardware deployment, software, applications, personnel, and expenditures related to information systems in the organization.
3. Diagnosis of current situation: analysis of the current situation and derivation of problems and needs.

4. Principles: by extracting from the organizational strategy and long-range planning, the chapter states the principles that underline any future plan (e.g., common data bases, distribution/centralization, end-user computing, etc.).

5. Application portfolio: a prioritized list and a short description of future applications.

6. Centralization/distribution aspects: centralization versus distribution of information systems resources and efforts is probably the most crucial problem in many organizations (see ch. 11). This chapter sets criteria for distribution policy and consequently allocates the applications presented in the portfolio among the pertinent parties.

7. Organizational implications: this chapter discusses the organizational structure of the bodies engaged with information systems in the organization, including functions required within user departments.

8. Policies: this chapter delineates the major policies related to such areas as personnel hiring and promotion, training, in-house development of software, hardware and software acquisition, end-user computing, information systems control, and information centers (see ch. 7 for an elaborate discussion on policies).

9. Budgetary implications: projection of future investments and expenditures related to information systems (hardware, software, personnel; distinction between development and maintenance costs).

10. Procedures for planning and development: this chapter portrays the procedures required to develop an annual short-range plan, and, if the organization lacks project development standards, sets the principles for an information system life cycle (see chs. 9, 10).

11. Action plan: this concluding chapter states concrete actions to be taken by management in order to accomplish the master-plan recommendations. The action plan should name functions of those who are to be responsible for the various actions, and specify a timetable for completion. This chapter serves as a checklist for top management to assure that the master plan is indeed carried out.

Participation in Master-Plan Development

Four groups should participate in the preparation and approval of the master plan. These are the information system unit, user departments, the *information system committee* (consisting of the top functional executives and the head of information systems), and senior management (chief executive officer and vice-presidents).

Senior management and the information system committee define the objectives of the organization, and the objectives and role of the information system unit. The information system unit provides current status information. User departments, together with the information system unit and committee, identify and assign priorities to projects. The information system unit and pertaining user departments develop specific project development schedules and requirements. The information system unit prepares the master plan document. The information system committee approves the plan or requests modifications to the plan. The information system unit coordinates plan modifications until the plan is approved. Senior management reviews the master plan and approves it, or returns it to one of the preceding steps for modifications.

As you can observe, the main emphasis is on the joint work of the users and the information system unit, the involvement of the information system committee, and the approval and commitment of top management to the final version of the master plan (see ch. 13 for further elaboration on the roles of users and top management in information system planning).

Among the four planning phases (strategic, long-range, master-plan, and short-range), the master plan is considered among many to be the most important phase. The first two are too broad and might become somewhat amorphous, particularly due to the rapid changes in information technology that make it hard for an organization to foresee more than five years ahead. For example, in 1981, could you foresee the organizational impact of microcomputers, office automation, and local area networks? Therefore, the master plan becomes the top strategic plan which is still tangible, concrete, and realizable.

Many organizations prefer to hire an external consultant or a consulting firm to perform the master-planning project. There are a number of reasons to justify that. First, domestic resources are usually occupied with on-going projects and thus are hard to fully free in order to carry out such a heavy project. Second, not every organization employs personnel who are competent to deal with master planning; it requires an intellectual capacity to comprehend the organization as a whole (systems approach) and to integrate organizational and information systems issues. Third, the preparation of a master plan requires a high degree of objectivity. Internal employees are suspect of being biased; external consultants tend to be more objective and less affected by internal politics.

Hiring an external consultant is certainly recommended, provided that two conditions are met: a steering committee is appointed to review the consultant's interim and final reports and to monitor the project; and a liaison person helps the consultant to find his or her way in the organization (the liaison is a technical helper; he or she should not participate in interviewing or in report writing).

Short-Range Information System Planning

Short-range operational planning concerns the performance targets and the specific tasks, schedules, and budgets to achieve short-range objectives. The time horizon is generally one to two years. Short-range information system planning is generally equivalent to the *information system annual plan.*

The top-priority projects from the master plan make up next year's annual plan. The difference in project description in the master plan and in the annual plan is only in detail. In addition to the relatively large identifiable new projects, the following two classes of information system projects have to be incorporated in the annual plan:

Enhancement projects—Defined as desirable to make an existing system more useful to the user.

Maintenance jobs—Defined as necessary to make an existing system function efficiently.

The annual plan is usually updated once a year. Sometimes rolling plans are used, where a new plan is prepared, for example, every quarter. During each planning cycle the plan for the quarter just completed is omitted, the existing plans for the next three quarters are revised, and a new plan for the fourth quarter is added.

The people involved in the short-range planning process are mainly part of the information system unit. They include the head of the unit, project managers, and managers of functions within the unit, such as operations, programming, system design, and technical support. Normally the initial phase of the short-range planning process requires extensive involvement of user management in order to accurately determine user goals and needs for information system services.

The final product of the planning process is the annual budget for the information systems unit. This is supported by an operating plan. These two, the annual budget and the operating plan, outline the activities that will take place during the year as well as the resources required to carry these activities out. The following list is a suggested format for the annual plan [7, pp. 41–46]:

1. Service objectives and overview—This section lists the assumptions on which the plan is based and states the objectives of the information system function during the year. It summarizes succeeding sections of the plan: overall resources needed, total expenditures, and major acquisitions of hardware and software.

2. Application development and maintenance plan—This section describes all applications to be implemented during the year. Each application is covered in terms of objectives, resources needed (people, computing time, budget), schedule, and key dates. The section also states resource demands for maintenance activities.

3. Operations plan—This plan describes the work load by major application of all work areas of the operations function: data entry, computing, output quality control, data storage, and data transmission. It shows the resources needed (people, equipment, materials) to handle the work load.

4. Technical support plan—This plan describes the activities and resources needed to give technical support to the activities of application development, maintenance, and operations. The plan may be subdivided into plans covering computer performance evaluation; installation of equipment during the year; installation of system software (e.g., new releases of operating systems and data base management systems); data base administration; communications network administration; system coordination; and miscellaneous technical assistance (to users, application development staff, and operations staff).

5. Standard practices program—This section states key dates and resources needed for the implementation of standard practices (e.g., design standards, programming standards, data standards, security standards, and auditing standards).

6. Staffing and organization plan—This plan shows any major changes in the organizational structure of the information system function considered necessary for future activities. It summarizes the total demand for personnel, by category, for each organizational unit, project, and activity. It also outlines a plan of action to acquire needed resources.

7. Education and training plan—This section outlines a plan of action for developing necessary skills of new employees and existing personnel.

8. Site plan—This section covers the gross plan for the accommodation of the new resources (equipment and personnel). The plan states the needs, key dates, resources required, and other matters of particular importance.

9. Financial plan—This plan shows the cost and, where relevant, the revenues associated with all the activities during the year. All the sections of the annual plan described in steps 1 to 8 are therefore prerequisites for the financial plan. The financial plan covers the operating budget, which is expressed in terms of costs and expenses distributed among projects and organizational units. Any expected revenues should, of course, be stated. If costs are charged to ultimate users, the operating budget has to outline the expected distribution to those users (see discussion on pricing policy in ch. 13). The capital budget is also a part of the financial plan. It states the projected expenses for the acquisition of fixed assets, such as machinery, equipment, furniture, and sites.

The final step in the comprehensive information system planning process is monitoring and *updating* the annual plan. The original plan tells where the information system function and management agreed they should be at any given time during the year. Since the environment of the information system function changes and constantly impacts the plan, the first step in preparing accurate plan updates is knowing what has been accomplished to date with planned resources. Without such updates, the plan soon becomes useless. Consequently, proper monitoring and updating of the annual plan are the cornerstones of an effective planning system. The plan updates are much more effective and helpful to management if each update includes a list of major changes from the previous plan and a brief description of trouble spots. Knowing about potential problems enables management and the information system unit to anticipate and take appropriate action.

Development Strategy for Information Systems

To consider *development strategies* for information systems, first imagine that you are the head of a family. Your spouse is a sculptor. You are a free-lance writer working at home. Your two children are, respectively, an accomplished tennis player and a swimmer. You own three expensive cars. You are moving to a new city where you have purchased a vacant lot. You hire an architect to design your new home. The architect can approach the design and construction of the house in different ways. Let us further assume that you represent several identical families, each one experiencing the trauma of living in a house developed on a different approach.

For family A, the architect designed a house that had a living room, three bed-rooms, a kitchen, and a dining room. One night your Mercedes, parked on the street, was extensively damaged by vandals. You called the architect and asked him to add a covered garage to the house. Two months later you discovered that your living room was full of sculptures. You then asked the architect to add a studio to the house. Your spouse was happy, but there was no room left on the lot for a pool and a tennis court, which your children wanted. You blamed the architect for using an ad hoc approach, and you started looking for another vacant lot and another architect.

The architect hired by family B spent a few days with them in their old home, observing and recording their activities and needs. The new house was seemingly a perfect accommodation for all members of the family. The architect succeeded in squeezing into the lot a tennis court, a pool, a studio, and office space, leaving not one foot of the lot unused. Soon you discovered that life in the house had become unbear-able: when the children swam and played tennis and your spouse chiseled, you could not do your writing. You blamed the architect for using a data-collection approach, and you started looking for a vacant lot and another architect.

The architect hired by family C started by charting the structure of the family and the functions of each member. He documented that one parent was a writer, one parent was a sculptor, and the children were college-age athletes. The new house you moved into was a dream. It had three study rooms, one for each of the children and for you, a big studio for your spouse, a tennis court, and a swimming pool. The kitchen was small and well equipped to prepare light meals. You soon found out that the children's study rooms were rarely used, and your spouse, who happened to be a gourmet cook, was raising hell. You summoned the architect and he told you that college students have to do a lot of studying at home and that a sculptor is assumed not to devote much time to cooking and entertaining guests for dinner. You blamed the architect for using an organization chart approach, and you started looking for a new architect and a vacant lot.

These anecdotes illustrate approaches adopted by many organizations for the de-velopment of their information systems. Obviously they are inappropriate. Current practices call for different approaches to developing information systems.

Inappropriate Approaches

The Ad Hoc Approach

An *ad hoc* approach, or fire fighting, has been adopted when the development of in-formation systems is carried out without preplanning and according to emerging needs. There is no master plan, and discrete applications without regard to any integration among them are made. The results of this approach are islands of computerized sys-tems. An ad hoc approach is justified only when the organization is under rapid or-ganizational change. When the organization stabilizes, such systems are normally redesigned.

The Data-Collection Approach

The *data-collection* approach assumes that systems are best developed after all the data is on hand. Representative samples of every kind of information that flows within an organization must be collected. A variant of this is the data-base approach, which leads to the establishment and maintenance of a giant data base with highly detailed data containing everything needed by all managerial and operational levels. The data base is shared among all users who access data relevant to their purposes. Data is collected, stored, and updated without a prior analysis of what use can be made of it. When a requirement for specific information arises, special processing has to be performed to produce this information.

The approach is usually justified on the grounds that not all information requirements can be projected, and therefore the only way to develop a system is to store all data and provide tools for its retrieval and processing. The approach presents tremendous practical difficulties because it is impossible to collect, store, and update all data, and then do special processing whenever a user needs information.

The Organization Chart Approach

The *organization chart* approach assumes that information systems generally follow organizational lines. Points of information interchange between systems are dealt with on an ad hoc basis. Basic transactions that are vital to many functions tend to be dealt with redundantly and separately by each functionally oriented system.

This approach, though common and plausible in theory, creates practical difficulties. Independent development of separate applications results in considerable duplication of design effort. Processing and information needs of the organization do not always coincide with existing organizational boundaries. For example, a sales transaction stimulates direct activities in sales, distribution, accounts receivable, finished goods inventory, and general ledger; and indirect activities in production and procurement systems. Distribution of monthly sales is certainly key data for managements of all these functions.

An information system conforming strictly to organizational boundaries has difficulty dealing with interdepartmental activities. Information along lines other than existing ones would be difficult to obtain, unless provisions were made to exchange information across boundaries using a common coding scheme.

Appropriate Approaches

The Top-Down Approach

The *top-down* approach, illustrated in figure 8.1, assumes that once the kinds of information that management needs have been determined, the systems necessary to supply the information can be designed. This approach begins by defining the objectives of the organization for which the system is developed. The activities of the organization are then identified, and the decisions necessary to operate them are specified. The major information requirements for those decisions are then determined. The next step

Figure 8.1 Steps in a top-down approach

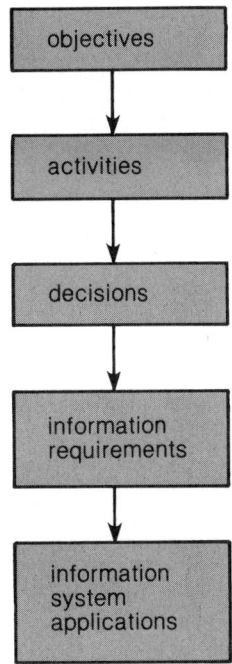

is to define subsystems (applications) and assign priorities for their development, with due regard to opportunities for integration. This constitutes the master plan. A frequently used top-down technique is the business system planning method developed by IBM [6].

The essence of the top-down approach is identification of the overall information requirements of the organization and development of information systems according to these requirements. The emphasis on identification before development facilitates integration of the various systems.

The Bottom-Up Approach

The *bottom-up* approach starts with the subsystems that produce operational information within some general conceptual framework and then adds the subsystems that produce management information. (Refer to ch. 5 for the distinction between these two types of information.) The resulting master plan thus reflects the orderly development and integration of the subsystems that grew in response to requests for information.

The approach, diagrammed in figure 8.2, begins by developing separate applications producing operational information, each with its own files. Related files are then integrated into a common data base supported by a data base management system. (See appendix A on the subject of data base management systems.) The next step is the addition of modules for planning and decision making that support the operational

Figure 8.2 The bottom-up approach

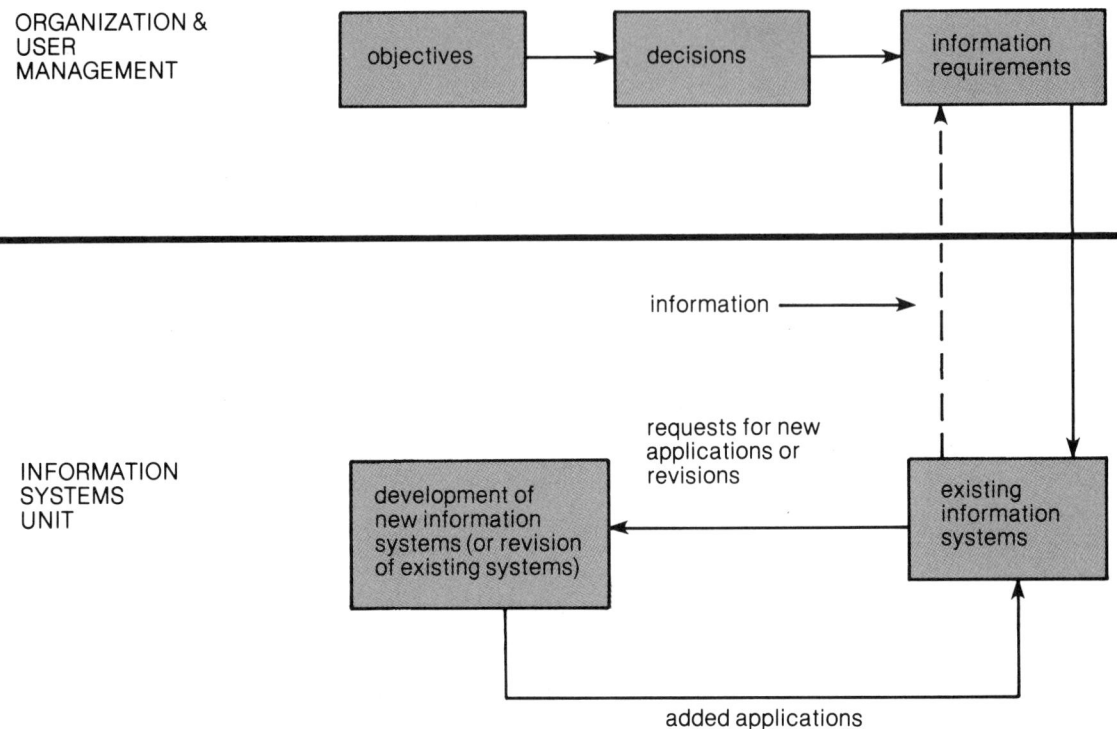

control and management control levels of the organization (see ch. 5). Finally the modules are integrated into a model base and the data base is expanded to include external data. At this stage the information systems can support decisions made by top management (the strategic planning level).

Bottom-up development expands in response to the real needs of the organization. Its main disadvantage is that the overall information requirements of the organization cannot be estimated in advance. The integration of the various applications, therefore, is not optimal. As information systems grow, they have to be redesigned because the initial design could not adequately account for the future scope of the systems.

The Evolutionary Approach

The *evolutionary* or modular approach is the most extreme form of the bottom-up approach. Like it, and unlike the top-down approach, the general model of the organization is undefined. But unlike the bottom-up approach, the evolutionary approach does not define even the general framework for the information systems. Not only does it develop systems on the basis of emerging operational needs, it also integrates them only as needs arise. There are two dimensions to the evolution: (1) the comprehensive information system evolves with the changing nature and needs of the organization; and (2) specific subsystems evolve over time in response to changing operational information needs and to the changing nature of the comprehensive information system itself.

Lest you think that the evolutionary and the ad hoc approaches are alike, we emphasize again that the former is devised by means of planning (long-, medium-, and short-range) whereas the latter is completely arbitrary.

The Parallel Approach

The *parallel* approach (see [3]) attempts to minimize the disadvantages of the bottom-up and the top-down approaches and to incorporate their advantages. In the first stage of this approach, operational information and management information systems are developed and operated independently. As both types evolve, efforts are made to use as much information as can be accessed from operational systems, as input to the management information systems. At the same time, management systems are developed to utilize the information available in the operational information systems that have been built. When this approach is followed consistently, the two types of systems will converge and will eventually become integrated into a total information system. This approach might be called an outside-in, or implosive, approach, since development begins relatively independently at both ends and the systems so developed undergo controlled evolution, each in the direction of the other.

The Middle-Out Approach

The approaches previously outlined have been advocated for the development of conventional TPS and SDS. Chapter 9 will introduce approaches for developing DSS that are specifically oriented to the technologies, environment, users, and information needs that are characteristic of DSS. We now turn to discuss one of these approaches, the *middle-out* approach, which is akin to the evolutionary approach, and can be adopted to develop conventional systems if the circumstances merit it.

Middle-out development (in contrast to top-down and bottom-up) relies on prototyping (see chs. 9 and 10), and designing-by-using. The approach begins close to the level of the problem at hand, and involves a cyclical process of generalizing (bottom-up) and specifying (top-down) at each stage of the development process [5]. Middle-out development begins with a much less global view of the environment than is conventional with most top-down approaches. In the top-down approach, there is an implicit notion of a wide-range plan, which structures the entire problem area being tackled. The approach and system plan must be completely developed before being implemented. Top-down analysis often means that a long period of time will be spent on global designs without ever getting down to concrete details. In decision support situations, the feedback obtained in the design and implementation process is crucial and means that extensive top-down analysis in the beginning has little value.

Bottom-up efforts, on the other hand, involve the development of building blocks (tools) that can later be used to construct solutions to information needs. However, this tool-building activity (e.g., constructing a data base) can cease to be a means to an end and become an end in itself. Bottom-up analysis generally suffers from distraction and from lack of decision-maker perspective. Many systems designers enjoy the task of building tools, even though the tools may not be well suited to the decision-making task at hand.

In middle-out development, a prototype system that supports an important but separable part of the overall problem is built quickly and used on the relevant part of the problem. The prototype helps solve that part of the problem immediately, and provides quick feedback on the structuring of the problem and on the use of the technique. The designer can use the feedback in refining that part, or in building other parts; or, the feedback may lead to a decision to abandon the whole project. The modules developed in middle-out mode may later be connected in order to solve some larger system problem, but this is not a precondition for building the modules. Another important purpose of a prototype is to establish the value of the system before many resources are spent on it.

A Concluding Remark

Now that the main elements of various acceptable approaches have been outlined, one might well wonder which is the best. As with other issues in information systems, no single approach is optimal for all organizations. Each approach has its advantages and disadvantages; each has its opponents and its proponents. The master plan for information systems can be prepared using any of the approaches. Although the top-down and the bottom-up approaches have been presented as alternatives, they are by no means mutually exclusive; the parallel approach, in essence, combines the two.

The top-down approach is generally favored by academics, who stress that information systems development should be a central mission of the organization, integrated into its objectives and strategy. Practitioners generally favor the bottom-up approach; it is more common in reality. We believe that each of the approaches presented in this section can provide a basis for a successful information system master plan when applied in appropriate circumstances. The approach adopted should depend on the structure of the organization, its complexity, size, environment, management philosophy, involvement of top management in the information system planning and development processes, and the organization's experience with computerized information systems.

Practical Conclusions for Information System Design and Use

The following conclusions are guidelines for information systems design and use.

1. Planning is a prerequisite to the successful development and use of information systems.

2. Strategic planning provides the framework for all information system plans.

3. Information system objectives must conform to and interrelate with organizational objectives.

4. There is a hierarchy of plans. This hierarchy is determined by the time horizon, detail, and operation.

5. Resources must be allocated to the planning activities.

6. Appropriate planning methodology at each planning phase prevents misallocation of resources at subsequent phases of the planning hierarchy.

7. The strategic plan should be developed by top management and not by the information system staff.

8. Schedules or priorities of project development should not be assigned in the long-range plan.

9. The long-range information system plan should be prepared by the senior executives and the information system committee and approved by top management.

10. The medium-range planning process should result in a master plan for information system development and information system activities.

11. The priority scheme for ranking projects to be implemented should be derived from overall organizational objectives.

12. A preliminary feasibility study must be conducted for each project before priorities can be assigned.

13. The priority scheme should be jointly developed by top management, user management, and information system management.

14. The master plan provides the framework for the annual plans and individual project plans.

15. The information system committee, user management, and information system staff should participate in preparing the master plan.

16. Top management should give final approval to the master plan.

17. The annual information system plan should be prepared by the information system unit and approved by the information system committee.

18. All stages of information systems planning should be thoroughly documented as a guide to subsequent planning and development, as a measure for control, and as a basis for evaluation and change.

19. There is no one optimal strategic plan for information systems. Each organization must develop the strategy that best fits its own situation.

20. A plan from the host organization that identifies its objectives is a prerequisite to effective strategic planning for information systems.

21. The planning process must be dynamic—i.e., flexible and adaptable to changing circumstances.

Summary

A comprehensive information system plan is vital to the successful development and use of information systems in organizations. The information system planning process has to be an integral part of the overall organizational planning efforts.

Information system planning begins with the establishment of a strategic plan, which provides a framework within which subsequent plans are to be developed. Strategic planning is the process of deciding on objectives for the information system function, on the resources required to obtain these objectives, and on the policies that are to govern the acquisition, use, and disposition of the resources. Implementation of the strategic plan involves the development of a hierarchy of plans, each being more detailed, concrete, and operational than the preceding one. The responsibility for preparing the strategic information system plan rests with top management.

With a time horizon of five to ten years, long-range conceptual planning for information systems is concerned with the general courses of action and broad types of resources to carry out information system strategies. No schedules or priorities of project development are assigned in the long-range plan. Only rough estimates of resource requirements exist. The plan should be updated annually, with the constraints imposed by the strategic plan. The responsibility for preparing the long-range plan rests with the senior executive in charge of information systems and the information system committee; it must be approved by top management. The long-range planning process consists of collecting background information, analyzing overall needs, and preparing the long-range plan document.

The medium-range managerial planning process deals with the medium-range information system objectives that can be achieved by specific projects within two to five years. The product of the process is the master plan for developing the information systems that are necessary to meet the present information needs of the organization. Given the objectives, needs, and constraints established in the long-range plan, the medium-range planning develops a portfolio of projects with assigned priorities; it defines resources and action plans for implementing the projects; and it prepares the master plan. Four groups participate in the preparation and approval of the master plan: the information system staff, user departments, the information system committee, and top management.

The short-range operational planning is generally equivalent to the information systems annual plan. It is concerned with the performance targets and the specific tasks, schedules, and budgets to achieve short-range objectives. The final product of the planning process is the annual budget for the information system unit, supported by an operating plan. The final step in the comprehensive information system planning process is monitoring and updating the annual plan.

Various approaches can be adopted for the development of the master plan or individual information systems. Inappropriate approaches are the ad hoc approach, the data collection approach, and the organization chart approach. Appropriate approaches include the top-down approach, the bottom-up approach, the evolutionary approach, the middle-out approach, and the parallel approach. Each has its advantages and disadvantages. The selection of an approach depends on the special circumstances of the organization.

Information system project implementation occurs within a framework of the objectives, strategies, and policies adopted by the organization. While the responsibility for strategic planning rests with top management, responsibility for implementing specific projects rests with the head of the information system function and the project managers. The next chapter is devoted to the phases and activities of developing and implementing an information system project.

Key Concepts

approach: ad hoc, bottom-up, data
  base, data collection, evolutionary,
  middle-out, organization chart,
  parallel, top-down
development strategy
enhancement projects
feasibility study
information system annual plan
information system charter

information system committee
information system plan updates
master plan
planning: conceptual, long-range,
  managerial, medium-range,
  operational, short-range, strategic
priority scheme
project portfolio

References

1. Anthony, R. N. *Planning and Control Systems: A Framework for Analysis.* Boston, MA: Graduate School of Business Administration, Harvard University, 1965.
2. Cash, J. I., F. W. McFarlan, J. L. McKenney, and L. M. Applegate. *Corporate Information Systems Management: Text and Cases,* 3d ed. Homewood, IL: Richard D. Irwin, 1992.
3. Ein-Dor, P. "Parallel Strategy for MIS." *Journal of Systems Management* 26, no. 3 (March 1975): 30–35.
4. Ein-Dor, P., and E. Segev. *Managing Management Information Systems.* Lexington, MA: D.C. Heath, 1978.
5. Hurst, E. G., D. N. Ness, T. J. Gambino, and T. H. Johnson. "Growing DSS: A Flexible Evolutionary Approach." In *Building Decision Support Systems,* edited by J. L. Bennett. Reading, MA: Addison-Wesley, 1983.
6. IBM. *Business Systems Planning—Information Systems Planning Guide*, Form GE20-052701. White Plains, NY: IBM, 1975.
7. IBM. *Managing the Data Processing Organization*, Form GE19-5208-0. Lidingo, Sweden: IBM, 1976.
8. Lientz, B. P., and M. Chen. "Long Range Planning for Information Services." *Long Range Planning* 13, no. 1 (February 1980): 55–61.
9. McLean, E. R., and J. V. Soden, eds. *Strategic Planning for MIS.* New York: Wiley-Interscience, 1977.

10. Miller, W. B. "Developing a Long-Range EDP Plan." *Journal of Systems Management* 30, no. 7 (July 1979): 36–39.
11. Rush, R. L. "MIS Planning in Distributed Data Processing Systems." *Journal of Systems Management* 30, no. 8 (August 1979): 17–25.
12. Schwartz, M. H. "MIS Planning." *Datamation* 26, no. 10 (September 1970): 28–31.

Questions

1. Differentiate among the following plans: strategic, long-range, medium-range, and short-range.
2. Describe the three steps necessary to devising a long-range plan.
3. What is meant by a "project portfolio" and what purpose does it serve?
4. What should be included in a master-plan document?
5. Explain why short-range information system planning can be considered equivalent to the information system annual plan.
6. Why are the ad hoc, data collection, and organization chart approaches inappropriate?

Problems

The Widget Manufacturing Company has decided to create a management information system for its company. The ultimate plan is to provide top management with detailed operational data that can be used in forecasting future development for the company. The initial plan is to set up a system for collecting, organizing, and storing the raw data. The company already has a large mainframe computer in-house, which was previously used for personnel files and manufacturing operations.

1. Write a charter for the Widget Manufacturing Company information system unit.
2. Stating explicitly any assumptions you have made, describe the long-range information system plan.
3. What possible information system projects might be contained in the project portfolio?
4. Create a short-range plan document.
5. Which approach would you use for developing the information system? Why?

Thornton County Office of Education

The Thornton County Office of Education is by contractual agreements the administrative agent for nine Special Education Local Plan Areas (SELPA). Each SELPA is composed of two to fifteen school districts and has responsibility for providing a full range of special education services to all of the disabled pupils who live within its geographical boundaries (see fig. 8.3). Pupil, staff, and financial data must be collected from each school district and aggregated at the SELPA level to produce state pupil counts two times per year, a federal pupil count once a year, and income reports three times per year. All of the required federal and state pupil reporting involves matrix aggregation of data by handicapping condition, age grouping, instructional setting, and ethnicity. The income reporting involves complex calculations based on staff counts and generates the special education income for each district and the SELPA office. In addition, pupil counts and teacher/pupil ratios are monitored on a monthly basis within each SELPA. Periodically, modified pupil and/or staff reporting are required by the State Department of Education due to legislative requests.

To meet the reporting requirements, the county office designed a special education management information system (SEMIS) in 1979 and implemented it in 1981. The current system involves online transaction processing and operates on a large mainframe computer with information stored in a relational database. The system has gone through numerous changes since it was instituted. Each district and SELPA office are connected through a terminal to the mainframe by dedicated telephone lines with communications handled by a network of four front-end processors (see fig. 8.4). Each district is responsible for entering its pupil and staff data through a terminal. At the district level, batch reports are produced on a monthly cycle or request basis to assist in the informational and administrative needs of the district. At the SELPA level, information can be monitored either by online summary screens or SELPA level batch reports. All required state and federal reporting is at the SELPA level. There are no required county level reports. There is also no structured decision making in the system, and the decision support function is limited to preprogrammed summary information with no ad hoc query capability. While thorough documentation is available for the system, there is no current master or operational plan. The SEMIS is one of seven online transaction processing systems operating on the county mainframe computer.

Within the county office, the Division of Special Education is responsible for communication between the district/SELPA staff and the County Information System Department. A division committee acts as the liaison between the technical staff and users. In the IS department, a systems analyst is assigned to the SEMIS with programming staff assigned as needed. Within each SELPA, a program council, composed of a program director from each district, meets monthly and is responsible for the ongoing decision making and planning. A superintendents' council meets on a quarterly basis to handle major financial and policy decisions (see fig. 8.5). An administrator, who is employed by the county office for each SELPA, acts as the executive secretary for each council and is responsible for submitting required reports.

Due to continual underfunding, it has become necessary to consider methods for cutting special education program costs. The current SEMIS system costs about $22.00 per pupil. The SELPAs are questioning whether a less sophisticated system could be developed to meet the

Figure 8.3 Current organization

CURRENT ORGANIZATION

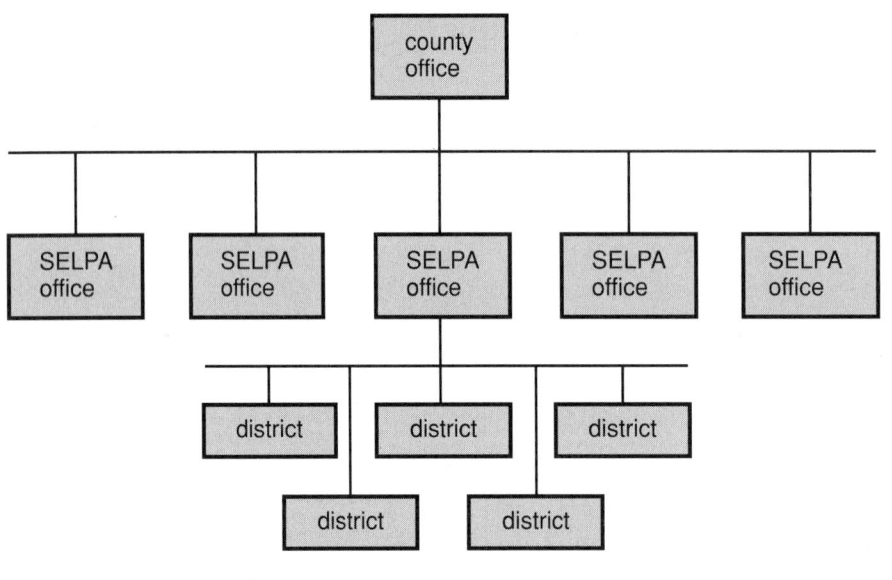

Figure 8.4 Current system configuration

CURRENT SYSTEM CONFIGURATION

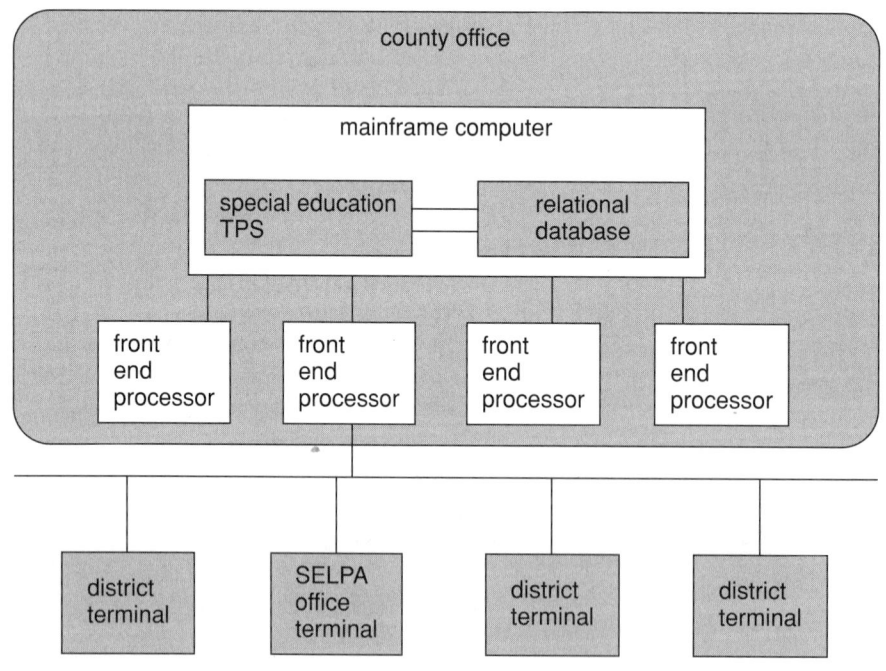

Figure 8.5 Governance structure

GOVERNANCE STRUCTURE

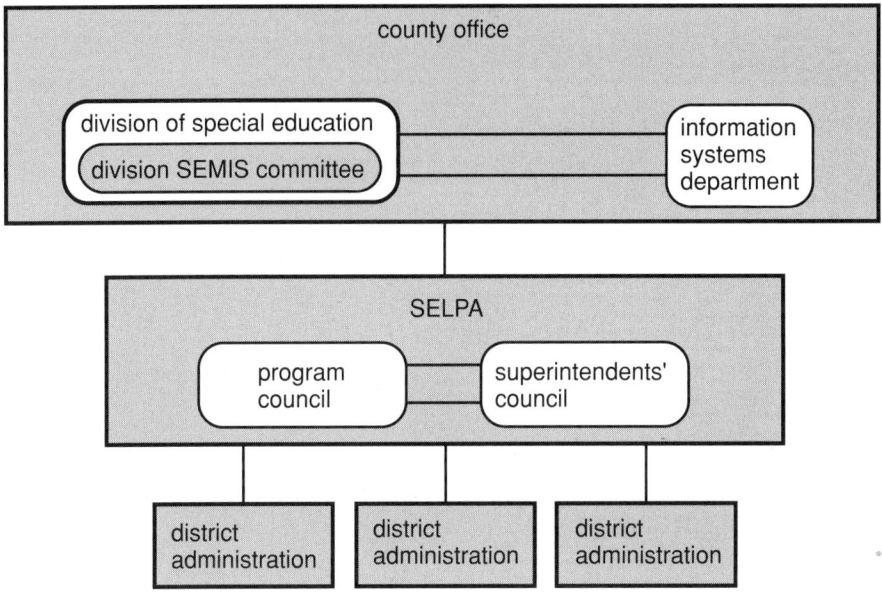

reporting and monitoring needs at a cheaper per-pupil rate with savings to be applied to program needs. Specifically, the following issues have been raised:

1. Based on current reporting requirements, is a transaction processing system really necessary to meet the information needs?

2. Given the advances in microcomputer technology, software, and networking, could a system be developed that would operate within each SELPA at a lesser cost?

3. Could a report-generating system be incorporated to allow each district to develop its own reporting formats and also perform ad hoc inquiries?

4. If a single SELPA is not large enough to support its own system, could two or three SELPAs join in operating a system?

Questions

Assume that you are an outside information system consultant who has been hired to assist in planning for possible changes.

1. Indicate the type of development strategy that you would utilize and why.

2. Briefly outline the activities that you would undertake in developing a master plan for change to the current SEMIS system. Include a list of personnel that you would contact in completing your project.

3. Assume that this case study is the analysis of the present situation. Provide a summary of the major sections that you would include in the remainder of a master plan, indicating the primary emphasis of each.

Chapter 9 *Information System Life Cycle*

Once the organization has established its information system policy and priorities for developing its individual information systems, it has a framework within which these individual applications can be developed.

This chapter describes the various phases and activities of an information system life cycle. It explains why information systems are periodically replaced by new versions. It outlines the various activities and emphasizes the different roles of developers, users, and management. And it indicates significant phases of the life cycle.

Introduction

Chapter 8 described how the organization establishes the strategy and policy for development and use of information systems. These culminate in the creation of a master plan that lists the priorities for developing individual systems or applications.

This chapter outlines the phases of development through which any individual information system goes. These phases are part of a *life cycle,* ranging from an initial information requirement—problem or opportunity—through the design, development, and operation of the system, to an eventual termination of the system, which triggers a life cycle of a new system. The approach taken is user-/management-oriented; it emphasizes the logical nature of *what* should be done, rather than the technical specifications involved in *how* the various steps of the life cycle should be carried out. The reader interested in learning more about techniques is urged to consult the references at the end of both this chapter and chapter 10.

The life cycle concept is not unique to information systems. An analogous concept applies to the development of a new product. The main idea inherent to the life cycle is that the development and operation of any system must evolve through the same consistent and logical process without ignoring any step. The development of an information system resembles the construction of a building. In most cases, buildings are not similar, but their construction phases are identical.

The sameness in the views of system life cycles is more likely to reflect recognition of an inherent logical sequence than borrowings from earlier writings. The logical progression from phase to phase appears so obvious that it is difficult to understand how system development could proceed in any other manner. Yet many organizations suffer schedule slips and cost overruns because stages in the life of a system are ignored.

This chapter discusses the following four major phases of a life cycle: *definition, construction, implementation,* and *operation*. Each phase produces its own set of documents. Often production and review of these documents form the milestones for determining completion of a phase.

Lest you be misled by the linear nature of the life cycle, we must point out that in practice it is an *iterative process*. Frequently questions arise during design that necessitate changes in requirements, or else design problems are detected during implementation. Generally it is desirable to reduce the looping back to previous stages as much as possible, implying that the people involved in each phase must possess some foresight into the next phase to know if their work is correct and complete.

There are many descriptions of the *phases* or steps involved in the information system life cycle, yet, surprisingly, the various writers (and organizations) do not present different approaches to the subject. They all start with a determination of what the system is to do; go through a design phase, an implementation phase, and operation of the system; and end with obsolescence. The similarity of different life cycle descriptions is illustrated in table 9.1.

The Reasons for a Finite Life Cycle

The life cycle of an information system is, on the average, four to ten years. This finite process begins and ends with a recognition that information needs are not being met effectively or efficiently by the existing information system. In between the beginning and the end are the phases of designing the system to meet recognized needs, building the system, and operating the system until it becomes obsolete. All systems eventually become outmoded due to various reasons. Paradoxically, the system that has just successfully completed the design phase is already on the road to obsolescence. More adaptable systems will last longer or require less extensive modifications, but even the most sophisticated system will eventually come under renewed scrutiny, and the information system life cycle will begin again.

You may recall the discussion in chapter 4 of the eight basic characteristics of a system: purpose, environment, boundaries, constraints, input, output, system components, and interrelations among the components. These characteristics are constantly affected to a greater or lesser degree throughout the life of the system. The result is that the effectiveness or efficiency of the system, or both, are reduced, thereby necessitating investments in modifications. As the pressures accumulate, modifications are patched one on top the other. Finally, the cost of modifying the system does not warrant the benefits gained, and the organization decides to replace the current system.

Assume that an organization developed in the past a computerized accounts receivable system that operated in a batch processing mode. Current transactions were recorded on manual forms and converted once a month by keying in to a PC and recording them on a diskette. The customer file was kept on a removable disk pack and updated monthly from the diskette. A monthly report was provided to the credit

Table 9.1   Comparison of Life Cycle Descriptions

Davis and Olson [6]	Jordan and Machesky [13]	Lucas [16]	Pressman [21]	Jalote [11]
Feasibility assessment	Requirements determination	Inception	System engineering	System feasibility
		Feasibility study		
Information analysis	Evaluation of alternatives	Systems analysis	Analysis	Requirements analysis and project planning
System design	Design specification	Design	Design	System design
		Specifications		Detailed design
Program development	Implementation	Programming	Code	Coding
		Testing	Testing	Testing and integration
Procedure development				
		Training		
Conversion		Conversion/ installation		Installation
Operation and maintenance		Operations	Maintenance	Operations and maintenance
Postaudit				

manager. This example illustrates the main technological, economic, and human factors that can affect the system's characteristics, including the following:

1. Increase in input quantities—The average annual rate of growth of credit sales was 20 percent. This led to more keying of transactions and more computer time to update the file. Initially the organization handled the increased loads by purchasing additional PCs, hiring additional data entry clerks, and using the existing computer on a night shift (requiring overtime pay to the operators).

2. Advances in technology—Advanced technology usually provides given outputs at lower costs or more outputs at the same costs compared to the old technology. In our example the organization decided to store the accounts receivable file on a new (faster and less expensive) fixed disk storage device and to record the transactions by means of online input terminals. This considerably reduced the cost of data entry, storage, and processing, and it enabled the accounts receivable department to cope with the constantly increasing data volume.

3. Changes in other related systems—The accounting department decided to switch from the preparation of a monthly to a biweekly trial balance. This meant that the accounts receivable system was required to change its updating cycle accordingly.

4. Changes in the environment—A software house offered to sell to the organization a sophisticated credit-scoring program that guaranteed a better rate of return on the investment in accounts receivable. This required a change in the layout of the records to include the moving average of monthly sales to customer.

5. Changes in user expectations and requirements—Initially, the system produced monthly and then biweekly reports to the credit manager and to the accounting department. One day the credit manager demanded the capability of immediate access to the account of every customer using terminals that were introduced to the organization. His demand was backed by the information system committee. The head of the information system department reported to the committee that this would require a major overhaul of the existing accounts receivable information system.

Obviously some of these events in the life of a system can be concurrent. It is typical that increases in data quantities are handled by the adoption of new technology, or that new technology triggers new user requirements. Note that information systems are constantly evolving. When the changes are relatively minor, we refer to them as maintenance activities. When they are more substantial, we refer to them as modifications. When the change is a major one, it may lead to the replacement of the existing system.

Figure 9.1 graphically portrays the accumulation of events occurring during the last phase of the system life cycle, the phase of operations. During the first period of the system in operation, errors and bugs and *requests for changes* follow a downward trend, reducing the costs of operation and maintenance. This is the period of infancy, or the takeoff period. In the second period of maturity, the errors and requests for changes are relatively stable. In the last period, old age, the costs of operation and maintenance point toward a new life cycle.

The life cycle phases engage various organization personnel. In the development process, many organizational elements are represented: professional, managerial, and status backgrounds. These include users of the specific application being developed, management, and various implementors. The people may work as individuals or in teams and committees, depending on the size and complexity of the application. This chapter reviews the roles, responsibilities, and functions of these people and organizational bodies and how they relate to each other. This state of affairs dictates an information system that can be divided into subsystems with clearly identified interfaces, treated with the knowledge that they will integrate into one harmonious system at the conclusion of the process.

Figure 9.1 Typical development of costs of system operation and maintenance

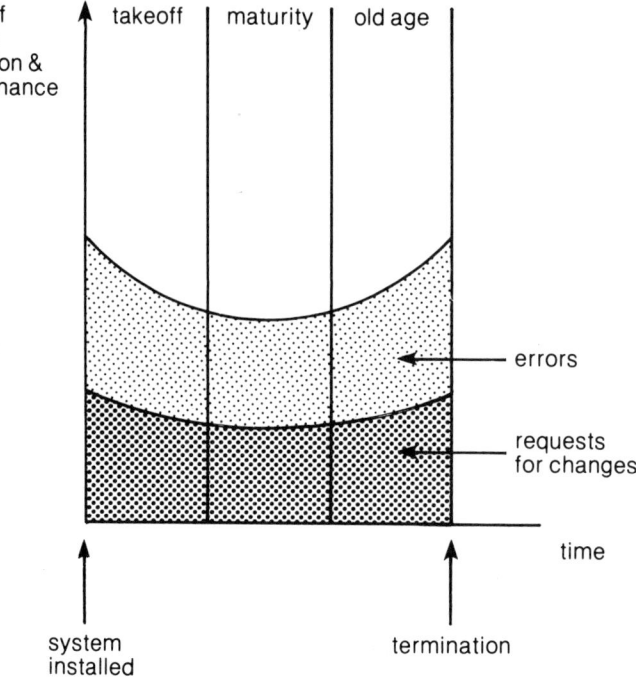

Common Problems in Developing Information Systems

Organizations that have developed computerized information systems have reported some common problems. The following list identifies some of these:

The investment in development and operation is greater than planned.

The timetable for development is too long.

The implementors of the system do not meet the planned schedule.

Major information requirements are not provided by the developed systems.

The installation requires great effort and experiences setbacks.

The outputs of the installed systems are unreliable.

The expected benefits from the systems are not achieved.

These reported problems are usually caused by the following reasons:

The scope of the information system to be developed is too large.

During development the large scope is reduced, so that the realized benefits from the system are less than the expected ones.

Insufficient time is devoted to the definition phase, resulting in incomplete specifications.

There is no comprehensive and consistent framework for controlling the development process.

General management and the future users of the systems are not involved in the development process.

To eliminate the problems so frequently encountered, the following two steps should be taken:

Structure the process of developing information systems.

Establish well-defined control points throughout the process and clear procedures for the activities to be performed at such points.

Phases of the Information System Life Cycle

The information system life cycle reflects the process of developing and operating computerized information systems. It encompasses the following subjects:

Characteristics of the environment in which the process takes place

Basic principles of the process

Activities and implementors of the process

Organization of the process

Environmental Characteristics Affecting the Life Cycle

There are several environmental characteristics that critically influence the development process, including the following:

1. Rapid advances in software and hardware technologies affect economic justification of computerized information systems. For example, prices of microcomputers dropped substantially during the 1980s. Even more significant was the dramatic increase in their capabilities: the speed with which they operate, the amount of memory they can use, the capacity of their auxiliary storage, and the quality and variety of their output devices. Consequently, a technical solution that was once economically unacceptable might turn out to be very economical in a short period.

2. A long time is needed to develop information systems, and today's systems are more complex and larger than systems in the past. Consequently, when the decision to develop a system is made, the decision makers cannot completely comprehend the nature of the system to which they will commit considerable resources.

3. The resources needed for developing and operating information systems are increasing with time.

4. The supply of expert personnel needed for developing and operating information systems is lagging behind the demand in both quality and quantity.

5. There are difficulties in communications between the systems developers and users. The difficulties appear during the phase of determining information requirements, during the development process, and during the operation of the systems.

The emerging conclusion is that decisions on system development are definitely made with uncertainty. The more complex the system, the higher the degree of uncertainty. The main purpose of structuring rigorous life cycle procedures is to reduce this uncertainty to the necessary minimum.

Basic Principles of Information System Life Cycle

The content, implementors, and documentation of the various phases of the life cycle that are described in the next section are derived from several basic principles whose application is of paramount importance. The following list of eighteen items outlines these principles.

1. Developing a new information system requires investment of resources, which should be justified, as for any other capital project. Some or all of the following factors should be taken into account:
   The net value of the system, including all present and future expenditures on it (i.e., costs of development and operation)
   The economic life of the system (remember that the system has a finite life span)
   The salvage value of the system to be replaced by the new system (i.e., what are the net additional benefits expected from the new system?)
   The net benefits of the system (does the new system produce the highest net benefits of all the alternative systems that can be developed?)

2. Every information system must have quantitative measures of its effectiveness—i.e., does the system achieve its purpose? The system itself should, preferably, produce information for such measures. Note that information systems serving the operations level of the organization (for example, transaction processing systems—see chs. 5 and 6) are characterized by more tangible benefits and, therefore, the measures of effectiveness can be assessed more easily than those of management information systems. The problem is amplified even more when the effectiveness of DSS and other small and personal systems is concerned. This is one of the reasons that the life cycles of TPS and other large systems differ from those of DSS and other small systems, as we shall see later in this chapter.

3. The system is being developed for a user. This implies that the user should be actively involved in the developmental process. Economic justification of the project is the user's responsibility. The logical specifications of the system

must be approved by the user before the construction phase (the user should, preferably, participate in defining the specifications). The user is responsible for implementing the system in his or her organizational unit (be it a department, a division, or an organization as a whole). The procedures for using the system must be approved by the user before being disseminated; this can be done by the user's active participation in procedure development.

4. Since the development process of a computerized information system is time consuming and complex, it must be partitioned into controlled segments. The end of each segment constitutes a checkpoint where the work done up to that point is evaluated and the planning for the remainder of the project is reviewed.

   The life cycle of an information system is made up of four major phases (these will be further subdivided into steps in the next section). These are

   Definition
   Construction
   Implementation
   Operation

   The first three pertain to the development process; the fourth to the operation and maintenance process. Controlling these processes raises some difficulties: a controller external to the development team does not have a good grasp of the preoperation phases of the system; the developers tend to vehemently defend their work; development is usually under time pressure; and there is a tendency to assign to the control activities relatively low-level employees who cannot withstand the pressures of the system developers. Recently, it has become common to delegate control over system development to electronic data processing (EDP) auditors (see ch. 14).

5. Those in charge should not hesitate to stop the development of a system if the situation merits this decision. Such a decision should preferably be made during the definition phase, while the investment is still relatively small. Figure 9.2 provides a rough idea of the proportionate allocation of investment in personnel in the three development phases of the life cycle. While the percentages will vary with different systems, those shown are indicative of the relatively small investment in the definition phase.

   There is another advantage to stopping the life cycle at the definition phase. The development of an information system involves several major risks, including the following:

   The system may be the wrong system (it does not solve the informational problems of the users).
   The system may be technically infeasible (the technology needed to implement it is not available).
   The system may be organizationally infeasible (the organization is not ready to accept its installation and operation).

   Figure 9.3 indicates that the definition phase is the most appropriate time to cope with these risks. This phase, which is the least structured of

Figure 9.2 Rough percentage of investment in personnel in information system development

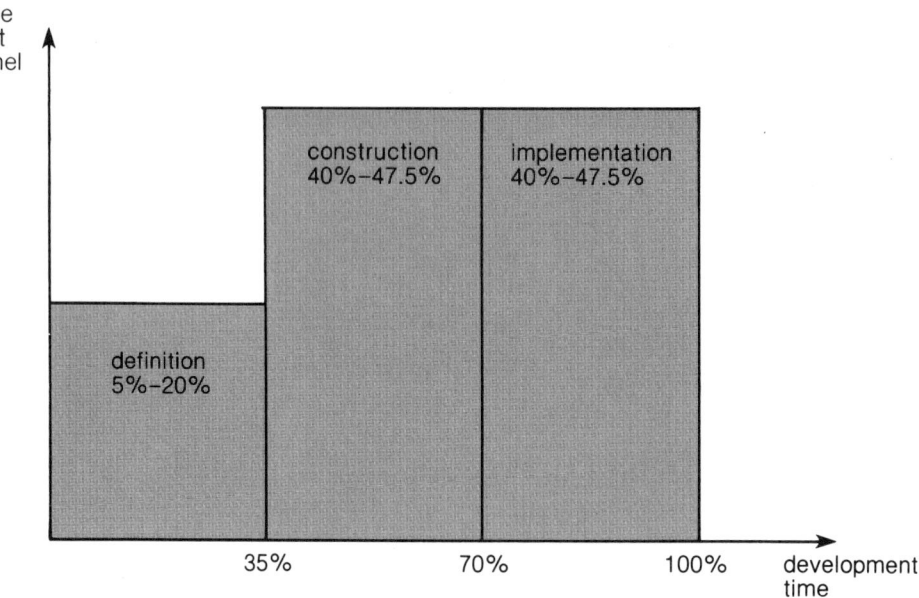

the development phases and the one involving the most creative work, should therefore be assigned the most qualified personnel. Being the least expensive phase, sufficient time should be allocated to it so that all potential risks are removed.

6. The active participation of the management of the organization in the life cycle must be mainly in the definition phase. Correct execution of this phase goes a long way toward ensuring success of the ensuing phases. In principle, directing the development phases and exercising control over the operation phase should not be left to the information system experts alone; management should assume responsibility for these activities and exert control over all of them.

7. The development of an information system is an iterative process. The top-down process starts with a macro perspective of the system and progresses to micro components. It is natural to find out while performing advanced-phase activities that there is an incompatibility between the detailed activities and the overall definition of the system. This will require returning to (iterating) an earlier stage in order to resolve the incompatibility. Virtually every one of the steps in the development process may produce information that can provide suitable modifications to one or more of the preceding steps. Thus, the step of system design can produce information that may revise the

Figure 9.3 Causes for failure in development versus cumulative development costs

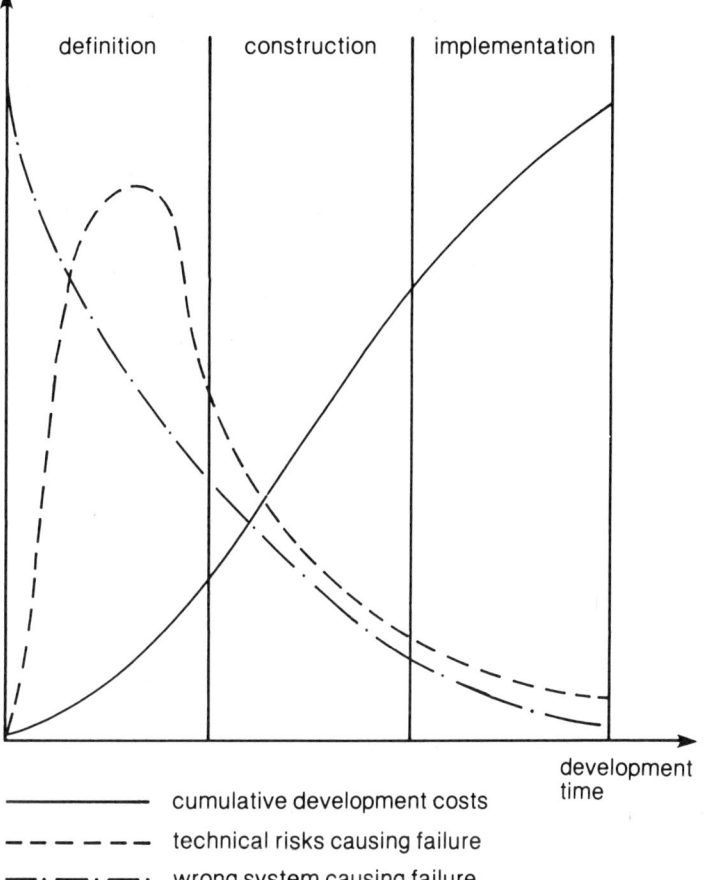

economic evaluation that took place in the information analysis step; it may even require revising earlier decisions about the basic feasibility of the system being developed.

The number of iterations should be kept as small as possible, since each iteration results in modifications and delays. The quality of the work in the early steps of the life cycle considerably affects the number of iterations. Judicious execution of early steps usually assures that when iterations are necessary, return to the starting point will not be required.

8. Several feasible alternatives, rather than one, should be investigated when computerized information systems are being developed. This investigation should be conducted during the definition phase.

9. Since information systems are an intangible entity, a major way to evaluate and control their products is through their *documentation*. Documentation has the following characteristics:

    The mere writing down, in clear and unambiguous language, helps on the one hand to identify weaknesses and gaps in the system; on the other hand, it serves as proof of the comprehensiveness of the design.

    Documentation is the tool used to manage the development process, to control its activities, and to plan future steps.

    Documentation provides backup for the system in its operation phase when system programs are potentially exposed to damage.

    The system developers are distinct from the persons who subsequently operate and maintain the system. The latter cannot function without adequate documentation. Documentation is thus vital for the operation of the system.

    Documentation is also vital for the postaudit stage of the system life cycle, since it enables people to compare expectations with actual performance.

    Like systems themselves, documentation is constantly evolving and degenerates slowly with time.

    Documentation is a vital training tool.

    The life cycle involves a large number of people. Documentation provides them the best communication medium.

10. There are various types of documentation. Each type has a unique mission, structure, and language. Each activity in the development process produces its own documentation.

11. Documentation does not only serve as a passive control tool or a communication tool. Documentation standards are used for structuring the development process. These standards serve as a checklist for the system developers and enable them to carry out their activities in a uniform and well-defined fashion. A development process based on detailed and comprehensive documentation standards is a predefined process that avoids the need to develop a framework for each newly developed system.

    Contemporary techniques of *software engineering* impose standard system analysis, design methodology, and documentation on the developing staff. In fact, some techniques make the documentation instrumental to the analysis and design activities. Such structured design techniques are recommended mostly because documentation becomes inherent to the activity rather than appended to the analysis and design activities after they have been completed.

12. Contemporary software packages (e.g., application generators) allow for fast construction of information system *prototypes*. Prototypes are extremely beneficial to reduce uncertainty and to clarify to users and management how the end product is going to look. System evaluation during the development period is thus based on more tangible and concrete impressions of both users and designers.

13. Many people take part in the development process. They come from different professional and organizational backgrounds: general managers, direct users, the information system department, information analysts, systems designers, programmers, and others. Various organizational bodies must be formed (special teams and committees) to facilitate their joint work.

14. The system development process involves a considerable element of creativity, which renders the planning difficult. However, advance planning is a prerequisite to the process being started. Segmentation of the process into steps and adoption of a timetable for each step will facilitate better planning than approaching the process as a whole.

15. The system construction phase produces computer programs and user procedures. The procedures are as important as the programs, for users tend not to use an information system without having fairly detailed procedures written in their language (i.e., not in the jargon of computer experts). The system developers must provide specifications for the procedures, must train the users to access the system by using the procedures, and must test the procedures before releasing them. The design and implementation of procedures thus resemble the design and implementation of computer programs.

16. *Conversion* from a current system to a new system constitutes a system of its own, which requires planning and control, writing of programs and procedures, and testing and training. The life cycle actually involves three systems: the existing system, the conversion system, and the new system.

17. The needs and capabilities of both the users and the organizational unit that will operate and maintain the computerized information system must be considered. This unit resembles a production shop where activities should be, as much as possible, routine, well defined, and streamlined. The information system should be designed in such a way that the constant requests for changes and modifications will not disrupt the smooth operation of the system.

18. The development of an information system is subject to the well-known law of diminishing marginal returns. Adding people to the development team will significantly contribute to the pace of development up to a certain point. Enlarging the team beyond that point will lead to a reduced product per person: a larger development team is not necessarily a prescription for faster development.

Activities and Implementors of the System Life Cycle

The life cycle of an information system consists of various, logically-linked activities. You may note that the discussion of who takes part, how, and in what activity has been incorporated in the preceding two sections on environmental effects and basic principles. This section is intended to provide a compact, overall description of the life cycle. Many topics outlined here will receive more extensive and illustrative treatment in the following chapters of this book.

Chapter 10 covers the subjects of feasibility study, conversion and implementation, training, testing, operation and maintenance, and postaudit. It also discusses some software engineering tools.

Chapter 12 describes the information system personnel and their role during the information system life cycle.

Chapter 13 discusses the role of the user during the various steps of the life cycle. It also presents some economic considerations regarding system development.

Chapter 14 outlines the documentation required in each step of the life cycle, and suggests control mechanisms that should be incorporated into information systems.

The development of every information system (or application) is a project-oriented undertaking that follows a uniform pattern consisting of a structured series of activities. Every one of these major activities (or development phases) can be broken down into smaller tasks; each of these tasks almost invariably occurs in every application development project.

Each development phase is a self-contained, manageable piece of work. A project cannot proceed to the next phase of development until it has successfully completed the prerequisite activities. If problems occur in a phase, work can be restarted in that phase without a return to previous phases.

The relative weight of the different phases can vary from one organization to another and from one system to another, but the order and completeness of a standard project structure should characterize the development of all information systems. Such an orderly structure minimizes the risk that important development activities are forgotten. It reduces project planning time because project managers need not go through the process of "inventing" their own list of activities. Each activity has a precise meaning and well-defined output; everyone therefore speaks the same language, which simplifies follow-up and review.

Each step (activity) in the life cycle is carried out by one or more *implementors (information analyst, system designer, programmer, user)*. Sometimes one person can assume the functions of more than one implementor; the information analyst and the system designer can, for example, be the same person in a small project. As a rule, in the ensuing discussion we will refer to the implementors in the singular. You should bear in mind, however, that when the project is complex and large, these may represent teams of specific functional implementors.

One of the basic problems encountered in the development process is the interface between the activities, particularly when responsibility is transferred from one person to another (e.g., when the development progresses from design to programming). The overall project manager must verify that the transfer is smooth and that all pertinent information is communicated from one activity manager to another, mostly via documentation, sometimes orally. There is, hence, a transition period between activities during which implementors of two successive activities work jointly to ensure the continuity of the project.

Every activity creates some product (output), usually in the form of documentation, that serves as input for the next activity. These products must be initially reviewed along the following points:

The functional aspect of the project at this stage of the development process

The economic, technical, and organizational feasibility of the project

Future timetable and resources required to complete the project

The review process itself should be well structured. Normally, it is first performed by peers in a formal session labeled *structured walk-through.* Only after the critique has been understood and the peers' suggestions have been considered is it time for a managerial review.

All information systems projects should be controlled by higher management in some way or another. The life cycle should contain predefined checkpoints at which management, users, implementors, and outside technicians formally review and evaluate the progress of the project. Each checkpoint represents a decision to be made: whether the project should be allowed to continue to the next scheduled checkpoint, whether it should be canceled, or whether it should be revised.

The logical times for reviews are at the end of each project phase. At the minimum, checkpoints should be scheduled at points in time when decisions about the continuation or revision of the development process are most critical. These typically occur during the definition phase, before programming begins, and after system testing. EDP auditors should also participate in the review meetings. The checkpoints in the definition phase assure management that the purpose of the system is fully understood before construction is started, and enable them to terminate the project while the incurred costs are still relatively low.

In conclusion, dividing the development process into phases and activities allows control of the process, delegation of responsibilities to appropriate expert implementors, optimal performance of required iterations, and ongoing economical evaluation of the developed system.

The Life Cycle

The *life cycle* of a computerized information system contains the following phases and activities:

    I. Definition phase
        1. Preliminary analysis
        2. Feasibility study
        3. Information analysis
        4. System design

Table 9.2   Relative Expenditures and Required Time to Develop a Computerized Information System

Phase	Expenditures %	Time %
Preliminary analysis	2	5
Feasibility study	1	5
Information analysis	10	15
System design	8	10
Construction	40	35
Implementation	39	30
	100	100

    II. Construction phase
        5. Programming
        6. Procedure development
   III. Implementation phase
        7. Conversion
   IV. Operation phase
        8. Operation and maintenance
        9. Postaudit
      10. Termination

As noted earlier, this suggested description of the life cycle is but one among many. However, all descriptions are similar in principle, and the differences have to do mainly with the level of detail. Table 9.2 presents a rough but typical distribution of the expenditures and time requirements associated with the main activities of the development process.

Table 9.3 describes the ten activities, the main work performed in each activity, the participating implementors, the authority approving the progress to the next activity, and the documented products of the activities. A companion diagram of the first three phases of development (definition, construction, and implementation) is presented in figure 9.4.

Preliminary Analysis

A *preliminary analysis* is usually conducted before an information system is designed and implemented. This can be triggered by any one of several initiation steps. A project can be initiated simply because it is scheduled to be developed according to the master plan for information systems development, or because a nagging information problem has been raised by users. The analysis is to determine if the problem or the subject due for development warrants further analysis. It also refines the problem statement and creates a preliminary plan for an in-depth analysis of the problem. Revealing the true nature of the problem, which may differ from the stated problem, is one of the most important aspects of this activity.

Table 9.3 The Information System Life Cycle

Activity	Content	Implementor	Approval for Next Activity	Documentation
1. Preliminary analysis	Information requirements Input sources System boundaries Location of system in organization	Information analyst and user	User and management	Preliminary conceptual report (in user's language)
2. Feasibility study	Economic Technical Organizational	Information analyst and user	User, management, and EDP auditor	Feasibility report (in user's language)
3. Information analysis	System specifications Project plan Resources required Project budget	User and information analyst	User and EDP auditor	Systems analysis report (in user's language)
4. System design	Specifications for programming; files; and conversion Review of economic feasibility Specifications for procedure development A system test plan Hardware/software selection schedule (if needed)	System designer	User, manager of systems development, management, and EDP auditor	Specifications of programs Specifications of procedures Conversion plan
5. Programming	Coding of programs Program testing and documentation System testing	Programmer	Chief programmer and system designer	1. Programs 2. Operators and input entry manuals
6. Procedure development	Instructions for users, input/output clerks, control personnel, and operating personnel Conversion procedures	User, system designer, and information analyst	User and EDP auditor	Procedures (manuals)
7. Conversion	Training Creation of new files Parallel running (if needed) Tune-up changes (if needed) Acceptance testing	All above—implementors plus operators and input/output operators	User and EDP auditor	Conversion log
8. Operation and maintenance	Operation of system Modifications	All above—implementors		Maintenance logs
9. Postaudit	Review of objectives and cost/benefits of system Evaluation of operational characteristics of system	User and information analyst, or EDP auditor	User and management	Postaudit report
10. Termination	A decision that current system should be (a) abandoned or (b) replaced by a new system	User and information analyst	Management	

Figure 9.4 Diagram of information system development process (to be read clockwise)

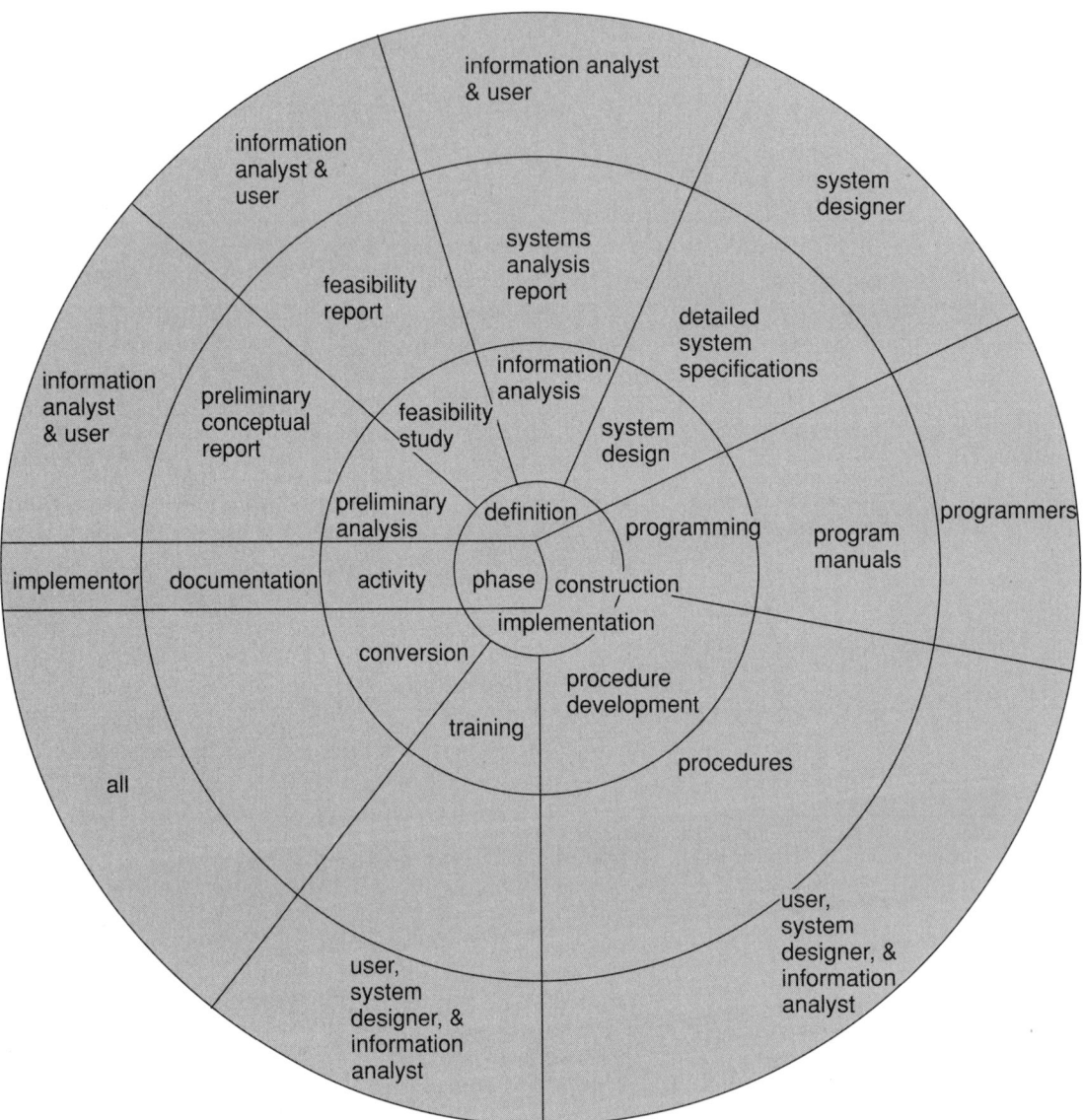

The main task of this activity is the collection of data needed to delineate the goals, scope, boundaries, and rough specifications of the proposed system. The outcome of this activity contains the following items:

Definition of the problem

Information requirements resulting from the problem (in brief)

Information recipients

Frequency of required information

Volume and sources of transactions to be processed by the system (the inputs to the system)

Scope and boundaries of the information system

This outcome comes in the form of a *preliminary conceptual report* to management. The report should include a recommendation concerning the need for further action (progress to the next activity in the life cycle), if deemed desirable.

During this activity the user plays an important role. Information systems are constructed to serve some user or users, and the user must have the ultimate responsibility for the products he or she asks of the system. (The user may be a number of individuals or even the organization itself.)

The *information analyst* also plays a prominent role during the preliminary analysis. The analyst may be an individual or a group of persons, depending on the size of the project. The title "information analyst," rather than "system analyst," is used to emphasize that this role involves the collection and development of information system concepts and requirements, rather than the design of the system. He or she is the one who communicates with users and management and who develops overall requirements and concepts of the system and its fit into the organization (more about these professions is discussed in ch. 12).

Feasibility Study

The major purpose of the *feasibility study* is to establish whether a project should be done and how it should be done if justified. This study should be performed by the user and the information analyst and reviewed by management. There have been many reported instances of users and information systems departments in organizations deciding what they wanted to do, and how they wanted to do it, without conducting a feasibility study. Then they set about putting together a document that outlined and justified their approach. This is clearly improper, for the *feasibility study report* should cover all the alternatives considered, the reasons for recommending one alternative, and the methodology by which successful implementation will be achieved. In short, the major purpose of this activity is to determine whether it is feasible to develop and install a system; if so, to suggest some acceptable scenarios; and, finally, to prepare a project charter that will be used to guide the project to its completion.

This activity should explore answers to the following questions:

What are the problems that the proposed system will solve?

How will the system solve the problems?

Is the technology required by the system available? (We label this *technical feasibility*.)

How will the system be accepted by the various users? (You may recall the resistance-to-change phenomenon discussed in ch. 2.) (We will label this *organizational feasibility*.)

Is the proposed system economically justified (do benefits outweigh costs)? (We label this *economic feasibility*.)

Is the system in line with the master plan and the priorities established by management?

What should be the next step in the development process?

The information analyst and the user participate in the feasibility study and submit the feasibility report to management. At this checkpoint, management can decide (a) to approve progression to the next activity; (b) to abandon the project; or (c) to revise it. (See ch. 10 for further details on the subject of the feasibility study.)

It is important to note that from the management's point of view, the feasibility study is the most crucial activity along the development life cycle. Until the end of this step, not too many resources have been poured into the project, so psychologically it is easier to abandon the project. The subsequent activities consume such a great quantity of resources (e.g., system analysis, design and programming personnel, and equipment acquisition) that management finds itself committed to completion of the project, even when it appears to be unjustified. Hence, we observe a common phenomenon: failing projects undergoing analysis, design, and programming activities cost more and more money in order to "resuscitate" them and to reduce the exposure to failure, while the best action would have been to call them off. Very seldom does management courageously cancel a project during the advanced stages of development. Thus, the conclusion of the feasibility study activity is analogous to the "point of no return" in a long-distance flight over the ocean.

Information Analysis

The *information analysis* activity is sometimes justifiably called the *logical* (or *conceptual*) *design step*, to distinguish it from the next activity of *system design*, sometimes called *physical* or *technical* design. The information analyst defines functional specifications of the proposed system (mainly from an external viewpoint) that are needed to meet the requirements and constraints defined in previous activities. The functional specifications are in the user's language, organizationally oriented.

The system defined in the preliminary analysis activity is partitioned into modules (subsystems), with the interrelations between the modules defined in detail. The technical and economical feasibility of the system is reevaluated. Because of the relatively large scope and importance of this activity, it usually consists of three parts: (1) analysis of present system, with the emphasis on *what* is taking place in the system; (2) determination of the information requirements, with the emphasis on *why* they cannot be provided effectively or efficiently by the current system; and (3) conceptual design of the new system. You will see in chapter 10 that the information analysis activity relies heavily on three similar parts analyzed during the feasibility study. The primary purpose of the information analysis task is to transform its two major inputs—user requirements (conveyed in the preliminary analysis report) and a project charter (conveyed in the feasibility report)—into structured specifications, reflecting in logical terms the system to be developed.

The information analyst and the user again play a dominant role in defining the specific functions of the proposed system that are needed to meet the requirements and constraints defined in the previous activities of the life cycle. They document their analysis and recommendation in a system analysis report. The report and a presentation of this activity will normally be given to management (to one of the committees established by management and described in the last section of this chapter). This presentation will normally include the definition of the problem, the recommended solution, and a project plan. Management must then review the presentation and the report and make a crucial decision: to commit the resources required for the detailed design, construction, and implementation of the system; to abandon it altogether; or to revise it (iterating to the beginning of this activity or to a previous activity). (The field of *software engineering* provides some techniques for the information analysis activity. This is discussed in ch. 10.)

The Project Plan

A detailed and comprehensive *project plan* is the basis for controlling all subsequent activities of the development process. It shows what the results of the project should be, how the project will be performed, when it will be done, and the resources required to do it. In fact, without the plan there is no control.

The content and level of detail of the project plan depend on the size and scope of the proposed system and on where the project lies in the development cycle. An initial plan usually emerges from the feasibility study activity. This is made more detailed and firm at the end of the information analysis activity. The plan may be modified in subsequent activities—subject, of course, to management scrutiny and control.

A possible standard project plan has the following elements:

1. *Overview*—Gives the background of the project, problems, and solutions, and states its objectives.

2. *Activity plan*—Defines the phases and activities of the development process, including dates and duration. Expected concrete results of the activities (such as documents and approvals) are also stated. To aid comprehension, the plan may take the form of a dynamic bar chart that can be updated as the project moves along. An example of such a chart produced in the feasibility study activity is shown in table 9.4.

Table 9.4 Activity Plan for an Information System Project

	JAN	FEB	MAR	APR	MAY	JUN	JUL	AUG	SEP	OCT	NOV	DEC	JAN	FEB
Information analysis	├─	─┤												
System design		├─	─	─┤										
Programming				├─	─	─	─┤							
Procedure development					├─	─	─	─┤						
Conversion							├─	─	─┤					
Operation									├─	─	─	─	─	─
Postaudit													├─	─┤
Management review		X		X					X					X

3. *Organization plan*—Defines the organization during the various activities of the project and specifies the functions and responsibilities of each group.

4. *Personnel plan*—Specifies for each individual (by name, if known, or by skill category) which activities are to be performed and when. Again, bar charts can be used (the personnel assignments can also be drawn on the bar chart describing the activity plan).

5. *Resource plan*—Details the resources (people, computer time for testing, materials, secretarial support) needed to complete the project and shows when these resources will be used (again, these can be graphically displayed by a bar chart). Because the development process is very labor intensive, the prerequisite for an accurate resource plan is the personnel plan.

6. *Budget*—Translates the consumption of resources into monetary terms related to the activities. It states the expenditures by cost element needed to complete the project and shows when the costs will be incurred.

7. *Review and reporting*—States the methods and tools to be used for formal reporting of project progress in terms of timing, scope, objectives, participants, and distribution list.

8. *Training plan*—Describes the training necessary for all those participating in or otherwise affected by the project. Includes the timing and the resources required.

9. *Documentation plan*—Outlines the documents to be developed during the project, including content, authors, deadlines, approval procedure, and distribution.

10. *Test plan*—Describes the tools, procedures, and responsibilities for testing at all levels—program testing, system testing, acceptance testing.

11. *Change plan*—Information system development is an evolving process beset by many changes. The change plan defines the types of change to be controlled and the procedures for coordinating and documenting them.

12. *Installation plan*—Defines the responsibilities of the user, the information system department, and the project team when the new system is installed.

System Design

System design is the creative activity of devising the program and procedure specifications for processing data by the new system. It involves the development of complete and detailed programming specifications from which the programmers can proceed with little or no additional outside reference. It also includes the development of plans and procedures for training users, for system and acceptance testing, and for conversion to the new system.

The activity of system design is concerned with identifying the proper hierarchy of system modules and their interfaces in order to implement the functional specifications resulting from the previous information analysis activity. That is why this activity is sometimes labeled the activity of *technical design, detailed design,* or *physical design.*

The implementor of this activity is the *system designer.* The system designer (again, one person or a team) receives a statement of logical requirements (i.e., the systems analysis report) and is then concerned with how best to fulfill these requirements. The designer breaks down the proposed information system into details, then prepares specifications for the various modules.

The system designer is responsible only for how, not for what. Unlike the information analyst, who is user oriented, the designer is concerned with the overall system performance. Yet, the designer is not a technician who almost mechanically produces a design. The design activity requires a high level of skill, creativity, and education in the face of evolving problems and technological advances in hardware/software. These characteristics are vital to the following main designer activities:

1. Design of the system output
2. Design of the system input
3. Design of the system files and data base
4. Design of the system processing methods
5. Preparation of specifications for programmers and procedure writers
6. Presentation of the system design to management and users for approval

A major tool in system design is *prototyping.* The purpose of prototyping is to create a system that will look very similar to the final system in terms of input and output screens, major reports, and other instrumental means of system operation. However, "behind the curtains" the system is still incomplete: it does not perform full data validity checks; it does not perform all the necessary variations in calculations; and it may not include many other routines (e.g., HELP routines). Nevertheless, the user can "feel" the system much better than when the system is presented only by means of documentation. In a way, a prototype is equivalent to model building in architecture, where the model is much more concrete than blueprints. Note that with present fourth generation software tools, such as *application generators* (see ch. 10), prototyping does not require too much effort and its merits are very high.

The functional specifications that were developed for the user during the information analysis activity in the user's language, and that were organizationally oriented, are now translated into technical specifications in the programmer's language, and are computer oriented. The system components to be automated are now designed for computerization. The system is partitioned into modules and programs within modules, and the following specifications are stated for each program:

Raw data sources—Where raw data originates; who generates it and when; how physical events are to be recorded; and whether it is necessary to use a written form or whether data can be keytyped online.

Input—The layout of the source documents; their origin, volume, number of copies, and frequency; their conversion to a machine-readable form; and input screen design.

Files or data bases—The files or data base tables; the storage devices; processing, organization, and access methods; and file or table sizes. (Appendix A extensively reviews these topics.)

Processing—Principles of processing, frequency of processing.

Output—The outputs, their layout, frequency, and production.

Testing and conversion—Test data, testing methods, measures for quality assurance of the programs, constructing the new files, and the method for verifying their contents.

Information flow—The general flow of data, namely, who gets what, when, and where. This should lead to transportation arrangements or a deployment plan for input and output equipment and for the communications network.

The system design report is the product of the system design activity. It normally contains the following items:

Flow charts of the system and its programs describing the processing flow, the inputs, outputs, files, and equipment to be used. The interface between the various programs in the system is emphasized.

A data dictionary that lists the titles of all the data (i.e., fields) belonging to the system, and delineates their characteristics in terms of field length, content (e.g., numeric, alphabetic), security level, and relationships to other items

Matrices that describe the interrelations between input data, files, and outputs (i.e., what data participates in which files and in which reports)

Layouts of source documents, input-entry forms, file records, outputs, and screens

Description of data validation tests

A narrative of every program, its function, and the principles of the processing performed by it

Detailed specifications for writing the procedures for system operation and use

A plan for testing every program and the system as a whole

A plan for constructing the files, either by collecting data from users or by converting current files

A system installation plan

A plan for the subsequent activities of programming and procedure development

An important aspect of the system design activity, which was implied in the previous discussion, and should be clearly stated, is the establishment of a comprehensive set of system controls. This is basically a plan to ensure that (1) only valid data is captured and processed; (2) processing is accurate; (3) the information generated from the system is accurate; (4) unauthorized access to the files and outputs is prevented; and (5) computer-related fraud is prevented. Several types of control should be considered and specified by the system designer (these are described in ch. 14 and are only listed here).

Input control

Processing control

Output control

Organizational control

Control of operations

Files control

Note that we did not include in the system design activity the issue of equipment selection and procurement. Usually the selection of computer equipment is related to many systems rather than to a single system. If a system requires selection of equipment, this will take place during the beginning of the system design activity. The system designer will then be responsible for preparing the specifications for the equipment. The selection policy of management may be such that the system designer communicates with vendors, prepares requests for proposals, selects one of the bids, etc. In principle, the system designer must consider the hardware and software configurations that the organization currently possesses, as well as their current work loads. The designer must estimate the capacity of the configuration to absorb the additional work loads implied by the new system. He or she must verify whether the operating system, the file organization, and the communications system can cope with the design requirements of the new system: are there software packages that provide solutions to input, processing, and output problems?

There are three possibilities facing the designer at the conclusion of this analysis. These are the following:

1. The current configuration is adequate for the system.
2. The current configuration is inadequate, but requires only additions of software and/or hardware.
3. The current system is completely inadequate and must be replaced.

The last two possibilities, of course, lead to the question of equipment selection and procurement, which should have been foreseen during the feasibility study. If this is not the case, revision of the feasibility report may be required.

Prior to submitting the system design report for final approval, it is common to have it reviewed by peers. This is performed with a structured walk-through— a formal procedure that ensures complete coverage of all the aspects of the system. (The structured walk-through is discussed in ch. 10.)

The final step in the system design activity is management's approval to proceed to the next phase of the project: system construction. The direct users of the new system, the information systems department, the *EDP auditor,* and higher management are all involved in this approval. The information systems department must concur that the system can be implemented as designed. The users must agree that the design is responsive to their needs. For higher management, this is a critical checkpoint; once the system enters the construction phase, large amounts of resources will be committed to the project.

Programming

The previous efforts to specify requirements and to design the system reach fruition during programming. Coding and testing of computer *programs* now take place. This is the time for faulty designs to be found out and for what is truly feasible to be determined.

The job of the programmer is to produce a computer program from the detailed specifications prepared by the system designer. The programmer is the main implementor of this activity, but the system designer is in continuous communication with the programmer, explaining the program specifications, preparing test data, sometimes testing programs, testing the system as a whole, and approving the progress to the conversion activity.

The programmer first reviews the program specifications received from the system designer, then develops the logic to solve the problem presented by the program. The programmer then codes the program in a programming language and removes any errors from the program caused by an improper use of the programming language (this process is called *debugging*). The program is then tested by actually executing it on the computer system. *Test data* is used to ensure that the program will process all actual inputs correctly. This is called *unit test* or *program* or *module test* (see [15] or [21] for more discussion of the various levels of testing).

It is highly recommended that another person, such as the system designer or a chief programmer, prepare the test data and compare the program results with manually calculated results. This prevents logical errors resulting from the programmer's misinterpretation of the program specifications. If the programmer prepares his or her own test data, the data will conform to the same misinterpretation.

After the programs in the system have been tested individually, the entire system of programs must be tested as a whole. This is called *system testing.* The integrated test normally focuses on the interfaces between individual programs and is conducted by the system designer or the head of the project team. If the system test is successful, the system is ready for the conversion activity and acceptance testing by the user.

A continuing part of the programming activity is documentation of the programs developed. This will guide the operating personnel and the maintenance programmers in the future. Program documentation includes all the information necessary for future use, understanding, and (where necessary) modification of the program. Typical program documentation usually includes the following items:

Narrative—Description of the purpose of the program and the solution used.

Logic display—Description of the logical steps in the program (often this is a program flowchart).

Program listing—A printed copy of the source program produced by the computer during program compilation.

Input/output layouts—Description of the data, file records, and reports showing the relative location of each field in each record.

Test data—A copy of the test data.

Operator instructions—All instructions necessary to run the program on a computer.

Procedure Development

While the programming activity results in computer instructions, the *procedure development* activity results in instructions for human involvement with the new system. Procedures for the various users and operators of the system are written and tested. This activity concurrently proceeds with the programming activity and is equally important.

The procedures are prepared by the information analyst or a special procedure writer along with the user and the system designer. It is important that the procedures are written in the user's language and that they are accurate and adequate. If they are not, the users of the system will be seriously affected.

Procedure development is not a popular task with computer experts, who would rather spend time on designing and programming than on instructing the user how to use and operate the system. This is why each procedure should be tested by the specific user (e.g., computer operator, input/output clerk, auditor, manager). Again, the procedure must be tested by a person other than the one who developed it.

The following elements illustrate the structure of a procedure for requesting a new report:

Purpose—To initiate requests for new reports.

User—Who may initiate a request? (A list of persons or managerial categories is provided.)

Form—What is the request form that has to be filled out? (A sample form is attached.)

Review—Who receives the request and initially reviews it? (The information system department in this case.)

Approval—Who approves (or rejects) the request?

Appeal—To whom can the initiator of the request appeal the decision, if necessary? (In this case the information system committee.)

Processing—Who processes the request, if approved? (In this case the programming unit.)

Budget—Who is to be charged for the expenditures involved?

Documentation—Where and how is the request to be recorded? (In this case in the change log of the affected application producing the report.)

Copies—Who gets copies of the correspondence involved in the procedure? (In this case internal auditing.)

Appendix—A flowchart of the procedure steps.

After procedures have been written and tested, the system is ready for computer implementation. The implementation should be a relatively smooth conversion from the old system (if one existed) to the new system.

Conversion

Conversion refers to (1) *training* the personnel operating and using the new system, (2) breaking the system in, and (3) acceptance testing by the user. In most cases conversion is associated with making changes from an old system to a new system. Should implementation of a new system not involve replacement or extensive modification of a current system—a situation seldom encountered—the difficulties are greatly reduced. Conversion constitutes a system of its own, which must be planned in detail, in advance, and with allocation of the necessary resources (personnel, capital, materials, machinery, space).

Conversion to a new information system may be undertaken in different ways. The old system can be replaced all at once, or the old and new systems can run in parallel paths for a time. Or the new system can be phased in module by module, or it can replace the old after a pilot module of the new system has been functioning for a while. (More on these approaches is discussed in ch. 10.)

Several components of the information system are subject to conversion. Completely new programs have to be broken in and run by the computer operators. Old programs may have to be changed. When programs are converted, they have to undergo the same testing procedures conducted for new programs. Procedures and documentation have to be converted to comply with the architecture and operating rules of the new system. Old files have to be converted to new storage media, new access mechanisms, and new methods of file organization. Sometimes a new system requires preparation of new facilities or improvement of old facilities, such as computer sites, offices, libraries of storage media (magnetic tapes and disks), and communications facilities.

Installing a new system normally involves changes in the old data processing methods, particularly manual ones. When the change is strictly a technical one within the same job category, it is introduced by the training program. For example, the data entry clerk can be trained to record input data online instead of offline. Sometimes, though, the change is more profound. For example, a new inventory reorder system that automatically issues reorder notices to suppliers means that reorder clerks are no longer needed and must therefore be reassigned to another function. In such a case the following steps should be taken:

The organizational implication (feasibility) of the new system must be evaluated during the feasibility study and the information analysis activities, and then reviewed by management.

The employees scheduled for conversion must be trained in advance for their new jobs, concurrent with performance of their old jobs.

The conversion on the scheduled date must be carefully preplanned in order to prevent disturbances.

It is a good practice for the user to perform an *acceptance test* of the system prior to its full operation. The test is prepared by the user and is performed by a joint team of the user and the project developers. The acceptance test consists of a checklist of conditions that are tested to verify the operating procedures of the new system. It is helpful to prepare scenarios of various possibilities that may occur in the life of the system and to test system performance in these scenarios. By approving the results of the test, the user endorses the system and the project team releases it for operation.

It is evident that many people participate in the conversion activity. The information analyst and the system designer are involved in training, minor modifications, program and procedure conversion, and acceptance testing. The programmers are involved in training computer operators and input/output clerks, and in converting and testing converted programs. Various data entry personnel, operators, dispatchers, schedulers, and computer librarians have to be trained. The direct users are trained to use the system and to take part in acceptance testing. Management keeps a close watch over the conversion activity, sees to it that conversion progresses according to the conversion plan, and is prepared to intervene if difficulties or disputes arise.

Although no formal piece of documentation is created during the conversion activity, all the significant events occurring during the activity must be duly recorded and filed for future reference in some kind of a *conversion log* book. The book may contain forms and entries reflecting users' complaints, minor modifications, actual conversion expenditures, results of acceptance tests, and the like. It is suggested that at this stage of the life cycle a project summary is prepared. This summary is really a document of the system development efforts and serves two purposes. First, it should help avoid future repetitions of mistakes made for this system. Second, it should serve as an index for topics of interest during the operation activity of the life cycle.

The costs of conversion should be estimated and accounted for during the feasibility study and the preparation of the project plan. These constitute a nonrecurring but relatively high expenditure that should be treated as a capital investment and included in the development costs of the new system. The components of conversion expenditures are personnel costs, computer time for parallel running and acceptance testing, materials, temporary physical facilities, and equipment.

At the conclusion of the conversion activity, the user becomes the owner of the system. The system then moves into the operation phase of life. The development activities of the information system life cycle are now terminated.

Operation and Maintenance

The system now operates like a production facility, processing data and producing information. *Maintenance* as an ongoing process is required for several reasons, including the following:

Errors in the system that were not discovered by the various tests—These errors may appear as a result of unforeseen rare events or an unexpectedly heavy load.

Requests for changes in the system—The changes can be initiated by users, by management, and sometimes by the environment (e.g., new IRS regulations requiring a new report for payroll deductions).

Changes in interrelated systems require changes in the relevant system.

Changes in the software/hardware configuration—An improved element put on the market may trigger a change in the relevant system in order to make it more efficient, or acquiring magnetic disk packs with larger tracks may trigger a change in the size of the blocks in system files.

Improvements initiated by the information systems department—Sometimes experience with the system or overutilization of computer resources generates the incentive to improve the efficiency of the system. For example, when the system was developed, plenty of slack computer time was available and programmers were not urged to develop very efficient coding; now computer time has become a more critical factor.

The various errors and requests for changes lead to *maintenance projects,* small-scale replicas of development projects that have similar life cycles as is evident in the following list (for more about software maintenance, see [21, ch. 20] or [3]):

1. Project initiation
2. Survey of the maintenance problem
3. Construction (analysis, design, development, testing)
4. Implementation
5. Final evaluation

Management of the operation and maintenance activity differs from management of the development activities and resembles production management. It reflects the following conditions:

Scheduling the promotion of system modifications within a set of changing priorities (because development projects usually have higher priorities)

Assigning work to a fixed number of available personnel resources as opposed to development management where personnel are preassigned to the work

Controlling a large number of relatively small projects

Typically, a whole new set of people interact with the system when it becomes operational. Maintenance activities require a great deal of the *maintenance programmers'* time; occasionally the user, information analyst, and system designer become involved in maintenance projects. The information system is operated by various computer center operators and *input/output personnel.*

Good documentation is imperative in program maintenance. Routine documents produced while the system is operational tend to be problem-oriented. They consist of *maintenance logs,* requests for change, and new (updated) program, user, and operator manuals. Also, experience with the systems during operation creates recommendations and insights for future projects and for the current system that need to be documented.

Postaudit

Periodic postinstallation reviews form control points throughout the operation of the system. These reviews are intended to evaluate the operational characteristics of the system, its operating costs, and whether any modifications are necessary to make the system operate more effectively and efficiently. These reviews reveal discrepancies that might require routine maintenance or that might be severe enough to indicate system obsolescence.

A formal, planned, and comprehensive audit of the system should normally be undertaken after the system has been in operation for about six months. The information analyst and the user play a major role in the audit. Management, internal auditors, and outside consultants may also participate in the study. The basic purposes of the *postaudit* are to compare the projected objectives, scope, costs, and benefits of the system as determined during development with the actual experience. The most important elements of the postaudit are

Extent of direct and indirect benefits produced by the system

Extent of direct and indirect costs associated with development and operation of the system

Evaluation of the information and reports generated by the system

Evaluation of the system personnel

Extent of top-management involvement in the postaudit

After the postaudit has been completed, the audit team should prepare a final postaudit report for management that reviews the system's history, projected and actual costs, and its projected and actual benefits. The report should also include recommendations for improvements, enhancement, revisions, or abandonment of the system. (A more detailed discussion of postaudit is presented in ch. 10 and in [1].)

Termination

Periodic evaluations of the system will indicate when the life of the current system is drawing to its close and a new life cycle is indicated. *Termination* is imperative when requests for changes and the number of errors reach a level where the continued operation of the current system is not worthwhile. The decision to replace the current system and begin a new life cycle is the final checkpoint for management. The decision by management should rely on an analysis performed by the user and the information analyst and their recommendations. Although no formal documents are created during the termination activity, the findings presented to management and management's decision should be documented. These constitute the last chapter (or epilogue) in the system book.

Figure 9.5 Life cycle activities along a time scale

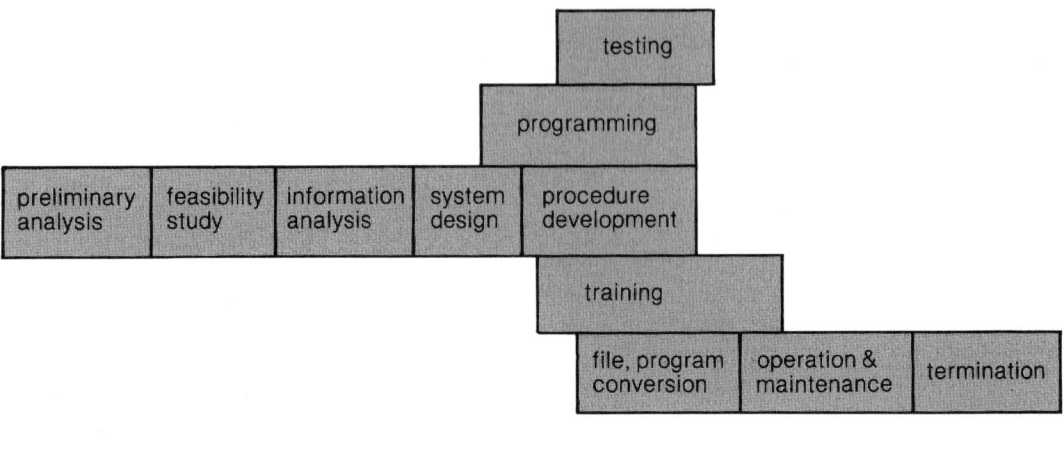

It is important to remember that there might be a long time lag between the decision to terminate and actual termination because it takes time to develop a replacement system. In fact, so long as the new system undergoes activities 1 through 7 in table 9.3, the old system is still intact. Therefore, a decision to terminate must take into account the foreseen circumstances under which the existing system will have to operate during the succeeding year or two. If management delays the decision until the current system is near collapse, the organization may well end up with a catastrophic situation.

A Final Remark

The structured life cycle of an information system may convey an impression of a completely linear process, where each step must terminate before the next one starts. To emphasize that this is not how information systems are developed in practice, we have separated the life cycle into "activities" rather than "steps." Not all activities are necessarily performed linearly. Some may overlap or be performed in a parallel manner. Others cannot be started before the conclusion of a preceding activity. The life cycle thus changes from organization to organization, from system to system, and from period to period. The only aspect that is completely linear is the succession of management checkpoints throughout the life cycle. Figure 9.5 displays one possible example of a progression of the activities. The last two sections of this chapter elaborate on the disparities in the life cycles of various systems and on the unique features of a DSS life cycle.

Organizing the Information System Development Process

We have to differentiate between managing an information systems department and managing an individual project. The information systems department has a lot of duties besides systems development, and managing it is discussed in chapter 12. An individual information system development project (hereafter called just "project") usually crosses departmental borders within an organization. For example, the development of a computerized system to monitor products distribution (following the example in figures 5.4 and 5.9) involves the department in charge of the central warehouse, the regional sales branches, the department in charge of the truck fleet, and possibly the production department. The system will have to meet requirements and procedures prevailing in all these departments, not to mention financial and personnel constraints imposed by other departments. Careful coordination of all the pertinent factors is necessary. Coordination and cooperation are obtained by the establishment of several bodies, most of which last only so long as the development project is alive. As soon as the system is implemented, these bodies vanish, and the participating individuals are assigned to new tasks. The main bodies are the *information system committee* (which is a permanent body), the *feasibility team,* the *steering committee,* the *development team,* and the *implementation team.* We will now describe the role and composition of each of these.

The Information System Committee

In chapter 8 we suggested that every organization should develop a master plan to delineate information systems development policy for a period of a few years. The establishment of a master plan is not a once-in-a-lifetime task, and the master plan will never be effective if shelved in the president's office. A master plan should be reviewed frequently and, if necessary, revised. This is performed by a permanent body termed the *information system committee.* This committee fosters the master plan and ensures that it is carried out.

The members of the committee belong to the top managerial level of the organization. A list of typical members includes vice-presidents (or their chief assistants) of finance, administration, marketing, and operation (production, distribution, services, etc.), as well as the head of the information systems department (who might also be a vice-president, as is more and more common nowadays), and representatives from the controller and auditing units.

The committee meets about every other month. It initiates feasibility studies of proposed systems; reviews feasibility reports and approves or rejects further development; reviews postaudit reports; sets priorities; and modifies the master plan.

The head of the information systems department, being a member of this committee, is responsible for carrying out the committee directives. Hence we may say that the information system committee plays the role of a board of directors for the executive who runs the information systems department.

The Feasibility Team

Suppose the information system committee is interested in developing a new information system, either to replace an existing one or to expand into a new application. Assume, also, that the preliminary analysis has indicated some promising results. Then an in-depth probe should be carried out by an ad hoc team—the feasibility team.

The *feasibility team* normally consists of at least three participants: a representative of the major user department(s) (the department(s) that will most benefit from the system should it be installed); a representative of the general management of the organization; and a representative of the information systems department, usually a senior information analyst. In a distribution system a feasibility team may include, for example, an assistant to V.P. finance (management representative); a veteran warehouse foreman and a regional sales manager (major user representatives); and a senior information analyst from the information systems department.

The composition of the team follows the trinity concept of the systems approach—designer, decision maker, user (see ch. 4). Besides reflecting the major interested parties, this composition also secures the check-and-balance mechanism during the feasibility study. For example, the user may have ambitious requirements that are not economically justified. The management representative may emphasize a global budgetary consideration and, hence, try to cut off the requirements. The information systems person may wish to push the study toward a highly sophisticated solution that would be more challenging to his or her professional peers, but perhaps not economically justified. Or, he or she might try to reduce the scope of the system, knowing the current heavy work load of the information systems department. The participation of all members of the trinity increases the chances of reaching a rational, economic solution (but it does not necessarily ensure this).

In many cases the feasibility team should be expanded, especially if there are several major users or if there is a need to consult an expert in a specific area. For example, suppose the distribution technique will be based on some operations research (OR) models, such as inventory control and/or networks. It might then be a good idea to involve an OR specialist in the study; an expert in computer networks may also be helpful. In cases where monetary transactions are involved, it is wise to have an auditor join the team.

Normally the team is headed by a user representative, provided that this person represents the most interested body. The way the study is conducted is discussed in chapter 10. The final report is submitted to the information system committee, which may decide on one of the following:

1. *GO:* Begin the development project
2. *NO GO:* Abandon the idea (temporarily or for good)
3. *ON:* Continue the investigation; the information so far is inconclusive

The ON type decision will, it is to be hoped, sometimes change to either GO or NO GO. If the decision is GO, then two bodies should be formed: the development team and the steering committee.

Figure 9.6 Involvement of various experts in the development team

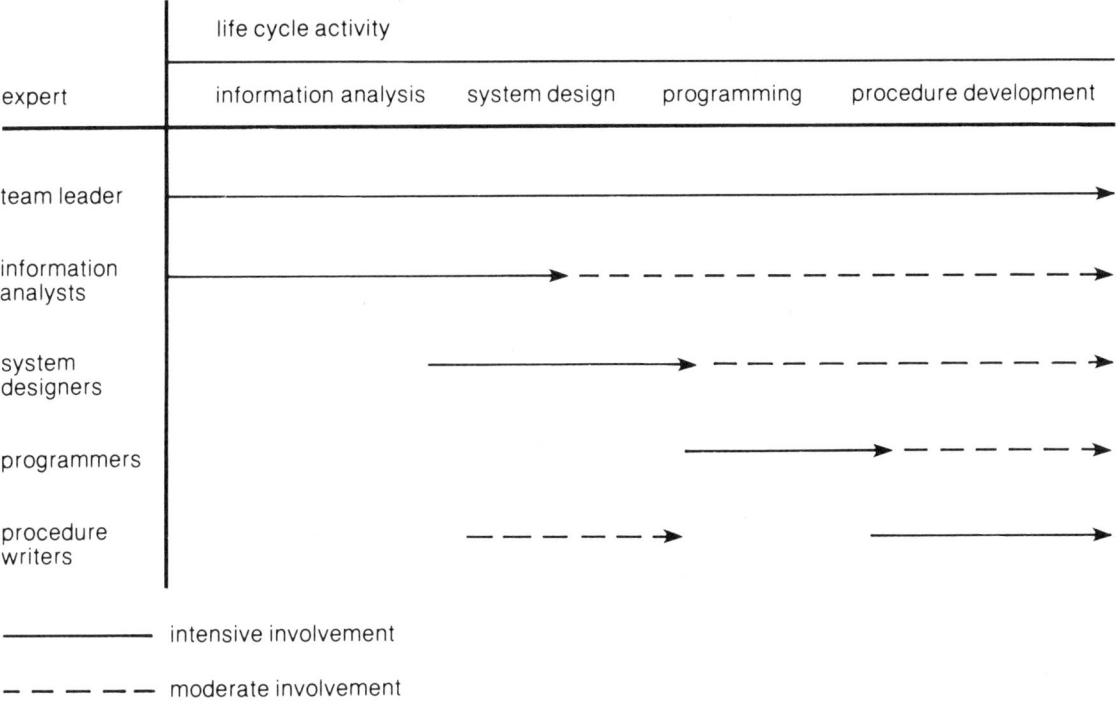

The Development Team

Development team is the title of a group formally established after a GO decision has been made. Its main goal is to develop an information system up to the point when it is ready to be installed (then it is supervised by the implementation team). The team is headed by a senior information analyst. This could be the same person who took part in the feasibility study; however, in many organizations the feasibility study and system development are performed by different people. The members of the team are information processing professionals employed by the information systems department; however, in organizations where user departments also employ information specialists or semiprofessionals, it is highly desirable that at least one of them join the team.

The composition of the team varies through time, depending on the activity at different points in the system life cycle. Figure 9.6 diagrams the involvement of various experts in the team. Clearly the team leader must run the show all the way through. During the initial information analysis, only information analysts are required. When the conceptual design of the proposed system is completed, system designers enter the picture in order to translate the conceptual framework into concrete specifications. The specifications then direct the programmers in writing and testing programs and simultaneously guide the preparation of procedures.

Figure 9.6 reflects an ''ideal'' case or circumstances such as might prevail in large organizations or large projects. In many other cases this outline would be modified due to local practices, particularly related to personnel. For example, some places do not differentiate between analysts and designers. Others combine the position of designer and programmer. Many departments do not employ special procedure writers; they assign the task to designers or programmers. Nevertheless, the idea of an ongoing body (i.e., development team) whose members vary is very common and, indeed, beneficial in maintaining efficient utilization of personnel.

The Steering Committee

The same line of thought that has led us to recognize the need for an information system committee should make us understand the vital role of a *steering committee*. This ad hoc committee does not produce a system, but monitors the development of a system. Its main purpose is to ascertain that the final product—the information system—conforms to the initial requirements that prompted the organization to undertake the project. In case the initial ideas fail to be completely applicable, the steering committee is responsible for modifying them by adopting new (or abandoning obsolete) ideas.

The steering committee consists of senior managers in the organization. It could certainly be a subcommittee of the information system committee. Its composition should follow the trinity concept already discussed: a senior executive representing general management (e.g., V.P. finance); senior manager(s) of the major user department(s); and the director of the information systems department. In some cases participation of an external consultant is helpful to express management and user views. The head of the development team also attends the committee meetings.

The steering committee is formed immediately after a GO decision has been made. The frequency of its meetings may vary; however, it must meet and review any major progress, in particular before the project moves from one life cycle activity to the next. These points are the major milestones of the project, but certainly there is a need for many more meetings. We suggest that one meeting per month is a reasonable frequency.

The major tasks of the steering committee are the following (the order of the items has no significance):

1. Approving and revising final and interim goals in the development process

2. Approving suggested performance of the proposed system (e.g., response time, reporting frequency, etc.)

3. Defining criteria by which the success (or failure) of the system will be evaluated after it is installed

4. Authorizing major acquisitions of hardware and software

5. Approving the appointment of key persons in the projects (e.g., project leader, senior professionals, consultants)

6. Approving the major framework of the project (e.g., subteams)

7. "Selling" the system to user departments and general management (the committee members are probably more familiar with the new system than anybody else in the organization, so they should introduce it to others and be the first to confront resistance to change; see ch. 2)

8. Periodically reviewing progress reports

9. Approving the project plan (i.e., modular development, if applicable, timetable, budget)

10. Determining priorities, particularly when the available resources dictate segmentation of the development

11. Reviewing cost/benefit analyses

12. Approving the results of prototype testing and system testing

13. Reviewing every major report (e.g., information analysis report, system design specifications, conversion plan) and authorizing progression to a subsequent activity

14. Coordinating conversion and implementation (this is done with the implementation team)

15. Reviewing postaudit reports

It is clear that the steering committee accompanies the project all the way to its implementation. In fact, even when the development team is replaced by an implementation team, the committee continues to exist. It may terminate its regular activities after the system has been installed, but then it resumes its meetings for a short period in order to evaluate the system (normally six months after installation). Only then does the committee adjourn.

The Implementation Team

In chapter 10 we discuss the implementation of a new information system and how to convert an organizational unit from a previous system to the new one. We hope that discussion will convince you of the importance of this activity. In fact, information systems that are technically perfect may fail due to poor implementation. That is why we advocate establishing a special team to handle that activity. This is not to say that the *implementation team* should be totally separate from the development team. On the contrary, it is a natural continuation of the development team and should consist of selected members of it, such as the head of the development team and some senior designers and programmers. However, since the main purpose now is to smooth the reception of the new system, the development group should be augmented by the following people:

1. *Users*—More representatives from user departments should join the team and should plan and perform training, conversion, tests, etc. Users should come not only from managerial levels but also from the operating ranks.

Figure 9.7 Hierarchical control of information systems development

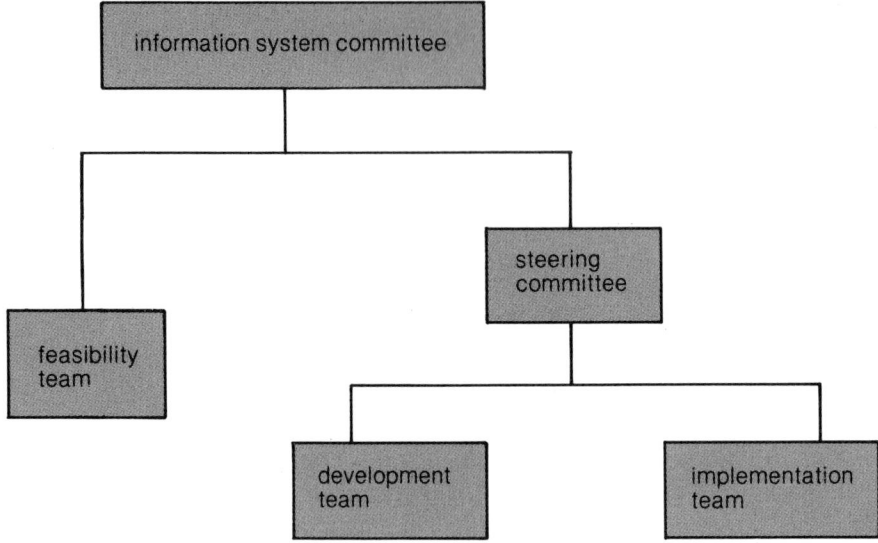

2. *Senior managers*—The delicate activity of conversion requires intensive involvement of senior managers (e.g., department managers and deputies) in order to provide sufficient authority to back up some tough decisions, which might hurt some employees. Particularly, the senior managers will have to cope with resistance to change. Despite being a skillful information processing professional, the head of the development team might not have sufficient authority or understanding of human nature to pursue such a complex operation.

In many organizations development and implementation are handled by the same team. We do not reject this; we only emphasize that new team members must be carefully selected when the development cycle enters its final activities.

Some Conclusions

Managing a development project is certainly not an easy task. One has to carefully balance development and control measures. Too much emphasis on control (e.g., too many committees and interim reporting requirements) might cause a significant delay in development of the information system. On the other hand, if developers are allowed to go ahead uncontrolled, the result might be a system not suited to specified needs.

The framework presented here maintains an appropriate balance between development and control. Figure 9.7 depicts the hierarchy of an information system development project, and partly summarizes the aforementioned concepts.

A Flexible Approach to the Development Life Cycle

While the previous sections in this chapter have stressed how imperative it is to impose rigid procedures on the information system development life cycle (ISDLC), this section intends to somewhat relax that gospel. The proliferation of information systems in organizations is so great that it has become impossible to attribute the same activities to every system *development project* in the same manner. We have to distinguish between in-house development and purchase of ready-made software; between transaction processing systems and decision support systems (see the next section); between mainframe applications and microcomputer applications; between centralized systems and distributed systems (see ch. 11); and between crucial applications and minor projects.

Do not misunderstand the message of this section. We do not advocate a return to a haphazard, individual, intuitive approach to ISDLC. On the contrary, a commonly accepted framework is absolutely essential. However, within this framework, some flexibility is allowed, provided that it is introduced in a systematic fashion. This flexibility is the issue of this section.*

Why Should the Traditional Approach be Reviewed?

The traditional development process and the system life cycle concept have been the backbone of systems analysis for years. Most project management systems and approaches are based on it.

The traditional ISDLC has always been a troublesome, complex, costly, and time-consuming process, primarily because of the nature of the systems that must be built with it. There is a general agreement [23, p. 138] that the volume of data, large files, high activity levels, multiple users, and predefined nature of tasks make some variation of the ISDLC a necessary and appropriate approach for transaction processing and traditional reporting systems, and that a complete replacement of the traditional systems development approach is not likely in the near future.

This traditional approach seems to advocate a rigid ISDLC, since it is probably the only tool to assure control over the development process. In practice, however, development processes are not that rigid. They vary with respect to the complexity of the system under development; with respect to the importance the organization attaches to the said system; and with respect to the user's environment. Moreover, in an era where canned software packages are mushrooming, there is a great difference between the ISDLC of a system developed in-house and a system acquired from an external supplier.

With waiting times for new applications running into several years, managers and users have been casting about for more efficient approaches to systems development.

---

*This section is partly cited from the article ''A Flexible Approach to Information System Development'' by N. Ahituv, S. Neumann and M. Hadass in *MIS Quarterly* 8, no. 2 (June 1984), pp. 69–78. Copyright 1984 by the Society for Information Management and the Management Information Systems Research Center. Reprinted by special permission of the publisher.

Gremillion and Pyburn [9] suggest that managers may have to abandon traditional patterns and evaluate projects by the criteria of commonality, impact, and structure in order to choose an appropriate development strategy.

McFarlan [17] notes that different projects require different management approaches in order to reduce exposure to the traditional risks of slippage in time, cost overrun, technical shortfall, or outright failure. McFarlan identifies three dimensions that influence the risk inherent in a project: project size (dollar expense, staff, number of departments affected), experience with the technology, and project structure. Consequently, he proposes a series of questions and forms that companies can use to build a risk profile that will help them choose a specific development process.

Here we take a similar line of thought, namely, that the emphasis placed on various phases of the ISDLC should depend on the nature of the specific project. Thus, we propose a flexible ISDLC. Each step in the ISDLC is characterized by several dimensions; it is possible that while a certain aspect (dimension) is highly emphasized, another aspect is somewhat de-emphasized, with both aspects belonging to the same step. For example, when an off-the-shelf software package is installed, testing can be de-emphasized while training should be highly stressed (where both aspects are part of the implementation phase of the ISDLC).

We distinguish between two categories of factors affecting the ISDLC: factors derived from the user and the environment requirements, termed *project/environment* factors; and factors derived from the nature of the development process, labeled *development-type* factors. We also distinguish between various dimensions (attributes) of the development process. The main message is that the ISDLC of a specific project should be tailored to the various affecting factors.

Project/Environment Factors

Project/environment factors are those derived from the requirements imposed on the system by users and other related bodies. Following is a list of factors and suggestions for their measurement (note that the measures are suggestive and not prescriptive):

1. Organizational Scope
The number of organizational units that are directly connected to the project. A project can involve only one or two departments (e.g., inventory control), or it can cut through most of the organizational entities (e.g., budget control, cost accounting). Measuring: Count the number of organizational units involved in the project (see [17, pp. 143, 149] and [9, pp. 135–36]).

2. Importance
The significance of the project for the organization. Does it substantially contribute to the operation of the organization? Measuring: Importance cannot be directly measured. However, it can be revealed through the expenditures the organization is willing to commit to the project, or through opportunity costs, such as cost decrease or profit increase. Thus, a surrogate variable for importance can be the project's budget relative

to similar activities, or the project's relative contribution to cost saving or profit making. These are usually assessed at an early stage of the ISDLC (see [17, pp. 143–45], [9, pp. 135–36], and [18, pp. 146–50]).

3. Organizational Maturity
The experience of the users in developing and operating computerized information systems. A more experienced organization can expect a smoother installation of a new system. Measuring: Although maturity is hard to measure, Gibson and Nolan [7] have defined stages of EDP growth. Associating the organization with one of these stages can represent maturity (see also [19, p. 113]). Another possible measurement is simply the number of computerized applications already installed in the organization.

4. Information System Policy
Organizations differ in the way they delegate the information processing activities to various departments. In some organizations, there is a central, powerful DP function; in others, many functions are distributed. The level of distribution affects the emphasis put on various activities of the ISDLC (see also ch. 11). Measuring: Level of distribution cannot be measured by a single variable. One should assess this by considering the many aspects of distribution. These are specified in two papers on profile distribution portrayal by Buchanan and Linowes [4, 5]. If we follow their assessment procedure, we may find out, for example, that while development is centralized, operation is decentralized, or vice versa. Any pattern of centralization and decentralization may have a different effect on the ISDLC (see also [19, pp. 115–19] and [2]).

5. Level of Structure
A transaction processing system is normally more structured than a system supporting managerial decisions. A more structured system may require less user participation during various ISDLC steps. Hence, system structure is an important factor in planning the development effort. Measuring: Structure can be assessed through an examination of the system's information processing performance. The lower the location of information processing within the organizational hierarchy, the more likely it is that the system is more structured. Consequently, its specification can be defined (see [17, pp. 143, 145, 147–50] and [9, p. 136]). Practical measurement can be attempted by identifying the location of the system's major users along the organizational hierarchy.

6. Technological Environment
Some development projects are based on advanced technology, while others are still anchored in the old conventional batch-processing mode of operation. The use of advanced technology is riskier than conventional modes, particularly when employees are not very familiar with it. In that case, more attention should be paid to various ISDLC stages. Measuring: The degree of technology advancement can be measured simply by the number of years elapsing since a specific technology was announced (see [17, pp. 143, 145, 147–50], [18, pp. 146–49], and [19, pp. 110, 115]).

Development Types

Any development project—be it in a large or small organization, in a centralized or decentralized environment—is typified by some traits related to the nature of the particular application under development. A development project can involve one of the following:

1. Development of a new information system
2. Modification (enhancement) of an existing system
3. Installation of an acquired new system (e.g., a canned software package)
4. Installation of a new version of an existing acquired system
5. Debugging or a minor change in an existing system

The type of project undoubtedly affects the various activities along the ISDLC. For instance, in an installation of an acquired system, the programming stage entails a relatively small effort while some aspects of the feasibility study are probably highly emphasized; in a bug-fixing project, more attention is paid to the time factor than is paid to the installation of a new version of an existing system.

The next sections present the various dimensions of the ISDLC in order to later show how these are affected by the project/environment factors and by the development type.

The Vertical Dimension of an ISDLC

The vertical dimension of an ISDLC is simply the sequence of steps that constitutes the development process. Starting with preliminary analysis, this sequence includes various steps (see the activities outlined in table 9.3) that culminate in the installation of a new system.

The steps along the vertical dimension are definitely influenced by factors that may increase or decrease the significance of a certain step. In an extreme case, a certain step can even be eliminated (e.g., using acquired software eliminates the need for programming).

Regarding each step as a rigid entity is an improper approach. Within each step there are various elements that can be altered due to the influential factors. For example, the degree of control that management has over a project is contingent on some factors (such as organizational scope), and may differ between different types of projects; it is also possible to have different levels of control during different ISDLC steps.

The elements that vary within each step are labeled horizontal dimensions, and are discussed next.

The Horizontal Dimensions of the ISDLC

The ISDLC is formal, gradual progress toward completion of an information system. The progress consists of steps; each step can be considered as a project by itself, including a list of tasks to be accomplished, a final product to be delivered (e.g., a feasibility report), and a sequence of checkpoints to be audited. There are some elements that are common to all the ISDLC activities. These elements can be emphasized or de-emphasized according to the status of the affecting factors.

The following list describes the various elements that are labeled the horizontal dimensions:

1. The activity dimension The process of developing a new system consists of many activities. The activities incorporated in the ISDLC are

Studying the organization

Information requirement analysis

Cost/benefit analysis

System analysis (logical design)

System design (physical design)

Programming

Procedure writing

Training

Testing

We usually associate activities with vertical steps; for instance, the programming activity is performed during the programming step. This, however, is not always accurate. Sometimes one has to perform a certain activity not only within its ''natural'' step, but within another step. For example, in a feasibility study of a very risky pioneer project, one may program a sample prototype module during the feasibility study step (i.e., a pilot program) in order to validate some assumptions. Another example is ''studying the organization.'' This activity is carried out during the feasibility study step and may be repeated during the information analysis step. Thus, the association of activities and steps is not necessarily a one-to-one or even a many-to-one relationship. Activities are iterated in various steps, although the depth of such an undertaking may vary throughout the ISDLC. Table 9.5 depicts activity intensity degree during the various steps in a ''normal'' project. In any particular project, the intensity is affected by the aforementioned factors, as we shall see later.

2. The control dimension There are a number of methods to assure that a system development project progresses in the right direction. This variety includes steering committee meetings, walk-through techniques, audit procedures, and quality control and inspection practices (for more details, see ch. 10). The selection of a set of assorted control tools for any particular project depends on the nature of the project, namely on the factors affecting the project. Moreover, control intensity may vary along the ISDLC. Thus, control can be regarded as a horizontal dimension of a flexible ISDLC.

3. The human resource dimension There are a number of professions involved in information system development (e.g., information analyst, system designer, programmer, procedure writer). A representative from every profession does not participate in every step. A programmer's skills, for instance, are not required in a feasibility study; or a system programmer's skills may not be required in a simple business

Table 9.5   Activity Intensity Degree during Performance of ISDLC Vertical Steps in a "Normal" Project

Step	Activity								
	Organization Study	Information Requirement Analysis	Cost/ Benefit Analysis	System Analysis	System Design	Programming	Procedure Writing	Training	Testing
Preliminary Analysis	M	M	L	L	L	L	L	L	L
Feasibility Study	H	H	H	M	L	L	L	L	L
Information Analysis	M	H	H	H	M	L	L	L	L
System Design	L	M	M	M	H	M	M	L	L
Programming	L	L	L	L	M	H	L	L	H
Procedure Writing	M	M	L	M	M	L	H	M	M
Implementation	M	L	L	M	M	M	M	H	H

(H = high intensity; M = medium intensity; L = low intensity)

application, but are essential in the development of a sophisticated real-time system. Thus, the type of human resources invested in a development project is a horizontal dimension of the ISDLC.

4. The nonhuman resource dimension   A development project consumes a lot of resources other than human, such as computer time, materials, and capital investment. Each of these is a horizontal dimension in itself because it may be affected by the various factors. For simplicity, they are aggregated here under the title "nonhuman resource."

5. The time dimension   It takes time to complete each ISDLC step. In some projects, management allows a long time; in others, a very short time is allotted to each step. Time may vary among projects and along steps, so it is a horizontal as well as a vertical dimension.

The horizontal dimensions characterize each step of the ISDLC. In fact, they shape the plan for an ISDLC that is uniquely tailored for each project. For example, a very complex system having a wide scope and a doubtful chance of success will probably trigger the following dimension values: high iteration of activities during the feasibility study, even to a degree where a pilot program is written and tested; high degree of control; high quality of human resources; reluctance to allocate large resources before concrete proofs of success are evident; and a long period of time allocated to a feasibility study.

The next section incorporates the influential factors and the various dimensions into a procedure that is essential for ISDLC planning.

A Practical Procedure for Planning and Reviewing an ISDLC

There is no magic wand to assist in shaping the ''optimal'' framework for any given development project, nor are we familiar with any mathematical formula that does. We do propose, however, a procedure that, based on two types of forms (working sheets), provides a systematic approach to adjust each ISDLC step to the project's specific circumstances. The procedure also enables the review of each step at predesignated milestones or upon completion in order to verify the initial anticipations and to revise plans if necessary.

The procedure is illustrated with the case of a real-life company in which the ideas presented in this section were used in developing an information system. The case involved a wholesale firm with a chain of regional warehouses that was interested in the possibility of installing a new online inventory control system to replace an existing batch-processing system. The firm was centrally managed, as was its computer department. The initial idea was to install terminals in the regional warehouses and to key in inventory transactions to a central system. The company did have long experience with EDP. Management predicted that the new system's main contribution would be to reduce costs of overstocking. The EDP department believed that there were adequate software packages in the market.

The first step in the suggested procedure was to construct a ''project profile,'' namely the level of risk associated with the project. This was performed by filling out form 1, which has a twofold purpose: to draw a ''project profile,'' and to provide inputs to subsequent form 2. The evaluator (the user of the form) had to mark, on a scale from 1 to 5, a preprinted assessment for each of the six project/environment factors and the development type. The closer the marks are to 5, the more ''risky'' is the project.

Table 9.6 illustrates the way form 1 was filled out during the preliminary analysis step for the wholesale firm. The profile emerging from table 9.6 (boxed attributes) is that of a normal development project, not too risky, but far from trivial. This finding affected the planning of the ISDLC, particularly the next step, the feasibility study.

We suggest that the first attempt to fill out form 1 be during the first step—preliminary analysis. Normally, great uncertainty prevails during this step, so the assessment of some factors will be questionable (for instance, before performing a feasibility study, it is difficult to tell whether a canned software package will be preferred to in-house development). Still, this is a first hint about the nature of the project. Revisions of form 1 can take place at major milestones along the ISDLC, particularly upon completion of each major step.

Table 9.7 presents form 2, which helps in planning the entire life cycle as well as each vertical step of the ISDLC. Form 2 is a simple tool that assists the evaluator in expressing his or her impressions of each horizontal dimension in each ISDLC step. In the two left-hand columns, there is a list of the influential factors and their marks (between 1 and 5, as determined in form 1). In the other columns, the evaluator is

Table 9.6 Sample Form 1 (Project Profile) for the Preliminary Analysis Step

	Low	Scale			High
Influential Factors	*1*	*2*	*3*	*4*	*5*
Organizational Scope	Very narrow	Narrow	Normal	[Broad]	Very broad
Importance	Very low	Low	[Normal]	High	Very high
Organizational Maturity	Very familiar	[Familiar]	Not so familiar	Unfamiliar	Extremely novice
Information Policy	Fully centralized	[Centralized]	Partly distributed	Distributed	Fully decentralized
Level of Structure	Fully structured	[Mostly structured]	Normal	Mostly unstructured	Very unstructured
Technological Environment	Very common	[Common]	Common and new	Mostly new	Extremely innovative
Development Type	Minor change; debugging	New version of a canned package	Modifications to an existing system	[New canned package]	New in-house development

supposed to write, qualitatively, the effect of each factor on the dimensions of activities, control, human resources, nonhuman resources, and time. The two lines at the top of form 2 indicate at which step the form is completed and to what step it pertains. The evaluator should fill out one form 2 for each step of the entire project.

Upon completion of a step, the entire set of these second forms is reviewed and revised. Every review provides a "fresh" view of the entire project.

Table 9.7 reflects the wholesale firm case. It illustrates form 2 as it was filled out by the evaluator during the preliminary analysis step relating to the feasibility study step. This is, in fact, a preconception of a step (note that the marks were taken from form 1 in table 9.6).

Since form 2 has to be filled out for each step, the aggregation of the forms (qualitatively, not mathematically) gives the evaluator some ideas about the nature of the ISDLC for this particular project at each given step of the ISDLC.

It is very important to note that the procedure presented here is based on an iterative process. The first time the set of forms is filled out is during the preliminary analysis step. Subsequently, whenever a step or a major activity is completed, reevaluation should take place, culminating in a revised set of forms. Thus, the suggested procedure serves for planning as well as for audit and review.

The Small or Personal System Development Life Cycle

This chapter started with a detailed description of the information system development life cycle. That approach characterizes the design process of "bread and butter" applications of organizations, such as billing, payroll, and inventory, where the emphasis is on computerized systems that periodically (daily, weekly, etc.) have to process a relatively large volume of transactions. These are the typical transaction processing systems and structured decision systems. We will refer to these as *conventional systems.*

Table 9.7 A Sample Form 2 (Step Characteristics)

Influential Factors		Possible Implications for Dimensions				
Name	*Mark in Form 1*	*Activities*	*Control*	*Human Resources*	*Nonhuman Resources*	*Time*
Organizational Scope	4	Wide scope—emphasize organization study	Carefully plan team's interviews so they won't waste too much effort	Team of 3 is enough: 2 EDP professionals + 1 user	Travel expenses and means	Need time to visit remote locations
Importance	3	Don't go too far in detailed design	Normal control procedures; i.e., one interim report	Select a good professional but not the "best"	Not relevant	No rush—2, 3 months is good enough
Organizational Maturity	2	No need to anticipate "resistance to change"; no need to emphasize aspects of training and procedure writing	Not relevant	EDP and user can provide experienced persons to feasibility team	Not relevant	No delays due to misunderstanding are expected
Information Policy	2	Inquire only into centralized systems	Team reports to EDP development manager	Limited user participation (maybe 1) in feasibility study	Not relevant	Not relevant
Level of Structure	2	Structured—no need to deeply involve users; no need to get into pilot programs at that stage	No need to double-check team's findings	Need good "technician"; no need for a DSS specialist	Not relevant	Shouldn't take much time to derive information requirements
Technological Environment	2	Nothing new; no need to inquire into technical feasibility	Check carefully only if the team recommends new technology	Include someone who knows telecommunication and online systems	Not relevant	No special problem is anticipated
Development Type	4	Survey software market for packages	Tight control over possible packages; beware of traps	Need someone who can check canned software	Provide testing facilities for canned packages	Might take time to survey the market

Filled during *Preliminary Analysis* Step
Relates to *Feasibility Study* Step

The previous section argues the need for introducing flexibility into the ISDLC. A high degree of flexibility must characterize the development life cycle of a class of *small or personal systems* for which traditional design methods are ill suited. This class of systems would particularly encompass most DSS development.

The term "small" is used here in reference to the scope of the particular system being developed, not in reference to whether it involves small or large computer equipment. A small DSS, for example, might very well run on a large mainframe. It might also be developed for the analysis of data extracted from a very large transaction processing system. (A very large information system might also be developed to run on a small personal computer or workstation.)

The word "personal" is also used to indicate scope. While the most obvious example would be a system developed to run on a personal computer, and possibly developed by the user, the implications of it being a personal system are more significantly derived from the limits placed on who the system must serve. Thus, a personal DSS might run on a mainframe to serve a particular individual's needs.

What characterizes the small and personal systems is both the need and the ability to respond to change. It could be argued that flexibility is desirable for all computerized systems. The maintenance costs during the life cycle of a conventional system are frequently more than its development cost. But there are several constraints that limit the flexibility for conventional systems. These constraints are related to the volume of inputs and outputs, file sizes, activity levels, number of people who must interact with the system, and the structured nature of the tasks. Therefore, frequent changes in conventional systems are troublesome. The small or personal systems, on the other hand, must be structured to facilitate a constant process of change in order to be effective in most cases. Their limited scope makes frequent and repeated change possible. The development life cycle of these systems emphasizes creating effective systems.

Not every DSS is a personal system (we reviewed institutional DSS ch. 6) and not every personal DSS is necessarily small. An institutional DSS, or one that is simply a large project, should be treated as a conventional system in terms of its life cycle view. Not every small or personal system is a DSS, but most will be. In the following sections we look at the life cycle for DSS as it exemplifies the development of small or personal systems, with special consideration for systems that are decision oriented.

Characteristics of DSS Development Patterns

Certain development patterns have been proposed as appropriate to DSS. Ginzberg and Stohr [8] summarize and discuss the common prescriptions for DSS development as follows:

It must include normative decision modeling.

It must induce change.

It must involve the user (to the extent possible).

The design process is flexible.

It focuses on the individual user, on roles, or on a problem.

While all of these characterize a DSS development process, the first two uniquely differentiate the DSS development from conventional system development.

A normative model specifies how a decision (or part of it) should be made. Normative modeling is the mechanism by which additional structure is imposed on unstructured or semistructured decision situations. Thus, if one purpose of a DSS is to bring structure to decision making, normative decision modeling is a necessary part of the DSS development process (you may want to review the discussion in ch. 3 on the normative value of information).

DSSs differ from most conventional systems in their orientation toward change. Conventional systems, with their emphasis on efficiency, attempt to avoid frequent changes and to concentrate on recording and processing relatively large volumes of transactions. DSSs, on the other hand, with their emphasis on effectiveness, attempt to alter the way people define and solve problems. This implies a different role for the DSS designer than that for designers of conventional systems.

The DSS designer acts more as a change agent, while the other designers act more as technicians (you may recall that the designer normally translates the logical design of the information analyst to very detailed technical specifications without much user involvement). As a result, the DSS designer must pay considerable attention to the organizational changes that are required, and must plan for more comprehensive training activities than are normally provided in conventional system development efforts.

We have stressed the need for user involvement in developing any type of a computerized system. User involvement in DSS development is more important than in conventional systems. DSSs are often less well defined, imply greater change, and require more training. As a result, user involvement is needed to help the designer resolve design uncertainties and to train the users of the new system. It should be noted that it may be difficult to involve the users during DSS development, sometimes because of the large number of users or because typical DSS users (e.g., senior-level executives) have limited time resources.

DSS literature has argued the need for an evolutionary, or an adaptive, design process for a DSS. This need follows naturally from the nature of the managerial and decision situations supported by a DSS. Ongoing management of DSS development and use, instead of just installation and use (as is the case of conventional systems), is necessary to address the need for the system's responsiveness over time. Obviously, not all DSSs experience rapid evolution in usage, while some conventional systems do. The key is to adopt a flexible development process (as argued in the previous section of this chapter) and to match the design approach to the needs of the situation. Where fairly stable usage patterns can be projected, a more traditional approach (i.e., ISDLC) is appropriate.

DSS may be oriented toward a particular individual, an organizational role (function), a specific problem, or a set of problems. This difference in focus has implications for the DSS development process.

An individual-oriented DSS should be designed with the needs and preferences of that individual in mind: which decisions should be supported, what models and data are appropriate, how data should be presented. In this case, the individual's cognitive style (see ch. 2) is a key factor in system design.

A DSS can be designed to support specific roles, such as one that supports decision-making behavior of people in certain positions (e.g., purchasing officers). Such systems can be designed with less attention to individual user preferences. Such a system also employs a normative model as defined by the organization, not by a user-designer dialog.

Problem-oriented DSSs are concerned with how certain problems should be solved, regardless of who is doing the problem solving. Such DSSs are also organizationally defined.

We hope that this discussion has convinced you that the very nature of DSS requires a different design technique from that for conventional systems. Most traditional systems analysis and design approaches are based on the assumption that the computerized system will have a well-defined process. But by their very nature, DSSs need to be independent of any imposed process because different decision makers approach problem solving in different ways.

DSS Development Approaches

There are a number of DSS design frameworks (approaches to construct a DSS). All approaches emphasize flexibility and recognize the need to build DSS with short, rapid feedback from users to ensure that development is proceeding correctly. The result is that the four major phases of an ISDLC (definition, construction, implementation, and operations) are combined into a single step that is repetitive.

Basically, the process is as follows: the user and the designer agree on a small but significant subproblem, then design and implement an initial system to support the decision making required by the subproblem. After a short period of use, the system is evaluated, modified, and expanded. This cycle is repeated until a relatively stable system is evolved. Although the frequency and extent of change will then decrease, the system will never be fully stable. It will always be changing.

The Iterative Design Approach

Sprague and Carlson [23, ch. 5] advocate the use of an *iterative design* in developing a DSS. It is the process by which flexibility is made operational in DSS. These authors describe it as a series of rapid cycles through the life cycle phases that are compressed and repeated. The development path of a specific DSS begins with version 0, the minimal usable system, moves to a satisfactory and relatively stable version, then changes in response to changes in the user, decision situations, and environment. The steps in the iterative process are as follows [23, p. 140]:

1. The user and the designer jointly identify a subproblem.
2. The designer develops a small but usable system to support the user. The designer and the user go through all the steps of the system development process quickly and on a small scale.
3. The system is refined, expanded, and modified in cycles.
4. At the end of each cycle, the system is evaluated by the user. With constant evaluation, the system can die when the need for it is over or when it proves to be of no value. Otherwise, a new cycle of analysis-design-implementation-utilization-evaluation starts.

The Adaptive Design Approach

The *adaptive design approach,* advocated by Keen and Gambino (see [14] for a detailed description of the approach and its use in developing a commercial DSS product), assumes that a "relatively" final system must evolve through usage and learning. Rather than the conventional focus on functional specifications, the designer relies on a prototype of a real system that provides the base for learning by using.

The adaptive design approach is based on the following principles:

1. Finding out quickly what is important to the user, as opposed to what the designer thinks ought to be important.

2. Providing something concrete with which the user (i.e., a prototype) can react and with which the user can experiment.

3. Defining a clear architecture for the DSS (i.e., linkages between the dialog, data, and modeling subsystems, in terms of the discussion in ch. 6), so that it can be easily modified and developed.

4. Paying careful attention to the user-DSS dialog and thus to the design of the dialog management subsystem of the DSS. This is why the adaptive design approach is also labeled the *linguistic approach.*

5. Emphasizing the importance of user learning in terms of the evolution of the system and the need for flexibility in the DSS.

6. Emphasizing getting started, rather than getting finished.

Notice that the principles of adaptive design stand in sharp contrast to the principles of the ISDLC. Also, notice that adaptive design is a joint venture between user and designer. The designer's job goes well beyond conventional systems design due to his or her need to

1. Understand the decision situation and user
2. Be able to humanize and customize the system for the user
3. Be responsive to the user and help stimulate exploration and learning

The Decision-Oriented Approach

The decision research focus addresses the prescriptive aspects of what decision makers should do (or how decisions should be made). A *decision-oriented approach* attempts to provide direction to DSS development by indicating what to monitor and what choices to make in order to direct the evolution of both decision making and DSS. In other words, this approach emphasizes the importance of the *D* in DSS. Proponents of the approach claim that, lacking a clear idea of the content and direction of changes to be achieved, an adaptive approach can lead to the development of systems that are usable and used, but not very useful.

The process of developing a DSS for a specific decision situation is shown here (for a detailed discussion and examples see [24]).

1. Choose a decision situation (e.g., how to invest surplus funds).

2. Collect data relevant to the decision situation.

3. Establish a coherent description of the current decision process.

4. Specify a norm for how the decision should be made—The activities of data collection and descriptive and normative modeling are highly interdependent. For example, a statement by the decision maker that only investment in bonds is considered implicitly tells that the decision norm is to consider a larger number of alternatives, such as investing in stocks. This, in turn, guides the collection of data (e.g., both data on bonds and stocks) in order to substantiate a tentative diagnosis, which is the next activity.

5. Diagnose and specify changes in decision making—For example, the designer may find that the decision maker relies on nominal rates of return only and disregards risks associated with the investment alternatives. The diagnosis might imply the introduction of DSS capabilities that support exploration of the rates of return and risk factors associated with various bonds and stocks. Diagnosis thus involves determining how decisions are currently made, specifying how they should be made, and understanding why decisions are not made as they should. Specification of changes in decision processes involves choosing what specific improvements in decision behavior are to be achieved and what DSS is required in order to achieve the specified improvements.

6. Provide the functional specifications for the desired DSS (e.g., output representations to the decision maker, operations on data, or commands that the decision maker can invoke).

7. Design and build the DSS: determine the nature of the dialog, data and modeling subsystems, and the DSS resources (see ch. 6).

8. Implement the DSS.

9. Monitor and evaluate changes in decision making and the impact of the current version of the DSS.

The decision-oriented approach is similar to the iterative and adaptive design approaches in that it also recognizes the need for cycling—returning from a given activity to prior ones until a relatively stable version of a DSS is obtained. Thus, the designer can go back from activity 9 (evaluation) to any of the activities 2 to 8; from activity 7 (designing and building the DSS) to activities 5 or 6; from activity 5 (diagnosis and specification of changes) to any of the activities 1 to 4.

To sum up, the three development approaches described in this section embody different strategies. The strategy behind the iterative and adaptive designs relies on computer-based technology developed as a simple, easy-to-use personal aid. It is primarily up to the user to decide when and how to use the system. This strategy will likely dominate as the market for DSS products grows.

The strategy behind the decision-oriented approach is based on improving decision-making effectiveness. It is a long-term effort, where the development of a DSS is viewed as one among several ways to increase the effectiveness of decision making. It is based on an effort to diagnose current decision making prior to the development of DSS. While the technology should not dominate the change process under this approach, it also needs to be kept simple, easy to use, and adaptable. For a study that surveyed DSS users' assessments of the importance of DSS development life cycle stages, see [20].

A Concluding Remark Concerning DSS

Most DSS literature has emphasized the differences between DSS and conventional systems. In contrast, we maintain that DSSs differ from conventional systems in degree, not in fundamental structure. For instance, the nature of large-scale and institutional DSSs are very close to conventional systems in design focus (efficiency of processing) and in implementation environment (anonymous users).

The main difference between DSS and conventional systems lies in the relationship between the DSS and its development process. The process is a cyclical system of activities (analysis, construction, implementation, evaluation) with interrelationships among three elements—the development process, the DSS, and the user and his or her decision situation. It is mainly in the analysis phase that DSS asserts its uniqueness by adopting a design approach that differs from the one used to develop conventional systems (e.g., the adaptive approach, the decision-oriented approach). It is this design approach that facilitates the following commonly accepted assertions about a *good* DSS:

It changes the decision situation.

It provides for the emergence of structure.

Other Approaches to Modeling the Life Cycle

We began this chapter by pointing out the general agreement that exists with regard to the phases that an information system development project goes through. While there are differences in the naming of those phases, each model of the ISDLC acknowledges their existence. Each recognizes that there are certain activities that must be performed in some organized way.

We described the traditional view of the ISDLC. While this is still an appropriate framework within which to analyze the life cycle, especially as it applies to large systems, we have said that a more flexible approach may be more suitable in actual practice. We have also looked at the matter of developing small or personal systems where there is greater emphasis on changes occurring within those systems.

Throughout the chapter we have emphasized the iterative nature of the development process. This iteration frequently results when something is discovered that requires changes to what was done at an earlier stage. In other words, the iterating is done to correct errors or omissions. Some variations on the ISDLC focus on intentional iteration as a tool of the development process.

Rapid Prototyping

One technique that has become widely used is that of *rapid prototyping*. As mentioned earlier, the value of prototyping is in getting the user involved more directly, thus gaining greater assurance that the design is responsive to the user's needs. In the rapid prototyping method, the first design is done quickly in the interests of building what is admittedly only a partial system. This provides the user something to respond to that is much more concrete than a document describing what the system is expected to do. With the results of the user's testing of this prototype, the developers can return to the specifications and refine them, produce a new design and implement it, and test a second prototype, then a third, and so on. Thus, these phases can be iterated until a final product is produced and put into operation.

There are numerous advantages to this approach. The first has already been mentioned—that of drawing the user into the development process in a more direct way. The result of this is to produce a system that can be put into operation in a much more satisfactory manner. This is particularly true of systems that involve much interaction between the user and the computer, either through a terminal or by the use of a personal computer. The prototype allows the user to get the feel of using the system while it is still being designed. In this way, any problems the user uncovers can be dealt with as a natural part of the development process, not as defects exposed after operation has begun.

Another advantage to this approach is that it is possible to detect, at a much earlier time, when a project is simply not going to be successful. An early prototype may make it clear that the development of the final product will be too costly, too time consuming, or for some other reason unsatisfactory. It is much easier for management to decide to cancel a project if such an opportunity is presented before a great amount of time and money has been invested.

Prototyping can be especially valuable in the development of brand new systems. In these situations, where there is no current manual or computerized version of the system on which to base the specifications for the new system, it is often a problem for even the potential users to visualize what the end product should be. The prototyping approach can provide "trial balloons" upon which to base further specifications.

Prototyping is not without its drawbacks (see [25]). It should not be viewed as a replacement for the more traditional approach, but simply as an alternative to be considered in many development situations.

Incremental Enhancement
Another variation on the iteration theme is that of *incremental enhancement*. In this approach the system is developed in increments, rather than in its entirety. Some portion of the total system is identified, completed, and put into operation. Then, an additional part goes through the entire cycle as an enhancement to the first version. In this way, a large system can be developed as a series of smaller projects rather than as just one large one.

Obviously, this approach can be combined with the prototyping approach. The first increment, especially, can be developed as a series of prototypes. Additional increments can also be prototyped on top of the existing system.

Technological Factors Influencing the ISDLC
There are other possible ways in which to view the ISDLC (e.g., the *cyclical model*) giving management additional flexibility in choosing the appropriate way in which to undertake a particular project. (For further comparison of the various models, see [12]

or [21]). We mentioned earlier some of the characteristics of the system being developed that make different strategies appropriate for different systems (e.g., mainframe or microcomputer, centralized or distributed, large or small, etc.). There are also some technological considerations that have had a substantial effect on system development. We will mention them here, and discuss them further in chapter 10.

1. Personal computers—Personal computers and workstations have had a profound effect on the kinds of systems that can be built where the system uses a PC or workstation as its computer, or as part of a larger system. The personal computer has also had an effect on the development process itself. Whether the system is being developed for PCs or for mainframes, the PC can be used as a development tool for programming, prototyping, documentation, and a variety of other support functions. This allows the development process to move forward more rapidly, more flexibly, less expensively, and with greater control.

2. Development software—Two kinds of software contribute to the desirability of strategies such as rapid prototyping. The first applies where programming is done in a conventional programming language. The fast and highly interactive program development tools that are available for personal computers and workstations make it practical to develop prototypes quickly, even in Pascal or C.

   An even greater contribution is made by the various *fourth generation* software packages for either PCs or mainframes. These 4GLs and related data base management software capabilities (see Appendix A) allow for much faster development of systems, and have been designed in such a way that prototyping or incremental development is a more convenient and natural process.

3. Reusable software—More and more emphasis is placed on building software that is *reusable*. This is an objective of many of the newer programming languages, and should be an objective of the design process. Clearly, the development of a new system can be made dramatically easier if substantial portions of it can be constructed from existing, reusable software modules. Such modules are already tested and documented. They may make it possible to develop the first prototype of a new system very quickly. Object-oriented programming languages (such as C++) focus on building programs around reusable objects. The package concept in the Ada programing language facilitates the reuse of program modules.

   Reusability adds another dimension to the ISDLC, since at the appropriate points in that cycle the developers must consider what available components might be reused. This means also that the reusable components must be catalogued and readily available. Hooper [10] examines the reusability issue from a managerial standpoint.

4. CASE tools—*Computer aided software engineering* (CASE) tools will also exert considerable influence on the way in which the ISDLC is formed for a particular project. Actually, the CASE tools that an organization has adopted will affect the organization's life cycle view on all of its projects. The CASE environment guides the analysis and documentation of a project and should make it easier to iterate the various stages in either the prototyping or enhancement strategies. Furthermore, it is claimed that the use of CASE tools tends to lead the developers into placing greater emphasis on the analysis and design phases, resulting in significantly less time to program and test the software [22].

Practical Conclusions for Information System Design and Use

The following are practical conclusions for information system design and use.

1. Every information system application follows a life cycle comprising the major phases of definition, construction, implementation, and operation.

2. The life cycle is an iterative process. The end of each phase and each activity constitutes a milestone for review and management decision on whether to continue, revise, iterate, or abandon the project.

3. Each activity in the life cycle is performed by specific implementors and produces specific documentation. The documentation serves as one of the inputs for subsequent activities of the life cycle.

4. The life cycle of an information system is finite. The system is terminated when it cannot efficiently cope with errors and changes.

5. The process of developing and operating an information system must be well planned and well controlled.

6. The life cycle is significantly affected by environmental factors, such as rapid advances in hardware/software technology; long time spans required to develop a system; constantly increasing amounts of resources required for developing a system; short supply of information system experts; and communication difficulties between system developers and users.

7. Active involvement of the system's user in its development is mandatory.

8. Sometimes the wisest decision is to stop the development of a system and to consider the expenditures on it as sunk costs.

9. Prototyping is a major tool to improve understanding between users and system developers.

10. The documentation generated with each activity serves as communication and as a control tool.

11. System development is a process of structured creativity.

12. Developing procedures for users and information system personnel is as important as developing computer programs.

13. The conversion activity should be regarded as a system itself and should be treated accordingly.

14. Three aspects are evaluated during the feasibility study activity: economic, technical, and organizational.

15. A project plan should be presented to management during the first phase of the life cycle. It should cover the proposed activities and their duration, required resources, personnel and budget, and training and installation plans.

16. The system design activity should establish a comprehensive set of controls for the new system.

17. The designed system should produce information by which the effectiveness and efficiency of the system can be measured.

18. Testing of individual programs and of the whole system should be performed by persons other than those directly involved in their development.

19. An acceptance test of the new system should be performed by the user before the system goes into operation.

20. Conversion and installation costs are capital expenditures and are included in the investment in project development.

21. Many maintenance projects take place during the operation activity and have a life cycle of their own.

22. A comprehensive review shortly after the installation of the system and periodic audits thereafter form control points for users and management throughout the operation of the system.

23. Depending on the system, the activities of the life cycle are undertaken in linear or in parallel fashion, or they may overlap.

24. The follow-up of a master plan is as important as the creation of it. An information system committee (or any other adequate body) must be established to serve as a permanent policymaker and to control the information systems in an organization.

25. Involvement of users and management in feasibility studies is essential. A feasibility team should not be staffed only by information systems specialists, but also by user and management representatives.

26. The development team should be headed by the same individual all the way through the development life cycle. Other members of the team may vary according to the needs of each specific development activity.

27. An ad hoc steering committee consisting of senior managers must monitor the development project and review major decisions.

28. The framework for information system development is always the same. However, each project is typified by a number of traits that might vary among different projects. Thus, some flexibility within the development cycle is highly recommended.

29. Traditional system design methods are ill suited for developing a DSS or other small or personal systems.

30. The DSS designer should act more as a change agent than as a mere technician.

31. User involvement in ISDLC is important. Techniques such as rapid prototyping can serve to increase that involvement.

32. User involvement in DSS development is even more important than it is in conventional systems.

33. The application of CASE tools not only helps to speed up the analysis and development, but (by shifting the emphasis to the analysis phase) tends to improve the design.

34. If it is advisable to cancel a development project, the sooner that fact can be discovered, the better.

Summary

The development and operation of an information system (or application) follow a life cycle comprising the major phases of definition, construction, implementation, and operation. The definition phase includes the activities of preliminary analysis, feasibility study, information analysis, and system design. The construction phase consists of the activities of programming and procedure development. Implementation concerns conversion and training activities. The operation phase includes the production and maintenance activities, postinstallation reviews, and the termination of the system life cycle. The concept of a life cycle structures this creative process and causes the process to be performed in a disciplined way, without overly constraining the process. It is intended to satisfy the following objectives:

To establish checkpoints for management

To develop backup documentation

To create a standard for evaluating the current status of a project

To set standard content for products of each activity

To define a common vocabulary of terms that can be used by all involved in the life cycle process

The major documents created during the various activities of the life cycle are the preliminary conceptual report; the feasibility report; the system analysis report; the system design report; various program, user, and operator manuals; and the postaudit report.

Maintenance projects are initiated during the operation activity of the life cycle because of constant requests for changes and the discovery of errors. These projects follow a similar life cycle process. At some point in time the system is abandoned or replaced and a new life cycle is initiated.

The development of information systems is pursued by five organizational bodies. (1) An information system committee is a permanent body that directs information systems policy and initiates new projects. (2) A feasibility team is established whenever the validity of a suggested application has to be verified. Its recommendations are submitted to the information system committee for a GO/NO GO decision. If a GO decision is made, (3) a development team assumes responsibility for the entire development, starting with information analysis and going through system design, programming, and procedure writing. Implementation and conversion are handled by (4) an implementation team. Both the development team and implementation team are monitored by an ad hoc committee of senior users and managers, (5) the steering committee.

The traditional approach to the development life cycle is very rigid. However, contemporary circumstances call for a more flexible approach. One has to distinguish between in-house development and the purchase of ready-made software; between transaction processing systems and decision support systems; between mainframe applications and microcomputer applications.

The factors affecting a development project are: the organizational scope of the project; the importance of the project to the continuity of the organization; the maturity and competence of the people involved; the policy toward information system development; the degree of structure of the problem; the technological environment; and the type of development (e.g., a new system and modifications in an existing system).

These factors may cause variations in a number of aspects, such as development activities, control, human and nonhuman resource allocation, and time limitations.

A practical approach to planning a development project is to construct a project profile in which all the factors are evaluated, to assess the factors' impact on the various aspects, and then to plan the project accordingly.

Small and personal systems present a different situation in terms of the development life cycle. Unlike large or conventional systems, these systems are characterized by the expectation of change. Therefore, the designer provides for a higher degree of adaptability in the system and a greater amount of flexibility in the ISDLC. Traditional design methods are ill suited for such small systems. Typical of these systems is the noninstitutional DSS. The DSS development must induce change, must deeply involve the user, must be flexible, and must focus on an individual user, on functional roles, or on a problem.

There are a variety of approaches to constructing a DSS. All emphasize flexibility and recognize the need to build DSS with rapid feedback from users to ensure that development is proceeding correctly. The result is that the major phases in the life of an information system (definition, construction, implementation, and operations) are combined into a single step that is repetitive.

There are other models of the ISDLC that emphasize the iterative nature of the development process. By intentionally iterating the cycle, or parts of the cycle, a number of advantages can be gained. Rapid prototyping ensures early involvement of the user resulting in important feedback into the development process. Iterative enhancement can reduce a large project into a series of smaller ones. Both methods contribute to an earlier determination that a project should be discontinued, if in fact the development is not going to be cost effective.

CASE tools are increasingly used to support and improve all phases of the ISDLC. The use of these tools tends to lead the developers into placing more emphasis on the design phase, with a resulting improvement in the time required to develop the system and in the quality of the software produced.

Key Concepts

acceptance test
adaptive design
application generator
conventional system
conversion
conversion log
computer aided software engineering
  (CASE)
computer: operator, selection
construction
cyclical model
debugging
decision-oriented approach
definition
design: conceptual, detailed, logical,
  physical, system, technical
development: project, team
documentation
electronic data processing (EDP) auditor
feasibility: economic, organizational,
  report, study, team, technical
horizontal dimensions: activity, control,
  human resource, nonhuman resource,
  time
implementation
implementation team
implementors
incremental enhancement
information: analysis, analyst
information system committee
information system development life
  cycle (ISDLC)
input/output personnel

installation
iterative design
iterative process
life cycle
linguistic approach
maintenance
maintenance: log, programmer, project
operation
personal system
phases
postaudit
preliminary analysis
preliminary conceptual report
procedure development
program
program test (unit test)
programmer
programming project
project plan
prototype (prototyping)
rapid prototyping
request for change
reusable software
small system
software engineering
system: analysis, analyst, controls,
  designer, test
steering committee
structured walk-through
termination
test data
training
user

References

1. Ahituv, N., D. Even-Tsur, and B. Sadan. "Procedures and Practices for Conducting Post Evaluation of Information Systems." *Journal of Information Systems Management* 3, no. 2 (Spring 1986): 61–65.
2. Ahituv, N., and B. Sadan. "Learning to Live in a Distributed World." *Datamation* 31, no. 18 (Sept. 1985): 139–48.

3. Arthur, L. J. *Software Evolution: The Software Maintenance Challenge.* New York: Wiley-Interscience, 1988.

4. Buchanan, J. R., and R. G. Linowes. "Understanding Distributed Data Processing." *Harvard Business Review* 58, no. 4 (July–Aug. 1980): 143–53.

5. Buchanan, J. R., and R. G. Linowes. "Making Distributed Data Processing Work."*Harvard Business Review* 58, no. 5 (Sept.–Oct. 1980): 143–61.

6. Davis, G. B., and M. H. Olson. *Management Information Systems: Conceptual Foundation, Structure, and Development,* 2d ed. New York: McGraw-Hill, 1985.

7. Gibson, C. F., and R. L. Nolan. "Managing the Four Stages of EDP Growth." *Harvard Business Review* 52, no. 1 (Jan.–Feb. 1974): 76–88.

8. Ginzberg, M. J., and E. A. Stohr. "Decision Support System: Issues and Perspectives." In *Decision Support Systems,* edited by M. J. Ginzberg, W. R. Reitman, and E. A. Stohr, 9–32. Amsterdam: North-Holland, 1982.

9. Gremillion, L. L., and P. Pyburn. "Breaking the Systems Development Bottleneck." *Harvard Business Review* 61, no. 2 (Mar.–Apr. 1983): 130–37.

10. Hooper, J. W., and R. O. Chester. *Software Reuse: Guidelines and Methods.* New York: Plenum Press, 1991.

11. Jalote, P. *An Integrated Approach to Software Engineering.* New York: Springer-Verlag, 1991.

12. Jones, G. W. *Software Engineering.* New York: John Wiley & Sons, 1990.

13. Jordan, E. W., and J. J. Machesky. *Systems Development: Requirements, Evaluation, Design, and Implementation.* Boston: PWS-Kent, 1990.

14. Keen, P. G. W., and T. J. Gambino. "Building a Decision Support System: The Mythical Man-Month Revisited." In *Building Decision Support Systems,* edited by J. L. Bennett. Reading, MA: Addison-Wesley, 1983.

15. Li, E. Y. "Software Testing In a System Development Process: A Life Cycle Perspective." *Journal of Systems Management* 41, 8 (Aug. 1990): 23–31.

16. Lucas, H. C., Jr. *Information Systems Concepts for Management.* 4th ed. New York: Mitchell McGraw-Hill, 1990.

17. McFarlan, F. W. "Portfolio Approach to Information Systems." *Harvard Business Review* 59, no. 5 (Sept.–Oct. 1981): 142–50.

18. McFarlan, F. W., J. L. McKenney, and P. Pyburn. "The Information Archipelago—Plotting a Course." *Harvard Business Review* 61, no. 1 (Jan.–Feb. 1983): 145–56.

19. McKenney, J. L., and F. W. McFarlan. "The Information Archipelago—Maps and Bridges." *Harvard Business Review* 60, no. 5 (Sept.–Oct. 1982): 109–19.

20. Meador, C. L., M. J. Guyot, and P. G. W. Keen. "Setting Priorities for DSS Development." *MIS Quarterly* 8, no. 2 (June 1984): 117–29.

21. Pressman, R. S. *Software Engineering: A Practitioner's Approach.* New York: McGraw-Hill, 1992.

22. Souza, E. "The Impact of CASE on Software Development." *Journal of Information Systems Management* 8, no. 1 (Winter 1991): 17–24.

23. Sprague, R. H., and E. D. Carlson. *Building Effective Decision Support Systems.* Englewood Cliffs, NJ: Prentice-Hall, 1982.

24. Stabell, C. B. "A Decision-Oriented Approach to Building DSS." In *Building Decision Support Systems,* edited by J. L. Bennett. Reading, MA: Addison-Wesley, 1983.

25. Weinberg, R. S. "Prototyping and the Systems Development Life Cycle." *Journal of Information Systems Management* 8, no. 2 (Spring 1991): 47–53.

Questions

1. Explain why all systems eventually become outmoded.
2. Select three problems common to the development of information systems and describe their causes and steps toward solution.
3. How does the environment affect the development process?
4. Explain why the definition phase is the most appropriate time to cope with risk.
5. Why is documentation important to the information system life cycle?
6. What are the phases and activities of the information system life cycle?
7. What questions should the feasibility study address?
8. What elements make up the project plan?
9. Describe the different roles of the information analyst, system designer, and programmer.
10. Differentiate by describing the members and the team or committee function of: (a) information system committee; (b) feasibility team; (c) steering committee; (d) development team; and (e) implementation team.

Problems

1. A life insurance company is considering an information system for all its client records. Using what you have learned about the information system life cycle, write a proposal for the definition phase.
2. Prepare the personnel plan and resource plan sections of a project plan document for a hospital information system. When preparing the plan, take into account the following items.
   a. The following information systems must be developed:
      Inpatient medical and billing records
      Outpatient medical and billing records
      Medical supplies inventory
      Operating room schedule
      Laboratories schedule
      Schedule of doctors, nurses, and administrative personnel
   b. There exists a hospital computer center with enough time, space, materials, etc., to meet the requirements of the new systems.
   c. The information systems staff consists of the department head, two systems analysts, and three programmers.
   d. The project is to last two years.
   Make any other assumptions necessary to complete the assignment.

School Districts Payroll

A county office is required by law to provide payroll processing for any school district within the county that desires the service. All basic processing must be provided at no cost to the school districts, and funding for this service will be provided by the state.

Currently the county is using a batch system to provide payroll warrants and reporting to 105 school districts over a four-thousand-square-mile radius. Data is submitted for capture to the county office five days prior to the warrants being issued. Most of the data is keyed in-house except during peak load periods when outside vendors are used to maintain the current level of service, with no more than a five-day turnaround. Payroll is processed every night, Monday through Friday, and warrants and appropriate reports are produced. The largest run is 50 thousand warrants, the smallest around 200. This equates to about 200 thousand warrants a month and over one billion dollars a year.

The current system was written in the early seventies and has been modified extensively to meet Federal and State requirements. The system also has to deal with individual demands made by districts as the result of contract negotiations. This may involve several different contracts per district.

As bargaining units become more active in the public sector, more demands are put on the payroll system. This, coupled with changing legislation, has resulted in a list of required changes needed and a wish list of desired changes to the current system. All parties have agreed that the system must have the following capabilities and that they will be provided:

1. Reducing the time frame from document submittal to warrant production is one of the most important capabilities. The districts are not averse to the time or to the cost of an online time reporting system.

2. Direct deposit to a variety of banks is also very high on the need list. This allows the district to pay either a portion or all of an employee's retirement benefits by bargaining units.

3. Cafeteria style benefits packages allow individuals to select how the dollar amount allocated for fringe benefits for each employee is spent.

All parties have also agreed that they will meet to discuss any other needs and wants that might be desired or anticipated at this time. These will all be evaluated along with the costs associated with each change. Additional meetings will be held to decide which wants are worth the costs.

Questions

1. Where in the life cycle is the current system and what criteria did you use to determine this?

2. What would be the next step for the data processing department to take, and how should they go about it?

3. Considering the critical nature of this application, if the decision were made to develop a new system, what considerations would be necessary for the conversion process?

JAVL: The Life Cycle of an Information System

You are about to take a journey through the life of a data communications system. The purpose of this system is to transfer graphics data between remote divisions of a large magazine corporation. It is hoped that the system will eventually assist in merging the company's graphics and text data bases in an effort to ease magazine production. With these goals in mind, we will begin our travels.

We are now entering the world of JAVL, Inc. This magazine company is composed of three divisions: International Productions, Domestic Productions, and Resource Management. All international and domestic operations are handled at the first two divisions respectively. However, the Resource Management division is somewhat complex. It houses the company's support departments such as Facilities, Administration, and Information Systems. Our travels will focus greatly on this latter department.

A review of some historical files reveals that the need for a cross-domain data communications system was initially envisioned by one of JAVL's first level managers in the Information Systems department. She saw that a single graphics data base could easily replace the two semiredundant data bases which currently existed at the company's productions divisions. Also, the need for nightly batch transmittals of graphics data could be totally alleviated. It would be more efficient if an editor could access a drawing from another division at any time of the day. Plus the hardware that supported the batch transmittals could easily be adapted for this new system.

After discussing the idea with her management and a few of the magazine's editors, it was determined that the idea should be pursued and eventually extended to create an integrated graphics and text data base. A couple of information system consultants were hired to conduct the major portion of the system's development. In an effort to establish control, they divided the development process into two major phases: Definition and Construction. They further divided these phases into steps that will become the life path of the system.

The first step of the Definition Phase was called the Preliminary Analysis. Here, emphasis was placed on determining the true nature of the problem the system was being designed to resolve. Pertinent data was gathered and information requirements were established. The consultants were assisted by IS management and the most experienced application program analysts and system programmers in the company. Minimum input was also received from a few editors. The research culminated with a Preliminary Conceptual Report, which included the scope and boundaries of the proposed information system along with a recommendation for future action. The document was presented to and approved by the IS management.

In the Feasibility Step of the Definition Phase, which from management's opinion is the most crucial step in the development life cycle, several alternatives were considered by the consultants. Questions were answered such as: "What are the problems with the batch mode?" "Is the proposed system affordable?" "Should users be receptive of the system?" Assistance was given by the same personnel, and the resulting Feasibility Report was approved by the IS management.

Our tour through the Definition Phase is now down to two steps. However, before these steps were approached, the manager who had envisioned the system was transferred to a foreign subsidiary. Once she had gone, much of the thrust behind the system vanished. Development continued nonetheless.

With the Information Analysis step came a lot of system, programming, and procedure specifications. As a result, the step was partially inclusive of the System Design step which was designated to follow. This time, only the consultants and the programmers participated in the analysis. Things were really getting out of hand now that the envisioning manager was gone. Steps were no longer being approved by even the IS management. It was becoming quite difficult to determine who the final user would be. As a result, efforts moved quickly to the Construction Phase so that the system would become available as soon as possible.

The first step of the Construction Phase was Programming. The well-defined specifications from the previous step were used to produce the computer programs needed by the system. Surprisingly, an appropriate amount of documentation was created. The consultants and programmers even conducted a little testing on the final system. The system then went into immediate production.

This is where the journey ends. There are no more records in the historical files to indicate how the system functioned in a production mode. Did it work? Did the users use it? Did it resolve the targeted problems? In an effort to answer these and a few other questions, I read the book *Principles of Information Systems for Management.* I learned that many of the life cycle steps in JAVL's communications information system were either not executed or else executed only partially.

Questions

1. Discuss some of the major principles and steps that were not followed in JAVL's communication information system life cycle.
    a. What type of problems should be expected as a result?
    b. What type of personnel would have participated if these steps had been completed?
    c. What type of control would have been inherent in these steps?

2. Develop a Project Profile for the JAVL communication information system.

Chapter 10 _Principles of Information System Development and Maintenance_

Information systems development is much more a skill than it is an art. The old days when programming and systems analysis were mystical and unquestioned are over. Nowadays an information systems developer must and should comply with well-structured procedures that smooth the development of systems. While the systems developer is encouraged to incorporate intelligence, experience, and intuition into the development, these qualities are in addition to, rather than in lieu of, standard practices.

A manager/user and even a layperson in the information systems profession should actively participate in the development of information systems that will later support his or her activities. While the previous chapter outlined the logical sequence of system development steps and emphasized their technical content, this chapter concentrates on those steps where the role of managers and others who are not information systems specialists is paramount.

Introduction

In chapter 8 we outlined some approaches to establishing and monitoring an organizational strategy of information systems development that resulted in a master plan. The substance of a master plan is a list of priorities for the establishment of information systems to be developed over a period of several years. In chapter 9 we narrowed the discussion to the life cycle of an individual system. Now, in this chapter, we concentrate on some stages of the life cycle, particularly those stages in which user and management involvement is imperative.

Table 9.3 in chapter 9 indicates that all the stages of the life cycle pertain in some way or another to users and general management. However, the stages of system design and programming are considered to be more ''professional-oriented'' in that the user and management roles are confined to passive involvement. In all other stages their roles are much more active. Since this book does not intend to train professional information analysts, systems designers, or programmers, we will elaborate here on the less "professional" stages and explain only briefly what you should expect the professionals to do in these stages. At the end of the chapter we present some system analysis and design methodologies and briefly discuss the contribution of software engineering to information system development. You may refer to any technical text [2, 3, 7, 8, 13, 14, 17, 21] if you want a taste of the vocational flavor of these skills.

The Feasibility Study

The *feasibility study* is one of the most crucial stages in the information system life cycle. Its conclusions determine whether the project is going to live or to die. The feasibility study is the first stage that is highly structured and formal (the preceding preliminary analysis stage is more superficial and intuitive). It is also the last stage that does not involve a considerable investment of money and time; subsequent stages consume a lot of human and physical resources. Although it is a good idea to reassess the cost/benefits and chances of success every now and then during the development cycle, in practice people are very reluctant to abandon a system after it has been designed or programmed. Since clear-cut cases are rare, people tend to find excuses to pursue the development. Therefore, psychologically, the feasibility study is perceived to be the last stage before reaching the "point of no return." It should therefore be carefully handled by both managers and implementors.

Aspects of Feasibility

Have you ever pondered the full meaning of the notion "feasible"? Suppose you consider acquiring a means of transportation between your home and your office. First you have to find out whether current technology offers possible solutions. In this case, the market probably offers various makes of cars, motorcycles, or helicopters. Then you have to check for reliability. Will the mode really fulfill the goal of getting you to your office, safely and on time? If that reliability is assured, does your inquiry end? Certainly not; you have to assess the economic aspects of each alternative. If riding a horse is found to be the most cost-effective way, you would have to find out whether this solution is acceptable to the society around you. Would people tolerate it? Has the infrastructure to support horse riding been prepared—e.g., horse lanes and stables in the downtown area?

Webster's New Collegiate Dictionary defines *feasible* as "capable of being done or carried out; capable of being used or dealt with successfully."* We believe that the adverb *successfully* should be emphasized. Success means not only a technologically reliable solution, but one that is economically worthwhile and organizationally acceptable. Thus, there are three major aspects of feasibility: technological, economic, and organizational. We will now elaborate on each.

---

*By permission. From *Webster's New Collegiate Dictionary* © 1981 by G. C. Merriam Company, publishers of the Merriam-Webster Dictionaries.

Technological Aspects

Whenever we face an information problem in an organization, we first have to inquire into the state of the art of current hardware and software technology in order to search for a possible solution. If current technology does not support any solution, and unless we have extremely solid reasons to invent new technology, we will probably drop the subject. Very seldom does an organization opt to devise a new information system having components that are not offered by manufacturers. Particularly, this would not be recommended to an organization that does not specialize in the information technology industry.

Technological feasibility is not a problem in operational information systems, particularly those supporting the low levels of the organizational hierarchy. For example, if you intend to computerize your general ledger or accounts receivable, you are not likely to find technological problems in either hardware or software. However, if you are looking for a more sophisticated application (e.g., a decision-support system, heuristic models), or if your application depends on advanced technology (e.g., computer networks, voice recognition, complex data bases, very fast transmission), you should thoroughly investigate the state of the art before taking any further steps.

Technological feasibility is a primary condition; existence of appropriate technology is mandatory for further investigation of the next aspects.

Economic Aspects

Provided that technological feasibility has been proven, the next facet to be verified is the economic feasibility. Simply, we have to estimate costs and assess whether the benefits merit the costs.

Cost estimate is not an easy task to perform because it has to incorporate development, capital, and operation expenditures prior to commencement of system development. However, it is considered to be simpler than benefit assessment, which may include monetary tangible, nonmonetary tangible, and intangible benefits (see discussion in ch. 3). Nevertheless, this must be evaluated by the feasibility team and reviewed by the information systems committee because both the organization and the development team should get a feeling for the extent of pertinent expenses. If the expense estimate appears to exceed management expectation, or if benefits do not merit costs, the project should be abandoned right away. (In ch. 3 we reviewed some theoretical foundations of this issue. In chapter 13 we provide some practical tools for evaluating the cost/benefits of information systems.)

Organizational Aspects

In the discussion of the psychological climate in chapter 2, we mentioned that information systems are not installed in a vacuum, but in a living environment. One of the purposes of the feasibility study is to predict how the environment (i.e., pertinent departments, customers, management) will react to the installation of a proposed system. Several questions should be asked.

1. Are the employees capable of operating the system, or is it too sophisticated for their capacities? For example, there was a known case where employees were required to key in very long sentences on a terminal keyboard. Although

they were certainly not illiterate, they were not trained in long verbal keying, which frustrated and consequently offended them. Finally they reached the point where they refused to cooperate.

2. Will the employees conceive that the system might risk their status (virtually or perceivably)? If so, we could anticipate serious resistance to change. A well-known example is found in eighteenth-century England, where textile workers demolished newly invented weaving machines because the machines threatened their jobs.

3. Do we anticipate major changes in labor conditions, such as additional shifts, extreme change of productivity, etc.? This might trigger demands for salary increases, which could lead to a labor conflict. For example, a new bar code recognition system that replaces one which requires keying in data at a keyboard could remain idle for months. Keying in continues because workers demand salary raises for expected improvement in productivity; management refuses.

4. Is the proposed system compatible with existing related systems? For example, you cannot design a system having input data that is supposed to arrive on magnetic storage media if the majority of your input sources are not yet computerized.

Organizational feasibility is normally a relative, not an absolute, term. We rarely find that a project is ultimately infeasible from an organizational viewpoint. The results of the investigation normally indicate the difficulties that might be anticipated and, hence, help us in preparing measures to eliminate or mitigate them. Still, without covering this facet of feasibility, the study would be incomplete.

Steps of Feasibility Study

Imagine being called to suggest a solution to a problem that bothers someone. You have been appointed to do that because of your general background and experience in the area, yet your involvement in the particular problem has not been intensive. First, you will want to thoroughly learn the current situation, trying to identify the causes of the problem. Your second step will be to determine the general requirements that, fulfilled, would reduce or eliminate the problem. Finally, you will design some alternative solutions, evaluate them, and come up with recommendations.

A feasibility study has the same phases:

1. Learning the current situation and identifying the problem(s)
2. Outlining the requirements of a desired solution
3. Roughly designing a few alternative solutions and evaluating them according to the feasibility aspects previously mentioned

As shown in table 10.1, some of these phases can be divided into specific steps. We will review now, step by step, *what* should be done and *why*. Since this discussion is management-oriented rather than vocation-oriented, we do not elaborate on *how* it is done.

Table 10.1   Phases of Feasibility Study

1. Problem recognition
   Objectives (quantified)
   Constraints (time, budget, personnel)
   Management policy (centralization/decentralization)
   Participating organizational units
   Conformity with the information systems master plan and interaction with other
     information systems
2. Study of the situation
   Organization, environment, industry, policies, objectives
   Study of physical flows
   Study of data and information flows
   Description of the existing situation based on a synthesis of physical and data flows
   Definition of problems that have to be solved
3. Information requirement analysis (data analysis or decision analysis)
4. Analysis of alternative solutions
   Technical, economic, and organizational aspects
   Determination of recommended alternative
5. Submission of the feasibility analysis report

Step 1: Define the Goals and Scope of the Feasibility Study

Imagine that you are taking part in the following scenario: Three people, including you, are sitting in a room. You have all been appointed to a *feasibility team* assigned to study a particular problem and to suggest solutions. Each of you is employed in a different department. You know each other by sight, but you have never had any close work or social relationships, nor are you familiar with the background and experience of each other. It is your first meeting. You have already ordered coffee and discussed the latest weather report. What would you do now as your first move?

We believe that the first move should be to examine whether you have some sort of common ground or agreement about the nature of the problem, the scope and goals of the study, and what you are expected to present as a product of your assignment. In short, you have to answer *Why are we sitting in this room?*

The following checklist may help you answer this question.

1. Review management objectives. Try to see what really bothers those who have assigned you to this committee. Do they have a long-range strategy (or a master plan) that has triggered this study, or is it a ''fire fighting'' task? If there is a master plan, how does the current problem conform with it?

2. Is it possible to quantify some of management's objectives? For example, suppose management complains that inventory is too large. Reduction in inventory levels is certainly an objective that could be quantified. Suppose management complains that it does not receive financial statements on time. ''On time'' is a quantitative term and should be expressed in such terms. As a rule, quantitative goals always facilitate understanding the scope and magnitude of problems, and thus they direct the team toward a common working base. (For further examples and clarifications see the discussion on tangible benefits in chs. 3 and 13.)

3. Is it possible to translate management objectives into specific performance measures? For example, can we designate the required response time of an online system? Can we designate the required frequency of reporting? Can we designate the required currency of displayed data? It is not likely that at this stage you will have accurate performance figures, but at least you will be able to narrow the range of your solution space.

4. Do we have any idea about the constraints imposed on a feasible solution— i.e., order of magnitude of expenditures (budget constraints), time horizon, availability and skill of personnel for development and operation? Normally, even under obscure conditions, one has some knowledge about a reasonably anticipated budget, time frame for development, and personnel capacity. Efficient conduct of the feasibility study depends on this type of knowledge.

5. Is there any written policy or unwritten style according to which the organization is managed? In particular, we refer to attitude toward centralization and decentralization. A highly centralized organization would be reluctant to accept a solution based on distributed data processing (see ch. 11), such as delegating computing power to local sites, whereas a decentralized organization might favor such a solution. Another example of a constraining policy is management's attitude toward software development. Does management insist on in-house development? Will it opt for subcontracting? Or will it accept recommendations to adjust current procedures to fit the requirements of a ready-made software package?

6. Some knowledge of the receptiveness of the departments involved may also be of great help to the team.

It is not likely that the team members will have the answers to these questions at their first meeting. It is more likely that after two or three sessions (which should take place in a few days) they will be able to agree on a common base for the study, and even write it down in a document entitled ''Problem Definition.'' This document may be submitted to the information systems committee. Upon its approval, it becomes the reference tool for the feasibility team.

Step 2: Study the Current Situation

The study of the current situation should be conducted using a top-down approach. Start by collecting background and general information, continue with interviews of key persons, and then get into the details of pertinent processes.

The background information should provide the team with sufficient knowledge about the type of operation involved. Such information includes relationships with the environment (customers, vendors, trade union, government, other departments), an organizational chart, relevant financial statements, volumes of operations and trans- actions, organizational policy and objectives, etc.

This introductory survey may take only a few hours if the team members are experienced employees of the organization and already have knowledge of its activi- ties. However, if some of the members are from outside the area under study, it might take a few days.

The next move should be to interview managers and key persons in the area. This has three potential benefits. First, you get their views of and attitudes to the problem. Second, they may refer you to other sources of information—people or written material. Third, you should try to get their blessing and cooperation because this would facilitate the study.

The last, but most involved, move is to study the current processes pertaining to the problem. We have to distinguish between physical flows and data (information) flows. The former involves the movements of physical entities (goods, materials, people); the latter involves the data generated and transferred from place to place. For example, suppose you study the production line in a cannery. The physical flow includes the handling of raw material such as fresh fruits and vegetables, cans, and chemicals, starting from their entry to the plant and ending at the finished goods warehouse. The data flow includes the generation of production transactions, reports on working hours, and consumption of materials. You have to trace the data in order to locate its origin and destination and then identify the information that comes in return—i.e., instructions.

This may sound relatively simple in a plant manufacturing ''concrete'' products. It becomes more complex in an organization performing clerical operations. For example, suppose you follow check clearing in a bank. Are the checks part of the physical flow or the data flow? They contain data that at a certain stage is read by a computer; on the other hand, check clearing and distribution are part of the bank's ''production'' process. The answer to this dilemma is that the check flow could be thought of as two parallel streams, material and data. Once the data is captured by the computer, the two flows go in different directions.

There are various methods of collecting data on the physical and data flows: interviews, questionnaires, samples or surveys of documents, reports and forms, or participants' observations. Selecting the appropriate method (or methods) will depend on the money and time allocated to the feasibility study, on the organizational climate, on the qualifications and experience of the members of the feasibility team, and on the nature and complexity of the problems under study.

The study of the current processes has several purposes. First, you understand the activities involved, but more than that, you understand how and according to which criteria and decision rules these activities are regulated. Second, by tracing the data flows, you can identify decision points (see ch. 5), communication channels, and procedures. In fact, destinations of data flows are supposed to be points where decisions are being made, and this is our main concern. Finally, the study might give you a clue to the cause(s) of the current problem(s). We can ask a general question: What could be the main reasons for the managerial problems that triggered your ''rescue'' assignment? Some managers probably feel they cannot pursue their objective because of unsatisfactory information (''they don't know what's going on down there''). In other words, the existing information system does not comply with their expectations; there is a mismatch between the operations (physical flow) and the knowledge about them (data flow). If you carefully study the current situation you are bound to find the true causes of the current problems.

This step should be concluded with a brief summary that delineates the current situation and emphasizes the problems and their causes as detected by the team. It is highly recommended that the current situation be described not only with narratives, but also with flow diagrams. In fact, the same techniques that are used for designing new systems (e.g., data flow diagrams, flowcharts—see the end of this chapter) are usually adequate to describe the existing physical and data flows. The study phase is thus concluded, and the team is ready for the next phase—information requirement analysis.

Step 3: Analyze Information Requirements

If we assume at this point that we already know the exact problems bothering the users and the causes of the problems (i.e., the deficiencies of the system currently used, be it manual or computerized), our next step is an *information requirements analysis* of any desired solution. It is important to note that we are not designing any information system at this stage; we only specify what a proposed system should be capable of doing. For example, suppose we examine a problem of a too-long credit period granted to customers. We may stipulate that any future information system for accounts receivable should include online access to each customer balance and its age. This does not suggest any technical specifications as to how to achieve these requirements.

The two basic approaches to deriving information requirements are data analysis and decision analysis. *Data analysis* takes the existing information flow as a starting point for the investigation, then determines information no longer required, information to be continued, and additional information required. The steps are summarized in Munro [16, p. 35]:

1. Examine all reports, files, and other information sources drawn upon by the manager.
2. Discuss with the manager the use of each piece of information examined.
3. Eliminate unnecessary information.
4. Determine unsatisfied information needs through interaction with the manager.

Decision analysis ignores existing information at the beginning and builds up information requirements from scratch. The method presumes that each organizational unit has some critical factors according to which its success is evaluated. These are called *critical success factors* (CSF) [18]. Maintenance of a satisfactory level of CSF requires support by certain information. Hence, the logical sequence of our inquiry should be first to determine the CSF, then to identify pertinent decisions, and finally to derive information requirements. This sequence is described by Munro [16, p. 36] as follows:

1. Determine major decision responsibilities through discussion with the manager.
2. Determine policy and organizational objectives relevant to decision areas identified.
3. Determine specific steps required to complete each major decision.

4. Develop a model (flowchart) of each decision.
5. Examine the flowchart to determine information required at each step in the decision.

We may add a sixth step to Munro's list:

6. Compare the outcomes of step 5 to the existing information system and determine whether (a) an enhancement could solve the problems or (b) there is a need for a major development.

To clarify the two approaches, suppose our feasibility study deals with the computerization of an accounts receivable department. If we select the data analysis method, we will first review the data flow in the department. How do invoices arrive at the department after a sale has been made? How is the invoiced information entered to customer accounts? How is payment entered to the account? How are customer statements produced? How are exceptional cases treated? What reports are prepared for various officers? After digesting this knowledge we will talk to managers and key persons to probe the usefulness of each data item and find out what is unnecessary (e.g., customer date of birth) and what is missing (e.g., age of balance). Finally, we will write down the information requirements, distinguishing between existing, on the one hand, and desired yet currently unavailable data on the other.

If we select the decision analysis method, we will first try to identify the CSF. Suppose it turns out that the department is judged according to its achievement in two critical factors:

1. Duration of credit lines
2. Number of bad (unpaid) accounts

Success is defined as not having an average credit duration higher than twenty days and not having more than 2 percent bad accounts in a year. These factors play an important role in decisions about granting credit to customers and supervising customers' payments. The next step would be to draw flowcharts depicting decisions on credit approval and decisions on some measures to urge customers to pay their bills. The flowchart would probably indicate that the history of customers' past payments and aged balances is highly important. The required frequency of reporting on aged balances should also be stated. This data now becomes part of the information requirements platform.

Each analysis method has some advantages and disadvantages. Data analysis is more structured and straightforward. However, being based on an existing system, it might overlook innovative ideas not currently in use. Decision analysis is oriented more to user needs, and therefore its consequences can be better tailored to managerial decision making. However, drawing the necessary information from decision makers might be a tough job because people find it difficult to explicitly formulate the way they make decisions, particularly when the decisions themselves are unstructured.

As a general rule, we would expect the data analysis method to be applicable in low levels of the organizational hierarchy (see ch. 5) while the decision analysis method seems to be more appropriate for developing information systems for higher levels (Davis [6] provides a survey of information requirement analysis methods; Pressman [17] details the underlying principles).

Step 4: Consider Alternative Solutions

At this stage we are prepared to consider some alternative solutions. However, the feasibility team faces a delicate problem here. On one hand, the team has to gain sufficient knowledge to be able to assess the costs, benefits, and timetable for each alternative. On the other hand, the team is not supposed to get into the nuts and bolts of each alternative; in fact, it would be a waste of time and money to do so because only one solution (if any) will be selected, and elaboration on the selected solution should be performed in subsequent stages of the life cycle. Setting boundaries to the thoroughness of the study such that it will not be too detailed, but will be sufficient for the *information systems committee* to make a decision, depends on the complexity of the problem and on the common sense and subjective judgment of the individuals involved—tempered by their experience.

A possible approach to this step is to roughly distinguish among several alternatives, such as (1) continue with the present system; (2) install a "traditional" batch system; (3) install an "online" system; and (4) go for a distributed solution. For each alternative, in particular the last three, you may then compare self-development vis-à-vis acquisition of ready-made systems. You can refine your comparison by doing separate analysis of hardware and software options. It is likely that you will have to meet some vendor representatives. These meetings are informal in the sense that the vendors do not have to make formal offers that commit them. They need only to provide information that may help in cost assessment. Estimates of the cost of internal resources (e.g., programmers, materials, computer) should be made by the feasibility team.

The findings should focus on three or four (at most) alternative solutions. Normally the current system is also considered an alternative, and serves as an anchor for comparison of the other alternatives. Each solution should be carefully checked for feasibility conditions. If they are met, then we are ready to write down and present the feasibility report.

Step 5: Report the Contents and Results of the Feasibility Study

The feasibility report is primarily for managers who are familiar with the organization and the problems; hence, it should be short. On the other hand, the managers are going to make some critical decisions (GO or NO GO), so it should be detailed enough to enable rational decision making. The team has to find a golden path between these extremes.

Generally the report should reflect the results of the previous steps, with more emphasis on solutions than on description of the current state. A reasonable table of contents could look like the following:

1. Description of current problems
2. Description of current system
3. Pertinent factors—users, management, customers, general public, governmental regulations, other restrictions
4. Requirements of any proposed solution
5. Outline of various alternatives (including retaining the current system)

6. Characteristics of each alternative—hardware, software, personnel for development, timetable for development, organizational implications
7. Costs and benefits implied by the preceding discussion
8. Recommendations of the feasibility team

The report is submitted to the information systems committee and supported by an oral presentation. If no further inquiry is requested, the feasibility team is dissolved.

The Scope and Duration of a Feasibility Study

We have elaborated on the feasibility study for two reasons. First, as already mentioned, the study is the last stage before large amounts of money are invested in the project. Therefore, careful handling of the study may save a lot of unwarranted expenditures later. Second, since intensive involvement of users and management in the study is very important, we believe that understanding the content of this stage is more essential than understanding the technicalities related to subsequent stages.

The feasibility study is not a lifetime project. On the contrary, it should be short and prompt. It is normally handled by three people over a period of weeks. For relatively simple systems, it should not take more than a couple of weeks. Complex systems might require two or three months; very seldom would more time be necessary. In fact, if the study takes longer, its recommendation might be outdated.

Sometimes it makes sense to propose two types of solutions for the same set of problems: (1) an interim solution to cope with the immediate pressure, and (2) a radical solution for the long term. This approach is particularly helpful when current problems demand quick solutions. However, interim solutions sometimes tend to become permanent once the organization's crucial daily problems are relieved. Therefore, watchful monitoring of the development of a long-term project is important.

Characteristics of a "Good" Development Project

As mentioned at the beginning of this chapter, the technicalities of systems analysis, design, and programming are beyond the scope of this text. (A brief discussion of system development methodologies is provided at the end of this chapter.) Our concern here is to shed light on the role of users and management during the most technical stages of system development. The major concern is the measures that should be taken by users and management to ensure the quality of an information system developed by a professional team.

Some of these measures have already been reviewed in the discussion of the steering committee in chapter 9. The emphasis in that discussion was on the committee's procedures and tasks. In this section we elaborate on the substance—what can and should be examined by the steering committee.

Software Quality Assurance

This aspect of information systems development has come to be known as *software quality assurance*. While this is the responsibility of the steering committee, it is so important that it often results in a specific organizational entity charged with overseeing, and assuring, the quality of the project. Quality must be designed into any product, and information systems are no different. Quality must also be monitored and measured. Herein lies the difficulty, since each project will be different in many respects, and the quality objectives and measures must be tailored to each system. These quality requirements must be spelled out from the beginning, forming a companion to the information requirements discussed earlier. For a full discussion of these matters, see [9].

Generally speaking, the *steering committee* should concentrate on two issues: the quality of the project management, and the quality of the system under development. Obviously, these two issues are not completely unrelated. A project that is poorly managed is more likely to produce an unsatisfactory system. However, for the sake of clarifying the discussion, we distinguish between these issues.

Quality of Project Management

Suppose you are asked to evaluate the quality of the management of a project in an area in which you do not have any particular expertise. You will probably try to find some facts that represent the performance of the manager you evaluate. For example, suppose you have to evaluate the quality of the sewage department in your city. You will look for facts that relate to the cleanliness of the city. You will combine them with budget and personnel figures and compare your findings to figures for similar cities. Consequently you may come up with an intelligent evaluation, even though it has not been prepared by an expert.

The same idea applies to a development project. However, the sewage case is a concrete system already in use; the development project is abstract, existing only on the drawing board. Can we find facts that reflect the quality of its management? Indeed we can. The best indicators for management quality are those called *management practices*. We will discuss some of the common ones.

Compliance with Life Cycle Stages
The *development team*, its leader in particular, should make distinctions between the various stages of the development life cycle (see ch. 9). The head of the team must report during and upon completion of each stage. If you poll team members and notice that nobody knows the current status of the project, or that later stages are carried out prior to formal approval of preceding steps, then the project is not managed as desired, and someone has to be called to account.

Use of Software Engineering Techniques
Many organizations have adopted analysis and design techniques rooted in software engineering and impose these on development projects being undertaken in the organization. Such techniques include structured analysis, data flow diagrams, data dictionary, and structured languages (more details are provided at the end of this chapter). A project leader who is both familiar with these techniques and willing to exercise them is preferred to one who sticks to traditional, haphazard development approaches. Even when management does not impose a specific technique, a consistent use of any of them will likely contribute to the success of the project.

Compliance with Budget and Timetable

Project budget and timetable reflect what the organization expects from the development team. Since the budget and timetable are based on prior estimates, some deviations are permissible and even considered natural. However, deadlines that are missed by a large margin and expenditures that significantly exceed budget guidelines indicate that there is a problem: either poor estimates or poor management. In any case, this calls for intervention by the steering committee. The committee may reassess the budget or timetable, or it may evaluate the project management. Sometimes individuals should be replaced; sometimes the project should be called off.

Documentation of Project Management

The notion of documentation is usually associated with technical material, such as system flowcharts, program listings, record layouts, printer spacing charts, screen layouts, and operational procedures. We tend to neglect the managerial side of documentation—i.e., keeping records of decisions and management aspects of a project. A good project leader should maintain files that encompass the supervisory facets of the project. Some of the major topics that should be recorded are personnel issues, plans and timetables, budget, progress reports, change requests, minutes of meetings, training, and acquisition of hardware and software.

Any decision that affects the progress of the project should be recorded and filed—particularly revisions in requirements and change requests. Very often the accumulation of many minor changes may have a major impact on timetable and expenses that later cannot be traced back due to lack of documentation. From the viewpoint of the project leader, it is good to have all these written in case he or she has to report and explain anything. From the steering committee viewpoint, having appropriate documentation is an indicator of the quality of management.

Frankness of Reporting

A project leader should report to the steering committee frequently and frankly. He or she should disclose any information pertinent to the progress of the project or to problems encountered by the team. If the committee detects incomplete information or reluctance to report, it should suspect that things are not as smooth as they seem to be, and should probe this deeply. In fact, the steering committee and the development team are sometimes responsible for huge project expenditures. If they do not control these costs appropriately, they may find themselves in big trouble when they have to justify them later.

Quality of System under Development

Good management of the project certainly contributes to quality improvement in the information system developed, but does not guarantee it. After all, analysts, designers, and programmers are the people who create the system, and their work should be carefully watched. The key issue to be monitored is the analysis and design of the system. Poor design generates sloppy systems, no matter how skillful the personnel.

We will now review some of the design attributes that should be watched and suggest how this can be done by management and users who are not necessarily information processing professionals.

Flexibility

Flexibility is defined as an information system's capability to cope with future changes in user requirements. Changes might occur because users who have learned the system's competence like to modify its processes: add more data items, prepare new reports, reformat existing reports, etc. Other changes may be imposed by the environment, such as new government regulations. Changes cannot be foreseen, otherwise they would have been built into the original version of the system. However, since a manager/user may have a good feeling for possible directions of change in his or her department, he or she should closely examine the design proposed by the development team, whose members are probably not as familiar with departmental activities.

The way to inquire into flexibility is by posing what-if questions. For example, suppose we would like to get a sales report itemized by products and not by customers. Is it possible, and what does it involve? Or suppose the government changes the income tax calculation. How long would it take to modify the payroll program?

Generally there are three types of changes that occur in information processing:

1. *Data change*—Changes in the processed data. These should never affect your system. For example, if you raise the salary of an employee, you do not expect to have any changes in the payroll system. An exception might be a change in the order of magnitude of data. [For example, the U.S. Postal Service changes its nine-digit Zip Code to a twelve-digit code. In such a case you may anticipate some troubles in the system if it has not been designed to handle this size code.] A more serious type of data change occurs when new data items are introduced into the system. For example, a new manager of the personnel department requests that some new fields be added into existing employee records (e.g., knowledge of foreign languages). This might entail some changes in existing programs. Note that contemporary software tools, such as application generators and DBMS (see appendix A), can better accommodate changes than programs dealing with "traditional" files. In any event, if you ask appropriate questions while the system is designed, you can avoid some of the troubles.

2. *Parameter change*—Changes in parameters and constants of relevant calculations. For example, if the government modifies the scale of income tax deduction, the formula remains intact, but its constants must be updated. A flexible design would eliminate the necessity to change programs in such a case by establishing parameter files that are external to the programs involved. If the design is not done this way, we might expect to have troubles whenever such changes occur. Programs have to be scanned to replace outdated parameters.

3. *Procedure change*—Changes in the formulas pertinent to some calculations. For example, if the government establishes a new method for income tax deduction, it is most likely that payroll programs will have to be modified. Such changes are more troublesome than any other type of change. However, structured and modular design of a system's components (programs and routines), accompanied by perfect documentation, may minimize the effort of inserting the changes.

Users and managers should have the capacity to ask the right questions about system flexibility and be able to interpret the answers they get. They should insist on getting simple answers that do not use professional jargon.

Simple Maintenance

When an automobile manufacturer designs a new model, one of the major motives for the design is to improve maintenance, such as simplifying access to the parts that are most commonly checked or replaced. We, as potential buyers, are very reluctant to buy a car if we know that its routine *maintenance* is relatively complex. Information systems are more abstract and less visual than cars; still, their internals have to be approached from time to time in order to correct a bug or to replace a subroutine. Standardized programming techniques (e.g., structured programming), standardized labeling conventions (e.g., field names, data directory, subroutine labels), and, above all, perfect documentation, facilitate maintenance. Users and managers should be able to probe these matters, and they must insist on seeing the documentation that accompanies the system.

Interface with Related Systems

Most information systems nowadays are no longer "discrete." They transmit and receive data from related systems using electronic and magnetic means. For example, an accounts receivable system is fed by sales and cashier systems; it feeds general ledger and cashflow systems. Another important example is office automation. Each office system will sooner or later communicate with other offices via electronic mail. Office system configurations are produced by various manufacturers. It is imperative to assure that they can "speak" with each other. *Interfaces* between systems are delicate points that might cause trouble. Systems should be designed to "converse" with related systems, either existing or planned. Users and managers should be able to question these matters.

Compatibility

Information processing technology advances so rapidly that we very often find ourselves designing a system for a certain configuration of hardware and software and later have to run it in a different configuration (upgraded or completely replaced). The likelihood of this phenomenon is even greater in organizations using service bureau facilities, for they may later switch to another server or acquire their own equipment. Management should know how compatible the systems are and should understand the possible implications of decisions to change data processing equipment.

Better *compatibility* can be attained by confining programmers to the use of universal programming languages (e.g., COBOL, FORTRAN), and by careful selection of ready-made packages for data base handling (see appendix A), online operations, or other common applications. If there are solid reasons for not using compatible features, management should at least be aware of future implications.

Expandability

Information systems are designed to handle certain volumes of data. The volume affects processing time, response time, auxiliary memory size, and other performance attributes. In practice, volumes fluctuate due to peak periods or seasonality. Systems should tolerate a certain degree of increase in volume—*expandability*. Management should set ranges in which a system is workable and be aware that demands above its threshold may cause the system to collapse. The well-accepted principle that transportation infrastructure (roads, highways, parking facilities) might be jammed if the number of vehicles using it exceeds a certain limit holds for information systems as well.

Efficiency

Efficiency is not a goal, as sometimes perceived by some professionals; it is a means to obtain effectiveness. (You may want to review ch. 4 on the aspects of effectiveness and efficiency.) For example, we design a system to respond within three seconds, not because it is nice and efficient, but because users would not use it otherwise. Sometimes users have requirements that would reduce efficiency, such as a special report that requires additional indexing or sorting. We prefer to comply with the requirement, or at least limit our arguing up to the point where we cannot persuade the user. Nevertheless, subject to satisfying user requirements, systems should be designed to operate efficiently—that is, to save computer resource.

Users and management can gain some insights on efficiency by asking about such things as elapsed time of processing, memory size, and disk occupancy, and then make comparisons with similar systems. Difficult though it is for laypeople to judge efficiency, it is worthwhile for them to try. (After all, have you never commented about the efficiency of the postal service though you are neither employed by nor an expert on the post office?)

Table 10.2 summarizes the discussion on factors contributing to the quality of the system under development. The factors that should be examined by users and general management are listed on the left side of the table. The center and right-hand columns indicate how these factors affect the success or failure of the developed system. Note that the center and right-hand columns are only indicators, and there may be exceptional cases. For example, a system may succeed even though (a) the project leader has not established a perfect method of documentation, or (b) the initial budget has been doubled during development. Still, the probability of success is certainly affected by these factors.

Table 10.2   Factors Contributing to Success or Failure of Information System Development

Factors	Will Increase Likelihood of Success	Will Increase Likelihood of Failure
Project Management		
Compliance with formal life cycle stages	Maintained	Not maintained
Compliance with budget	Maintained	Not maintained
Compliance with timetable	Due dates met	Overdue
Management documentation	Clear and formal	Unclear
Reporting	Frequent and frank	Irregular and reluctant
System Characteristics		
Flexibility	Obtained	Not obtained
Maintenance	Easy	Difficult
Interface with related systems	Smooth	Rough
Compatibility	Obtained	Not obtained
Expandability	Possible	Impossible
Efficiency	Achieved	Not achieved

Conversion and Implementation

Suppose you have a date with a person you really like. You plan the evening very carefully. You select a good restaurant with fine food. You proceed to a quiet night club. But when you reach the conclusive part of the evening, you discover that you have lost the key to your apartment. Then, after you finally manage to enter the apartment, your living room is a mess, your stereo does not work, and your mother shows up for an unexpected visit. How would you like that? In the same spirit, you can design and program an excellent information system, but if you do not plan its implementation, you might ruin the entire project.

The stage of conversion and implementation deals with the actual installation of the newly produced information system in the organization. This stage is, in fact, a potpourri of issues, such as training, testing, file conversion, and procedural changes. Each of the issues requires delicate and careful treatment. Most of them involve users of various ranks who might not be familiar with information technology, and therefore could be sensitive or even hostile.

The involvement of senior managers is of great importance. This is the main reason for the elaborate discussion that follows. We intend to convince you that this stage is a project by itself. Hence, it merits establishment of a special team (*implementation team*) and should be treated with a lot of care and patience. Otherwise even the most technically perfect system might fail. We will now review some of the major issues related to conversion and implementation.

Training

In chapter 2 we mentioned that introduction of a new information system to an organization is often perceived as a major change and may easily trigger negative reaction. Negative reaction can be weakened or suspended if the people involved understand the purposes and benefits of the system and also know how to operate it. People become much less afraid of something if it stops being mysterious. Therefore, training programs should have two targets: providing general understanding of the system and acquiring technical skills to run it. We call these *"ideological training"* and *"operational training."*

Ideological Training

Ideological training is primarily directed at managers and at those who are in command of the operational staff. But it is necessary to convey some capsule material to the operational ranks also.

The major components of the training are the following:

1. *System's goals and benefits*—Why was the system installed? How does its installation improve decision making and managing capacity? How would it enhance current processes and procedures?
2. *System's constraints and limitations*—What can the system do? What can it not do? What should be the expectations regarding response time, data currency, data accuracy, and other attributes of information (see chap. 3)?
3. *Organizational implications*—Are there any implications for organizational structure and authority? If so, in what direction?
4. *Functional implications*—What changes are anticipated in human roles and activities? How can they be controlled?

Operational Training

Operational training familiarizes the appropriate personnel with the information system's operational aspects that pertain to their tasks. Obviously they do not have to master all the nuts and bolts of the system internals, but they do have to recognize every means by which they interact with the system. This would imply the following:

1. Understanding how to fill out every form submitted to the system
2. Understanding the content and interpretation of every report produced by the system, on a screen or a printout
3. Recognizing errors and correction procedures
4. Mastering update procedures
5. Understanding time constraints related to the submission of input data, the receipt of reports, and the currency of information

In summary, employees have to learn all the technicalities contributing to smooth and fluent operation of the information system. The best way to accomplish this is by conducting hands-on workshops in which dry runs are performed. In this way employees acquire both formal knowledge and some rules of thumb that may be very helpful. For example, they get a feel for the order of magnitude of various numerical

Table 10.3 Training Emphasis for Managers and Operational Staff

	Ideological Training	Operational Training
Managers	Highly emphasized	Moderate
Operational Staff	Moderate	Very thorough

figures and hence learn to become suspicious when the figures exceed a reasonable range; they may recognize that certain figures may never be negative, and if they are, then there is an error somewhere. Hands-on workshops make the new system more touchable—and thus less threatening.

Training of Managerial Versus Operational Staff

Managers have to be familiar with *operational* material to the extent that they are able to supervise their subordinates. And it is very important to stress the *ideological* background for the managers, because if they are not convinced that the system contributes to their performance, they will be reluctant to enforce its use.

Operational staff should get some ideological background to motivate them to accept the system, but for them greater emphasis should be placed on the practical issues. Table 10.3 summarizes the difference in training for the two groups. To put it bluntly, if you overload managers with technical details, or if you burden the operators with too much ideology, you might lose your audience and ruin the training. An appropriate mix of both should be carefully blended in a well-planned training program.

Conversion

Every new information system replaces something that prevailed before, be it an old computerized system or a set of manual procedures. The transition from the old to the new system is extremely delicate because there is a hidden conflict of interests between the implementors and the rest of the organization. The implementors would like to have some sort of intermission that they can use to prepare the system for use; the organization handles many activities, of which the information system is only a small segment; the organization cannot afford a break; it must maintain the continuity of its operations. Since the implementors must comply with the organizational interests, they have to plan the conversion so the continuity will be preserved and interruptions of normal activities will be minimal.

Issues of Conversion

Three issues should normally be dealt with when conversion is planned: files, programs, and working procedures.

New files should be completely ready prior to installation of a new system. For example, if a bank installs a new information system to handle its customer accounts, each customer's balance (effective as of a certain date), must be recorded and ready for the first run of the new system. Otherwise the system will not be able to update customer records and calculate new balances.

The problem of file conversion is not very severe when the new system replaces a computerized system and there are no significant changes in the data used. Usually there are ready-made utility programs that perform the conversion. Still, we have to run special programs to do the job. These programs have to be either coded or acquired. In a way, we have here a miniproject that requires analysis, design, programming (sometimes), and particularly careful scheduling.

When the new system replaces a manual system, file conversion might be a difficult problem. Imagine that you have to convert a bank's customer accounts from manual to computerized bookkeeping. You have to code and key in the customer details of all the accounts. Then you have to verify the recorded data. This might take weeks. Meanwhile, you have to continue the manual bookkeeping. This would imply that some changes in data already recorded (e.g., address change) may happen during the preparation period. You have to establish a procedure for interim updates. Finally, one night (literally), or perhaps one weekend, you have to merge the current balances with the data already recorded. And Monday morning you run your new system. Again, we could notice here that a special set of programs has to be written—i.e., a miniproject has to be conducted.

Program conversion is less likely to take place because a new system normally involves new programs. But it might happen from time to time that we wish to convert and use some existing programs or subprograms. For example, suppose you replace a traditional batch-processing payroll system with a new online system. Since the formula according to which salaries and deductions are computed does not change, you may consider adapting some existing routines in order to save some reprogramming efforts. Another example is an organization that replaces its hardware equipment. Normally many of its information systems will not be redeveloped, but only converted to suit the new equipment.

A prerequisite to efficient program conversion is availability of good program documentation. Otherwise it is difficult to understand old programs that were mostly written by other programmers. In any case, you have to compare carefully the cost and effort of reprogramming to the cost and effort of converting existing programs. Some manufacturers have some conversion aids, such as a program that translates source programs written in one manufacturer's version of COBOL to the version used by another manufacturer. Such aids may certainly affect decisions to convert or to rewrite.

The conversion of working procedures is an involved task. It includes preparation of new input forms and new preprinted continuous sheets; establishing new timing for transmission of inputs and outputs; installing terminals; and adjusting human activities to the requirements of the new system. It involves contacts with draftspersons, printing houses, transportation departments, telephone companies, and suppliers of training facilities. Each individual activity is not particularly complicated, but the collective volume and variety make it a fairly complex operation.

Methods of Conversion

There are several ways to approach conversion, as is shown in the diagram in figure 10.1. The preferred way, though most costly, is the *parallel* approach. Both the old and the new systems run in parallel for a limited period. At the beginning of the period

Figure 10.1 Methods of system conversion

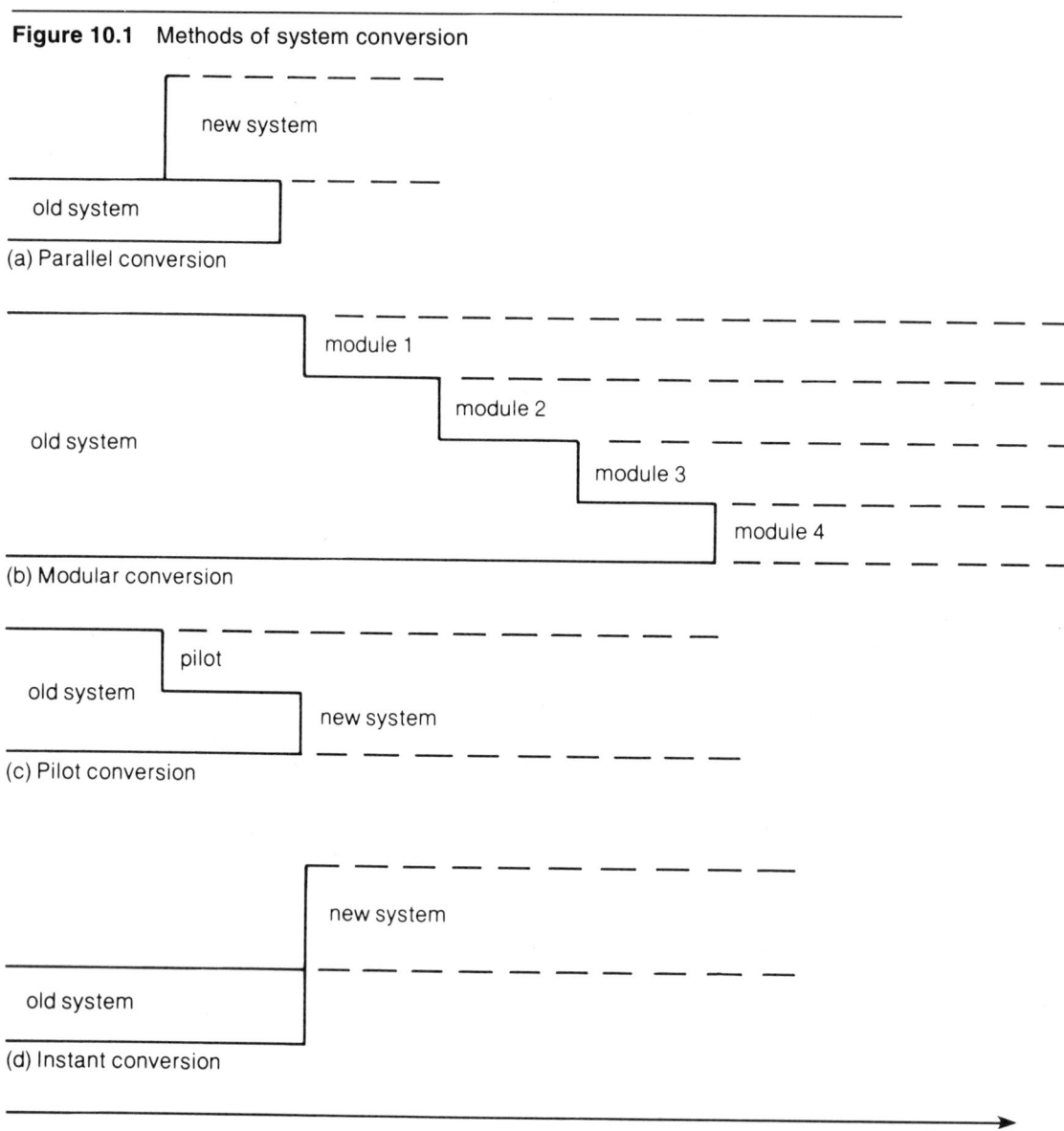

(a) Parallel conversion

(b) Modular conversion

(c) Pilot conversion

(d) Instant conversion

time

the old system is still the "live" one and the new system is only dry run in order to verify its results. At the latter part of the period the new system becomes the "real" one, but the old one is still maintained for backup and control. Only after the new system performs satisfactorily is the old one scrapped. This approach is very safe, but it is expensive because operating costs are nearly doubled during the conversion period. It is common to use the parallel approach for accounting and bookkeeping information systems, where possible errors might cause fatal monetary implications.

Another conversion method is the *modular* (phased) approach. The system is divided into relatively small modules and each module is tackled separately, one after the other. This approach is feasible only if segmentation is viable—i.e., there is a logical division of the system and each module is independently workable (or, at most, depends on preceding modules). For example, a new inventory system can start with the conversion of files to a data base and the installation of appropriate processing programs, while input may still continue to arrive in batches. Only later can input be converted to online data entry. Another comparable example can be borrowed from conversion to the metric system. This system has been divided into subtopics, such as weights, distances, temperatures, and volumes. Each topic is handled separately. In fact, a parallel approach is undertaken within each topic.

A variant of the modular approach is the *pilot* conversion. A module that adequately represents the complexity of the various modules of the new system replaces a parallel module of the old system. If that module performs satisfactorily, the other modules of the new system are installed, incorporating the lessons gained during the conversion of the pilot module. For example, suppose a multibranch bank wishes to introduce a new information system for its tellers. A recommended approach would be to select one branch for experimental installation of the new system, then expand the use of the system to a few additional branches, and only after the experiments appear to be successful, launch a full-scale conversion of the entire bank.

The worst, but sometimes necessary, approach is the *instant* (crash) conversion. One night, out of the blue, the new system replaces the old one. This approach is very troublesome, but sometimes is a must. A comparable example is conversion of a transportation system from left-side driving to right-side driving as was done in Sweden during the sixties. The amount of preparation is enormous: signs, lights, public education, etc. When the due date comes, the conversion must be instantaneous, within a minute. Nobody would like the idea of having half the drivers driving on the right side of the roads while the other half are still driving on the left side.

While parallel conversion is operationally preferable, it is not always feasible and it might be costly. These conversion cost factors are the next topic.

Conversion Costs

When they design a new system, developers sometimes overlook the costs involved in the conversion. This might be a fatal mistake since these costs are far from negligible. In fact, in a real case an organization considered a conversion from "traditional" file organization techniques to a data base management system. Conversion costs were assessed for two alternatives: purchasing hardware from the current hardware vendor or purchasing hardware from another vendor. It turned out that costs of conversion were 25 percent of the equipment price for the first alternative and 50 percent of the equipment price for the second.

Let us examine now the major components of conversion costs:

1. *Personnel for conversion planning*—The cost of personnel involved in designing and monitoring the conversion.

Table 10.4   Conversion Components and Costs

Conversion Components

1. Programs
2. Files
3. Procedures (input, output)

Conversion Costs

1. Personnel: Planning and performing the conversion; overtime for other participating personnel
2. Computer time: Parallel runs and preparations in-house; use of outsourcing or alternate computer centers
3. Special equipment: Remote entry terminals, rental of communication lines, air conditioners, etc.
4. Construction: Site preparation for parallel conversion
5. Materials: Paper, forms

2. *Personnel for performing the conversion*—The cost of programmers, operators, instructors, and others who carry out the conversion. Sometimes other participating personnel are paid overtime, particularly when parallel conversion is carried out.
3. *Computer time*—The cost of additional time for parallel runs and preparations.
4. *Outsourcing*—Sometimes part or all of the conversion operations are performed by an outside service provider or at other computer sites.
5. *Special equipment*—You may have to install remote entry terminals and rent communications lines for the conversion period.
6. *Construction*—Sometimes you have to carry out some construction changes in order to install more equipment while the previous equipment is still required for the conversion period.
7. *Materials and supplies*—Forms, paper, etc.

Obviously we do not advocate that these costs prohibit system development. We merely suggest that they should be taken into account as part of the total system development budget. Table 10.4 summarizes our discussion of conversion components and costs.

Testing

It is part of human nature to test anything new. We taste a new cereal before we decide if we like it; we road test a new car before we buy it. In fact, we refrain from testing only things that are familiar; we intensify tests whenever the product examined is considered to be unique and particularly if it is costly. Every new information system is unique for the organization involved, and it is most likely costly. Therefore, tests should be carried out during the system development cycle.

There are three types of tests: program tests, system tests, and acceptance tests. The first two are handled internally by the development team; the latter is conducted by the user.

Program Test

Every program should be tested separately prior to integration into a system or a subsystem. When a programmer claims that a program has been debugged and is now ready, the programmer's superior should verify the claim. This is done with a *program test:* preparing *test data,* running the data under the new program, and comparing the program results with results that have been manually calculated.

It is important that a person other than the programmer prepare the test data because the programmer might have misinterpreted the requirements from the very beginning and, hence, would not recognize a certain error in the program. In other words, we have to distinguish between program debugging, which is normally done by the programmer, and formal testing, which should be conducted by an "objective" judge.

System Test

After programs have been individually tested, the entire system should be examined. The integrated test normally focuses on interfaces between programs, particularly the transfer of data from one program to another and the handling of files shared by two or more programs.

System test is also an internal task for the development team. Responsibility is assumed by the head of the team. Only after the system test is successful is the system handed over for an acceptance test.

Acceptance Test

In a way, the *acceptance test* is a symbolic act designating the handing over of an information system from the development/implementation team to the user. By approving the results of the test, the user actually endorses the system.

From the user viewpoint, an information system is much more than a collection of computer programs. It involves procedures, documentation, trained personnel, maintenance, etc. Therefore, an acceptance test is, indeed, a checklist of conditions that should be tested prior to approval of the new system by the user:

1. *Smooth run*—Programs are bug-free; interfaces are ironed out; runs of test data exhibit correct results.
2. *Full documentation*—Programs and files are accompanied by clear, detailed, and updated documentation.
3. *Trained personnel*—Training programs have been completed and employees understand their roles.
4. *Clear operating procedures*—All the operating procedures for the system—procedures for normal operation, recovery, backup, input entry, changes, and output distribution—are clear and well documented.
5. *Liaison persons*—A liaison officer and a maintenance programmer have been appointed in the information system department (see ch. 12).

In summary, the user has to determine the criteria for acceptance and then take an active part in the acceptance test. If the test is completed successfully and all other conditions are satisfied, the system is ready for operation.

Conclusions

You have probably noticed that implementation and conversion constitute a complex stage involving a variety of activities and individuals located in various departments. The approach toward conversion (parallel, modular, pilot, instant) should be planned at an early stage of the system development. Any change occurring during development stages might have implications for the implementation plan and, therefore, should immediately trigger a review and perhaps a revision in the plan. Moreover, even if the implementation plan is perfect, unforeseen changes should always be anticipated during its execution. Hence, tight coordination is mandatory for this stage. Maintaining an implementation logbook is also necessary.

We began our discussion by claiming that a special team has to be committed to the implementation and conversion stage because this stage is a project by itself. We hope you are now convinced.

Operation and Maintenance

After an information system has passed the acceptance test, it enters into what one hopes will be a long period of operation. Unfortunately, information systems are not closed systems (see ch. 4); they interact intensively with their environment. This implies that changes might be required and errors might occur.

The major problems usually identified during operation are in (1) the division of responsibilities between the users and the professional information systems (or data processing) department, and (2) the treatment of change requests. We will now discuss these problems.

User Responsibility

Suppose you dine in a restaurant. It is the chef's responsibility to provide you with appropriate food that has been carefully stored and nicely prepared. However, it is your responsibility to know how to eat the food, and to refrain from ordering dishes that might disturb your digestion. The same applies to information systems. The information systems department should provide the user with adequate data; however, the user is responsible for the right "digestion" of the data.

There are two different views regarding user responsibility for an information system. One view regards the user as an outside customer whose responsibility is confined only to submission of input data and receipt of outputs. According to this view, the entire data processing is handled by the information systems department while user roles are minimal. The second view suggests that users should assume responsibility for operations and the information systems department only provides processing facilities and technical support.

In most cases we favor the second approach because we believe that intensive user involvement is beneficial. However, we have to note that the second approach necessitates appointment of a coordination officer in the user department. It also presumes that the user has reached a certain degree of maturity in understanding information systems.

Sometimes the second approach is not feasible, usually because there are many scattered users—e.g., a multibranch bank. In such cases the information system is better off if the operation is centrally monitored by the information systems department.

Information System Department Responsibility

The professional department in charge of information systems operation (hereafter called the *IS department*) is responsible for carrying out normal operations and handling changes requested by users. Practically, these tasks are handled by different individuals: normal operations by operating staff; analysis of change requests by an information analyst; program changes by a programmer. This division of duties might confuse users because it means they first have to classify their problems according to these categories and then approach the appropriate function. A liaison officer could be appointed in the IS department to serve as the sole address for any request coming from the users of a particular system. The liaison officer would activate other employees, depending upon the type of problem addressed to him or her.

A liaison officer is usually an information analyst whose liaison duties are only part of his or her regular occupation. In some cases an IS department may appoint a full-time liaison officer to serve several users or to support extremely complex operations.

In addition, each information system should be maintained by a maintenance programmer. This programmer must be familiar with the programs so that whenever there is a need to change a program or check its correctness, it will not take him or her too long. Maintenance programming may be a part-time job of a regular programmer. However, in many organizations this is a full-time job through which every programmer has to pass along his or her career path (see ch. 12).

Handling of Changes

Change requests are like rain; they are certain to come but we can never tell exactly when and in what magnitude. In other words, every information system is expected to require changes during its life cycle. Changes may be required because of environmental dynamics—e.g., governmental regulations. Changes may be requested by users after having learned more about the system's capabilities. Changes may be initiated by IS professionals because of installation upgrading or in order to improve efficiency. There is no use fighting change requests. A better idea is to regulate them in a rational manner by establishing a formal procedure for handling them.

Usually most change requests are so minor that there is a natural temptation to discuss them in a short conversation at the nearest cafeteria and then carry them out in a couple of hours. Such a "procedure" would be a fatal mistake because the accumulated number of minor changes introduced in this manner may very soon bewilder anyone who wishes to keep track of what is going on within the system.

A better, yet somewhat longer, way to introduce changes is through a formal procedure:

1. The initiator of the change fills out a change request form.
2. An information analyst (who could be the liaison officer) analyzes the cost/benefit implications of the request. If the request incurs costs above a certain level, a higher level manager (or the information systems committee) reviews the case.
3. If a GO decision is made, an appropriate sequence of design-program-test is carried out.
4. Documentation is accurately updated.
5. The revised version is released for use after being announced to and approved by potential users.

It is human nature to try to shortcut such procedures, particularly when the change is very minor or very urgent (e.g., ''we will certainly remember it when we have to further examine the programs''). But in a few months nobody can recall what has really happened, and the disparity between the unupdated documentation and the revised programs is so wide that any minor change becomes virtually major.

Postaudit (Postevaluation) of Information Systems

The amount of money and effort invested in the development of an information system is usually very high. Yet because of the long time it takes to develop a system, there are always some deviations between the initial planning and the final product (i.e., the information system installed). The combination of large sums of money, deviations in the final product, and a variety of interested parties implies that the newly arrived system would likely be controversial: some parties are satisfied while others are disappointed. Even if this is not the case, it is a good practice to evaluate an information system after it has been installed and periodically thereafter. The conclusions of such a probe may benefit the organization in both managerial and personal aspects.

Postaudit Practices

When Is It Conducted?
Field observations indicate that immediately after the installation of a new information system there are many change requests and maintenance problems. It takes time to stabilize a system and learn how to live with it. Therefore, an early *postaudit* inquiry might come up with premature conclusions. On the other hand, if the postaudit is delayed too long, the usefulness of the conclusions may be in doubt. Hence the optimal time to conduct a postaudit is about six months after installation of the information system. If by then the system is still shaky, it may indicate that something is inherently wrong because stability should be obtained by that time. After the first postaudit inquiry, a frequency of once a year is normally sufficient for subsequent inquiries.

Who Conducts It?

A postaudit is initiated by the information systems committee, which appoints an individual or a team to undertake the task. It may reassemble the steering committee and ask its members to *postevaluate* the system.

The main advantage of having the steering committee undertake the evaluation is that its members are probably most knowledgeable about that particular system, so they would not have to learn as much before they start. On the other hand, these people might be biased because they have been involved with decisions made during development of the system. Other individuals may be more objective. The information systems committee should consider the trade-off between objectivity and learning period before making any appointment.

In many organizations there is a special function called *EDP auditor,* which specializes in the auditing of information systems (see ch. 14). Sometimes this function is confined to accounting aspects of information systems. If the function is expanded to other aspects, it is natural then to assign an EDP auditor to perform the postaudit.

Data for Postaudit

The major motive of postaudit is to compare prior planning with its realization. The evaluator should obtain all the estimates related to development and operation costs, timetables, performance, and benefits, and compare them with reality. The pertinent data is likely to be found in various reports, such as the feasibility study report, system analysis and design reports, and other documentation prepared by the project management. The data describing reality can be partly measured and partly retrieved from bookkeeping and budget records. Intangible factors can be assessed by interviewing several key officers.

Aspects to Be Investigated and Reported

The main purpose of the postaudit is to learn from the past in order to improve in the future. It may also initiate some acts to improve the system that is evaluated, but the chances of reviving a failed system are low. The aspects to be examined are:

1. Quality of the system
2. Quality of the project management
3. Quality of the planning process

The first two aspects have been discussed in a previous section of this chapter. The third aspect requires some elaboration.

It is not unlikely that the actual time and money invested in the project will deviate from the initial estimate. It is also not unlikely that the actual performance and benefits do not exactly match the expectations. Unexpected factors could have caused these deviations, and nobody should be blamed for that. Poor project management and/or poor professional qualifications could be the main reason. In that case, some personal and organizational measures must be considered. However, it could be that nothing was wrong during the development cycle—the initial plan was just unrealistic. This

Table 10.5 Outline of a Postaudit Report

1. Findings:
   Development costs: planned vs. actual
   Implementation costs: planned vs. actual
   Current operations costs: planned vs. actual
   Timetable: planned vs. actual
   Performance: planned vs. actual
   Tangible benefits: planned vs. actual
   Intangible benefits: planned vs. actual
2. Significant deviations from plans:
   Causes
   Explanations
   Consequences
3. Conclusions related to:
   Staffing
   Planning
   Organizing
4. Recommendations:
   For the current system
   For future projects

may be due to lack of experience in the area or to unique characteristics of the system involved. For example, an information analyst might underestimate the amount of programming effort required for a certain program; a project leader might underestimate the complexity of a system when he or she develops for the first time a system based on new technology (e.g., local area network, voice recognition).

The process of postaudit has to be systematic and detailed. The evaluator should scan the initial estimates and compare them to the actual findings. Each unreasonable deviation is marked and checked. Interviews with key persons may help a lot. Only after the details have been clarified is a comprehensive evaluation made.

The major findings and conclusions are reported to the information systems committee in a written report. A possible outline of such a report is suggested in table 10.5.

The report may be accompanied by an appendix (possibly confidential) in which evaluations of certain individuals are attached. The report is submitted to the information systems committee, which may then initiate some actions. It is important to note that the recommendations of the report constitute an important factor in long-range planning of information systems. For example, if the report doubts the ability of the system to last for a long time, a revision of the master plan is required so a new system can be developed sooner than initially anticipated. A detailed methodology for conducting postaudit of information systems is provided in [1].

System Development Tools and Techniques

Imagine that the methodology of constructing buildings was left to the complete discretion of each individual builder in terms of planning material standards, sequence of activities, safety arrangements, etc. Would you like to step into a building like that?

Similar situations prevailed in the area of information system development for many years. However, the increase in the cost and in the social and commercial importance of software turned out to be so high that it was necessary to establish some rigid (structured) standards and procedures to control the involved process of development.

To understand the growing impact of software development, you have only to examine some statistical figures. Some eight million people worldwide are categorized as professional programmers. The number more than doubled during the 1980s [19, p. 21]. Annual spending for software in the U.S. is estimated to be $225 billion by the mid-1990s, $450 billion worldwide [4]. Clearly when any sector of our economy reaches such proportions, formal practices become a must. These practices are dealt with by the discipline labeled software engineering.

The establishment of a formal information system life cycle in the late sixties can be considered as the early budding of software engineering (even though the term itself was not existing yet). Since then, many tools, techniques, and procedures have been proposed and utilized. These can hardly cope with the fast growth in software production. It is believed that 60 percent to 80 percent of software cost is spent on maintenance, rather than on development of new systems [17, p. 667]. It is also believed that two-thirds of maintenance problems are caused by incompetent analysis and design.

What is the major problem of system analysis and design? Figure 10.2 portrays a sequence of activities selected from the system life cycle. The arrows connecting the boxes relate possible errors to the time they are likely to be detected. For instance, an error in programming is normally detected during testing. An ill-designed procedure is usually identified during the conversion period. However, the most serious type of mistake, misunderstanding the system, can only be recognized after operations have begun. At this stage it is very costly to change, which is why formal information analysis practices are so vital.

Software Engineering

During the seventies, users and information system professionals realized that the problem of increasing software maintenance cost was not due primarily to programming, but to the long trail leading from the conception of a system to its specification. They suggested the adaptation of engineering methodologies to software development processes. Consequently, the term *software engineering* became prevalent [5].

Software engineering deals with a variety of issues, such as systems analysis, systems design, programming, testing, time estimate of development activities, and management and control of software projects. We will now briefly mention some of the principles guiding the practical tools.

Analysis and Design Principles
The traditional approach to describing an information system was based on a narrative text accompanied by flowcharts. There were no rules regarding the format of the narrative or the level of flowchart detail. This approach suffered from a number of deficiencies. The definition of a system was not very clear, which could lead to ambiguous

Figure 10.2 Relationship between errors and their detection along a system life cycle

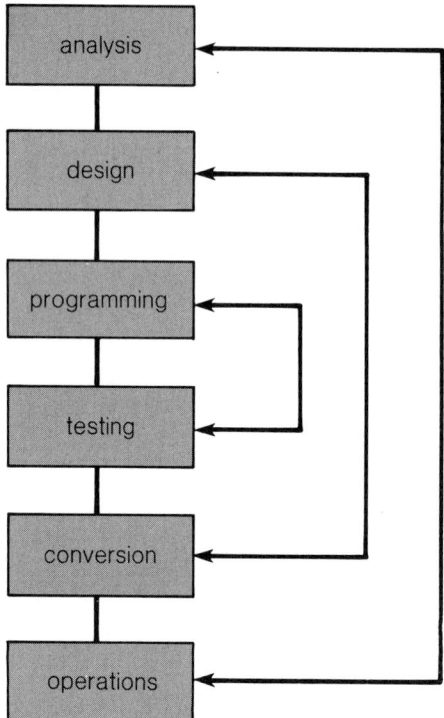

interpretation by programmers who had to translate the analysis and design specifications into programs. There were no measures to ensure that a system analysis report was complete, namely, that the analyst had not overlooked a ''dark corner'' of the system. Above all, the traditional approach provided the analyst only with means for presentation (e.g., flowchart); it did not focus on tools aiding performance of the analysis activity itself. Therefore, the entire task of analysis and design was left to intuition, experience, and common sense. Not that these traits are unimportant. On the contrary, they are absolutely required, but they should not exclude a systematic approach.

A major principle in system analysis asserts that documentation produced after the analysis has been completed is inferior to documentation produced while performing the analysis and design task. Otherwise, it states, documentation is always incomplete.

Another major principle is that communication between the analyst and the designer and between the designer and the programmer should be as smooth as possible. This can be achieved only if they ''speak the same language,'' namely, they use similar techniques.

The following section briefly reviews some techniques that adhere to these principles.

Software Engineering Tools

The most common term in software engineering is *structured system analysis (and design)* [7, 12, 21, 23]. The structured approach consists of a number of techniques that together constitute a systematic approach. The major ingredients of the structured approach are mentioned here.

Data flow diagrams (DFD)   A data flow diagram is a graphical presentation of the flow of data between processes and data files in the system under analysis. The DFD delineates the sources that generate data, the processes which data undergo, the files where data is stored, and the destination of information that is provided. All these are portrayed according to rigid rules. The most important principle is that the DFDs are arranged in a hierarchy of detail level. In other words, the entire system is described by a general DFD; each ''box'' (or process) is further elaborated in a more detailed presentation; each component of the second-level DFD can then be broken down into more details, and so forth, until a satisfying level of depiction is obtained. Note that the same technique can be used for any step along the analysis and design; the difference lies in the amount of detail.

The symbols used for drawing DFDs vary among writers. Some of the most prevalent sets of symbols are those that have been suggested by Yourdon [23] (who is considered to be a forerunner in this area), DeMarco [7], and Gane and Sarson [12].

Data dictionary   The data dictionary is a formal description of every data item (field) associated with the information system. Each field is assigned a unique title (e.g., CUSTOMER-NAME, EMPLOYEE-SALARY). The major properties of the field are mentioned (e.g., numerical field; data field), as are the users that initiate and update the field, its security level, the files and reports it belongs to, and any other pertinent information about the data item. The data dictionary is instrumental in successfully coordinating the various people developing the same system. Its use is highly recommended even when other complementary techniques (e.g., DFD) are not imposed on the development team.

Immediate access analysis   Immediate access analysis helps to decide which immediate accesses to each data item (field) are needed by the user. Each data item is characterized by the type of operations performed on it and by the list of users and processes accessing it (e.g., generate, update, or request the item). This analysis is instrumental in designing the system files and processes.

Program design language (PDL)   Program design language is a narrative technique that describes the processes in the information system. However, the language in use is not natural English, but a special subset of the language that has to obey rigid ''grammatical'' rules. The common term for this language is *''structured English,''* and the rules are somewhat similar to the rules of programming logic. The result is a ''free-style'' program; namely, paragraphs that are written like upper-level programming languages, but without the distracting details of programming syntax. The PDL is very helpful in clearly communicating ideas from analysts to programmers via designers.

Configuration Management

Configuration management is a common tool for managing the development and maintenance of information systems. The term *configuration* here does not relate specifically to hardware but to all the components of an application system, including, in particular, programs, data-files, and documentation. Each item of the configuration is recorded by the configuration manager, who may be assisted by a special software package for that matter. The relationships and the mutual connections among the items are also recorded. Any change in an item or an addition of new items is recorded, and its impact on other items is checked. Interested parties are then notified, and their reaction is received and noted. In this way, it is assured that pertinent relationships are not overlooked when changes occur [20].

There are many other techniques and methods in software engineering. The Warnier-Orr methodology and the Jackson System Development method are both techniques that focus on data structure rather than data flow. Structured Analysis and Design Technique (SADT) has been commonly used, and several newer, object-oriented methods are attracting interest. For descriptions of these, see [17].

Many software engineering tools are computerized. They include software packages that handle the analysis, design and documentation of a new system, as well as the coordination among the members of a development team. The general term for these tools is *CASE (Computer Aided Software Engineering)*[11].

CASE tools (see also ch. 9) are usually directed toward the analysis and design stages, but sometimes generate the necessary program code from the design specifications. For example, a CASE tool may provide for the interactive design of a computer screen format for data input, and once the design is complete, generate the code to display the screen and capture the input data.

Software products available for CASE range from specialized programs to support a single aspect of the development effort to quite comprehensive support systems that package a variety of integrated tools for all stages of the process. This integration ensures consistency and compatibility that might otherwise be more difficult to accomplish (see [2] and [15]).

Because CASE implements the structured techniques that have been discussed, the analysis and design processes are improved, and thus fewer errors are introduced. These tools also improve and reinforce the management of these development activities by standardizing the methodology and by automatically generating documentation. For a good management overview of the subject, see [10].

Before concluding this section, we want to emphasize that an important part of the structured approach is not only the development itself (e.g., analysis, design, programming), but also the comprehensive review of the interim products generated in each life cycle activity. This is achieved by a *structured walk-through,* a term used for a formal session of peer evaluation [22]. The document to be reviewed is distributed among a number of professional colleagues, and, after a short period, they orderly specify their comments and suggestions. Negative reactions of the participants may cause modifications in the product under discussion and even a second walk-through when this is deemed necessary. Only after the reactions are generally positive is the project team granted permission to proceed to subsequent activities.

In summary, we stress that software engineering is not a certain set of tools and methodologies for system development. It is rather a way of thinking that emphasizes an orderly and systematic approach to information system development. The variety of methodologies is enormous; each organization has to select a certain mix of techniques that is believed to be consistent with and adequate for its needs. More important than the selection of specific techniques is the managerial skill to impose their use and to control the quality of the systems under development.

Practical Conclusions for Information System Design and Use

The entire chapter deals with actual practices of information system design and use, so if you are especially interested in practical conclusions, you better read it all. The following is a list of the most significant conclusions of the chapter.

1. Feasibility study is the last stage that still does not involve a relatively large investment of money and effort. A thorough study can save future hazardous adventures.

2. A project is feasible only if three conditions are met: (1) it is technologically possible; (2) it is economically worthwhile; and (3) it is likely to be accepted and properly handled by the potential users. A feasibility study must address these aspects.

3. A feasibility team must first agree on the problems; second, acquire sufficient knowledge of the present situation; third, outline the characteristics that would be required from any proposed solution, and only then design and propose some alternative solutions.

4. There is nothing wrong with the feasibility team expressing its own opinion about various proposed solutions. However, the feasibility report should be objective and not biased in any direction.

5. Users, management, and a steering committee do not have to supervise the daily activities of a development team. There are methods to assess the quality of projects without interference. One can inquire into management practices and characteristics of the basic system and get a fairly good feeling for the quality of the development project.

6. Implementation and conversion constitute a crucial stage. It is therefore recommended that these be handled by a special team, which may be, in fact, a reincarnation of the development team.

7. An appropriate training program is essential to the success of system implementation. Training should not be confined to technical matters, but should also address the concepts and goals that have influenced the installation of the new system.

8. Conversion has to be planned far ahead of the installation date; in fact, it has to be planned during the information analysis stage.

9. Try to avoid instant conversion—make it gradual and modular.

10. Conversion costs may be very high compared to the total development costs. They should be estimated and incorporated in the cost/benefit analysis of the project.

11. Testing of programs and systems is first handled by the professional team. However, when the team claims that a system is ready for installation, the user has to prepare and conduct an acceptance test. Only after successful completion of the test is the system endorsed by the user.

12. System acceptance depends not only on successful tests, but also on the completion of many other tasks, such as documentation, training, and written procedures.

13. During the period of normal operation of an information system it is important to define precisely who is responsible for what—particularly to define the responsibility of the user vis-à-vis the authority of the information systems department.

14. Requests for changes in an existing system should be submitted and handled in a formal manner. In a way, a change request has to undergo a mini-development life cycle.

15. Postaudit is essential to the organization because it may lead to modification of the audited system and its conclusions can assist in future projects.

16. The use of software engineering techniques (e.g., structured analysis, data flow diagrams) is essential to the development of information systems because it directs the development life cycle through a rigorous sequence of activities and facilitates communication between analysts, designers, programmers, and users.

17. It is important to select a comprehensive and consistent set of analysis, design, and programming techniques. It is no less important to impose the chosen techniques on the project development teams.

Summary

This chapter has concentrated on the concerns of users and management during the information system life cycle. Therefore, it has emphasized stages and activities in which user and management involvement is especially important.

The feasibility study is a crucial stage because it is the last chance to halt commitment to major expenditures—to stop before a full-scale development project is launched. Representatives of users, management, and the information systems department take part in the study.

The notion of feasibility consists of three aspects: technological, economic, and organizational. The technological inquiry verifies the existence of technical solutions to the problem. The economic inquiry evaluates whether the costs merit the benefits. The organizational inquiry examines the capacity of the organization to accept various technical solutions.

The feasibility study is based on the following steps: definition of goals and scope; study of the current situation; analysis of information requirements; consideration of alternatives; and submission of a feasibility report to the information systems committee.

During system development, users and management concentrate on the quality of the work, but they do not get into the details of the system being developed. Quality can be assessed by examining project management practices and various system characteristics.

The quality of project management is evaluated by analyzing several indicators: project management compliance with formal life cycle stages and milestones; compliance with budget and deadlines; appropriateness of documentation; frequency and frankness of reporting; and use of software engineering techniques.

Major qualitative characteristics that should be examined are flexibility; simplicity of maintenance; interfaces with related systems; compatibility with other types of hardware and software facilities; expandability in case of future growth; and efficiency of system performance.

Conversion and implementation is a complex stage, encompassing many different issues. The major issues are training, conversion, and testing.

A training program must address managers as well as operational staff. The program has to cover general background and "ideology" as well as operational skills.

Conversion refers to files, programs, and human activities. Files have to be ready before the new system can operate. Programs are normally rewritten, but sometimes it is worthwhile to adopt some programs or routines from previous systems (there are some tools that aid in accomplishing this). People have to modify activities and work according to new procedures.

There are various methods of conversion. The best approach, yet the most costly, is parallel conversion: the old and the new systems run in parallel for a while. Another approach is modular conversion: the new system is gradually introduced, module by module. A variant of this method is pilot conversion: one module only is introduced and then the rest of the new system is installed. The least desirable approach is instant conversion; nevertheless, sometimes the nature of the system necessitates instant conversion. Another possibility is conversion based on a combination of these methods (e.g., a pilot module runs in parallel).

Conversion costs might be high and may include personnel, computer time, outsourcing charges, equipment, special construction (if needed), and materials. The costs should be incorporated in the cost/benefit analysis of the feasibility study.

Testing of an individual program is done by the superior of the programmer who wrote it. A system, or a system module, is tested first by the project leader (i.e., the system test) and finally by the user (i.e., the acceptance test).

An information system can be accepted by users only if several conditions are met: smooth operation is exhibited; full documentation exists; training is completed; procedures are written; and a liaison officer and maintenance programmer(s) are appointed.

During the operation period of an information system, it is important to define strictly the responsibility of the user and the information systems department. In most cases it is preferable to make the user responsible for normal operations while the IS department provides only processing facilities and technical support. However, there are cases where users are not able to assume responsibility; they only send inputs and receive outputs while the entire processing is handled by the IS department.

A delicate matter during system's operation stage is the treatment of changes. This should be systematically handled as follows: a written change request is submitted; the request is analyzed by an information analyst; if it is decided to undertake it, appropriate design, programming, and testing are carried out; and documentation is updated. Only then is the new revision approved for use. Abiding by this procedure is the only way to keep the system neat and maintainable.

Postaudit of an information system is performed by the steering committee or a professional auditor. It is usually undertaken about six months after the system is installed and periodically thereafter. The purpose of postaudit is to examine the quality of the audited system, the quality of the project management, and the reliability of the organizational planning process. The evaluation is based on comparisons between plans and their realization regarding budget, timetable, system performance, and benefits. The conclusions are submitted to the information systems committee, which may trigger system modification and revise future plans.

For many years, the system development life cycle was carried out in an intuitive, ill-structured fashion. Software engineering has been developed to resolve the problems of haphazard system analysis, design, and programming. Software engineering consists of a large number of methodologies devised to assist information system professionals in undertaking and managing the various activities of the development life cycle. Some of the most noted techniques are structured analysis and design, data flow diagrams, data dictionary, and structured walk-through. An organization has to select a set of methodologies that is most adequate for the organizational needs and its professional staff competence. It is very important that the methodologies be strictly imposed on the development teams.

Key Concepts

CASE
change requests
compatibility
configuration management
conversion: instant, modular, parallel, pilot
critical success factors (CSF)
data analysis
data dictionary
data flow diagram (DFD)
decision analysis
development team
EDP (electronic data processing) auditor
efficiency
expandability
feasibility: study, team
flexibility
immediate access analysis

implementation team
information requirements analysis
information systems committee
IS (information systems) department
interface
maintenance
management practices
postaudit
postevaluation
program design language (PDL)
software engineering
software quality assurance
steering committee
structured English
structured system analysis and design
structured walk-through
test: acceptance, program, system
training: ideological, operational

References

1. Ahituv, N., D. Even-Tsur, and B. Sadan. ''Procedures and Practices for Conducting Post Evaluation of Information Systems.'' *Journal of Information Systems Management* 3, no. 2 (Spring 1986): 61–65.
2. Anderson Consulting, P. O. Flaatten, D. J. McCubbrey, P. D. O'Riordan, and K. Burgess. *Foundations of Business Systems.* Chicago: The Dryden Press, 1989.
3. Awad, E. M. *Systems Analysis and Design.* 2d ed. Homewood, IL: Richard D. Irwin, 1985.
4. Boehm, B. W. ''Improving Software Productivity.'' *Computer* 20, no. 9 (Sept. 1987): 43–50.
5. ———. ''Software Engineering.'' *IEEE Transactions on Computers*, C–25 (Dec. 1976): 1226–41.
6. Davis, G. B. ''Strategies for Information Requirements Determination.'' *IBM Systems Journal* 21, no. 1 (1982): 4–30.
7. DeMarco, T. *Structured Analysis and System Specification.* Englewood Cliffs, NJ: Prentice-Hall, 1979.
8. Eliason, A. L. *Online Business Computer Applications.* 3d ed. New York: Macmillan, 1991.
9. Evans, M. W., and J. Marciniak. *Software Quality Assurance and Management.* New York: John Wiley & Sons, 1987.
10. Fisher, A. S. *CASE: Using Software Development Tools.* New York: John Wiley & Sons, 1988.
11. Gane, C. *Computer-Aided Software Engineering: The Methodologies, the Products and the Future.* Englewood Cliffs, NJ: Prentice-Hall, 1990.

12. Gane, C., and T. Sarson. *Structured Systems Analysis*. Englewood Cliffs, NJ: Prentice-Hall, 1979.
13. Gilb, T. *Principles of Software Engineering Management*. Wokingham, England: Addison-Wesley, 1988.
14. Jordan, E. W., and J. J. Machesky. *Systems Development: Requirements, Evaluation, Design, and Implementation*. Boston: PWS-Kent, 1990.
15. Mercurio, V. J., B. F. Meyers, A. M. Nisbet, and G. Radin. "AD/Cycle Strategy and Architecture." *IBM Systems Journal* 29, no. 2 (1990): 170–88.
16. Munro, M. C. "Determining the Manager's Information Needs." *Journal of Systems Management* 29, no. 6 (June 1978): 34–39.
17. Pressman, R. S. *Software Engineering: A Practitioner's Approach*. 3d ed. New York: McGraw-Hill, 1992.
18. Rockart, J. F. "Chief Executives Define Their Own Data Needs." *Harvard Business Review* (Mar.–Apr. 1979): 81–93.
19. Time-Life Books. *The Software Challenge*. Alexandria, VA: Time-Life Books, 1989.
20. Vallabhaneni, S. R. *Auditing the Maintenance of Software*. Englewood Cliffs, NJ: Prentice-Hall, 1987.
21. Yourdon, E. *Modern Structured Analysis*. Englewood Cliffs, NJ: Yourdon Press, 1989.
22. Yourdon, E. *Structured Walkthroughs*. 4th ed. Englewood Cliffs, NJ: Yourdon Press, 1989.
23. Yourdon, E., and L. L. Constantine. *Structured Design*. Englewood Cliffs, NJ: Prentice-Hall, 1979.

Questions

1. Describe the three major aspects of feasibility.
2. Why should the current situation be studied with a top-down approach?
3. Compare the two basic approaches to deriving information requirements: data analysis and decision analysis.
4. How can one evaluate project management quality?
5. Characterize the features of a quality information system.
6. Differentiate between ideological and operational training.
7. Conversion impacts files, programs, and working procedures. Explain why and how this is true.
8. What types of tests must be conducted and when?
9. How can the information system procedures be designed to allow for changes?
10. Which aspects of the system should be evaluated in a postaudit?

Problems

1. Imagine your local supermarket. Describe the physical flows and data (information) flows both in narrative and graphic form.
2. A large real estate office is planning to automate. Select either a data analysis or a decision analysis approach. Explain your rationale for choosing that approach and detail what you expect to discover.
3. A library is considering automating its catalog. Among other considerations, the team must select the conversion approach and estimate costs for each approach. What factors must the team consider?

ABC Corporation Sales Order System

ABC Corporation is a large aerospace company employing approximately 10,000 people. ABC manufactures a variety of components for military and commercial aircraft. Thus far, the company has generated approximately 2,000 sales orders. Each week about 50 more are created. The problems encountered using the current sales order system are as follows: 1) The information entered by the Contract Administrator (C.A.) is not edited or validated other than by the scrutiny of the C.A. or by the approving authorities. There are no methods of verifying that a sales order is complete or accurate. 2) The efforts expended by Contracts in keying sales order data do not concurrently service any other organization. Each functional organization must themselves reenter the same data into their own systems. Sales order file maintenance procedures to support such systems as Common Payroll, Personnel System, and Labor Distribution System do not ensure a timely update from sales order release to updating the computerized files. The leadtime for these tasks ranges from one to two weeks and has a significant impact on the labor validation process. 3) Revisions, inquiries, and reports on sales order data require a physical retrieval of the master sales order from file cabinets and then extracting and transferring information from one form to another. This is a tedious and time consuming process, especially if the sales order has been misfiled, pulled out by another C.A., or lost in an approval cycle. 4) The current approval cycle consists of attaching a routing slip to the sales order and hand-carrying it through four other functional organizations. During the one-to-two-week approval cycle, there is no efficient method for tracking its status. 5) Sales orders enter the distribution cycle multiple times. Approved sales orders are initially distributed, revised with "Intent to Close" and "Final Closeout," and at times, revised to stop work, to release stop work, to cancel, or just to correct or change the information already disseminated. Each time it is revised, Graphics reproduces the entire sales order for distribution. Over a million pages are processed through Graphics and Correspondence Control each year. Each time a sales order reenters the distribution cycle, it faces the possibility of being lost or misdirected. The excessive paper volume and lack of ready access to the latest sales order information results in daily trouble to Contract Administration.

Current System Description

Sales orders are initiated by Contract Administration. Upon receipt of an order from the customer, the C.A. phones Cost Accounting of his intent to create a sales order. He verifies usage of the next available sales order number found within a preassigned block of numbers issued by Cost Accounting. The number is noted by Cost Accounting and is documented in a Sales Order Log maintained by Contracts. The C.A. initials a handwritten sales order which is later either typed or keyed into the word processing system.

Through either method, a hardcopy is produced on a preprinted sales order form. The C.A. reviews and signs the printed sales order. A copy of the sales order is produced and released in advance to Cost Accounting, while the original sales order is logged and routed for approval signatures from Contract, Program Controller, Program Office, Pricing, and Cost Accounting. Upon a one-to-two-week approval cycle, the sales order eventually returns to Contracts and the authorization dates are documented into the Sales Order Log. A Graphics Work Order is filled out and the original sales order is sent to Graphics for reproduction. All copies are then sent to Correspondence Control for distribution to the functional organizations. Graphics returns the original sales order which is filed for later reference. From this point on, all questions or revisions regarding the sales order require a manual retrieval from the master sales order file in Contracts.

Sales Order Revisions are sales orders annotated with changes to a previously released sales order. These changes may range from minor typographical errors to major changes to the work statement. They include authorizations to stop work, to resume work, or to notify the intent to close, to cancel, or final closeout of the sales order. A revision alphabet together with revision notes are written directly onto the original sales order. The revised sales order is attached with a routing slip and reenters the same approval cycle as the original sales order. Instead of a full signature, the authorizing representatives acknowledge the revision notes by entering their respective initals next to the note. Upon completion of the approval cycle, the sales order is returned to Contracts where the revision number and date are entered into a Sales Order Log. A Graphics Work Order is completed, and together with the original revised sales order are sent to Graphics for reproduction and distribution. This time the Sales Order Revisions are printed on a variety of colored paper: Work Stop Orders (blue); Work Stop Release (white); Notice of Intent to Close Sales Order (green); and Sales Order Cancellation and Final Sales Order Closeouts (pink). Revisions are distributed to the recipient of the original sales order.

The information requirements of the new computerized sales order system are as follows: sales order number, revision number, customer, title, description, date sales order was opened, date sales order closed, target close date of sales order, cost account numbers, contract code, contract/authority number (if applicable), contract type (if applicable), digitized signature logo, and whether recurring or nonrecurring.

The hardware currently at ABC includes the following: IBM 4381 Mainframe, IBM 3274 Front-end Processor, IBM PC and Compatibles, Apple/MacIntosh, and Sun Workstations running CAD/CAM software.

The software currently at ABC includes the following: CAD/CAM software, dBASE IV, Lotus 1-2-3, VersaCAD, AutoCAD, and Patran.

Questions

1. If you were conducting a feasibility study, discuss the various alternative solutions. Which one would you choose and why? Did you use a data analysis approach or a decision analysis approach? Why?

2. Which conversion approach would you select and why? What factors would you consider in making your decision?

Chapter 11 Distributed Information Systems

For many years, computer technology was based on central mainframes and underdeveloped communications equipment. These factors imposed severe limitations on information system development, operation, and control. Organizations had to comply with technological constraints, rather than having technology serve management philosophy. Particularly, decentralized organizations had to operate centralized systems; end users were deprived of computing equipment.

Present technology does not set any technical limits on the degree of information systems distribution. The technological advances in minicomputers, microcomputers, communications networks, and supporting software, combined with the incredible decrease in hardware costs, have brought managements to a position where they can select any degree of distribution of information systems. This chapter mainly focuses on managerial aspects of distributed information systems.

Introduction

There is a prevailing misconception of the term *distributed information system* (DIS). Many people associate the term with the dispersal of hardware equipment. This, however, is not necessarily accurate. For instance, in a large, multibranch bank operating an online system, terminals are deployed all over. However, transaction processing can still be performed on a central mainframe. In this case, input and output facilities are distributed, whereas processing and data bases are centralized, not to mention that application development and managerial control are definitely centralized.

Another example is a supermarket chain in which each store possesses an independent computer attached to the cash registers. In this case, routine operation is completely distributed; however, since neither the local manager nor the local cashiers write their own computer programs, we can assume that software development and maintenance are extremely centralized. A counterexample is almost any university or college, where nobody dictates any programming standards to scholars, and the acquisition and allocation of hardware is centrally managed. Here, development is distributed, but some aspects of management and control are centralized.

In summary, total distribution or total centralization are usually nonexistent. Information systems perform many activities. While some activities can be highly distributed in certain cases (e.g., data capture), others are still strictly centralized (e.g., programming). Management has to articulate a clear policy regarding the various aspects of distribution. With the rapid development of front-end workstations (terminals and microcomputers) and with the fast expansion of end-user computing, devising an appropriate distribution policy has become one of the most crucial issues in information systems management. Well-managed distribution is a blessing; anarchical deployment of hardware and software is a curse. This is the principal message of this chapter. We start, however by discussing some relevant concepts and looking at some illustrative examples.

Computerized information systems conventionally start with transaction processing applications, may evolve into structured decision systems, and then develop decision support modules. Along this route of upgraded services, many activities of the information system change form. These include changes in hardware, software, applications, programming, personnel, systems analysis, control operations, data bases, and the like. We are concerned here with the various ways these information system activities can be organized. The activities may be centralized, decentralized, or distributed.

Client-Server Architectures

The terms *client* and *server* originated with *local area networks* (LANs) developed for the purpose of allowing simple user workstations (personal computers) to share more expensive resources, such as file storage or printers. Thus the network connected these workstations to a more powerful server computer (but usually still a microcomputer). This server provided the service of storing files for the workstations or printing output from the workstations, acting as a *file server* or *print server*. The other computers in the network, the workstations, were then the clients of this server (see [19] for a more extensive treatment of this and related topics).

Such networks thereby allow workstations to share data (files), providing some degree of transparency as to where the data physically resides. Each workstation runs its application programs, and the file server delivers records or entire files to the workstation upon request.

From these beginnings have developed a multitude of relationships among the hardware and software components of a network—local or otherwise—which are termed *client-server*. Most such systems currently involve the use of some relational data base management system running on the server (microcomputer or mainframe), with application programs running on the client computers and requesting data base services through queries formulated in SQL (structured query language). On the other hand, the term client-server may very well be applied to other forms of data base management systems and other kinds of relationships between client and server.

One important variation is the existence of multiple servers within the network, and the fact that a particular computer may function both as a client and a server. This architecture results from placing portions of a data base at different locations (a distributed data base), or actually having multiple data bases within the network.

Any computer in the network might house some data for which it acts as server to other network nodes, and at the same time it processes applications which are clients for data located at other computers (servers) in the network. Every node might be both a client and a server. Thus, the terms *client-server system* and *distributed system* are synonymous when both are taken in the broadest sense.

Downsizing

Downsizing is the term given to a form of distribution that does not necessarily have any implications about geographical dispersion. Downsizing comes about because of the apparent cost-effectiveness of microcomputers or workstations when compared to mainframe computers [9, 10]. This form of distribution is undertaken because of the practicality of allocating the work that might be done by a single large computer to a network of smaller ones. It may also be motivated by the possibility of a reduced hardware expense, or by the expectation of reduced development expenses and faster turnaround times on new applications resulting from the use of smaller, simpler computers [17]. In any case, downsizing has become a significant factor in many decisions concerning the distribution of information systems.

Inter-Organizational Systems

Increasingly, the information systems of an organization may be in direct communication with the information systems of other organizations. Such systems are frequently motivated by an interest in gaining competitive advantage. For example, if Company Z's customers can enter their orders directly into Company Z's computer, Z gains advantage over other suppliers who must send a salesperson to get the order. At the same time, if Company Z can order directly from its supplier's computer, Z can more efficiently keep its inventories at minimal levels. These systems that cross organizational boundaries carry extra technical considerations (see, for example, the discussion of EDI in ch. 15) and managerial concerns, but they are becoming a common adjunct to the distributed information system milieu.

A Historic Example

The Hyatt Hotel Corporation [14] began operation in 1957 with its first hotel in Los Angeles. By 1979 it had 51 hotels in 42 cities. The company established its first data processing operation based on an NCR Century computer, at Hyatt's corporate offices in Burlingame, California, in 1971. The centralized DP center used a batch-mode system, with keypunching of data and round-trip mail and courier deliveries to and from the center. As the chain's operations expanded, deliveries took too long to produce meaningful reports, so Hyatt moved to entering the data at terminals in the hotels, replacing the mailing and key-punching.

By 1975 Hyatt's data communications and centralized processing problems were becoming too much to handle. It then ordered a Datapoint Corporation distributed system, based on a Datapoint 5500 minicomputer which provided time-sharing, disk storage, fast printer, and remote terminal input. Processing was done as follows: When a data entry sequence was completed, the data was transmitted to a 5500 for preprocessing and editing. The data was then transmitted via a dial up line to another 5500 in Burlingame. There it was placed on disk, and subsequently converted to tape. The tape was then introduced into the central Century mainframe computer, which handled the final processing. To get reports, journals, and other documents back to the hotel, the data flow was reversed, with tapes going back to the 5500 and its disk, then back to the hotel's minicomputer which generated the hard copy documents. Subsequently, the mainframe computer was replaced by minicomputers in the headquarters and in regional locations.

This example illustrates the typical movement of many information systems—from complete centralization to considerable distribution of information activities. Initially it was a completely *centralized information system,* from data entry to generation of output. As Hyatt expanded operationally and geographically, data entry activities were the first to be *distributed.* Later, data validation activities were distributed to dispersed minicomputers. Data base maintenance and data processing activities were next distributed to regional and local centers. Some activities remained centralized, such as program development and overall control, and these were overseen by the corporate staff and the vice-president of management information systems. It could have become a completely *decentralized information system* had its nodes been completely autonomous, rather than being linked by a telecommunication network with management of the nodes subordinated to the corporate DP staff and executives.

The purpose behind Hyatt's adoption of a distributed information system was the desire to improve operations, i.e., to put the necessary information in the hands of the local hotel's management in a more timely fashion. An additional result was a substantial savings in operating costs, particularly from the replacement of the mainframe by minicomputers. This is an early example of a benefit accruing from downsizing, although the term was not used at the time and the concept was not well understood; it was an era when people believed that large computers provided greater benefit through economy of scale.

Some Current Examples

United Airlines [4] has added to an already distributed system by installing local area networks of workstations at its major terminals. For example, at O'Hare Airport in Chicago, 400 diskless client workstations are networked to 40 servers. The servers are networked together and in turn are tied to a variety of mainframe host computers. Thus, each workstation can access centralized data, while also providing a number of local functions aimed at getting passengers onto their airplanes more quickly.

From their workstations, United's employees can access the Apollo reservation system, as well as systems for operations, maintenance, and administration of the airline. Each system is on a different mainframe configuration. The major motivation for the LANs, however, is the ability to perform a number of activities that do not require access to these systems. An example is the ability of the workstation to read the passenger's magnetic striped ticket and to print luggage tags without the agent having to do any writing by hand. Coupled with similar applications, a 30 percent reduction in passenger processing time is expected.

By contrast, the Orange County (Florida) Assessor's Office has moved to a distributed system in what appears to be a downsizing move. A mainframe system was replaced by a local area network with seven servers. The seven server machines (486 based systems) are connected to 150 personal computer workstations serving the Assessor's office and 500 additional county computers.

This move to a network of small computers was chosen in lieu of adding to the previous IBM 4381 mainframe configuration. This was done in anticipation of significant hardware cost savings, and—probably more importantly—with the expectation of lower software costs. The Assessor's office has experienced shorter lead times for new software development for the microcomputers, and trying out new software products from vendors means risking hundreds of dollars instead of tens of thousands of dollars.

The New York State Department of Civil Service [12] has installed a distributed system with the objective of reducing turnaround time on changes to the health plan data of 1.2 million state employees. The previous system required changes to be typed on paper forms and transmitted to different personnel for entering into a mainframe computer.

In the new system a mainframe is still used, but the mainframe acts as a server, and a network of personal computers is used to make inquiries and changes to the health care data base. Actually, several different modes of access to the server are provided. A local area network in Albany connects hundreds of Civil Service employees to the server. The server is a large mainframe provided by an outside service and located in Omaha. The Civil Service people can inquire and make changes while interviewing the insured person concerned. In addition, other personal computers can have the same type of access through dial up connections. Inquiry capability is supplied to health care providers and pharmacies through special terminals, personal computers, or even touch-tone telephones. In the previous system changes often took weeks to be reflected in the data available for these inquiries, which providers make to check eligibility. Now any changes entered will be reflected in inquiries made the following day. While this inter-organizational system extends only inquiry capability to users outside the state government, those users and their terminals are parts of the system, and were a driving force behind the movement to a greater degree of distribution.

Development of Technology

The Hyatt example is important because it parallels some important developments in the underlying technology. As Hyatt expanded it increased the geographic dispersion of its hotels and the volume of transactions to be processed. With that expansion came the need to distribute its information system activities. This distribution became economically feasible because of a number of technological advances:

Improvements in cost/performance of central processing units and memory

Improvements in cost/performance of auxiliary (disk) storage devices

Improved system software

Improved system and program development methodologies

Development of data base management systems (DBMS)

Improved reliability and effectiveness of data communications

Improvements in application software

Development of specialized terminals for use at the point of transaction

Of course, we continue to see improvements in each of these areas as the technology continues to advance (see ch. 15 and appendix A). The technology has been and continues to be both an enabler of and an incentive for the development of distributed information systems.

The issues raised with regard to distributed information systems are neither new nor unique to the computer era. Historically, the relative balance between distributed and centralized information processing has depended partly on the goals of those needing the information and partly on the technology available to implement those goals. When technology is available to serve those needing centralization, the balance tends to shift in that direction. When technology becomes available to serve decentralized goals, the balance shifts in that direction.

These relationships between goals and technology tend to fluctuate over time. Prior to computerized information processing, manual distributed processing was necessary because of the technical barriers to centralized collecting, processing, and storing of large volumes of data. With the information technologies of the 1950s and 1960s, the balance shifted toward centralized processing. With current technologies, it makes good economic sense to distribute data collection, storage, and processing toward the end users. This trend also supports a growing demand by users for autonomy, creativity, and decision-making power.

A distributed system is best viewed as a hybrid between centralized and decentralized systems. It can provide many of the advantages of both systems and avoid many of their disadvantages. It is useful, therefore, to briefly list the advantages and disadvantages of these diametrically opposed approaches in their purest form (i.e., complete centralization and decentralization). Advocates of centralization usually base their arguments on the improvement of overall efficiency; those arguing for decentralization claim improvements in effectiveness. Literature is full of the pros and cons, and both types of presentations are equally impressive [11; 8, pp. 29–34; 7, ch. 5; 15; 13, ch. 17; and 1].

Centralization Versus Decentralization

A completely centralized information system handles all processing at a single computer site; maintains a single central data base; has centralized development of applications; has central provision of technical services; sets development priorities centrally; and allocates computer resources centrally. The system's remote users are served by transporting input and output data physically or electronically.

A completely decentralized system has no central control of system development; no communication links among autonomous computing units; and standalone processors and data bases in various sites. Each unit funds its own information processing activities and is totally responsible for all development and operation.

Advantages and Disadvantages of Centralized Systems

The main advantages of centralized information systems lie in *economies of scale.* Large centralized systems reduce the need for multiple hardware, software, space, personnel, and data bases. These systems provide better opportunities for recruiting qualified personnel and maintaining training programs. They enable management to impose tight control over the information function activities in terms of standardization and security provisions (see ch. 14). Coordination of development efforts and budgets under the guidance of an overall organizational master plan (see ch. 8) is facilitated. Small or remote organizational units can benefit from accessing a broad repertoire of large mainframe software that would not be available to them had they installed a small independent system. Finally, utilization of system resources can be more efficient.

On the other hand, there are some disadvantages to fully centralized systems. These require high initial investment in mammoth hardware, a sophisticated operating system, widespread communications equipment, and complex application software. Centralized systems require highly qualified personnel for development and maintenance. A system failure might paralyze the entire organization unless an expensive backup system is guaranteed. Most importantly, users are usually less satisfied and poorly motivated because they are less involved and feel less responsible for their application systems. And, due to many interdependencies, the software is much less flexible and cannot be tailored to any one user or function (see [15]).

Advantages and Disadvantages of Decentralized Systems

The pros and cons of decentralized systems reflect a mirror image of the discussion on centralized systems. In other words, almost all the advantages and disadvantages mentioned there turn into disadvantages and advantages here, and vice versa.

Observations indicate that user motivation and satisfaction is increased under a decentralized environment. This is attained because users feel more involved and more responsible, systems are better customized to their specific needs, and they usually get better response time in routine operations as well as in requests for changes.

The organization as a whole can benefit from decentralized systems in a number of aspects: users become directly responsible for the IS budget, therefore their demands are probably more restrained; costs of physical and electronic transport of data are reduced; the risk of a total breakdown of information processing equipment vanishes.

The main disadvantages of completely decentralized systems involve coordination and control. Users tend to develop small, local "empires" and it becomes hard to impose standardization, security measures, and sharing of data and professional knowledge. It is not easy to obtain integrated information for corporate management, nor to access a local data base for the use of another local user. Consequently, duplication of data and development effort is most likely, entailing diseconomy of scale in hardware, software, personnel, and other resources.

A Concluding Remark

A comprehensive study of centralization versus decentralization is described in King's paper [15]. However, you can easily learn from the preceding sections that we cannot designate a preferable approach. This is why we prefer the term "distributed systems"; namely, systems that are partly centralized and partly decentralized.

Distributed Systems

It is sometimes hard to understand the distinction between a distributed system and a decentralized system. We will try to illustrate the difference using a pictorial example. Suppose you take a watermelon to the top floor of the Empire State Building and throw it over the side. After the watermelon has reached the ground, it will be "decentralized." However, if you carry the watermelon in both hands down the elevator or stairs, place it on the ground, and carefully slice it into pieces, it will be "distributed." In other words, the term "distributed" connotes controlled and policy-guided decentralization. With this in mind, we can turn to a more systematic discussion.

Broadening the Scope of Distribution

The common definition of a distributed system implies the spread of hardware and data to multiple sites around an organization, interconnected by a communication network. This definition is deficient, however, because it overlooks a wide range of other activities associated with managing information processing:

> A broader definition acknowledges that data processing is an organizational resource consisting of many areas of activity, each of which may be executed or controlled by various individuals. These activities, or areas of responsibility, can be spread across an organization in a variety of ways, and a manager should carefully consider the appropriate degree of decentralization for each of them [6, p. 145].

Two areas of information system activities are usually identified [6, p. 146]. The first is categorized as execution, and subdivided into development activities and operation activities. Development activities consist of data base administration, applications programming, information analysis, systems design, system documentation, user training, procedure development, conversion, and feasibility studies. Operation activities consist of hardware operations, telecommunications, systems programming, applications maintenance, data entry, and reporting. In most companies the execution activities are associated with technically trained personnel, such as information analysts, system designers, programmers, data base administrators, and operators.

The second area of information system activities is categorized as control. These activities involve regulation of the budgets, costs, people, time, quality assurance, and plans for delivery of information system services. The items usually fall under the responsibility of various managers, rather than information experts. They may consist of security provision, priority setting, standardization of tasks, accessing of data, scheduling tasks, budgeting, personnel planning, and evaluation of computer products.

Armed with these delineations of activities, we can now state that a distributed information system is one where authority over one or more information system activities has been distributed—i.e., delegated. A completely centralized activity is one that is wholly undertaken by a central information system. A completely decentralized activity is one that is wholly undertaken by a user unit. A distributed activity is one that is somewhere on the spectrum between these two extremes.

For example, consider the activity of applications programming. As a centralized activity, the application can be turned over to the user as a turnkey system. As a distributed activity, the user can communicate his or her needs to the center's programmers, or participate in the programming team, or supervise development, or do the application testing. If the user takes care of all the stages, this activity is considered decentralized. Another example is hardware operation. If all the processing is done at the center, the activity is centralized. If all the processing is done at the user's site, the activity is decentralized. The activity is distributed when the user performs data validation on his or her minicomputer, then transmits the validated data to the larger computer at the center for file updating.

There is, therefore, a wide variety of distributed systems. They vary along two dimensions: (1) How many activities are distributed? and (2) What is the degree of distribution for each distributed activity? Each type of distributed system leads to a different information system structure, each of which possesses some of the advantages and disadvantages of centralized and decentralized systems.

It is beyond the scope of this book to describe every possible structure with its pros and cons. At most, we can briefly list several principal alternative structures (described more extensively in [11]; see also [5] and [6]).

1. *Distributed processing with central data base*—Some processing takes place at local minicomputers (for instance, data entry and validation) but without support of a local data base.

2. *Hierarchical system with local data bases*—Processing is done locally and a local data base is updated from local transactions and also, periodically, from the central data base. Summary data is sent to the central computer for global processing and central data base updating.

3. *Distributed data base with limited sharing*—In addition to having local processing and local data bases, the local center can access other local data bases for low-probability events (e.g., verifying the balance of a bank customer wishing to cash a check at a branch other than his own).

4. *Multiple-level hierarchical distributed system*—Any local processor of the distributed system is a central node of lower-level distributed systems. The Hyatt information processing system was such a system. It had four regional nodes, based on Datapoint ARC systems, each one distributing processing and data bases to various hotels using Datapoint 5500 minicomputers and local data bases.

5. *Fully distributed network*—Composed of multiple autonomous processes and partitioned data bases that have equal control status. This is a nonhierarchical structure without central control and with no single computer playing a central role. It permits sharing of resources (primarily programs and data) among network sites by using telecommunications.

Management Role in Distributed Systems

Distributed systems are not a panacea for every organization. The structure to be selected—i.e., the degree of distribution—depends on the circumstances of the specific organization. The best approach is the one that best matches the philosophy, structure, strategy, and goals of the host organization (see [2]). After all, you should not forget that an information system is a means to an end and not an end in itself. General management plays a major role in the choice of structure—and that involves trade-off between the advantages of centralized and decentralized information system activities.

Information systems are control and coordination devices that should fit an organization's structure and facilitate achievement of its goals. The philosophy of management about how the organization should be managed must dictate the information system structure. The general organizational approach must be consistent throughout, including information systems. It is inconceivable that information systems would be decentralized in an organization that is primarily centrally oriented; and, vice versa, that a centralized system would be in a decentralized organization. A single-product company with functional divisions (e.g., an airline) will tend to have a much less distributed information system than will a conglomerate with completely autonomous divisions producing unrelated products.

A distributed system must be designed from a central management perspective. Its development and subsequent operation must be planned and controlled by the various organizational bodies associated with information systems—the information system committee, the various steering committees, the overall manager of information systems, and the corporate information system staff (see chs. 9, 12, and 13 for a more detailed discussion of these).

The next sections suggest a systematic approach to distributed systems.

Distribution Spectrum and Profile*

In an earlier section, we mentioned that information system activities can be classified into three categories: development, operation, and control. The most elementary stage in establishing a policy for distributed information systems (DISs) is to list the activities pertaining to the particular organization. Table 11.1 presents a typical list, taken from the authors' experience of a real case in the banking sector. You can also refer to [5] or [6] for a similar list.

You may have noted that there are differences between some titles of the activities cited here and those mentioned in the system life cycle in chapters 9 and 10. The reason for this should be obvious since organizations tend to devise a private terminology. The general framework, however, is similar.

Once the list of activities is made, it is time to write down responsibility spectra. For each activity, you designate the most centralized mode and gradually move to the most distributed state. Table 11.2 presents responsibility spectra for the activities listed in table 11.1. The left-hand side of each spectrum suggests an extreme case of centralization; the right-hand side is an extremely distributed mode; in between are the intermediate states. A similar approach had first been suggested by Buchanan and Linowes [5,6]. Note that the definitions along each spectrum might vary among different organizations.

---

*The following sections are partly cited from the paper, "Learning to Live in a Distributed World" by N. Ahituv and B. Sadan, *Datamation*, (Sept. 15, 1985): 139–148. Copyright 1985 by *Datamation*. Reprinted by permission.

Table 11.1   Information System Activity List

Category	Activity
Development	System definition System analysis System design Application programming Data base administration Documentation User training
Operation	Hardware operation Communications network operation Systems programming Application software maintenance Input preparation File handling Output distribution to departmental users Output distribution to customers
Control	Providing security Priority setting Setting working procedures Accessing data Controlling routine data processing cycle Scheduling development tasks Professional personnel management Budgeting Review and postevaluation

Using the Distribution Profile

The responsibility spectrum table (table 11.2) is a useful tool in a number of cases, including the following:

1. For individual systems that are already in operation, it is used to document the status of the system in terms of its *distribution profile* (i.e., its position along the various spectra). One table like this can replace one thousand words of narrative explanation. Moreover, a survey of all existing systems can be assisted with these spectrum tables, and the resulting profiles can be categorized, analyzed, and aggregated for clear demonstration to management.

2. For individual systems under development, a spectrum table is used to deliberate the desired level of distribution in each activity, and thereafter to review and to possibly revise the distribution profile whenever deemed necessary.

3. For corporate management and the information system management, the spectrum table is an excellent vehicle to express a distribution policy. They can classify information systems into a number of categories (e.g., accounting systems, office systems, DSS), and determine the degree of distribution for a certain category just by drawing borderlines on each spectrum row. The borderlines will designate the minimum and maximum degrees of distribution allowable for each class of information systems.

Table 11.2 Responsibility Spectra

Activity	Very Centralized	Spectrum			Very Distributed
System Definition	User raises preliminary requirements	User defines requirements	User selects a solution among proposed alternatives	User participates in definition team	User performs system definition
System Analysis	User is not involved	User reviews system documentation	User defines detailed requirements	User participates in analysis team	User performs analysis
System Design	User is not involved	User reviews physical design	User defines physical requirements	User participates in design team	User performs design
Application Programming	Turnkey system	User forwards programming requirements	User participates in programming team	User supervises programming	User writes programs
Data Base Administration	User only controls source documents	User sets data requirements	User performs logical design of DB	User performs physical design of DB	User manages independent DB
Documentation	User receives functional guidelines	User writes user manuals	User participates in technical documentation	User prepares detailed description of all manuals, programs, and DB	
User Training	User gets training from others	User sets training requirements	User prepares training material	User conducts part of the training	User is fully responsible for training
Hardware Operation	User does not operate hardware equipment	User operates terminals and/or data entry	User operates local front-end computer	User operates local computer as part of a centralized system	User possesses independent computer center
Communication Network Operation	User gets central services	User operates a network supported by staff personnel		User is in charge of own network	
Systems Programming	User applies given operating system	User accommodates application programs to a given operating system	User maintains own operating system	User develops and maintains an operating system	
Application Software Maintenance	User complains of errors in programs	User requests changes and modifications in application programs		User corrects errors and makes changes in application programs	
Input Preparation	User prepares source documents	User keys into a central data entry system	User keys into a local data entry system	User possesses a local independent input and file system	
File Handling	All data files are central	User is responsible for data located in a central site	User handles local files as part of a network	User possesses independent local files	

Table 11.2 *Continued*

Activity	Very Centralized	Spectrum			Very Distributed
Output Distribution to Departmental Users	Central output production	Combination of central and local output facilities	Local output facilities connected to a central computer	User operates a local independent output system	
Output Distribution to Customers	Central report printing and mailing	Central printing and user mails to customers		User prints out and mails to customers	
Providing Security	Security arrangements are central	User operates local security subject to central guidelines	User devises local guidelines subject to central policy	User in charge of local security guidelines and operation	
Priority Setting	Priorities are imposed by central unit	User places requirements	User rank-orders requirements	User sets priorities	
Setting Working Procedures	Working procedures are imposed by center	User suggests working procedures	User modifies central working procedures according to local circumstances		User sets working procedures
Accessing Data	User does not decide on access privileges	User suggests access privileges	User approves privileges for data accessing		User sets privileges for data accessing
Controlling Routine Data Processing Cycle	User only keys-in input	User dispatches own programs			User is fully responsible for correctness of input, processing, and output
Scheduling Development Tasks	User presents needs	User prioritizes needs	User suggests timetable		User approves timetable
Scheduling Operational Tasks	Timetable for operations is centrally scheduled	User prioritizes tasks	User suggests scheduling		User schedules operational tasks
Professional Personnel Management	Personnel needs are centrally dictated	User presents requirements for personnel	User hires few liaison officers		User hires, fires, evaluates, and promotes professional employees
Budgeting	User presents needs but not in monetary terms	User sets constraints to expenditures	User details budgetary requirements		User is in charge of resource budgeting and control
Review and Evaluation	User is not involved in evaluation	User collects data on performance	User sets performance criteria	User participates in performance evaluation	User evaluates system performance

A major question is how the distribution decision is made. What are the criteria for determining the degree of distribution? These are discussed in the next section.

Criteria for Determining Distribution

There have been a few attempts to adopt quantitative models to solve distribution problems [3,18]. These models are limited, however, to distribution of hardware. We do not know of any magic wand in the form of a mathematical formula that optimizes distributed systems when the term is perceived in its broader sense, as used here. Nevertheless, we provide an arbitrary list of criteria that facilitates the policy-making process in such cases.

1. *Relationships to mainline IS systems*—When a new proposed system is supposed to be tightly connected to principal organizational systems (e.g., accounting and bookkeeping), it is unlikely that a high level of distribution will be suggested; when a new system appears to be detached from the mainline (e.g., payroll, word processor), distribution of various activities can be seriously considered.

2. *Data uniqueness*—When the system's data is unique to the particular system and the user department (e.g., personnel file), the organization will favor a higher distribution level, particularly with respect to the data base; when the data is shared by many systems and by various users (e.g., bookkeeping), centralization is more likely favored.

3. *Number of users*—As the number of users increases (e.g., bank tellers), there is more need for central control over the development and for the central coordination of the operations.

4. *Existent independent computer system*—When a user already operates an independent computer, it is more likely that development and operation activities will be delegated to the user.

5. *Cost considerations*—Factors pertaining to economies of scale, communications costs, equipment acquisition and deployment cost, personnel requirements, and the like play an important, but not dominant, role in a distribution decision. The rapid decrease in the costs of hardware (particularly microcomputers and terminals) may encourage a decision to distribute; still, the cost factor should be seriously considered.

6. *Availability of ready-made applications*—When a similar application has been installed elsewhere and is offered for acquisition, a decision to purchase that system rather than to develop one may impose a certain level of distribution that is dictated by the proposed solution.

7. *Application uniqueness*—When the application to be computerized is unique to a certain function in the organization (e.g., macroeconomic forecasts), it is more likely that development and operation power will be delegated to the direct user of the system.

8. *Data security*—If the data is more confidential (e.g., personnel file), it is more likely that control and maintenance functions will be handed over to the direct user.

9. *Requirements for data availability*—Sometimes it is vital to have the data available at any moment (e.g., foreign currency balances); hence, it is advisable to maintain the data and the pertinent software on local equipment, rather than to depend on external or remote services. Consequently, distribution will be favored.

10. *Organizational factors*—The organizational structure of the firm or the amount of power delegated to subsidiary companies in a conglomerate may highly affect decisions about the level of distribution.

11. *Exogenous factors*—Governmental regulations, laws (e.g., Privacy Act), competition, infrastructure conditions (e.g., vendor location), or backup systems (e.g., location of compatible equipment in case of emergency) may influence the decision on how far to distribute.

The impact of each criterion on the final decision cannot be universally assessed. It may vary among organizations and among systems. Still, the list of criteria is very instrumental in reaching a formal, documented decision rather than an intuitive one.

Establishing a Policy for Distributed Information Systems

Due to the rapid proliferation of microcomputers and communications networks, the following "horror" scenario very often takes place in a large number of organizations. The top executive in charge of the information system function discovers one morning that a number of distributed (or decentralized) information systems have been installed all over the place and are already in full operation; yet, there is no policy monitoring the proliferation of those systems, nor have there been established formal measures controlling existing distributed systems. In a panic, the executive summons some staff members and orders them to devise a clear policy. The following nine steps are those that lead to the establishment of such a policy.

Step 1: Revise IS Activities

The list of activities presented in table 11.1 is not "a list for all seasons." It must be adjusted to the circumstances of the organization under study. This adjustment process involves two activities. First, the person in charge of constructing a distribution policy (hereafter, the analyst) has to review in depth all the procedures and practices related to information system development, operation, and control. This review should result in a tentative revised list of activities. The second action is to interview a number of key persons in the organization and to request their comments on the suggested list. Following the interviews, a "conclusive" list is generated. Note that the term "conclusive" stands only for the preparatory steps until management approves the suggested policy. It is not necessarily a final list.

Step 2: Revise Responsibility Spectra

After a list of activities has been formulated, the centralization/distribution (C/D) scale within each activity has to be determined. The various spectra must be tailored to suit the specific organization.

A suggested method to undertake this step is to prepare proposed spectra based on the analyst's best judgment. Then the analyst has to try to portray the C/D profile of a few existing information systems that are prone to distribution. This will facilitate the definition of the various grades along each spectrum row.

Step 3: Set Distribution Boundaries

The C/D profile is meant to characterize individual application systems. Nevertheless, it is likely that an organization will set limits on the degree of distribution it is prepared to allow in each of the C/D areas. For instance, an organization may decide that personnel management of IS professionals is always centralized, regardless of the department or system with which they deal; hence, the "circle" on the spectrum of personnel management will always be drawn on the left side. An organization may be inclined to delegate the responsibility for system operation to the end users; hence, the C/D profile of Operations will tend to the distribution side.

Generally speaking, the spectrum table is a useful tool for the organization to exhibit its overall policy towards C/D by drawing borderlines on each activity row. At this step, the analysts only suggest the C/D limits that will be discussed and approved in a later step. The benefit from drawing the suggested limits so early is in identifying exceptions; namely, existing systems that have already exceeded the limits.

Step 4: Setting Distribution Criteria

The C/D profile is a descriptive technique that helps in understanding and standardizing a DIS. It cannot, however, substitute for a decision-making process in which the level of C/D will be analyzed for each system entering the development cycle.

The major requisite for making an intelligent decision on C/D level is to have a list of criteria by which a decision maker can judge how far a certain system is to be distributed. Undoubtedly, the criteria vary among different organizations.

Step 5: Setting Procedures and Milestones

The C/D profiles and criteria aid in making the decision on the degree of distribution. But there is also a need to determine the timing of the decision and to schedule milestones at which the decision should be reviewed.

Assuming that the organization develops new information systems in compliance with formal system development life cycle standards and procedures, it is recommended that the C/D aspects be analyzed and reviewed along the normal SDLC, as illustrated in figure 11.1.

As suggested in figure 11.1, there should be at least one activity that is centrally handled. This activity is the preliminary analysis, where the initiative to develop a new system is examined. During this step, a tentative C/D profile is constructed with particular emphasis laid on the development part of the profile. The study report and the

Figure 11.1 Centralization/distribution decision procedure

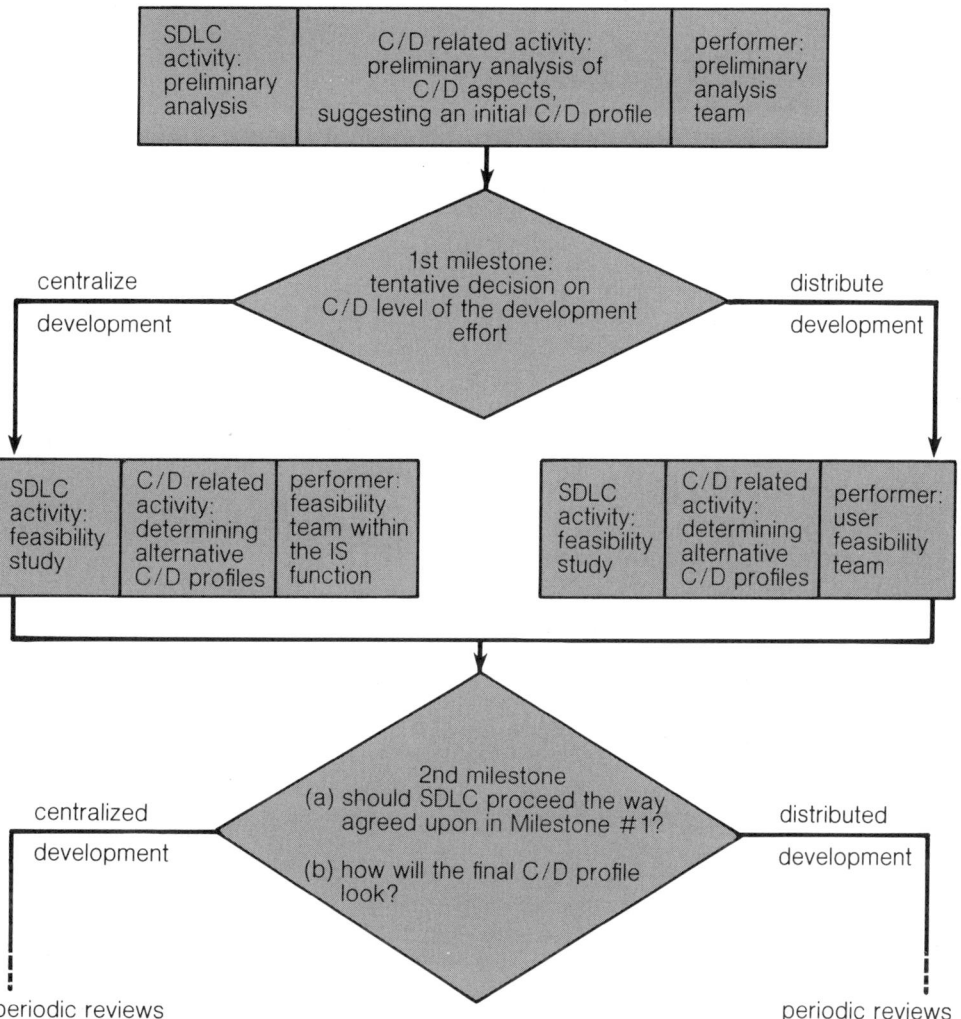

suggested profile are given to the IS committee (see ch. 9) that is responsible for the GO/NO-GO decision. Part of a GO decision is to determine whether the feasibility study activity will be centralized or delegated to the user.

In any event, the feasibility study report will have to include alternative C/D profiles covering all aspects of distribution. These will be discussed during the second milestone, where the decision on the C/D profile should be finalized (as far as any system architecture decision *is* finalized at this stage).

Later, whenever the steering committee is assembled for a periodic review of the project, part of its time should be devoted to C/D profile review. These periodic reviews continue until the system moves from the development to the operation phase.

Step 6: Interim Report to Top Management

At this point, the team responsible for devising distribution policy should have the following items already at hand:

1. A list of IS activities pertinent to the particular organization
2. Responsibility spectrum table
3. Suggested boundaries within which the organization should tolerate any degree of distribution
4. A list of criteria on which a distribution decision should rely
5. Suggested procedure for the distribution decision-making process

This material is substantial enough to call for an interim report to management. Management should review and approve (or modify) the suggested policy, and give its blessing to proceed to the subsequent steps. This is specifically required at this point since the next step incurs more cost than the previous ones.

Step 7: Survey of Existing Distributed Systems

Once the C/D documentation standards (i.e., the C/D profile) has been approved, it is essential to survey all the existing systems suspected of being more or less distributed. The team that carries out the survey should use the agreed spectra. This has the following merits:

1. The suggested spectra will be reexamined and possibly revised if necessary.
2. The team will obtain updated and well-organized knowledge on all the distributed systems.
3. Extreme exceptions (with respect to the agreed boundaries) will be noted and reported to management.

In addition to these three advantages, the survey findings will serve as the basic data for the subsequent step, where system classification should take place.

Step 8: Establishing Control Procedures

A major cornerstone in a distribution policy is the control procedure, or the rules by which DISs are governed when they are under development as well as when they are in operation. Because of the variety of viable C/D profiles, it is impossible to establish a single control procedure that will be usable for all of them. On the other hand, it is impractical and undesirable to devise a tailor-made control procedure for each system. The golden mean is to classify the C/D profiles into a small number of major categories and to establish a control procedure for each major category. Following is an example for one such major category.

Table 11.3 suggests a control procedure for an information system development cycle that is suitable for a profile of an *extremely* distributed case. In this table, which is adopted from a real case, there are four organizational bodies involved in distributed

Table 11.3 Responsibilities during System Development—Extremely Distributed Project

Phase	Activity	User Professional Team	User Management	IS Function Professional Staff	IS Function Management
Definition	Analysis of Existing System	Performs	Approves	—	—
	User Requirement Definition	Performs	Approves	—	—
	Feasibility Study	Performs	Approves	Assists and reviews	Approves
System Analysis	Logical Analysis	Performs	Approves	—	—
	Conversion Requirements Definition	Performs	Approves	Assists	—
	Control and Security Requirements	Performs	Approves	Assists and reviews	—
	Resource Requirements Definition	Performs	Approves	Assists and reviews	—
	Testing Requirements	Performs	Approves	Reviews	—
	Final Report	Performs	Approves	Reviews	Approves
System Design	Detailed Design	Performs	Approves	Assists	—
	Conversion Design	Performs	Approves	Assists	—
	Control and Security Design	Performs	Approves	Assists and reviews	—
	Testing Design	Performs	Approves	Reviews	—
	Interfaces to Other Systems	Performs	Approves	Assists	—
	Program Specifications	Writes	Approves	—	—
	Final Report	Prepares	Approves	Reviews	Approves
Implementation	Programming	Writes	—	Assists	—
	Testing and Integration	Performs	Approves	Assists	—
	Operation Procedures	Writes	Approves	—	—
	User Procedures	Writes	Approves	—	—
	Training	Assists or performs	Approves	Assists or performs	—
	Conversion	Performs	Approves	Assists	—
	Acceptance Test	Assists	Performs and approves	Assists and reviews	—
	Declaring Completion of Development	—	Reviews and approves	Reviews	Approves
Postaudit	Postaudit	—	Reviews and approves	Performs	Approves

Table 11.4   Responsibilities during System Operation—Extremely Distributed Case

Activity	User Department			IS Function		
	Professional Staff	*Operational Staff*	*Management*	*Professional Staff*	*Operational Staff*	*Management*
Normal Runs	—	Performs	Sets priorities	—	Coordinates with other systems	—
Failure in a Normal Run	Assists in identifying cause Suggests solutions	Identifies causes and recovers	Is informed of serious events Coordinates with other units Discusses future implications	Assists if required	Coordinates backup facilities	Is informed of very serious cases
Bug(s) in a Program	Identifies and corrects	Calls for help	(as above)	(as above)	—	(as above)
Changes and Additions to Software	Analyzes the request and suggests a solution Performs tests	Reviews Tests and approves test results	Approves	Assists if required	Is informed for backup needs	Is informed in major cases
Changes and Upgrading to Hardware	Analyzes the request and presents requirements	Reviews requirements and coordinates installation	Approves and forwards to IS function	Assists in analysis Orders equipment	Assists in installation if required	Approves

system development. These are the professional team and the management of a user department, and the professional staff function and the management of the information system function. Table 11.3 designates the responsibilities of each body along the development cycle.

In a similar fashion, there is also a need to establish control procedures for activities related to systems under normal operations. Table 11.4 designates five typical operational activities and determines responsibilities of various organizational bodies for the case of an *extremely* distributed system.

As mentioned earlier, procedures similar to those in tables 11.3 and 11.4 should be prepared for the most prevalent C/D profiles. Note that the two tables only summarize what should be included in such procedures. In reality, they should be more detailed.

Step 9: Obtaining Management Approval
At this stage, the distribution policy is ready for final approval. In addition to the items that were available at the interim report (see step 6), the team should now have a revised version of the responsibility spectra based on a survey of existing systems. There is

also a list of criteria and a number of control procedures devised for the most typical C/D profiles in the organization. It is time for management to review and to endorse the entire policy.

A Final Remark

It is vital that management promulgate the policy among all users to stress its importance. It is likely that users will comply with the DIS policy only if they are convinced that the issue is truly important. One necessary step upon approval is to appoint a highly ranked officer to take charge of DIS coordination. This officer should make sure that the policy is appropriately implemented.

Practical Conclusions for Information System Design and Use

The following list contains practical conclusions for information system design and use.

1. A distributed system can realize many advantages of both centralized and decentralized systems while it avoids many of the hazards.
2. Information system distribution refers to the degree of responsibility over any information system activity that is shared by the central information system function and the user groups.
3. The structure of a distributed information system has to match the organization's strategy, structure, and goals—not the other way around.
4. Organizations possessing a distributed system should, as a rule, maintain central control that is exercised by an overall information system manager and staff.
5. Distribution policy should be based on a list of criteria that is devised for each organization.
6. Distribution policy should be assisted by decision aids, such as a spectrum table and decision milestones.
7. The establishment of a distribution policy should be carried out step-by-step in a systematic approach.

Summary

Information systems can be structured in different ways, varying from a centralized to a decentralized structure. A completely centralized information system is one in which resources (hardware, software, personnel, applications) are concentrated at one central site. A completely decentralized system is separated into autonomous sites, each one fully controlling its resources, without any interaction between the units or without any central control. Each of these extreme configurations of information systems has its advantages and disadvantages. The proponents of a centralized system focus on the efficiency that results from economies of scale. Advocates of a decentralized system favor the effectiveness achieved by having autonomous units customized to local user needs.

Advances in information technologies (minicomputers, microcomputers, telecommunications, sophisticated system and application software, data bases, and low-cost processing and storage devices) make possible information system structures that constitute hybrid systems. These can realize many advantages of both extremes, yet avoid many of their disadvantages. Such systems are called distributed information systems. All are located on the spectrum between complete centralization and complete decentralization.

The many activities inherent in an information system are categorized as execution activities or control activities. Execution activities involve development (data administration, system design, training, applications development) and operation (applications maintenance, processing, data entry). Control activities have to do with the planning and control of information system resources (setting priorities, security, budgeting, or scheduling tasks). An activity can be handled by a central information system staff or by a user. Distribution of an activity has to do with the degree of responsibility over the activity delegated to a user. A distributed information system is, therefore, one in which the responsibility over at least one activity has been delegated to some extent to a user. It follows that there is the potential for multiple distributed information systems.

Corporate management plays a major role in determining the structure of the information system because this structure has to fit the organization's strategy, structure, diversity, and goals, as well as the management's philosophy. Management has to consider the various information system activities and decide on their desired degree of distribution. These considerations should be a part of the information system master plan, which should also specify priorities for developing and implementing the distributed system. The information systems committee, various project steering committees, corporate information system staff, and the corporate information system manager should be used by corporate management to control the implementation of the distributed system.

There are several major configurations of distributed systems. They reflect distributed processing facilities with or without a large central processor, distributed data bases with or without a common data base, and distributed communications networks. In all types, including a fully distributed system, some central control must be exerted by a central information system manager and staff. Otherwise, the distributed system will tend to become an unplanned decentralized system.

A systematic approach to describe distributed systems is to use a spectrum table. A spectrum table lists all the activities pertinent to information system development, operation, and control. For each activity, the distribution spectrum is delineated. An analyst can document each system by drawing its profile on the spectrum table.

The spectrum table can be used for a number of purposes: profiling existing systems; planning the degree of distribution for future systems; and expressing management policy in terms of distribution boundaries.

There are many criteria that assist in determining the degree of distribution. Some of these include relationships to other systems, data uniqueness, number of users, existence of local hardware, cost, availability of software, application uniqueness, security, response time requirements, and organizational climate.

Management policy towards DIS should be established in a systematic manner through a number of steps. First, the IS activities are listed and a distribution spectrum portrayed for any one of the activities. Distribution boundaries, criteria, and decision-making procedures are set next. Finally, after surveying existing systems, control procedures are established. Management has to accompany the entire process and give its blessing to the suggested policy. A highly ranked officer should coordinate the distributed information systems in an organization.

This chapter completes part 2 of the book. In this part, we started from information system theory and gradually moved into practice. Our main purpose is to convince you that the theoretical framework can also be implemented. We hope we have done so.

The third and last part of the book deals with issues related to organizing and managing the information systems in an organization.

Key Concepts

centralized information system
client-server architectures
decentralized information system
distributed information system (DIS)
distribution policy

distribution profile
distribution spectrum
downsizing
inter-organizational systems

References

1. Ahituv, N., and B. Sadan. "Learning to Live in a Distributed World." *Datamation* 31, no. 18 (Sept. 1985): 139–48.
2. Ahituv, N., S. Neumann, and M. Zviran. "Factors Affecting the Policy for Distributing Computing Resources." *MIS Quarterly* 13, no. 4 (Dec. 1989): 389–401.
3. Akoka, J., ed. *Management of Distributed Data Processing.* Amsterdam: North-Holland, 1982.
4. Booker, E. "United Takes Distributed Approach." *Computerworld* 26, no. 13 (Mar. 30, 1992): 1.
5. Buchanan, J. R., and R. G. Linowes. "Making Distributed Data Processing Work." *Harvard Business Review* 58, no. 5 (Sept.–Oct. 1980): 143–61.
6. ———. "Understanding Distributed Data Processing." *Harvard Business Review* 58, no. 4 (Jul.–Aug. 1980): 143–53.
7. Burch, G. J. G., F. R. Strater, and G. Grudnitski. *Information Systems: Theory and Practice.* 3d ed. New York: John Wiley & Sons, 1983.
8. Cortada, J. W. *EDP Costs and Charges.* Englewood Cliffs, NJ: Prentice-Hall, 1980.
9. Douglass, D. P. "Putting Large Systems on PC Networks." *I/S Analyzer,* 28, no. 1 (Jan. 1990): 1–16.

10. "Downsizing: The Application Migration." *Datamation* 38, no. 23 (Nov. 15, 1992): 38–48.

11. Emery, J. C. "Managerial and Economic Issues in Distributed Computing." In *1977 IFIP Conference Proceedings,* edited by B. Gilchrist, 945–55. Amsterdam: North-Holland, 1977.

12. Ferranti, M. "Benefits System Brings Together Mainframe, Client/Server Technology." *PC Week* 9, no. 20 (May 18, 1992): 25.

13. Hussain, D., and K. M. Hussain. *Managing Computer Resources.* 2d ed. Homewood, IL: Irwin, 1978.

14. "Hyatt Hotels Moving to Decentralized DP." *Computerworld,* Special Report/23 (July 30, 1979).

15. King, J. L. "Centralized Versus Decentralized Computing: Organizational Considerations and Management Options." *ACM Computing Surveys* 15, no. 4 (Dec. 1983): 319–49.

16. Lindquist, C. "County Thinks Small, Dumps 4381 for LANs." *Computerworld* 26, no. 14 (Apr. 6, 1992): 1.

17. Martin, J. "Faster, Cheaper, Smaller is Still the Trend in Hardware." *PC Week* 7, no. 19 (May 14, 1990): 74.

18. Streeter, D. N. "Centralization or Dispersion of Computing Facilities." *IBM Systems Journal* 12, no. 3 (1973): 283–301.

19. Summers, R. C. "Local Area Distributed Systems." *IBM Systems Journal* 28, no. 2 (1989): 227–40.

Questions

1. Compare centralized and decentralized information systems.
2. What are the characteristics of the two areas of information activities?
3. Define the term "distribution."
4. Define the term "distributed information system (DIS)."
5. What is a distribution profile?
6. What are the main uses of a distribution profile?
7. Why is it essential to classify DISs into a small number of categories?

Problems

1. Using one of the DIS examples described in this chapter, consider what additional assumptions would need to be made about activities not mentioned, then prepare a distribution profile for that system.
2. Previous chapters (particularly 5 and 6) have distinguished between a transaction processing system (TPS) and a management information system (MIS). Try to relate this distinction to DIS; show how a distributed TPS looks; and how a distributed MIS should function. Are there significant differences between the two in terms of distribution attributes?
3. What are the hardware and software components that are necessary to obtain some degree of distribution?

Walker Manufacturing Company

Walker Manufacturing Company (WMC), with its headquarters in Chicago, Illinois, is the leading manufacturer of exhaust systems. An exhaust system includes mufflers, pipes, and clamps. WMC's products are used for passenger cars and trucks, domestic and foreign, of almost all makes, models, and years.

WMC has six manufacturing facilities strategically located around the nation: Chicago, Illinois; Seattle, Washington; LaMirada, California; Denver, Colorado; Aberdeen, Mississippi; and Harrisonburg, Virginia (see fig. 11.2). Each manufacturing center has a warehouse. The manufacturing facilities in Chicago reside in the same vicinity as the head office. The customer orders are normally filled by the closest warehouse. All the shipments of goods are contracted to nationwide trucking companies.

At the present time, WMC has a mainframe computer in the headquarters and a minicomputer in each manufacturing center, except for the one in Chicago. Each minicomputer supports the application systems for a manufacturing center and its associated warehouse. The applications include manufacturing, inventory, distribution, purchasing, accounts payable, bookkeeping, personnel, and payroll. In addition to supporting these applications, the mainframe computer at the head office supports the customer order processing, invoicing, accounts receivable, and marketing systems. There are no communications between the computers in the manufacturing centers.

WMC's customers include car manufacturers (e.g., GM), big retailer stores (e.g., K Mart), discount installers (e.g., Muffler King), and independent garages. All customer orders and invoices are handled by the head office, either by telephone or by mail. Each evening, the order information is transferred from the head office to the manufacturing centers, and the manufacturing centers transfer the manufacturing, shipping, and inventory information to the head office (see fig. 11.3). The customers' orders are normally shipped the day after the order information is received by the warehouse.

With these computer systems, the company encounters the following problems:

1. The customers constantly request the option of placing orders through the warehouse/manufacturing center, especially those who prefer to place orders by phone and live in different time zones from Chicago.

2. The customer's order is shipped at least one day after the order is placed. This slowness in shipping causes some customers to turn to WMC's competitors.

3. The noncurrent inventory information for each warehouse causes some orders, which could have been filled immediately, to be put into backorders, and vice versa.

4. When there are shortages of some products in one manufacturing center, the other manufacturing centers may have a surplus of those products.

5. When one manufacturing center has a labor dispute, shipments normally handled by that center cannot be easily handled by another center.

6. The price of purchasing raw materials would be lower if the needs of all manufacturing centers could be batched together.

Figure 11.2 The manufacturing centers of WMC

7. The specifications of parts are set by each manufacturing center. The specifications of parts to be used for the same make, model, and year may not be the same for all manufacturing centers.

8. Maintaining programming staffs for five remote manufacturing centers is too costly.

The management is eager to correct these problems, but mandates that although the orders can be placed through the warehouses as well as the head office, the invoice will still be handled by the head office. The management also emphasizes that a "crash" of the computer at the head office should not impact the normal operations of other manufacturing centers and their associated warehouses.

Questions

You are assigned by the MIS director to analyze the situation and to produce a report for the following problems:

1. Set distribution boundaries for Walker Manufacturing Company.

2. Propose a centralized/distributed policy for an inventory system which you think is "perfect" for WMC. The inventory of a product is updated when it is produced, and when it is shipped. Up-to-the-minute inventory information is very important to the customer order system.

Figure 11.3 WMC organizational structure

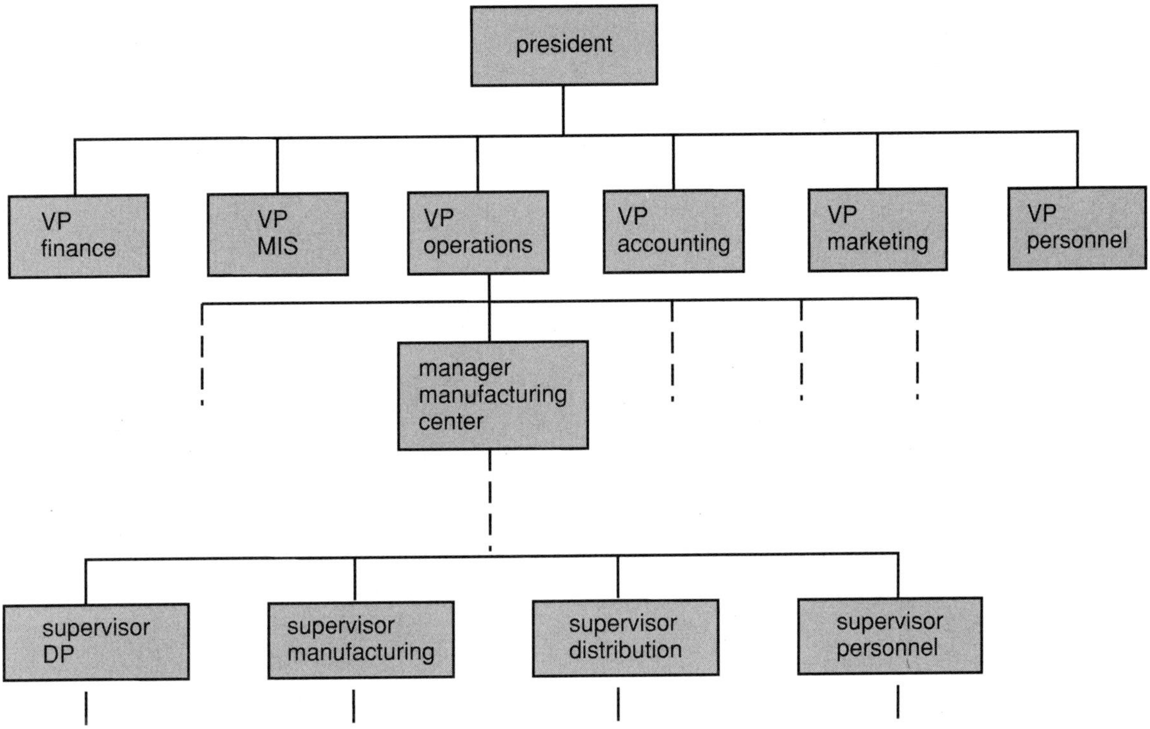

Figure 11.4 *a.* Balance sheet of WMC as of December 31, 1992 (in thousands)
b. Consolidated income statement for 1992 (in thousands)

A. Balance Sheet of WMC as of December 31, 1992 (in thousands)

Assets		Liabilities	
==============================		==============================	
Current		*Current*	
Cash and short-term		Acct payable	$ 900
investment	$ 12,050	Note payable	$ 20,000
Acct receivable (net)	$ 12,560	Salary payable	$ 890
Inventory	$ 35,890		
Prepaid expense	$ 1,300	*Long-term debt*	
		Long-term liabilities	$ 30,300
Fixed		Mortgage payable	$ 23,350
Buildings (net)	$ 33,050		
Land (net)	$ 60,000	*Stockholder's equity*	
Equipment (net)	$ 29,140	Common stocks	$ 50,500
		Paid-in capital	$ 45,000
	========	Retained earnings	$ 13,050
	$183,990		========
			$183,990

B. Consolidated Income Statement for 1992 (in thousands)

Operating revenue	$400,000
Interest and other revenue	$ 30,200
	========
Total revenue	$430,200
Less:	
Expenses:	
Cost of goods sold	$343,500
Administrative expenses	$ 5,000
Depreciation	$ 13,300
Maintenance	$ 1,400
Interest expenses	$ 4,500
Advertising expenses	$ 3,200
	========
Total expenses	$370,900
Net before tax	$ 59,300
Income taxes	$ 23,720

Net income	$ 35,580
	========

Haphazard General Hospital

Mike Masson has just taken over as president of HGH. He is very concerned that HGH has no DIS (Distributed Information Systems) policy. To make matters even worse, HGH has two different IS departments (Clinical Systems and Management Systems) whose managers can agree on very little, much less a DIS policy. Mike has finally given up trying to get a solution from his IS people and has come to you for help.

Mike explains:

In the 1980s even though the hospital had an IBM mainframe computer, several of the hospital's clinical departments purchased minicomputers and hired and trained their own programmers. These people developed specialized applications and supported their systems independently out of their own budgets. These systems include both highly specific clinical applications as well as more generic billing and personnel systems. The departments include the Clinical Lab, Respiratory Care, Epidemiology, Physical Medicine, and the Pharmacy.

These departmental clinical systems were nearly all developed in a language for which it is difficult to find programmers. As a result, these systems were eventually consolidated into the Clinical Systems Department. The department consists of one programmer/analyst for each system and two operations support people for nights and weekends. Each programmer/analyst is responsible for every aspect of his or her system (e.g., hardware, systems software, applications, user support operations, etc.). The Programmer/Analysts report directly to the department head. They meet with the user department and together decide on projects, priorities, and budgets. User departments seem very satisfied with this relationship. The Clinical Systems Department has also begun to develop many of its newer applications on PCs.

The Management Systems Department is responsible for most of the overhead departments in the hospital (e.g., Accounting, Payroll, Medical Records, etc.) and is organized in a more traditional way. It is composed of both development and operations groups. The development group includes a Data Base Administrator, Programmers, Analysts, and Project Leaders. The operations group includes Systems Programmers, a production support team, Operators and Supervisors, and a data entry team. Programmers, Analysts, and Project Leaders are assigned to specific projects as needed by the department head. Projects are determined by the Management Systems department head and his boss (the VP of Finance). Users must write formal requests to be reviewed by them. Users are very dissatisfied with this system. All of the Management Systems applications are on the IBM mainframe computer.

This situation has created several problems: 1) patients may receive several bills (one from each department) after a single hospital stay; 2) each of the clinical departments uses different methods for calculating and reporting management information which may come in a variety of forms and rarely matches; 3) many of the clinical system applications are redundant; 4) the clinical system applications only communicate via tape, requiring hospital census data to be manually transcribed from the mainframe to the mini when it needs immediate update on the mini.

Questions

1. Which of the IS activities (identified in ch. 11) need to be centralized? Why?

2. Which of these IS activities need to be distributed? Why?

3. Can the two IS departments remain separate and still implement a successful solution to the DIS problem?

Part III

Organization, Management and Control of Information Systems

Chapter 12 Organizing the Information System Department

Information is a vital asset in every modern organization. It is not enough just to have information stored somewhere; it has to be provided to users accurately and on time. An organization nowadays spends around 5 percent of its annual budget on information systems. This may be a lot of money so it is of paramount importance that it is efficiently utilized. Moreover, in many organizations 60 to 70 percent of the employees are "computer-dependent workers"; namely, they can hardly operate when the computer systems are stumbling.

Therefore, for the same reasons that we allocate resources to manage materials, personnel, sales, and capital, we have to carefully plan and allocate resources to manage information. The way these resources are motivated and organized is the main issue of this chapter.

Terms of Reference

Every organization has its own approach to organizing information systems resources. Some organizations centralize the resources under a single organizational unit; others prefer to delegate authority to functional units (i.e., an information department within accounting, within marketing, within personnel, etc.). Some organizations possess powerful computing equipment and maintain a strong professional staff in their main office; others distribute equipment and staff among various geographical locations (see ch. 11).

In McLean and Soden's book [14], twenty key persons of large organizations in the United States presented the way they planned MIS in their organizations. If you scan their presentations, you will find that almost every organization handled its information systems activities differently. This particular characteristic has not changed in the years since the survey; there remains great diversity among organizations in the structuring of the IS function. There is nothing negative in this observation; on the contrary, it indicates that organizations tailor information systems units according to their particular needs. It does mean, however, that we cannot generalize or portray a model for information systems organization.

The multiple approaches also imply multiple definitions for similar functions. In some organizations, information systems units have become independent divisions reporting directly to a vice-president. In others, they are still departments or sections managed by a middle-level executive. Job titles also vary, and it is not easy to tell whether an information analyst in one place is the same as a senior system engineer in another place.

In the discussion that follows, we refer to the organizational unit dealing with information systems as the *information systems department* (hereafter ISD). Also, we regard the ISD as a central body that is responsible for information systems all over the organization. However, you can easily modify our model to fit a local unit that provides information services on a regional or functional basis. As for professional titles in information systems, we adhere to the most frequently used terms, but mention synonymous terms whenever they are applicable.

In keeping with the idea of an information systems department, we have used the term *director* for the head of the ISD. In many large organizations today, the importance of this position is recognized by the use of the term chief information officer (CIO). Whatever the title or organization, the vital nature of the information resources makes it critical for the head of the ISD to report at the highest possible level.

Professions Related to Information Systems

In the old happy days of the 1950s and the beginning of the 1960s, the ordinary specialist in information systems (then called data processing—DP) was some sort of genius with comprehensive knowledge in hardware, software, analysis, design, programming, and implementation. That person—perceived by laypeople as a combination of Mr. Spock, Superman, and Einstein—analyzed a problem, designed the ultimate solution, wrote programs, and even ran the system, since nobody else knew how to do it. Written practices, life cycle stages, and formal working procedures were not considered necessary—casting doubt on the specialist's supernatural genius was out of the question.

To illustrate, here is a real example. In the first half of the sixties, a well-known computer series, the IBM 1400, had a memory size of 16,000 characters; therefore, the saving of memory was a dominant consideration in programming. Coincidentally, the operation code (OP code) of the READ command was the character *1*. Hence, if you had to use a constant of *1*—say, ADD *1* to a counter—you would scan your program, find the location of a READ command, and add the content of the OP code to your counter. In that way, you saved one character (byte) in memory. Sooner or later a change request would show up, compelling you to patch the program and, consequently, to shift the READ command to a different location. If the ADD command was not modified accordingly, the entire program would turn into a mess. Imagine how intimate the relationship between a programmer and his or her programs would have

Figure 12.1 Information systems professionals as a bridge between user and equipment

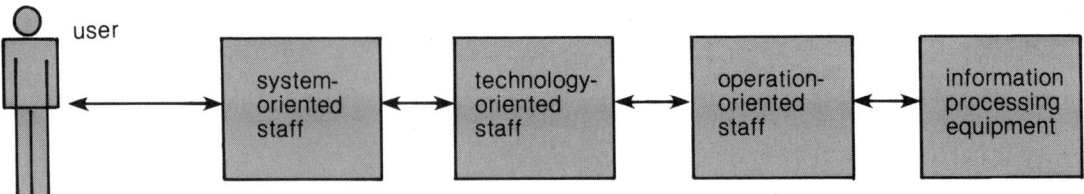

to be in order to maintain normal operations. If a programmer quit his or her job, or went on vacation, an enormous effort was required to convey his or her knowledge to a successor.

The old myth of computer specialist has now perished. The former know-all genius has branched into a variety of different professions, each so well defined that it can be handled by ordinary human beings. These professions can be divided into three job orientations:

1. Operation-oriented
2. Technology-oriented
3. System-oriented

The role of each class is better understood if we first state the general goal of the information systems profession. On the one hand, there are users who, presumably, know their needs but cannot operate a large mainframe computer. On the other hand, there is a computer that is capable of processing data, but has to be instructed. Information systems professionals bridge the gap between users and information technology—as illustrated in figure 12.1.

In the old days, the three ''staff'' boxes in figure 12.1 were all handled by the same individual. Today the user appeals to a system-oriented specialist for help in meeting his or her information requirements. The specialist translates the user's requests into technical specifications that can be used by technology-oriented personnel to create a system. The system created is run by operation personnel.

This framework normally applies to mainframe applications in which a formal life cycle procedure is to be maintained. The framework also applies to networks of smaller computers being used in lieu of a mainframe or as some other form of a distributed system. Some modifications to this are common when the user is supposed to use his or her own *personal computer* (PC). (These modifications will be discussed at the end of the chapter.) The next discussion pertains primarily to mainframe or network environments.

We will now elaborate on each category and then discuss promotion and career paths within and across categories.

Figure 12.2 Professions involved in information processing operations

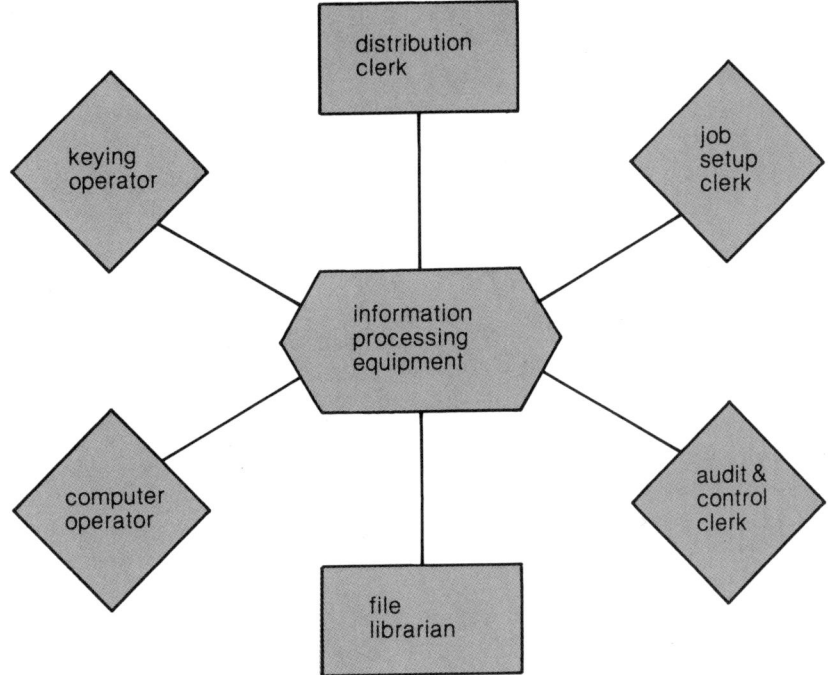

Operation-Oriented Professions

The operation-oriented professions are those involved in normal operations of information systems. Individuals in this category do not design or develop new systems, but perform duties related to the execution of existing systems. Figure 12.2 illustrates the major functions included in this category, which we will now briefly discuss.

Keying Operator

A *keying operator's* main duty is to key in data recorded on written forms to produce a computer-readable form.

The keying device may be an offline device—not connected to the main computer(s). For example, a diskette is an offline device. Or the keying device may be online—connected to the main computer(s). For example, an online terminal is an online device.

The performance of keying operators is measured by the rate and quality of their keying—how many characters (or records, or forms) are keyed in per unit of time and the percentage of errors among them.

Computer Operator

A *computer operator* normally works in the computer room and takes care of its routine operation. This person mounts magnetic tapes and disk packs, handles printers, etc. The operator is supposed to understand the system's messages and know how to react to them using the console.

A computer operator does not necessarily have to master programming, but should certainly have some background in information systems and a good command of the particular operating system with which he or she works. Skilled operators can often prevent a lot of trouble in recovery and reruns; the better trained and educated they are, the better for the organization employing them.

File Librarian

Almost every ISD accumulates a huge number of magnetic tapes, diskettes, and disk packs that have to be cataloged and stored. Sooner or later the storage problem warrants employment of a *file librarian*. The librarian takes care of the catalog (which normally parallels a computerized catalog), and he or she separates scratched from reserved volumes, cancels old files, and marks new reels and packs. A qualified librarian should have a general background in information processing, but no special technical skill is required.

Audit and Control Clerk

In many organizations, particularly where transaction processing (see ch. 6) involves huge amounts of data, a distinction is made between a keying operator and an *audit and control clerk*. The former keys in data, while the latter is responsible for correcting errors and complementing missing items. Even if the keyed data is validated online, complex errors that cannot be instantly corrected must still be handled. For example, if the accumulated total of a batch of transactions does not match a precalculated control figure, and the error is not from incorrect keying, it is probable that one or more transactions have been dropped off the batch. Someone has to check this and perhaps contact the source of the submitted data. This is not usually done by the keying operator, who continues to key in, but rather by an audit clerk, who has been trained to clear up data irregularities.

An audit clerk should have certain knowledge of bookkeeping and information processing and extensive knowledge of the procedures and practices pertinent to the information systems with which he or she is dealing.

Job Setup Clerk

In large computer installations that have a significant volume of batch processing, a *job setup clerk* receives job requests from users (or programmers) and dispatches them to the computer while checking out the technicalities of the requests and verifying certain details regarding accounts and priorities. This function is, in effect, the reception desk for the computer room. The setup function may be fulfilled by an operator. In a decentralized environment, particularly where users possess remote terminals, this function is performed by the user's employees.

Figure 12.3 Technology-oriented professions and their association with information systems' technical components

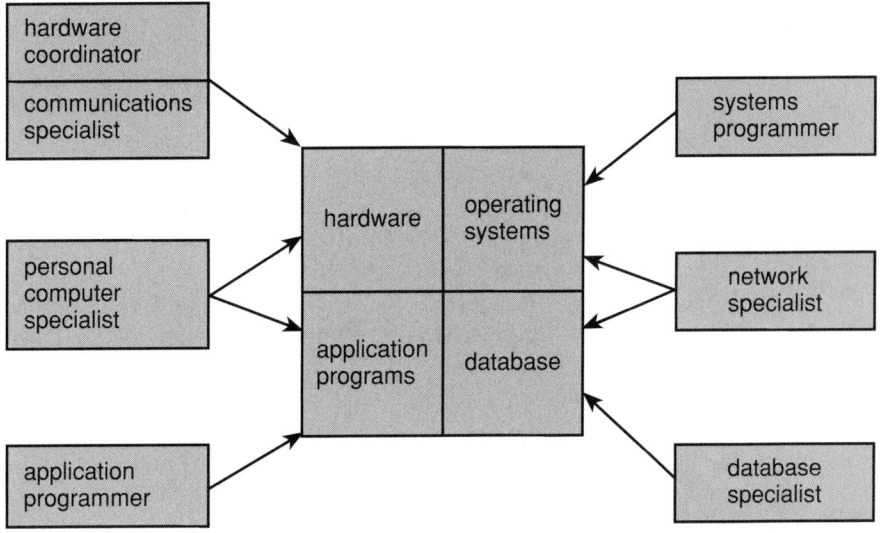

Distribution Clerk

A *distribution clerk* handles and distributes outputs of information processing. In large organizations that are oriented to batch printouts (e.g., banks, utility companies), distribution is a large-scale function that involves separating, collating, and shipping tons of paper. No special qualifications are required for an individual to hold this position.

Technology-Oriented Professions

Individuals in the technology-oriented category are skilled persons who have mastered extensive knowledge of information technology, hardware, and software. They deal with system development and also with maintenance and operation activities that require a high degree of skill and professional education. They may be found in various sections of the ISD and report to different superiors. For example, an application programmer would probably report to the head of a development project, whereas a systems programmer may belong to an operation section and report to the head of operations. Their common denominator is thorough knowledge of the bits and bytes that make up information processing technology. Figure 12.3 illustrates the major technical components of an information system and the professionals qualified to handle it. We will now discuss each profession briefly.

Application Programmer

An *application programmer* makes his or her living by writing (coding) programs for user applications. This person has mastered one or more common programming languages (e.g., COBOL, Pascal, C) to the extent of transforming program specifications to concrete programs, and compiling, debugging, and testing them.

An application programmer is usually a college graduate and may very well have some background in the type of business for which he or she is working. (See Teichroew [21] for a discussion of the education of information system professionals.)

An application programmer works closely with system designers (see discussion later in this section), who submit program specifications to him or her and test the finished programs. The performance of application programmers is evaluated primarily by program quality (e.g., frequency of bugs), efficiency, and compliance with prevailing standards and practices in the organization (see ch. 10 for software engineering methodologies). It is evaluated secondarily by the number of coded instructions per unit of time.

Systems Programmer

In a way, this title is misleading because a *systems programmer* has nothing to do with users' information systems (applications). A systems programmer is an expert in operating systems and other utility software, which are the basis of every computer configuration. This software is extremely complex, and sometimes written in low-level languages (e.g., Assembler). It consists of many tables, pointers, and switches. The handling of this software requires great programming skill.

Typical tasks of a systems programmer may include the following:

Tracing and correcting malfunctions in the operating system

Installing new versions of software packages

Instructing application programmers on new options in the operating system

Instructing application programmers on using the computer hardware and software in an efficient manner

Tuning the operating system to gain better performance

Writing sophisticated software programs or routines

A systems programmer would likely be a computer sciences graduate and/or an experienced and highly competent programmer. He or she works closely with operators, application programmers, and vendor support technicians, and very seldom interacts directly with users.

In many organizations, the systems programming group belongs to the operation section of the ISD, rather than to the development section, since its main task is to assure smooth functioning of the computer software. This may very well cause some managerial and social problems because operations and systems programming staff have different backgrounds. Careful managing can prevent or resolve such problems.

Network Specialist

The *network specialist* might be considered as a systems programmer who specializes in the network aspects of the system. However, the task goes beyond the systems software that provides the network with its connectivity. The network specialist must also be well-versed in the communications hardware and work with the more general communications specialist (see below). Additionally, the network specialist (or network administrator) must be cognizant of the applications implemented on the network, and the other software in use—especially data base management software. It is the role of this specialist to oversee the security and integrity of the network and assure its smooth operation, even in a dynamic environment in which network nodes are added and removed. Since there may be a very large number of computers involved, and they may be widely dispersed, this person generally will make use of special software devoted to the management of the network (see [12] and [15]). Thus, this specialist even has his or her own "application."

The network specialist is likely to have a background and qualifications very similar to those of the systems programmer, and will work closely with operations, programming, and vendor personnel. Unlike the systems programmer, the network specialist is likely also to have contact with users.

Hardware Coordinator

The *hardware coordinator* is required mainly in organizations equipped with large-scale computer facilities, particularly where equipment components are from different manufacturers. Such configurations necessitate employment of an expert who understands the technicalities and characteristics of various hardware options, and who can advise management and system developers whenever an acquisition or an interface is considered. In short, the hardware coordinator is supposed to know which nut can be attached to which bolt, and what should be required from and examined in vendor proposals.

A typical hardware coordinator will normally have a solid background in electrical engineering and communications, as well as knowledge of software. The function is usually a staff position in the ISD, but it may belong to a supporting group of experts in software, communications, or data base management systems (DBMS).

Personal Computer Specialist

The *personal computer specialist,* might be considered a special form of the hardware coordinator above, although with more emphasis on software knowledge and less requirement for an engineering background. This person would be expected to know about the various configuration possibilities for at least one type of personal computer, to know about the software packages available for those computers, and about hardware-software compatibility considerations.

Since these personal computers, or workstations, may be or may become part of a network, this specialist will work closely with the network specialist described above. He or she will also work closely with users, providing the software advisory and hardware consulting services discussed later in the chapter.

Communications Specialist

The rapid growth in the distribution of processing power (mainframes, microcomputers, front-end terminals, office automation equipment, CAD/CAM systems) has generated the need for *communications specialists*. This profession requires a technical knowledge of such communications equipment as local-area networks, computer networks, computerized switchboard devices, voice and data communications equipment and protocol, network security and control, and the like.

A communications specialist should have a solid background in hardware (e.g., electrical engineering). However, knowledge in operating system software is also essential.

The major role of the communications specialist is to optimize and coordinate the communications network(s) in the organization. This includes data communications as well as voice communications. Other tasks are to advise management on planning and acquisition of communications equipment, to interact with vendors and verify their proposals, and to help other ISD employees when they face communications problems in system development and in routine operations.

In very large organizations, the communications specialist reports to a communications director (see [22]). In most cases, the communications specialist is part of the technical services department (see discussion on organizational structures of ISD later in this chapter).

Data Base Specialist

It is necessary to distinguish between two professions related to data base management systems (DBMS): data base administrator (DBA) and data base specialist. The former is involved in the content design of a data base and therefore belongs to the system-oriented category of professions. The latter is more involved in the structure and internals of a DBMS and hence belongs to the technology-oriented category.

A *data base specialist* may be considered the systems programmer of the DBMS. This person knows the physical structure of the DBMS's internals, including all its routines, tables, and files. Therefore, he or she is qualified to maintain the DBMS, to insert new data, to reorganize files, and to tune up the DBMS in order to improve performance. The tasks are similar to those mentioned for systems programmers. Obviously, the background and qualifications of the two professions are alike. Yet, data base specialists are usually not positioned in the operation section, but with the DBA group, which may very well be a different section of the ISD (see discussion on organizational structures of ISD later in this chapter).

System-Oriented Professions

Individuals in the system-oriented category are mainly concerned with users and how to respond to their information needs. These individuals should adopt a holistic approach to information problems, rather than concentrate on the detailed technicalities of information processing technology. At the same time, they have to sufficiently master the technological aspects so they understand what could and should be handled by a computerized system, and to what degree.

Figure 12.4 Working relationships among various professions

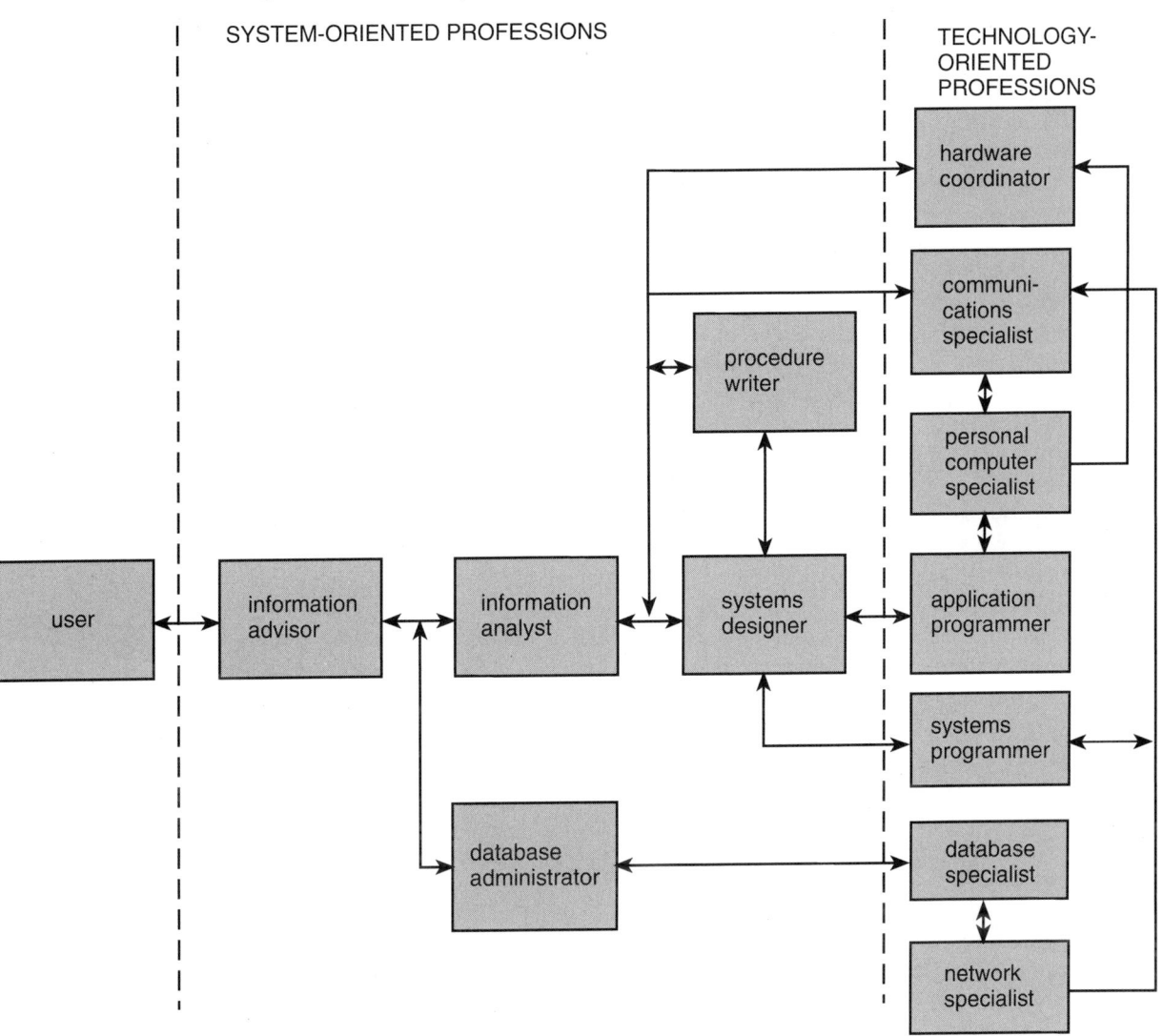

The professions in this category have close working relationships with each other and with the technology-oriented professions. These relationships are illustrated in figure 12.4.

As figure 12.4 shows, users are normally represented by information advisors. The requirements they submit may involve data design (i.e., affect the data base) and processing design (i.e., modify or expand the model base). The possible effects on the data base require the involvement of data base personnel—namely, the data base administrator (planning, design) and specialist (physical alterations, tuning). Model base change, in many cases, implies the development of a new system(s). The change is analyzed by an information analyst, who also coordinates the development project (including designers, programmers, procedure writers) while being advised by experts, such as hardware coordinator, systems programmer, data base specialist, and communications specialist.

Obviously, this hypothetical scheme is, in reality, altered according to circumstances. Yet, it generally portrays the formal working relationships among various professions. We will now elaborate on each profession in the system-oriented category. (See a related discussion in [21].)

Information Advisor

Traditionally, interaction between users and professionals was carried out through information analysts employed by the ISD. As use of computerized systems expanded from transaction processing to managerial decision making (see ch. 6), which requires deep understanding of user objectives, a need arose for *information advisors* within user departments. The main concern of these advisors is the information requirements of the users. Their task involves preparation and submission of requests for new system development; participation in feasibility studies and implementation teams; acceptance testing; recommendations to accept, change, or reject new systems; planning and modifying user policy on information systems development and use; and participation in budget preparation.

A qualified information advisor could be a former information analyst who has had appropriate management education and who has developed a comprehensive view of the organization and its information needs. Or this person could very well be a user's employee whose relationships with computerized systems have been extensive enough for him or her to acquire sufficient knowledge in the area. In any case, this person has a systems approach to problems; he or she does not have an inclination to deal with small technical details.

Information Analyst

An *information analyst* is the person who assumes major responsibility for information systems development. He or she represents the ISD in feasibility studies. If the decision is to carry on, he or she analyzes user requirements and derives their hardware, software, personnel, and budget implications. The information analyst devises the logical skeleton for a new system; the designers, programmers, and others will fashion its flesh and skin. A senior information analyst normally heads development teams during the information systems development stages (see chs. 9 and 10).

Skill in information analysis requires the uncommon combination of management and technical education with emphasis on the former. An ideal background for an information analyst is an M.B.A. degree with concentration in MIS. Nevertheless, a person with technical experience (e.g., a programmer) who can comprehend the wide spectrum of nontechnical organizational issues may very well make a good information analyst.

It is important to note that excellent programmers do not necessarily become competent information analysts because the nature of these two professions is dissimilar. Programmers are occupied with details, while information analysts are concerned with essence. Although an information analyst has to master some basic knowledge of programming, at least to the extent of being able to manage programmers, wide experience in programming is definitely not a prerequisite. However, experience in system design and in organizations in general is almost a must. (For a humorous description of an incompetent information analyst, see Martin [10] and [11].)

System Designer

A *system designer* is the intermediary between the system-oriented and the technology-oriented professionals. This person transforms the logical framework created by the information analyst into detailed specifications, such as program structure charts, files, input forms, and output layouts. Therefore, a system designer has to comprehend the overview of the system as well as the fundamental methods of programming, operating, keying, and pertinent clerical procedures. Knowledge of software engineering methodologies is also required.

A typical system designer may be an experienced programmer who wishes to pursue his or her career in information analysis and/or managerial positions in information systems. Or the system designer may be a college graduate (preferably in management) who acquired some programming knowledge in college and has just begun a career in information analysis. Another possibility is to have an experienced user's employee trained in information systems for a while and then appoint him or her to a position in system design.

In addition to designing systems, a system designer may supervise a few programmers or procedure writers. In any event, a system designer should prepare test data and validate programs written according to his or her specifications.

System designers (and information analysts as well) should be familiar with prototyping techniques (see ch. 9 for more details on prototyping).

Procedure Writer

The essence of the *procedure writer's* profession is preparation of the written procedures used by computer operators, keying operators, user's clerks, distribution clerks, and others to run the system during its operation stage (see discussion on life cycle in chs. 9 and 10). In many organizations, this task is assigned to system designers; in others it is given to programmers as soon as they finish coding the pertinent programs. Either way, the organization benefits by obviating additional learning time; both designers and programmers are presumably familiar with the system. However, system designers and programmers are likely to find reasons for delaying this job to the next day, the next week, or the next month because procedure writing is not very exciting. Finally, you find yourself with a complete system, but without any written working procedure. It is, therefore, a good idea to appoint full-time procedure writers whose sole task is to write procedures and test their applicability.

The qualifications and background required for a procedure writer are almost the same as for a system designer; good technical styling capacity is certainly an advantage. In fact, rotation arrangements between these two positions are not uncommon.

Data Base Administrator

A data base administrator (DBA) is the system-oriented counterpart of the data base specialist, just as an information analyst and a system designer are counterparts of programmers. In other words, the DBA plans the data base and devises it for user requirements, while the specialist tunes, maintains, and modifies its software. Murch [16, p. 18] defines the DBA's function in the following way: "to ensure the integrity and controlled, well-planned development of the corporate data resources." Given the complexity of today's multiuser, and frequently distributed, systems and the necessity of sharing data among users, Awad and Gotterer [3] say that the DBA's "most important task is to resolve conflict and ensure a smooth-running database environment."

The DBA function is a must when an organization possesses a data base management system (DBMS). However, even when files are still traditionally organized, the organization might appoint a DBA. In that case, the DBA keeps track of the various files, standardizes record formats and data item labels, and maintains a data directory and a uniform currency of redundant data. This may well be a preliminary foundation for a future DBMS. (See appendix A on information system technology for more details on DBMS.)

The DBA duties include participating in development teams and steering committees of pertinent systems; consulting information analysts and system designers on data base aspects; consulting with management on acquisition of pertinent hardware and software; planning data base structure and content based on organizational objectives and master plan; developing standards related to data and files; and carrying out education programs for users and professionals.

In addition to these duties, one of the main concerns of the DBA is the security of the corporate data base. Since the data base is a resource usually shared by many different users, its security might become a critical problem. We would not like to separate the data base into several discrete fragments, but we want to prevent access to all data. For example, we may want to prevent the salary field from being accessed by most users of the personnel file while other data items are kept open for interested users. The DBA resolves such problems by devising software passwords, regulations, logbooks, or alarms. Large organizations, particularly those possessing sensitive data, tend to appoint a special information security officer who assumes responsibility for the above issues.

In some organizations, the DBA group operates independently as a staff function in general management. However, in most cases, the DBA is an officer in the ISD. In any case, this is a senior position, usually staffed by a senior information analyst or an experienced data base specialist who has acquired greater perspectives on the organization and its information needs.

Career Paths in Information Systems

When talking about career paths, we have to distinguish between the operation-oriented category, on one hand, and the technology- and system-oriented categories, on the other. Professions belonging to the former are technical or clerical and do not require any particular college education or business experience. A career in one of these professions is normally confined to that profession and does not differ, in nature, from any other clerical or technical career. For example, a computer operator who has gained some experience may be promoted to shift foreperson and later get a managerial position in the operations section. The same holds for keying operators. Some positions may lie in a single career path. For example, computer operator, file librarian, and job setup clerk may belong to the same path; distribution and audit and control clerk may also be part of a predetermined career path.

A person in the operation-oriented category may move to another category provided that he or she exhibits the necessary skills to do so. However, this switchover is not automatic and certainly cannot be viewed as a promotion path.

The technology-oriented and system-oriented categories have some common traits. First, the starting point is often the same: some programming knowledge and experience. Second, transfer from one category to the other is not rare.

The network illustrated in figure 12.5 describes some alternate career paths in these classes. Unidirectional arrows represent possible promotion; bidirectional arrows represent possible transfer, which can be considered promotion, though not necessarily. In general, we notice two career routes. The one in the technology area includes programming (application and systems) and data base expertise. The one in the systems area includes procedure writing, design, analysis, and data base administration. Figure 12.5 does not include higher steps in the promotion path; however, you may assume that the next steps are either in management of various sections of the ISD (see the discussion later in this chapter) or in general management (a staff or a managerial function). Note that the hardware-oriented professions (i.e., hardware coordinator and communications specialist) are omitted from figure 12.5. This is because the origin and career path of these professions are different.

We refer the reader to some additional professions relating to information system control and security assurance that are mentioned in chapter 14. In particular, we refer you to the EDP auditor and to the security specialist.

Each organization probably develops promotion paths that differ from the general scheme in figure 12.5. And there are many individuals whose careers have undergone exceptional routes. Yet, figure 12.5 reflects the usual career paths in information systems.

Organizational Structure of an Information System Department

The personnel associated with information systems includes individuals whose skills vary from clerical to extremely technical, and whose cognitive style varies from an extreme sensitivity to details to an extreme holistic perception. It is not an easy task to organize and direct such a diverse group. On top of that, an information systems

Figure 12.5 Possible career paths in information systems programming, design, and analysis (read from left to right)

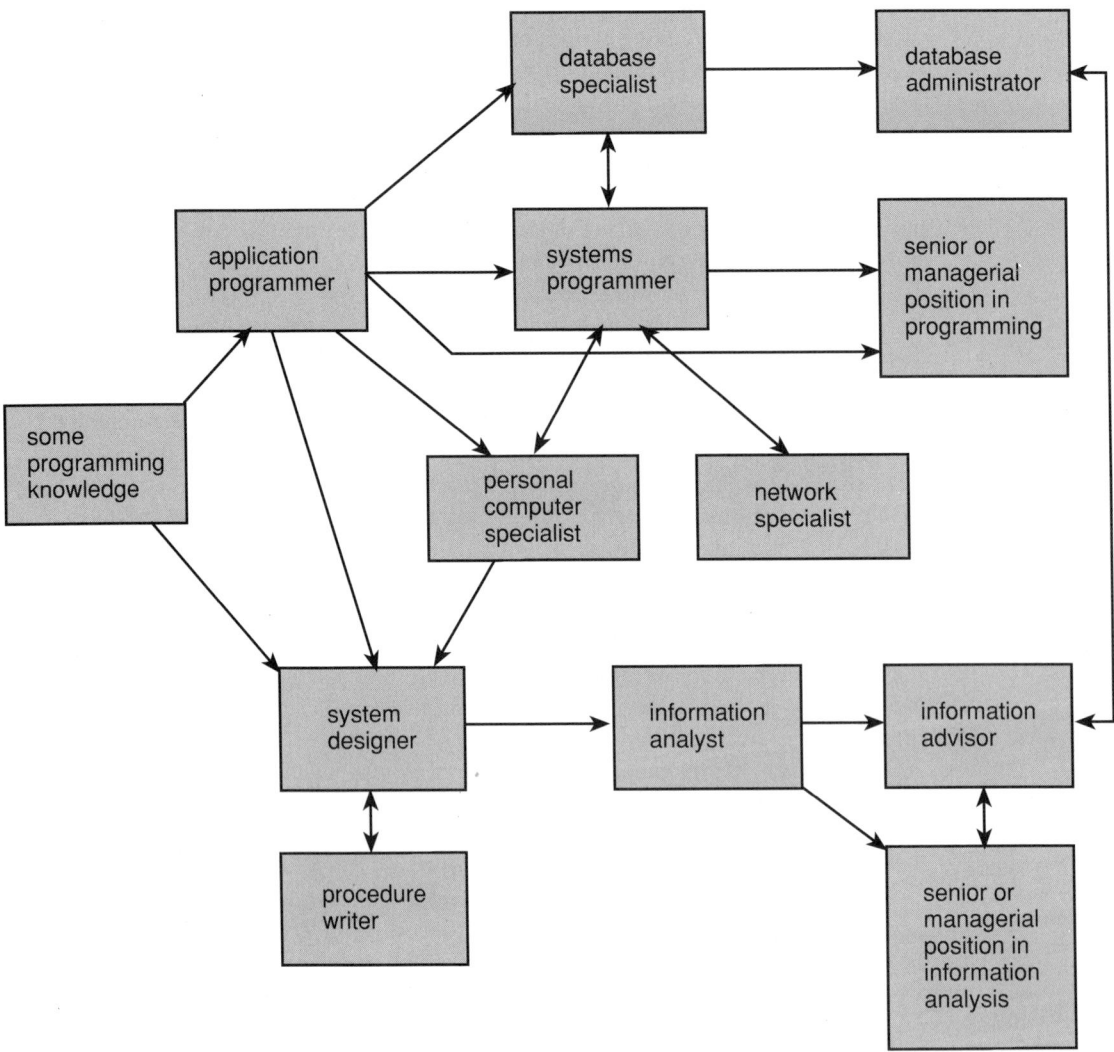

department (ISD) is usually equipped with sophisticated and expensive machinery; it maintains a lot of interactions in a dynamic environment (with users, management, etc.); it usually deals with mass production (zillions of transactions and printouts); and it controls a powerful commodity (information). That is why it is so important to organize and manage the ISD appropriately.

We said at the beginning of this chapter that it is almost impossible to portray a universal model for organizing an ISD. Each organization has its own problems, preferences, and unique solution [14]. The discussion that follows assumes that most of the information processing and development resources are located in a central organizational body (ISD). This does not mean that we advocate this approach; it is only a more compact way to present the pertinent material. You may easily relate the discussion to a less centralized situation.

We will first outline the functions of an ISD, then present some "traditional" organizational structures, and finally discuss structures that are likely to cope better with contemporary technology and the information requirements of higher-level management.

Functions of an Information System Department

An organizational structure is a means to incorporate various functions in order to pursue some predetermined objectives. Hence, according to the systems approach adopted in this book (see ch. 4), any discussion of the organizational structure of an information systems department must be preceded by a clear definition of its objectives and functions.

For a centralized situation, we define the primary objective of the central ISD as providing computerized information services to the entire organization in which it operates [2]. This is achieved by three major functions.

1. *Systems development*—Carrying out all the activities of the information systems development life cycle (see chs. 9 and 10): feasibility study, analysis, design, programming, and implementation of new computerized information systems.

2. *Information production*—Undertaking or assuming responsibility for activities pertinent to routine runs of information systems: data capture and validation, computer operation, output distribution, job setup, supplies procurement, etc.

3. *Systems maintenance*—Ensuring prompt and reliable running of existing information systems: detection and correction of bugs, modification and enhancement of programs and procedures, keeping updated documentation, etc.

Successful accomplishment of these functions requires the support of two supplementary functions.

1. *Technical support*—Expert assistance in special areas, such as systems programming, DBMS, communications, and hardware.

2. *Administration*—Handling all administrative work stemming from the aforementioned activities, such as secretarial services, personnel management, training, and budget planning and control.

Obviously, effective organizing and managing of all these functions are important. As you may expect, organizations have adopted different structures to handle their information systems; no one alternative is ultimately preferred. The next section presents some of the more common structures.

Figure 12.6 An applicational organization of an ISD in a manufacturing business

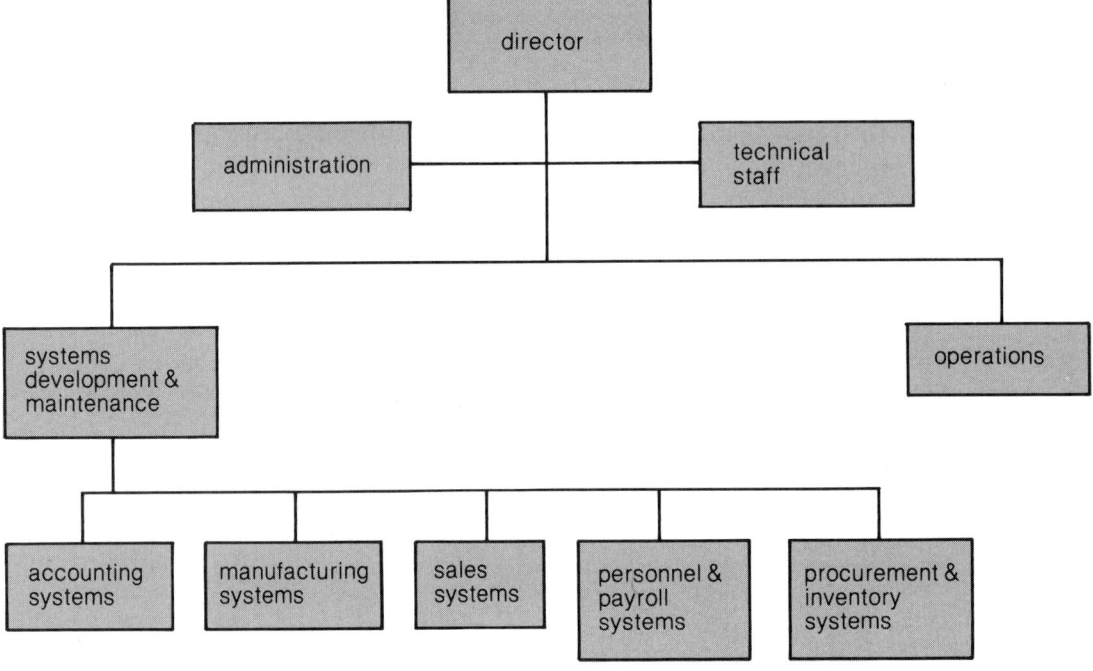

Traditional Structures of Information System Departments

We will describe how the structure of the ISD evolved historically. There are certainly many exceptions, but most organizations followed a similar route. (Gildersleeve [6] supplements the following discussion.)

Applicational Structure

The first business computer applications dealt solely with transaction processing (TPS—see chs. 5 and 6). Thousands of bookkeepers, warehouse clerks, and production clerks were replaced with computers that performed virtually the same job, only faster and more accurately. Since information for middle- or high-level management was not required, integration of information from different systems was not needed. Most systems were designed and operated in a "discrete" mode—namely, without coordination among them. This naturally led to establishment of ISDs organized in correspondence with different applications or classes of applications—the *applicational structure.*

Applicational ISDs, at least the development and maintenance portions, are replicas of the organization as a whole. Figure 12.6 illustrates a typical applicational structure of an ISD in a manufacturing business. Note that each section handles the development and maintenance of systems serving a different department (or division) in the organization. Consequently, there are groups of application experts: analysts, designers, and programmers for bookkeeping applications, for personnel applications, for inventory applications, etc. Each group develops, modifies, and maintains its own systems. Supporting functions, like systems programming or administration, are organized as staff functions. The operations function is usually, but not necessarily, handled centrally. We will elaborate on the structure of the operations section later.

Pros and cons of the applicational structure   The advantage of the applicational structure lies mainly in the specialization it creates. Each team becomes highly user-oriented in the sense that it understands the user's activities, problems, and jargon; thus, introduction of new applications does not consume long learning periods. Apparently, this structure often evokes good relationships between user and developer.

The main disadvantage of the applicational structure becomes apparent when it is time to integrate data from different areas in order to provide management with information for tactical or strategic decisions. Often it turns out that each team has exercised different computerization conceptions, as is revealed in programming practices, file organization techniques, data definition, record identification, etc. For example, suppose you have to develop a cost accounting information system to support pricing and sale decisions. The manufacturing system keeps track of production inputs, such as worker-hours, machine-hours, and raw materials consumed for certain production processes. The payroll system stores salary data. The procurement system records the purchase cost of raw materials. The sales system "knows" the marketing costs of finished goods. But when you probe deeply into each system, you find the following:

Finished goods are identified differently in sales and manufacturing systems.

Employee numbers in the payroll file are not used when worker-hours are recorded in manufacturing, so no one can tell exactly who spends time on a particular job.

The identification keys for raw materials in manufacturing and procurement are different.

The procurement system measures some raw materials by volume while the manufacturing system uses weight as the standard measure.

The difficulties arising from this situation are enormous. It will probably take at least a year just to tie up all the loose ends. The reason for this mess is that for many years each team developed systems adequate for its own user, while no one was concerned with future integration.

Another possible disadvantage of the applicational structure is that "some application groups become inundated with work while other groups, subject to lower demands, have little to do" [6, p. 46]. If each group has established a "sovereign kingdom," it is not easy to transfer personnel from one group to another.

To recapitulate, the applicational structure appears to be the fastest way to lay down the infrastructure of transaction processing systems in an organization, provided that future needs for integration are not ignored.

Figure 12.7 A functional organization of an ISD

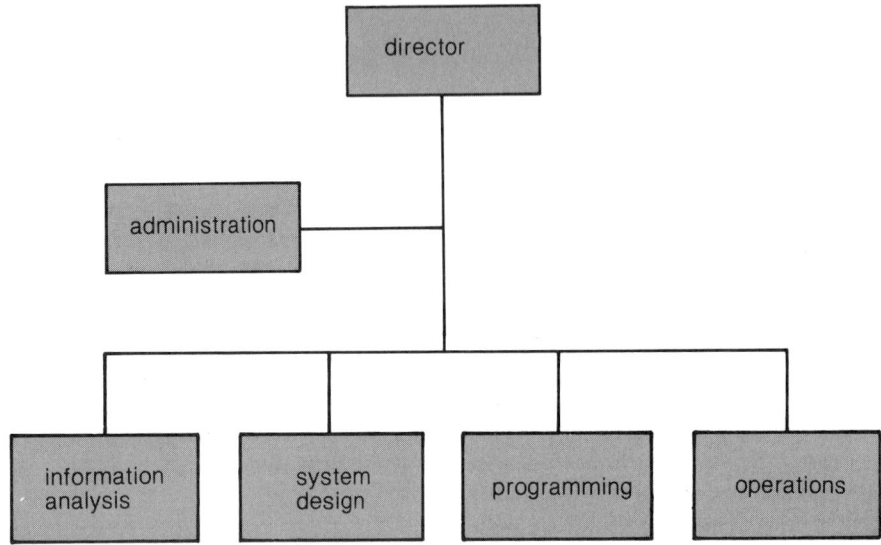

Functional Structure

Sooner or later coordination of different applicational areas becomes a crucial problem and the need for integrated information becomes a top priority. This usually happens at the same time that the complexity of the system information begins to require the kind of professional expertise unlikely to be acquired in applicational teams made up of individuals of different professions. Organizations at this level of maturity tend to adopt a functional structure for their ISD.

In a *functional structure,* employees are grouped according to professions (functions) rather than applications. Thus, we can observe an information analysis group, a system design group, a programming group, etc. Figure 12.7 illustrates a functionally organized ISD.

Each unit in the functionally organized ISD specializes in a few activities of the information system life cycle (see chs. 9 and 10). Feasibility studies and information analyses are performed by the information analysis unit; detailed design, specification preparation, and procedure writing are done by the system design unit; programming and testing are done by the programming group; and normal runs are handled by operations. Note that, unlike the applicational structure (fig. 12.6), there is no need here for the technical staff function since each unit may employ its own supporting staff— e.g., systems programmers in the programming unit, standards and procedures officers in the system design unit. With the help of its own staff, each unit is able to develop uniform working standards that obligate all its professional incumbents.

Pros and cons of the functionally organized ISD   The great advantage of functional organization is specialization. Programmers, designers, and analysts work among colleagues doing the same kind of work. This, inevitably, stimulates diffusion of knowledge and creates the kind of professional competition that encourages individuals to enhance their skills.

Another advantage is the standardization that can be imposed on the systems under development. All the programmers have to comply with the same programming practices (e.g., structured programming); all the designers have to use the same set of forms and notations; all the analysts have to refer to the same data definitions. This should provide solid foundations for data integration and data bases. Standardization is, in fact, obligatory in functional organizations because the responsibility for a development project varies along the system life cycle. Hence, programmers may refuse to write programs if the instructions are poorly specified, and system designers may refuse to detail specifications if the system analysis report is poorly documented or does not comply with a software engineering methodology.

The inherent bureaucracy of functional organization is, however, a significant disadvantage. It takes a lot of time, a lot of memoranda exchange, and many formal meetings (and cups of coffee) until you manage to "roll" a project from one functional group to the next. Since the pace of development is slow, urgent projects are frequently assigned to special task forces that bypass obligatory formalities.

Another and more serious disadvantage results from the relationships between users and system developers. Since responsibility varies from stage to stage, a project is not supervised by a single individual in the ISD. The user therefore has to communicate with different persons during the development life cycle. Each person may have a different view or might fail to recall previous arrangements agreed upon by his or her predecessors. Imagine the frustrations of a naive user simultaneously involved in various development projects, each in a different stage of system life cycle, when he or she tries to identify who is responsible for changes requested in programs, and who takes care of changes requested in source documents.

In essence, functional organization might lack individuals who specialize in user areas and problems. Therefore, too much emphasis might be placed on technical perfection of information systems while responsiveness to user needs is put aside.

The functional structure is more likely to prevail in organizations that have matured with respect to their information processing. Such organizations usually have large volumes of data, many applications already installed, and sophisticated information requirements. This would inevitably necessitate rigid standardization and coordination of data, files, and programs. In addition, users are mature enough to take care of their own interests.

Matrix Organization

To continue the evolutionary process, the pendulum that swung from the user-oriented to the profession-oriented approach now swings back toward the user. This is because of the need to "compensate" the user for the disadvantages of functional organization by establishing a structure that facilitates responsiveness to the user's needs. This structure is often called *matrix organization*. Matrix organization retains the basic structure of the functional organization, but project orientation is enhanced by super-imposing project leaders or liaison officers upon the functional structure. Figure 12.8 illustrates the way this is handled in a manufacturing business.

The functional structure can easily be identified in the background of figure 12.8. However, each user has an "envoy" in the ISD; an ISD employee who takes care of the user affairs in the ISD. In some cases, particularly when the development project is relatively complex, this envoy is a project leader who focuses only on a specific project while the team members alternate from stage to stage. In most cases the liaison officer takes care of several projects, all related to the same user or group of users.

In the matrix organization, the expert work is still handled by functional groups and projects move from group to group as development progresses. But one person is the liaison between the user and the ISD, the sole addressee for any user request. He or she would transfer the request to the appropriate function and follow up on the outcomes. The liaison officer is also responsible for informing the user about the status of pertinent projects and for coordinating any irregular runs of existing systems. The authority and status of a liaison officer should at least equal that of a senior information analyst or a development team leader.

Pros and cons of matrix organization   A matrix structure certainly reduces some dis-advantages of functional organization, especially by establishing better contact be-tween the users and the ISD. And it maintains the advantages of functional organization (e.g., standardization, data integration).

The disadvantage of the matrix structure lies mainly in the managerial problems it creates. Most of the professional employees have to report to two supervisors. For example, a programmer who regularly reports to the programming supervisor must also obey instructions from the project leader or the liaison officer. Moreover, the programming supervisor and the liaison officer might have conflicting interests; the former is interested in efficient allocation of his or her staff; the latter is willing to push his or her project hard. This may lead to competition to obtain the most desirable programmers.

Operations

So far we have focused on the development and maintenance functions in an ISD. In other words, the discussion has concerned organization of the system- and technology-oriented personnel. The production function, around which most of the operation-oriented personnel are positioned, is generally represented by a single box labeled "operations." We now elaborate on this portion of the ISD.

Where operations are fully centralized, the operations unit is responsible for un-dertaking the following functions:

1. Running the computer shop, including the pertinent environment, like file library, supplies, etc.
2. Routing the flow of data into and out of the computer shop, including keying in, batching, distribution, and control.

Figure 12.8 A matrix organization of an ISD in a manufacturing business

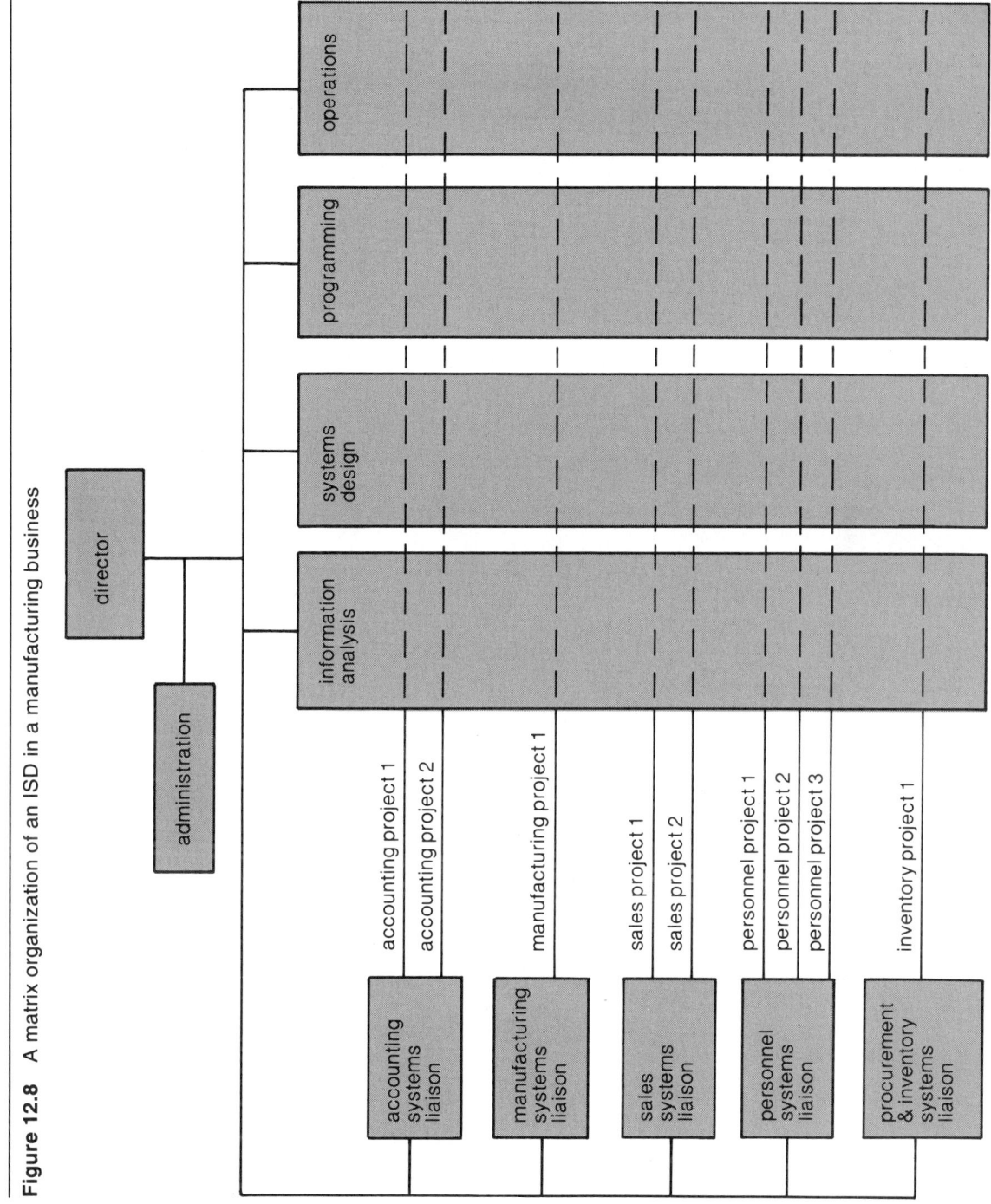

Figure 12.9 An organizational structure for the operation function of an ISD

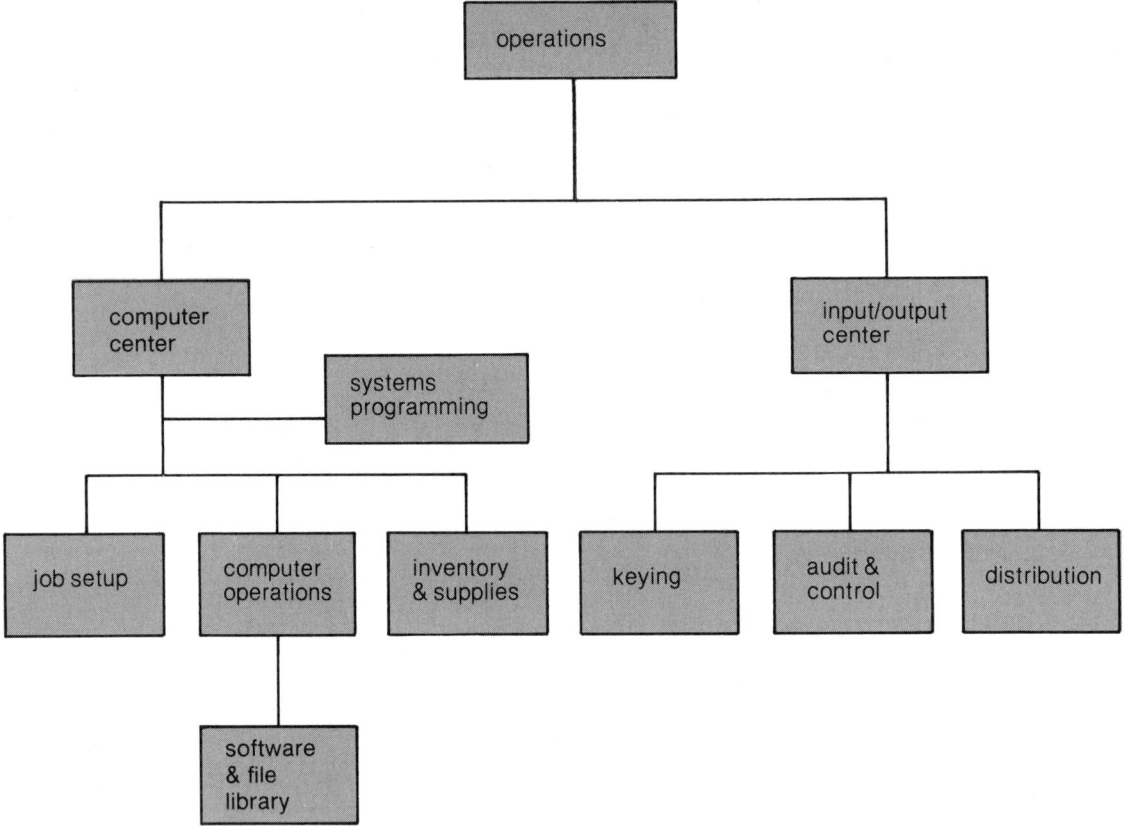

A possible organizational structure for an operations unit is suggested in figure 12.9.

The structure in figure 12.9 distinguishes between two major functions: the computer center and the input/output center. The input/output center deals with the following:

Keying in—Includes offline magnetic devices (e.g., diskettes), direct keying through terminals, magnetic ink encoding, etc.

Distribution of reports and microfilms and possibly storage in an archive or return of source documents (e.g., sorted checks that have to be returned to the various branches of a bank).

Audit and control of inputs and outputs—For instance, batch balancing, checking, and correction of data irregularities, etc.

Coordination of remote input/output facilities.

The computer center handles all activities related to operation of the hardware and software of the computing equipment. This includes operation of the computer(s) and its peripheral devices; the job setup; the file library; and procurement and storage of supplies, such as continuous forms and diskettes.

In some organizations the systems programming group is a part of computer operations. This seems logical because the principal duty of the group is to maintain the operating system. However, it may lead to some human relations problems because systems programmers tend to be affiliated with the more specialized environment of programming. Mutual alienation might arise between this group and the rest of the operations employees. That is why in many cases we observe that the systems programming group is a staff function in the programming section of the ISD.

Organizing a Large-Scale Information System Department under Contemporary Requirements and Technology

When the volume of information processing increases beyond a certain level, organizations tend to distribute their information processing among various departments or geographical locations. This would constitute a hierarchy of information systems, each of which involves a different degree of data aggregation and serves a different organizational level (see discussion on distributed information systems in ch. 11). Consequently, the central ISD is split into several local departments, each perhaps having an organizational structure similar to any of the aforementioned. The organization headquarters will then employ a staff function to coordinate the local activities. It may also possess a separate ISD to handle its own informations systems (assuredly of MIS or DSS type—see ch. 5). See the discussion of hierarchical organization structures later in this chapter.

However, there are still many cases, particularly when management is reluctant to relinquish power, in which information systems are kept centralized. "Traditionally" structured ISDs appear to be unable to cope with large-scale operations of this type and should, therefore, be revised. This section proposes a revised approach, based on the previously described organizational structures, but with a few modifications. We will first briefly define the notion of "large-scale operations under contemporary requirements and technology," and then examine the proposed organization. The discussion follows Ahituv and Hadass [2].

Characteristics of Large-Scale Operations

The terms "large scale" and "small scale" are relative. What would be considered large scale in one instance (a regional car dealer) might be considered small scale in another (General Motors Corp.). Nevertheless, the following properties characterize large-scale information processing:

1. A volume of daily transactions measured in hundreds of thousands, at least

2. Data processing equipment with a monthly rental that is at least a six-digit figure

3. Computing equipment acquired from several manufacturers

4. Decentralized input/output equipment located in various sites

5. Computer applications are numerous and involve many different users; their nature and requirements are heterogeneous

6. The ISD employs many individuals (hundreds at least) of different professions and skills

These characteristics are certainly not obligatory; some may not exist some places but the operations would still be considered large. For example, an organization that acquires most of its equipment from the same manufacturer can still maintain large-scale operations; or the number of daily transactions might be relatively small but the variety of applications is enormous. As a rule of thumb, we propose that if any four characteristics out of the list hold, the scale of operations is indeed large.

Characteristics of Contemporary Requirements

Contemporary requirements normally derive from top-level management, whereas "traditional" requirements are those that have characterized transaction processing systems since the advent of business computers. Recalling the discussion in chapters 5 and 6, we will review typical information requirements of middle- and top-level management.

1. A typical manager/user may want to implement structured decision systems (SDS) or decision support systems (DSS). This implies the need for a thorough analysis of decision-making processes; in other words, there is a need to employ skilled information analysts and to develop information systems that are original, flexible, and user-oriented.

2. Operations research models and heuristic techniques are likely to be essential for many applications. This implies the need for collaboration between information systems professionals and experts in other disciplines.

3. Many requirements are ad hoc in nature. This implies development of software for immediate responses, such as interactive programming and query languages.

4. Responses to information requests should be quick and on location. Therefore, terminals and other online features are usual.

5. The managers—or, more normally, their support staff—would like to have hands-on computing equipment or handy terminals by which they can "play" with figures and examine various alternatives. Easy-to-handle software and hardware are almost a must to allow for end-user computing.

Again, these characteristics are not obligatory and the degree to which they exist in an organization will vary. However, the existence of at least a few of them indicates that the organization is on a contemporary track with respect to its information requirements. (See also ch. 7 for the strategic importance of information technology.)

Characteristics of Contemporary Technology

In appendix A we review the major components of modern information processing technology. Most of these are likely to be present in a large-scale ISD.

The hardware components of contemporary technology would probably include online terminals, telecommunication equipment, a large mainframe, and a wide spectrum of peripheral devices, such as graphic display units and optical reading devices, as well as traditional input/output devices (disks, tapes, etc.).

The software components would probably include data base packages (DBMS), query languages, interactive programming tools, fast-reporting languages, simulation and other operations research packages, fourth generation languages, etc.

Principles and Framework for the Complex Organizational Structure

These characteristics certainly create complexity and difficulties that are inherent to the nature of a modern ISD. They can never completely disappear; however, they are reduced if an appropriate organizational structure is set up and is then well administered. This is the *complex organizational structure*.

Following the systems approach, we will first propose some principles for an ISD and then suggest an appropriate structure. The principles are derived from the problems detected in the ''traditional'' organizations and from the characteristics previously mentioned.

Principle 1. Applications are user-oriented rather than technology-oriented.

Principle 2. Management information systems (SDS and DSS) are handled by specialized team(s).

Principle 3. Users do not have to be aware of the different functions of the ISD; each user deals with a sole ''agent'' in the ISD who takes care of the user's needs.

Principle 4. Because of their large scale, operations are centrally administered.

Principle 5. Because MIS (besides transaction processing systems) share data coming from various users, data bases are centrally administered.

Principle 6. Corporate policy directs development planning by means of a master plan (see ch. 8); development decisions are based on economic considerations that take into account the cost/benefits of the organization as a whole in addition to the cost/benefits of individual users.

Principle 7. A core of technology experts (e.g., systems programmers, data base specialists) is kept separate from the application teams, but closely supports them; this group is managed by an individual who can fluently communicate with his or her subordinates.

Principle 8. Administrative and control functions of the ISD are the tools to facilitate managing, and, therefore, are reported directly to the ISD management.

Figure 12.10 Organizational structure of a complex ISD

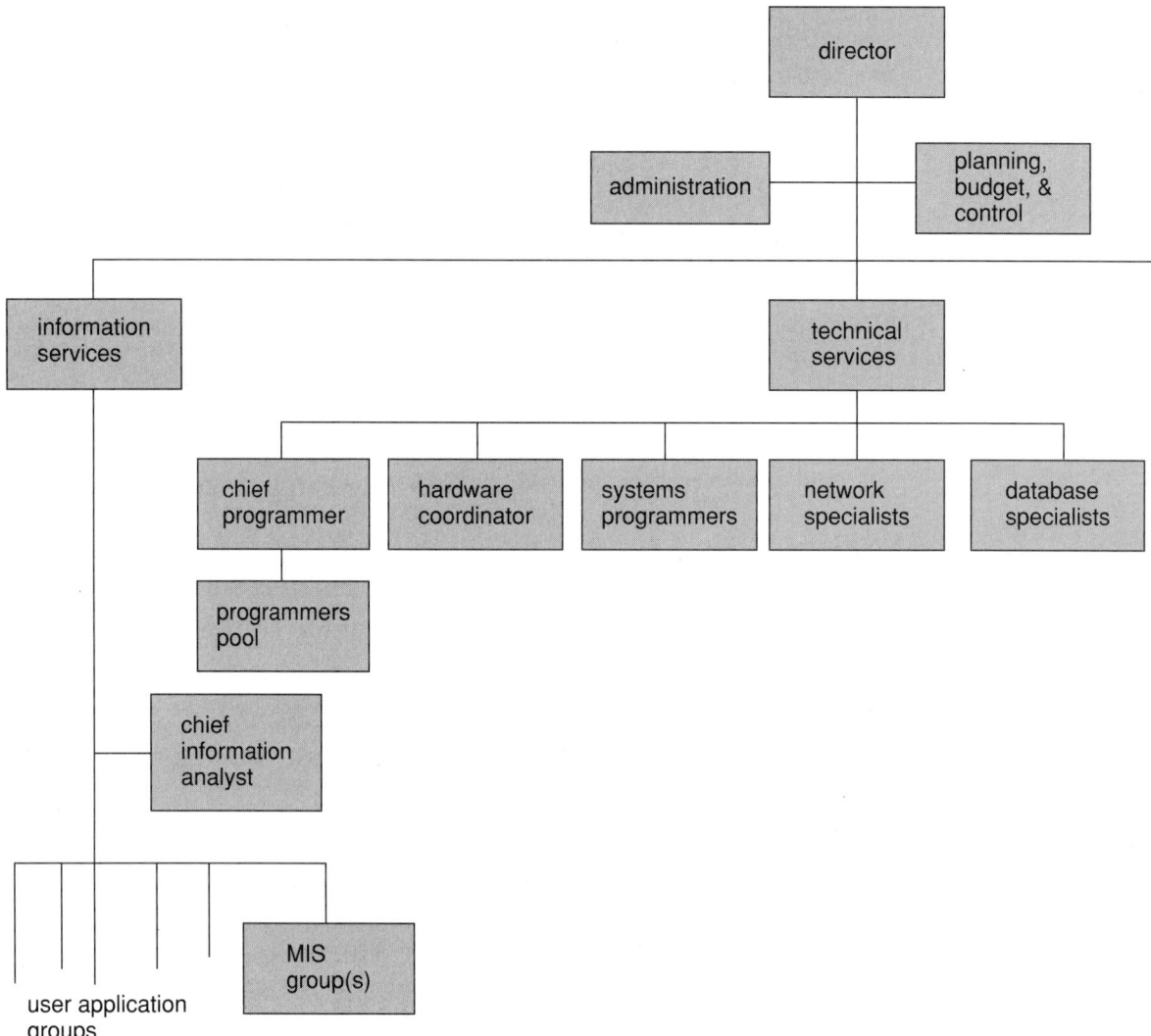

Principle 9.   The various groups composing the ISD use appropriate standards and
working procedures; these are maintained by special functions
dedicated to establishing and controlling standards and procedures.

Figure 12.10 suggests an organizational structure that complies with these principles. In the next section we elaborate on the major components of this structure.
Figure 12.10 does not include an information center; this will be discussed later in this
chapter.

Figure 12.10 *Continued*

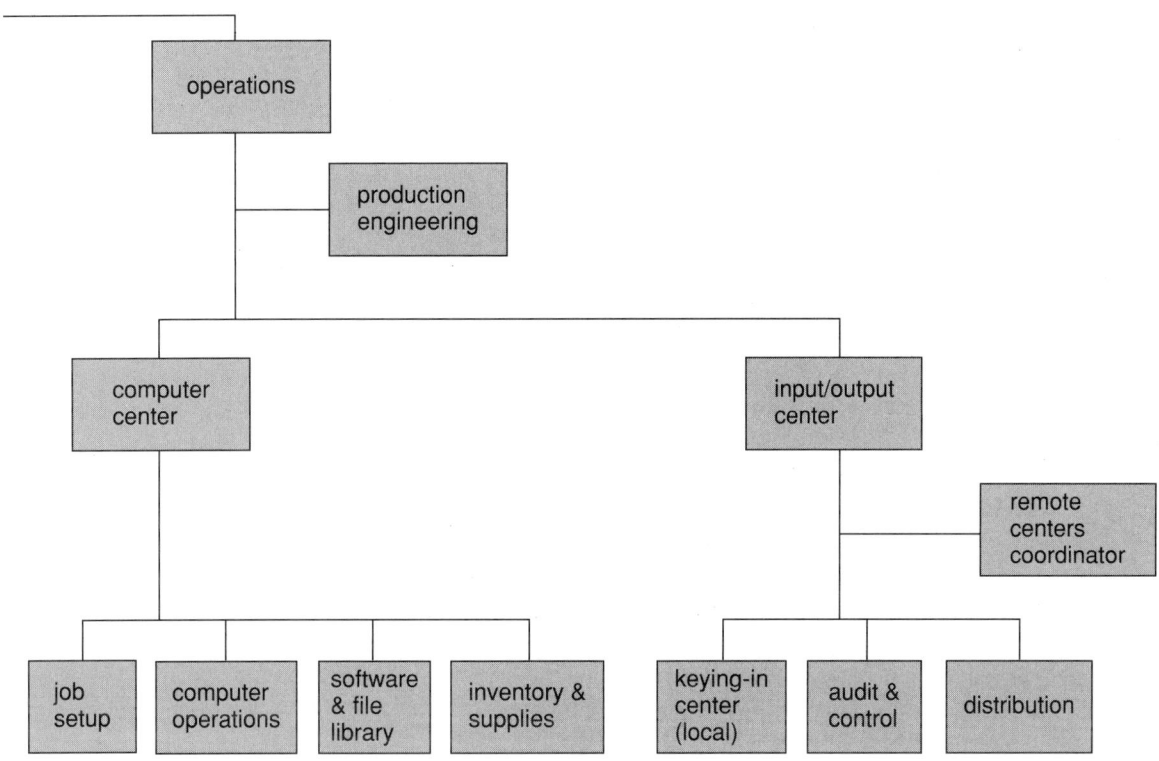

The Role of the Various Units

In general, the ISD is composed of four major units—information services, technical services, operations, and management. Each is set up to cope with different types of problems.

''Information services'' is the unit that deals with the users. It consists of application groups, each of which deals with a different user or group of users. Each group develops and maintains the software that directly serves its user. The head of each group is the sole addressee for any request from the users associated with the group. For example, an accounting applications group would be responsible for all bookkeeping and accounting systems; a sales applications group would be responsible for all the systems dealing with sales, distribution, etc. A special group is responsible for systems that support top-level management (MIS and DSS). The latter group may be expanded or divided into subgroups, depending on the spread of MIS use in the particular organization. Standards and procedures are devised and controlled by the office of the chief information analyst.

"Technical services" is the unit that handles the hardware/software technology and copes with the problems stemming from its installation, upgrading, and use. The unit employs technology-oriented individuals who are acquainted with the bits and bytes of information processing equipment. They include a data base administrator and his or her subordinates (data base specialists); a systems programming group; a hardware coordinator and experts in telecommunication; and, finally, a chief programmer who devises and controls programming standards and who is responsible for the quality of programming jobs. This person directs and coordinates the programmers. Of course, the programmers are always assigned to application groups as needed, so the programmers' pool is just an imaginary, transient area through which programmers pass between assignments. (Some reject this idea and assign programmers to application groups on a permanent basis.)

The manager of technical services must have a broad technical background. Otherwise, he or she might not be respected by subordinates. The manager could be a former technology-oriented professional with management capacity who knows how to present the technical jargon to top-level management.

The technical services unit is a key function in the ISD because it has to provide essential support to both information services and operations. The former has to be advised on technological characteristics that affect systems analysis and design; the latter has to get support to handle the computer hardware, software packages (e.g., operating system), and data bases.

"Operations" is the unit that copes with the mass production of information processing. Its structure is very similar to that presented in figure 12.9. The following additions would help adjust such a unit to large-scale operations:

1. A staff function entitled "production engineering." This function is required to efficiently plan the enormous flow of documents and materials through the unit. Since operations is nothing but a large production plant, it must utilize production engineering methods for scheduling production and maintenance, inflow and outflow of materials (source documents and printouts), inventory management, etc. Production engineering may also aid information services and technical services in designing procedures and forms.

2. The huge amount of files (data bases) requires a file library unit that is not subordinated to computer operations anymore. In fact, this unit is closely coordinated by the data base administrator.

3. Because input is, in some cases, keyed in, or because output is printed out in several locations where there is no professional staff, a coordinator is needed to establish and maintain input/output standards and advise remote users how to operate the equipment.

Table 12.1   The Involvement of Various Departmental Units in Systems Life Cycle

Stage	Unit Assuming Responsibility	Other Participating Units	Consulting Units
1. Preliminary analysis	User	Application group	
2. Feasibility study	User	Application group; planning/budget/control	Technical services experts (as required)
3. Information analysis	Application group	User	Technical services
4. System design	Application group		Technical services; production engineering; user
5. Programming	Application group	Programmer pool	Technical services
6. Procedure development	Application group	Production engineering	User
7. Conversion and implementation	Application group	User; operations; administration	Technical services; planning/budget/control
8. Operation and maintenance	Operations or user (depending on prevailing practices)	Application group	Technical services
9. Postaudit	Planning/budget/control or EDP auditor		Internal audit
10. Termination	Management		

The ''management'' unit of the ISD consists of several functions in addition to the executives (a director and possibly a deputy). ''Administration'' handles all the routine activities of any organizational unit, such as personnel, bookkeeping, secretarial support, etc. The only special requirement here is that the personnel function is aware of the different professions involved in an ISD and also takes care of promotion and training. ''Planning/budget/control'' is unique in the sense that it has to translate corporate policy into concrete periodical planning and then monitor the realization of the planning. Development programs, budgeting, budget control, and participation in feasibility studies all must be monitored. This unit provides information to the ISD director so he or she can make appropriate decisions.

These are the essence of a complex ISD. In the next section we outline the way information systems undergo their life cycle within this kind of structure. Interrelationships among the various components of the complex structure will be clarified.

Monitoring the Information System Life Cycle

Chapter 8 outlined the information system life cycle and designated the various functions taking part in it. In this section we follow the same life cycle stages but discuss involvement of departmental units during the life cycle. This will shed light on the respective roles and interrelationships of each unit. The discussion is summarized in table 12.1.

1. *Preliminary analysis*—The initiation of new, insightful ideas can be sparked by anyone. However, the first inquiry and preliminary report are undertaken by pertinent users and application groups. The report is submitted to management (normally represented by an information systems committee), which may appoint a feasibility team.

2. *Feasibility study*—The user is responsible for the study. Other members of the study team are taken from the relevant application group (ISD representative) and from the planning/budget/control unit. The latter group is presumed to represent management since the unit is not committed to projects of specific users. Technical and other experts assist the feasibility team if required. The feasibility report is submitted to the information systems committee.

3. *Information analysis*—At this stage, a development team is established and the application group takes charge throughout the entire development. Users still take active part in the information analysis stage (e.g., information requirement analysis—see ch. 10). The technical services unit provides assistance when the team has to consider the properties and constraints of various hardware/software features.

4. *System design*—The detailed design of the information system is carried out by the application group, which continues to staff the development team. However, support for procedure planning and form design is given by the production engineering unit. Technical advice can be given by data base administration, systems programming, etc.

5. *Programming*—In this stage, some programmers join the development team on ad hoc assignment if they are not permanently assigned to application groups. The technical services unit continues to support the development team with programming practices and hardware/software technicalities.

6. *Procedure development*—This stage has a great impact on future operations; therefore, it is jointly carried out by the development team and production engineering unit. The latter has to see that operational considerations are sufficiently observed.

7. *Conversion and implementation*—This stage, the most involved and delicate, requires the collaboration of many functions. Responsibility is still assumed by the application group through an implementation team (see chs. 9 and 10). However, user participation is ultimately required, particularly in training and conversion; the operations unit should be involved in training and scheduling; the administration unit schedules and provides facilities for seminars and courses; the technical services unit sees that all the technical aspects are ironed out; planning/budget/control prepares the mechanism for bookkeeping and budget follow-up of the new system.

8. *Operation and maintenance*—In chapter 10 we mentioned that responsibility for normal operations may be assumed by either the major user or the ISD. That is why table 11.1 presents two alternatives in this stage. In any case, for maintenance and changes, the application group takes charge. The liaison officer for the user(s) of the particular system is a member of the application group and is the sole addressee for any user appeal.

9. *Postaudit*—This stage is the responsibility of planning/budget/control. If carried out by a team (e.g., the "revived" steering committee), there may be participants from other units, too (e.g., major users). However, planning/

budget/control is responsible, and the findings are reported to ISD management and the information system committee. Organizations that employ EDP auditors should certainly assign one of those to carry out the postaudit activity.

10. *Termination*—An information system is scrapped only with management approval.

To sum up the discussion, we identify here two major executing bodies: the application group, which carries out the development; and operations, which undertakes the daily production. The administration and technical services units support these bodies as required. Planning/budget/control is a staff unit that takes care of the organizational perspective as well as activity follow-up. Users express their desires via their counterparts in the application groups. All that's needed now is a competent manager to run the shop.

Hierarchical Organization Structures
A very large organization might tend to have a number of separate, independent IS organizations as mentioned earlier. However, it is important for most organizations that the efforts, and most especially, the *information* of these individual IS departments be coordinated as a part of the overall business plan of the enterprise. This may involve a firm with a number of separate business units in multiple locations. Increasingly, organizations exist with multiple business units that span more than one country. An example of such an organization is Air Products and Chemicals, Inc. (see [9]).

APCI previously had a heavily centralized IS organization, with all development and operation centrally controlled. A reorganization placed more responsibility within the business units but retained functional oversight at the corporate level (see fig. 12.11). Obviously, for such an organization to be successful, the person at the top of the hierarchy must be placed at a very high reporting level—in this case a vice president of MIS who in turn reports to a vice chairman and chief administrative officer.

A major benefit to this hierarchical organization, as seen by its vice president, is that distributing more of the developmental work into the operating groups provided him with more time and opportunity to engage in substantive discourse with the group vice presidents about the role of IS in meeting corporate objectives.

Some Other Organizational Considerations
Most of the foregoing discussion has been based on the idea of an IS function that is completely internal to the organization. Two particular exceptions to that notion need to be discussed.

In the first case, an organization may make use of purchased software for all or part of their IS activities. In this situation, it is suggested that the form of the organization does not change. Rather, in the applicational organization, *systems development and maintenance* becomes *systems acquisition and support* for one or more applications, with a reduction in the level of staffing required. Similar comments apply to the functional organization.

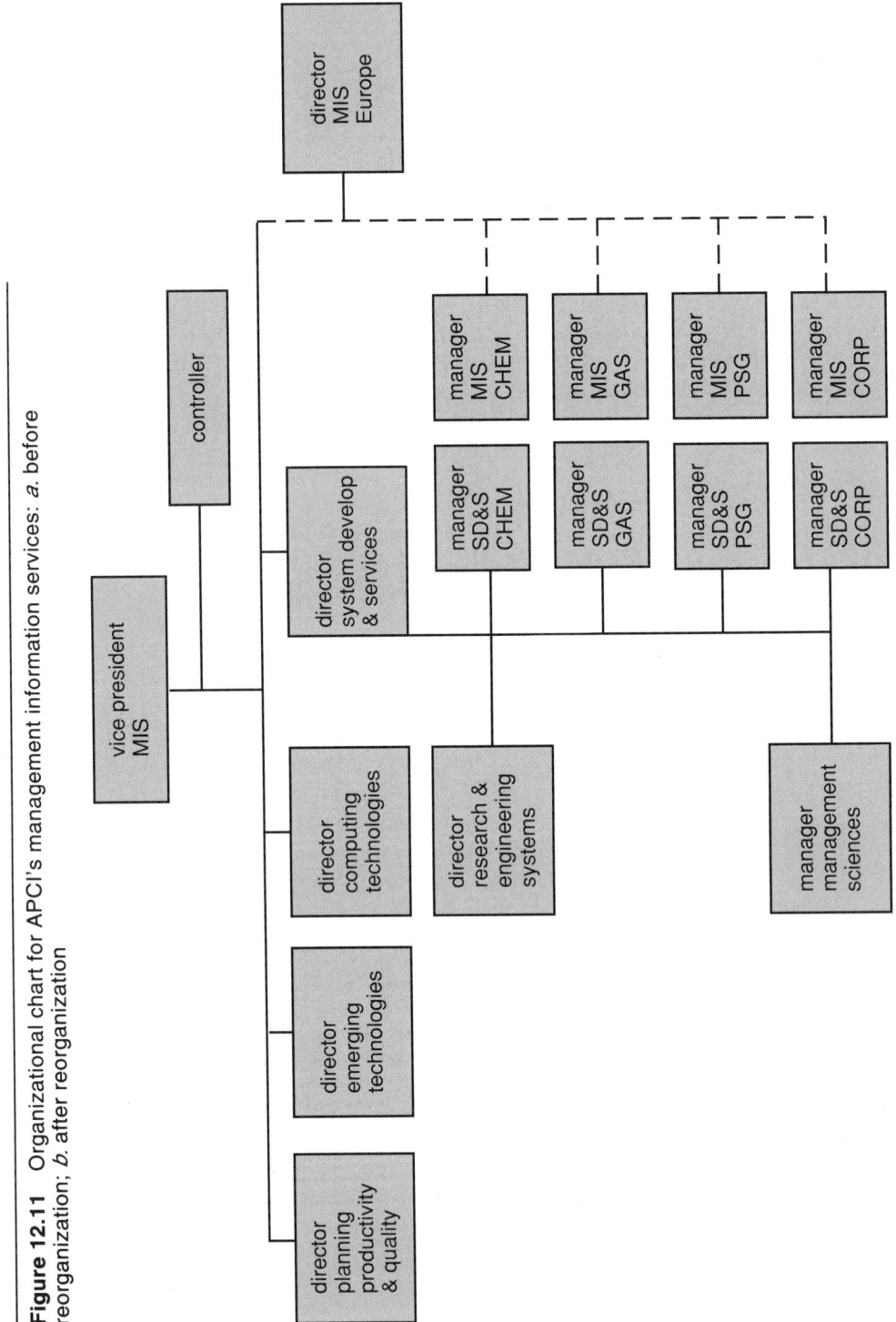

Figure 12.11 Organizational chart for APCI's management information services: *a.* before reorganization; *b.* after reorganization

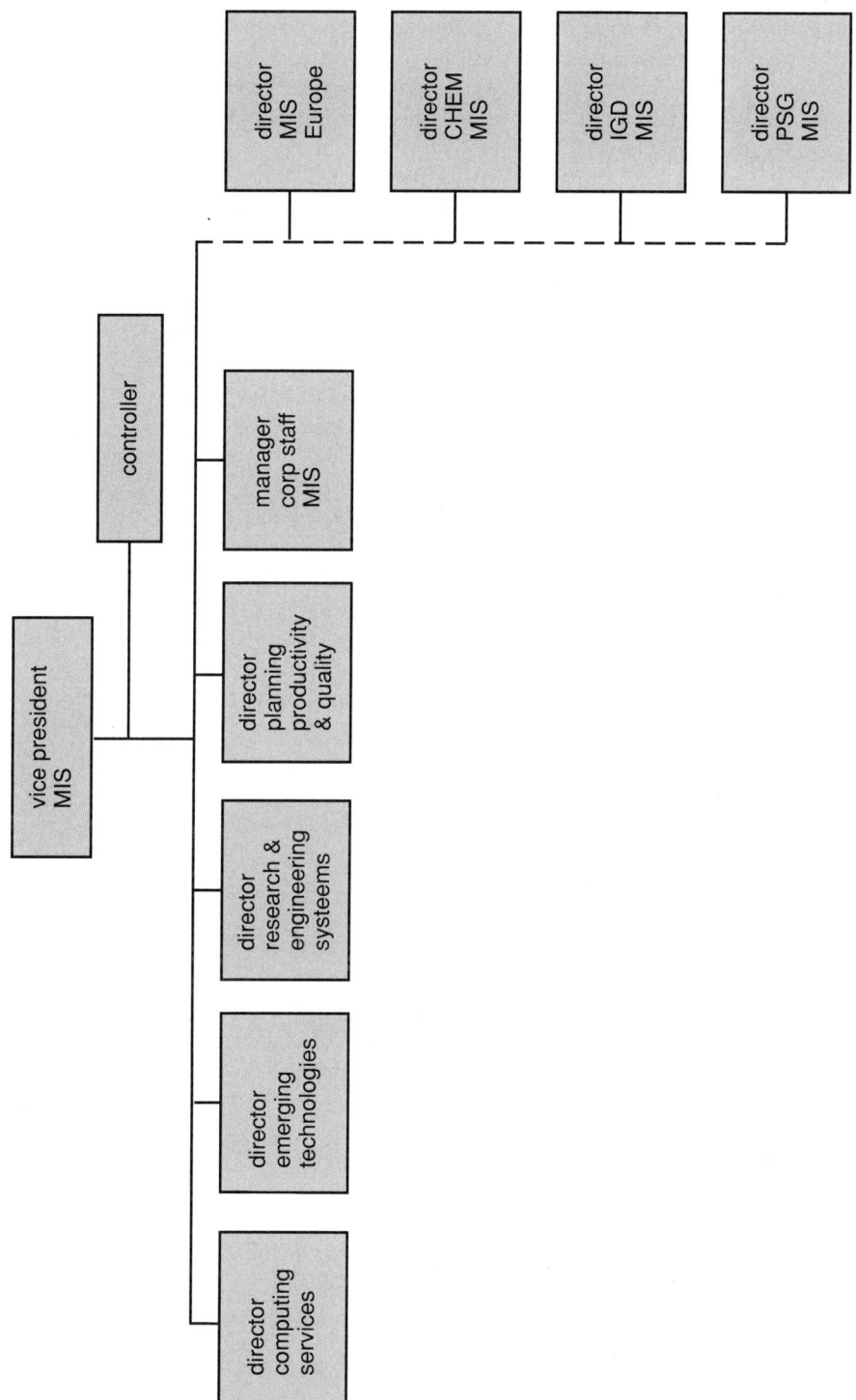

Organizing the Information System Department   433

In the second case, an organization may go to an outside vendor for the provision of the hardware and operating personnel (see discussion of *outsourcing* in ch. 13). In this event, *operations* might be retitled, with some personnel being required to maintain liaison with the vendor and to handle transmittal of data to and from the vendor's location.

In summary, the use of outside vendors for software, hardware, or personnel will reduce the number of people required in the IS organization, but will not substantially change its form and certainly not its reporting level.

End-User Computing

The widespread use of personal computers and computer-based workstations has brought with it the so-called Age of the End User. This age brings with it not only new hardware and software facilities, but also a new responsibility for end users to guide the application of information technologies in the direction that will be truly useful for them [17, 20, ch. 11].

Contemporary information system literature tends to designate end-user programming and end-user computing as a departure from conventional information processing. We tend to view *end-user computing* (EUC) as a generic term for any information processing activity performed by direct end users who actually use terminals or microcomputers to access data and programs (either programmed by them or by others). While conventional information processing (mostly TPS) is directed at raising organizational productivity, EUC is directed at raising individual productivity. Thus, EUC has been growing rapidly over the past two decades and accounts for an ever larger share of total IS budgets [4].

Who are typical end users of an information system? Rockart and Flannery [18] suggest six distinct classes of end users who differ significantly from each other in computer skills, method of computer use, application focus, education and training requirements, and support needed. These classes include the following:

Nonprogramming end users—Only access data through software provided by others.

Command-level users—Need to access data and manipulate it for their own purposes. They understand the available data base(s), and are able to manipulate data by most often utilizing a set of commands from software tools, such as spreadsheets or DBMSs.

End-user programmers—Develop their own application programs.

Functional support personnel—Sophisticated programmers supporting other end users within their particular functional areas.

End-user computing support personnel—Most often located in a central support unit, such as an information center. In addition to aiding end users, they may also develop software for them [1].

Data processing programmers—Provide service to end-users departments wishing to get contract programmers for a specific application.

EUC is a continuation of the historical trend of disengaging the end user from the direct reliance on the information system professional (programmers, input-output clerk). While end users still indirectly get services from the information systems personnel (maintenance of corporate data bases, technical support), they continuously break away from the information system unit's responsibility for planning and implementing much of the new information technology. This historical trend is reflected both in hardware and in software technologies. In hardware, the move from central site mainframes to time-shared dumb terminals, and then to intelligent networked terminals (i.e., microcomputers) have a host of user-friendly input-output devices (such as mice, touch-sensitive screens). In software, the progression from machine languages to user-oriented high-level languages, and then to off-the-shelf-packages, DSSs, DBMSs, natural language processors, and other user-friendly software tools.

The importance of facilitating and managing EUC is being widely felt. The information system literature indicates an increasing concern about the end-user issue. During the 1980s, the facilitation and management of EUC was already considered an important issue for management attention. In the 1990s, that concern continues as the technology provides greater opportunity for EUC and as existing end users seek to broaden their roles [13].

EUC is changing the role of the information system units in organizations. The applications being requested and developed by end users are no longer transaction-oriented, automating clerical functions with well-structured procedures. They are higher level systems attacking unstructured problems in which the end user is an integral and dynamic element. Many of the functions traditionally under the information systems unit will move to end-users departments. As initiative and responsibility for automation passes to the user community, information systems professionals will have to alter their roles, to be less experts than facilitators.

Information system managers used to be wholesalers, providing services to a small number of large organizational units, such as departments and divisions. They ran the computing system as a production shop. With the emergence of EUC, they are becoming service-oriented retailers, with a large number of customers. These customers are, in many instances, as sophisticated as the information systems staff. Many of them are quite knowledgeable about microcomputers, networking, local-area-networks, spreadsheets, application generators, and DSSs. Another factor beyond *knowledge* is *opportunity:* the cost of getting involved in EUC is constantly decreasing. These, plus the friendly hardware and software devices, put technology within every end user's reach.

The growth in the end-user demands implies a different management control process for information systems. With EUC we are moving from what may be called the management of the supply, where the information systems unit controls the supply of the information resource, to the management of end users' demand at appropriate cost and service levels. The traditional structure of an information systems unit—with a central computer and remote dumb terminals—made sense back when computing configurations were expensive. In the 1990s, an organization often has more computing power in its desktop microcomputers than in the central computing site, and this will considerably increase in the future.

This is not to say that central computing will become obsolete. The bulk of information processing in most organizations will continue to be transaction-oriented, with heavy volumes of inputs and outputs and with responsibility for maintaining the integrity and security of the common organizational data base. However, the future central site may become a warehouse of raw materials (data) and of finished goods (updated files, information). Such a site will be responsible for collecting, maintaining, and storing data, and distributing information (analogous to the way the central finance department collects, maintains, saves, and distributes capital resources). Like a telephone exchange, the central site will act more and more as a switcher of data and information of all types—internal and external (from public data bases), voice, image, numeric, graphic, and textual.

There are various issues and challenges facing the information systems management with regards to EUC. These have to do with security and privacy, control procedures, cost justification of hardware and software products, training and support of end users. These have to do with the organizational structure and processes used to manage EUC.

The first area of EUC management with which information systems management must be concerned is EUC strategy. A strategy and derived policies aimed at developing and managing EUC must be defined and promulgated as part of the overall information systems planning process (see ch. 8 on planning). The second area of concern is that of supporting the end user. This has to include the provision of hardware and software products, consulting services by the central information systems people, the development of an education and training program (see [1, 19]), and the development of procedures for access to internal and external data by end users. A third area of concern is the need for well-defined control processes in the end-user area, specifically those that pertain to the justification of end-user systems.

The computerized workstation may be the best vehicle for EUC. We emphasize computerized, since most people in organizations have always worked at a manual (or mechanical) workstation. Like many terms in the information system area, workstation is a glorified label for a simple concept: the computerized desk, bench, or board of different types of end users—typists, secretaries, executives, engineers, accountants, draftsmen, and the like.

Basically, the workstation is a computer-based configuration of hardware and software components. The configuration can vary from just a dumb terminal with a keyboard and a monitor (screen), hooked up to a processor, to a sophisticated supermicrocomputer with a printer, secondary storage devices, various input devices, a graphics monitor, communications port, and appropriate software.

Thus, different end users will have different workstations. The manager can have an *executive workstation,* including a DSS package and access to a public data base; the typist can have a workstation with a hard-copy printer and a word processing package; the secretary can have a *secretarial workstation,* with an electronic mail and a calendar management package; the design engineer can have an *engineering workstation,* with graphics, plotter, digitizing pen, and an electronic tablet; the accountant or financial expert can have a *professional workstation,* with a spreadsheet package. Each one of these workstations is an intelligent desk that will better support the user functions that have evolved over centuries.

The computerized workstation can be a stand-alone system, or be part of a network; a single-function, or a multifunctional workstation. Single-function workstations are on the wane. Organizations seeking to provide technological support to the full range of tasks and workers find the multifunctional workstation more desirable. Clerical and secretarial workstations, formerly restricted to word processing, are a good example: they are increasingly likely to require electronic mail, calendar, and access to local corporate data bases. Another example is executive workstations: executives seldom work at one task at a time. They are interrupt-driven, and their workstation should emulate that environment. They may be involved in making a decision (using a DSS), then switching to writing and distributing a memo (word processing and electronic mail), then receiving a phone call (telecommunications), followed by scheduling a meeting (using a calendar package), and then back to decision making.

The Information Center

The end user may be equipped with a terminal or microcomputer as a part of a planned (top down) implementation of an information system. On the other hand, the end user may equip him or herself, or be equipped by a department, with a personal computer. When this is the case, the organization must be prepared to support, and to some extent control, such usage. In other words, there must also be a plan for a bottom up integration of end users into the organization's information processing activities.

It may also be the case that a workstation provided as part of a planned system may also be employed by the user for other activities that were not a part of the original plan. For example, a manager who is supplied a microcomputer for use as an electronic mail terminal may find that he or she wants to use it for a variety of other tasks. The manager or professional with access to a microcomputer will find it instrumental for such things as quick engineering calculations, trend analysis, "what if" questions, examining major accounting and financial figures, and budget planning.

The dividing line between *personal computer* and *workstation* is not a clear one, and in many cases a particular computer may be used as both. If an individual has access to a computer and may exercise his or her own discretion as to its uses, then it becomes a personal computer for the purpose of this discussion.

Typical users usually utilize their PC in two types of modes. The first mode is a stand-alone machine, which offers such useful and friendly software as electronic spreadsheet programs (e.g., LOTUS 1-2-3®), DBMS (e.g., dBASE®), word processors (e.g., WORD®), statistical packages (e.g., SAS®), graphic packages, integrated software packages (e.g., WORKS®), and application programs for specific uses (e.g., PERT). The second mode is a terminal communicating with a mainframe or with other PCs. This mode enables the user to access central or remote data bases for data retrieval. In many cases, the user wishes to download extracted data from a central computer to his or her own PC, and thereafter to process the data in a stand-alone mode. In other cases, the data may flow in the opposite direction, namely uploading PC files for storing and processing on a mainframe computer.

Regardless of the exact mode of operation, there are some factors common to many of the front-end users: they do not wish to become technical experts in microcomputer operation; they are not prepared to comprehend the horrific jargon, technicalities, and acronyms of communications specialists; and they do not want to write programs in BASIC or any other programming language. They do look for a friendly, easy-to-use tool that will improve their decision-making process and the effectiveness and efficiency of their job. They expect that somebody else—a computer professional—will resolve the technical problems.

This is the origin of the concept of *information center* (IC). We now elaborate on its functions and location in the organizational structure (see also [8, ch. 18]).

Functions of the Information Center

The principal objective of the IC is to assist PC users in all aspects of operation in order to increase the effectiveness of these machines. This mission is carried out by providing a number of services.

A major function is performed in the IC by the *software advisor*. This individual should learn user needs and suggest appropriate software. In particular, the advisor has to verify that the software is compatible with the user's hardware, that it can interface with other pertinent programs, and that it can read in and produce data files in an appropriate manner.

The software advisor has to be familiar with packages available in the software industry. He or she has to understand the constraints imposed by the hardware and communications equipment on the possible use of various software packages.

In many cases, users prefer to develop their PC application by themselves, provided that the software is indeed friendly. However, sometimes users would rather have an application delivered to them. Hence, another function in the IC is *application development*. Fulfillment of this goal requires a special breed of information system professionals. These individuals are a combination of information analyst and application programmer. The information analyst aspect is essential to understanding user requirements and needs; the application programmer competence is required to select and use the most adequate software. We stress that emphasis on efficient programming is not necessarily an advantage here. A programmer who delights in saving two commands out of a routine of twenty and spends five days to achieve this will probably serve the users very poorly. In most cases, a "quick and dirty" solution is preferred to an efficient and prolonged one.

Complementary to software-related functions, the IC has to also provide *hardware consulting* services. In many organizations, standardization of hardware equipment is imposed by management. In such cases, the hardware consultant is responsible for the recommendation and selection of the standard equipment. Even when users can select any PC they want, there is still a need for someone to advise them on the capacity of the PC and on various characteristics of CPUs and peripheral units. The hardware consultant is supposed to perform this task, assuming that he or she is up-to-date on the hardware industry.

A major role of the IC is user *training*. Lay users are somewhat reluctant to operate PCs (particularly when their children are doing it faster at home). This phenomenon is much amplified when the PC is located in a public space where subordinates can watch their boss "mumbling" on the keyboard.

All of the above consulting and advising functions may be carried out by one or more *personal computer specialists*. Depending on the size of the organization and the extent of personal computer usage, these services might simply be provided by persons who have this as a part of their duties, or there may be several personal computer specialists, each specializing in a particular area such as hardware, applications, or training.

A common solution to the problem is to establish a microcomputer shop and a training program in which managers and their staff can take elementary courses in PC operation and software. Computer shops can also be used for individual practice and to develop pilot applications (prototypes) before a final acquisition decision is made.

Note that some large organizations offer a take-home program for potential PC users; namely, a PC is installed in the user's home for a limited practice period. In this way, users manage to overcome the initial fear and hesitancy of operating the PC at the office. (For more on user training, see [1].)

Last, but undoubtedly a paramount function, is the *data supply* function. Most PC users need data extracted from central files, either on a periodic basis or for ad hoc purposes. Had they been required to personally communicate to the central mainframe and learn about file formats and DBMS specifications, they would likely refuse to use the PC. They need a go-between; someone who is familiar with the formats and locations of central files and who can transfer data to diskettes or other handy means in a format that is easily read by the PC. Observations prove that without this assistance, users become frustrated and eventually quit using the PC. Needless to say, the data supply function is also responsible for the flow of data from PCs to mainframes (the severe problems created by flows in this direction are discussed later in the chapter).

The Control Function of the Information Center

In addition to supporting lay users, an IC should also include some control functions. It has to establish procedures for operations and maintenance of front-end equipment, software, and files. These include backup arrangements, security provisions, publication of operating manuals, and inspection of distributed equipment.

The wide use of front-end equipment might pose very serious threats to the integrity of central files. If lay users start to update the central data bases of the organization, it will not take more than a few days until all those files contain totally unreliable data. It is the duty of the computer center to protect its files; however, it is the role of the IC to educate the users regarding what they should and should not communicate with the central computers.

The best approach to the problem is to adopt the *unidirection principle*. This principle states that the user may retrieve data from central systems; and the user can never update, delete, or add data to central files (note that this principle does not exclude saving user's private files on a central system). Maintaining the unidirection principle increases the likelihood that central files will remain clean.

Broadening the Scope of the Information Center

Until now, the discussion on the IC focused mainly on PC services. This, however, is not a necessary limitation; many ICs do not limit their services to PC-related activities. In fact, it is common to broaden the IC activities so it caters to any type of request for information. According to this line of thought, user requests are classified into two categories: large-scale requests that require the development of a full-size information system or introducing major changes in an existing system; or minirequests that can be provided in a short period with a relatively small effort. Requests of the first category are diverted to the ISD; minirequests are served by the IC by means of application generators, query languages, PC applications, and the like.

The great advantage of this approach is that users are not turned down as often as they might be were they working directly with the ISD. For the ISD, minirequests are nothing but a pain in the neck. They deal with the big things and are usually disturbed when they have to allocate an analyst or a programmer to a small job. Thus they tend to assign very low priority to these requests. Unlike the ISD, the IC is founded in order to fulfill the small requests; it is much more versatile in its ability to respond, so users are more satisfied.

Organizational Location of the Information Center

A grave mistake is common among many ISD managers. They perceive that the PCs compete with the central computer so they try to block the introduction of the smaller computers. Users, then, continue to acquire PCs clandestinely. Sooner or later the ISD manager realizes that the battle against the PCs is in vain, but by then it might be too late. There are already many PCs around, but there is no standardization, no control, no procedure, and no IC. When an IC is eventually established, it takes a great effort to regain control.

As the old proverb says, "If you can't beat them, join them." A recommended strategy for the ISD is to encourage the use of PCs, but to do so under a controlled and rational policy. Establish an IC; develop criteria and formal procedures to purchase hardware; select a number of models that will become the corporate standard equipment; advise the users in software selection and application development; and smooth the way for users, rather than placing obstacles in their way.

The IC should be affiliated with the ISD, but it should not be an organizational unit under the hardware or the software sections. These functions are too technical; they tend to be bit- and byte-oriented. The IC should be affiliated with the information services unit (see fig. 12.10) because this unit has a tradition of responding to user requests. If an organization follows this strategy and appoints an appropriate IC manager, the chances of success are high. (For a more extensive discussion on the information center environment, see [5], [7], and [8, ch. 18].)

Some Examples of Information Centers in Organizations

To recapitulate, the rapid growth of minicomputers and microcomputers operating independently within user departments has led various organizations to find more effective ways of addressing user needs. The information center concept is the development of readily available information systems consulting staff and affiliated computer access equipment.

The IC is usually staffed with several experienced user-oriented individuals. It also employs people who are able to assist users in problem solving. This assistance is offered in the form of user programming, computer operation, and access to data bases that are needed to gain use in fast access to information.

A substantial number of organizations that have used information centers for several years report some impressive results in alleviating overloads in the data processing department and in solving users' problems.

Practical Conclusions for Information System Design and Use

The following list contains practical conclusions for information system design and use.

1. Clearly defined job descriptions and professional qualifications are essential for every position in the ISD. Poorly defined functions and obscure boundaries between functions result in poorly designed information systems that are irregularly used.

2. Development and operation of information systems require the employment of individuals of many different professions. Training, promotion paths, and apprenticeship tracks must be carefully planned for each profession. Otherwise, employees' confusion will reduce their productivity and quality.

3. Maintenance programmer is a vital position, without which an existing application might collapse. Since it is not a sought-after position, it could be assigned to programmers on a rotating basis, and thus integrated into the promotion path.

4. ISD managers, when short of application programmers, are tempted to assign systems programmers to application development. This may turn out to be a wrong decision because poorly maintained system software might delay all the operations of the entire ISD.

5. A clear distinction between system-oriented and technology-oriented personnel is essential. The former pursue user needs; the latter cope with technical problems. If the distinction is not made, we might end up with technically perfect systems that do not serve any user.

6. In general, the organizational structure of an ISD should comply with management philosophy (e.g., centralized or decentralized) and with the maturity of the organization with respect to information system use (e.g., basic transaction processing compared to advanced MIS).

7. Applicational organization is better for development of basic transaction processing systems (the infrastructure of information processing). However, future integration needs should not be overlooked; a guiding master plan is always a must.

8. Functional organization better serves an organization during the stage when information systems are being more extensively used and when the need for data integration requires formal procedures to be introduced. However, user needs must not be ignored while housekeeping is being done.

9. Matrix organization seems to be a golden compromise between the applicational and functional structures. However, it might create some managerial problems concerning coordination of personnel and definition of responsibilities.

10. The three aforementioned structures seem to be inappropriate for large-scale operations in a contemporary environment. The structure suggested in figure 12.10, although more complex, appears to offer a better fit.

11. As the use of information systems in an organization becomes more involved and voluminous, the need to devise and maintain rigid procedures increases.

12. Establish an Information Center (IC) that assists users in acquiring and operating personal computers (PCs) and software packages.

13. An IC can develop into an organizational unit that specializes not only in PCs, but in all kinds of user requests that do not call for the initiation of a full-scale development project.

Summary

This chapter has dealt primarily with managerial aspects of information processing—in particular, issues of personnel and organizational structure.

The personnel who deal with information systems are divided into three categories: operation-oriented, technology-oriented, and system-oriented.

Operation-oriented personnel mostly take care of normal runs of existing applications: keying operator, computer operator, file librarian, audit and control clerk, job setup clerk, and distribution clerk.

Technology-oriented personnel must be closely acquainted with the bits and bytes of hardware and software: application programmer, systems programmer, hardware coordinator, data base specialist, and communications specialist.

System-oriented personnel must understand user information requirements and transform them to workable specifications: information advisor (affiliated with the user department), information analyst, system designer, procedure writer, and data base administrator.

Career paths in the operations-oriented category are different from those in the other two. In operations, an individual is normally promoted in the same occupation—e.g., from operator to shift foreperson—as in any other clerical career.

Career paths in technology- and system-oriented professions are interrelated. The starting point is usually some programming knowledge, with which a person may branch to a technical career—for instance, in programming—or to a system-oriented career—say, in system design and information analysis. However, switchovers from a technology- to a system-oriented career are very common.

There are many approaches to organizing an ISD. They derive from different managerial conceptions (e.g., centralized vs. decentralized); from different intensities of information utilization; and from different institutional circumstances. Nevertheless,

ISD functions are almost constant: systems development, information production, and systems maintenance. These functions are supported by technical and administrative functions.

The discussion in this chapter presumes centralization of information services (for the sake of simplicity) and describes various organizational structures in correspondence with the historical development of the use of information systems in organizations.

The initial organizational structure is usually applicational. The ISD personnel are grouped according to the departmentalization of the parent organization (e.g., accounting applications, production applications, etc.). This structure speeds up establishment of basic transaction processing systems, which are the infrastructure for any future use of MIS. The main disadvantage of the applicational structure is revealed when it becomes necessary to integrate information handled in different application groups; the systems developed by different groups may not be able to "converse" with each other.

Functional organization involves grouping the ISD employees according to their professional function—i.e., information analysis, system design, programming, and operations. Standardization is thereby improved and data integration is facilitated. The main disadvantage lies in separating users and ISD professionals.

The matrix structure is an attempt to overcome some of the previously mentioned disadvantages by superimposing liaison officers and project leaders on the functional structure. This arrangement may resolve some problems, but it may also create conflict between liaisons and line managers in the ISD.

Organizing the operations portion of an ISD is less debatable. Normally it consists of two units: one runs the computer site and all pertinent activities (job setup, file library, computer room, supplies); the other handles inflows and outflows of documents and reports, including keying, validation, and distribution.

Organizations that are very mature in the use of information systems find it difficult to get along with any of the "traditional" structures. They have to cope with large-scale operations, sophisticated information requirements, and contemporary information technology. Any organizational solution to problems stemming from these conditions should comply with the following principles. (1) Information systems ought to be user-oriented. (2) MIS should be easily incorporated in the repertoire of applications. (3) Users must have a representative in the ISD. (4) Operations should be centrally coordinated. (5) Data bases should be centrally managed. (6) Systems development plans should follow corporate strategy and be subject to economic reasoning. (7) Technical experts should support development and operations units in a coordinated fashion. (8) Powerful administration, planning, and budgeting entities should exist and report directly to the ISD management. (9) Working standards and formal procedures should be established.

The organizational structure in figure 12.10 complies with these principles. It concentrates the technical support staff in a special technical services unit. The system development unit is user-oriented, but with means established to ensure consistency and standardization. The operations unit is attuned to cope with large volumes of information processing. The management unit exercises its authority through the administration function and a powerful planning/budget/control unit.

The systems life cycle in a complex organizational structure is formally regulated through clear definition of responsibilities (table 12.1). Although responsibility alternates along various life cycle stages, continuity is preserved through constant involvement of the user and the application group.

An information center (IC) is a special organizational unit that deals with personal computer (PC) applications and with many other user requests that do not necessitate the initiation of a full-scale development project. The IC performs a number of functions. It helps users in software selection and operation; it develops PC and other instant applications for end users; it consults with users in hardware selection; it is responsible for user training; and it provides users with extracts of data files retrieved from central data bases. The IC also takes care of control procedures among end users, such as, file backup, software backup, and security. The IC should be affiliated with the information services unit in the ISD.

This chapter has focused on internal aspects of an information systems department. In the next chapter, we move our attention to general management, information systems users, and their interactions with the ISD.

Key Concepts

clerk: audit and control, distribution, job setup
communications specialist
data base: administrator, specialist
end user computing
file librarian
hardware coordinator
information: advisor, analyst
information center (IC)
information systems department (ISD)

network specialist
operator: computer, keying
organizational structure: applicational, complex, functional, matrix
personal computer (PC)
personal computer specialist
programmer: application, systems
procedure writer
system designer

References

1. Ahituv, N., J. J. Baroudi, and B. Ronen. "The Characteristics of Microcomputer Support Personnel: A Normative Perspective." *Human Systems Management* 7, no. 4 (1988): 321–31.
2. Ahituv, N., and M. Hadass. "Organizational Structure of a Complex Data Processing Department." *Information and Management* 1 (1978): 53–57.
3. Awad, E. M., and M. H. Gotterer. *Database Management.* Danvers, MA: Boyd & Fraser, 1992.
4. Benjamin, R. I. "Information Technology in the 1990s: A Long Range Planning Scenario." *MIS Quarterly* 6, no. 2 (June 1982): 11–31.
5. Gabel, D. "Keeping Corporate Computers Personal." *Personal Computing* 8, no. 3 (Mar. 1984): 68–79.
6. Gildersleeve, T. R. "Organizing the Data Processing Function." *Datamation* 20, no. 11 (Nov. 1974): 46–50.

7. Hammond, L. W. "Management Considerations for an Information Center." *IBM Systems Journal* 21, no. 2 (1982): 131–61.

8. Hussain, D., and K. M. Hussain. *Managing Computer Resources.* 2d ed. Homewood, IL: Irwin, 1988.

9. Ives, B., and S. Jarvenpaa. "Air Products and Chemicals, Inc.: Planning for Global Information Technology." *International Information Systems* 1, no. 2 (Apr. 1992): 77–99.

10. Martin, M. P. "The Instant Analyst." *Journal of Systems Management* 26, no. 2 (Feb. 1975): 12–19.

11. Martin, M. P. "Instant Analyst Education." *Journal of Systems Management* 27, no. 7 (Jul. 1976): 6–9.

12. McCusker, T. "Uniting IBM/DEC Net Management." *Datamation* 38, no. 17 (Aug. 15, 1992): 28–34.

13. McGann, J. A. "Meeting the Challenge of End User Computing." *Journal of Systems Management* 41, no. 3 (Mar. 1990): 13–16.

14. McLean, E. R., and J. V. Soden, eds. *Strategic Planning for MIS.* New York: Wiley-Interscience, 1977.

15. Moad, J. "Client/Server Management Arrives." *Datamation* 38, no. 23 (Nov. 15, 1992): 28–33.

16. Murch, R. "Taking an Organizational Approach to Data Base Administration." *Canadian Datasystems* 7, no. 10 (Oct. 1975): 18–24.

17. Panko, R. R. "Directions and Issues in End User Computing." *INFOR* 25, no. 3 (Aug. 1987): 181–97.

18. Rockart, J. F., and L. S. Flannery. "The Management of End User Computing." *Communications of the ACM* 26, no. 10 (Oct. 1983): 776–84.

19. Sein, M. K., R. P. Bostrom, and L. Olfman. "Training End Users to Compute: Cognitive, Motivational and Social Issues." *INFOR* 25, no. 3 (Aug. 1987): 236–55.

20. Sprague, R. H., and B. C. McNurlin. *Information Systems Management in Practice.* Englewood Cliffs, NJ: Prentice-Hall, 1986.

21. Teichroew, D. "Education Related to the Use of Computers in Organizations." *Communications of the ACM* 14, no. 9 (1971): 573–88.

22. Willmott, T., and J. Pierce, Sr. "The Emerging Telecom Director." *Computerworld on Communications* (Jan. 18, 1984): 83.

Questions

1. Differentiate among the following three job categories: operation-oriented, technology-oriented, system-oriented.
2. Compare the job functions of an application programmer, systems programmer, hardware coordinator, and data-base specialist.
3. What is the role of the information analyst?
4. How does the data-base administrator differ from the data-base specialist?
5. What are the functions of an information system department?
6. How do traditional ISD structures compare with contemporary structures?
7. What are the advantages and disadvantages of the applicational structure as compared to the functionally organized or matrix organization ISD?
8. How would you characterize a large-scale operation?
9. Describe the four units which comprise the contemporary ISD.

Problems

1. Keeping in mind the proposed principles for an ISD, design a scheme for the organization of a bank's information systems department. Assume that the bank has many branches, has commercial as well as individual accounts, offers various checking and savings plans, offers loans, has an automated teller machine network, etc.

2. A large insurance company is considering going "paperless," i.e., automating all clerical and secretarial activities as well as supporting management decision making online. Describe the various stages this project would involve. Who would assume responsibility for and be involved in the various stages? Use examples throughout.

The EMC Group

The EMC Group of companies is headquartered in Fountain Valley (F.V.), California, where one of the Group's IBM (4300) mainframe computers is located. Another IBM (4300) computer is located in Santa Ana (S.A.), CA. The F. V. computer has, until early 1992, supported production processing for the Electronics division (Pomona, CA), the Phoenix division (Phoenix, AZ), and all application development and testing activities for Southern California and Arizona. Also, prior to that time, the S.A. computer supported production processing for the Mil/Aero (M/A), Components (C/I), and Central (corporate) divisions. Then and now the Electronics and Phoenix divisions communicated with a mainframe via remote job entry (RJE) equipment, a DEC VAX and an IBM AS/400, respectively. Due to the small size, the Speciality and Chad divisions each had a stand-alone IBM AS/400 (see figure 12.12). These comprise the North America portion of EMC.

Each division is organized along groups of product lines with different mixes of commercial vs. government customer bases.

The IS function was centrally organized (see figures 12.13, 12.14, and 12.15) until mid-1992. The IS manager reported to the EMC North America Comptroller. The IS manager's line responsibility included Southern California with dotted line responsibility for the Electronics and Phoenix divisions. These two divisions and the M/A, C/I, and Central divisions (located in Orange County, CA) shared a pool of Systems Analysis and Programming resources. M/A and C/I shared many common applications and data base. Pomona and Phoenix maintained separate applications and data base.

The divisions were not completely content with the entire IS structure. Until mid-1992, when the profitable M/A division made IS application requests, the IS department had to poll the C/I division to gain their support in order to standardize the shared applications and data base. Often the less profitable C/I division would balk and/or refuse to sponsor the M/A project and schedules were extended. The M/A General Manager was often foiled in an attempt to enhance the division's systems and could not influence the direction of IS. When one of the divisions felt that they were not getting an equitable share of the programming/analyst resources, the centralized pool would be balanced by the IS manager to accommodate and pacify the divisions for a short while. In addition, both divisions felt that they lacked IS ownership and that they had very little control over the escalating IS cost allocations and wanted much more. The divisions were generally satisfied with the level of IS operations service, online response time, report distribution, etc.

The M/A division became more profitable and sales grew along with the M/A General Manager's clout, which was used to mount pressure to separate M/A applications and data base from the C/I division and, in turn, to divisionalize the IS department personnel and hardware. The resultant IS organization (see figures 12.16, 12.17, 12.18, and 12.19) dramatically altered reporting relationships. The former IS Manager (So. CA) became the Director of IS for the EMC Group Worldwide with no line responsibility. The Worldwide scope came with recent international acquisitions, all of which have independent IS resources. The former Computing Services Manager obtained responsibility for all of the IS function, under the M/A division reporting to the division Comptroller. A former Information Center (IC) specialist obtained responsibility for the C/I division, reporting directly to the division Comptroller. The Central division remained on the M/A computer (few shared applications). Some common applications shared with all divisions remained on the M/A computer (i.e., Payroll, Accounts Payable). The C/I division did not want to service the Phoenix division because of a small C/I IS staff, so Phoenix was shifted to the M/A mainframe. Since these changes the following conditions exist:

- The C/I mainframe is underutilized (from 65–75% to 40–50%) and the allocated costs have nearly doubled (from $468/cpu-hr to $864/cpu-hr). The Electronics division is not happy with this, either.
- The C/I mainframe users are unhappy with their service level, related to the small IS staff, which is adversely affected by normal employee absences and vacation. The inexperience of the IS supervisor contributes to this, too.

- The M/A General Manager remains unhappy with IS since he envisioned having total control of these resources but finds that he is in contention for them with his own Comptroller. As a result, the Comptroller often influences IS project priorities, hence, favoring the financial systems to the detriment of other project schedules.
- The payroll application requires extensive modification to service the Pomona division, yet they perceive that they have less access since it resides on the M/A mainframe.

Questions

1. Describe the IS (Southern California) organizational structure of EMC prior to and after 1992 in relation to chapter 12 of the text. Include a description of the advantages.

2. Suggest and describe an alternative IS (Southern California) organizational structure which may have addressed divisional management's concerns and would perhaps help avoid the problems described in the case.

Figure 12.12 EMC computer network

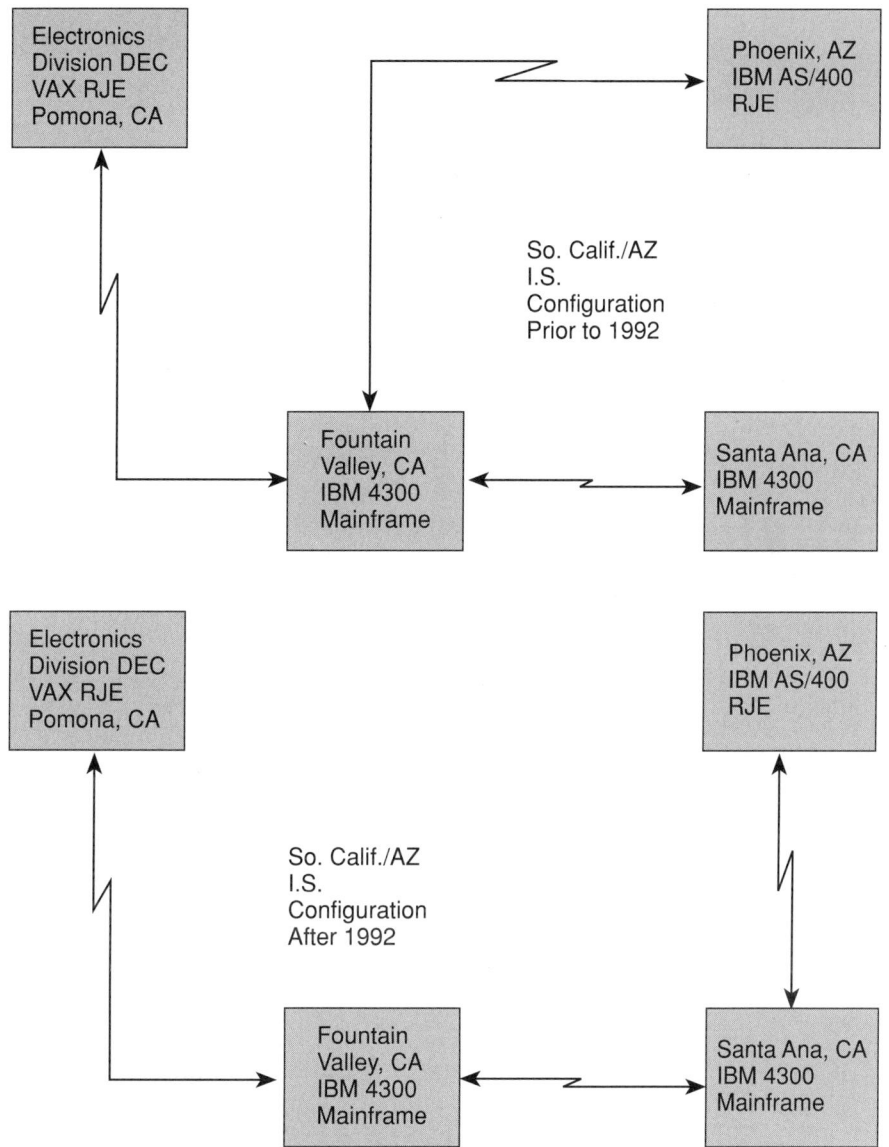

Electronics Division DEC VAX RJE Pomona, CA

Phoenix, AZ IBM AS/400 RJE

So. Calif./AZ I.S. Configuration Prior to 1992

Fountain Valley, CA IBM 4300 Mainframe

Santa Ana, CA IBM 4300 Mainframe

Electronics Division DEC VAX RJE Pomona, CA

Phoenix, AZ IBM AS/400 RJE

So. Calif./AZ I.S. Configuration After 1992

Fountain Valley, CA IBM 4300 Mainframe

Santa Ana, CA IBM 4300 Mainframe

NOTE: The mainframe link is primarily for transferring software into production after development/testing and allowing access to shared applications on the S.A. mainframe.

Figure 12.13 Information services

INFORMATION SERVICES – SOUTHERN CALIFORNIA

INFORMATION SERVICES:
    administration
    information center
    office systems

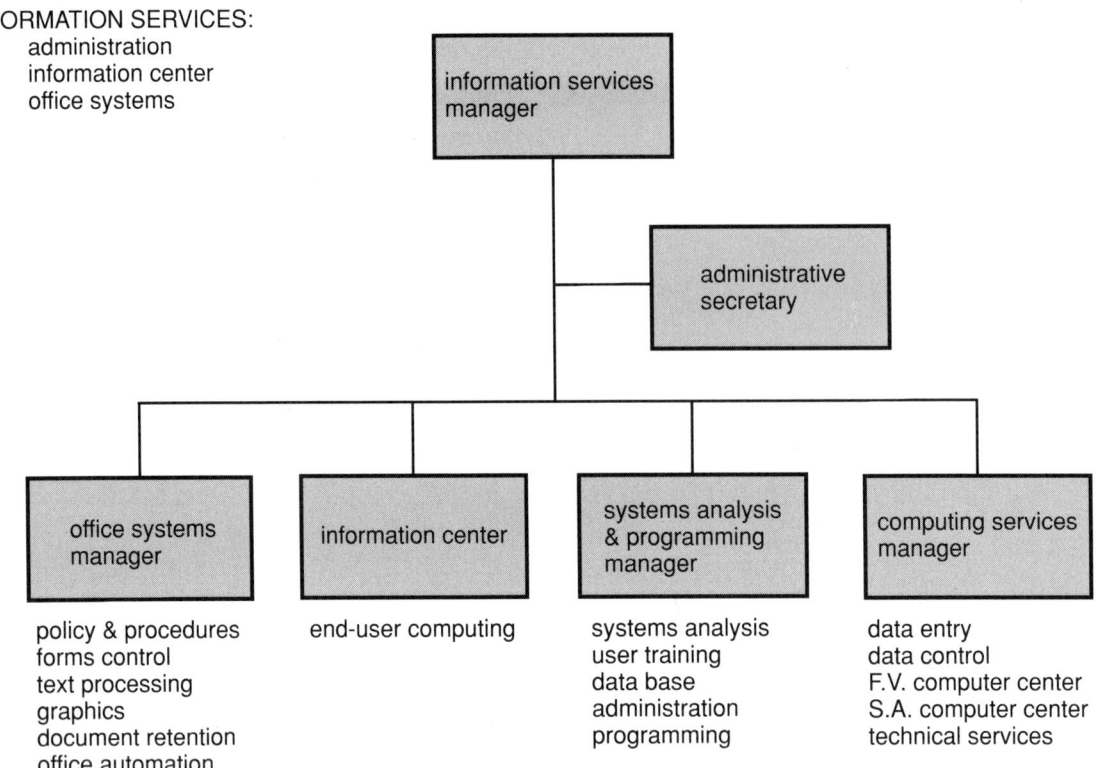

office systems manager	information center	systems analysis & programming manager	computing services manager
policy & procedures	end-user computing	systems analysis	data entry
forms control		user training	data control
text processing		data base	F.V. computer center
graphics		administration	S.A. computer center
document retention		programming	technical services
office automation			

Figure 12.14 Computing services

COMPUTING SERVICES:
    Santa Ana Computer Center
    Technical Services
    Fountain Valley Computer Center

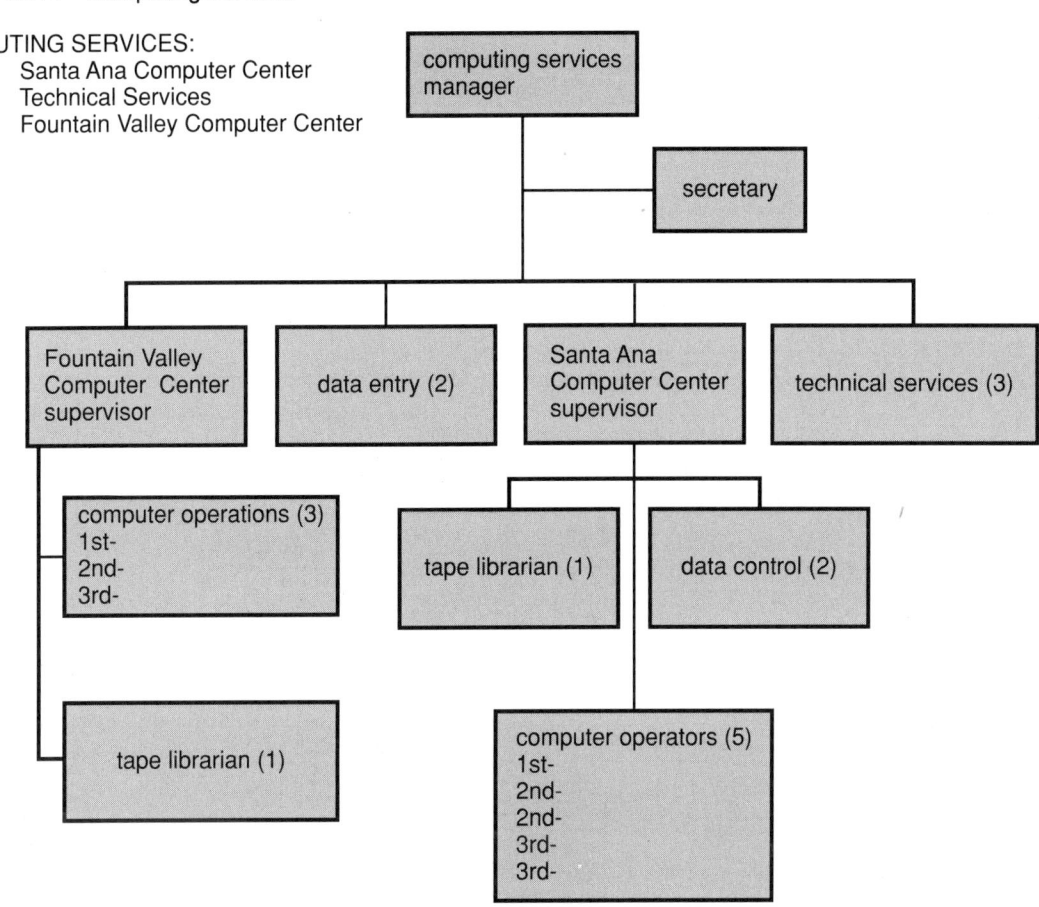

Figure 12.15 Systems analysis and programming

SYSTEMS ANALYSIS & PROGRAMMING
C/C 2061 - systems analysis & programming
C/C 2063 - data base administration

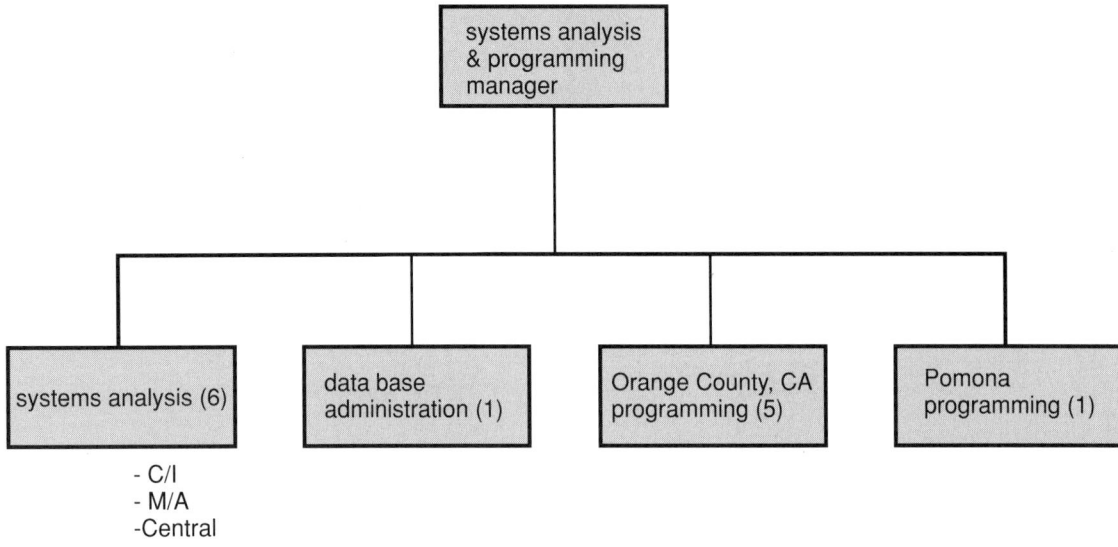

Figure 12.16 Information systems

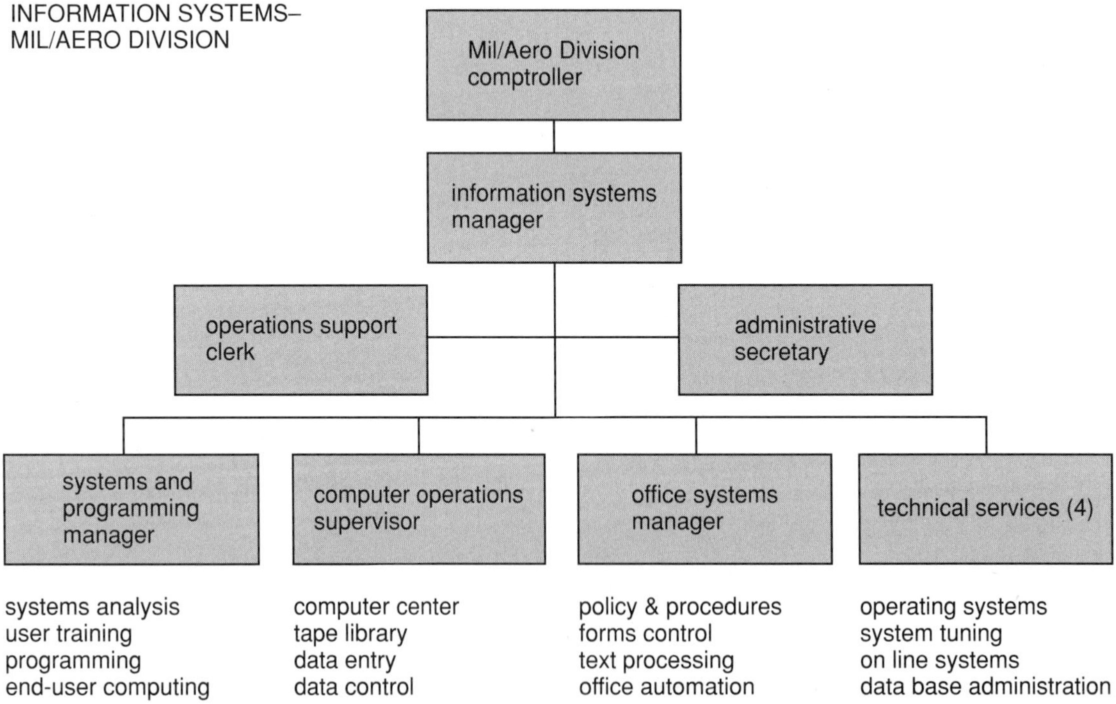

INFORMATION SYSTEMS–
MIL/AERO DIVISION

Figure 12.17 Systems and programming

INFORMATION SYSTEMS –
MIL/AERO DIVISION

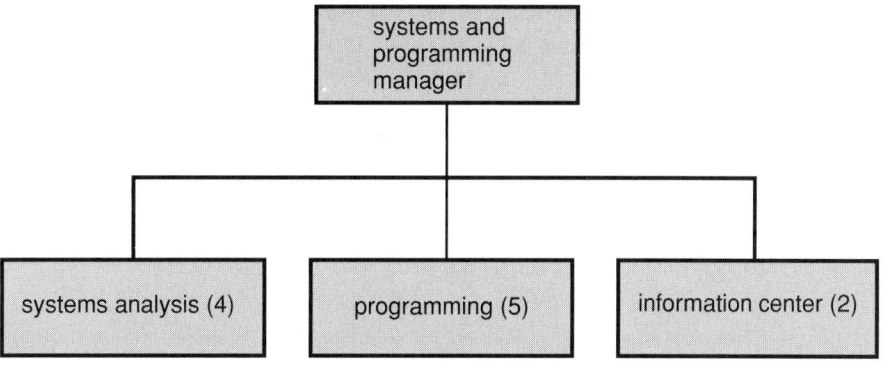

Figure 12.18 Computer operations

INFORMATION SYSTEMS –
MIL/AERO DIVISION

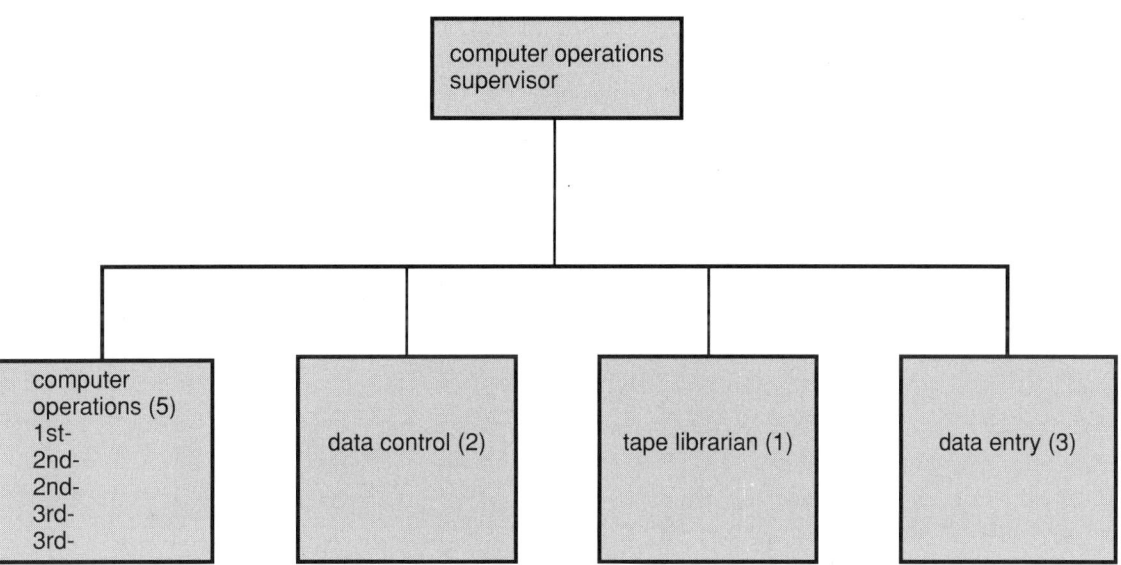

Figure 12.19 Information systems for the components division

INFORMATION SYSTEMS –
COMPONENTS DIVISION

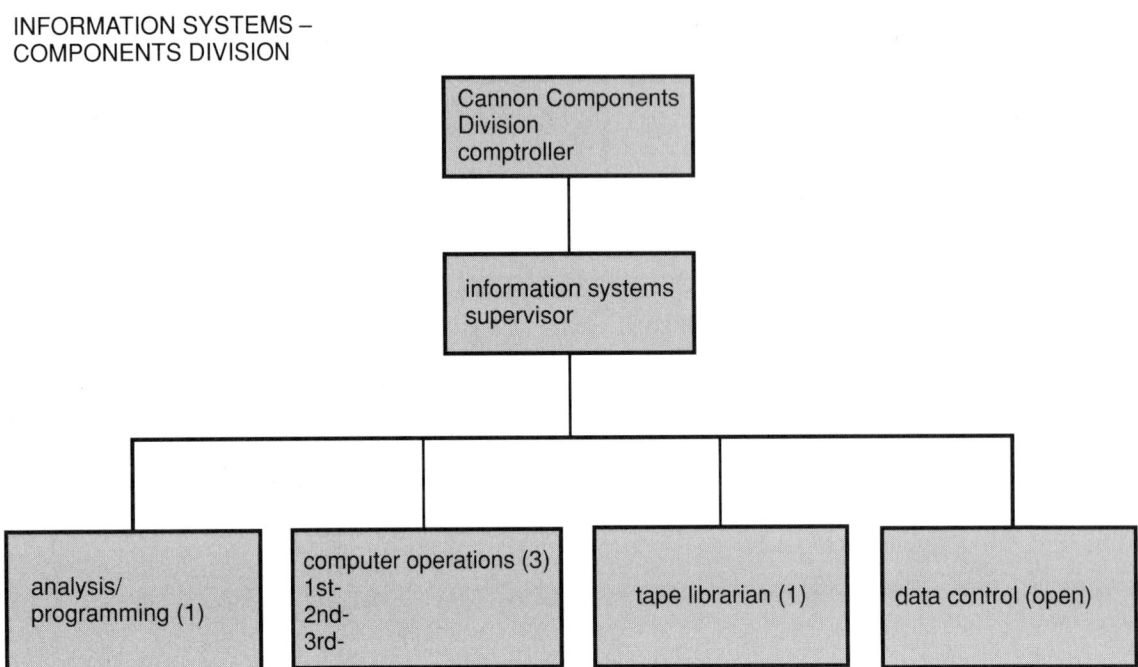

Figure 12.20 Comptroller organization

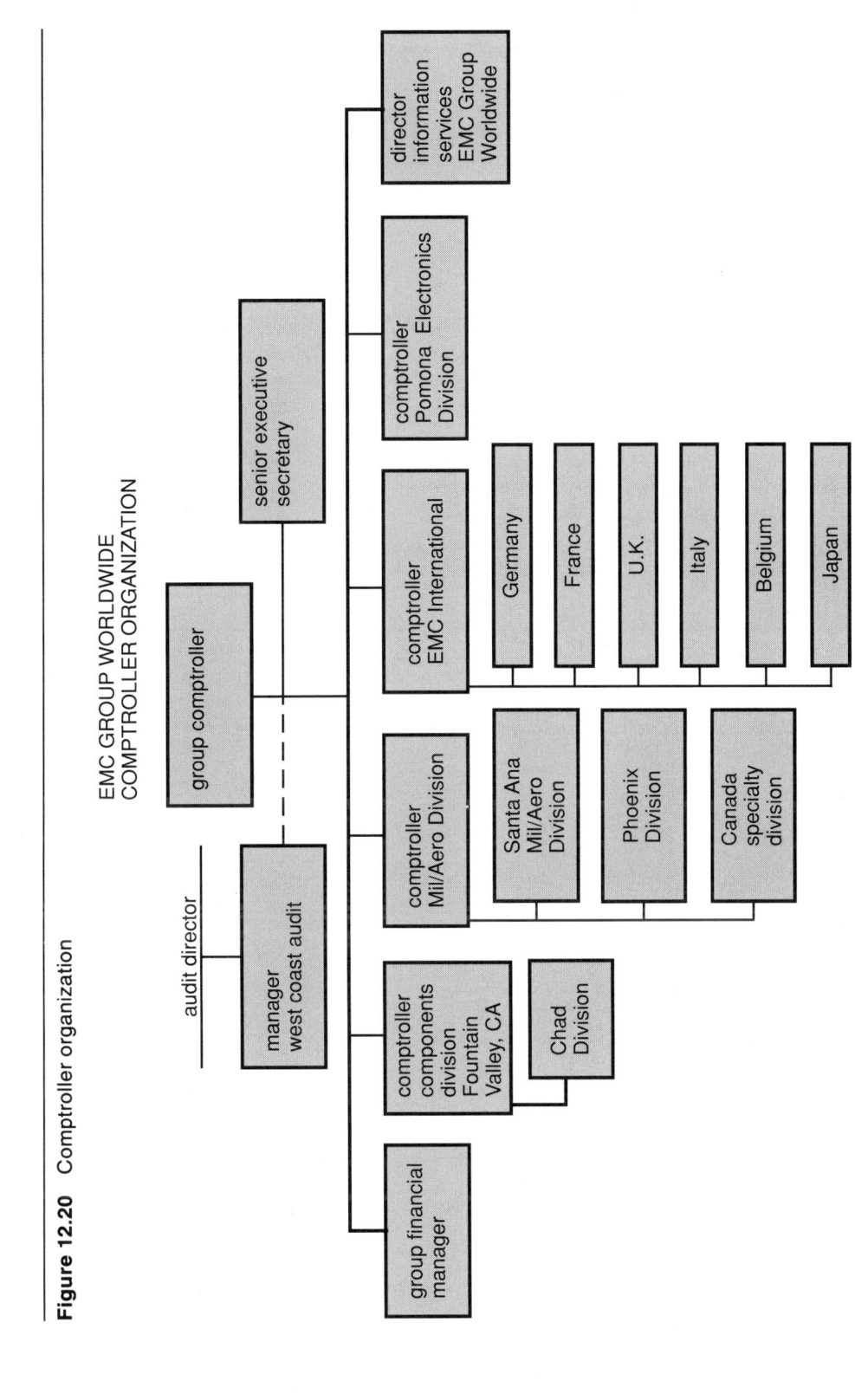

EMC GROUP WORLDWIDE
COMPTROLLER ORGANIZATION

group financial manager

comptroller components division Fountain Valley, CA

Chad Division

manager west coast audit

audit director

group comptroller

senior executive secretary

comptroller Mil/Aero Division

Santa Ana Mil/Aero Division

Phoenix Division

Canada specialty division

comptroller EMC International

Germany

France

U.K.

Italy

Belgium

Japan

comptroller Pomona Electronics Division

director information services EMC Group Worldwide

Figure 12.21 Information systems for EMC Group Worldwide

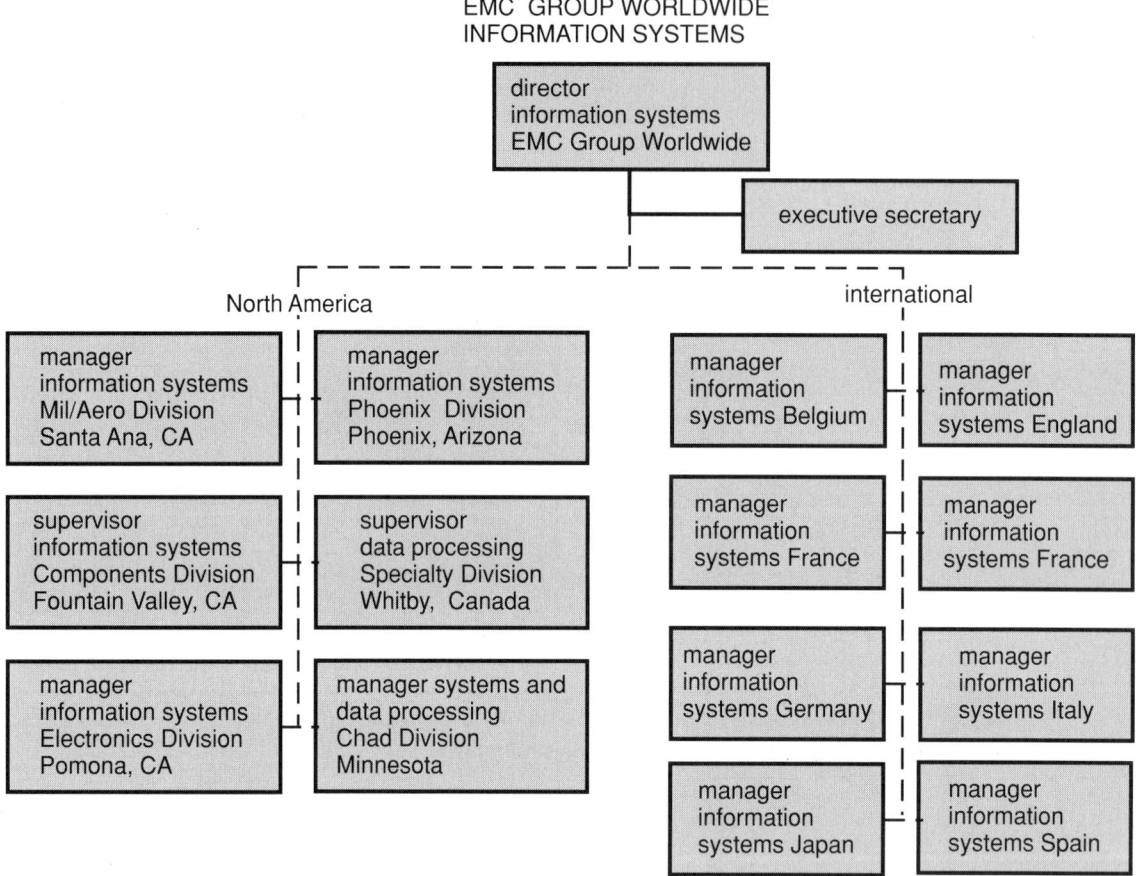

EMC GROUP WORLDWIDE
INFORMATION SYSTEMS

director
information systems
EMC Group Worldwide

executive secretary

North America

manager
information systems
Mil/Aero Division
Santa Ana, CA

manager
information systems
Phoenix Division
Phoenix, Arizona

supervisor
information systems
Components Division
Fountain Valley, CA

supervisor
data processing
Specialty Division
Whitby, Canada

manager
information systems
Electronics Division
Pomona, CA

manager systems and
data processing
Chad Division
Minnesota

international

manager
information
systems Belgium

manager
information
systems England

manager
information
systems France

manager
information
systems France

manager
information
systems Germany

manager
information
systems Italy

manager
information
systems Japan

manager
information
systems Spain

Figure 12.22 1992 year-end divisional statistics

1992 Year End Divisional Statistics

Division		Net Sales (in $,000)
Mil/Aero (M/A)		$ 111,485
Commercial (C/I)		37,253
Phoenix		32,192
Electronics		17,037
Total		$197,967

		Net Income (in $,000)
M/A		$ 2,249
C/I		(992) loss
Phoenix		1,856
Electronics		2,501
Total		$ 5,614

	Total No. Personnel	No. I.S. Personnel
M/A	1,450	32
C/I	172	7
Phoenix	302	6
Electronics	138	4
Total	2,062	49

* I.S. Budgets for each division approximates 2% of Sales.
**The Chad and Specialty divisions have similar profiles as that of the Electronics division; however, each has a stand-alone I.S. facility.

Chapter 13　*General Management, Users, and the Information System Function*

Appropriate organizing and skillful staffing of the information systems function are not the sole factors contributing to the success of information systems in an organization. Dedication of general management and appropriate involvement of users are equally important.

Management should foresee organizational needs, guide the information systems function accordingly, and control its progress. Users should understand pertinent systems, participate in development processes, and exert control over routine operations.

The previous chapter concentrated on the internal affairs of the information systems function. This chapter focuses on some aspects pertaining to general management and users of information systems.

Introduction

There is a short science fiction story that describes in detail how an unmanned bomber aircraft lands at a military airbase; there, computer-controlled machines fuel and prepare the bomber for its next mission. An automatic conveyer arms the aircraft with a nuclear bomb, the aircraft's automatic navigator is programmed to carry out the next task, and the bomber takes off. Only toward the end of the story does the reader realize that there are no human beings around. Civilization has been exterminated from earth long before by a doomsday system that continues to automatically manufacture and bombard the planet with nuclear bombs.

This story illustrates a system that does not serve any user, nor has it any management. The government (the management that ordered the system) did not foresee all the possible outcomes. The developers, therefore, did not devise the necessary controls. Consequently, the military forces (users) could not exert control over the system. Eventually the system outplayed its originators.

Similarly, information systems might turn out to be perfect, nonpurposeful machines if executives and users do not exert the power delegated to them by the organization. You may recall that we have frequently mentioned the important role of management and users throughout previous chapters. We stressed this point in relation to the system's trinity (ch. 4); information systems planning (ch. 8); system life cycle (ch. 9); and system development (ch. 10). This chapter collates and recapitulates many of the points already mentioned, and then arranges them more compactly. It also incorporates some new issues, mostly related to information system evaluation.

We use the terms "executives" and "*general management*" to signify the top-level management that assumes responsibility for the entire organization. We use the term "user(s)" to describe departmental units that directly use certain information systems. The term "*user management*" is, hence, the top-level management of a user department. The term "*information systems department (ISD) management*" stands for the top-level management of the information systems function.

It is important to note that these terms are conceptual and sometimes may refer to the same entity. For example, when a decision support system (DSS—see ch. 6) is developed for general management, users and executives coincide; when the ISD develops a programming aid to facilitate program debugging, user management and ISD management roles coincide. In most cases, however, the terms would probably correspond to separate entities.

We will now reexamine user roles in information systems planning, development, and operation.

The Role of Information System Users

The users of an information system are those organizational functions and individuals to whom the outputs of the system are directed. Users, even if they belong to the same department, are not necessarily a homogeneous group of individuals. There are various managerial levels (top, middle, low) and operating ranks. Each views the information system and its outcomes differently. For instance, an efficient computerized system that is supposed to save half the current manual labor may be highly appreciated by user management, yet detested by the lower ranks.

The set of pertinent information systems varies over time: there are existing systems, systems under development, and systems under conceptual planning. This implies that there are current users, future users, and potential users.

In most cases, we refer to user management. The level of management ascends as the horizon of planning widens. For example, long-range planning involves top user management; the design of a customer order form may require the involvement of a low-level manager; scheduling tomorrow's deliveries is settled with a senior clerk. In the same spirit, potential users take an important part in devising the information systems master plan (see ch. 8); they do not have anything to do with scheduling night shifts of keying operators.

We will now scan the planning and development process of information systems and designate users' roles.

Users' Contribution to Information System Planning

In chapters 8 and 9 we distinguished between overall planning of information systems in an organization and development of an individual system. Following the same distinction, this section discusses users' parts in corporate planning of information systems; the next section deals with users' involvement in the development of individual systems.

As you may recall (ch. 8), the overall planning process is composed of a hierarchy of plans. At the top stands the organizational strategy for information systems. At the next lower level is long-range planning (five to ten years ahead). The level below that refers to medium-range planning—i.e., the master plan (two to five years ahead). The bottom level is the operational plan for the coming period (usually an annual plan). Each planning level influences the subordinate plan; each level is constrained by directives imposed by a higher plan.

The disparate characteristics of each planning level call for different types of user involvement in each level. We will now elaborate on the various modes of involvement.

User Involvement in Strategic and Long-Range Information Planning
The two top levels of information systems planning are launched by corporate management. The plans do not designate specific projects, nor do they dictate exact schedules. Planning is confined to outlining long-range objectives and routes to achieve those objectives.

Although it is the general management that undertakes long-range planning, there is no doubt that user management has to affect the planning process by submitting its long-range requirements. Clearly, this should be handled by the top management of user departments. Very often these senior managers are inclined to undervalue the importance of this "obscure, nonobligatory rubbish called long-range planning." They overlook the fact that the systems they get this year are, in a way, a result of resources allocated due to prior long-range plans. Similarly, their inputs to the current planning process will benefit future development. Therefore, sloppy treatment of long-range plans at present might result in grief in the future.

When asked to submit inputs to long-range planning, user management examines two types of future needs. First, it considers the linkage between the user department and the entire organization under alternate scenarios delineating possible directions of the organization as a whole. This would help determine future requirements of data integration. Second, user management predicts the degree of additional computerization or enhancement of current computerized systems that will be required for various areas within the department. The latter type of need is affected by organizational progress as well as by internal developments.

For example, suppose the top management of the production division in a minicomputer manufacturing firm is asked to submit its long-range needs. The firm's general management indicates that a desired strategy is to expand operations to overseas markets (right now they operate only in North America). This implies that some production lines would be installed abroad in order to benefit from lower labor costs in certain countries. The implications for the division's information systems are quite obvious: they should be distributed rather than centralized; they should be closely tied to personnel files to enable better cost accounting. Unrelated to that, the division management deems the existing production management system outdated because it operates in a batch mode and does not provide prompt information. In addition to that, the division management would like to establish tighter connections between the production management information systems and the CAD/CAM systems. In conclusion, the production division management recommends the following:

1. The replacement of batch systems by online systems is a major goal in long-range planning.

2. The integration of personnel and production data is a requisite of overseas expansion plans.

3. The integration of managerial information systems and CAD/CAM systems is a primary long-term goal to establish computer integrated manufacturing (CIM).

Note that in the spirit of long-range planning, neither timetables nor specific projects appear in the recommendation list.

User Involvement in Master Plan Preparation

A master plan for information systems reflects medium-range planning with a horizon range of between two to five years (see ch. 8 on this subject). A master plan contains a list of projects (or areas of development) and some rough estimates of required resources, ranked by priority. Unlike annual operating plans, master plans do not get into details. The master plan is prepared by ISD management, reviewed by the information systems committee (see ch. 9 on this subject), and approved by general management.

User management participates mainly in two areas of master plan preparation. First, while the master plan is being constructed, user management submits input to those who sketch the plans. Second, while the master plan draft is being examined by the information systems committee, user management, by virtue of its membership in the committee, certainly contributes to shaping the final version.

Following the previous example (the production division in a minicomputer manufacturing firm), suppose it has been decided that a switchover to online information systems for production management is a major goal. The division management knows better than anyone else which particular system should be converted first, second, and so on. The priority is determined by the nature of the applications (e.g., prerequisite conditioning) and the severity of current problems. For example, if data capture is transformed to online mode first, then outputs become more updated even if they continue to be produced in a batch mode for a while; hence, an online data-capture system should be ranked higher than an online reporting system. Subsequently, the information systems committee reviews the master plan draft of the entire organization. At this stage, the production division representative wants to be sure of the following:

1. Production information systems are not deprived in comparison to other divisions' applications.

2. The divisional planning conforms to the overall direction of organizational planning.

3. Adequate and enhanced resources are allocated, and some other parties (e.g., general management) share the costs if the application required by the production division is a pioneering project for the ISD (e.g., the first online system to be installed or the first use of a DBMS).

In summary, user management undoubtedly has to consider the overall perspective of the entire organization. It is assumed, however, that overall interests are sufficiently preserved by general management. Therefore, the main role of user management is to keep an eye on the divisional interests because these might not be taken care of by anyone else.

User Involvement in Operating Plan Preparation

An operating plan specifies projects due for the coming period (usually a year), schedules development efforts, and allocates resources (see ch. 8 on this subject).

Users are wrong if they think that their role in this stage is just to submit detailed requirements to the ISD. In a way, submission of requirements is a commitment as well as a request because user management has to provide complementary resources of its own. For example, if a feasibility study is due next month, a senior officer of the user department is committed to participate and must be available. If a conversion from an old to a new system is due in the spring, the user should anticipate many interruptions during that period and be prepared to cope with them. Therefore, when user management prepares the requirements for the coming period, it should take into account the information needs as well as the available resources within the user department.

To follow our ongoing example, suppose the development of an online data-capture system is the hot issue during the coming period. The first two months will be dedicated to conducting a feasibility study. The production division management guarantees that a senior deputy will substitute for the production line manager for a couple of months so the manager can take part in the study. It must also make sure that no new products are scheduled to enter production during that period. Otherwise, it is likely that the production line manager will have to spend time resolving unexpected problems instead of collaborating in the study.

Some Concluding Remarks

Ein-Dor and Segev [11, ch. 7] specify some variables that are related to a user's contribution to the success or failure of MIS. The following variables pertain to information systems planning:

1. *User requirements* should be thoroughly identified and described.

2. The *rank* of user representatives should be adequate to the nature of the planning process; it should be high enough to enable a comprehensive view of departmental issues and to ensure pursuit of agreed upon plans.

3. The *motivation* of user management to pursue information systems matters should be high.

Table 13.1 Rank of User and Nature of User Requirements Involved in Information Systems Planning

Level of Planning	Rank of Participating User	Nature of User Requirements
Long range	Top user management	Very general; goals and directions
Medium range (master plan)	Top user management	List ranked by priority of areas to be dealt with
Short range (operating plan)	Senior officers (approval of top management is required)	Detailed list of projects, schedules, and allocation of resources

Table 13.1 relates these variables of rank and requirements to various levels of planning. It suggests that the longer the planning horizon, the higher the manager involved should be; the shorter the planning horizon, the more detailed the user requirements should be.

User Involvement in the Information System Life Cycle

Chapters 9 and 10 describe the information system life cycle, starting from initiation of a new system through all stages of development and operation until the system "passes away." While users take part in every activity of the life cycle, their role is sometimes more active (e.g., in the feasibility study) and sometimes more passive (e.g., in programming). We will now reexamine user involvement in the various life cycle activities.

User Role in Committees
Chapter 9 suggested that information systems be monitored by two committees: the information systems committee and the steering committee.

The information systems committee is a permanent body that devises the master plan and monitors its realization. Appropriate representation of top user management is essential to the effectiveness of this committee. (Since the committee is involved primarily in overall planning and monitoring, user roles in it have already been mentioned in the previous section, so there is no need to elaborate here.)

The steering committee is an ad hoc body formed to monitor the development of a particular system. It is important to have a senior officer of the user department take an active part in the committee's work. The user representative actually has two jobs: he or she monitors the development processes to be sure the system conforms to needs and requirements, but also promotes the embryonic system within the user department so that when the time comes for the system to be installed, its reception will be facilitated.

Practically, this would require that the user representative attend all committee meetings, review all the reports, and consider departmental aspects prior to making any decision that commits the department. In his or her backyard, the representative makes sure that related departmental decisions do not contradict future implications from the system under development, and that sufficient resources are allocated to support conversion and implementation when the need arises.

User Involvement in Preliminary Analysis and Feasibility Study

As you may recall, the preliminary analysis—when ideas are first discussed and presented to management or to the information systems committee—is the most informal stage in the system life cycle. Since the user is not always the initiator of new ideas, it is important to have the user endorse them, or at least agree to further analysis. Very seldom does an organization decide to develop an information system in spite of solid user objections. Note that from the user viewpoint, it is too early to reject a new idea at this stage because the in-depth inquiry is yet to begin and the system may later appear to be useful.

A more crucial stage is the feasibility study because its results will grant the project life or death. The feasibility study is carried out by an ad hoc team (see chs. 9 and 10) whose members represent users, general management, and the ISD.

The user representative should be an information advisor (see ch. 12) employed by the user department. If this function does not exist, a senior officer with appropriate background in information systems might do well. Note that active participation in a feasibility study is a full-time job; therefore, the user representative should be released from all other duties for the duration of the study.

User Involvement in System Development

A simple rule can be applied to user involvement in a development project: the deeper into technical details the development, the more moderate the involvement. However, the user never stops being involved since control and monitoring functions must be maintained.

In the information analysis stage, the user works closely with ISD personnel in order to specify requirements and desires. If the user employs an information advisor (see ch. 12), then the information requirements analysis rests completely in his or her hands. Otherwise, the analysis is pursued in collaboration with users and information analysts. In any event, the user takes a very active role at this stage.

When it comes to system design, the user role is reduced to approving proposed forms, output layouts, and working procedures. In the programming stage the user role further diminishes. However, all the way through, a user representative attends the meetings of the steering committee to monitor and control.

User Role in Implementation

The user role in conversion and implementation is of paramount importance; in fact, it becomes central. During preceding stages only a few employees of the user department really took an active part in the project. However, at the implementation stage many employees participate in testing, training, coding, verifying, or coordinating.

User management should be aware not only of the many interruptions that might occur during implementation—such as software malfunctions or wrong procedures—

but, above all, of resistance to change. It is essential that a senior officer of the user department take charge of the implementation and that some other user employees join the implementation team.

User Role During Normal Operations

In chapter 10, we mentioned that there are two different approaches to operations handling. One is that the user should assume full responsibility for normal operations, including data capture, job setup, output distribution, etc. The ISD in this case is only the provider and caretaker of data processing facilities. The other approach is that responsibility for operations should rest with the ISD, while the user is just a lay customer who submits input and receives final outputs. Note that the latter approach is not feasible in an environment based on deployment of online terminals at user departments; by definition, this setting requires high user responsibility.

Whatever the approach selected, several conditions should always be monitored by users, including the following items:

1. The quality of input data—User management should make sure that input forms are correctly filled out.

2. Timing—The user should prepare and submit data on time (even a perfect information system cannot produce output from nothing).

3. Advance notification of exceptional circumstances—Whenever the user thinks that a forthcoming event might affect information processing, advance notice should be given to the ISD. For example, many accounting systems generate an extra volume of transactions at the closing date of the annual balance sheet, due to clearing of transient accounts. This might require extra use of information processing equipment (keying in, computer time, printers). Advance notice may help the ISD with job scheduling during that period so the user will not get upset on the crucial days.

4. Constant watch over data validity—Although control mechanisms (hardware, software, and manual) are built into most information systems (see ch. 14), there is always a slight chance that a certain angle has not been completely covered—that a mistake could happen or a felony be committed. Because users are likely to be more familiar with the content of the data than ISD employees, they should constantly examine the outgoing results.

5. Formal handling of change requests—Every request for a change must be formally handed in to ISD through regular procedures. Impatient users may often consider this a nuisance, but in the long run they can only benefit from having a fully documented system. (See ch. 10 on the subject of change handling.)

6. Constant watch over system adequacy—As time passes, the system's performance might degenerate due to too many patches or the performance may simply not be adequate for increasing volumes of data. This may call for the initiation of a new system life cycle. Users should be able to foresee

needs for a new system long before an existing system collapses. They can use some simple indicators that do not require special expertise. For example, constant follow-up of some performance measures, such as elapsed time, file volumes, number of read/write operations, etc., may indicate whether the system is still in good shape. Similarly, significant changes in computing charges may be an initial alarm signal.

Outsourcing

An increasing number of organizations are having some of their IS requirements filled by outside vendors. This *outsourcing* of part or all of the IS developmental or operational functions is an important option to be considered.

The idea is not new, certainly. IS management has always been able to use service bureaus, facilities management firms, and providers of consulting and contract programming. What is new is the important role that outsourcing has acquired as a means of meeting market pressures and coping with rapid changes of technology [13].

Outsourcing really encompasses any service that is obtained from outside one's own organization. It includes buying application software in place of programming your own, or even accessing the data bases offered by *online service* companies. However, most of the issues about outsourcing relate to doing it on a much wider scale, by contracting to have an outside source provide at least a major portion of the equipment and personnel required to carry out the IS mission.

There are several possible benefits. Some benefits are economic ones derived from consolidating the IS activities of one organization with those of many others. Economy of scale no longer results from using large computers, but it is obtainable by making use of larger facilities and larger organizations. Many of the sources of outsourced services are very large companies that can more readily take advantage of the advances in hardware that offer greater benefits at lower cost. They can also afford to have all of the experts and specialists required to keep up with changes in technology. These larger firms can make a heavier investment in backup equipment, security provisions, and personnel training.

Other possible benefits are strategic ones. Management may feel that outsourcing the IS function enables their organization to better focus on its primary business objectives. Management might also decide that the only way to obtain access to a necessary technology or expertise is to go to an outside source.

On the other side of the coin there are potential losses. Perhaps the most obvious is the loss of some control [13]. An internal IS activity can be given as high a priority as management desires. If the activity is being performed by an outside vendor, that vendor's priorities will prevail.

There is also the possibility that IS loses its strategic importance within the organization. There is the danger of an "out of sight, out of mind" attitude developing in which the outsourced function becomes a routine with little thought given to new or innovative approaches to its role in enhancing productivity, competitiveness, or flexibility.

Outsourcing on a large scale may be at least temporarily disruptive. It means a shift of personnel, frequently with some of the IS staff being changed to employment by the vendor. This not only is a problem for those directly concerned, but may also cause morale problems for those employees who remain. Clearly, much advanced planning and preparation is required to deal with this kind of transition (see [19]).

The important role that outsourcing will continue to play is evidenced by the fact that it is predicted to result in a $50 billion industry by the mid 1990s [29]. The extent to which it will be considered by any particular organization will depend on a great many factors, but management must be aware of its possibilities. Dué [9] describes some steps to be taken to prepare for making the right decision if and when the time comes.

General Management and the Information System Function

General management may be a user of certain information systems, such as budget planning or macroeconomic forecasting. As an information user, its management duties do not differ from those of any other user, and thus have been covered in the previous section. In this section we address issues directly related to its managerial role.

Henry Fayol's definition of management functions, mentioned in chapter 5, includes planning, organizing, staffing, directing (coordinating), and controlling. The organizing and staffing aspects of the information systems function are discussed in chapter 12. Here we will elaborate on the planning, coordinating, and controlling functions. First, however, we will discuss the rank and location of the director of information systems.

Rank of the Information System Director

In every organization that maintains computerized information systems there is a certain point on the hierarchical ladder where a professional director of information systems reports to an executive who is not an expert in this area. For example, the ISD director (the ''professional'') may report to the controller (the ''nonprofessional''). This point of interaction is delicate. It is analogous to a sensitive electrical fuse that can easily be short-circuited.

In part, this is because of a behavioral pattern of information systems professionals. Ein-Dor and Segev describe it this way [11, p. 152]:

> Computer technicians form a separate subculture that has its own extensive and incomprehensible vocabulary and jargon, a subculture which delights in technical sophistication and tends to prefer complex to simple solutions.

Robert Townsend, former chairman of the board of Avis is even more blunt:

> Most of the computer technicians that you're likely to meet or hire are complicators, not simplifiers. They're trying to make it look tough, not easy. They're building a mystique, a priesthood, their own mumbo-jumbo ritual to keep you from knowing what they—and you—are doing [27, p. 36].

These descriptions may exaggerate. Even so, they clearly illustrate a communication problem. Of course management, afraid of revealing its ignorance, has often left the floor to computer professionals and not exercised any control over their products.

Ackoff [1] wrote a lively discussion on this subject. That was quite a number of years ago, but the problem still exists and sometimes underlies a move toward outsourcing (see [23]).

But rather than trying to allocate blame, we should try to prevent recurrences of past mistakes. This can be done if we accept two important rules:

1. Management can exercise control over information systems even if the responsible executive is a layperson in the area.

2. Computer professionals can establish communication channels to top management if ISD top management is close enough in rank to general management.

We will elaborate on the second rule. The first rule is discussed in the sections that follow.

It is extremely important that the managing director of the ISD (often called the CIO or chief information officer [21]) be close enough to the level where overall organizational strategic decisions are being made so that he or she can present professional aspects that might affect forthcoming decisions before they are made.

For example, suppose that, due to tight market conditions, general management decides to adopt a more rigorous pricing policy based on cost accounting for each marketed product. This decision would necessitate development of a costing information system, which would be based on integrated data taken from production, procurement, personnel, cashflow, and general ledger applications. The ISD director who participates in management meetings can point out that it takes ten months to develop the desired system. He or she can then suggest an interim solution that is eventually accepted. Meanwhile, being exposed to the severity of the problem, the director pushes the development team hard so the system is ready in eight months. Everyone is satisfied. If the ISD director were far down in the organizational hierarchy, the decision to incorporate rigorous costing in pricing policy would have been made without his or her presence. The ISD director would be summoned to hear the decision a few hours later, and only then could mention the ten-month development period. General management would be upset and feel that ISD was trying to undermine management policy; the interim solution would be devised under protest, and the credibility of the ISD would be shattered.

In summary, it is vital to have the information systems director report directly to a senior executive. This is especially important when the development of systems for medium- and high-level management (MIS) is in the offing. Ein-Dor and Segev [11] suggest that two hierarchical levels allow reasonable "distance" between the top executive and the individual in charge of information systems.

Location of the Responsible Executive

Granting a decent rank to the person in charge of information systems is only a partial solution to the communication problem because the problem may have another angle—the orientation of the ISD. Historically, most ISDs were established within functional units whose demand for transaction processing had outgrown their manual capacity to handle the data. That explains why frequently an ISD reports to the executive in charge of bookkeeping (controller). This convenient "fostering" environment is satisfactory during the ISD infancy, but it may prove to be limiting once the use of information systems reaches maturity. The fostering functional unit tends to influence the orientation of the ISD toward its immediate needs by assigning lower priority to the applications of other functions. An ISD director would also tend to satisfy his or her boss (the functional unit director) at the expense of the requirements of others.

A mature ISD should become an independent unit within the organization and report directly to a senior executive at the general-management level. The professional director of the ISD can then be a vice-president, or at least report directly to a vice-president who is, perhaps, in charge of information, planning, and operations research.

The placement of the CIO is no less important when some or all of the IS function has been outsourced. The focus of attention of this executive will change, to be sure. In place of planning for equipment, software, and personnel, the CIO's responsibilities shift to the selection of vendors, management of contracts, and monitoring of performance of the outsourced services. He or she must have no smaller role in assuring that the organization's IS requirements are met, and that the strategic importance of IS continues to be considered even though it may be less visible.

Management Role in Information System Planning

General management plays a leading role in strategic planning, a very active role in long-range planning, and must approve medium- and short-range planning.

General management has to set objectives for information systems strategy in the same manner that it is supposed to direct any other organizational activity. For example, suppose the management of a regional manufacturing business wishes to expand its activities nationwide. The objectives set for the production division involve planning distributed production; the objectives set for the marketing division probably involve the buildup of a national sales network. Similarly, the information systems function will have to consider distributed information systems (see ch. 11) as part of its long-range planning.

Long-range planning involves a horizon of five to ten years and indicates, in general, the areas to be emphasized and the resources required. The initial draft is prepared by top management of the function(s) concerned, but the final version is prepared by general management. As in the nationwide expansion example, the information systems function would prepare an initial draft portraying alternative information systems deployment—e.g., distributed computing facilities versus a central, powerful computer site connected to many front-end terminals. Organizational and economic implications of each alternative are an important part of the initial draft. General management would discuss the draft, perhaps reiterate the planning process, and end up with a long-range plan.

The long-range plan stimulates preparation of a master plan that describes the projects to be developed, their priorities, and the implications concerning personnel, capital investment, and operating cost for a period ranging from two to five years. The master plan is prepared by top ISD management in collaboration with the information systems committee (see ch. 9). Again, formal approval of general management is required to authorize the plan.

The same process repeats itself for the short-range planning. However, the short-range plan is much more detailed, particularly with respect to budget considerations. Often such a plan is not submitted to general management but is finalized with the information systems committee.

In summary, the broader the range of planning, the more active the role of general management; the shorter the range of planning, the more power delegated to individual executives, directors, and subcommittees.

The Coordinating Role of General Management

Users are not always eager to have new information systems for their departments (see ch. 2 on the subject of resistance to change). Information systems professionals might also be reluctant to devise new systems, particularly when a certain application is not challenging. General management is often the only group that comprehends the overall direction of the organization and understands the long-range consequences of installing or abandoning certain information systems. Also, general management has the power to impose decisions and pursue matters believed to be essential.

General management can exercise its power in several ways:

1. Direct orders—e.g., written policy, written plans, oral instructions, etc.

2. Indirect coordination by means of resource allocation (budget).

3. Indirect coordination by means of incentives to collaborate. For instance, a development team is rewarded if a new information system is completed before its due date; accounts receivable clerks get an extra bonus if they can cope with an increased volume of transactions without additional personnel after a computerized system is installed.

Even if general management handles planning and development tactics appropriately, routine activities may still raise a lot of coordination problems. Remember that information systems professionals and users constitute different subcultures. While both parties may be devoted to their duties, frequent conflicts are almost unavoidable. These difficulties are usually settled at low- or middle-level management, yet if the conflicts should increase, a senior executive may have to step in. This is not to say that the president of a company has to arbitrate between a programmer and an accounts receivable clerk. But if conflicts become a daily habit, it indicates that policies and working procedures should be examined. General management should appoint someone (if necessary, an external consultant) to study the problem and suggest remedies.

Managerial Control over the Information System Function

General management should not get involved in the details of information systems. To do so would get in the way of its mission, which is to lead the entire organization. Also, senior executives who do not specialize in information systems may be embarrassed because they find it difficult to understand the details. Information systems professionals might interpret detailed inquiries as a lack of confidence in what they are doing. General management need only understand the implications of various technical characteristics on the organization: for instance, how the installation of interactive terminals affects response time in certain activities. If management finds it necessary to learn the details of a certain case, it can get them indirectly by appointing an EDP auditor, by hiring a consultant, or by employing a permanent information advisor in the head office.

General management control over the ISD can be maintained by examination of several apparent indicators that reflect the quality of the information systems function.

Indicators Reflecting the Quality of Information Systems Management

Suppose you employ a nanny who takes care of your children while you are at work. Certainly you are concerned with the quality of treatment your children are getting while you are away from home. Nevertheless, because you cannot observe the nanny during working hours, you look for some representative indicators that can be easily observed. For example, are the children clean? Do they eat enough and on time? Do they behave well? Do they complain?

Similarly, if you are an executive whose responsibilities include information systems, yet you are not the direct manager of the ISD and cannot spend most of your time scrutinizing it, you must adopt some representative indicators that will help you assess the overall quality and performance of the ISD. We list here some characteristics that might be of assistance.

1. *"Law and order"*—This somewhat obscure indicator refers to the way the ISD is administered. For instance, follow the development cycle of certain projects to check whether development teams report upon reaching predetermined milestones (see ch. 9). Examine the documentation produced upon completion of various life cycle activities to see whether standards are met. Glance at various reports (e.g., an information analysis report of a system under development) to see how they look; visit the computer room to check on whether the operators possess written, updated procedures. If you maintain this kind of probe on a random, yet frequent enough basis, and from time to time you look into the progress of a specific project (see ch. 10 on the subject of evaluating the quality of a development project), you will get a feeling of how your subordinates run the information systems shop.

2. *Users' satisfaction*—Talk to users in managerial and operational ranks and listen to what they say. They will probably not spell out explicit, blunt grievances unless the situation is really gloomy, but you will sense the atmosphere. Just remember that users' bad moods do not necessarily mean that the performance of the ISD is weak, particularly during the infancy of information systems (see ch. 2 on the subject of resistance to change). However, if experienced users complain about mature systems, the situation calls for further attention (see Streeter [26] and Ein-Dor and Segev [11, p. 157–58] for a discussion of *computer-dependent workers*).

3. *Personnel utilization*—In chapter 9 we indicated that the nature of information systems development is such that individuals are involved intermittently along the project's life cycle. This fact introduces slack into staffing plans. Moreover, if the organizational structure of an ISD is applicational (see ch. 12), certain teams may have peak work loads while other teams can go fishing. These phenomena are natural, so long as they do not recur often or last long. If they become an ongoing syndrome, then something is wrong.

4. *Productivity*—The overall productivity of an ISD is not difficult to determine. You just count the number of new projects developed in a period of time, say a year, and the number of existing systems maintained by the ISD and compare those to the number of professional employees to see whether the figures make any sense. This is obviously a rough assessment since it ignores the quality of the systems produced and the complexity of the projects. But examining these figures may reveal something. For example, in a real case that we know of, a consultant was called in to investigate a large ISD (two hundred employees, one hundred of whom were professional analysts, designers, and programmers) that had failed to satisfy both general management and users. A quick inquiry revealed that the department had produced only three or four new major systems during the previous year. This led to a more thorough survey, which found that 90 percent of the professional personnel were permanently involved in maintenance-type jobs, such as change inserts, reprogramming of certain routines, debugging of old programs, and reformatting reports and source documents. The underlying reasons for the problem rested in poor handling of life cycle practices and in poor documentation. Productivity was not the real problem, but examining it led to the disease causing the symptoms.

5. *Equipment utilization*—General management frequently encounters demands to upgrade information processing equipment or to have it replaced with machinery of more advanced technology. This normally involves significant capital investment, and therefore necessitates thorough scrutiny prior to any major decision.

The following checklist should be part of the scrutiny.

- Has the ISD exploited the option of using extra shifts?

- Does ISD management attempt to level work-load peaks by establishing a discriminating pricing policy? This could involve discounts to nonurgent requests, favoring jobs left overnight, encouraging efficient programming by overcharging jobs that consume large memory size (see discussion on pricing later in this chapter).

- Are there routine scrutinies into the necessity of various reporting requirements, or do many printouts find their way directly to neighborhood nursery schools where children draw on their backside? (A bold move could be to suspend the production of suspect reports and wait until someone complains. If nobody does, you have saved a little.)

- Has ISD management encouraged redesign and/or reprogramming of some critical applications suspected of being inefficiently devised in the first place?

- Often applications were developed under time pressure and/or while equipment capacity was not restricted. Redesign may significantly reduce resource consumption.

- Is it possible that a certain resource is the sole bottleneck of the entire configuration? For example, perhaps acquisition of an additional line printer will do away with the bottleneck.

- Maybe the overload is temporary or has been caused by atypical requirements that do not merit the cost of changes. If so, you should consider the use of service-bureau facilities instead of a major acquisition.

We are not advocating turning down requests to upgrade equipment nor are we claiming that information processing equipment should always be 100 percent utilized. On the contrary, every computer installation must contain some slack in order to cope with peaks and to meet unforeseen demands. A computer that works twenty-four hours a day, seven days a week, without having any components idle, should probably be augmented. We are recommending that executives be sure that requests for upgrading are not given only perfunctory examination (for an extensive discussion on performance evaluation of computer systems, see Borovits and Neumann [8], Ahituv and Igbaria [4], and Kant [15]).

Indicators of Management Quality—An Overview

The list of indicators is typical of any evaluation problem where high-level managers are judged. The indicators are not quantitative; they are not linked to rigorous measurement; they are based on subjective judgment and intuition to some extent. The manager's performance, similarly, is not quantitative; it cannot be measured by short-term outcomes and it involves decisions based on subjective judgment.

Note also that the indicators are not independent of each other; they may overlap. For example, lack of "law and order" and low productivity may very well be interpreted as a cause-and-effect phenomenon. Nevertheless, if an ISD is poorly managed, it does not really matter which is the hen and which is the egg; appropriate measures have to be taken anyway.

Table 13.2 summarizes the direction of the indication provided by the various indicators with respect to the quality of ISD management.

General Management and Information Systems Policy Issues

Conventionally, general management should not intervene in routine decisions and regular activities of the information systems function. General management pursues its interests by means of the following measures:

Setting clear objectives and monitoring long- and medium-range planning (the planning function)

Deciding on organization of the information systems function (the organizing function)

Table 13.2   Indicators Reflecting the Quality of ISD Management

Indicator	Indication of Proper Management	Indication of Poor Management
"Law and order"	Kept	Loose
Users' satisfaction	High to medium	Low to nonexisting
Personnel utilization	Efficient, balanced	Inefficient, unbalanced
Productivity	High	Low
Equipment utilization	Moderate, with reasonable slack times	Extremely high or extremely idle

Appointing competent persons to senior positions in the information systems
  function (the staffing function)

Coordinating users and information systems (the directing function)

Establishing appropriate control mechanisms (see ch. 14)—e.g., EDP auditing,
  information systems committee, periodical reviews (the control function)

A few other issues require policy promulgation by general management or by
senior executives. Those issues have a common denominator: money. They all involve
significant monetary commitments (e.g., computer acquisition) or financial policy (e.g.,
internal pricing for computing services). We will now review a potpourri of such topics.
(For an elaborate discussion on information systems policy, see ch. 7.)

Cost/Benefit Analysis

We have repeatedly emphasized the importance of employing economic criteria in
information systems planning and development. Chapter 12 assigned the practical task
of economic evaluation of information systems to a planning/budget/control unit. On
the other hand, chapter 3 stressed the theoretical and practical difficulties involved in
assessing costs and (particularly) benefits of information, which raises two questions.
First, if the difficulties are so great, how can cost/benefit analysis be performed?
Second, why should general management be concerned with this?

To answer the first question, we will present a practical approach to cost/benefit
analysis. The answer to the second question is straightforward: cost/benefit analysis of
information systems is still virgin territory, without theoretical and practical foundations. The results of analyses are highly sensitive to initial assumptions and might
depend on the method chosen and the technicalities of the calculations performed.
Therefore, we do not suggest that executives perform the analysis, but we do recommend that they understand it thoroughly, and sometimes even get into details. An
extensive discussion of the subject is found in King and Schrems' survey paper [17];
a theoretical framework is provided in [2].

Steps of Cost/Benefit Analysis

Cost/benefit analysis of an information system serves either as a planning tool to evaluate proposed alternatives or as an auditing tool to carry out a postaudit of existing systems (see ch. 10). In both cases, the analysis involves the following steps:

1. *Selecting an analyst*—Potential sources of an analyst (or a team) can be found either in-house, if the organization is large enough to employ such persons (e.g., in the planning/budget/control unit), or externally (i.e., hiring a consultant). A local analyst may have a better starting point due to his or her better grasp of the particular organization. An external consultant may be more experienced in methods and techniques, and, conceivably, more objective, yet more expensive.

2. *Identifying alternatives*—The analyst, in collaboration with other appropriate individuals, specifies the objectives of the desired system and roughly sketches a few alternative ways to obtain them. Alternatives that appear to be acceptable are further elaborated. (Obviously this step is bypassed if the situation is a postaudit.)

3. *Identifying the factors contributing to costs and benefits*—The analyst identifies all the elements constituting the cost and all the outcomes considered to be benefits. For example, computer time is always a cost factor; programming effort is a cost factor in projects where the software is developed in-house; reduction in inventory levels is a benefit gained from a new warehouse information system. Note that at this stage, no measurement is being done; in fact, it is not yet known whether all the identified factors are measurable. The prime purpose of the step is to collect all the pertinent factors (we will elaborate on cost and benefit attributes later).

4. *Devising measurement criteria*—The analyst decides how to measure each factor. This appears to be relatively easy with respect to costs (measured in dollar terms); however, it might be a severe problem when benefits are considered (see ch. 3). Maintaining consistency of measurement units and time horizon is important. For example, if the life cycle of one alternative is expected to be five years, and another alternative will be intact for eight years, the analysis must reconcile the difference. We will elaborate on measurement problems later.

5. *Measuring costs and benefits*—Once the measurement criteria are resolved, the analyst estimates the costs and benefits associated with each alternative. In a postaudit, the system's costs and benefits can be measured or assessed from accumulated data; in a before-the-fact analysis, they have to be estimated. In fact, this stage is mainly a combination of collected data and intelligent judgment.

6. *Calculating cost/benefit values*—The analyst consolidates the cost and the benefit figures to get net cash flow figures for each alternative, then introduces the time element by employing a discount factor.

Table 13.3 Dollar Costs and Benefits of Two Alternatives—an Example

Year	Alternative A			Alternative B		
	Benefits $	Costs $	Net Flow $	Benefits $	Costs $	Net Flow $
0	0	10,000	−10,000	5,000	15,000	−10,000
1	10,000	10,000	0	8,000	500	7,500
2	12,000	500	11,500	8,000	500	7,500
3	12,000	800	11,200	8,000	800	7,200

7. *Comparative analysis*—The analyst selects criteria by which several alternatives can be compared; for instance, net present value and return on investment are very common criteria. Then he or she substitutes the figures previously obtained into the formulas derived from the chosen criterion to get the "bottom line." The results, together with narrative explanation and reference to intangible aspects, are presented to management.

Later we will elaborate on the more difficult problem of identifying and measuring cost and benefit attributes. At this point, let us illustrate the computational portion of the analysis with an example.

Suppose an organization considers two alternate information systems (table 13.3). Alternative A reflects an in-house development of software. This incurs most costs during a longer development period, but is better tailored to organizational needs and therefore provides higher benefits. Alternative B proposes to purchase a ready-made software package, which is less costly; however, the price is a lump sum that has to be paid immediately and the benefits are lower. Both alternatives will last for four years. (Remember that after a while, the benefits become stable but the costs increase toward the end due to increasing maintenance problems—see fig. 9.1 in ch. 9.)

The analyst has decided to exercise the criterion of net present value for purposes of comparison. The controller suggests that 8 percent is an adequate discount rate, hence the net present value (PV) is calculated using the following formula:

$$PV = \sum_{t=0}^{3} \frac{\text{net flow}}{(1+0.08)^t}$$

The resulting figures are $8,750 for alternative A and $9,090 for alternative B. Note that this calculation is somewhat simplistic because in reality the inflows and outflows of cash are distributed over the year, whereas here it is assumed that they occur at the beginning of each year.

In addition to the monetary figures, the analyst lists the intangible benefits (and disadvantages) of each alternative. For example, the ready-made package has probably been better tested due to its widespread use. On the other hand, the company will need maintenance services provided by an external software house, whose priorities do not always concur with those of the organization.

This example also illustrates the sensitivity of the analysis. The difference between the bottom lines of the two alternatives is relatively small in proportion to the absolute figures involved. Minor modifications in cashflow estimates or discount rates could reverse the results. This reaffirms the point that top management should be aware of the details of cost/benefit analysis.

Identification and Measurement Problems

Selecting comparison criteria and performing numerical calculations are the easier part of cost/benefit analysis. The harder part is identifying all the elements that constitute cost and benefit and determining how to measure or estimate them.

The difficulty lies in two areas. First, when proposals are to be evaluated, one has to predict costs and benefits that will occur after certain circumstances have been altered due to the introduction of the new system (not to mention inflation and other exogenous factors). Second, not all the elements are expressed in or are transformable to monetary values.

Cost approximation is regarded as simpler than benefit approximation because only the first of the difficulties holds. King and Schrems [17, p. 24] list some typical cost factors, grouped into the following major categories:

1. *Procurement costs* (e.g., equipment purchase)
2. *Start-up costs* (e.g., personnel searches and hiring activities)
3. *Project-related costs* (e.g., software development, training)
4. *Ongoing costs* (e.g., rental, depreciation)

The first three cost categories may be treated as capital investment (though not necessarily in a single lump sum) or as nonrecurrent expenditures. The last category belongs to operational cost accounts. The main problems are (1) to make sure that the cost list is, indeed, exhaustive; (2) to avoid redundancy (e.g., do not include both computer rental fees and charges for CPU time in ongoing costs); and (3) to figure out proper estimates of future expenditures. If these are resolved, the numerical calculations are simple. In short, the major obstacle facing cost assessment is the identification; measurement is normally straightforward.

Unlike costs, the benefit side of the analysis poses severe measurement problems in addition to the identification problems. In chapter 3 we classified benefits into three categories:

1. Tangible monetary benefits
2. Tangible nonmonetary benefits
3. Intangible benefits

Tangible monetary benefits do not present any problem that is additional to those mentioned in relation to cost. For example, suppose you consider installing an information system to assist in portfolio management and you expect that the use of the system will increase the annual yield. If the increase can be assessed and compared to the system's cost, you can easily obtain the profit (or loss) margin due to installation of the new system.

The second category (i.e., tangible nonmonetary benefits) can be subdivided into two—*transformable into monetary* terms and *nontransformable into monetary* terms. For example, suppose a new inventory management system will reduce the level of certain inventory items. The reduction in quantities implies less storage space utilization, less money invested in inventory, and perhaps fewer personnel to deal with reordering, counting, paperwork, and distribution. This may also result in lower frequency of special deliveries (with fewer shipments, less truck utilization, less gas consumption, less overtime pay, etc.). Once all the pertinent factors have been identified and quantitatively assessed, the transformation to monetary equivalences is not difficult. The procedure then continues in the manner applied to monetary benefits.

Nontransformables create a severe problem. Such intangible benefits are often the most important in public services. For example, suppose a computerized dispatching system for an ambulance service is considered and it has been proven that response time to calls will be improved by six minutes per call on the average. According to known statistics, this may save the lives of 28.6 people a year (on the average, of course). A more sophisticated system would probably save the lives of 39.1 people, but its cost is twice that of the inferior alternative. Granted that you have quantified all the tangible benefits, but could you calculate cost/benefit in this case? If not, then the tangible benefits should be treated in the same way we treat intangibles (more later). Still, it is better to provide decision makers with tangibles as much as possible.

The problem of how to handle *intangible* or tangible nontransformable benefits is not so difficult so long as the monetary analysis results in positive figures (i.e., net profit). In such cases the nonmonetary benefits are the icing on the cake and can only reaffirm the profitability of the project. That is not the case if the monetary analysis provides negative results or if several alternatives significantly differ in both monetary terms and intangibles. For example, two alternative dispatching systems differ in the operational costs of ambulances and personnel (monetary benefits), in the average response time they promise (tangible yet nontransformable to money), and in the information they provide for long-range planning of ambulance services (intangible). A consolidated comparison is not possible because the various attributes are incomparable. All you can do is provide decision makers with the relevant data. They will have to assess whether a certain difference in dollar terms justifies certain marginal benefits. (For example, does the saving of 10.5 lives per year merit spending $78,322 more? What is the political worth of human life?)

Value Analysis

Keen has proposed [16] an evaluation technique that he terms *value analysis*. It is similar to cost/benefit analysis, but with some important differences. First, the emphasis in value analysis is on benefits, based on the assumption that these are of primary interest to decision makers and that computing cost/benefit ratios is unnecessary if the benefits meet some threshold and the costs are within some acceptable limits. Second, the method attempts to reduce risk by requiring prototyping as part of the evaluation process; prototyping is assumed to be a relatively inexpensive way to obtain relatively accurate evaluation data.

While value analysis is more applicable to the evaluation of a DSS development project (see ch. 9), it may be used to evaluate any type of information system. The technique entails four steps.

1. Establish the operational list of benefits that the system must achieve to be acceptable.
2. Establish the maximum cost that one is willing to pay to achieve the benefits.
3. Develop a prototype of the system.
4. Assess the benefits and the cost.

The advantages of value analysis are that it is simple, is integrated with an installation approach (prototyping), and seems very close to the intuitive approach that many managers use to evaluate an information system. The main disadvantages are that it is a limited form of evaluation, which may not include all the measures that are relevant, and that it is a much less rigorous method than the cost/benefit technique.

Note that the value analysis is basically an evaluation technique that starts with users and/or management establishing the values (benefits) they expect to get from the system.

A Final Remark

The problems of cost/benefit analysis are profound. The concept is rooted in still-debated theories (e.g., multiattribute utility theory), imperfect methodologies (e.g., what is the discount rate pertaining to capital investments?), and technical difficulties of estimation and measurement (e.g., what is the cost of writing a 1,000 line COBOL program?). In spite of the problems, some sort of cost/benefit analysis must be done for every information system undergoing a development or an audit process. There is no universal (magic) formula dictating how to do that. (King and Schrems [17] provide an adequate starting point, though.) You will always have to use your judgment and to customize known techniques to suit the specific case under analysis.

Financing Methods for Computer Acquisition

The discussion that follows refers to any acquisition of information processing components, be it hardware equipment or software products. However, since the acquisition of an organization's main computing equipment usually involves large expenditures, we prefer to put the common term "computer acquisition" in the title of this section. Nevertheless, the following discussion can theoretically be generalized to apply to any acquisition of hardware/software components.

We emphasize *theoretically* because with the current proliferation of hardware and software products and vendors, not all financing options are necessarily applicable. On the hardware side, there are big mainframe computers, mini- and microcomputers, high- and low-priced printers and storage devices, and the like. The financing options that are available for high-priced equipment may not exist for low-priced equipment. For instance, many microcomputers and peripheral devices are sold only and never rented or leased.

On the software side, there are again high-priced products (e.g., a complex CAD/CAM software package) and low-priced products (e.g., PC word processors). Also, there is a multitude of vendors, ranging from IBM to a one-person software house. Again, some products are sold only, while others can be rented or leased. To complicate the picture even further, software, unlike hardware (unless a user manufactures his own computer), can be developed in-house or acquired from an external supplier.

Therefore, this section attends to situations where hardware/software products enjoy several financing options. This is the case with most large and minicomputer mainframes and many large mainframe-oriented software products (e.g., DBMSs). The next section will attend to software issues—make or buy—and software selection considerations.

The large amount of money usually required for computer acquisition warrants active involvement of general management. But money is not the only thing at stake in choosing a computer. There are implications regarding information systems strategy, and the flexibility to change strategy should it be desired. Were it not for such implications, the issue of financing computer acquisition boils down merely to considerations that are well covered in introductory finance textbooks (e.g., the acquiring firm's cost of capital, cashflows, tax advantages).

We will review options pertaining to financing computer acquisition and discuss the monetary and organizational aspects of each option. (See also related discussions [3, 10].) We will present a comparative analysis of various options.

Purchase

The list price of a piece of equipment is not the only *purchase* cost. The vendor will probably mention shipment cost (if applicable), but you have to take into account insurance and maintenance costs as well. These services are usually provided by the vendor, but are not free. (We assume that installation costs, such as construction, air conditioning, special electrical attachments, etc., are similar for every acquisition option, so we omit them from the discussion.)

In return for your money, you get a computer that is yours forever, to use as long as you wish. It might even carry a residual value should you find a buyer at the end of its economic life cycle. (The end of the equipment life cycle in your organization does not necessarily mean that someone else would not find it useful. Thus, we distinguish between *economic life cycle*—duration of profitable use for a particular organization—and *physical life cycle*—how long the equipment can reliably operate.) On the other hand, it might happen that you need a new computer because your volume of data processing rises sharply or information requirements become much more sophisticated, but you cannot find a buyer for your outdated computer because technology has advanced rapidly; so you are stuck with an old, inefficient computer that has not recovered its initial cost.

Rental

If you acquire a computer through *rental*, you can return or replace it whenever you wish.

Some vendors charge fixed monthly rental fees without regard to the amount of time the equipment is used. Others charge a basic fee for a certain number of hours of use and an additional fee for overtime. A maintenance fee is normally included in the rental payment; however, some vendors specify this separately. We label as *pure rent* the net figure representing total rental minus maintenance fee.

The vendor may, of course, modify rental fees at times, and this introduces some uncertainty to profitability evaluation. On the other hand, risk is reduced because the customer is free to return or replace the equipment should it be found unsatisfactory or not economical. Of course, once they are installed and are being used widely, computers cannot be returned in the twinkling of an eye. Conversion to another computer has to be planned and might become very complex, particularly when the replacement is acquired from a different manufacturer. Renting does not completely release you from commitment to use a certain computer, it only reduces the extent of the commitment. Renting is also a way to defer expenditures over time.

Lease

Computers can also be obtained with a *lease*—i.e., the customer pays a series of monthly payments at the end of which the computer can be either returned or purchased for a predetermined sum of money. While not every vendor offers a lease option, almost any computer can be obtained through a third party whose business is purchasing computers from manufacturers and leasing them.

The lease option incorporates some of the advantages of both purchase and rental. Yet, if you lease from a third party, you have to carefully examine the terms of the contract in order to make sure that you get the same level of services that you would have gotten had you acquired the computer from the original vendor.

Purchase Option

Some vendors offer an arrangement that is similar to, but not exactly like, leasing. According to this arrangement, labeled *purchase option*, the customer rents the computer and may decide to purchase it later. If so, a certain percentage of the already paid rental fees is deducted from the purchase price at the time the purchase option is exercised. Usually the vendor will limit the period of time during which the option is valid, and will set an upper boundary to the accumulated amount that can be deducted from the purchase price. This may vary for different hardware components.

For example, suppose the monthly rental fee is $1,000, purchase price is $48,000, and the accumulated percentage of rental payments applicable to the purchase option is 60 percent. If the customer opts to purchase after twenty months of rental, the customer will pay a purchase price of

$$\$48,000 - (20 \times 1,000 \times 0.6) = \$36,000.$$

However, if the option stipulates that the customer cannot exercise the option after more than, say, thirty-six months, nor can the deductible amount exceed 50 percent of the purchase price, the customer would have to pay at least $24,000 for purchase (see Ahituv and Borovits [3] for a detailed analysis of the purchase option).

The main advantage of the purchase option is that it allows deferment of a purchase decision. Many customers hesitate to purchase data processing equipment, especially when it is the first installation in their organization or when it is unfamiliar equipment, even if the purchase alternative is better than the rent alternative. After they have tested the new equipment for a while, they are better able to judge its adequacy. Hence, even if in the first place purchasing appears to be more financially attractive than any other alternative, customers might be willing to allow extra cost in order to reduce the uncertainty surrounding a purchase decision.

Comparative Analysis of Acquisition Methods

Selecting the appropriate finance method for computer acquisition is typical of decision making under uncertainty. When the economy is unstable, when inflation prevails, and when interest rates fluctuate, no one can be sure of the right decision. Moreover, computer manufacturers may increase or decrease monthly rental fees and purchase prices on short notice. In fact, Ein-Dor and Borovits [10] showed that the ratio between purchase price and rental fee of various hardware components (of IBM, in that particular paper) was not constant over time; it was even counter to that predicted by the life span of the equipment and prevailing considerations in the capital market. They concluded that IBM's purchase-to-rent ratio appeared to be determined primarily by marketing considerations, such as competition with third-party leasing companies [10, p. 103]. Obviously the ordinary customer does not possess enough information to predict future trends.

Perhaps the most crucial factor is the anticipated life cycle of the acquired equipment. Whether you expect to utilize the computer for one year or for ten years makes a lot of difference. Renting tends to be less advantageous than purchasing as the expected duration of use grows longer.

If all the relevant parameters are obtainable, comparative analysis becomes simple. For example, suppose a purchase price of $48,000, a pure monthly rental fee of $1,000, an interest rate of 1 percent per month (compounded monthly), and a life cycle of four years (forty-eight months). Since we deal with pure rent, we may eliminate maintenance cost from the calculation of the various options. For simplicity, we will also ignore any additional factors. The net present value of the series of rental payments would be

$$\sum_{t=1}^{48} \frac{1,000}{(1+0.01)^t} = \$38,350,$$

which is less than the lump sum of $48,000. Thus, renting is preferred. However, if the expected life cycle is five years and the monthly compounded interest rate is only 0.75 percent, the net present value of the rental payments is $48,530. Rental is approximately the same as purchase price. Assume now that you consider exercising the purchase option after one year of rent and that 60 percent of the accumulated rental

Table 13.4   Comparative Figures of Purchase, Rent, and Purchase Option Methods

Life Cycle	48 months		60 months	
Monthly Interest Rate	0.75%	1.0%	0.75%	0.1%
Net Present Value of Rent	$40,480	$38,350	$48,530	$45,400
Net Present Value if Purchase Option Is Exercised after 12 Months of Rent	$48,820	$47,570	$48,820	$47,570

Purchase price: $48,000
Deductible percentage of rental payments: 60%
Monthly rental: $1,000

payments are deductible from the purchase price. The option will equal a net present value of $47,570 under monthly interest rate of 1 percent, and $48,820 under 0.75 percent. Table 13.4 exhibits some selected figures comparing the methods of purchase, rent, and purchase option (extensive comparative tables are presented in [3]). Note that the rental value is affected by the length of the life cycle and the interest rate; the purchase option value is affected only by the interest rate (and the option preconditions); and the purchase price is affected by neither the life cycle nor the interest rate.

This illustrates that the selection of a financing method is sensitive to some parameters whose certainty is in doubt. General management involvement in such decisions is imperative, particularly when large sums of money are at stake.

Software Acquisition

General management faces several policy issues related to acquisition or development of software. The policy directives should guide the decisions on software made by users or by the information system function in any software evaluation process. Such a process includes definition of needs served by a specific software, the decision to make or to buy, identifying vendors, evaluating vendors, evaluating the software package, evaluating the vendor's support and service offerings, and assessing the impact of the package on the organization.

Computer software can be divided into three categories (see appendix A for more specific categorization). The first is *system software,* also called the operating system. This software is used to manage the computer resources so as to maximize their utilization or to provide a particular level of service to the users. These include scheduling routines, memory allocation schemes, language compilers, and other functions that must be performed to keep the system running.

Another category of software products is utilities. These can be independent programs or part of the operating system. Utilities perform some of the routine work of a computer, such as keeping track of user libraries, sorting and merging, copying of files, and accounting of resource usage.

The third group, *applications software,* is written for the user's needs. These programs can be purchased, leased, or developed in-house by the user organization. Unlike operating systems, which are usually obtained from the computer manufacturer at the time of installation and are rarely written by the individual user, applications software is often a result of in-house programming efforts. Utilities may be of either type and can be classified as such.

Custom software can be developed to meet the needs of a single customer or a small group of customers (i.e., engaged in the same activity). Standard (systems and application) software can be sold by vendors to a large number of customers, and hence can be priced at a fraction of their development cost. They are not tailored to the needs of any single user, but can be obtained for much less than the price of customized software. A standard (commercial, off-the-shelf) program may meet the basic requirements of a user, but not provide the necessary detail. On the other hand, a customized program should provide all the options and detail requested by the user. The only way to acquire a standard package to meet these details is by in-house modification or by outside vendor support in making adaptive changes.

Bear in mind that the discussion here does not apply to all sizes of organizations and all sizes of computer installations. Almost all small-business users of microcomputers purchase *off-the-shelf software packages* (e.g., spreadsheets, file management, word processing). Such users have neither the expertise nor the resources to develop more than the simplest application program. Other users may totally rely on outsourcing to provide for their information processing needs. It is the organizations with an established information system function and equipment that are most likely to have an in-house programming staff and so are required to make a decision between purchasing software or developing it themselves.

Acquisition Options

It is possible sometimes to lease software for in-house use. Whenever this option is taken, the application is usually very specific and no programming changes are necessary to adapt it to the user's needs. Usually, the source code is not even supplied to the user, so no changes can be made.

Other alternatives for software acquisition include purchase of a commercially available product, contracting for a tailor-made application, or developing the software in-house. The acquisition of *proprietary software* packages is an alternative to user development of the application programs. With packages, the application usually can be implemented more quickly and frequently at a lower cost. However, the package may not exactly meet the needs of the user. Particularly, a small computer user may not be able to justify application development costs to make the application exactly what is needed, whereas a larger user is more likely to do so.

Management faces here a typical business problem of make versus buy. To put the issue into some perspective, bear in mind that although the trend is strongly in favor of proprietary packages, expenditures on these in the early 1980s represented less than 5 percent of the software expenditures for nonmicro-based computer applications. This may indicate that the nontangible benefit/cost ratio of a "make" decision outweigh the tangible ratio for many organizations.

Each of the alternatives has advantages and disadvantages that have to be considered. The decision process involves a number of criteria that are commonly used. It is beyond the scope of this book to review these in detail, so we will merely list the major ones (for an extensive discussion see [6, ch. 3]). It is worthwhile to repeat here what was stated in the discussion on the system development process (ch. 9); namely, the starting point for such a process is the determination of user's information requirements. You should define the problem to be solved, specify the basic processing functions (inputs, processing, and outputs), and identify the requirements for interface with the operating system and existing applications. The requirements can be used in preparing cost estimations for in-house software development and for requesting vendors to present their packages for considerations.

We now contrast the alternatives of *buy, make* or *contract* with an outside software company, with the decision criteria of cost, availability of package, maintenance, specificity of the user's requirements, necessary modifications, documentation of the software, and utilization of user's information system resources.

Purchase of a packaged software product from a vendor costs, in many cases, less than developing it in-house. This is due to the fact that the vendor can spread the development costs over many buyers. The product is immediately available and is usually easily implemented. Often the vendor charges a fee of up to 10 percent of the purchase price for maintenance of the product; maintaining in-house developed software can amount to more than 50 percent of the development cost. Modifications to purchased software are very common, since it may not exactly meet the buyer's specific requirements. The vendor can offer assistance, but almost always at a cost. If the documentation associated with the package is poor, it will be difficult for the in-house programmers to modify and maintain the package. Another important criterion is availability of user's information resources (i.e., hardware, information analysts, system designers, programmers).

The decision to *develop in-house* must initially rest on a fair estimate of all costs associated with the analysis, design, programming, testing, and implementation. With this alternative, the product will not be available for use for some time. Any maintenance and future modifications (i.e., corrective and adaptive changes, respectively) will be the responsibility of the programming staff. Since the requirements analysis will be in-house, the system can be designed so that it will meet the specific requirements of the users. A key criterion in the decision is the current utilization of resources. If resources are being fully utilized, it is unlikely that new development projects could be undertaken without causing other tasks to suffer.

The alternative of *contracting* the software project to an outside software house (tailor-making) has some of the advantages and disadvantages of both the buy and make alternatives. Information requirements analysis would be necessary to exactly determine what the software needs to do. The software, once completed, will therefore meet the specific needs of the users. However, as with in-house development, the software will not be available immediately. It may be possible to contract for maintenance, but it is more likely that this will be performed in-house. Modifications, too, will be done in-house; therefore, the contract should include a clause about documentation. There are five methods for procuring contracted software: cost plus fixed fee, cost plus award fee, cost plus incentive fee, fixed price plus incentive, and firm price.

Once all the acquisition alternatives have been examined, they have to be compared and ranked on the basis of some common criteria. You can refer to the section on cost/benefit analysis in this chapter for a discussion of the possible methods of conducting such analysis and reaching a decision.

The Software Acquisition Process

When a decision to purchase a software package has been made, the most judicious way to conduct the process of evaluation and selection is to break the task into stages and develop a checklist of procedures for each stage (such a checklist is provided in [14]). The following is a suggested sequence of stages:

1. Determine the requirements—This has usually already been done when considering the acquisition alternatives.

2. Gather information about available packages and their associated vendors. The information can come from buyer's guides, trade publications, the software vendors themselves (responding to a request for information or a request for proposal), consultants, and users of the packages.

3. Narrow the field to packages that meet mandatory requirements (e.g., a given budget or a given hardware configuration).

4. Perform a detailed evaluation and comparison of the remaining candidate packages. There are several criteria that should be carefully considered in evaluating and comparing the merits of specific packages. You should demand information from each of the prospective vendors, then try to verify them through written agreements, talks with other users, or benchmark tests. Borovits [6, ch. 5] suggests the criteria of functionality, capacity, flexibility, usability, reliability, security, performance, maintainability, ownership rights, minimization of operating and maintenance costs, and minimization of purchase and installation costs.

5. Confer with present users of the packages that have emerged as leading contenders.

6. Conduct benchmark tests on your own computer system or demand a benchmark demonstration (on benchmarks, see [8]).

7. Decide which package will perform the necessary functions and satisfy all the evaluation criteria at the lowest overall cost (including the indirect costs of modifications, installation, conversion, training, maintenance, documentation, etc.).

8. Negotiate a sound contract with the vendor (or modify the vendor's standard contract, if possible and if necessary).

9. Conduct an acceptance test of the package.

10. Install the package and integrate it fully into the organization's overall operational environment.

11. Perform a postinstallation audit of the package.

Note that these stages very much resemble the development stages of an information system (see chs. 9 and 10). This is not surprising since a software package is a major component of such systems.

Charging for Computer Services

Since computer services nowadays use a substantial portion of organizational budgets, and this portion tends to increase over the years, it is essential that management is aware of how these costs apply to users of such services. Appropriate mechanisms of costing and/or internal pricing for computing services constitute a frequently used tool by which management can monitor computer use.

This is not to say that management should design charging mechanism in detail. However, it should recognize some alternative techniques and should set principles and guidelines for devising a charging method. This is the main concern of this section. (For a comprehensive discussion of theory and practice in costing and pricing for computing services, refer to McKell, Hansen, and Heitger [20], Borovits and Neumann [7], and Pick and Whinston [22].)

Overhead (Indirect) Costing

Some organizations charge the costs of computing services against various overhead accounts of the organization. In doing this, they avoid the difficult problems of creating a "payback" mechanism through which users recover the costs of computing services rendered to them. This means that the computing services budget is set by general management without direct correlation to user demand. Certainly, general management, while deciding upon the budget, recognizes and considers the users' needs; however, on a day-to-day basis, users do not feel they have to pay for the services they get.

Although *indirect costing* is undoubtedly an easy approach relative to those discussed later, it is strongly criticized. The criticism is nicely summarized thus [20, pp. 106–7]:

> In such cases the users tend to view computing services as being "free," since they are not charged in direct proportion to actual usage of those services. This can result in the system becoming unnecessarily crowded with jobs of questionable worth and/or inefficiently programmed jobs using more computing resources than necessary. Since the computer can only provide a certain amount of service in a unit of time, a crowded system can result in longer turnaround times to all users, and a subsequent request to management from the computer department for a larger budget.

We should add that a larger budget would not remedy problems, but only relax them for a while because the overhead costing method inherently leads to expanded work load.

Principles of Direct Costing

Imagine that you patronize a health spa that renders such services as sauna, massage, and the like. When you pay your bill you certainly want to understand the charging method. You would like to know that you always pay the same amount for the same (or equivalent) services unless fee or tax changes have been announced. Most of us would also like to know that all customers are equitably charged—i.e., that the charges do not discriminate. The management of the establishment would like to ensure that all services rendered are recovered through the billing system.

These, in fact, constitute the basic principles of direct costing for computing services [20]:

1. *Completeness*—All service resources are included.
2. *Reproducibility*—Equivalent charges result from equivalent services.
3. *Understandability*—Charging method is clear.
4. *Equitability*—The method does not discriminate between customers.

A basic premise of these principles is *measurability*—i.e., that there are viable ways to exactly measure the services rendered.

Management may deliberately drop one or more of the principles in order to pursue certain goals. For instance, jobs that can be held overnight are granted a discount, in order to even out the work load of the computer. The principle of reproducibility is thus relaxed. However, this particular practice would relate more to pricing policy than to costing, and will be discussed later.

Practice of Direct Costing

Prior to the era of multiprogramming, *direct costing* was not a big problem. Every program, while being run on a computer, occupied virtually all the computing resources because no other program could run in parallel, even when some resources were kept idle. For example, even though a certain program did not utilize a printer when it was running, the printer was still virtually unavailable to users because no other program could get into the CPU. It was reasonable, therefore, to adopt the elapsed time of a run as a sole measurement for cost. This is not true anymore because with multiprogramming, several programs can simultaneously share the same resources. In fact, the elapsed time of equivalent runs may even vary, depending upon the arbitrary mix of jobs run concurrently in the CPU. Inevitably, more sophisticated costing methods had to be devised.

The most common method of direct costing involves the following steps [24]:

1. *Identifying measurable activities*—The analyst identifies all the measurable computing activities and assigns measuring units to each activity; for example, CPU time, memory size, number of channel operations, number of lines printed out, connect time of a terminal, and number of disk tracks occupied by a file.

2. *Allocating direct costs*—The analyst assigns the cost factors of the computer configuration to the various measurable activities. For instance, CPU rental fee would be assigned to CPU time; printer rental fee would be assigned to lines printed out.

3. *Allocating overhead costs*—The analyst assigns related overhead costs to the various activities in proportion to the amount of services required to execute them. For example, the building depreciation would be allocated in proportion to the floor space occupied by various devices; operating personnel's costs would be allocated in proportion to the time it takes to operate and handle various devices.

4. *Predicting the consumption*—The analyst estimates the work load of each component during a standard period, say a year. For example, it is predicted that a certain terminal will be connected for twelve hours a day, twenty-five days a month, or 3,600 hours per year.

5. *Determining standard rates*—The analyst divides the sum of the direct and overhead costs assigned to a certain activity (steps 2 and 3) by the predicted work load (step 4), giving the cost per unit of utilization. For example, suppose a terminal is rented for $1,500 per year and relevant overhead costs are $1,200 per year. Suppose the estimated connect time is 3,600 hours. Then the standard rate for one hour of connect time would be $(1,500 + 1,200)/3,600 = \$0.75$.

Once the standard rates are set, the computation of the charge for each job is simply performed by counting the consumption of each measurable activity, multiplying it by the associated rate, and summing up the results.

This method complies with all the aforementioned principles. It is complete (provided that the analyst has not ignored any cost factor). It is reproducible (the same job will always incur the same charge independently of the job mix). It is clearly understood. And different customers are equitably charged for equivalent services.

Despite this, the method still has some deficiencies. First, if actual consumption does not match predicted consumption, costs may not be recovered or revenue may outweigh costs. The latter problem is resolved in some organizations by granting rebates to customers at the end of the year. However, if you try to set a similar arrangement for deficit recovery (i.e., surcharging customers at the end of the year), you are doomed to a noisy confrontation with all computer users who will complain, with some justification, that you encroach on their ability to administer budget planning and control.

The second deficiency lies deep in theoretical grounds. The method does not account for considerations of marginal utility and marginal cost. For example, suppose a new application requires major and costly upgrades in hardware, upgrades that do not significantly benefit anyone besides the user of the particular application. For instance, a regular line printer has to be replaced with a fast, sophisticated, expensive one. Other users may gain slight benefit, but do not necessarily need the new printer. Still, everyone will have to share the additional cost per printer line, so long as the increase in total printing work load does not fully compensate for the additional cost.

There are some theoretical solutions for the marginality problem, but they appear to be impractical. For an extensive discussion of theoretical and practical problems, see [7, 20].

Pricing

Unlike costing, pricing policy does not necessarily have to endorse all these principles. The pricing mechanism operates in essentially the manner previously described—i.e., each hardware component is assigned a standard rate and the user pays the accumulated sum of utilization units times rates. However, the rates are set to pursue management goals rather than to recover costs. We will now illustrate this by a few examples.

Suppose management wishes to discourage large programs that occupy big portions of internal memory. A progressive rate for memory occupancy can be set, such as a basic rate for the first 100K, a double rate for the next 100K, and so on.

Suppose, on the contrary, that memory size is not a constraining problem but that channel capacity is an apparent bottleneck. An increase in the rate for channel use accompanied by a decrease in memory rate will encourage users to exercise larger blocking factors, with, consequently, more moderate traffic in channels (see [4] for a pertinent discussion).

In general, many computer components (though certainly not all) maintain some sort of trade-off relationships. For example, printouts, and terminals are exchangeable to a certain degree. When management wishes to push reluctant users toward more intensified use of certain resources, it can use the pricing mechanism as a tool to achieve such purpose.

Binding Policy

An issue closely related to pricing policy is whether to compel departmental users to run their applications only on an in-house computer or to let them select an outside service.

If management equalizes in-house computer rates to market prices, it would also be logical to allow departmental users to "test" the marketplace prior to making any commitment to use internal computing services. However, this may be troublesome with respect to security, future integration needs, etc. Sometimes it is almost infeasible, particularly when data is confidential.

On the other hand, if management binds departmental users to in-house facilities, the computer services department monopolizes the service; this might evoke inefficiency, surcharges, and other symptoms that characterize lack of competition. A possible remedy is to let the computer department offer its services to external users, too, and encourage it to make profits, provided that departmental users and external customers are equitably charged. This would create incentives to improve efficiency and to adjust rates to meet market prices.

We do not have definite answers to the binding problem. However, the issue certainly merits a thorough consideration by general management.

Some Concluding Remarks

The problem of allocation of information services among departmental users in an organization does not differ, in principle, from any other problem of allocation of scarce resources. In that respect, the fundamental principles of microeconomic theory should be applied to problems in evaluation, allocation, and management of information services. However, microeconomics itself suffers from some theoretical barriers. Consequently, informational problems inherit those barriers. For example, an organization as a whole and departmental users within it cannot be treated as individuals with respect to prioritizing preferences and assessing a utility function. Therefore, it is very difficult, if not impossible, to determine universal criteria by which alternative plans for allocation of information services will be ranked.

Information processing technology has progressed very rapidly during the last four decades, far ahead of the theoretical economic grounds that are supposed to support it. Hence, reality usually places on managers the responsibility of selecting hardware and software, setting priorities for development projects, setting prices, financing computer acquisition, and the like.

The collective wisdom of theoretical and pragmatic contributions to this area is labeled *information economics*. The previously discussed topics are only a part of that discipline. They were discussed here because they normally require extensive involvement by general management. Other related subjects are computer selection [12, 25], software selection [5, 6], computer performance evaluation [8, 15], and more. A pioneering effort to formulate theoretical grounds and to generalize pragmatic approaches in the area of computer economics was done by Sharpe [24]. Sharpe's text was published in 1969 and lacks, therefore, some reference to contemporary technology. Still, it is recommended to those who wish to advance their knowledge in this area. Also recommended is a more recent book by Kleijnen [18].

Practical Conclusions for Information System Design and Use

The following list contains some practical conclusions for information system design and use.

1. Information systems are primarily devised to serve users, subject to corporate objectives dictated by general management. Therefore, it is imperative that management and departmental users take an active role in the planning and development of information systems.

2. The "community of users" includes, besides users of existing information systems, potential users of future systems. Hence, potential users should not be overlooked while long- and medium-range planning processes are undertaken.

3. User management should anticipate future needs, assess them, and submit requirements to general management before long-range plans are completed. User management should not rely on general management and the ISD to do the long-range requirement analysis on their behalf.

4. Setting priorities for future projects to be included in a master plan (medium-range plan) is performed by user management.

5. Not only is the ISD committed by an operating plan (short-range plan), but also by departmental users. Therefore, user management must guarantee that desired resources (e.g., senior officers and clerical personnel) will be allocated in compliance with the operating plan schedule.

6. User management has to appoint officers to various committees and teams involved in project development. The competence and rank of officers should be adequate to guarantee sufficient authority to pursue new (and perhaps controversial) projects.

7. User representatives normally assume responsibility for the following life cycle activities: preliminary analysis; feasibility study; information requirement analysis (as part of information analysis); implementation (particularly acceptance testing, training); and normal operations. However, users should participate in all the rest of the activities as well.

8. The manager of the ISD must rank high enough in the organizational hierarchy that he or she influences the decision-making processes, on the one hand, and directs organizational strategy toward information system planning and development processes, on the other hand.

9. In organizations that have reached maturity in their use of information systems, the ISD should report directly to an executive within general management.

10. Although general management focuses on strategic and long-range planning, it maintains approval authority over medium- and short-range plans.

11. General management exerts control over the quality of an ISD by means of observing various representative indicators: "law and order," users' satisfaction, utilization of personnel and equipment, and productivity. Constant observation may indicate whether the ISD is functioning properly.

12. Every information system project must undergo a cost/benefit analysis. The results should be carefully examined because usually they are very sensitive to initial assumptions. The analyst reports on tangible outcomes as well as intangible variables. The latter are qualitatively evaluated by management and users.

13. Economic justification of various computer acquisition options might alternate over time. Therefore, compatibility of computer applications with different hardware/software environments is an important factor in information system design.

14. Direct charging for information services is a necessary tool to impose economic considerations on users of information systems. Therefore, direct costing is highly preferable to indirect (overhead) costing.

15. Pricing policy is an effective tool to ensure management objectives—i.e., to encourage or discourage use of various resources. From a user's and designer's viewpoint, information systems should be flexible enough to facilitate rapid switchovers to alternative resources (e.g., alternative auxiliary storage media, alternative input/output devices, larger or smaller memory size, etc.).

16. General management and ISD management should keep informed about the possibilities of outsourcing some or part of the IS functions. The potential for reducing costs should be appreciated, and the implications to the organization must be understood.

Summary

Relationships between general management and users and implementors of information systems are the main concern of this chapter. The chapter focuses mainly on users' and general management's roles. The basic premise is that success of information systems is very dependent on appropriate collaboration of all parties involved.

The first part of the chapter deals with user involvement. The user "community" includes those who are using existing systems, as well as potential users who may subscribe to future undertakings. Both parties should take part in long- and medium-range planning processes.

Strategic and long-range planning is undertaken by general management. However, management of departmental users must foresee future needs and submit requirements accordingly so that the departments will not be overlooked during planning and, consequently, deprived in resource allocation. Future requirements are derived by assembling departmental (internal) needs as presently foreseen, and needs stemming from exogenous implications, i.e., development of other departments, strategic direction of the organization as a whole, and trends in the relevant environment.

When the medium-range plan (master plan) is drafted, users define the areas and projects they wish to be developed during the planning period. The list is assigned priorities in accordance with departmental and organizational preferences. A senior user representative must watch the departmental interests during the approval process of a proposed master plan.

Operating planning (short-range planning) determines and schedules budget, personnel, equipment, and other resources to be allocated during the coming period. The operating plan is a mutual commitment of users and the ISD to accomplish certain projects in a certain time using predetermined resources. User management has to guarantee that required internal resources will be available on time to pursue the various undertakings.

Some major user-related factors that affect success or failure of planning are clarity of user requirements; adequate rank of the person(s) representing a departmental user in planning activities; and motivation of user management.

The user plays an important role in the development of individual systems. A departmental user is represented in the information systems committee, which guides information systems development on a continuous basis. The user is also represented in the ad hoc steering committee that monitors each specific project. By participating in the steering committee, the user representative can influence the development direction as well as promote forthcoming information systems within the user department.

The intensity of user involvement fluctuates during the information system life cycle. The user presides over the preliminary analysis and feasibility study; is very often responsible for the information requirement analysis carried out as part of the information analysis stage; is still active in system design and procedure writing, but becomes more passive during programming; again has primary responsibility when the system reaches implementation—i.e., conversion, training, testing, and installation.

During normal operations, the user is in charge of the quality of the input data, the timing of data processing activities, and the arrangement of irregular runs. The user has to constantly monitor the adequacy of the system, the validity of the produced information, and the appropriate handling of change requests.

Outsourcing has become a major factor in the IS operations of a growing number of organizations. Management sees in outsourcing a very real opportunity to reduce costs. There is also an advantage to be gained from the vendor's ability to acquire the latest technological advances and to retain a large technical staff. At the same time, there are dangers to be aware of, ranging from loss of control over IS operations to a downgrading of its strategic importance in the eyes of management.

The second part of the chapter focuses on general management's involvement in information systems. General management has a vital role in monitoring the information systems. Because the subject is full of technical and complex terminology, which is sometimes perhaps exaggerated by information systems practitioners, it is especially important for the manager of the information systems function to rank high enough to report directly to senior executives and, in return, communicate their ideas to professional staff. It is also recommended that a mature information systems function be independent—namely, not affiliated with any functional department, such as accounting, production, marketing, etc.

General management plays a leading role in strategic planning, a very active role in long-range planning, and is concerned with approval authority of medium- and short-range planning.

General management sets objectives for information systems strategy. Long-range planning is jointly undertaken by the executive in charge of information systems, the top management of departmental users, and the top manager of the information systems function, in accordance with the strategic objectives. General management gives final approval to the proposed plan.

The preparation of a master plan (medium-range planning) and a short-range operating plan is administered by the information systems committee, which is advised by departmental users and the ISD. General management would usually prefer to confine its involvement at this level to review and authorization.

General management also coordinates departmental users and the ISD. This is done by means of written policy, instructions, and directives; budget is another important tool for directing and coordinating. Management can also establish incentives to award certain achievements and, thus, encourage interdepartmental efforts. General management does not deal with day-to-day minor disputes between users and developers. However, if such conflicts become common, they may indicate severe problems that call for thorough scrutiny.

General management can exert control over the information systems function without having to get into details of projects and daily activities. It can examine some simple indicators reflecting the quality of ISD operations. These indicators are degree of ''law and order'' maintained in the ISD; level of user satisfaction; efficiency of personnel utilization; overall productivity of the ISD; and efficiency of equipment utilization.

The last part of the chapter raises some policy issues that normally require general management's decision making. These issues usually involve large capital investments and/or financial policy.

Cost/benefit analysis of information systems is difficult to carry out because solid theoretical grounds are lacking (e.g., how to consolidate nonmonetary benefits and costs), as are uniform practices. Since most analyses are performed in order to assess future outcomes, the results are very sensitive to initial assumptions and depend upon questionable predictions. General management must look closely at cost/benefit reports.

Reality, nevertheless, compels us to perform cost/benefit analysis frequently, either for postaudit purposes or, more likely, as an aid in selecting a project among several alternatives. The analysis involves the following steps: identifying alternatives; identifying cost/benefit factors; devising measurement criteria; measuring costs and benefits; calculating consolidated cost/benefit figures; and presenting a comparative report, which should include intangible as well as tangible variables.

We distinguish four categories of variables: monetary; tangible nonmonetary that can be transformed to monetary terms; tangible nonmonetary that cannot be expressed in money; and intangible. Only the first two categories can be quantitatively analyzed; the last two must be qualitatively evaluated by those who make the final decision.

Four methods of financing computer acquisition are discussed: purchase, rent, lease, and purchase option. The last enables the customer to rent first and purchase later if that seems worthwhile. If the purchase option is exercised, a predetermined percentage of the rental payments are accounted as part of the purchase allowance.

Selection of a financing method could be a simple exercise in finance if all the parameters could be determined. However, since expected life cycle, future interest rates, future rental fees, future purchase prices, and some other factors may vary over time, the decision is complicated. Moreover, the financing method may have an impact on the organization as a whole. Information systems development might be decelerated if an organization is stuck with an outdated computer that cannot be abandoned because it has not recovered its initial cost. For this reason, besides the relatively large amounts of money that are usually involved, management has to be concerned with such decisions.

There are several policy issues related to the acquisition or development of software. These include the decision to develop software in-house, to purchase it, to lease it, or to contract out for it. Each of these alternatives has advantages and disadvantages that have to be considered based on a set of criteria. Once a decision to acquire proprietary software is made, a process of evaluating and selecting among the packages (and their vendors) has to be adopted by the organization.

Costing, internal pricing, and charging for computing services may be an effective tool for directing use of information systems in an organization, provided the method is wisely used by management.

The indirect (overhead) costing method charges the computing costs against various overhead accounts. This method is not recommended because users feel they get free computing services, so do not base their requirements on economic considerations. This method can lead to surplus demand and a jammed computer.

The direct costing approach charges users for their proportional consumption of the total use of computing facilities. This method requires that the equipment (hardware and software) be equipped with features to measure the work load of components. If measurement is possible, any direct costing method should be (1) complete (it should include all consumable resources); (2) reproducible (it should produce equivalent charges for equivalent jobs); (3) understandable (it should be clear to the users); (4) equitable (it should not discriminate between users).

The most common direct costing method is based on the following procedure: direct and indirect costs are allocated to the various hardware components; annual work load is estimated for each component; the total cost allocated to a component is divided by the estimated work load, giving a standard rate for a unit of utilization. Each job is then charged according to the actual use of each component. While the method has some deficiencies, it is practical, and thus very popular.

The internal pricing method for charging departmental users for computing services is normally congruent to the costing method, but can serve to influence departmental users toward destinations desired by management. For instance, night jobs may be granted a discount in order to level work load.

If users are bound to use in-house services, the computing center, as a virtual monopoly, might become less economically efficient due to a lack of competition. On the other hand, a nonbinding policy may cause severe problems of data security and data integration. In any case, this matter must always be reviewed and settled with general management rather than at lower ranks.

All the decision problems mentioned are part of the discipline labeled information economics. Some other topics discussed within the framework of this discipline are computer selection; computer performance evaluation; and computer contracting. Despite theoretical gaps, information economics does provide some theoretical grounds and practical tools to aid in managing scarce information resources. Further material on this subject is in the reference list at the end of this chapter.

Key Concepts

applications software

benefits: intangible, monetary, tangible, transformable to money

chief information officer (CIO)

completeness

computer-dependent workers

cost/benefit analysis

costing: direct, indirect (overhead)

costs: ongoing, procurement, project, start-up

custom software

equitability

information economics

"law and order"

lease

life cycle: economical, physical

management: general, ISD, user

measurability

off-the-shelf packages

outsourcing

productivity

proprietary software

purchase

purchase option

pure rent

rental

reproducibility

systems software

understandability

user: motivation, rank, requirements, satisfaction

utilization: equipment, personnel

value analysis

References

1. Ackoff, R. L. "Management Misinformation Systems." *Management Science* 14, no. 4 (Dec. 1967): 147–56.

2. Ahituv, N. "A Systematic Approach Towards Assessing the Value of an Information System." *MIS Quarterly* 4, no. 4 (Dec. 1980): 61–75.

3. Ahituv, N., and I. Borovits. "Analysis of the Purchase Option of Computers." *The Computer Journal* 21, no. 2 (1978): 105–9.

4. Ahituv, N., and M. Igbaria. "A Model for Predicting and Evaluating Computer Resource Consumption." *Communications of the ACM* 31, no. 12 (Dec. 1988): 1467–73.

5. Anderson, E. E. "Choice Models for the Evaluation and Selection of Software Packages." *Journal of Management Information Systems* 6, no. 4 (Spring 1990): 123–38.

6. Borovits, I. *Management of Computer Operations.* Englewood Cliffs, NJ: Prentice-Hall, 1984.

7. Borovits, I., and S. Neumann. "Internal Pricing for Computer Services." *The Computer Journal* 21, no. 3 (1978): 199–204.

8. Borovits, I., and S. Neumann. *Computer Systems Performance Evaluation.* Lexington, MA: D. C. Heath, 1979.

9. Dué, Richard T. "The Real Costs of Outsourcing." *Information Systems Management* 9, no. 1 (Winter 1992): 78–81.

10. Ein-Dor, P., and I. Borovits. "The Purchase-to-Rent Ratio: Inferences Concerning a Pricing Policy." *Management Datamatics* 5, no. 3 (1976): 101–3.

11. Ein-Dor, P., and E. Segev. *Managing Management Information Systems.* Lexington, MA: D. C. Heath, 1978.

12. Gable, G. G. "Consultant Engagement for Computer System Selection." *Information and Management* 20 (1991): 83–93.
13. Gupta, U. G., and A. Gupta. "Outsourcing the IS Function" *Information Systems Management* 9, no. 3 (Summer 1992) 44–50.
14. Kamoji, D. "A Checklist for Acquiring Applications Packages." *Computerworld* 17, no. 41 (Oct. 10, 1983): ID/33–ID/40.
15. Kant, K. *Introduction to Computer System Performance Evaluation.* New York: McGraw-Hill, 1992.
16. Keen, P. G. W. "Value Analysis: Justifying Decision Support Systems." *MIS Quarterly* 5, no. 1 (March 1981): 1–16.
17. King, J. L., and E. L. Schrems. "Cost-Benefit Analysis in Information Systems Development and Operation." *ACM Computing Surveys* 10, no 1 (March 1978): 19–34.
18. Kleijnen, J. P. C. *Computers and Profits: Quantifying Financial Benefits of Information.* Reading, MA: Addison-Wesley, 1980.
19. McCusker, T. "There is Life After Outsourcing." *Datamation* (April 1, 1991): 62–64.
20. McKell, L. J., J. V. Hansen, and L. E. Heitger. "Charging for Computing Resources." *ACM Computing Surveys* 11, no. 2 (June 1979): 105–20.
21. "Management's Newest Star: Meet the Chief Information Officer." *Business Week.* (Oct. 13, 1986): 160–65.
22. Pick, R. A., and A. B. Whinston. "A Computer Charging Mechanism for Revealing User Preferences within a Large Organization." *Journal of Management Information Systems* 6, no. 1 (Summer 1989): 87–100.
23. Ryan, H. W. "Can IS Avoid Marginalization?" *Journal of Information Systems Management* 8, no. 3 (Summer 1991): 57–59.
24. Sharpe, W. F. *The Economics of Computers.* New York: Columbia University Press, 1969.
25. Shoval, P., and Y. Lugasi. "Computer System Selection: The Graphical Cost-Benefit Approach." *Information and Management* 15 (1988): 163–72.
26. Streeter, D. N. "Productivity of Computer-Dependent Workers." *IBM Systems Journal* 14, 3 (1975): 292.
27. Townsend, R. *Up the Organization.* New York: Knopf, 1970.
28. Veryard, R., (ed.) *The Economics of Information Systems and Software.* Oxford: Butterworth-Heinemann, 1991.
29. Weber, J. "Computer Services for Hire." *Los Angeles Times* (Aug. 2, 1992): D1–D2.

Questions

1. Describe the user's contribution to information system planning.
2. How does the information advisor participate in the information system life cycle?
3. What conditions should be monitored by the user during the operation cycle?
4. Why is it important that the information system director be of a rank where overall organizational strategic decisions are made?
5. How can general management help coordinate the acceptance of new or modified information systems?

6. Characterize those indicators reflective of quality information system management.
7. What steps make up a cost/benefit analysis?
8. Give examples of typical cost/benefit categories of analysis.
9. Compare the advantages and disadvantages of purchase, rental, lease, and purchase option of computer equipment.
10. Why is indirect costing frequently criticized?
11. What is the difference between costing and pricing?

Problems

1. Compare the costs and benefits of two alternative information systems over three years. Alternative A involves the purchase of an in-house microcomputer system at $15,000 and includes all necessary and optional software. Extra disk storage will need to be added after the first and second years at a cost of $2,000 each year.

   Alternative B involves use of the company's mainframe and requires purchase of two intelligent terminals for $900 each. Most of the necessary basic software, but hardly any of the optional software, exists. Also, the company requires that each department pay for monthly use of the computer. This is estimated at $500 a month the first year, $700 a month the second year, and $900 a month the third year. Assume an 8 percent discount rate.

2. Describe the tangible monetary benefits, tangible nonmonetary benefits, and intangible benefits of a recently computerized real estate office that previously had only file cards and a monthly listing. Are any of the tangible nonmonetary benefits transformable into monetary terms?

3. Calculate the net present value of renting or using the purchase option of a computer configuration that costs $105,500. The pure monthly rental fee is $1,800, interest is 4 percent (annual) compounded monthly, and the life cycle is 5 years. The purchase option allows 50 percent of the accumulated rental payments to be deducted from the purchase price, but the deductible can not exceed 55 percent of the purchase price. Is it worth using the purchase option, and if so, when? How would this change if the monthly interest rate were one percent?

Gold County Payroll System

Gold County (see figure 13.1, exhibit A, for background information) has been using an outside service for their bimonthly payroll preparation for the past 5 years. In the last negotiations with the twenty-eight separate union groups, several complaints concerning the current payroll system arose from the union representatives. County officials working on the negotiations also had several complaints regarding the flexibility of the system. Examples of complaints were:

1. The unions complained that it took several days to obtain information on personnel classifications' actual pay rates. This hampered their ability to negotiate with the full information allowed them by law.

2. The county officials complained that it took at least two days to receive a forecast as to what a proposal would mean in dollars within the payroll/personnel system. They also complained about the escalating costs to run the system.

3. Both organizations complained about the lack of flexibility in the system, the frequent problems in running the "standard" system each month, and the tremendous cost estimates for any changes desired to the system.

The current software package used by the service vendor is a CICS version of a payroll/personnel system. In discussion with current information systems management, they have agreed to present a proposal for purchasing, installing, modifying, and implementing the CICS payroll/personnel system in the central computer center. The ISD charges county users for all services.

Exhibit B, figure 13.2, shows the last year's detail charges from the timeshare company and a 5-year history of charges.

Exhibit C, figure 13.3, shows an estimate from IS for future 5-years costs as requested.

Questions

1. Given the past 5-year costs for the service, what do you expect to see in the future 5-year costs if Gold County continues to use the current service?

2. Compare the answer to #1 to exhibit C. Which is the most cost-effective option for Gold County?

3. Recalculate exhibit C given the fact that IS is not currently supporting CICS and estimates one-time costs of $350,000 ($25,000 can be capitalized) and annual costs of $90,000 for support.

4. Recalculate exhibit C with Gold County funding all capitalized costs. If the vendor offers to install the payroll/personnel package for $225,000, which includes all modifications, and this cost can be capitalized, what changes would you make to your costing?

5. Prepare a recommendation for Gold County for their payroll personnel system. Include tangible as well as potential intangible benefits. Recommend terms and conditions for the selected approach. State any and all assumptions.

Figure 13.1 Gold County exhibit A

Exhibit A
Gold County
April, 1992

Gold County is located in Southern California near a large metropolitan population. Its current population is one million residents with a 20 percent growth annually for the past three years which is expected to continue for the next five years. The majority of the county's residents commute to neighboring counties for employment. Gold County is 5,000 square miles in area. Only one-third of the county is considered well populated.

The county government is governed by a Board of Supervisors. There are five supervisors on the board, and they are elected for four-year terms. Every two years, two or three of the board members seek reelection. The county has been in existence for 85 years and currently has 10,000 full- and part-time employees. The number of employees has grown from 8,000 to 10,000 in the past three years. The county employees are located at the administrative center, at the 350-bed county hospital, at one of the four jails which range from 50 to 350 cells, or at one of the dozen or so smaller offices throughout the county. Several of the facilities are 24-hour, 7-day-a-week facilities. The county has a large administrative complex in the county's biggest city and several smaller offices throughout the county.

Gold County has suffered from increasing financial difficulty because of Proposition 13 (passed in 1979), which limited property taxes of 1 percent of assessed value and provided additional benefits for senior citizens. Additional financial burdens have come about because the federal and state governments have delegated programs to local control and administration without funding. The majority of county departments have not had an increase in budgets for three years despite the negotiated raises and increased expenses. To further complicate matters, the Board of Supervisors has decreed that there will be no lay-offs of county employees.

Figure 13.2 Gold County exhibit B

```
Exhibit B
Gold County
April, 1992

TOTAL Service Cost Re-cap

January 1 to December 31, 1991

CPU Hours              150 at   $300 per hour              $45,000
Disk I/O's          41,040 at     .176 each                 7,223
Tape I/O's           9,272 at     .25 each                  2,318
Print Lines        407,430 at     .156 each                63,559
Forms Bursting      16,844 at     .105                      1,769
Maintenance Hours      348 at   $ 50.                       17,400
Modification Hours
   FLSA                997 at   $ 50.                       49,850
   Union Requests      326 at     50.                       16,300
   Other Requests      550 at     50.                       27,500

                                TOTAL                     $230,919

January 1 to December 31, 1990  TOTAL                     $188,551

January 1 to December 31, 1989  TOTAL                     $113,444

January 1 to December 31, 1988  TOTAL                      $79,411

January 1 to December 31, 1987  TOTAL                      $65,227
```

Figure 13.3 Gold County exhibit C

Exhibit C
Gold County
April, 1992

INFORMATION SYSTEMS PROPOSAL ESTIMATES

Capital Items (can be fiananced over 5 years at 7.75%)

Software	$125,000
3390 Disk Drive	280,000
3390 Disk Controller	325,000
Laser Printer	38,690
6 Terminals	7,250

First Year Costs Estimate

Analyst	1700	Hours at $38.	$64,600
Programmer	3250	Hours at 38.	123,500
Data Analyst	680	Hours at 38.	25,840
Network Support	204	Hours at 38.	7,752
CPU Hours			48,875
Disk I/O's	115	at $425.	7,275
Tape I/O's	48,500	at .15	1,800
Print Lines	10,000	at .18	62,500
Forms Purchase	500,000	at .125	900

Second Year Costs Estimate

Analyst	1700	Hours at $39.50	$67,150
Programmer	2250	Hours at 39.50	86,900
Data Analyst	325	Hours at 39.50	12,838
Network Support	100	Hours at 39.50	3,950
CPU Hours	92	at $450.	41,400
Disk I/O's	39,000	at .17	6,630
Tape I/O's	8,250	at .19	1,568
Print Lines	400,000	at .15	60,000
Forms Purchase			950

Third Year Costs Estimate

Analyst	1700	Hours at $40	$ 68,000
Programmer	2200	Hours at 40	88,000
Data Analyst	350	Hours at 40	14,000
Network Support	75	Hours at 40	3,000
CPU Hours	100	at $460.	46,000
Disk I/O's	46,800	at .18	8,424
Tape I/O's	9,900	at .19	1,881
Print Lines	425,000	at .15	63,750
Forms Purchase			1,000

Figure 13.3 *Continued*

Exhibit C Page 2

Fourth Year Costs Estimate

Analyst	1700	Hours at $42.	$ 71,400
Programmer	2550	Hours at 42.	107,100
Data Analyst	400	Hours at 42.	16,800
Network Support	100	Hours at 42.	4,200
CPU Hours	120	at $475.	57,000
Disk I/O's	58,500	at .19	11,115
Tape I/O's	12,500	at .20	2,500
Print Lines	510,000	at .16	81,600
Forms Purchase			1,250

Fifth Year Costs Estimate

Analyst	1700	Hours at $43.50	$ 73,950
Programmer	3400	Hours at 43.50	147,900
Data Analyst	500	Hours at 43.50	21,750
Network Support	125	Hours at 43.50	5,438
CPU Hours	150	at $500.	75,000
Disk I/O's	76,050	at .20	15,210
Tape I/O's	16,250	at .22	3,575
Print Lines	575,000	at .175	100,625
Forms Purchase			1,500

NOTES: Management and operational overhead costs are included in hourly and equipment rates. Rates are calculated annually based on actual costs and usage. Rates for the past three years have risen 17% (1990), 13% (1989), and 11% (1988).

Chemicals Research, Inc.

Chemicals Research Inc. (CRI) is a chemical manufacturing company located in Southern California. It is a privately held company whose owner, Mr. Smyth, founded, based on chemical patents he obtained in the late 1950s. CRI specializes in the manufacturing of bonding chemicals. Sales in 1990 totaled 75 million dollars, of which 8 million was spent on R&D. Mr. Smyth built the company based on the idea of cutting-edge technology in bonding chemicals as CRI's market nitch. Until the late 1980s, this strategy worked admirably, with steadily increasing sales and profits for CRI. For the last three years, sales have held steady while profits have decreased. Mr. Smyth attacked the problem as he always did in the past, by increasing the R&D budget. This did create several new products with great sales potential, but so far it has not materially increased sales.

Eighteen months ago, Mr. Smyth's grandson and only heir, Mr. Richmond, took the position of Vice-President of Manufacturing immediately after finishing a Masters Degree in Chemical Engineering (see fig. 13.4). While attending school, Mr. Richmond worked summers in various manufacturing areas, and although he planned on joining CRI for years, Mr. Richmond finds himself in increasing conflict with Mr. Smyth. The source of conflict is computerization. Mr. Richmond feels he has done all he can do without the addition of computers to at least the production and inventory control processes, and preferably the sales and order entry operations as well. Mr. Smyth feels computers are a waste of time and money and adamantly refuses to consider these ideas, even though other changes introduced by Mr. Richmond in the production and inventory control areas have increased productivity 20 percent while holding costs steady.

Both CRI's Vice-President of Sales and Vice-President of Finance helped found the company in 1959 and distrust computers as well. The Controller has been with the company for twelve years and installed a batch system ten years ago to handle Accounts Payable, Accounts Receivable, and the General Ledger. He has been trying for the last three years and just succeeded, with the help of Mr. Richmond, in convincing Mr. Smyth that it would be cheaper to replace the old accounting system with a new one, than to continue to pay the constantly more costly maintenance contracts on outdated machines and the extra labor costs that a batch system imposes. Because the ISD staff consists of the manager, one programmer, four computer operators, and three key-punch operators, you have been invited to make a proposal.

Questions

You have only been asked to update the accounting system, when obviously the entire company needs to be placed online.

1. Just how much do you propose at this point in time?

2. How do you deal with upper management reluctance?

3. Assuming an expanded solution is approved, what steps need to be taken to minimize negative impacts during implementation?

Figure 13.4 CRI organizational structure

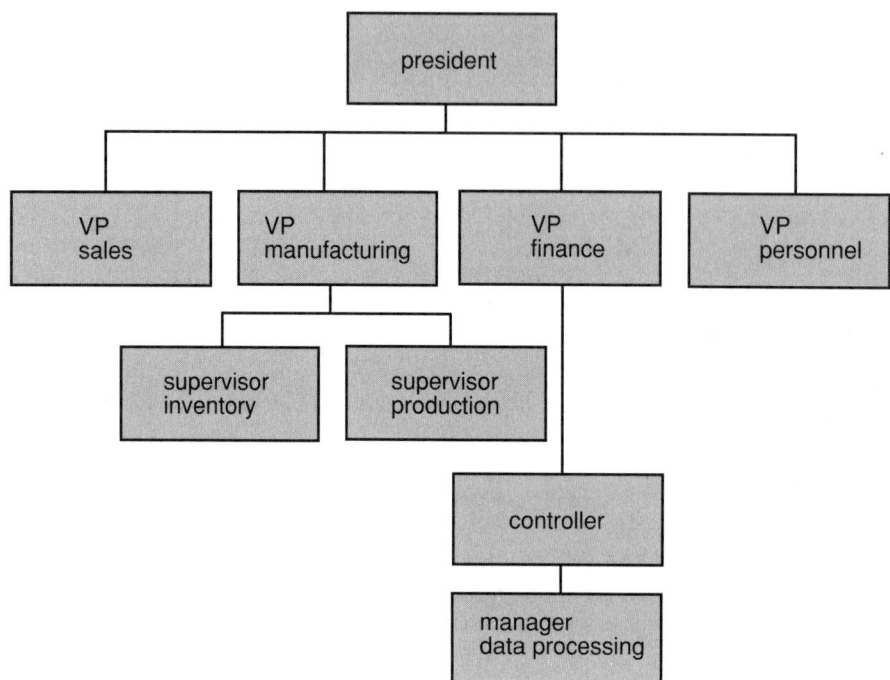

Chapter 14 Information System Controls

Information systems are by nature open systems: they interact with a dynamic environment surrounding them. Information systems are by and large complex: they comprise many components having different traits—people, machines, programs, etc. Being open and complex, information systems are highly vulnerable to inadvertent or deliberate imperfection.

Since we cannot watch every single transaction all along the processing cycle, we have to devise control provisions to guarantee information reliability—if not to perfection, then at least to an acceptable degree. Control measures are the main concern of this chapter.

Introduction

In chapter 4 we presented some concepts related to systems theory. A major proposition was that any purposeful system must be regulated by a control subsystem in order to guarantee that the system performs within the boundaries imposed by predetermined purposes. Every purposeful system can, in fact, be subdivided into an executing subsystem and a control subsystem (see fig. 4.8).

Control is obtainable only by a flow of data designating the system's status from the executing to the control subsystem and, in return, a flow of corrective instructions from the control to the executing subsystem. Hence, information systems are, in the most general sense, control tools to monitor other systems. This applies to a home thermostat as well as to the national import/export statistics processed and stored on a mammoth computer. Both instances are examples of data that is used to determine system status (heat, national economy) and to exercise certain corrective measures (turn on the furnace, increase tax on import) if so desired.

Unfortunately, control systems in general and information systems in particular are not foolproof. They are subject to malfunctioning, either bona fide or due to wrongdoing. Therefore, we have to devise means *to control the control; namely, to control information systems, which control other systems.* How far should we proceed? Should we establish means to control the control of the control, and so on? This is mainly an academic question because, in practice, we have to stop somewhere—or else have the entire national labor force engaged in exerting control, one over the other.

In the ensuing discussion we examine two layers of control: first, control measures that are superimposed on information systems to warrant better reliability; second, human control by means of auditing, where one of the auditor's tasks is to verify the adequacy of other control measures. We will not discuss how the auditor can be controlled; however, we will specify the background and training required for information system auditors (hereafter, EDP auditors). First we designate the types of control pertaining to information systems.

Control Classification

Imagine that you possess some very expensive paintings by prominent painters that you hang on the walls of your living room. Since you are aware of the high value of the paintings, you ask a security company to install alarms all over your house. One night while you are away, a burglar breaks into your house. Immediately all the alarms sound, but the burglar grabs a magnificent Picasso from the wall and escapes. The stolen painting is never retrieved. The system detected the burglary, but could not prevent the loss.

You go to the security company and complain. They suggest that for an extra charge they will install an automatic shut-off mechanism that locks and electrifies all the exits of your house once an alarm has been triggered. Dispirited and frustrated, you install the shut-off mechanism but, being skeptical, you also increase the coverage on your insurance policy. The next time a burglar breaks in, he is trapped inside your house until the police arrive. The system has proven effective, not by preventing the break-in, but by correcting the consequences.

This anecdote illustrates two of the three elements that make up control: prevention, detection, and correction [25]. Complete control is attainable only if all three elements are covered.

Preventive control averts faultiness or wrongdoing. For example, posting a notice on an entrance gate that the house is wired and protected may by itself restrain certain intentions to break in. Similarly, recording, totaling, and cross-checking of individual transactions may discourage potential embezzlers (of small scale); a password might prevent unauthorized use.

Detective control signals an error or wrongdoing once it has occurred; for example, the alarms installed in the house. A detective control is an edit (validity check) program that verifies input data.

Corrective control provides means to correct the fault once an error has been detected. For example, the automatic shut-off mechanism and a *backup* procedure are corrective controls.

These control categories are conceptual rather than physical. In reality, it is often difficult to place a certain control measure in a specific category. More often a control measure will incorporate elements associated with all the categories. For example, the use of a check sum (a precalculated total of a batch of transactions) may prevent potential embezzlement. It certainly indicates the occurrence of some errors, and it may well hint at the source of a problem by means of the difference between the check and the actual sums. Hence, it is usually more convenient to specify how a certain control measure helps to improve each control category than to tag the measure with a specific category label.

Responsibility for Control

The reliability of a system is the responsibility of management. In other words, if anything goes wrong, management will have to account for it. Thus, management has to make sure that adequate control provisions are implanted and imposed on information systems. This is particularly true for errors and wrongdoings that are predictable, hence avoidable, because if management can identify a possible loophole, anybody else can do the same and abuse it.

This is not to say that management should attempt to achieve perfect control. First, we doubt whether this is possible. Second, planning control is, after all, a matter of cost/benefit. Additional control incurs additional costs. An organization might pay for certain control measures much more than it might lose by not having them if the cost/benefit analysis of control is not appropriately carried out. In general, we may say that any organization must meet generally accepted accounting principles and common audit practices. On top of that, it has to evaluate its own unique circumstances to see whether they merit the installation of additional provisions, and if so, how far they should go.

Let us take, for example, the concept of redundancy. In data processing, redundancy is almost synonymous with a "bad word"; it contrasts with efficiency; it entails consumption of more disk space; it complicates programs that have to update files. In many software product brochures, particularly those for DBMS, you will find that one of the most praised features of the product is the elimination of redundancy. However, when it comes to control, redundancy is not necessarily bad. It helps in reconciliation and in recovery.

This example demonstrates the main problem of control; it contrasts with efficiency. The more control features you pour into an information system, the less efficient the system is since it has to spend time and other resources on control procedures. Selecting the golden middle is management's responsibility.

Types of Control

Control is attained by exercising a large variety of measures, which can be classified into three categories:

1. *Administrative control*—Includes all sorts of regulations, procedures, and practices imposed on employees in the various departments (e.g., segregation of duties).

2. *Built-in control*—Includes many features inherent to software and hardware components of a computer center. These are for "public use" and do not pertain to any specific application (e.g., a parity bit).

3. *Application control*—Includes measures that are superimposed on specific applications in order to conform with the characteristics of the particular application (e.g., *audit trail,* encryption).

We will now briefly discuss each type of control.

Administrative Control

Before the advent of computerized business systems, departmental bookkeeping was usually handled by each operating department. Since most business transactions involve several departments, it was much easier to detect discrepancies by means of reconciliation between various departmental books (provided that the books were properly handled). For example, a sale transaction would be recorded in sales, finished goods, and accounts receivable. If discrepancies in those accounts were found, one could trace back for the cause.

Computerized systems usually maintain similar accounting books (i.e., files). The data is stored on a computer that, in many cases, is centrally managed. However, unlike manual systems, the data is neither visible nor concrete; in order to access the data, you have to be assisted by computer professionals. No layperson can tell exactly what is stored in the ''black box.'' Moreover, the extensive use of data bases in order to reduce data redundancy may, by the same token, impair the reconciliation capability. In short, centralization of data has merits as well as disadvantages. Many people think that, with respect to control, the disadvantages are potentially harmful.

Administrative control is a set of regulations and procedures that attempt to cope with problems caused by the centralization and invisibility of data. It is believed that by imposing certain rules on the personnel involved, information systems will be less exposed to carelessness or abuse. We will now discuss some of these regulative provisions.

Segregation of Duties

As mentioned, concentrating all the accounting data of an organization in a single computer installation is a potential danger because it may permit realization of malicious purposes. Since we cannot afford to separate the data, we try to gain satisfactory control by separating the individuals who have access to the data during capture, processing, storing, and retrieval activities. This separation is labeled *segregation of duties.*

The basic premise of this is that if duties are strictly segregated, malicious intents can be subtly realized only by applying ''collective wisdom''—in other words, the collaboration of several individuals. Naturally, such a collusive effort is difficult to coordinate, if initiated by one person.

Segregation of duties is a basic principle of internal control. It should be applied to information systems development and operation activities.

In development, segregation of duties is made possible by instituting strict distinctions among the following:

System design

Program writing

Program review

System test and approval

System installation (handing over to operations)

In operations, segregation of duties is made possible by instituting strict distinctions among the following:

Source document preparation

Computer input preparation and balancing to source documents

Input error correction and irregularity inquiries

Computer operations

File library

Balancing inputs against printouts

Output distribution

Systems programming

Data base administration

Hardware maintenance

Note that segregation is mainly a preventive provision. However, detection and correction are facilitated too, particularly for inadvertent errors because the likelihood of an error not being detected while passing through so many different hands is fairly small, provided that control measures are appropriately undertaken.

Implications of Segregation of Duties on the Organizational Structure

In chapter 12 we presented an organizational structure for a large-scale information systems department (ISD) (see fig. 12.10). The structure suggested there satisfies the constraints dictated by the need to segregate duties; we will not repeat the discussion here. However, some organizations have augmented their ISD by an additional unit that may be called the *quality control section* (QCS).

QCS serves as an interface between system development and operation. Every information system, upon completion of its development, is handed over to the QCS, which tests the system and examines its compliance with common standards of design, programming, and control. If these are met, QCS installs the system and transfers responsibility to the operational function. This procedure is repeated whenever a modification is made in an existing system. Figure 14.1 illustrates the way this procedure is exercised in practice.

According to the framework shown in figure 14.1, each function maintains its own software. For instance, a project development team may have space on disks where all the programs under development are stored. When the system is ready for installation, the pertinent software is copied to a test library on which it will be stored for testing purposes until it is approved. Then QCS copies the software to the production library. Only QCS is allowed to store or replace programs in the production library, which

Figure 14.1   Accessibility of ISD functions to software libraries

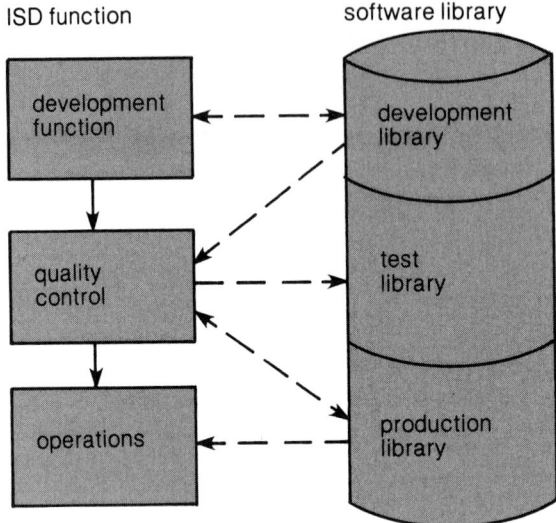

comprises operational programs. In fact, development personnel are not permitted to access any program cataloged in production, while operation personnel are not allowed to intrude into software under development.

These restrictions are supported by means of *passwords,* logbooks, etc. They are not foolproof, but they may improve control. The procedure may cause delays in the pace of development, particularly when it comes to inserting minor modifications in existing systems; but that is the price we have to pay for proper control.

Other Administrative Control Measures

Segregation of duties is only one measure among many that constitute administrative control. In fact, every established procedure, be it in system development or operation, is an element in the fabric of administrative control. In development, administrative control includes the following:

Formal life cycle procedures

Formal reporting to committees

Standards for system analysis and design (e.g., structured design)

Programming standards

Implementation practices and logbooks

Testing regulations

Change handling procedures

Postaudit (see [2])

Documentation standards (this will be discussed later in the chapter)

In routine operations, administrative control provisions include these items:

Exact procedures for error detection and correction

Operating procedures (in writing)

Backup and recovery arrangements

Routines for balance check and reconciliation

Regulations for hard-copy storage and archive management

Limitations on the accessibility to software libraries

Limitations on admittance to the computer room, to the file library, and to other privileged places

These are only samples of possible ways to exercise administrative control. If you use them, you will reduce the likelihood of abuse or faultiness in your systems. However, constant watch over development and operation is a must, in addition to establishing formal procedures. For a discussion of these matters, see [10, 21, 25].

Built-in Control

Most computer installations are equipped with control features that are built in the hardware and software of the installation. Many of these features are automatically activated whenever the computer performs a relevant action (e.g., a parity check). Virtually, nothing is required of us but to know of their existence. However, there are some features whose activation is optional (e.g., password), so we have to learn when and how to use them.

We classify built-in control measures as hardware and software features and will briefly mention some of the usual ones.

Hardware Controls

Information processing equipment is inlaid with control features that check the validity of various operations performed along the cycle of data processing. Control features are installed not only in the computer and its peripheral devices, but also in offline machines used for keying, communication, and the like. Let us follow the cycle of data processing and highlight some of the major features.

Most input media are equipped with control features. For example, you may duplicate the input data encoded on forms to be read in by an optical reader; the optical reader will then have two equivalent data lines to read in. In case one of the lines has been physically damaged, the data can still be read in without human intervention.

More "intelligent" input media, like diskettes, are usually mounted on programmable devices so control can be obtained by means of a software program; this will be discussed later. However, one has to know the technical capability of these machines before acquiring them.

Whenever input data is transferred from remote locations to a central computer, the data passes via telecommunication networks. Those are normally geared with hardware features that check for completeness and validity of transmissions. There are various modes of data transmission. Each mode is characterized by different control disciplines that may affect the reliability of the conveyed data. Moreover, the topology (structure) of a network can be designed in different manners (see appendix A). A certain topology may allow transmissions to be redirected through alternative routes once a certain link has been found inoperative. Another topology might not provide a fallback alternative. Hence, a user of such technology, even a layperson, should understand the control aspects of various proposed telecommunication networks.

Telecommunication networks can also be equipped with *ciphering* devices [5]. These devices scramble the data flowing through the network so only a designated station equipped with a certain *deciphering* code can "understand" the content of the messages. Ciphering is very common in commercial systems (e.g., EFTS—electronic fund transfer systems) as well as in military systems.

The central computer installation has plenty of control measures installed within the hardware. Most are beyond our direct concern as users. For instance, we do not really care how the *parity bit,* which is attached to each memory byte, is working, so long as we know that this aspect of control has been addressed. However, there are features having more important implications. For example, some computer models will terminate a program whenever the program attempts to divide a number by zero; other models will produce a quotient, usually the largest number that can be stored in memory, and then proceed (business as usual) without letting anyone know of the (potential) error. Some computer models will terminate a program if it has encountered a calculation overflow; others will proceed without any indication. The overflow problem may be very important for scientific applications, but of less significance for business applications.

An important control aspect is the tolerance of hardware equipment to fluctuations in temperature, humidity, and electrical power. Some models have more tolerance than others, and therefore can be installed in less than desirable environmental conditions (e.g., in a production shop, on mobile equipment). Sometimes we have to devise fallback features to level uncontrollable fluctuations—say, in electrical voltage. For example, standby batteries or emergency generators may be required in certain cases. Such measures are costly, thus management has to assess the cost vis-à-vis the damage that might occur if they are not adopted.

External storage and output devices should also be considered in light of the degree of control they provide. For example, would it be better to acquire one fast line-printer, or should we install two slow printers that can perform an equivalent workload? The latter alternative provides better backup, but waiting time for urgent printouts may be longer.

There are some simple measures worth knowing. For instance, magnetic tapes can be secured from undesired rewriting (i.e., destruction of current records) by simply inserting a plastic ring onto a certain slot on the reel. In a similar fashion, you can protect a diskette from rewriting. Since this measure is optional, you have to designate it explicitly in the operating procedures so it will be carried out. Another example is terminals that can be locked so no one can use them without an appropriate key. Again, this is an optional feature that should be specially ordered.

This discussion has not covered all the hardware control features by any means, but it highlights a few and directs our attention to the fact that such measures exist. Many times we can adopt a simple hardware feature and save a lot of effort in manual or computerized activities (e.g., a plastic ring instead of a double backup).

Software Controls

We should distinguish between software features that are ''public domain'' and can be utilized in any information system and measures that are specially tailored to the particular traits of a specific application. The former are discussed in this section; the latter are presented in a subsequent section.

Software controls include provisions that may improve the quality of programs under development, as well as software measures to exert control over operations. Programming quality can be improved by using debugging aids, structured design techniques, and the like. The best way to stress the importance of this issue is to cite from a report prepared by the Comptroller General of the United States [13, pp. 16–17]:

Management Control Can Be Improved
Projects to develop and maintain computer software can be very lengthy and involve many people. The possibilities for errors in the computer programs and poor management of the efforts are high due to extreme technical complexity and the lack of standards and common practices. By requiring proper use of software tools and techniques, ADP managers and supervisors can substantially improve control over software development and maintenance.

For example, requiring independent inspection by a software quality control group will help ensure that programming language standards and programming practices standards are followed by the systems analysts and programmers. Appropriate software tools can aid management control by automating much of the manual effort needed to evaluate unfamiliar programs.

Another means of improving management control is to adopt a carefully considered group of software tools and techniques to yield more predictable software costs and provide better documentation. For example, we visited a private sector company which develops software. The company has adopted, and requires the use of, a group of modern programming tools and techniques including structured programming, a program support library, structured design, concurrent documentation, and preprocessors. The benefits reported to us include improved project control, better end products, better organization for the maintenance phase, and estimated annual savings of $1 million in the development and maintenance of systems.

This quotation emphasizes the importance of exerting control over software while it is being developed. There is nothing more enraging than having an entire system suspended at 2:00 A.M. while programmers dig into certain subroutines to look for a disruptive bug. Moreover, opportunity makes the thief; namely, uncontrolled software may be a gold mine for computer abusers.

A different angle of software control is the usefulness of software features to exert control over operations. For instance, most operating systems contain an option that users will be identified by confidential *passwords*. This would prevent unauthorized users from accessing the computer. Another software feature is the logbook, in which each interaction with the computer is recorded. Most computer manufacturers offer recovery routines that may be useful after encountering a system failure, so that all the programs do not have to be restarted from the beginning.

Files can also be protected by various software features. It is very common to begin and to end a file with labels called *"header"* and *"trailer."* These labels contain information related to the file, such as record length, blocking factor, expiration date, file name, number of blocks, etc. Upon request, standard software routines will check whether the content of the header and the trailer records matches predetermined parameters that have been designated by the user. If not, the file will not be processed and the operating system will notify the operator.

Most operating systems maintain a file catalog (directory). The catalog contains the name, the physical location, the number of generations required to be preserved, and some other parameters pertaining to data files. A file catalog facilitates the work of computer operators and file librarians as well as prevents, at least partly, premature deletions.

Many data base packages (DBMS—see appendix A) contain automatic recording of all the transactions passing by. This would make it possible to trace back updates and recover after system failures. It is a good idea to devise a similar system for conventional files, too, particularly when an update is performed in an online mode.

Most of the aforementioned means are activated only upon request; namely, they are optional. For instance, the computer will not check header and trailer labels unless directed to do so. Hence, you must first learn of the existence of software features, and then learn to incorporate them into your system in order to strengthen the overall control. This is, in fact, the main idea behind application control, which is discussed next.

Application Control

While it is true that control should be imposed on every information system, the particular measures employed may vary in light of the specific traits of each application. For example, the control exerted over a monetary information processing system (e.g., cashier transactions) would be tighter than that applied to data collection for national statistics on production in the food industry. The former system is vulnerable to potential abusers, whereas an error of a few thousand dollars does not make a meaningful difference for the latter system.

The notion "application control" refers, therefore, to provisions employed to meet the specific requirements of a particular application. Application control may incorporate administrative, built-in, and ad hoc measures. It should interlace preventive, detective, and corrective provisions [14].

We will now mention some traits often found in many applications and will present some commonly used control measures that may fit. We will go along the *data processing cycle*—i.e., from the stage of data creation to the stage of output distribution, as illustrated in figure 14.2 (a similar figure is A.1 in appendix A). We will emphasize problems related to monetary data.

Figure 14.2 Data processing cycle

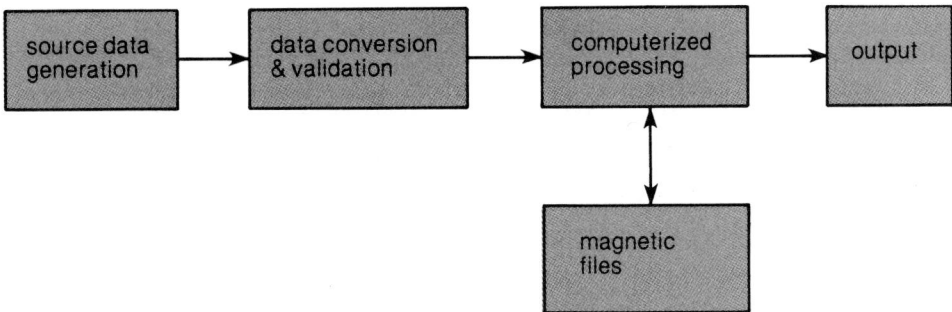

Handling of Source Data

Source data is usually created as a result of a physical transaction—a sale, a payment, a withdrawal. The description of the activity is recorded on a form, a source document (a written transaction). At this point, control problems generally fall into the following categories:

1. *Authorization*—Is the initiator of a certain transaction authorized to perform and record the said transaction? The problem can be partly resolved if transactions are handled by at least two persons: one who prepares the source document and another who reviews and authorizes it. Transactions that are keyed in directly to a computer (online) should be accompanied by a requisite password and the identification of the initiator.

2. *Authentication*—Is the initiator of a certain transaction (or query) the person whose identification has been keyed into the system? Maybe it is an impostor. In simple cases, this problem is solved by attaching a unique password to each user and preventing the password from being displayed on the screen. When sensitive data is involved, additional features are required such as encrypted password or even physical authentication devices (e.g., magnetic card, fingerprint identification, voice identification) [4].

3. *Completeness*—Have all the pertinent transactions been recorded and forwarded for further processing? There are several ways to ascertain completeness. One is *batching*—i.e., grouping of a large number of transactions into small batches. Each batch can be accompanied with any or all of the following control figures: a *record count* that designates the number of records (transactions) constituting the batch; a *control total* that accumulates the total monetary amounts of the batch's transactions; and a *hash total* that accumulates the values of an arbitrary data item such as an identification number. Later, when the transactions are keyed in or read in by a computer, the control figures can be recalculated and compared to the original figures so that any discrepancy will signal that some transactions are suspected of being missing.

Online input cannot be checked for completeness by any of these control figures. Hence, a common method to overcome the problem is to store all the daily transactions on a file and run a comparative program at the end of the business day. Another way to assure completeness is to have all the source documents preprinted with consecutive serial numbers so that any skipped number is immediately detected. This method requires rigid procedures for transaction recording and submission, particularly when transaction sources are scattered, so it is exercised only for delicate data. For example, some police departments use this method to make sure that traffic tickets are not "washed out" after they have been issued.

4. *Accuracy*—How can we make sure that the recorded data is not erroneous? There are certain ways to check for accuracy. However, extensive verification usually takes place during the conversion of data from human- to machine-readable form, a subject that is discussed later. Accuracy can also be improved simply by effective design of the source forms. This is discussed in the next section.

What Makes a Good Form?

The design of a source document, particularly when it has to be filled out manually, is crucial for the smoothness and correctness of operations. Poorly designed forms call for mistakes, misunderstanding, and irritation and may cause significant deterioration of system performance and control capacity. So we will interject a few remarks about what makes a form effective.

Have you ever filled out an income tax return? Was it clear? Have you ever filled out a course enrollment card? Was it easy? Suppose you are the manager of an operational function that intends to adopt a new computerized application for some of its major activities. A system designer enters your office with a draft of a proposed form to be used in your department. You have to evaluate the adequacy of the design. How would you evaluate the proposed form?

Here are several criteria of quality.

1. *Self-explanatory*—The form has to guide the recorder, so each item is clear, well defined, and without ambiguity. This is imperative for documents that are not used frequently (e.g., an income tax return, which is normally filled out once a year).

2. *Exhaustive*—The form should contain all the pertinent data items so there will be no need to add missing data later. This implies that a designer knows exactly the output requirements before shaping any input form.

3. *Logical sequence of items*—Forms are often filled out while a person is interviewing someone or scanning other documents. Make the sequence of questions logical and in a reasonable order; for example, personal details first, personal history second, monetary information third, etc.

4. *Limited redundancy*—It is boring and irritating to have to repeat data, so the form should minimize repetitions. However, some redundancy may help in verifying and double-checking. For example, on checks we are requested to

specify the amount of money twice—once in words and once in figures—in order to maintain better control. Hence, data redundancy is not always bad, but it has to comply with common sense.

5. *Stick to necessary information*—Do not overload the form with items that will not be useful for any future purpose. For example, if the date of birth of the applicant's mother is not a vital data on a job application form, omit it.

6. *Easy to key in*—You have to remember the keying-in operator who will have to scan the form. If the sequence of recorded data items does not match the keying-in sequence, probability of errors goes up.

7. *Easy to handle manually*—Sometimes we tend to forget that documents are transferred, filed, retrieved, and handled by clerks in addition to being keyed in. Thus, we have to recognize the prevailing clerical practices and adjust the form to fit those.

8. *Spacious*—Writing the whole Bible on one eggshell is an art rather than a common clerical practice. Allow sufficient space for the data requested.

It is certainly not easy to satisfy all these criteria simultaneously. Some may even be contradictory at times. For example, compliance with the spaciousness and self-explanatory criteria would enlarge the size of a form, whereas ease of manual use may require a reduced size. Nevertheless, we have to bear these criteria in mind when we design source documents in order to facilitate control thereafter. Thus, proper form design may be viewed as a preventive control aid.

Screen Design

The widespread use of visual displays with terminals and personal computers has altered the way in which forms are used, and in some cases replaced them altogether. Forms may now be used for recording data that will be transcribed to a computer screen. Necessarily, the form and the screen format will need to be coordinated. In some cases, data will be entered directly without a form.

For example, a customer order may be taken through the mail, using a preprinted form supplied. Upon receipt, the information will need to be keyed in to a computer or terminal. On the other hand, the order may come in over the telephone, and the information entered directly into the computer without the creation of an intermediate form.

Most of the foregoing discussion about form design applies to screen design as well. However, there are some differences. For one thing, the size of the screen is fixed and limited (often 25 lines of 80 characters). It may take more than one screen, and unlike paper forms, the user can only see one screen at a time. Screens are more flexible, however. A paper form may have to be very large in order to handle a variety of possibilities. A screen can have its format altered dynamically in response to data entered so that only the necessary "blanks" are presented to be filled in. Screens also have other advantages in the use of color, graphics, and highlighted or blinking fields. All of these can be used to enhance understandability and increase the accuracy of the data entered.

Guidelines for form and screen design are presented in [9]. Specifically it mentions the following with relation to screens:

1) Consider the nature of the user. Instructions may have to be very explicit if the user uses it infrequently or is from outside the organization (a customer, for example).

2) Instructions should be consistently displayed and only displayed when relevant (no instruction about going to the next screen when the last screen is displayed).

3) Avoid displaying terms like "error" that the user sees as disparaging.

4) Provide constant feedback. Messages should be provided that confirm the correctness of data entered, or that keep the user informed about the progress of the processing that is taking place.

Data Conversion and Validation

We return now to application control along the data processing cycle (fig. 14.2). The next stop in the journey is at the activities of *data conversion* and *data validation*. Data conversion is the process of transforming data from a human-readable to a computer-readable medium (e.g., keying in). Data validation is the process of error detection and correction. This process is always carried out before new transactions serve in update and calculation activities.

In the old days of offline keying and batch processing, conversion and validation activities were handled separately. First the data was keyed and subsequently a computer program (usually labeled "edit program") read in the keyed data and verified correctness. Errors were printed out on a special report, which initiated clarification and correction activities. This usually resulted in repetitive keying and a rerun of the edit program until the data was error-free. This process is illustrated in figure 14.3.

Figure 14.3 outlines a process that is somewhat more complicated than this narrative description. The figure designates an additional file labeled "invalid data," which keeps a record of all the erroneous transactions, so that in subsequent reruns, the edit program will be able to check for completeness of the input material.

Contemporary technology allows consolidation of conversion and validation activities, either by online keying on terminals attached to a central computer, or by utilizing programmable devices for offline keying (e.g., diskettes mounted on microcomputers). In both cases, the keying operator communicates with an edit program that constantly monitors the validity of the keyed data and instantaneously signals an error.

The extent of validity checking depends on the capacity of the machine that hosts the edit program. In general, we distinguish between four degrees of depth in validity checks:

1. *Individual data items*—The program examines whether a data item (hereafter, a field) meets certain conditions related to its content. For instance, a "customer name" field cannot contain numerals; the "day" attribute of a "date" field cannot exceed thirty-one, nor can it be a nonpositive number; a "quantity" field cannot contain alphabetic characters.

Figure 14.3 Data validation and correction in systems based on offline keying and batch processing

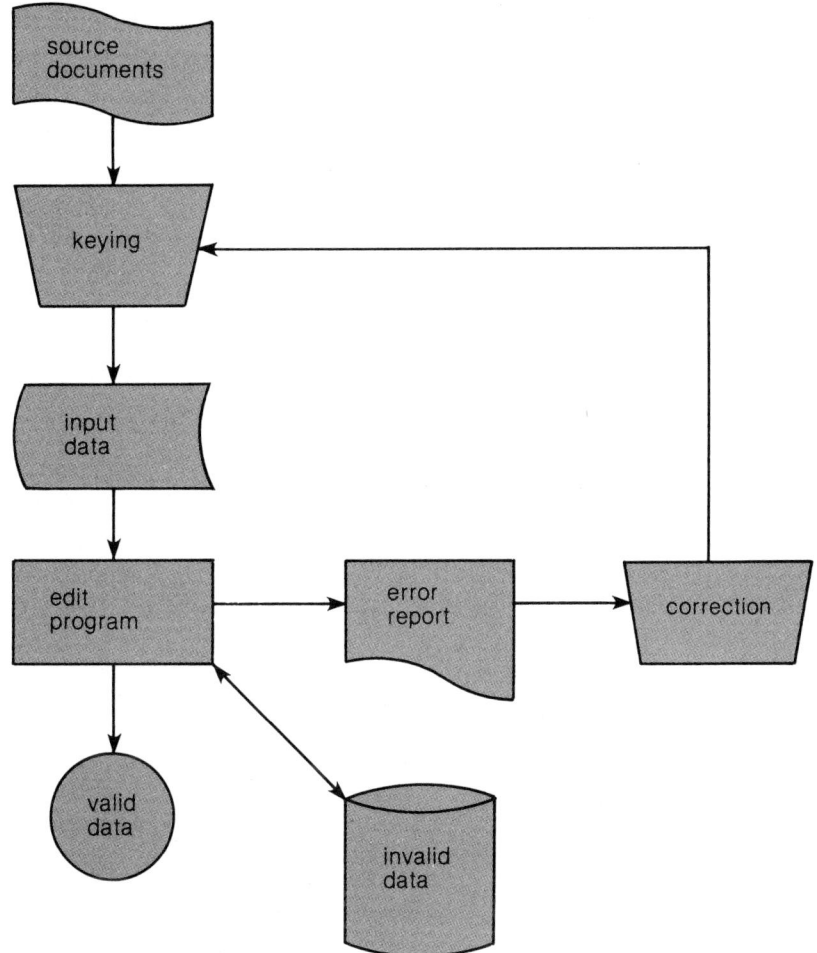

2. *Relations between fields*—The program examines whether relations between two or more fields belonging to the same record meet some predetermined conditions. For example, if the ''month'' attribute is two, the ''day'' attribute cannot exceed twenty-eight; however, if the ''year'' attribute is divisible by four, the ''day'' attribute may not exceed twenty-nine.

3. *Relations between records*—The program examines whether several input records satisfy some predetermined conditions. For example, does the accumulated total of all the amounts designated in individual transactions balance the figure designated in a batch-control record? Note that detection of unbalanced sums cannot point out the exact location of an error, but can only indicate the existence of an error.

4. *Relations between input records and existing files*—The program compares input data to data stored on existing files in order to check for consistency. For example, do we have this account number in our files? Is this customer entitled to credit? Is the student qualified to enroll in a certain course?

It is obvious that if you wish to exercise more in-depth validity checks, you will have to employ more capable ("intelligent") machines. For example, in order to accomplish validity checks of the fourth degree, you have to attach existing master files to the computer hosting the edit program. This may require engaging a relatively large computer for the purpose of data conversion and validation. We may conclude once more that control is basically a cost/benefit matter.

Control over Computerized Processing

The computerized processing is probably the most difficult segment to control relative to other portions of the data processing cycle. Actions taken by a computer program are not visible, thus wrongdoing can be cleverly camouflaged. Moreover, computerized processing usually consists of a sequence of programs, each handing over data to its successor, so it might be difficult to identify the origin of a certain error.

It is, therefore, quite common to center application controls at this point on external measures, mostly administrative. For instance, if we maintain rigid programming standards; if we impose strict segregation of duties; if we insist on complete, detailed, and up-to-date documentation; if we clearly distinguish between development and operation functions (see fig. 14.1); we may partly relieve the anxiety over what happens inside the black box.

Still, there are some ways to implant control measures into computerized processing. This is achieved by adding control routines to operational programs. For instance, we can keep forwarding control figures along the entire process; namely, each program will accumulate record counts, control totals, and hash totals so long as the process goes on. These figures will be forwarded from program to program and reconciled with newly calculated figures. We can also insert validity checks along the process, for instance, to assure that a payroll system does not produce paychecks in an amount exceeding, say $6,000 or less than $0.01.

Ahituv and Zelek [8] describe a sophisticated control technique performed right after a program completes its execution. The technique is based on checking some statistical characteristics of the program performance.

Output Control

Some concerns regarding output control include the following:

Is it correct?

Is it complete?

Does it reach the right destination?

Is it secured?

The cause for incorrect output is not likely to be found in the stage of output preparation but, rather, in preceding steps of inputting or processing. However, since output is normally more visible and concrete than intermediate results, and since it is also the last opportunity for verification before control is taken away from the ISD, we have to utilize control options as much as possible. This would include reconciliation of output data with previously produced control figures, such as totals and counts; visual scanning of reports and screens to reassure data reasonableness; comparisons between different reports and also between outputs and inputs. Output completeness can also be checked by means of control figures. In addition, consecutive numbering of pages is a simple yet effective tool.

Prompt distribution of output is attained if the distribution function is provided with sufficient resources and regulated by well-defined procedures. Tools aiding distribution may include computerized address labels, clear and large headings, up-to-date mailing lists, and the like.

Output security is obviously a function of the output content. Confidential data should be guarded and isolated from nonprivileged reports. Output security should also be regulated by clear policies and procedures and maintained by competent personnel.

Security of online output (e.g., terminal display) is more involved than that of printouts because users may possess terminals at remote and scattered locations and it is difficult to make sure that only authorized personnel push the buttons of a terminal. It is more feasible to limit access to online output by frequently changing passwords, identification requirements, and ciphering. [5, 6].

File Control

As stated earlier, most of the file control measures are built-in controls. To realize file control, one has to select the control options that will warrant decent control. This may include the use of passwords, labels (see [25], pp. 253–55), catalogs, and ciphering of stored data [5]. A statistical method to assess data reliability based on checking data samples is presented in [1].

In addition to these, each application requires complementary means depending upon its specific traits. A very common control provision is to preserve previous generations of master and transaction files. In fact, each sequential update of a master file (see appendix A for more on file organization techniques) maintains, as a by-product, the input files that have been used to create the last version of the master file. It is, therefore, a matter of establishing the right administrative procedures should one wish to avoid deletion of a few previous generations. The process is illustrated in figure 14.4.

Each sequential update produces a new master file, while the previous master file becomes virtually obsolete. Yet, if the previous master and transaction files are kept intact and the new master file is accidentally damaged, it can be restored by replicating the last update process. The number of previous generations that are preserved may vary in relation to the nature of the application. Some computer installations keep a few generations intact, while important data from older generations are extracted and condensed in files held for a longer period.

Figure 14.4 Generations of files in a sequential update

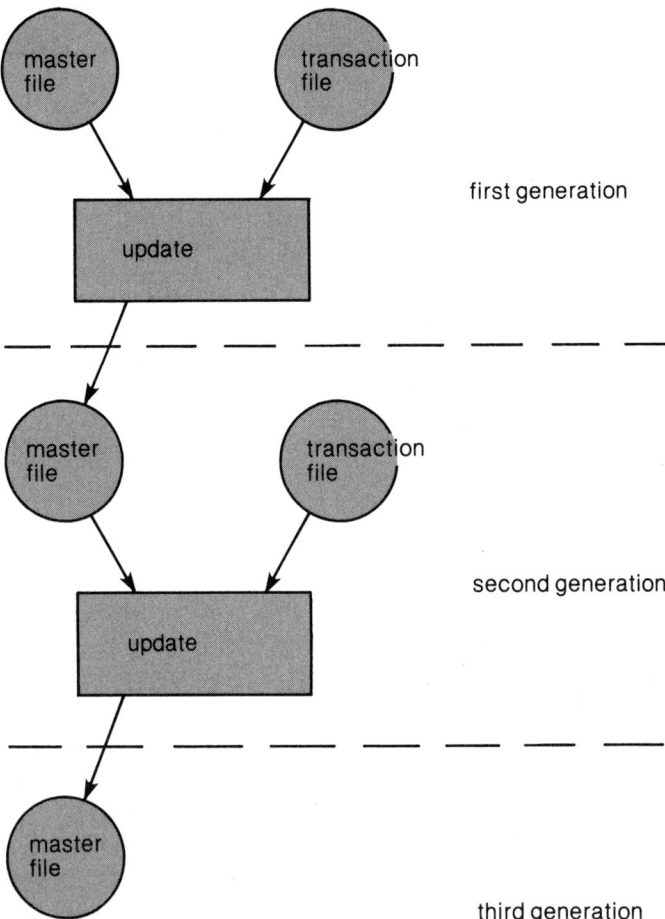

first generation

second generation

third generation

This technique is not similarly applicable to direct (random) updating because in direct access files, records are updated in place (see appendix A). Therefore, preservation of previous generations is possible only if master files are copied and the copies are kept separately. Such procedures, accompanied by continuous backup storing of transaction records (particularly in online applications), make it possible to restore master files in case of file destruction.

Another measure of file control is to place backup files in fireproof vaults, or even at a different location. In other words, every new master file is immediately copied and the copy is taken elsewhere.

Note that many of these provisions are administrative, hence require the establishment of appropriate procedures. Since the provisions are costly, they should be selected in the light of the specific application and the characteristics of the data involved.

Audit Trail

Of particular import is an aspect of control that pertains to the data processing cycle as a whole, the *audit trail*.

Most business applications deal with monetary transactions (e.g., payroll, accounts receivable) or with activities having monetary implications (e.g., inventory movements). Such business applications are subject to generally accepted accounting principles and auditing requirements. A prominent principle is the availability of an audit trail. This means that an auditor is able "to trail an original transaction forward to a summarized total or from a summarized total backward to the original transaction. Only in this way can it be determined whether the summary accurately reflects the business' transactions" [25, p. 256].

System designers must be aware of the audit trail requirement and its implications for system design. In short, each transaction must be preserved along the processing cycle; moreover, mutual references must be established between transactions and outcoming aggregations. These implications are valid not only for computerized data (i.e., magnetic files) but also for "paper" data, such as source documents and printouts.

An audit trail is obtainable if the designer devises a systematic numbering method for accounts; namely, each account number must indicate major and super-major accounts into which this account is accumulated. Very often the designer will have to attach pointers to records. Obviously, the preservation of old generations of files and an archive of source documents is vital.

Some Concluding Remarks on Application Control

The audit trail concept is a good demonstration for the argument that application control is much more a problem of appropriate design than of operation. It is inconceivable that an information system can first be designed and implemented, and thereafter controls can be superimposed on the already existing system. Controls have to be superimposed during the design and then incorporated into program writing, procedure writing, implementation, and operation, so that control measures become an integral part of the entire system. This would imply that information analysts, system designers, and project leaders should be conscious of control aspects; and auditors should take an active part in system development to guarantee sufficient solutions to control problems.

When auditors and system developers disagree on the degree of control that should be applied, the final decision rests with management. Management should be able to assess the cost of controls vis-à-vis the probable costs implied by not adopting certain measures. The probable costs would include not only monetary outcomes, but also factors of goodwill, legal implications, privacy, and confidentiality. As usual, it is a problem of cost/benefit analysis where tangible and intangible variables are intertwined (see ch. 13).

A possible control aid is to devise a permanent statistical system that collects and analyzes data about errors. For instance, if data about the frequency of keying errors is continuously analyzed, distributed by data item, type of form, keying operator, keying location, and the like, it is possible to be better prepared to recognize certain control problems and to diagnose their causes. Again, a statistical system of this sort should be developed in parallel to the principal system so the latter can produce the input data for the former.

Information System Documentation

Information system *documentation* is probably one of the most prominent means of control. Proper documentation has a great influence on all aspects of control. It forces system developers to carefully examine each segment of the proposed system before its structure is final; hence, it is a preventive measure. It may detect design errors while the system is still on the drawing board. Later, during operation, it facilitates comparisons between real and expected outcomes. Thus, it is also a detective measure. Proper documentation also speeds up tracing an error, so it makes an efficient correction aid. There is no doubt, therefore, that the quality of documentation is as important as the quality of the information system it is supposed to describe.

The Problem of Documentation Timing

Everybody preaches the importance of proper documentation, yet not many do something about it in their own organization. In fact, most information system professionals regard documentation as the "dark side" of their job—a must that should be done superficially in order to get rid of it as quickly as possible.

The main reason for this prejudice lies in the timing of the documentation. In many information systems departments (ISD), system developers first complete a development activity and then have to supplement it with requisite documentation. For example, a system designer is supposed to design a system and then wind it up with documentation; an application programmer writes a program (at most draws a scratch flowchart on a wrinkled, greasy piece of paper before commencing the coding) and then outlines what the program does and how. Consequently, documentation is the least creative task of system developers' work.

Because documentation is perceived as an after-the-fact task, after the "real thing" has been completed, it is neither exciting, nor stimulating, nor creative. No wonder resentment arises.

System Development and Documentation in Parallel

A possible solution to the resistance-to-documentation problem is simply to impose documentation practices—i.e., a "law enforcement" approach. It is certainly a workable approach; however, tight and frequent supervision would be required. It may succeed if employees learn that transfer to a new project as well as promotion in the long range depend on completing satisfactory documentation.

An alternative approach is to make documentation an integrated part of the development process. In other words, design and programming progress together through preparation of certain worksheets that serve as design and programming aids, and they simultaneously constitute the appropriate documentation necessary for the system. In this way, documentation becomes a by-product of the development process; in fact, development cannot proceed without supporting documentation. Eventually antagonism to documentation will perish.

This principle guides the analysis, design, and programming techniques that have been developed in software engineering (see ch. 10). A prominent example is structured analysis, where documents lead to structured design, which provides input documentation to structured programming.

Modern approaches to system development that are known by the general term CASE (computer aided system engineering—see ch. 10) incorporate the documentation in the software that is used for the analysis and design of the information system. In such cases, the creation of documentation is almost automatic. Still, one has to make sure that the documentation is updated as the system undergoes changes.

Principles of System Documentation

Almost every textbook on system analysis or software engineering provides the reader with guidelines for the form and content of system documentation (see, for example, [9], [20], or [26]). Such texts also suggest symbols to be used for flowcharts, data flow diagrams, and other standard means of communicating among the developers and users of the system. Other texts are specifically devoted to the methods of developing good documentation (see, for example, [27]). Glass [16] provides a broad view of the skills needed and standards to be followed.

Increasing use is made of *online documentation*. Such documentation exists as files, or as part of a data base, such that users can retrieve the documents for viewing on a display or for printing hard copies on demand. Some of this documentation is embedded in the software in the form of *help screens* that can be called up, as the programs are being used, to answer questions as they arise. Other documentation may be available as tutorials or reference material. Horton [19] provides an extensive coverage of the preparation of effective documentation in this form.

Whether documentation is done online or with external paper documents or in both forms, some basic principles apply:

1. *Consistency*—Documentation should maintain consistency in labeling and reference to common terms and prevailing activities. For instance, each form should mention the information system for which it is used; each form should use the same title for the same function (e.g., once the person who analyzes systems has been labeled ''information analyst,'' do not use the term ''system analyst'' on the heading of pertinent forms). Consistency refers also to the use of file names, data item labels, program labels, etc.

2. *Complete headings*—All the different forms constituting the documentation should consist of complete headings to facilitate identification of the system to which a form belongs and the person who prepared it. Date of preparation is a vital datum to facilitate documentation updates.

3. *Agreed set of symbols*—All documents, particularly those containing data flow diagrams and flowcharts, should use the same set of symbols so every person involved in a project will comprehend the documentation created by his or her peers.

Not only the forms, but also any narrative document relative to any activity during the system life cycle should adhere to these principles. This would include feasibility reports, information analysis reports, design specifications, program specifications, operating procedures, change requests, and the like.

Proper handling and maintenance of the documentation is no less important than is appropriate design of system documentation because even the most adequate form is worth nothing if its content is obsolete. Hence, it is vital that ISD management impose and enforce strict regulations regarding system documentation. The regulations encompass the following aspects:

1. *Complete and strict filling out*—Management should ensure that all forms and documents are completely filled out and that system developers and operators do not overlook or ignore certain forms or items within forms.

2. *Update*—Documentation must be as current as the system it describes. Whenever a change is inserted into an information system, a parallel update should be made in the documentation pertaining to it. Otherwise, the documentation stops reflecting the status of the system and becomes useless or hard to use. (Have you ever tried to locate a bug in a program when the program listing does not display the last version of the program?) Thus, change procedures should refer to both system and documentation handling.

3. *Accessibility*—Documentation must be collated and filed. In other words, when we need to glance at a document, we must know exactly where it is located and who may provide it. Documents that are randomly scattered all over the ISD premises do not provide any help.

It is therefore advisable to manage the documentation by using contemporary software engineering techniques, such as configuration management (see ch. 10), or CASE.

As mentioned, the particular documentation convention selected is not important as long as it adheres to these principles. However, it is incorrect to believe that system documentation relates only to the ISD. Users and management also have a say, and they should insist on appropriate documentation; without that input, when a system goes down and poor documentation fails to reveal a cause, users and management will be the first to suffer.

EDP Auditing

With the computer becoming more complex through the development of sophisticated multi-programming capacity, coupled with telecommunication links and a wide variety of new input and output devices, another dimension has been added to the role expected of the auditor. In order for him to fulfill his professional responsibilities, the auditor must now be able to perform a wide variety of tasks which, until recently, did not exist or were not considered within the auditor's scope.

For example, when manual systems were audited, a wide variety of approaches were generally available and the most appropriate would be selected for the given circumstances. If there were control weaknesses, corrective changes were easily formulated and suggested. However, it is now possible to produce a data processing system with such poor controls that neither the auditor nor the manager can place reliance on the system's integrity. For this reason, audit review during the design and development process of an automated system has become crucial if management is to be provided needed assurance that auditable and properly controlled systems are being produced.

Moreover, once systems are placed in operation, the auditor has a continuing requirement to review both general controls and application controls. Such reviews are to assure that systems support management policy and produce reliable results. For a system already in operation when an audit is scheduled, the auditor should determine whether the system's objectives are being met [12, p. IV].

This passage has been quoted from EDP audit standards that were published in 1979 in recognition of the important role that auditing had assumed in relation to information systems. In fact, most organizations of any size today channel their monetary transactions via computer applications. Therefore, a lack of or inadequacy in EDP auditing may result in the qualification of an accountant's opinion on financial statements. A qualification of this sort might occur when an accountant is unable to verify compliance with generally accepted accounting principles.

A modern EDP auditor does not limit concern to postaudit. To do so may result in suggestions that are too late to carry out, either because modifications to existing systems might be very costly, or because abuse has already been committed. The auditor's duties have to be expanded, therefore, to preimplementation activities; the auditor must take part in system design and development. The auditor has three different duties:

1. The auditor has a say during system development.
2. The auditor serves as a ''watchdog'' of all the controls—i.e., makes sure that overall control provisions are established and kept.
3. The auditor performs an audit of existing systems.

This is well described in the Comptroller General's standards [12, p. 2]:

1. The auditor shall actively participate in reviewing the design and development of new data processing systems or applications, and significant modifications thereto, as a normal part of the audit function.
2. The auditor shall review general controls in data processing systems to determine that (A) controls have been designed according to management direction and legal requirements, and (B) such controls are operating effectively to provide reliability of, and security over, the data being processed.
3. The auditor shall review application controls of installed data processing applications to assess their reliability in processing data in a timely, accurate, and complete manner.

In summary, an EDP auditor has a dual task. The auditor is, in a way, a control measure, since he or she carries out some control activities (e.g., periodic auditing of certain systems). At the same time, the auditor activates all the controls—namely, he or she exerts control over the control (e.g., checks for segregation of duties). We will now discuss these audit facets.

Control Activation

Remember the story we told at the beginning of this chapter about an alarm system that did not prevent a valuable painting from being stolen? Let us go back to that story, and imagine that you have installed the best alarm system available in the market, equipped with every possible gadget. One night when you return home from a concert, you find that burglars have stolen some of your most valuable paintings without causing any reaction from the police or the security company. The melody of Brahms that has been echoing in your head is now replaced by crescendos of fury. How come? After you calm down, you discover that your children, who left the house a couple of hours after you did, forgot to turn on the alarm system. In fact, you had forgotten to remind them to do so. In other words, the control system was satisfactory, but control over the control was never exerted.

A few weeks later you return to your home at night and find a fabulous Rembrandt missing. One window is open, but the alarm system did not operate at all. On the verge of crying, you discover that the wiring around that open window had never been connected properly; thus the break-in did not even trigger the alarm. You blame yourself for not watching the system installers closely. In other words, your involvement in preimplementation activities was not sufficient.

Lest you start wondering how many more paintings are left for further examples, we assure you that this is our last use of the anecdote. The story is meant to illustrate that installation of control measures is not the end of the road. Auditors have to participate in the development of the information system to make sure that the measures are designed and devised properly [14]. In addition, auditors have to make sure that the measures are activated as required while the system is in operation.

Auditor Participation in System Development

During system development, the auditor does not substitute for an information analyst or a system designer. The auditor acts as an observer and a reviewer. The auditor advises the developers on accounting principles and audit requirements that have to be considered by them. The auditor must be assured that the developers understand and take those considerations into account. The auditor reviews the design and the programs to guarantee compliance with control requirements.

The Comptroller General's standards mention six objectives for the auditor's involvement in system development [12, pp. 5–8]:

1. *Management policies*—"To assure that systems/applications faithfully carry out the policies management has prescribed for the system."

2. *Audit trail*—"To provide assurance that systems/applications provide the controls and audit trails needed for management, auditor, and operational review."

3. *Controls*—"To provide assurance to management that systems/applications include the controls necessary to protect against loss or serious error."

4. *Efficiency and economy*—"To provide assurance that systems/applications will be efficient and economical in operation."

5. *Legal requirements*—"To assure that systems/applications conform with applicable legal requirements."

6. *Documentation*—"To provide assurance that systems/applications are documented in a manner that will provide the understanding of the system required for appropriate maintenance and auditing."

These objectives certainly broaden the scope of the auditor's mandate beyond traditional postaudit.

In summary, we may say that an EDP auditor has two roles during the system development phase. One role is the "watchdog," to assure that the development process is in compliance with life cycle practices. Note that the development of a DSS does not resemble the traditional life cycle, hence it may imply some differences in auditing. This is described in [3]. The other role is that of a user: the EDP auditor submits information requirements the same way other users do; the requirements designate the control measures that should be incorporated into the system, and the reports, log files, and access techniques that are to be used in the future by the auditor in order to facilitate routine audit during the operation phase.

Supervision of Existing Control Provisions

Another facet of EDP auditing is to see that control provisions are strictly kept. This refers mainly to administrative provisions set by management for preventive purposes.

It is a normal human trait to be lenient with employees who inadvertently break some administrative regulations. Managers may not understand the necessity of some formal restrictions because they are not aware of potential danger. For example, a manager may let a talented computer operator insert changes into an application program in order to apprentice the operator in programming in preparation for future promotion. This defies the rule of segregation of duties; the manager has obviously never understood the reasons for this rule.

Very often time pressure is used as an excuse for a deliberate omission of administrative control provisions. For example, a project leader may let a programmer skip formal testing procedures provided that the programmer completes debugging on time. A program may then be handed over to a user without having undergone all the required formal tests, but the due date is met.

The EDP auditor has to play the role of a mean watchdog and try to avoid such actions, or complain loudly when they happen.

It is recommended that EDP auditors prepare a checklist of control provisions. This checklist may be useful whenever an audit is carried out over the ISD or part of it. A sample checklist and control questionnaire are shown in [25]. Sample cross-check matrices are provided in [14].

Auditing a Computerized Application

Suppose you were asked to examine the reliability of the postal services. You could send a large number of letters from many different locations to many other locations and follow up the outcomes: count how many letters arrive at the assigned destination; how many letters are lost; how long it took for letters of various mailing classes to arrive; how many letters whose addressees are unknown are returned to the senders. Collecting and processing these statistics could give you an indication of the reliability of the postal services.

Another approach is to examine the internal processes of the postal services. You can spend some time with the system, inquire about procedures, observe sorting equipment, follow up transportation lines, interview key persons and operations staff, check control mechanisms, and the like.

You could also exercise a combination of the two approaches by sending a sample of letters and analyzing the results and simultaneously examining the internal processes of the postal services.

The first approach regards the postal system as a "black box" and tests its reliability by means of input/output analysis. The second approach evaluates the system by scrutinizing its components.

Similarly, an audit of information systems can be based on either of these approaches or a combination of them. In EDP auditing, the "black box" method is labeled *auditing around the computer;* the second approach is called *auditing through the computer.*

Auditing around the Computer

The fundamental idea of auditing around the computer suggests that extensive examination of a system's inputs, outputs, and intermediate data by means of controlled samples will indicate whether the system is reliable. The process is briefly described in [11, p. 816]:

> Typically, the auditor selects source documents; traces associated entries through intermediate computer printouts; and finally examines resultant entries in summary accounts.
>
> The basic advantages of this technique are: its low cost; low level of requisite technical expertise; and ease of comprehension by all persons involved—auditors, management and EDP personnel.

The major criticism of this approach centers on its alleged superficiality: it can hardly cope with systems of voluminous data; it is based on intermediate and final printouts that may not reflect what is really being done inside the computerized process;

intermediate printouts are not always automatically available, hence, if they are requested ad hoc, the auditor is at the mercy of designers and programmers. This is a thoroughly undesirable situation.

The auditing-around-the-computer technique was most common at the beginning of the computer era, mainly because auditing of computerized applications became a must, but also because auditors lacked the extensive expertise required; hence, this approach was better than not doing anything. These days, while the method has not been ruled out, it is acceptable mainly as a complement to more subtle techniques.

Auditing through the Computer

Auditing through the computer is an approach that can be realized by various techniques. The basic idea is that the auditor assesses the reliability of a system by running controlled tests and examining closely the system's components.

The simplest technique is called *test decks*. The auditor prepares test data, which encompasses every possible variation in the processing, including erroneous data. The test data is run through the examined information system while the auditor observes and analyzes intermediate and final results and compares those to the "should be" results that have been calculated beforehand.

A possible extension to the test-data technique is the *dummy company* technique. The auditor gets all the pertinent programs and runs them on test data and artificial files. In other words, the auditor creates a dummy company with dummy files and channels dummy transactions through the real programs to see whether the process is performed as intended.

Another technique is *parallel simulation*. According to this technique, the auditor simulates the client's application by generating programs that are supposed to perform the same functions that are handled by the examined programs. The auditor can then run data (test data or real data) through both systems and look for discrepancies. This technique, however, is relatively costly.

There are many more related techniques that are not reviewed here (see [11], for example). The use of networks, distributed information systems, and interorganizational data flows add additional considerations for the auditor (see, for example [17]). Hansen and Hill [18] examine the special problems of auditing systems that incorporate *electronic data interchange* (EDI). The auditor should also make use of special auditing software packages. Such software is designed to aid the auditing process with programs that give auditors easy access to files and auditing procedures [23].

It should be noted that in addition to the various possible techniques, the auditor has to examine all other related aspects. This will include program and system flowcharts, program listings, operational procedures, backup/recovery procedures, administrative provisions, and the like. Only a comprehensive examination can provide the auditor with enough evidence on the degree of reliability of an information system. (For comprehensive texts on EDP audit, we recommend [29] and [15].)

Auditing with the Computer

With the computer around, the internal auditor's task can be greatly improved. Many activities that once consumed a lot of humanpower and took long periods of time can now be performed easily by computers. For instance, random sampling by computers is almost instantaneous; screening of files to look for exceptions becomes very easy; comparisons and cross-checks between files are quite possible.

In a way, computers can facilitate internal audit activities rather than complicate them. The only condition is that the internal auditor learn to utilize these machines and their software.

Some Concluding Remarks

The fast expansion of computer applications has created a great demand for competent EDP auditors. Apprenticeship of EDP auditors is prolonged and involved because an expert in this area has to master several different disciplines: accounting, auditing, information systems, computer business applications, and information processing technology (hardware/software characteristics). Sufficient practical experience is definitely a must to achieve competence. This is, therefore, the main reason why demand for competent personnel outgrows supply in this area.

In addition to supply and demand problems, the profession of EDP auditing has to cope with rapid progress in technology. For example, auditing information systems based on traditional file organization techniques is not like auditing systems based on a DBMS. Auditing online systems is different from auditing batch-processing systems. Interested readers may refer to several references [7, 15, 21, 22, 28, 29] for further information.

Information System Security

With the rapid growth in the use of computerized information systems, it has become evident that computerized information requires protection like all other organizational assets. The problems related to information security are difficult to resolve, since most information systems are normally built to facilitate data dissemination rather than to limit it. The purpose of this section is to highlight some risks and possible security measures. For more details, the reader can refer to textbooks dealing specifically with this issue (e.g., [24] and [21]).

Causes of Risk

Risks to information systems can stem from various sources, such as nature, human beings, or technology. We will now discuss some of the main sources of risk.

Natural disasters can happen anytime and almost anywhere. These include fire, flood, earthquake, and the like. Any might damage computer centers, communication lines, and data files, or they can hurt key persons without whom it is difficult to operate the systems.

Humans can also generate risks, inadvertently or deliberately. For instance, employees can go on strikes; programmers can overlook bugs; keying-in operators can falsify monetary transactions; competitors can hook up to a communication line.

Technology is a risk factor in itself. A new piece of hardware can be unreliable; a new software package can fail to work properly; communication lines can be of low quality.

Sometimes the organization that uses the systems generates risks by imposing incorrect procedures or by not imposing appropriate procedures.

Risks can be internal—posed by the organization itself (employees, buildings, procedures); or risks can be external—caused by outsiders (criminals, industrial espionage, computer hackers). Risks can be physical and tangible, such as damages to computer sites, or destruction of files. However, risks can also be intangible, or at least hard to quantify, such as loss of goodwill, or loss of confidential data. The next section lists possible areas that should be reviewed in order to avoid or reduce exposure to risks.

Where Do We Search for Risk?

Good guesses and intuition are certainly helpful, but they should not substitute for a systematic effort to identify potential risk factors. The first step toward risk avoidance (or reduction) is conducting a comprehensive survey to identify potential risks. The survey should include the following areas:

1. *Personnel*—Procedures of hiring, screening, promotion, firing, and resignation; training requirements; quality and qualifications of employees.

2. *Physical environment*—Location of buildings, neighbors, topographical and weather conditions, power supply, access to the building and to the computer floor.

3. *Hardware and software systems*—Maintenance agreements, reliability, vendor support, documentation, and backup.

4. *Communications*—Reliability, backup, security, verification, and control procedures.

5. *Operations*—Backup procedures, data security, input/output controls, process controls, and administrative controls.

6. *Contracts*—With vendors as well as with customers.

7. *Laws and regulations*—Privacy acts, national security, etc.

This list is certainly not exhaustive. It is presented only to demonstrate the width of the scope. The next sections will discuss some measures to improve information *system security.*

Security Measures

Very similar to control measures, security measures are also composed of administrative, technical, and human elements. Prerequisites to security arrangements are the appointment of an information *security officer* and the preparation of a *security plan.* We will now elaborate on these two.

Information Security Officer

The *New York Times,* in a special supplement on jobs published October 16, 1983, described computer security specialists as ''a new breed of computer professionals . . . who mix the technical knowledge of a programmer with the suspicions of an auditor and the sleuthing instinct of Hercule Poirot. The combination of the talents is rare, and good computer security experts are in short supply.'' There is a special-interest group on security, audit, and control, which is affiliated with the Association for Computing Machinery (ACM).

Similar to the EDP auditor, the security officer is responsible for a number of issues: preparing an organizational security plan for information systems; implementing the plan; and controlling the daily activation of the security measures. We will turn now to the security plan and to some prevailing measures.

Information System Security Plan

An information system security plan is an overall approach to security issues. The plan should comprise the following sections:

1. Objectives and goals
2. Identification of potential risks and assessment of their possible damages
3. Proposal of a set of measures and provisions to reduce or eliminate the risks
4. Economic justification of the proposed measures
5. Steps of implementation, including timetable and resources required
6. Provisions for maintaining the security measures after they will have been established

The plan is submitted to top management for approval. Management has to realize that approval of the plan entails allocation of resources for implementation and maintenance. Resources include personnel, hardware and software features, training facilities, and the like.

It is recommended that in addition to appointing a security officer, management will form a permanent committee to govern these issues. The committee plays the role of a ''board of directors'' vis-à-vis the information system security officer.

Information Security System

An information security system is a software package that deals with various security problems. It performs a number of functions; the major ones are here.

1. *Identification*—The system should be able to identify each terminal by its location; it should be able to identify a communications line that transmits or receives data; it should be able to identify each user by matching codes to passwords.

2. *Authorization*—The system should determine whether a certain request is allowed when it comes from a certain terminal, on a certain line, by a certain user, giving a certain password, and referring to a certain file or data item. Any request that does not comply with such an authorized pattern should be denied.

3. *Data security*—The system should control the distribution of outputs and ensure that reports are not diverted to wrong locations. It should protect files, maintain catalogs, and delete obsolete data. Advanced systems are capable of performing ciphering and deciphering if so required.

4. *Communications security*—The system should be able to disconnect any line whenever it suspects that the line is being abused. It should be able to verify lines and terminals. Above all, it should log all the activities initiated by end users.

5. *Assistance to the security officer*—The system has to provide information to the security officer in terms of exceptional activities, reports on classified processes, statistics, and the like. Moreover, the system should activate alarm calls whenever there is a repetitive illegal attempt to intrude.

Security systems are available in the software market. They are very useful for computer centers based on large mainframes and widely used communications. They are less commonly used in microcomputer environments.

Contingency Plan

A cornerstone in security arrangements is the *contingency plan.* A contingency plan deals with the following issues:

1. *Emergency plan*—This plan tells exactly what should be done in case of emergency, such as fire, flood, or terrorist activity. The plan should detail the files that are to be evacuated, the rooms and floors that should be secured, and who is to do what.

2. *Backup plan*—Unlike the emergency plan, which is rarely activated, the backup plan is continuously drilled. It deals with routine arrangements made for an emergency situation. These include file backups, computer backup, and training of backup personnel. If the security officer fails to monitor the daily execution of the backup plan, the other plans will not help when they are needed.

3. *Recovery plan*—The execution of the recovery plan follows the emergency plan. Once files have been saved and backup equipment is available, it is time to reconstruct the system. However, very often the backup installation lacks the required capacity in terms of computing power, communications lines, etc. The recovery plan sets priorities and determines the sequence of recovery activities.

Note that all the components of the contingency plan should be drilled from time to time, and they have to be modified in accordance with changes in the organization and the environment. If the plan is shelved and not tested periodically, it is most likely that it will not be adequate when needed.

Practical Conclusions for Information System Design and Use

The following list details some practical conclusions for system design and use.

1. Control must be built into an information system. Therefore, it should be considered part of the design and the build-up of a system, rather than an after-the-fact activity.

2. Information systems should incorporate all aspects of control: preventive measures to avoid faultiness and potential abuse; detective features to signal incorrectness; corrective procedures in case an error or a suspected felony is identified.

3. Management and EDP auditors should continuously examine and review design outlines to ensure compliance with control standards.

4. Control should not be exaggerated. It should adhere to generally accepted accounting principles and audit requirements. Beyond that, any additional measure should be subject to cost/benefit considerations—i.e., how much does it cost in comparison to the potential loss it may prevent?

5. Administrative control includes a set of procedures and regulations imposed on the information system function. Development and operation of any application should first conform to overall control provisions.

6. The cycle of system development is usually long, costly, and under time pressure. These characteristics may lead management to relax control measures at times, which might help short-range problems, but could hurt in the long range—and therefore should be avoided.

7. Segregation of duties is an example of a measure that might lengthen development and operation time. Still, this rule is necessary for preventive (and perhaps detective) control.

8. Establishing a quality control function in an ISD is recommended.

9. Computer software and hardware are usually enriched with plenty of built-in controls, many of which are optional. Management, EDP auditors, and system developers should be familiar with built-in control measures so they can incorporate them into information systems as they see fit.

10. Application control includes three categories: administrative controls relevant to a certain application; built-in controls useful to the application; ad hoc measures specially tailored for a particular application. System developers should subtly blend controls from all three categories.

11. Control design encompasses the entire data processing cycle. For source documents, it institutes arrangements to maintain data completeness and accuracy, and to assure that transactions are initiated only by authorized personnel. For data conversion and validation, it states the checks necessary to assure validity. For computerized processes, it designates the built-in controls that should be activated and the extra checks that should be inserted into application programs. For output handling, it outlines distribution and security provisions. For file control, it regulates file expiration and backup.

12. Design of source documents and visual display screens is directed by a few guidelines: the document or screen should be self-explanatory, i.e., guide the person in the process of filling in the information; it must cover all pertinent data items; the sequence of data to be entered should be logical; some redundancy may help in control, however, exaggerated redundancy is undesired; the document or screen should not contain anything that is unnecessary. For paper forms, the convenience of manual handling and transcription of the data is of paramount importance. For screens, the interaction with the user must be considered, and instructions kept explicit, consistent, and friendly.

13. Bookkeeping applications must comply with audit trail requirements, which state that an auditor must be able to trace any summary figure backward to its originating transaction and any individual transaction forward to an accumulative account. This imposes rigid design constraints relative to transaction and master file preservation and account numbering.

14. Documentation is an integral part of information system development. Management should allow for the time required to document a system.

15. Various design and programming techniques allow system development and documentation to proceed together. This may improve the quality of both development and documentation; hence, indirectly, users, developers, and management will all benefit from adopting such techniques.

16. Information system documentation should be consistent, complete, and adopt an agreed upon, common set of symbols.

17. Management should make sure that documentation is up-to-date, completely filled out, accessible, and well-ordered.

18. EDP auditors participate in information system development in order to emphasize control aspects. They may require installation of special features in a system under development so that audit will be facilitated during operation.

19. Organizations should establish an information system security plan and make sure that the plan is implemented.

20. It is recommended that organizations employ an information system security officer whose job is to plan and implement security provisions and to look after security arrangements on a routine basis.

Summary

This chapter has dealt with information system controls. Its main premise is that since information systems are open, complex, and heterogeneous with respect to components, they are highly exposed to erroneous or malicious doings. Therefore, each information system should be interlaced with a congruent control system. Control is obtained by an appropriate blend of technical means, administrative provisions, and human supervision.

Control is classified into three categories. Preventive control refers to measures to prevent errors or wrongdoings. Detective control refers to measures installed to detect incorrectness. Corrective control refers to procedures devised to correct faultiness. In practice, many control measures incorporate preventive, detective, and corrective traits.

Responsibility for control rests in management hands. Management should ensure, first, that information systems comply with accounting and auditing principles. Beyond that, control is a matter of cost/benefit—i.e., how much does it cost vis-à-vis the loss it may prevent?

Information systems are subject to three types of controls: administrative, built-in, and application control. Administrative control includes a set of procedures and provisions that regulate all aspects of system development and operation. These regulations do not refer to any particular application, but rather institute rules for the way each activity is to be carried out.

A paramount administrative provision is the segregation of duties. This implies that employees do not handle activities they are not initially assigned to. For example, a programmer shall not enter the computer room; a computer operator shall not write programs; a keying operator shall not correct errors except for keying errors.

Another administrative control measure is the establishment of a quality control function and assurance that every new information system or change in an existing system is tested by that function on its way from development to operation. In addition, developers shall not access applications in operation, while operation personnel shall not access programs under development.

Other administrative provisions involve institution of formal procedures, reporting practices, and the like.

Built-in control refers to hardware and software features that are normally incorporated into the information processing equipment by the manufacturers. Many of these are permanent features that do not have to be activated, but we should know of their existence. However, some of the measures are optional, so their use should be explicitly designated.

Hardware control features include reading double-check, "intelligent" keying-in devices, communication controls and rerouting procedures, parity bits, automatic detection of invalid arithmetic operations, and file protection mechanisms. Equipment tolerance of temperature, humidity, and voltage fluctuations and features that allow recovery from fluctuations are also part of hardware control.

Software controls include software mechanisms to improve control, such as passwords, logbooks, and restart procedures, as well as aids to facilitate control over software development, such as programming, testing, and debugging tools. Software handling of file labels is another example of software control.

The notion of ''application control'' refers to a variety of control measures taken to face the central problems characterizing a specific application. The control mix may include administrative, built-in, and ad hoc controls. Application control encompasses the whole data processing cycle of a computerized application. It deals with appropriate handling of source data—i.e., maintaining data completeness and accuracy and assuring proper authorization of transactions. It covers data conversion and validation. Contemporary technology permits simultaneous data conversion and validation.

Validity checks may be superficial or profound, depending on the capacity of the keying equipment. Validity checks range from simple examination of individual data items, through comparative checks of a few items or several records, up to screening new transactions against existing records to verify certain data items.

Computerized processing is controlled by means of special routines and by transposing various control totals from stage to stage.

Output control is intended to assure completeness, proper distribution, and security of the system outputs. These are accomplished by various means, including numbering, labeling, and safeguarding.

File control is obtained by copying backups, preserving previous generations of files, physical protection, passwords, labels, transaction logbook, and the like.

Proper design of forms and documents facilitates control. An appropriately designed form is self-explanatory, exhaustive, logical in its writing sequence, not too redundant, not overloaded with unnecessary data, easy to key in, easy to handle manually, and spacious.

Visual display screens must also be designed properly, following most of the guidelines for paper forms. In addition, it must be considered that multiple screens may be required rather than a single form, and that the user may need much instruction and reassurance.

An imperative factor in bookkeeping systems is the audit trail. This is an audit requirement built into the system which allows auditors to trace transactions forward to a summary account and to trace summary accounts backward down to the exact transactions which constitute the account. This has significant implications for system design.

The second part of the chapter discusses information system documentation. It claims that problems of misdocumentation normally arise when system developers are required to complete documentation after a development activity (e.g., design, programming) has been finished. The best way to mitigate the problem is by adopting design and programming techniques that generate documentation as a by-product of the development activity.

System documentation should be consistent, complete, and use agreed-upon symbols and notation.

Management should see that documentation requirements are strictly met, up-to-date, orderly, and accessible.

The next part of the chapter discusses some aspects of EDP auditing. An EDP auditor has a triple function: participation in system development, controlling the use of every control measure, and auditing computerized applications. During system development, the auditor reviews design and programming products to make sure that control aspects are not overlooked and that the system under development complies with predetermined objectives. These may include management policies, audit trails, control requirements, efficiency and economy, legal requirements, and documentation standards.

The auditor's ongoing responsibilities are to institute and maintain control provisions, particularly administrative controls.

At times the auditor may select one or a few information systems and carry out a full-scale audit. There are two approaches to an information system audit. A relatively simple one is "auditing around the computer." The auditor analyzes the inputs and outputs of a system to look for any discrepancies.

A more subtle approach is called "auditing through the computer." The auditor runs application programs on test data or real data to check for appropriateness. Several techniques and tools have been developed to execute auditing through the computer. This approach appears to be more reliable than auditing around the computer but requires a high degree of professional competence.

Internal auditors can be assisted by computers for normal internal audit activities, such as sampling, exception detection, and cross-checking. For such purposes, computers are faster, more efficient, and cheaper than human labor.

The tremendous growth of computer use in business application has created an overwhelming demand for EDP auditors. Since apprenticeship of skilled auditors is a prolonged process, the demand for them continues to exceed the supply.

Securing the organizational information systems has become an important issue. Information systems are vulnerable to many risks emerging from natural causes (e.g., fire), human causes (e.g., computer-related crimes), technological malfunctions, and inappropriate procedures. The first step in handling such risks is identifying them. Then an overall security plan should be devised and implemented.

A major function related to this issue is the information system security officer. This person has an important role in planning and maintaining security arrangements.

Other key security components are the security software package and the contingency plan. The software should be able to deal with problems of user identification, authorization data, and communications security, and to provide assistance to the security officer. The contingency plan should deal with emergency, backup, and recovery planning.

Key Concepts

accuracy

auditing: around the computer, through the computer

audit trail

authentication

authorization

backup

batching

ciphering

completeness

contingency plan: emergency, back-up, and recovery

control: administrative, application, built-in, corrective, detective, preventive

data: conversion, validation

data processing cycle

deciphering

documentation

EDP auditing

encryption

file label: header, trailer

parallel simulation

parity bit

password

quality control section (QCS)

record count

security: officer, plan, system

segregation of duties

total: control, hash

References

1. Agmon, N., and N. Ahituv. "Assessing Data Reliability in an Information System." *Journal of Management Information Systems* 4, no. 2 (Fall 1987): 34–44.

2. Ahituv, N., D. Even-Tsur, and B. Sadan. "Procedures and Practices for Conducting Post Evaluation of Information Systems." *Journal of Information Systems Management* 3, no. 2 (Spring 1986): 61–65.

3. Ahituv, N., and I. Getz. "An Auditing Approach to Iterative Development of Decision Support Systems." *The EDP Auditor Journal,* 1986, no. 3: 34–37.

4. Ahituv, N., Y. Lapid, and S. Neumann. "Verifying the Authentication of an Information System User." *Computers and Security* 6, no. 2 (Apr. 1987): 152–57.

5. Ahituv, N., Y. Lapid, and S. Neumann. "Processing Encrypted Data." *Communications of the ACM* 30, no. 9 (Sept. 1987): 777–80.

6. Ahituv, N., Y. Lapid, and S. Neumann. "Protecting Statistical Data Bases Against Retrieval of Private Information." *Computers and Security* 7, no. 1 (Feb. 1988): 59–63.

7. Ahituv, N., and D. Lee. "Control Concepts and Evaluation Techniques for Use in Auditing of Advanced EDP Systems." *The EDP Auditor Journal* 4 (1984): 45–53.

8. Ahituv, N., and M. Zelek. "Instant Quality Control of Large Batch Processing Jobs." *MIS Quarterly* 11, no. 3 (Sept. 1987): 313–23.

9. Anderson Consulting, P. O. Flaatten, D. J. McCubbrey, P. D. O'Riordan, and K. Burgess. *Foundations of Business Systems.* Chicago: The Dryden Press, 1989.

10. Boockholdt, J. L., and D. H. Li. *Accounting Information Systems: Transaction Processing and Controls.* Homewood, IL: Irwin, 1991.

11. Cash, J. I., A. D. Bailey, and A. B. Whinston. "A Survey of Techniques for Auditing EDP-Based Accounting Information Systems." *The Accounting Review* 32, no. 4 (Oct. 1977): 813–32.

12. Comptroller General of the United States. *Auditing Computer-Based Systems.* Washington, D.C.: General Accounting Office, 1979.

13. Comptroller General of the United States. *Report to the Congress: Wider Use of Better Computer Software Technology Can Improve Management Control and Reduce Costs.* Washington, D.C.: General Accounting Office, 1980.

14. Fitzgerald, J. *Designing Controls into Computerized Systems.* Redwood City, CA: Jerry Fitzgerald and Associates, 1981.

15. Gallegos, F., D. R. Richardson, and A. F. Borthick. *Audit and Control of Information Systems.* Cincinnati: South-Western Publishing, 1987.

16. Glass, R. L. *Software Communication Skills.* Englewood Cliffs, NJ: Prentice-Hall, 1988.

17. Hansen, J. V. ''Audit Considerations in Distributed Processing Systems.'' *Communications of the ACM* 26, 8 (Aug. 1983): 562–69.

18. Hansen, J. V., and N. C. Hill. ''Control and Audit of Electronic Data Interchange.'' *MIS Quarterly* 13, 4 (Dec. 1989): 403–13.

19. Horton, W. K. *Designing and Writing Online Documentation.* New York: John Wiley & Sons, 1990.

20. Macro, A. *Software Engineering: Concepts and Management.* New York: Prentice-Hall, 1990.

21. Moeller, R. R. *Computer Audit, Control, and Security.* New York: Wiley, 1989.

22. Mullen, J. B. *The Practitioner's Guide to EDP Auditing.* New York: New York Institute of Finance, 1990.

23. Perry, W. E. *A Standard for Auditing Computer Applications: Using Audit Software Packages.* Pennsauken, NJ: Auerbach, 1987.

24. Pfleeger, C. P. *Security in Computing.* Englewood Cliffs, NJ: Prentice Hall, 1989.

25. Porter, W. T., and W. E. Perry. *EDP Controls and Auditing.* Boston: Wadsworth, 1987.

26. Saldarini, R. A. *Analysis and Design of Business Information Systems.* New York: Macmillan, 1989.

27. Simpson, H., and S. M. Casey. *Developing Effective User Documentation.* New York: McGraw-Hill, 1988.

28. Watne, D. A., and P. B. B. Turney. *Auditing EDP Systems.* Englewood Cliffs, NJ: Prentice-Hall, 1990.

29. Weber, R. *EDP Auditing: Conceptual Foundations and Practice.* 2d ed. New York: McGraw-Hill, 1988.

Questions

1. Classify control into three conceptual categories.
2. Compare the functions of administrative, built-in, and application control.
3. Describe types of administrative control measures.
4. Give examples of types of hardware controls.
5. How can source data be controlled?
6. What are the four degrees of depth in validity checking?
7. Describe the backup measures that ensure file control.
8. Why should documentation be written in parallel with other information system functions?
9. What are the functions of the EDP auditor with regard to system development?
10. Give examples of various techniques of auditing through the computer.

Problems

1. Design a form or set of forms to be used by a bank patron applying for a loan to buy an automobile and by the bank employee in approving or disapproving the loan.
2. Assume that you were asked to examine the reliability and efficiency of a credit rating service. Describe how this might be accomplished by (1) auditing around the computer and (2) auditing through the computer.

BT Industries

The privately held BT Industries is a maker of trendy home appliances such as coffee makers, small microwaves, toasters, automatic defrosters for frozen food, and other kitchen accouterments. The essence of marketing for BT (Burnt Toast) Industries is aimed at the ''Yuppie'' market where two-income families have made time more precious than money. For this market, the emphasis is on up-to-date styling and perceived quality for traditional appliances. The company is also doing extensive research and development for more exotic labor-saving applications for the home market such as a machine/robot, which on command clears a table of dirty dishes, cleans them, and stacks them in the cupboards. Other projects include an automatic vacuum cleaner system, an automatic supper preparation device, and a dust free environmental home system. Progress in this area has accelerated with the advent of easily accessible microchips.

The gross income of BT Industries is approximately $250 million with a projected growth rate of 10 percent a year. Profits are not expected to keep pace with growth (about 5 percent growth per year), but market share is expected to increase (from 4 to 12 percent in a highly competitive market). These projections are based on an established group of designers who have proven their abilities over the last 5 years to anticipate and design successfully for the BT market segment and the ability of the manufacturing sector to translate those designs into easily manufactured

items. Quality control and design have historically taken precedence over cost for BT Industries. Continued success in these areas will support the ambitious development program sponsored by the firm's egotistical founder and principal shareholder, I.M. Uge. Uge foresees and is planning for a series of breakthroughs in the home appliance field.

The firm has just added a CAD/CAM system to its home office in Boston with communications links directly to its four assembly plants in Los Angeles, Seattle, Miami, and Boston. The purpose of this system is to accelerate the design process of currently sold appliances from the inception of the idea to the actual manufactured product. Each manufacturing plant represents a computer controlled state of the art assembly process. The Boston system is based on a DEC VAX/VMS 9000 system with identical systems in the four assembly plants, which are separate from the main office in Boston. The Boston Manufacturing branch is used for prototyping usually in the early morning and on weekends. Communications are presently accomplished over leased lines. The problem of security is to keep the designs secret until the products actually appear on retailer shelves. An additional problem is introduced here with orders for long lead items (items defined here as the components which must be ordered prior to the actual dissemination of the design to the assembly plants) from outside suppliers. These items include such things as microchips, heating elements, special hardwoods, and a variety of special metal casting devices. It is the intention of BT Industries to keep the final design of its products as secret as possible especially from Far East Asian competitors.

Accounting for the company is done on an IBM 4300 also centralized in Boston with remote terminals at all manufacturing plants. Communication is accomplished with batch updates on a twice-weekly basis over commercial phone lines. The accounting packages are bought commercially, but there is a foreign exchange series of programs that are unique to the company and are considered necessary for the continuing competitive capability of the company.

There is a strong systems analysis and programming staff for the company also based in Boston. Because of the computer intensive approach of the founder and the heavy investment in new plant and equipment, approximately 11 percent of all company revenues are controlled by the DP VP who generally draws his staff from the Boston area. Almost all of the staff calls Boston their home. Each of the four major plants have only a few applications programmers to "trouble shoot" on site. Expertise for these programmers is maintained by rotating them out of the four sites on a biannual basis and returning them to Boston for work in either new developments or for maintenance of the considerable investment already made. Documentation for the staff continues to be a major problem both in the Research Area and in the area of programs which have been developed by BT Industries to customize their CAD/CAM packages.

One problem with the CAD/CAM system is that it is new to the company and initial estimates for a quick payback do not give it a large margin for error before it has the potential to force the company into the red. The main reason for CAD/CAM effort is for BT to remain ahead of its competitors on a time scale rather than cut costs in manufacturing.

Another area of extreme BT sensitivity is the research done for possible new areas such as the "automated baby watcher." The research for new projects has been extremely expensive but the founder of the company perceives a major untapped market. The research itself is done in a "locked" environment in Boston with a captive VAX 6000 with a strong communications research link to the outside. The developers of futuristic products for the company have indicated an extreme need to stay current with the latest trends in AI, electronics, and computers. The founder is alarmed that a casual perusal of his developers' requests for abstracts may give competitors strong indications of possible trends.

Still another source of continuing aggravation for the company's CEO is the behavior of the "trendy" design group for the current line of appliances. The CEO is concerned that his design group not ignore budgets and deadlines as they attempt to top last year's successes. The particular concerns of the CEO are keeping the design groups happy so that they will not "defect" to a competitor, keeping the designs secret, and keeping the reproducibility of the product lines intact. A small additional worry is the resistance of some of his designers to the new CAD/CAM system.

Questions

1. Design administrative and systems development control systems for the BT Industries that reasonably satisfy I.M. Uge's paranoia in completeness but are not ruinous in cost.

2. Devise documentation standards appropriate for the different types of development, and indicate how these standards would be implemented.

The Accidental College Computer Problem

In 1987, the computing needs of the student body at Accidental College were small. The student computer system was used exclusively by math and science majors. This small minority of the student body (Accidental College is a liberal arts college specializing in nontechnical fields of study) used canned, field-specific software to study chemistry, biology, physics, mathematics, and programming. As a group, these would-be hackers enjoyed the benefits of a computing facility larger than their needs or demands. Many of the hackers studied the system closely and became quite proficient with its manipulation. The head of the student computing facility, Dr. Slobko, took interest in these hackers and formed a cliquish relationship with them. The students learned a great deal from Dr. Slobko, who provided them with unlimited access to system manuals and documentation.

At one point, the hackers expressed the desire for a word processing program, an application not currently provided by the PRIME 550. Since funds were not available for the purchase of word processing software, Dr. Slobko decided to develop his own program. The system was developed piecemeal in Slobko's spare time. Since the software was viewed as a "toy" for the exclusive use of system hackers, it was written without attention to modern programming practices. The result was a poorly-documented piece of software that had no user's manuals. Surprisingly, the word processor, dubbed Acciwriter, was effective and relatively easy to use. Occasionally enhancements to Acciwriter were requested, and Dr. Slobko or one of his hackers would make improvements or add additional features. In time, Acciwriter became a capable program, and the hackers used it for all their collegiate word processing needs.

As might be expected, other students heard of this new system by word of mouth and took interest. The hackers, who took pride in their superior knowledge of the PRIME system, were delighted to demonstrate their expertise to any interested party. Word of the school's new word processing system traveled quickly through all departments until the use of Acciwriter was far more widespread than ever initially intended. The result was that Accidental College found itself in the business of providing free word processing to the student body. As use of the system increased, so did the need for more terminals, printers, and processors. The once-uncrowded computer center was now filled past capacity. System failures affected a significant portion of the student body. The system was out of control. To compound these problems, Dr. Slobko died, leaving the maintenance of his spaghetti code to inexperienced subordinates and student hackers.

Meanwhile, the students who were quick to embrace the benefits of the new system were even quicker to complain about system inadequacies. The Student Services Committee studied the problem and sent the following list of problems to the President of the College.

Hardware Complaints

The number of terminals is inadequate to support student demand for them. Long lines in the computer center are the norm, not the exception. There are 100 terminals to support a campus of 1600 students. The original terminals were designed for math and science applications and are therefore less appropriate than ones designed for word processing. Yet, when additional terminals were requested, the same inappropriate ones were purchased. System failures are frequent, especially during peak demand periods. (On one occasion, almost 100 students lost their midterm papers the night before they were due.) Access time is painfully slow during peak demand. Printing a file can take over an hour during peak demand. Finding a terminal to print from during peak demand can be impossible.

Software Complaints

There is no user manual or class available from which to learn the system. Students learn the system by word of mouth. The online help system is unfinished. A common response to a help query is "no more information available at this time."

Complaints about Students

Students use the system as a Xerox machine, thus exhausting supplies of paper, printer ribbon, and patience. Students compose papers on the terminals, tying them up for anywhere from 1 to 12 hours. Students hold terminals for friends by using terminal hold programs. There is no official student queuing system for those waiting for a terminal. "Catch as catch can" is the rule of thumb. The system is now used almost exclusively for word processing. Science students are hard pressed to find available terminals for number crunching. Students knowledgeable about the PRIME system (hackers) have infiltrated "secured" areas, stealing passwords, erasing files, posting obscene mail messages through other account names, tying up display screens, and forcing log outs. It is even rumored that one such hacker crashed the system the night before papers were due in the hopes of getting an extension (he did).

Questions

You are interviewed for the job vacancy created by Dr. Slobko's untimely (timely?) demise. The College President has informed you of the current situation. The President wants to make sure that you are the right person for the job, so you have been asked to prepare a short analysis of the problems.

Examine the list of system problems.

1. For each of the problems listed under *hardware* and *software,* identify the *types* of control that could have prevented the problem. Explain *how* the specific control would have avoided the trouble.

2. For the problems listed under *students,* develop a security/control policy that will fix/prevent all problems listed. Include a penalty scheme for students who break system regulations.

Chapter 15 Organizational and Social Implications of Advances in Information Technologies

Since the introduction of the first computer in 1944, computer technology has progressed at an astounding rate. Today's computers are faster, smaller, more reliable, and cheaper than earlier computers. Consequently, computers are found in almost every aspect of our daily lives.

In addition to use in organizations, computers have become affordable for home use. Perhaps no other device invented by humans has had such a profound and rapidly pervasive effect upon our society.

This concluding chapter reviews current and future developments in various technologies of our information age and traces the organizational and social implications of these developments.

Introduction

An anecdote was told some years ago to illustrate the amazing rate at which technological advances in computing systems had been achieved. It said that from 1955 to 1980 the cost of performing 100,000 multiplication operations by computer had dropped from $1.26 to $0.01. Had other products and services improved by the same ratio, an automobile would cost less than $200 and one could fly around the world for $3.

Since 1980, the costs of computation have decreased again by at least a factor of 100. That additional improvement applied to the foregoing transportation costs would make transportation today essentially free. We can only wish that this had happened.

Some other facts serve to underscore the current state of information technology:

An IBM RISC workstation can perform 100 million instructions in one second. Large, multiple processor computers can perform up to a trillion instructions per second.

In the last four decades, the amount of work that a single computer processor can perform in one second has increased by at least a factor of 10,000. That is an order of magnitude improvement for each decade.

In the 1960s, only the most expensive computers would have as much as a million bytes of memory. In general, memory was one of the most expensive components of a computer system, and software was designed to use as little memory as possible. In 1992, an inexpensive *personal computer* routinely has several million bytes of memory, and the cost of the memory is nearly negligible.

The early magnetic disks used for data storage were one or two feet in diameter, or larger, and could store about one million characters. Personal computers can now store tens of millions of characters on disks that are less than two inches in diameter. Instead of spending tens of thousands of dollars for a disk storage unit, a user may spend only tens of dollars.

A typical disk in 1992 can store 62 million bits of data per square inch. This means that a square inch can store an amount of information equal to that found in 250 pages of the Manhattan telephone directory. A single computer can easily access more than 100 billion bytes of disk storage.

Computers are no longer limited to accepting input data from keyboards or from specially prepared documents. Handwritten information, video camera images, and even the human voice can all be interpreted and processed by computer. Computers can output data in a variety of graphic forms, voice messages, or printed documents. Computers can communicate with users or with each other by a wide variety of land-based or satellite communication services. Transmission rates of over a million bits per second are offered at a reasonable cost.

In 1950, only a few experimental computers existed in the United States. By 1960, a few thousand computers were in use, mostly in relatively large organizations. In 1970, there were about 100,000 computers including the *minicomputers* introduced in the 1960s. By 1980, the number of computers had risen to over a million, largely due to several hundred thousand of the new ''personal'' computers. In 1990, over 50 million computers were in use, with several million more being sold yearly.

The discussion in the previous chapters of this book reflects the state of the art of *information processing technology*—its development, use, and control of organizations—as we approach the 21st century. Rapid changes of major significance in information processing technology have always affected its use. All predictions of things to come suggest that the changes in our future will be at least as spectacular as those in our past. A vast literature predicting future developments in information technology and the impact on individuals, on organizations, and on society at large is found in books, in newspaper and magazine articles, and in radio and television programs. It takes the form of scientific forecasts, lay predictions, and horror stories as well.

Early large magnetic disk packs and a small internal disk drive. (top) © Walter Bibikow/The Image Bank; (bottom) © G. K. and Vikki Hart/The Image Bank

It is beyond the scope of this book to even try to summarize all facets of future information technology. But we will attempt to identify and review general trends that are of importance to information systems users, to information system managers, and to general management.

One concern that all of these parties must have in common is that the difficulty of managing information systems will continue to increase. The importance of managing information as an organizational resource (asset) has been recognized, but the emphasis on this will increase. Information systems have to be managed the same way that other resources (capital, personnel, materials) are managed.

We first examine four areas of information system technology: hardware, software, applications, and people (see [20] for more detailed facts and figures regarding trends; [53], [7], and [33] for more discussion of the implications of these trends).

Trends

Hardware Trends and Implications

The accomplishments in hardware technology could not have been predicted, and it remains difficult to predict what the future will bring. It does seem likely however, that more performance at less cost will continue to be the trend. These developments are the result of need, and the need continues to grow. It has been said that our appetites for computing power grow faster than our ability to satisfy them. Applications have been identified that will require processors ten orders of magnitude more powerful than are presently available.

We have seen an enormous growth in the use of information processing technology. In recent years, that growth has been described as "explosive." However, with that growth the proportion of an information system budget spent on hardware has declined steadily, and that trend also seems likely to continue. The cost of processing power goes down but the costs for people to use that processing capability go up.

The greatest improvement in cost/performance ratios has been with the personal computers and workstations. This has led to a trend known as *downsizing,* in which large computers are replaced by a network of smaller computers. Such networks have greater flexibility in terms of physical placement, provide increased availability through redundancy, and cost less. In addition, they provide a simpler software development environment than a large mainframe computer system, and this can lead to smaller software costs in the bargain.

External storage devices also continue to exhibit a dramatic decline in cost, with improved speed, capacity, and reliability. These devices provide very high storage capacity even for the very small computers. This enhances the ability of these small computers to be applied to a wide variety of very sizeable applications. It also contributes to the ability to downsize a mainframe application, or to distribute an application and its data to a number of dispersed locations.

There is no longer any assumption of economies of scale where computer hardware is concerned. Much of the tendency in the past to concentrate information processing resources in a centralized mainframe installation was based on the desire to obtain the best value by buying the "large economy size" computer. Since small computers and their associated storage devices offer as good or better cost/performance, organizations are free to distribute these computers to the locations where they will do the most good, and distributed systems and distributed databases are receiving more and more favorable attention and use.

In recent years impact printing technology has been seriously affected by the introduction of laser and inkjet printing devices, with tenfold increases in speed over older devices. The printers of the future will provide better resolution, less noise, and less maintenance—all at reduced costs. With the expanded use of online applications using terminals, the amount of printing may actually decline in the future as more data is stored on inexpensive and directly accessible units rather than in the form of printed reports. On the other hand, computers are increasingly used to produce quality documents with high resolution graphics and color as a more effective means of presenting

Portable computers go where the manager goes. Courtesy of Apple Computer, Inc./ John Greenleigh, photographer

information for human consumption. At the same time, very small, very inexpensive printers make it possible for every small restaurant to prepare your credit card bill online to the computer that checks your credit.

More and more use will certainly be made of CD-ROM storage devices. The ability to store sound and pictures along with text is opening the way to a host of *multimedia* applications, with education being perhaps the most obvious. Currently most CD-ROM usage is in a *read only* environment; in other words, it is a form of publishing. As it becomes more of a two-way medium, its effect on information systems will be significant as it provides new and powerful ways to communicate information to users.

Specialized terminals have become pervasive in our daily lives: automatic teller machines, bar code scanners, badge readers, credit card readers, fast food ordering keyboard devices, and others. They will continue to be developed and enhanced because they reduce or eliminate the amount of data that has to be input by people using conventional keyboards. This not only saves money, but is more accurate, more reliable, and faster.

Contributing to the growing use of terminals and distributed processing will be the improved reliability, improved capacity, and reduced cost of telecommunication facilities. Digital transmission services are replacing the use of conventional voice lines for communications. Using fiber optics, *integrated services digital networks* (ISDNs) provide the ability to transmit voice, data, and images in whatever combination the user needs, and at rates in excess of a million bits per second. It is estimated that this technology has reached less than one percent of its potential.

Another hardware development that will potentially impact information systems in general is the increasingly "portable" computer. The laptop computers were the first to be genuinely portable. The notebook computers are those small enough to fit in a briefcase, but still have a full keyboard. Pen computers use a stylus in place of a keyboard; along with hand-held computers, they will be even more convenient to carry. As this ability to take the entire computer from place to place increases, our view of distributed applications may change significantly.

What are the implications of these trends in the development of hardware? Greater numbers of individuals in an organization and more of the functions of that organization will become dependent on direct and immediate contact with information processing applications. Together with the proliferation of computers of all sizes, this close contact will require greater concern by management for security, backup, compatibility among hardware devices, consistency of data and applications, and proper accounting for costs. The organizational environment of the future will be more dependent on information processing than ever before.

Information has become an organization's resource, to be planned, controlled, and used to provide better and less costly services. Management concern with the information resource may surpass the attention currently placed on other resources, such as personnel, capital, machinery, and materials.

As the cost of hardware components decreases, software costs will become an even larger percentage of the total cost of information systems. The acquisition or development of software will become a more important issue for information systems managers and general management. More and more emphasis will be placed on the evaluation, planning, and control of the development and maintenance of application software. The next section discusses some of the trends on the software side of information technology.

Software Trends and Implications

The cornerstone of the software in use in any information system is the systems software (operating system) with which all of the applications must interface. This software may either be provided by the hardware manufacturer, or obtained separately. The major manufacturers have traditionally developed their own systems software, but again the personal computer brought new forces into play.

For a number of years, some users have chosen to use the Unix operating system instead of the one provided by their hardware's manufacturer. Unix was developed at AT&T's Bell Laboratories, was written in the C language, and was thus easily portable to other computers. Because of its portability, it was chosen by a number of smaller manufacturers to be used for their personal computers and workstations. Unix has therefore risen to prominence as a standard environment that provides compatibility for applications across a variety of hardware platforms. In a similar vein, a group of manufacturers has formed an alliance to provide an *open systems* interface, i.e., a standard to which each will develop its own operating system while maintaining compatibility for application development. Thus a user will have greater freedom in the future to select his or her hardware and application software independently from one another.

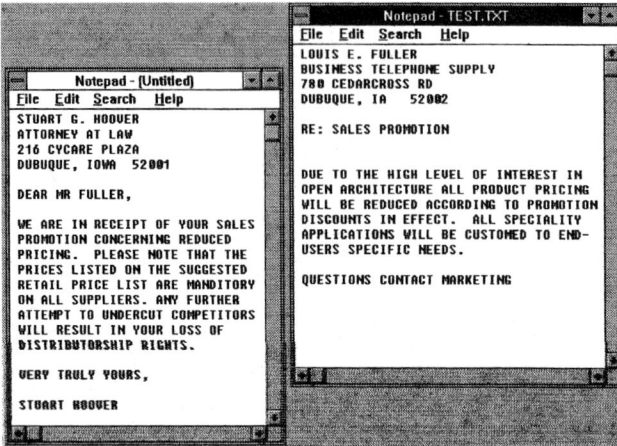

In part due to the increasing number of computer users without a long background of computer training, operating environments are being developed with simplified, more graphical interfaces. These interfaces are termed *windows,* and they provide the user with the ability to "see" a number of things that the computer may be doing concurrently, as well as to direct its activity by making choices from a menu or a set of icons. Some kind of windowing software will become a fixture of most information systems.

Most applications are centered around a data base; increasingly, users are turning to a software supplier for a data base management system. Again, this may be obtained from the hardware manufacturer or from an independent supplier. Examples of the former are IBM's DB2 relational data base management system, used only with their larger computer systems; and DEC's Rdb, usable only with VAX computer systems. An example of the latter would be Oracle Corporation's Oracle system. Versions of this exist that can be run on a wide variety of computer hardware, and under different operating systems.

Most of the relational data base products use a fairly standard language, called SQL (for Structured Query Language), to define and maintain the data and to make inquiries about it. This makes possible the use of a great quantity of available software involving different hardware and even different data management systems. This in turn has helped foster the client-server environments that are so important. Most data base software also emphasizes the ability to respond to a variety of needs for ad hoc reporting through an easy to use query language. This contributes to the growing trend to expect software to provide more support for decision making.

Increased attention will be given to software engineering. More and more use will be made of *computer aided software engineering* (CASE) tools to develop information systems. More attention will also be given to programming languages that promote reusability and reliability. Increased use will be made of existing software packages

Excelerator CASE tool. Courtesy Index Technology Corporation

as they become more flexible and more adaptable. The cost of purchasing such software will decline as competition increases and as standardization leads to bigger markets for these products. All of these approaches will contribute to better information systems, and at the same time will permit achieving these systems with costs which are lower than those resulting from the older methods.

Application Trends and Implications

Especially as the result of the proliferation of small computers, virtually every organization is in some way touched by information technology. Larger organizations have all had information systems for some time. They continue to expand those systems into new areas by incorporating new technologies and finding different and innovative applications to advance the organization's goals. Smaller organizations are finding the advantages of computerizing some of their information handling. In some cases, an information system may actually be a necessity for a small organization to remain viable.

So what we will see in the future is mostly a matter of organizations of all sizes using computers to perform or support additional functions, and changing the ways in which they utilize the technology.

A great deal of software has been developed over the past several years resulting from, and contributing to, the growing use of personal computers. Much of this personal computing paradigm, such as the spreadsheet, is being integrated into the mainstream information system environment with the development of mainframe and network versions. Thus users will retain the ability to do "personal" computing while sharing software and data with others in the organization.

Some applications continue to lend themselves to batch processing. Operations that are cyclical, such as the issuing of paychecks, utility bills, or credit card statements remain rather naturally jobs that are done by computers in batches. The nature of many of these batch jobs is changing, however. Direct deposit of paychecks and the rendering and payment of all kinds of bills are readily handled by electronic funds transfers. A person's bank and his or her debtors and creditors can make the transaction by means of their computers.

Other kinds of interorganizational computer applications will increase also. The ability of a user organization to order the products of a supplier organization by directly accessing the supplier's computer was introduced to give the supplier a competitive edge. In addition to helping the supplier, this capability can also be advantageous to the user organization by providing a key component in the *just-in-time* inventory strategies. This kind of computer to computer ordering-billing-payment arrangement has the potential for great benefit for both organizations; at the same time, it obviously must be undertaken with extreme care (for security matters, for example) because of the involvement of two (or more) organizations.

Online applications will continue to replace many operations that were formerly done in batch mode. In many cases, this online operation is made possible by the introduction of the specialized input devices discussed earlier, such as the bar code

CAD system. Courtesy Norsk Data A.S.

scanner or the devices that read encoded plastic cards. Because of the advantages these devices provide, their use will surely increase. In other cases, online applications will result from the ability to simply use any computer to access another computer to effect a transaction. For example, using one's personal computer to pay a bill or order a product. Online processing of these transactions not only saves creation of documents, it provides a more immediate and more satisfactory completion of the transaction. The bill is paid without the delay and uncertainty of the mail. The product ordered is known to be in stock, or an immediate alternative can be pursued.

Specialized output devices also contribute to the continued trend toward online applications. Probably the most popular such device is the automatic teller machine with its output of cash, but perhaps the most important has been the high quality graphics display. This has made possible the *computer-aided design* (CAD) of many products such as automobiles, appliances, and even computers. CAD tools are also used by architects in the design of buildings, by marketing people in the design of packaging, and in any situation where the ability to visualize the finished product is important. This high quality graphics output may even be an end in itself, as particularly exemplified by animation or special effects in movies. This technology is still in its infancy, so a substantial increase in its application is to be expected.

Computerized communications in various forms have become a fixture of organizational and personal life, and will continue to be expanded and enhanced. At least one form of this is familiar to everyone: the computer that calls you at home to sell you something. We can only hope that this will be enhanced in some way to make it less obtrusive.

Another form that everyone has experienced is the computer that answers your telephone call. This is sometimes annoying, but more beneficial, in analyzing the purpose of your call and directing it to the person (or computer program) that can respond most directly to your need.

As discussed in chapter 6, many large organizations use some form of *voice mail,* the large scale counterpart to your home answering machine. Many also have some form of *e-mail* by which members of the organization can communicate using their computers or terminals. Many also have access to other organizations by connection to an interorganizational network such as *Internet.*

All of these uses of computers to handle communications will continue to grow because they are cost-effective compared to the use of people to perform these same functions. We will see an integration of these capabilities with computers accepting, storing, transmitting, receiving, analyzing, and delivering voice, facsimile, pictures, and text for the purpose of human communication among people and organizations.

Personnel Trends and Implications

The experts in the area of information systems agree, and salary surveys substantiate, that personnel costs are the fastest growing component of an organization's expenditures for its information systems. This trend can be expected to continue. Hardware costs continue to decline, so that even as more hardware is used, its expense becomes relatively less. Similarly, even though more software is purchased, its costs continue to decline. But as information systems grow to encompass new and broader areas of an organization's activities, the demand will remain strong for information analysts, system designers, and system and application software specialists, as well as for programmers and operations and support persons. As the technology changes, personnel will need to be trained in the use of new hardware and software products, and in new analysis and design tools and techniques. As applications become more extensive and more sophisticated, a higher level of training will be required.

Three ways to contain or to reduce information systems personnel costs are: (1) automate manual activities to reduce the need for people; (2) increase the productivity of those people involved; and (3) increase the user's share in information system activities. Care must be taken in the latter case that total costs for the organization do not increase, masked by being moved into a different budget.

Much has been done to automate activities that were formerly manual tasks or otherwise consumed people's time. Operating systems have taken over many of the functions previously performed by computer operators. High capacity disk storage and data base management systems have reduced the need for tape and disk librarians. Data entry terminals capture and validate data that was previously handled by data entry clerks. Communications networks eliminate the need for manual transmission of documents.

Much has also been done to improve the productivity of information systems people in every area. Better user interfaces make everyone's use of a computer or terminal more productive. The *graphical user interfaces* (GUI) that are now commonly used will become more prevalent, more standardized, and even more efficient. Highly interactive programming tools have enhanced the productivity of programmers using the traditional programming languages; the newer languages emphasize the creation of reusable program modules, with an obvious benefit in terms of personnel costs. System design and development tools (CASE tools) will increasingly provide the environment in which new applications are originated and existing applications evolved. These products enable a design process that is more controlled and much less demanding of people's time and effort. We can expect to see these tools expanded greatly as more use is made of expert systems, decision support techniques, and group work support software as a part of the CASE environment.

The use of these design and development aids will help to produce systems more efficiently, but even more important is the effect they will have on their maintainability. Systems developed in a CASE environment can be expected to be better structured, more uniform, and certainly better documented than systems developed in the traditional way. This results in less effort being required to maintain these systems. The savings that result from this are substantial since the cost of maintenance has typically been more than half of the total cost of a system.

It is unlikely that improvements in productivity can ever be as dramatic as the improvements in hardware costs have been and will continue to be. It is also unlikely that the ability to automate information systems personnel functions will keep pace with the expansion of those functions. Consequently, if personnel costs are to be kept in check, some attention must be given to enlarging the role of the users to take on some of the activities formerly left to information systems professionals.

Some of these tasks are operational, and we have previously discussed how interactive and specialized terminals capture data directly from the user. Thus, the user can be expected to take a larger role in the entry and validation of data. As more users interact with the system directly, rather than through documents, they can take increased responsibility for determining which programs are run and when. But the greatest benefit comes from the user becoming more participative in determining the nature of the system in the first place. Through their more direct involvement, they are in a position to provide a better definition of their needs. With the design tools that can be used (e.g., an online data dictionary) they can become part of the design team. Development strategies such as prototyping give them the opportunity for *real-time* input to the development process while relieving the information systems personnel of some of the burden of testing and evaluation.

Actually, what will happen in a great many organizations is that there will be a blurring of the distinction between the activities of the information systems professionals and the well-trained, experienced users. This can result in enormous benefit to the organization, but may lead to a distortion of what are the real costs associated with the information resource.

Implications of Trends for Information System Management

The advances that have occurred in information technology, and those yet to come, have vast implications for the management of the information system function in organizations. A helpful framework for understanding the implications of technology trends and of organizational reaction to those trends can be found in Nolan's *stage hypothesis* put forward in the 1970s [39]. Though some observers doubted its validity as an explanatory model [4], it has been a well-known and widely cited model of computing evolution in organizations [27]. It attempted to describe the stages that an organization went through in adopting and adapting to data processing technology. Since computing technology currently exists in virtually every organization, perhaps it is most useful to view it simply as a description of the evolution of the IS function over the past few decades, and not as a model for what to expect in any particular organization.

Nolan described six stages of "growth." Let us think of these as six stages in the maturation of organizations in relation to their information systems.

Stage one, "initiation," was marked by low expenditures for computers and related equipment, small user involvement, lax management control, and functional applications implemented simply to reduce costs.

The second stage was "contagion." Applications proliferated throughout the organization, users were superficially enthusiastic about using the fruits of data processing, and budgets grew rapidly. Most management viewed the computer simply as a machine, and were even more neglectful in exercising control over the DP activities. Computer usage grew rapidly, but crisis after crisis arose.

In stage three, the "control" stage, general management got involved and tried to control the DP functions. At this point management realized that computers were here to stay and would become increasingly important. The DP operation rose higher in the organization, and centralized controls were established. Management had to face the implications of trying to integrate different applications using different programming languages and incompatible hardware and software. Data communications were employed to tie together computers and their users, and attempts were made to use databases that could provide common data for multiple applications. Much experimentation was endured, and users were frustrated.

Stage four was the stage of "integration." It featured the rise of control by the users, who began to exercise more influence on the applications being serviced. Users began to demand access to databases and other online services. The DP department began to operate more as a computer utility, with account teams to interface with users and respond to their needs. More planning and control was exercised within the DP department, and users were held accountable for their applications. Users established steering committees to guide the DP activities, and DP departments began to use a chargeback mechanism to place the financial responsibility with the users. Management controls became more effective, relying on greater standardization, cost accounting, and project management.

Stage five was the phase of "data administration." The application portfolio was integrated into the organization, and the DP department served more as an administrator of data resources than of machines. This is why the term "information systems" is preferable to "data processing."

Nolan's last stage was that of "maturity." Organizations began to use their data resources to develop competitive and opportunistic applications, not just those that would make their own internal operations more efficient. The IS organization at this stage is viewed solely as a provider of the information resources, and IS management concentrates on strategic planning for the management of that resource.

Large organizations that began using computers in the early days of their existence may have gone through each of these stages (perhaps more than once, in some cases). Now we can look back at these stages as historical developments. The IS function as a discipline is "mature," and if an organization is a mature organization, the IS component of that organization will be at that stage.

Management in general will find its role becoming increasingly difficult as organizations continue to face a more complex, more dynamic, and a more competitive world. Information systems managers may be presented with even more challenges as they find their responsibilities, and opportunities, changing within their own organizations. The importance of the information resource and of information systems will only increase as managers rise to the challenge of competing in world markets. The importance of the IS function may surpass the traditional functional areas of finance, marketing, personnel, production, accounting, and the like; those areas are all permeated by and dependent upon the information system. The paramount concern: information is a vital organizational resource with accompanying costs and benefits, and must be accorded appropriate management attention at all levels.

We turn now to several specific technological developments that have particular significance for individuals, organizations, and society in general.

Videotex

In chapter 6 we reviewed some of the facilities provided by public data bases. A growing technology that builds on the use of such data bases is *videotex*. Videotex is not a new technology; it adapts existing technologies to fill some needs for enhanced two-way communication. Television is an excellent way to transfer information, but it is unidirectional. The telephone is excellent for two-way communication, but it cannot accommodate graphics. Videotex has been a generic term for a variety of proposed, experimental, and existing combinations of technologies designed to serve markets that telephone and television left untouched. The concept was born in the United Kingdom in the early 1970s, and several experimental and operational systems in Europe and in the United States met with limited success over the next few years.

A number of possibilities exist. For example, the service could be provided over a cable or other television network, either as a one-way (receive only) service, or with special television receivers that could both send and receive information. TV sets could be manufactured with this capability, or adapters could be provided. A deterrent to wide customer acceptance of such a system has been the cost of these special terminals or adapters (on the development of these early systems, see [52]).

Then came the personal computer. A PC equipped with a modem provides the kind of two-way communication required for these services, using the telephone network. Interactive use of databases such as described in chapter 6 was possible from any such computer by subscribing to the service for a monthly fee plus time and telephone charges, and services such as CompuServe (a service of H&R Block), GEnie (General Electric), and America Online began serving a wide audience of users.

On-line services like CompuServe allow users to shop at an "electronic mall."
Courtesy of CompuServe Incorporated

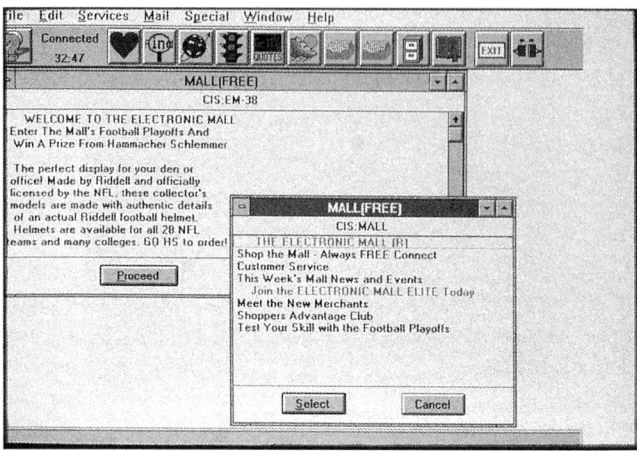

Those computers equipped with graphics displays could also receive pictures, thus advertising and home shopping became an impetus for the development of new services. Prodigy, a joint venture of Sears Roebuck and IBM, has been very successful (hundreds of thousands of customers) by emphasizing the graphics aspects of communication, and by adding advertising revenues to its financing base. For retailers, this opens up new possibilities for marketing, and at least one retailer came into existence just to exploit this new sales approach [45].

These companies generally provide their subscribers with access to databases, news, games, and such things as shopping and airline reservations (for a comparison, see [14]). They also offer software that can be downloaded for use on the user's computer, usually at little or no cost. Popular features of these services include the ability to send electronic mail to other subscribers, and to join in ''conferences'' where questions and comments on a particular topic are collected and may be viewed and responded to by the users. While principally targeting the computer user at home, many of the capabilities provided are also useful to businesses.

Some of these systems are very inexpensive to use. Pricing methods vary among providers, but an example is the Prodigy service, which could be had for a flat fee of under ten dollars per month in 1992. This entitled the user to unlimited use, paying only telephone charges in addition to the monthly rate. Most of the service providers were accessible by means of a local call.

One of the reasons for referring to this topic as ''videotex,'' and for discussing other possibilities, is that much remains to be exploited in this area. The current success of the online databases is only the beginning. It still is not ''television,'' even though graphics capabilities are provided. Imagine home shopping where you could see (on request) a movie of the product in action rather than just pictures. Imagine a marketing research project where the ''encyclopedia'' entry for some emerging market country is accompanied by real-time television pictures of its cities, its people, etc.

In a companion development, use of the telephone in two-way communication involving people and computers is achieving new levels. IBM offers a product line (CallPath) which includes voice processing [25]. This enables a caller to interact with a computer by answering the computer's questions with voice responses. Applications include leaving and receiving voice messages, filing reports or claims without mailing forms, and using data base inquiry or other *audiotex* kinds of activities. Thus, we will see new interactive systems that include voice processing for a more natural and easily usable video/audiotex environment.

Further developments such as those using television require higher speed transmission than is provided by the current telephone network. High speed transmission is provided by television cable and is available from regional telephone companies and other providers. Thus, future developments will depend in part on the relative roles of telephone companies, long distance communications companies, cable television networks, and others. In Canada, a major videotex service called Alex is provided by a regional telephone company [47]. In the United States, the telephone companies have been been slower in developing videotex gateways because of legal limitations on the nature and scope of services they can provide.

The possibilities for the use of videotex in business, industry, government, and the home are almost unlimited. Some of the benefit will come from what will be provided by the videotex "utility" companies. Other uses will be tailored to the needs of a particular organization as a part of its information system development (see, for example, [31]). Its impact will undoubtedly interact with the future course of *telecommuting* [59]. The directions taken by all concerned will depend on legal and social issues as well as on perceptions of market potential and personal and organizational benefits. The technology exists and its use in business is certain to expand significantly in the years ahead.

Anywhere: Another Name for Office of the Future

In 1981, when the first edition of this book was written, the title of this section was "Office of the Future." In 1989, when the third edition was written, the title was changed to "Home: Another Name for Office of the Future." For this edition, the title has been changed again. Within the span of these few years, the future has become the present. Office information systems have become an integral part of organizational information systems, and were, therefore, discussed in chapter 6. The focus of this section has shifted to a newer, and still evolving, phenomenon involving the *remote work* of professionals and office workers. Remote work generally refers to organizational work performed outside the normal confines of location and time. Telecommuting refers to the substitution of communications capabilities for travel to a central work location [40]. Many workers whose activities are centered around the use of a computer can perform those duties anywhere that access to the computer can be provided.

The idea of remote office work began in the 1970s as the use of terminals and distributed processing became more widespread, and some small scale experiments were begun. The publication in 1980 of Alvin Toffler's book *The Third Wave* [56]

Seven microcomputers feed information from around the world into the "trading room" located at the home of this couple—investment professionals who do not need to "go to" work. © Fred R. Conrad/NYT Pictures

brought the idea of working at home to a large number of people. One of its chapters, entitled "The Electronic Cottage," described in detail the concept and its prospects. While this telecommuting has not become the norm, it has been employed with increasing frequency.

We have met an editor of a monthly trade journal who claims that the journal does not have an office. The editor, a number of reporters, the secretary, and the sales manager, all work at home or on location. The reporters transmit material to the editor via electronic mail and fax; after reviewing the material, the editor transmits it to the secretary who is responsible for arranging the manuscripts for print. She is aided by desktop publishing software and equipment, and by a graphics expert who also works at home. The so-called "business phone number" is the secretary's home number from which she can divert calls or record messages as needed. This arrangement works well for a small-scale journal, thus saving office rental fees and transportation costs. A large scale enterprise would probably not be able to adopt such a complete strategy, but in many cases it has some parts of the organization that could, or already have, turned to this mode of operation.

Of course there are many important social, psychological, organizational, and economic issues involved (see [22], [15], or [10]). These issues should be resolved by three groups: the user (i.e., the department with the telecommuters), general and personnel management, and the information system unit (recall the system trinity concept in ch. 4). The issues and their ramifications are too numerous to discuss here, other than to provide a less than comprehensive list: security provisions, remote supervision, individuals' life-styles, need for social interaction in the workplace, economies of scale in providing services, costs of equipment and communications, equipment selection, the nature of office jobs, self-discipline, job satisfaction, career paths, family relationships, management control, and the relationship between work and leisure. These issues result from the socio-technical nature of office and information systems (whether remote or not) that include people in addition to hardware and software.

The telecommuting or teleworking idea has generally been thought of in terms of people who have been referred to as *information workers* or *knowledge workers*. One implication is that the use of a computer or information system is their primary job— word processing, data entry, computer programming, etc. In addition to these occupations, however, a growing number of people use a computer as an ancillary to their primary duties. Field workers such as sales representatives, investigators, and inspectors can do their "paperwork" from home rather than travelling to a central office at the end of each day.

This section might also be called something like "computers on the move." Information systems will be increasingly influenced by the portability and mobility of the computers that are provided. This mobility provides a new dimension to the telecommuting paradigm that has associated remote work with the notion of some alternate "place" (such as the worker's home or a service center near the worker's home), where non-commuters, possibly from different organizations, would share facilities. The early efforts at telecommuting and the early predictions about it were rooted in the notion of a telecommuter using a terminal connected to a computer at the office site. The terminal would not have been easily moved, and if leased line communications were involved, those would not have been movable either. Telecommuting was certainly given a substantial boost by the personal computer. Rather than only having a terminal, the worker has the full capability of a computer, with printer, and may only need to communicate at times to upload or download information.

This still ties the worker to particular places where a personal computer is available, but even so enables that worker to use more than just one specific computer or terminal. Data and programs can be transferred from one computer to another by means of floppy disks. The advent of the truly portable laptop computers and the notebook computers frees the worker to move about at will, using his or her own computer, working wherever the computer can be connected to a communication line. Inexpensive modems have helped with this. Disk storage that is inexpensive, small in size, and increasingly large in capacity lets the telecommuter take not only the computer, but large amounts of data wherever he or she needs to go.

It is estimated that upwards of five million workers participate in some form of telecommuting or telework for at least a part of their normal work schedule [36]. Nevertheless, the idea of a nationwide landscape of ghost downtowns surrounded by electronic cottages is clearly premature. Few innovations of this scope are adopted smoothly and quickly—even in small organizations. It is safe to assume, however, that these new possibilities will change the face of the workplace as it offers alternatives to—not a replacement for—office work as we have known it. Different organizations will utilize it in different ways. The point is that the technology provides the freedom to respond to the needs of the organization and its individual workers without being constrained by considerations of access to the information resource.

Artificial Intelligence

A group of scientists spent years working on the ultimate computer, a machine with so much knowledge that it could answer the questions that had intrigued people for centuries. Finally, the day came when they were ready to plug in their creation. One of them turned the machine on and, standing nervously at a terminal, typed in the first question: "Is there a God?" The machine thundered back, without hesitation, "There is now."

Jokes like that were popular in the fifties and sixties. The fear that computers would become smarter than people has eased in recent years as computers have become commonplace in the plant, the office, and the home; and as computer scientists have gained more knowledge of the complexities and limitations of the field.

Getting computers to do more than just routine data processing tasks is the focus of an area of computer science called *artificial intelligence,* or AI. Broadly, AI involves the programming of computers with traits normally associated with human intelligence; or, with getting a computer system (i.e., hardware and software) to perform acts we think of as the province of humans. Of course, when we see how it is done, we realize that it is just a mechanical process (otherwise the machine could not do it). But if you do not know how the "trick" is performed, it does seem as if the machine can think. The field of AI is thus involved with different human activities as imitated by machine. The main contribution of AI research has been not so much to solve problems of information handling (such as translating from a foreign language), as to show what tremendously difficult problems they are. For more information about the general subject of artificial intelligence see [21], [30], or [65].

Research in AI can be divided into two main categories. The first may be called the *engineering approach.* The researcher in this case wants to create a system that is able to deal with interesting and difficult intellectual tasks, regardless of whether the methods and techniques used are similar or identical to those used by humans. The objective of such a system is simply to accomplish the task efficiently and reliably. Examples of this approach include pattern recognition tasks (such as recognizing handwritten characters), translating text from one natural language to another, composing music by computer, and locating warehouses across the country in an optimum manner.

The second may be called the *modeling approach.* This approach has the basic objective of trying to gain an understanding of the internal mechanisms of a real-life system and to explain and predict its behavior. This category includes, for example, projects that simulate human experts' problem solving, decision making, or learning behavior by building models of these processes.

The three basic motivations for research in AI have been to (1) replace human intelligence because it is expensive, scarce, and often less than reliable; (2) establish theories of human intelligence in the form of simulation models; and (3) assess the AI capabilities of available software and hardware. Within these, AI research has covered a wide range of topics—theorem proving, pattern recognition and picture processing, robotics, learning and problem-solving techniques, natural language processing, question-answering systems, speech recognition, computer-aided design and manufacturing, automatic programming, and knowledge-based or expert systems. Some of these have been implemented in organizations; most of the others that are still largely theoretic in nature have an immense potential.

Research in artificial intelligence has been conducted since the earliest computers were put into use, but the practical applications were slow in coming. In some areas, progress has been slow because of the heavy demands that these applications place on computing power. In other areas, there was not a large enough market for AI products to spur development. These markets are developing, computing power is becoming cheaper, and products are appearing and being used in increasing numbers. This acceptance of the products leads to new products, and *AI based* applications will become commonplace in a very short time.

One area that has perhaps not received a great deal of attention as an AI contribution, but does fall within its realm, is that of the *fourth generation languages* (4GLs). These have come into widespread use, and while not providing a very ''natural'' language interface, they do permit the user to communicate in a way that is more natural than the use of a conventional programming language. We will undoubtedly see an expansion of these capabilities, and more powerful *natural language* capabilities, as more end users take a direct role in shaping their information systems. Some other important developments in artificial intelligence are discussed in the following sections.

Expert Systems

One of the most active areas in AI has been and continues to be that of *expert systems* (ES). These systems embody knowledge of a particular subject or activity combined with inference mechanisms that enable the system to use this knowledge in problem solving situations. By the 1980s, prototype systems were in use in a number of fields such as medical diagnosis, mineral prospecting, and computer system configuration. Major efforts are underway in industry and science to exploit this technology, and to extend it to new applications where human expertise is expensive or in short supply (see [28] for concepts and methods pertaining to expert systems).

An expert system is a computer program that has built into it the knowledge and capability that allows it to operate at the level of a human expert. Expert performance means, for example, the level of performance of a medical doctor in making a diagnosis, or of very experienced people doing engineering, scientific, or management tasks. Expert systems make use of an extensive set of decision rules used by professionals in a certain discipline (e.g., medicine or law) to assist the user in diagnosing, discovering, or carrying out some activity. They simulate problem-solving human experts in a specific problem domain (see [60]).

Expert systems allow trained end users to interact with the computer iteratively until a likely answer or result is obtained. In these cases, the expert is the collective knowledge and wisdom of the theorists and practitioners who have contributed to the particular field of interest. Expert systems are usually built so that they can explain the lines of reasoning that led to their decisions or outcomes. Some can even explain why certain paths of reasoning were rejected while others were selected.

An expert system is also known as a *knowledge-based system* because it relies on its base of knowledge of the particular subject matter to be dealt with. Thus an expert system may also be viewed as a knowledge-based decision support system. The two terms are frequently used interchangeably, although there is a subtle distinction between them. A DSS is designed to assist its human user in arriving at a decision. An expert system may be viewed as leading the user through a process by which the ES arrives at the decision. It is a narrow dividing line at best.

The knowledge-based DSS, or expert system, has a knowledge base in addition to the components (described in chapter 6) which compose an ordinary DSS. The knowledge base generally consists of a set of application-specific rules and parameters, and procedural information regarding their use. The rules may take the form of ''if-then'' statements, or may be expressed in a variety of other forms.

Once the knowledge base is created, the use of that knowledge involves processing the rules to determine how they apply to the particular case at hand. A program must see which rules are ''satisfied'' (i.e., what conditions are met) and what the implications are (i.e., what can be inferred from these conditions). Thus the program is referred to as the inference system, or *inference engine*. The inference engine is not application specific, but is specific to the particular way in which the knowledge is represented. Thus there can be a class of expert systems that have a common inference engine, each with its own knowledge base.

The construction of an expert system begins with knowledge acquisition. This involves the transfer and transformation of problem-solving expertise from some knowledge source into the computer program. Potential sources of knowledge include human experts, textbooks, data bases, and one's own experience. The expertise to be elucidated is a collection of specialized facts, procedures, and judgmental rules about the narrow domain to be dealt with. The process of acquiring this information and transforming it into program form is called *knowledge engineering,* and a person who claims this specialty is known as a *knowledge engineer.* Human experts have acquired their expertise not only from knowledge found in textbooks and lectures, but also from experience: by doing things again and again; failing, succeeding, getting a feel for a problem, or learning when (and when not) to go by the book. They therefore build up a repertoire of working rules of thumb, or heuristics (see chapter 3), which, combined with ''book knowledge,'' makes them experts in their particular domain.

The knowledge engineering process involves interrogating these experts to extract their knowledge and entering that expertise into the knowledge base. Progress in expert systems has always depended on the ability to invest in the development of persons who have the skill to do this. Therefore, much of the pioneering work was done by large universities such as Carnegie-Mellon, Stanford, and MIT, and by large computer manufacturers such as IBM and the Digital Equipment Corporation (DEC).

One of the best-known expert systems is the system developed at Carnegie-Mellon University under contract with DEC. (see [55] for a detailed discussion of this project). The system, which DEC calls XCON (for eXpert system CONfigurator), has been used by the company's sales personnel to take orders, and by order processing clerks to check and complete incoming customer orders for VAX computers. It takes anywhere from thirty minutes to three days for a person to configure an order and to achieve an

80 percent accuracy rate (i.e., 80 percent of the orders being configured correctly). It has been claimed that XCON takes three to five minutes and is 90 percent correct. This system was put into operation in 1981, resulting in substantial savings in labor costs, faster order processing, better manufacturing and purchasing information, and the release of senior technicians to tasks too difficult for XCON. This pioneering work, and its resulting publicity, paved the way for subsequent developments because of its success.

More recently, DEC has developed a system called CANASTA (Crash ANAlySis Troubleshooting Assistant) to aid in analyzing computer operating system failures. It has been estimated that this program saves DEC over $2 million per year [5]. DEC also provides its users with an expert system, Rdb Expert, to assist in the design of Rdb relational databases.

A type of software referred to as an *expert system shell* was introduced in the 1980s and provided great impetus to the development and use of expert systems in a wide variety of organizations [42]. A *shell* provides an interface to allow the user to enter the knowledge for a particular application, and provides the inference processing program to utilize that knowledge base. The fact that these software products could be used on personal computers made them widely available, and made expert systems— at least on an experimental basis—accessible to virtually any organization that wanted to use them. These tools have been continuously enhanced, providing in some cases a complete software development environment that includes provisions for an integrated data base, spreadsheet, text processor, rule base, procedural language, user interface building tools, and even natural language capabilities (see, for example, [24]). These products have enabled users with little experience in AI or in software development to create expert systems; at the same time, the more extensive tools have been used to build elaborate and comprehensive knowledge-based information systems.

Expert systems have clearly become a part of the main stream. A survey of 500 diverse organizations at the beginning of the 1990s showed that 70 percent had some form of expert system in use [2]. The most frequently identified barrier to more extensive use was the lack of knowledge engineering capability within the organization; thus future progress may depend more on training personnel for this task than on technological developments.

The Factories of the Future: Computer Integrated Manufacturing Enterprises.

Artificial intelligence has had a substantial impact on the state of manufacturing technology today. *Computerized vision systems* and *robots* are playing important roles in what we have thought of as *factory automation*. As with the "office of the future," much of what was predicted some years ago for the "factory of the future" has already come to pass, but the continued achievements in AI promise much more to come.

Robots are devices that can sense their environment and intelligently manipulate it. In general, their sensing of the environment might take any of the forms of human sensory perception, but seeing and hearing are the forms that are most highly developed so far.

Computer vision systems consist of electro-optical devices that act as sensors, and interpreters that can automatically identify specific patterns and trigger appropriate action of associated mechanisms or systems. An intelligent robot might have such a vision system to enable it to perform specific tasks in response to known, but randomly occurring, external factors.

Computer vision is not just a TV camera strapped to a mechanical arm that records images on tape. The system must be able to digitize the image for processing, compare it with specific patterns stored in its memory, and make some decision about what it "sees." It must be able to do all of this in *real time:* process the images and interpret them with enough speed to keep up with the actual events being observed. Advances in specialized VLSI processor chip fabrication, and in the use of lasers, opens up new opportunities for computerized vision systems that are very fast, highly specialized, and cost effective. Such systems are being used in conjunction with robots, but also for simpler tasks such as inspection and measurement applications on a production line.

Computer vision in a much more restricted sense has been widely implemented for some time in the form of systems for optical character recognition. Such systems are capable of reading special type fonts or bar codes. Still, computer vision and sound (voice) recognition are in their relative infancy. We can expect much more in the way of these products in the future.

To the general public the most interesting application of AI has always been *robotics*. The most serious research and development in this area has been toward their use in automating various activities in manufacturing, space exploration, and military operations. While access to such tools has not been as widespread as with expert systems, the availability of relatively inexpensive simple robot "arms" has enabled a sizeable body of research to take place. A robot is usually an analog mechanical device with digital control, often used to perform work that humans find difficult, boring, or dangerous (e.g., bomb defusing), or that humans perform slower or at higher costs. It is these attributes that ideally suit the robot for work in manufacturing or chemical processes, and the early application of these devices was frequently isolated to automate a particular task. Thousands of robots have been installed in automobile manufacturing plants, for example.

Along with the automation of some of these activities, computers have been used for other, related parts of the manufacturing process. In particular, *computer-aided design* (CAD) has been a major contributor in streamlining the design stages of product development. A number of software products are available that allow a CAD system to be implemented on virtually any workstation or personal computer that has adequate memory, processor power, and a suitable graphics display. Access to a printer or plotter is required for output of the end product of the design process. The user can design and analyze components of physical systems and solve problems in the engineering of such systems (electrical, chemical, mechanical, etc.), or in mapping, architecture, or even packaging and advertising. Furthermore, the user is relieved of the tedious tasks of producing the drawings and documentation. With CAD, the original drawings are composed on the computer, spatial information is digitized and stored so that it can be retrieved and modified. The use of CAD systems can reduce production lead times and enhance productivity. These benefits result from a substantial cut in design and drafting time, and the ease with which previous work can be reused or modified. CAD can also result in a reduction in material usage (for the creation of physical models), quicker introduction of new products, and improved quality of the design and the resulting products.

Computer-aided manufacturing (CAM) refers to the use of computers to automate the manufacturing process. Using the output from the CAD stage, the CAM tools assist in a number of steps—from the short-term scheduling of particular pieces of equipment, to the programming of numerically controlled or computer-controlled machines and robots.

The introduction of CAD, CAM, and a variety of computer-controlled devices, including robots, brought significant changes to the manufacturing environment and naturally raised organizational questions that are still being dealt with (see [1] or [58]). These new flexible manufacturing systems (FMS) led to what has been termed "islands of automation" in factories. The efforts to bring these separately automated parts of the process together in a coherent fashion were the beginnings of *computer-integrated manufacturing* (CIM). This integration recognized the necessity to link product data bases resulting from a CAM operation, manufacturing data bases maintained by a transaction processing system, and the various computerized manufacturing operations (see [44] or [35] for more on CIM).

The result should be a single system, not a collection of different systems. However, the need for *integration* extends beyond just the factory operations. Inventory control, cost accounting, and project management have all been *computer aided* for years. A truly integrated system encompasses all these and more. Hence the use of terms like ''computer-integrated enterprise'' to indicate that the integration must extend to all facets of the organization, not just the factory floor. An increasing emphasis is being placed on the need for such integration as a part of the pursuit of Total Quality Management. There is also interest in extending the system beyond the enterprise itself to include suppliers and customers. Just-in-time inventory strategies, for example, benefit from such inter-organizational systems. Nevertheless, nearly two-thirds of a group of manufacturing firms surveyed in 1992 said that they did not yet have a strategy in place for implementing a CIM program [50]. As the hardware and software products relating to CIM become more plentiful, more compatible, and more affordable, this picture will surely change in the next few years. Information systems managers in manufacturing organizations will clearly need to keep abreast of these developments.

The Fifth-Generation Computer

Through much of the decade of the 1980s, attention was focused on the coming of the fifth generation of computer systems. The anticipation of this generally began with the announcement of Japan's *Fifth Generation Project,* a collaboration of industry and government, dedicated to producing a radically new kind of computer system.

The first three generations of computers have traditionally been identified as those using vacuum tubes, transistors, and integrated circuits, respectively. The fourth generation was never so clearly delineated, but has generally been associated with the use of large scale integrated circuits and the microprocessor chips. The next major deviation in computer technology, therefore, could be considered to be the fifth generation.

All of the mainstream commercial computers to date have followed very much in the footsteps of the original stored program computer, the EDVAC, attributed to John von Neumann. Thus, this conventional computer architecture is referred to as ''von Neumann.'' It has been generally accepted that the computers of the future would need to break away from this traditional, sequential processing in order to achieve the kinds of speeds necessary to accommodate the applications expected to be wanted or required. It is expected that future computers will need to be more intelligent: providing natural language interfaces, being able to ''see'' and ''hear,'' and having a large store of knowledge. The amount of computing power required to support these capabilities will naturally be immense.

Thus, the announcement of the Fifth Generation Project was greeted with enthusiasm. This would produce a computer projected to be very ''non von Neumann,'' having a great deal of parallelism and possessing all the traits of the intelligent machines just described. It was also greeted with a great deal of apprehension: if the Japanese were successful, they would enjoy a tremendous competitive advantage over the world's other computer manufacturers [16].

The Japanese project was proposed to span ten years. The objective was a machine with three major components: a problem solving and inference processing unit; a knowledge based management system; and an intelligent interface. Each machine would then be able to simulate some form of human behavior such as: diagnosing illnesses and recommending treatments; providing legal or financial advice; diagnosing and repairing faults in computers; or running factories.

Performance targets were established in accordance with anticipated needs. They included the ability to process 100 million to one billion logical inferences per second (LIPS), whereas computers of 1980 were only capable of 100,000 LIPS. This would be achieved, in part, by using up to 1,000 parallel processing elements. The system was to have a vocabulary of 100,000 words with a 99 percent accuracy rate in the syntactic analysis of written natural language; a speech recognition system capable of recognizing up to 50,000 words with 95 percent accuracy; and a graphics system capable of storing and using up to 100,000 graphic images.

Formally, the project was a failure. At the end of the ten-year period, the program was terminated without having met its goals [43]. Nevertheless, there have been a number of benefits from the project. The apprehension felt in other countries when Japan announced this project sparked similar large scale efforts elsewhere. The European Strategic Program of Research in Information Technology (ESPRIT) is a major cooperative effort among European high technology firms to share research and development efforts toward a fifth generation computer system. In addition, individual countries, primarily France and the United Kingdom, have ongoing government-funded research projects with similar goals.

In the United States, the major response to the Japanese project was the formation of the Microelectronics and Computer Technology Corporation (MCC). This is a consortium of several major companies formed to conduct long-range research and development related to advanced computer systems. It has undertaken a wide range of projects, ranging from the packaging of integrated circuits to the development of knowledge-based systems. In Japan and elsewhere, the project has served to focus attention on needs for the future, thereby providing incentives for a great deal of innovative research, for the funding for that research, and for the training of a great number of computer scientists.

Perhaps one lesson to be learned from this project's failure is the difficulty of planning so many years into the future in a world in which the technology, and its application, are rapidly changing. The Japanese did achieve a system with 1,000 processors working in parallel; however, U.S. firms are marketing systems with tens of thousands of processors. Yet the real problem is that user attention has largely turned away from huge machines with specialized capabilities—however intelligent they might be—and has focused on the powerful small workstations that have become available in the course of that ten-year period spanned by the Fifth Generation Project.

Virtual Reality

Virtual reality is currently the most popular name for something that has been around for a long time under a variety of names. As a "simulated environment," we can associate it with such things as the flight simulators that have been used to train pilots for many years. The difference is simply the price tag. Computer hardware is now inexpensive enough to encourage development of products with wider appeal.

Most of the current attention for research and development in this area is focused on the product's entertainment value. As a new form of a super video game, the market potential is enormous. For example, Nintendo sold 32 million of their "first generation" eight-bit video game machines before moving on to their sixteen-bit improved version [57]. While still largely experimental, virtual reality arcade games are being developed and used, and products for home use are not far behind. The investment required is substantial, but the possible returns are attractive enough to stimulate a great deal of interest (see [9]).

One way for a person to experience a virtual "reality" is to wear a headset that provides a tiny screen for each eye, giving the illusion of three-dimensional vision. Head movement causes the images being displayed to change, as though the wearer were looking around. The "realness" of this virtual reality depends on the level of detail present in the display and the speed with which it changes in response to movement (for a more detailed explanation see [3]).

It is easy to see applications of virtual reality that go beyond its entertainment value. As a way of creating scenes of proposed events, or re-creating scenes of past events, it could have great value in training, investigation, and research. In real time it could be extremely useful to improve the remote control of robots in dangerous situations, or even to enhance the telecommuting or teleconferencing environment.

While business applications of this technology are probably still some time away, they will surely arrive. One reason for mentioning this technology is that we have learned how difficult it is to predict how long a new technology will take to develop. Just a few years ago, who could have foreseen what the personal computer would evolve into and what effect it would have on the world. The point is, again, that computer technology is responding to markets that are much larger than they were in the past. The effects of that continue to be astounding.

Final Remarks Regarding Artificial Intelligence

For a time it seemed that major strides in AI would depend on significant new computer architectures that would be designed around the use of *LISP* or *Prolog,* languages that have been widely used for AI programming. Undoubtedly, developments in that direction will continue to be pursued, but meanwhile there is great progress being made with conventional architectures and with conventional programming languages. Increasingly, expert systems software is being developed using the C or C++ programming languages. Software compatibility among AI and related products is achieved by developing systems to run under Unix. The personal computers and workstations have become so powerful and so plentiful that surprising advances have been made and will continue to be made.

The significance of this to the information systems manager is largely in the changing nature of those information systems. As AI becomes more pervasive, and as systems become more "intelligent," the support that they provide at all levels becomes more active as compared to the passive TPS and DSS. As the information systems take on more of the activities that are presently carried out by humans, the role of the humans involved changes. The human role is no less important, and perhaps it is even more important, in connection with these more comprehensive information systems; however, effective use of AI technology may require new organization structures, new marketing and management styles, different product strategies, and different distribution methods.

AI has certainly emerged from its previous position as a purely research issue and is taking its place as a very real component of current information systems. Nevertheless, it is still in its infancy relative to what we can expect in the future. Natural language interfaces will allow us to talk to systems with extensive knowledge bases and the ability to sense their physical environment. These systems will understand complex situations and learn from their experience. Information systems managers will need to do the same.

Communications

Much has been said in this book about the role of data communications in information systems. Some current and evolving developments deserve special mention for the impact that they are likely to have in the years ahead in all of the areas we have discussed.

One movement, already well underway, is the use of Commercial Internet. In a sense, Internet is the "original" network, beginning as ARPANET in 1968. ARPANET was a project of the U. S. Department of Defense, linking together a number of disparate computers at various government agencies and university research centers. Its purpose was to share different kinds of computing resources, programs, and data. Each *host* computer on the network might in turn have its own local network of terminals or other computers. ARPANET evolved into today's Internet, sponsored by the National Science Foundation, and its growth is currently exploding. In 1981 there were 213 connected host computers. By 1991, the number had grown to 376,000. In 1992 the number was over 700,000 and still growing.

Although originally designed for research and education (virtually every U.S. university is on the network), Internet is currently growing because commercial organizations are joining the network [48]. Businesses are attracted to the network because it offers a standard, compatible, accessible means of communicating with other computers of their own and others' organizations. As more and more organizations join, everyone benefits—including the research and education communities—because costs of connection and transmission decrease with higher volume. Also, it can be expected that a number of new services will evolve to tap this market of easily accessible customers.

Internet is a network of networks, and at least one of those networks provides access to individuals on a toll free, dial up basis. Its services extend to thirty-eight countries; it also has gateways to other networks, extending electronic mail capability to over fifty countries. It has become another sort of "public utility" available to provide organizations with a ready-made communications service.

Many of the capabilities planned for information systems involve the processing of voice and images as well as simply data. In the past the transmission of voice, data, and images involved the use of separate networks. Future networks will integrate the transmission of all three over the same digital communication lines [34].

The transmission of data is already moving toward the use of high speed digital links rather than using the conventional telephone network designed to carry analog voice signals. The use of fiber optic connections between cities has increased the transmission capacities, and one result of higher capacities and higher speeds is a lower cost per bit of information. An *integrated services digital network* (ISDN) provides the capability for a business to connect two (or more) locations with a single line to be used for data and fax as well as ordinary telephone traffic. The economic benefit can be substantial.

There are also efforts to provide an *electronic data interchange* (EDI) standard. Such a standard would make the encoding and exchange of data uniform among businesses and among types of data. Thus far, these standardization efforts have concentrated on specific industries [8]. Say, for example, that within a particular industry a standard format is established for a purchase order. Then any company's program that sends a purchase order can send it to any other computer's program that receives purchase orders, not just to a ''compatible'' program that matches the sending program. Of course, the underlying network (ISDN or otherwise) would have to be standard. More widely applicable standards are clearly an objective, as they provide communication possibilities for even more innovative inter-organizational applications.

Global Information Systems

As we approach the end of the century, there is little doubt that information technology will diffuse throughout the world and will become the backbone of an increasingly interdependent global economy.

Doing business on a global scale was common before the widespread use of information systems. However, it has largely been the influence of recent advances in telecommunications and computer technology that has turned businesses of every size and type into global competitors. Multinational corporations now account for most of the world's economic activity. Global competition was, just a short time ago, only suitable for large companies. Now, even small, domestic firms can suddenly find themselves pitted against a non-domestic competitor. For example, a U.S. auto body parts supplier could find that its competition is Japanese, rather than a firm down the road in Detroit.

Often a non-domestic competitor will be larger, have greater financial resources, lower production costs, or greater product sophistication. Increasingly, it also could be a modest size firm with a carefully crafted information system. The rapid infusion of information technology into the world economy has had profound impacts. Existing businesses are being reshaped, while new types of businesses are being created. Fewer businesses than ever are immune to global competition. Fewer still can avoid the strategic use of information technology. In 1992, the majority of firms did not have an international IT strategy coupled with a worldwide network, but the number that do is increasing.

Along with their considerable benefits, global information systems pose difficult and unique problems. The issue is not just scale. Large global systems are more difficult to create and manage than domestic systems of equivalent size. Other problems that are inherent to doing business abroad include different languages, cultures, and customs. Some of these problems are merely annoyances. Others can stymie an integrated global network. Different regulations and regulatory agencies world-wide can make creating a single network an infuriating puzzle. Independent post, telephone, and telegraph operations in some countries can block network hookups or inflate their costs beyond recognition. Lack of local computer supplies and service technicians, coupled with restrictive import regulations in developing countries, can transform simple hardware breakdowns into logistical nightmares. Regulation of transborder data flows can hinder—or even block—the movement of both basic transaction data and critical management information. Even internal company barriers can hinder global IS deployment. Independently minded subsidiaries may resist new systems for fear of losing autonomy or control. Home office staff, on the other hand, may resent how IS resources are drained away to support remote sites.

Although burdened with such implementation problems, global IS are still the wave of the future. One payback of the rapid growth of global systems is that as more systems are established, implementation barriers will begin to fall. As for cultural barriers, global trade builds bridges between cultures and homogenizes customs. When MacDonald's serves Big Macs on Red Square in Moscow, one can be sure that some consumers are similar the world over. While society may bemoan the loss of cultural diversity, the job of technologists becomes easier as worldwide cultures blend. Furthermore, as countries, states, and cities realize that they, too, are competing in the international marketplace for the manufacturing plants and offices that will support their future economic health, they will surely move to lessen the existing barriers to international systems, and to improve the communications infrastructure.

Another barrier to the implementation of global IS is the lack of international standards. An example is videoconferencing technology, which has not yet made the metamorphosis from a boardroom technology to a common communication vehicle. What hampers this is the lack of an audio compression standard to make various vendors' equipment inter-operable, and to allow customers to take advantage of price and feature competitiveness. Another example is the need for developing universal gateways that enable integration and collaboration among different hardware and different networks as easy to accomplish and as transparent as possible.

One danger in global information systems is that they are exposed to more risks than domestic systems, being composed of a variety of nodes operating in different environments—the system is as good as its weakest link (for instance, the exposure to a political upheaval in a given country). Therefore, much more flexibility and redundancy may be required in the design and operation of a global IS.

A lot of concern is expressed by both researchers and practitioners about the poor IT infrastructure in many countries, and the issue of geographical boundaries that impede information flow. More attention, however, should be paid to the overall sociotechnical environment. The state and diffusion of information technology in a country can be analyzed within the conceptual framework of a web (or sandwich) model [33]. Web models view IT developments as complex social objects which are constrained by their socio-political-cultural context, infrastructure, and history.

Briefly, the state of IS implementation depends on the technological infrastructure of a country (hardware, software, peopleware, telecommunications), and the social-cultural-political superstructure of the country. Many developing countries are not only lacking in terms of infrastructure, but, unfortunately, have political, social, and cultural norms that do not foster global information systems. A good example is the pre-Yeltsin USSR: in a planned economy, with mandated production quotas and no profit objective, real-time information was not important, appreciated, or even welcomed.

The important thing to remember is that technology was the key enabling factor in creating multinational businesses. It continues to be so today. Now, the technology most likely to influence the expansion of global business is information technology. As communication and coordination costs drop at a breathtaking rate, the new challenge is to create strategies that optimize the concentration or dispersion of critical resources. It is no longer necessary to choose exclusively between concentration and dispersion when designing a global organization. Those who exploit information technologies will earn competitive advantage by finding the best balance between these two modes. Building products in a variety of locations based on the most favorable conditions is known as *rationalizing* operation. Although costs are a primary driver of rationalized operations, availability of labor and materials, or favorable regulations, can also influence task distribution.

Not only is IT an enabling factor in international trade, it is also a great equalizer. By using it, even small companies can become global, especially if it is a company that sells products or services with a high information content. In the international arena, one can say that IT is the great equalizer and enabler.

Global firms have only become possible because of the stunning advances in telecommunications and transportation. Without these technologies, the coordination costs and problems of centralized control would be nearly insurmountable. Becoming a global firm requires more tightly linked information systems. In some industries, such as financial services, transportation, and communications, global strategies linked to global IS are essential. Since most airlines now serve international routes, their systems must be global, too. Producers of bulk and commodity items have long competed on a global scale without integrated information systems. Now, however, rapid changes in markets, currency, and prices make the use of IT to support global sales and production a necessity.

A lot of research and discussion of global IS issues focuses on two extremes—the large global companies (American, German, Japanese) on one hand, and the developing countries on the other hand. A rich area for business opportunities pertains to small developed countries and how they can effectively use global IS strategies—countries such as Israel, Denmark, Belgium, or Singapore; these countries that have no comparative advantage in terms of raw materials or capital stocks, but they have achieved high levels of education, domestic use of IT, and a skilled and multi lingual labor force. Such countries possess the advantages of nimbleness, flexibility, and specialization in a niche market.

With IT, history may repeat itself: after all, the great trading nations were once the Phoenicians, the Greeks, and the Dutch, who exercised to the fullest the technology of ocean navigation, had cultural norms that facilitated international trading, and were also supported by the national policies of their rulers. While ocean-going vessels and sailors were needed in the past to carry physical products, telecommunications networks and IS professionals are needed today. For the small developed countries, less capital is needed to invest in installing the information infrastructure today than was needed in the physical infrastructure in the past.

Organizational and Social Implications of New Technology

Videotex and telecommuting demonstrate how new technologies give management the opportunity to consider new approaches to managing and controlling their organizations. Managers spend most of their time communicating—by telephone, by written correspondence, in meetings, and in conferences. By utilizing new technology in these areas, management levels can be eliminated, spans of control extended, and better coordination introduced (see [13] for more on new organization structures).

Future information systems in organizations will be supported by *data processing* (focused on the processing of numbers), *word processing* (focused on the processing of text), *image processing, graphics processing,* and *voice processing.* Underlying them will be local and wide-area communications networks. Coordination of these facilities will be increasingly important to the efficiency of organizations. Sharing hardware, software, and support personnel makes such economic sense to these organizations that a new breed of information system manager may arise as a result of reorganizing the information function to incorporate these technologies under a common organizational roof [53].

The key factor for successful implementation of the new technologies is making the technologies acceptable to employees. Within an organization people communicate through informal communication as well as through more formal channels. Studies have shown that informal communications are vital to keeping the morale of workers at a productive level. Automation may upset the informal communication mechanisms, possibly causing the information system to fail. The problem of retaining social contact among workers is as yet unresolved. The next steps in automation will probably take more account of the importance of maintaining informal communication channels.

It is a well-observed phenomenon that people resist change (see ch. 2). Also, it is still a fact that some people are intimidated by computers. If the new technologies are to bear fruit, they must be successfully installed in the environment of people. Care must therefore be taken by management and by information system personnel to help users of new technologies to see the benefits of the changes. Behavioral aspects are as important as technical and economic aspects (recall the discussion of technical, economic, and organizational feasibility in ch. 10). A key factor in the acceptance of change is the friendliness or unobstructiveness of the interface between people and machines. Although much can be done to improve physical interfaces (such as screens, keyboards, or printers), ''friendliness'' is largely a function of software. Current trends toward the use of *windows* and *icons* is a step in this direction. Future developments of *natural language interfaces* offer additional hope.

Successful implementation of new technologies will thus depend to a great extent on organizational and human factors. Organizations should therefore adopt a strategy that will include the following:

Provisions to educate users in the benefits of the new technologies

A continuing focus on the importance of "friendly" hardware and software interfaces

Provisions to educate the information system professionals in the potential of the technologies as well as the methods to implement them

A thorough understanding of organizational entities in terms of the types of work performed and the probable opportunities these represent

A program to educate general management in the benefits to be realized and the organizational changes necessary to effect this realization

Personal ("Home") Computing

We have talked a lot about "personal" computers simply in the sense of a computer designed for use by a single person. We have also discussed the use of computers at home (or elsewhere) to do "office" work through telecommuting; and we touched on the use of videotex services for such things as home shopping, travel arrangements, and games. But let us look further at the use of personal computers for these and other truly personal reasons—letter writing, household expense accounting, name and address lists, and the like.

The original vision of the personal computer was as a "home" computer—small enough and inexpensive enough to use at home for activities associated with the home. The very first microcomputers were largely used at home, by hobbyists, and few people (if any) could have foreseen the effect that the personal computer would have on information systems in business. Many of the initial uses of microcomputers in business were the result of these hobbyists bringing their "home" computers to work.

Now there are more than 50 million of these personal computers in use in offices and homes. While the computer is not yet as prevalent in the home as the TV set, a large percentage of households are now "computer equipped," and this has important consequences for business information systems as well as for our personal life styles.

Probably the most important fallout from the personal use of computers has been the creation of mass markets for products. Software has been particularly affected by vendors responding to the opportunity to sell tens of thousands, if not millions, of copies of a particular program or package. There is little doubt, for example, that the current popularity of the C programming language and the Unix operating system are a result of the development of software products to sell to the large market of individuals using computers at home for personal reasons. If virtual reality products develop quickly, it will be because of a large market for games software and related hardware, not because such products may facilitate bomb disposal.

Perhaps less obvious has been the effect of mass markets on the production of books and magazines. Contributing to the success of personal computers and the more popular software products has been the ability to buy books describing and explaining them, rather than having to rely on the vendor's manuals. An author who produces a book about personal computers or about a particular word processing package has a large potential market—much larger than the market for any one computer book before personal computers came on the scene. The vendor-produced documentation has always had a usually well-deserved reputation for inscrutability, but even that has improved as a result of competition and the opportunity to significantly affect sales by producing good manuals.

In the early days of computers, "computer utilities" were envisioned that would make computing power from large mainframe computers available to terminals in the home. It is no longer necessary to acquire computing power from a utility, but other kinds of services do lend themselves to this approach. The Prodigy service was clearly designed to appeal primarily to the home-user market, and would certainly qualify as an "information" utility. The service they sell is embodied in the information and programs to which they provide access.

A part of the service offered by the online database or videotex utilities is simply the exchange of information. These conferencing, or *bulletin board,* services are popular enough that large numbers of small entrepreneurs have come onto the scene. Most of these are free, or charge just enough to cover expenses, so the system operator ("sysop") is doing it for his or her own enjoyment. While the users are usually those who can dial for the charge of a local call, the sysop may also give them access to other bulletin boards in other locations. The users can carry on conversations, look for helpful information by category, or ask questions for any interested person to answer. The large number of these services, and the amount of traffic involved in using them, are indicators of the amount of personal use being made of computers.

One of the popular uses of the bulletin board is the exchange of *shareware,* software that is available free or for a small charge (on the honor system). A programmer may make his or her product available for others to download to their own computers, with the expectation that if they like the product and use it they will send a few dollars to cover the programmer's expenses or furnish a small profit (a small profit multiplied by lots of customers could equal big profits).

So what we have is a blend of people using computers at home: for strictly personal reasons (utility and amusement); as small business entrepreneurs; or for professional reasons associated with their employment. Frequently the same person uses a computer for all these reasons. Much of this home use depends on communication: with other users, with videotex utilities, or with the office. The impact of this on communications facilities is bound to be significant, and the development of new, high speed, less expensive communications capabilities will spur growth in each of these uses.

One other social implication of this relates to telecommuting. A growing number of people use a computer at work and also have one at home. These people do not officially telecommute, but their work day is geared to the fact that they can take some of their "computer work" home at night and do it on their own computer. At home their job-related work and their personal computer use may blend together so as to be indistinguishable. Some limitations on this have resulted from the necessity to have either a communications link between office and home, or to have the ability to transfer data from one place to the other on a floppy disk. The new portable computers with their huge disk storage capacities will undoubtedly have an effect. The information

worker and other professionals may simply use the same computer at work and at home, so the distinction between professional use and personal use will become blurred even further. Clearly the computer is changing people's lives in all kinds of ways.

Security of Information Systems

In 1979 an accidental activation of the U.S. Census Bureau's main computer center sprinkler heads caused the center to be flooded with several inches of water. Two large computers were destroyed and two others were damaged [17].

Two computer centers in Toulouse, France, were burned and their contents destroyed in 1980, with two terrorist groups claiming responsibility, although the centers were involved in routine business applications, not government or military operations. Damage included the burning of computers, client records, archives, and programs [19].

The San Francisco earthquake of 1990 caused extensive damage to the computer systems of the city of Oakland. Twenty-five percent of the personal computers were disabled in addition to other damage. Oakland made the best of the situation by replacing the lost equipment with a better designed, more integrated system [64].

In 1991, a large computer installation in New Jersey lost its power due to a flooded parking lot and a resulting short in the local power station. This was especially embarrassing and somewhat frightening because this installation was designed to provide backup service to other users in the event of some disaster at their sites [6].

These events colorfully illustrate the need to protect information systems from a variety of hazards of nature, accident, or violence. While these hazards are very real and must be considered in the planning of a system, there are even greater (and more probable) threats from a number of other sources. The use of computer systems by more people, the wider distribution of those systems, and the extensive use of communications to connect people and computers make information systems susceptible to dangers other than fire, flood, and earthquake (see [11] for an extensive discussion of this).

Lack of *security* is a growing problem because organizations have become more dependent on their information systems. While hardware can be destroyed and replaced relatively painlessly (although often at great cost), much information, once destroyed or maliciously manipulated, is irretrievable. This brings us to the perpetrators of such damage—people. While the intruder from the outside is a real threat to information systems, what such a person can do is insignificant when compared with the damage that can be done by employees, through error and neglect and through fraud and abuse.

Several trends in the nature of information systems are making the problem of security increasingly important, and these same trends are making security more and more difficult to deal with. Probably the most significant trend is simply the fact that information systems are so integrated into most businesses that the IS-related risks are simply risks to the business itself. Other trends include [38]:

Increasing use of data bases of personal information, such as medical and financial records

Wider use of computers in safety-critical applications where peoples lives may be at stake

Proliferation of networks and computers embedded in other systems

More widespread ability to use (and to abuse) computers and information systems

Growing networks, public and private, that extend worldwide while the international political environment remains unstable

Security planning must guard against four basic hazards to the information system: loss, theft, damage, and misuse. In the early days of computers, the computer—along with its programs and data—could be secured by locking the room where all of it was kept, and by protecting the room from fire, flood, and other disasters. Only authorized persons were allowed to use the computer or even to be near it. Contrast that with today's information system, which might consist of a network of personal computers used by dozens or hundreds of persons, each using different computers at different times and at different locations, and each transferring data and programs from place to place within the network. Or, think about an executive whose notebook computer is in a briefcase with large quantities of sensitive data in its disk storage. The potential for loss, theft, damage, or misuse is staggering.

The security plan for an information system must assure three characteristics of that system: confidentiality, integrity, and availability. Confidentiality, or secrecy, only allows access to authorized persons. Integrity requires that changes be made in specific, authorized ways. Availability means ensuring that the system is accessible when needed by authorized parties. All of the system's assets (hardware, software, data, people) must be protected against the hazards mentioned above in order for security to be maintained. Security safeguards must be an integral part of the information systems plan, and a number of them were discussed in chapter 14 (for a more extensive treatment of the subject, see [38] or [41]).

Much remains to be done in terms of the security characteristics of software (and hardware) supplied by vendors. A survey of managers responsible for information systems security resulted in the following list of features that should be considered essential when evaluating vendor-supplied products [38]:

User Identification
Unique ID for each user
Automatic suspension of ID upon unauthorized attempt at use
Ability to prevent simultaneous uses of same ID
Display of date, time, and place of last use of ID at log on
Ability to assign an expiration date to an ID

User Verification or Authentication
Prevention of reuse of expired passwords
System-enforced password changes
ID and password verification always required at log on
Passwords of six or more alphanumeric characters required
Passwords stored in encrypted form
Automatic elimination of "easy" or obvious passwords

File Access Control
Ability to limit access to files, programs, and data bases
Ability to limit access to a specific time or day
Virus detection and protection capability
Vendor certification that product is virus free
Ability to purge or erase a deleted file
Capability to encrypt data
Ability to destroy the plain text during encryption
Required use of a secure production library of programs

Terminal Controls
Prevention of display of passwords on screens or reports
Automated timeout capability
Identification of terminals
Terminal locks

Telecommunications and Networking
Network security monitoring
Bridge, router, and gateway filtering
Dial-in user authentication
Modem locks
Call back modem authentication
Automated data encryption and decryption capabilities
Automatic disconnect of unneeded modems

Detection Measures
Audit trails provided for all invalid access attempts
Violation reports with time, type, who, what
Ability to query system log for selected data
Network intrusion detection

Some of these are common and expected features of current software products. Many are not yet uniformly provided, if at all, but will be—especially if management makes sure to look and ask for these in the products they acquire. Of course, all of these capabilities should be design objectives in any systems created internally.

What are the other implications for management? Where computer security programs have been ineffective in the past, it has been because of an unprofessional approach and a lack of management support. Better understanding by general management and a commitment from information system managers are indispensable for effective security. The solution must include greater emphasis on computer security training, the establishment of security policies and standards, commitment of resources, and "designed-in" security measures in both hardware and software.

It is essential to recognize that the security program needs complementary elements. For example, rigid entry controls at the entrance to the computer room are not effective if a remote terminal provides easy access to any program or data file. Also, costs and benefits of each security mechanism must be evaluated. Absolute security is not attainable, and the cost of successively higher degrees of security rise rapidly. Consequently, trade-offs are necessary, based upon a comparison of the potential cost and probability of each type of loss, with the likely cost of providing additional security against it. To conclude, computer security is a management problem, and it is amenable to management solution.

The Privacy Issue

Data security includes the mechanisms for protecting the privacy of individuals and organizations. No other topic has been so thoroughly associated with computing in the public imagination as *privacy* of personal information [18]. But why should we be concerned with this issue in a textbook on information systems? By now it should be apparent that current information technology, paradoxically, poses an increased threat to privacy (compared with the older technologies) and at the same time provides the means to ensure a greater degree of privacy. The threats are increasing because the potential for inexpensively collecting and sorting vast amounts of data on specific individuals in huge data bases is increasing—not to mention the improved electronic accessing of these data bases through terminals and personal computers linked by communications networks. Yet the same technologies, wisely used, can provide hardware and software features that maintain the integrity and security of files and data bases and prevent the unauthorized and malicious accessing of them.

The following excerpt from *Time* reflects the threat to individual privacy:

> The U. S. Government alone maintains some 3 billion personal computer files, a treasure trove through which any army of bureaucrats can search and snoop. Even more extensive are the records maintained by local governments, private credit agencies, banks, insurance companies, schools, and hospitals. It is hard to live in a modern society without leaving a long, broad electronic trail. . . .

New efforts by lawmakers to address concerns about computerized invasion of privacy are still embryonic. A bill to create "data integrity boards" to oversee Government matching programs is expected to pass Congress this year. But civil libertarians argue that tighter restrictions are needed. The alternative, they say, is a frightening drift toward an Orwellian society in which Big Brother is always watching [12].

We are by now well aware of the all-pervasive presence of computers and electronic files. Many government agencies and public and private organizations store our personal data items in these files. The following list is an obvious one, by no means exhaustive: Internal Revenue Service; Social Security Administration; electric, gas, and telephone utilities; insurance companies; banks; colleges; motor vehicle departments; police (maybe); credit card and credit rating companies; physicians; and employers. There are some intuitive questions that we may want to raise about these files containing our records:

Who has the right to keep data pertaining to us?

Who has the right to access our records?

Who has the right to update and change our data?

How do we know that the data is accurate?

How can we guarantee that our data is not maliciously or erroneously accessed and used against us?

How can we prevent one organization from divulging information about us to another organization without our permission (e.g., the police transferring data to a college admissions officer)?

The media have long frightened us with visions of a giant universal data base containing stored information about all individuals and open to access by Big Brother [61]. From the point of view of securing our privacy, such a data base might be a very positive step. Safeguarding one giant file would be easier than designing security mechanisms for many files with different structures, locations, and access mechanisms. However, the chance of a central data base of complete information about us is fairly remote because of economic, technical, legal, behavioral, and political considerations.

What exactly does privacy mean when applied to computer systems and their data? Westin defined privacy as

the right or claim of individuals, groups, or institutions to determine for themselves when, how, and to what extent information about them is communicated to others [62].

Rubin modifies this somewhat in limiting the right of an individual to withhold information if the withholding would cause harm to another [46]. As with many other rights, there must frequently be some compromise.

Most organizations require privacy to operate (e.g., industrial and trade secrets), and in many cases to lose it would spell disaster. The major difference between an individual and an organization is that the individual has little or no control over the security of the data about him or her used by others, whereas the organization can better manipulate the information it wants others to have. But unauthorized access to vital organizational data by employees, outsiders, and other organizations would be a serious problem if it were not controlled. Thus, modern organizations have to guard the privacy not only of individuals, but of their own organizational data and practices.

The public perception of the privacy problem is primarily focused on the credit reporting industry: the collection and dissemination of information relating to the financial status of individuals. Virtually every adult in the United States has such data stored in the data base of one or more of the three large organizations that dominate this business. Just one of these organizations—TRW Credit Data—is said to have data on over 100 million people. In the past, credit reports have constituted the major complaint to the Federal Trade Commission, but firms are now taking steps to improve the methods by which consumers can verify the accuracy of data being reported about them [49].

These companies exist because there is a need. Increasingly, our complex society requires the computerization of data about people. Merchants could not extend credit to people they do not know without some means of verifying that they are credit worthy. Taxes could not be fairly collected without computer verification that people are filing their returns and reporting the income they received.

A data base concerning income or taxes is frequently used by a government agency in a practice referred to as matching, in which the contents of two data bases are compared. For example, this may be used to determine if a person applying for welfare does in fact have an income that would make him or her ineligible. The matching might be on the basis of name, social security number, or some other means of identification. Again, the complexities of our society make such practices inevitable, but they also raise considerable questions about the rights of individuals to privacy where such data is concerned [46].

Public concern over privacy issues has led governments at all levels, in this country and in many others, to pass a variety of *privacy protection* laws. Privacy protection refers to a set of rights that individuals can claim under the law versus the collection, storage, processing, use, and dissemination of personal data in record-keeping systems. The following objectives have been proposed for such legislation:

There must be no secret data bases that collect personal information.

Individuals must be able to determine what information about them is being recorded and how it will be used. They should be permitted to correct or amend this information.

The individuals whose records are on file must be made aware of the existence of the files and of their contents.

Individuals must be compensated for damages caused as a result of data being stored.

A regulatory board must give permission for data bases to be set up and for personal information to be issued from them. The board also must have the authority to inspect computer centers.

No one responsible for a file may disclose any of its personal contents unless authorized.

Information collected for one purpose should not be used or made available for any other purpose without the consent of the individual.

Any organization maintaining, using, or disseminating personal information must ensure the reliability of the data and must take precautions to prevent its misuse.

Unfortunately, these objectives are not very uniformly met. Some data bases are regulated by federal laws, some by state laws, and some are not covered by any laws [46]. At the federal level, moves to protect privacy began with the Privacy Act of 1974. For a long time the federal legislation was narrowly applied to financial institutions, electronic communications services, and federally funded educational bodies. Thus, in most states there is no regulation of employers records, insurance records, or any of the other data bases not covered by the federal statutes. In fact, most states do not even regulate the data bases kept by the states themselves. At the federal level, the Computer Matching and Privacy Protection Act of 1988 was a move to provide safeguards in the computer matching activities of federal government agencies.

Pressure continues, however, for increased legislation and greater uniformity. As the use of data communications and computer networks becomes the norm, there is increasing concern about the impact of those communications on matters of privacy [66]. In any case, organizations must be concerned about their obligations under existing or proposed privacy laws. Not to be taken lightly are the considerable costs of complying with these laws and regulations. They include costs for:

Establishing procedures to inform individuals of the data collected and disseminated about them

Ensuring that information systems have security safeguards to prevent unauthorized access (review the preceding section on security)

Verifying the accuracy, validity, and currency of the data being collected and disseminated

Making changes when data is found to be incorrect

Reporting to regulatory agencies supervising compliance with privacy protection laws.

Management would be well advised to consider all these matters in the data planning stages, rather than to wait until forced to think about them when new laws are enacted.

Computer-Related Crime

There is a new class of criminal: the white-collar criminal who uses the computer, or any other part of an information system, as the object or the tool of a crime. The popular term ''computer crime'' is a misnomer. It implies that the computer is committing the crime, which is not the case. A computer is only a tool, much as a gun is a tool in an armed robbery. Hence, a more appropriate term would be computer-aided crime or *computer-related crime.* In effect, computer-related crime can be defined as any illegal act for which knowledge of computer technology is essential [37]. Most crimes aided by computer are just old crimes with new technology.

This section is purposely placed at the end of this book to reward you for toiling bravely through its pages: knowledge of information system technologies and uses may help you reap great personal benefits—psychic, intellectual, and even financial. If you are a student majoring in one of the functional areas of management, it may take you years to climb the organizational ladder and become financially secure. If, alternatively, you major in computers and information systems, you may have immediate fringe benefits. We say this, of course, with tongue in cheek. Here are three illustrative cases.

Case one. A young computer whiz stumbles upon the computer program used by Pacific Telephone Company in California to record and process sales transactions. With the help of a friend in the phone company's data processing department, he uses the telephone to place phony orders for expensive equipment. He has the equipment delivered to warehouses where it comes into his possession. Naturally, he enters the correct information into the computer so it appears that the goods have been paid for. Next he proceeds, again through the computer, to sell more than a million dollars of the equipment back to Pacific Telephone. But he is not willing to quit while he is ahead. He gets greedy, tries for too much, and is eventually detected by the phone company. He is up for prosecution and a stiff jail sentence, right? Wrong. Pacific Telephone is worried because its security has been breached and they don't know how. They hire the 21-year-old computer crook as a security consultant. Pacific Telephone won't prosecute if he will keep other people from breaking into the system as he did.

Case two. A computer programmer for a large bank in New York slips a few extra instructions into the program that figures each depositor's interest for the month and automatically credits the account. Now when the program rounds off each amount to the nearest penny, it deposits the tiny sum left over to the account of the programmer's friend. The programmer is finally caught by accident: the police raided the programmer's bookie, and the bookie's records showed that the programmer had lost over $100,000 in a few years. Natural suspicions led to an extensive check of the programmer's records, and the fraud was discovered. Although just a miniscule sum was taken from each account, the total was staggering. The bank decided to be discreet, fearing that if it became known that a junior computer programmer could rip off the bank, the bank would be in serious trouble. Thus, the programmer was quietly dismissed, and was only asked to turn over the unspent portion of the ill-gotten gains.

Case three. The computerized air traffic control system of New York's Kennedy International Airport suspiciously malfunctioned and nearly caused a midair collision involving an airliner carrying the Soviet ambassador to the United States. Some observers have speculated that the equipment failure resulted from human tampering.

These three stories have become nearly legendary, but they are true. They highlight some of the aspects of computer-related crime (in the last case it would have been computer-related murder) that are of growing concern to organizations and law enforcement agencies. One aspect of these crimes is the fact that so many perpetrators go unpunished, and even uncaught. It has even been estimated that as few as 10 percent of these crimes are detected. Consequently, there is little quantitative data on which to base any measurement of the severity of the problem. The examples certainly stand out as severe: for any particular organization, it would probably take a much less dramatic episode to represent a very serious problem.

Computer related crimes may involve a number of different kinds of activities. The following categories are based on ones suggested by Sieber [51]:

Embezzlement. Changing the data or the program for financial gain
Theft. Stealing the data or the program
Sabotage. Causing damage to the physical computer components or to data or programs
Theft of Service. Unauthorized use of system for gain
Unauthorized Access. Remote use of a system just for ''fun''
Traditional Business Crimes. Use of a computer system to commit fraud against other organizations or individuals

Each of these categories poses its own problems in terms of prevention, detection, and recovery. The embezzlement, or ''internal fraud'' category is of extreme importance because of the opportunity for severe financial loss to an organization (see [29]). Two other categories deserve special mention because they have thus far been particularly problematical.

Unauthorized access to use a system ''just for fun'' is popularly called *hacking*. Hackers use a remote terminal and gain access to a computer or to a network by means of systematically or accidentally determining a valid user's code and password, or by discovering some loophole, or *trapdoor* through which to enter. Since this is frequently random and purposeless, it is all the more difficult to deal with, and frequently does no harm. However, it is very easy for this crime to spill over into another category as the hacker finds that he or she has looked into a file of credit card account numbers, or other sensitive data. A book by Cliff Stoll [54] provides a great deal of insight into this problem in the context of a real life spy ''thriller.''

The other category is that of sabotage, and is currently exemplified by the ''epidemic'' of computer ''viruses.'' These are programs that attach themselves to other programs for the purpose of doing some kind of mischief (sometimes just displaying a harmless message, sometimes doing serious damage to programs or data). When an ''infected'' program is run, the *virus* program may copy itself onto other programs, and thereby spread its infection. These viruses can be carried from computer to computer on floppy disks or over communication lines. The effect may be quickly noted, or it may show up at some later time (a *logic bomb*). A related problem (in this case actually called a *worm*) received a great deal of publicity when it spread to several thousand computers, including government and military terminals, over the Internet [38] (see [23] for a discussion of viruses, worms, Trojan horses, and other ''rogue'' programs).

There are measures to be taken against this form of sabotage or vandalism. For example, programs are available that will examine files to detect and remove viruses. As an indication of how bad the problem is, one such detection program is able to identify over 1,200 different virus programs and their variants. The number is growing, and the problem will only get worse as there is more interchange of programs and data among computers.

Prevention and detection of computer-related crimes are the responsibility of senior management, boards of directors, and regulatory and criminal justice agencies. The need for laws directly applicable to computer-related crime has long been recognized, and at least 47 states have enacted some statutes to combat this form of crime [63]. At the federal level, three pieces of legislation have been adopted: the Computer Fraud and Abuse Act of 1986, the Electronic Communications Privacy Act of 1986, and the Computer Security Act of 1987. Since much of this legislation and its subsequent amendments have focused on areas involving federal government interests, the real burden of prevention and prosecution lies with the state laws.

What are the implications for management? It is possible to build safeguards into the development and operation of information systems—such as those described in chapter 14, and in the section on computer security in this chapter. Obviously, these safeguards imply costs that should be evaluated vis-à-vis potential losses (for a discussion of risk analysis, see [41]). Organizations will be faced with the dilemma of deciding when an information system is secure enough. If an organization goes too far, no one will be able to use the system. The only safe system is one that is not used, since any security system can be breached with proper know-how. Many organizations are in a hurry to get new information systems operating, so they skip safeguards. Some fail in their security because they believe that if they have not been ripped off yet, their system is secure. Others find it too costly to change their systems to incorporate safeguards. The lesson is clear: security has to be designed into the system from the start.

Summary

This concluding chapter has dealt with current and future developments in various information technologies. It attempted to draw organizational and social implications from these developments.

The cost of computers has dropped continuously while their performance has improved. Technological trends suggest that the cost/performance ratio for all computers will continue to improve. Although at present it is improving more rapidly for the smaller personal computers and workstations, the larger computers will continue the trend as well. External storage devices are also declining in cost; their speeds are improving, and their storage capacities are increasing. These same trends hold for input/output devices and for communications services. Computers may be accessed by a variety of general or special purpose terminals, and may be readily networked together in client-server networks or in other cooperative relationships. These developments support the distribution of data and of processing power to any part of an organization that needs it. More and more processing of information will be done online, interactively, by those directly concerned with the creation, use, and interpretation of data.

As the relative costs of hardware and communications decrease, software costs become a larger percentage of the total expenditures for information systems. As a result, increasing emphasis is placed on the cost/benefit evaluation of system software and application packages and their maintenance. Applications packages will become more plentiful and more generally suitable as greater standardization and emphasis on open systems interfaces becomes commonplace. Applications will generally center on one or more data bases, and the use of more natural and less technical languages will extend their use to more people within an organization.

Personnel costs will be the fastest growing element of the total information system cost. Efforts to control these costs will rely on increasing the productivity of both the IS professionals and of all other personnel using the system, as well as on automating manual activities wherever possible.

A rapidly evolving technology builds on the use of public data bases. These interactive services center on the use of personal computers to communicate with a service provider and with other users. While these providers are currently exploiting the market of "home" users, many of the available services have business uses and that aspect is certain to grow. In addition, extending these videotex services to include the use of television is likely to emerge. Businesses will also find many uses for private, personalized applications of this technology.

The developments in communications services—along with the widespread availability of increasingly portable personal computers—has made the possibility of remote work in a variety of forms a reality of today's business environment. Further development of these capabilities and organizational adaptations to exploit them will make some form of telecommuting even more common in the future. People will tend to do their information work wherever it is most convenient.

Artificial intelligence is an area of computer science that is concerned with using computers in performing acts that we normally think of as the province of humans. Some fruits of this research are already at work in organizations, while others have an immense potential. Some of these products are purely software; others involve special hardware.

The two software areas that have received the most attention are natural language processing and expert systems. Natural language is of particular interest in allowing users to interact with information systems without resorting to technical computer language. These interfaces may include handwritten or spoken words as well as typed text. Expert, or knowledge-based, systems automate the way that human experts solve complex problems. These systems provide advice to their users by building up a chain of reasoning from basic premises to a conclusion. The rules for this reasoning are obtained from experts by specialists called knowledge engineers.

The use of vision systems and intelligent robots in manufacturing is the result of hardware devices that have emanated from AI research. Another component of these automated factories are the computer-aided design (CAD) and computer-aided manufacturing (CAM) systems. CAD systems enable the engineer or other designer to use a graphics terminal and interactive software to design products or their components, relieving the user of much of the tedious detail of drafting and documentation. CAM uses CAD data to automate the manufacturing process through computer-controlled machinery. Tying all of these systems together with the related information systems leads to computer-integrated manufacturing (CIM) and the computer-integrated enterprise.

The interest in AI and the belief that new systems architectures were required to support the applications of the 1990s and beyond led the Japanese to institute their Fifth Generation Project. While this project received much attention during the 1980s, it did not succeed in producing a revolutionary new computer. The project did have an influence on technology, however, largely by providing incentives for research in other countries.

One incentive for continued developments in AI is the vast market that exists for electronic games. Virtual reality provides highly responsive three-dimensional displays that convey to the user the sense of actually being in a particular environment. This market will lead to the development of capabilities that have uses in business, industry, and other organizations.

Many developments are taking place with regard to communications. The Internet network is rapidly connecting commercial organizations as well as educational and research institutions. It extends communications capabilities to organizations throughout the world. Integrated services digital networks carry voice, data, and images over the same line. This simplifies communications for organizations and will lead to information systems in which the use of all three media is more highly integrated. Electronic data interchange (EDI) will standardize the way in which transactional data is represented, facilitating transmission of such data both within and between organizations.

Personal (home) uses of computers will continue to have an impact on organizational uses of computers. The large markets for hardware, software, communication services, and information services will provide incentives for development in each area. All these products and services will apply to organizational requirements, and information systems will benefit from technology that responds to large consumer markets.

Information technologies give rise to several major societal issues that entail benefits as well as social costs and the need for associated safeguards. People will tend to make fewer distinctions between personal and business uses of their computers. Organizations will not tend to depend on where the information-based work gets done.

The trends toward distributed processing, huge data bases, widely available communication links, and ubiquitous personal computers will pose greater dangers to software and data security. Lack of security will continue to be a growing problem because of the enlarging role of information systems in most organizations. The risks of breaching the security of information systems can be handled by various safeguards, both external and internal to the operation of the systems. The installation of safeguards must be viewed from a cost/benefit perspective.

Data security includes mechanisms for protecting the privacy of individuals and organizations. Information technologies pose increased threats to privacy because of the potential for economically storing vast amounts of data about persons or organizations, and because of improved electronic access to this data. Privacy is the right of people or organizations to determine when, how, and to what extent information about them is communicated to others. Modern organizations have to deal with these privacy issues. Increasingly, privacy protection legislation is being passed to require that privacy rights be recognized. Compliance with such legislation implies costs to organizations, but non-compliance may result in even greater costs through lawsuits.

New information technologies foster computer-related crime, a term that covers any illegal act for which knowledge of computer technology is essential. Computer-related crime is of growing concern to organizations and law enforcement agencies. The need for laws directly applicable to these crimes has been recognized and is leading to more computer-related crime legislation. Organizations should incorporate safeguards against such crime into the development and operation of the information system, wherever the costs are justified by the prevention of potential losses.

This final chapter includes explicit practical conclusions for information system design and use. Therefore, unlike the preceding chapters, it does not end with a section listing these conclusions. Instead, we close with the following commentaries:

> Information processing technology will advance rapidly, challenging our ability to utilize it fully. . . . Achievement of these technological advances brings huge opportunities for managers in all lines of work. These opportunities can be exploited by many managers; their employers will obtain advantage from the exploitation of technology. The employment of sophisticated technology is not an optional activity. In our competitive global economy, failure to stay technologically current will be a high-risk option [20, p. 147].

> We are firmly locked into a cycle of technology driving strategy driving technology. Each opportunity that new technologies create demands in turn more technology. There is no end in sight—in how widely and deeply technology is driving the transformation of how we do business and the performance potential from companies that truly understand the nature of the revolution and the power it can provide [32, p. xii].

> The issue is management, not technology. Obviously, over the next decade we will see new and unanticipated business, technical, organizational, political, social, and economic challenge, opportunity, stress, and uncertainty. Information technology will be a constant cause or correlate of much of these. There are no easy answers to the many questions they raise, and managers will continue to find IT a source of frustration and problems. They will also find it a source of excitement and solutions [26, p. 236].

Key Concepts

AI based software
artificial intelligence (AI)
bulletin board
computer-aided design (CAD)
computer-aided manufacturing (CAM)
computer-aided software engineering
  (CASE)
computer-integrated manufacturing
  (CIM)
computer-related crime
computer vision
electronic data interchange (EDI)
engineering approach
expert systems (ES)
factory automation
Fifth Generation Project
fourth generation language (4GL)
''friendly'' software
graphic user interfaces (GUI)
hacking
image processing
inference engine
information (knowledge) workers

information processing technology
integrated services digital network
  (ISDN)
knowledge-based systems
knowledge engineering
logical inferences per second (LIPS)
modeling approach
natural language
open systems
personal computing
privacy
privacy protection legislation
remote work
robotics
security
shareware
shell
stage hypothesis
telecommuting
videotex
virtual reality
viruses
windows

References

1. Ahituv, N., and B. Ronen. ''Centralization and Distribution of CAD/CAM Systems.'' *Human Systems Management* 5, no. 4 (1985): 301–8.
2. Ansari, A., and B. Modaress. ''Commercial Use of Expert Systems in the U.S.'' *Journal of Systems Management* 41, no. 12 (Dec. 1990): 10–13.
3. Arthur, C. ''Did Reality Move For You?'' *New Scientist* 134, no. 18 (May 23, 1992): 22–27.
4. Benbasat, I. ''A Critique of the Stage Hypothesis: Theory and Empirical Evidence.'' *Communications of the ACM* 27, no. 5 (May 1984): 476–85.
5. Blanchard, D. ''Conference Report.'' *Expert Systems* 8, no. 3 (Aug. 1991): 204–5.
6. Booker, E. ''Comdisco Rationalizes Outage.'' *Computerworld* 25, no. 11 (Nov. 11, 1991): 12.
7. Cash, J. I., Jr., F. W. McFarlan, and J. L. McKenney. *Corporate Information Systems Management.* Homewood, Illinois: Dow Jones-Irwin, 1992.
8. Cerf, V. G. ''Prospects for Electronic Data Interchange.'' *Telecommunications* 25, no. 1 (Jan. 1991): 57–60.
9. Cook, R. ''Serious Entertainment.'' *Computer Graphics World* 15, no. 5 (May 1992): 40–48.
10. Cunningham, S., and A. L. Porter. ''Communication Networks: A Dozen Ways They'll Change Our Lives.'' *The Futurist.* (Jan.–Feb. 1992): 19–22.

11. DeMaio, H. B. *Information Protection and Other Unnatural Acts: Every Manager's Guide to Keeping Vital Computer Data Safe and Sound.* New York: American Management Association, 1991.

12. DeWitt, P. E. "Don't Tread on My Data." *Time* (Jul. 6, 1987): 84.

13. Drucker, P. F. "The Coming of the New Organization." *Harvard Business Review* 66, no. 1 (Jan.–Feb. 1988): 45–53.

14. Duffus, J. R. "Going Online: The Bottom Line." *Consumers' Research* 74, no. 10 (Oct. 1991): 11–16.

15. Duxbury, L. E., C. A. Higgins, and R. H. Irving. "Attitudes of Managers and Employees to Telecommuting." *INFOR* 25, no. 3 (Aug. 1987): 273–85.

16. Feigenbaum, E. A., and P. McCorduck. *The Fifth Generation: Artificial Intelligence and Japan's Computer Challenge to the World.* Reading, MA: Addison-Wesley, 1983.

17. "Flooding of Census Bureau DP Room Probes." *Computerworld* (Oct. 8, 1979): 9.

18. Freedman, W. *The Right of Privacy in the Computer Age.* New York: Quorum Books, 1987.

19. "French DP Center Burned, Terrorist Groups Take Blame." *Computerworld* (Apr. 28, 1980): 1, 8.

20. Frenzel, C. W. *Management of Information Technology.* Boston: Boyd & Fraser, 1992.

21. Genesereth, M. R., and N. J. Nilsson. *Logical Foundations of Artificial Intelligence.* Los Altos, California: Morgan Kaufman Publishers, Inc., 1987.

22. Goodrich, J. N. "Telecommuting in America." *Business Horizons* (Jul.–Aug., 1990): 31–37.

23. Hoffman, L. J., ed. *Rogue Programs: Viruses, Worms, and Trojan Horses.* New York: Van Nostrand Reinhold, 1990.

24. Holsapple, C. W., and A. B. Whinston. *Manager's Guide to Expert Systems Using GURU.* Homewood, Illinois: Dow Jones-Irwin, 1986.

25. "Interactive Voice Response Units Debut." *Data Communications* 20, no. 11 (Sept. 1991): 133–34.

26. Keen, P. G. W. *Shaping the Future: Business Design through Information Technology.* Boston: Harvard Business School Press, 1991.

27. King, J. L., and K. L. Kraemer, "Evolution and Organizational Information Systems: An Assessment of Nolan's Stage Model." *Communications of the ACM* 27, no. 5 (May 1984): 468–75.

28. Klein, M., and L. B. Methlie. *Expert Systems: A Decision Support Approach—With Applications in Management and Finance.* Reading, MA: Addison-Wesley, 1990.

29. Kuong, J. F. "Computer Fraud—Points of High Exposure You Should Focus on When Controlling and Reviewing for Fraud." *Computer Security, Auditing & Controls* 19, no. 1 (1992): 1–8.

30. Kurzweil, R. *The Age of Intelligent Machines.* Cambridge, Massachusetts: The MIT Press, 1990.

31. Kusekoski, G. "Corporate Videotex: A Strategic Business Information System." *MIS Quarterly* 13, no. 4 (Dec. 1989): 447–56.

32. McGowan, W. G. *Revolution in Real Time.* Boston: Harvard Business School Press, 1990.

33. McHenry, W. K., and S. F. Goodman. "MIS in Soviet Industrial Enterprises: The Limits of Reform from Above." *Communications of the ACM* 29, no. 11 (Nov. 1986): 1034–43.

34. Mayo, J. S. "The Future is Integration." *Datamation* 36, no. 6 (Mar. 15, 1990): 35–37.

35. Mitchell, F. H., Jr. *CIM Systems: An Introduction to Computer-Integrated Manufacturing.* Englewood Cliffs, NJ: Prentice-Hall, 1991.

36. Mokhtarian, P. L. ''Telecommuting and Travel: State of the Practice, State of the Art.'' *Transportation* 18, no. 4 (1991): 319–42.

37. National Criminal Justice Information and Statistics Service of the Law Enforcement Assistance Administration, U. S. Department of Justice. *Computer Crime: Criminal Justice Resource Manual.* Washington: U. S. Government Printing Office, 1979.

38. National Research Council. *Computers at Risk: Safe Computing in the Information Age.* Washington: National Academy Press, 1991.

39. Nolan, R. L. ''Managing the Crisis in Data Processing.'' *Harvard Business Review* 57, no. 2 (Mar.–Apr. 1979): 115–26.

40. Olson, M. H. ''Remote Office Work: Changing Work Patterns in Space and Time.'' *Communications of the ACM* 26, no. 3 (Mar. 1983): 182–7.

41. Pfleeger, C. P. *Security in Computing.* Englewood Cliffs, NJ: Prentice Hall, 1989.

42. Philip, G. C. ''A Case Study in Selecting An Expert System Shell.'' *Journal of Systems Management* 42, no. 1. (Jan. 1991): 33–35.

43. Pollack, A. ''`Fifth Generation' Became Japan's Lost Generation.'' *New York Times* (June 5, 1992): D1-D3.

44. Ranky, P. *Computer Integrated Manufacturing.* Englewood Cliffs, NJ: Prentice-Hall International, 1986.

45. ''Retailers and Videotex.'' *Stores* 72, no. 2 (Feb. 1990): 30–31.

46. Rubin, M. R. *Private Rights, Public Wrongs: The Computer and Personal Privacy.* Norwood, NJ: Ablex Publishing Corporation, 1988.

47. Saunier, F. ''Alex Spreads Its Reach in Canada.'' *Telephony* 218, no. 20 (May 14, 1990): 11–12.

48. Schrader, W., and M. Kapor. ''The Significance and Impact of the Commercial Internet.'' *Telecommunications* 26, no. 2 (Feb. 1992): 17, 21.

49. Schwartz, J. ''Consumer Enemy No. 1.'' *Newsweek* 118, No. 18 (Oct. 28, 1991): 42–47.

50. Sheridan, J. H. ''The CIM Evolution.'' *Industry Week* 241, no. 8 (Apr. 20, 1992): 29–51.

51. Sieber, U. *The International Handbook on Computer Crime.* Chichester: John Wiley & Sons, 1986.

52. Siegel, E. *The Future of Videotex.* Englewood Cliffs, NJ: Prentice-Hall, 1984.

53. Sprague, R. H., and B. C. McNurlin. *Information Systems Management in Practice.* 2d ed. Englewood Cliffs, NJ: Prentice-Hall, 1989.

54. Stoll, C. *The Cuckoo's Egg: Tracking a Spy Through the Maze of Computer Espionage.* New York: Pocket Books, 1990.

55. Sviokla, J. J. ''An Examination of the Impact of Expert Systems on the Firm: The Case of XCON.'' *MIS Quarterly* 14, no. 2 (June 1990): 127–42.

56. Toffler, A. *The Third Wave.* New York: William Morrow & Co, 1980.

57. ''Top of the News.'' *Business Week,* no. 3231 (Sept. 16, 1991): 30.

58. Umar, A., R. Krachenberg, and T. Lyons. ''Organizing for Computer Integrated Management.'' *Information and Management* 20 (1991): 355–62.

59. Valovic, T. ''Electronic Information Services: The Impact on Corporate Users.'' *Telecommunications* 24, no. 10, (Oct., 1990): 51–56.

60. Walters, J. R., and N. R. Nielsen. *Crafting Knowledge-Based Systems: Expert Systems Made Realistic.* New York: John Wiley & Sons, 1988.

61. Wessel, M. R. *Freedom's Edge: The Computer Threat to Society.* Reading, MA: Addison-Wesley, 1974.
62. Westin, A. *Privacy and Freedom.* New York: Atheneum Books, 1967.
63. Wilson, D. C. "Viewing Computer Crime: Where Does the Systems Error Really Exist?" *Computer/Law Journal* 11, no. 2 (Apr. 1991): 265–85.
64. Winkler, C. "Oakland's Forced IS Lesson." *Datamation* 36, no. 17 (Sept. 1, 1990): 93–94.
65. Winston, P. H. *Artificial Intelligence.* 3rd ed. Reading, MA: Addison-Wesley, 1984.
66. Wolinsky, C., and J. Sylvester. "Privacy in the Telecommunications Age." *Communications of the ACM* 35, no. 2: (Feb. 1992): 23–25.

Questions

1. How does the trend toward lower cost, greater speed, and greater capacity of hardware impact information systems?
2. Why does standardization improve the availability and price of "off-the-shelf" software products?
3. What are the implications of future developments for information system personnel?
4. Describe Nolan's six stage hypothesis of data processing growth.
5. What happened to the "Fifth Generation" computer? Why?
6. How can information technology substitute for energy?
7. What potential risks affect the security of information systems?
8. Why should information system designers be concerned with the privacy issue?
9. Describe the changing role of the information system manager.

Appendix A *Information System Technology*

To make a theory applicable, technology has to provide tools to implement it. For instance, space travel would have remained an academic (and science fiction) issue had engineers, physicists, biologists, metallurgists, mathematicians, computer scientists, and many others not collaboratively endeavored to devise concrete tools for that enormous undertaking. Similarly, information systems, particularly for management (i.e., MIS), are realizable only as a result of the rapid progress of information processing technology. In fact, technology advances so rapidly in this area that we sometimes wonder which comes first: theoretical foundations or technological achievements.

This appendix briefly reviews information processing technology. Its main purpose is to illustrate to the reader how the concepts and ideas presented in the book are achievable by means of existing technology.

Introduction

Several statistics in chapter 15 have demonstrated the magnitude of the revolution that computing technology has undergone during the last four decades. The rapid progress is reflected not only in cost and performance terms but also in qualitative traits. Computers nowadays can communicate directly with "naive" users; can support managerial decisions; can perform office work; and can access, retrieve, and integrate large volumes of data. In other words, they can be of assistance to operational ranks as well as to managerial echelons in organizations.

The problem facing a modern manager/user is not whether to use computers at all, but rather how to optimize their use—namely, how to use them most effectively, efficiently, and economically. A somewhat different aspect of the same problem is how to comprehend computer usefulness without having to learn all the technicalities of hardware and software internals.

We believe that these problems are solvable. To analogize: we make decisions on how to use available transportation methods (drive a car, take a train or a bus, fly in an airplane) without having to understand fully the way they are constructed. Similarly, by understanding major traits of information processing equipment, we can satisfactorily make use of it without getting into nuts and bolts.

This appendix reviews a variety of hardware and software features associated with information system technology. It will emphasize traits that may have an impact on potential use and application. Also, it will limit the discussion of technical characteristics to what is necessary for an understanding of the applicational implications. We will refrain from presenting an extended review of computer history, and, rather, stick to recent and present technology. (Interested readers may refer to [9] for an overview of that history, or to almost any introductory text in computers and *data processing* (*DP*)—(see [3] or [6]).

The first part of this appendix reviews information processing equipment (hardware and software) as it applies to the *data processing cycle,* i.e., input, processing, output, and storing. This part centers on the role of individual computers, both large and small, in carrying out that cycle. Subsequently we will discuss two other topics of paramount importance to information systems: *data bases* and *data base management systems* (DBMS) software; and data communications and *teleprocessing* concepts.

The Data Processing Cycle

In the beginning there is a physical transaction—an event that may have an impact on the status of the organization. For instance, a client buys merchandise; a customer deposits cash; a production shop completes a job; a company hires a new employee; raw materials arrive.

Unfortunately, computers cannot always recognize a physical transaction; in many cases the transaction has to be recorded. A recorded transaction, often called a *source document,* is thereby generated.

Creation of written transactions is not always a must and may be skipped in certain instances. For example, computers that navigate airplanes, or computers that monitor vehicle traffic in a city do not wait until the users record and key in every pertinent event (e.g. aircraft coordinates, traffic volumes in a certain intersection). Those computers employ electronic detectors to directly capture data about relevant events. Similarly, in business applications it is possible to capture a transaction without preparing a written document. For example, when you withdraw cash from an automatic teller machine you do not fill out a form prior to performing this activity. However in business applications, the use of hard copy source documents is still common, particularly in monetary (bookkeeping) applications, where the documents also serve control purposes (see ch. 14). In some cases, the source document can be read by an optical or magnetic sensing device such as we will discuss later; these documents are said to be *machine readable.* If this cannot be done, then the document must be translated into a computer readable form. This is called *data conversion.*

Next, the machine-readable data is read in by means of *input devices.* After being read in, the data is processed in computer memory; this is the processing stage. The processed data can thereafter be displayed and/or stored. Data is displayed on a human-readable medium when humans have to react and make decisions; this stage is labelled *output.* Data is stored on computer-readable media when the data is required for further processing; this is called *storing.*

Figure A.1 The data processing cycle

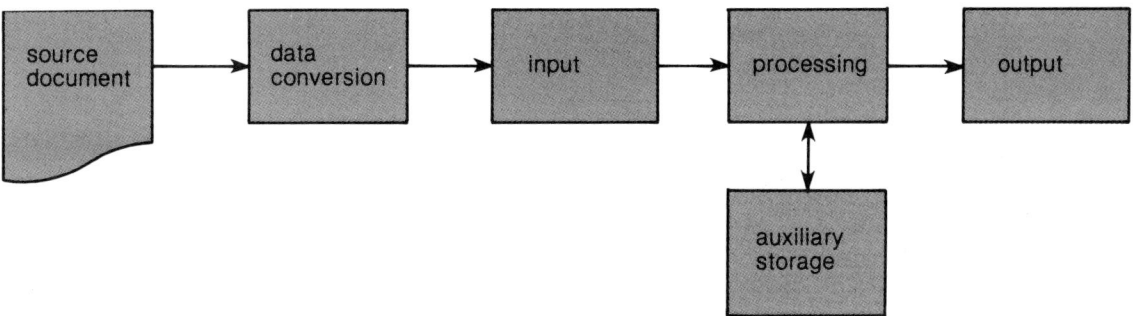

Figure A.1 diagrams the data processing cycle (similar figures appear in chapter 14, where the control over that cycle is discussed, and in chapter 6, where the transaction processing cycle is more extensively described). We will now present the major hardware/software components that participate in the data processing cycle.

Data Conversion and Input

The data processing cycle starts with the creation of source documents. In some cases, these source documents are themselves created by computers, as we will see shortly. Otherwise, you may refer to chapters 6 and 14 for a discussion of design and handling of source documents. The two topics of conversion and input are discussed together because of the way they are interrelated.

Data Conversion and Input Equipment

This section reviews some prevailing input and conversion methodologies. The following section will propose some criteria for selection and use of a particular method.

Data conversion is really the act of a person making the translation from what he or she reads on the document into keystrokes to enter the data into a computer or computer terminal. Thus, the conversion and input blend into a single activity, with the keyboard being the input device. Since the conversion is done under computer control, validity checking can take place as the conversion takes place; errors can be detected and corrected as a part of the process, and *data capture* and *validation* coincide. If the data is keyed in to a terminal connected to the computer that will ultimately use it, the conversion is online and complete validation can be done at that time. In some cases, the conversion will be done using a microcomputer, with the converted data being subsequently transferred to a larger mainframe computer by means of a diskette. In this case, the diskette becomes the machine readable input to the mainframe computer, and the conversion is said to take place offline. Some validity checking may be done by the microcomputer, but it would tend to be more limited.

Figure A.2 Magnetic ink characters on a bank check

A keyboard contains keys for alphabetic characters, numerals, punctuation and other special characters much the same as a typewriter. It also has special function keys that a computer can recognize as relating to operations to be performed, saving key strokes and reducing the likelihood of error. Other keyboard characteristics relate mainly to human engineering, and if a person is to use a keyboard extensively, these should be considered.

A common source document is the bank check, and these documents have special *magnetic ink character recognition* (MICR) encoding. They are readable by special devices that recognize numbers and special characters printed with ink containing magnetizable particles. In the case of a check, most of the data is known when the check is printed (bank number, account number, check number) and only the dollar amount needs to be encoded (converted from the handwritten figure to MICR) to make the document itself machine readable. Characters encoded in magnetic ink are exhibited at the bottom of the check in figure A.2. The amount is printed on the check when control totals are formed in the processing of deposits. Since only part of the data undergoes conversion, complete validation must be a separate activity performed later.

Optical character recognition (OCR) also uses special readers that can recognize preprinted characters. In this case, special ink is not required, only a special type font that is recognizable by the OCR reader. OCR is frequently used to input documents that were prepared by a computer printer—for example, telephone and utility bills, credit card customer statements, and the like. The dominant trait of all these cases is that the data (account number, billed amount, etc.) is completely known when the bill or statement is prepared, so there is almost no need for supplementary human writing in the payment of the bill, and no need for data conversion. The computer has prepared its own input, as the portion of the bill to be returned with payment. Figure A.3 exhibits a telephone bill containing OCR characters near the bottom.

Figure A.3 A telephone bill printed in the OCR technique

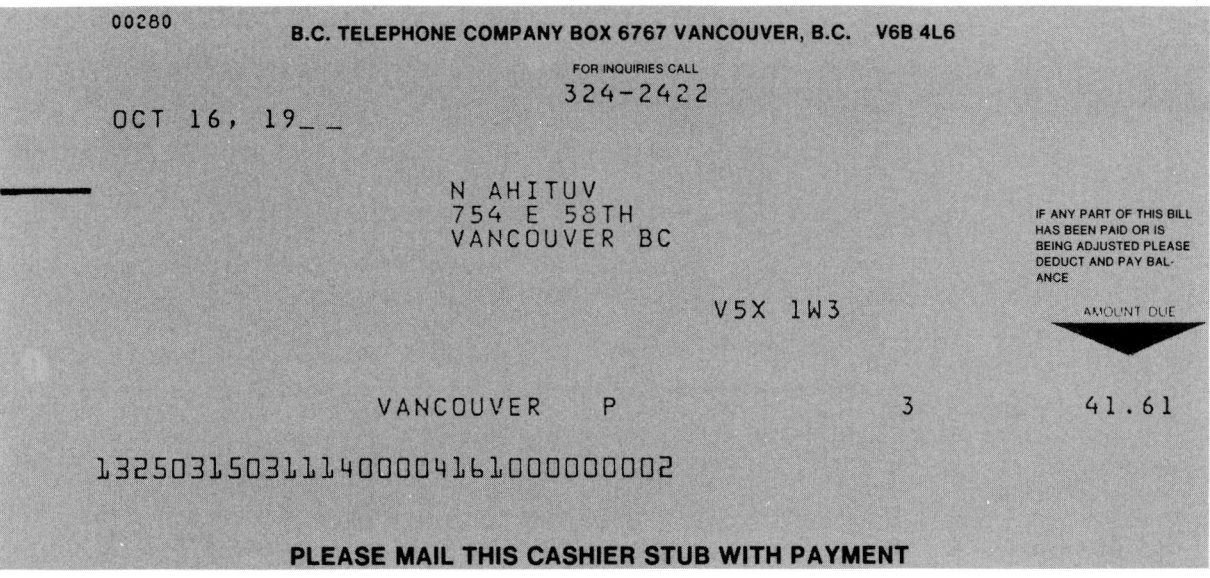

Another form of optically recognized encoding is the *bar code*. It is common for supermarkets and department stores to make use of such codes preprinted on the merchandise package or price tag. Figure A.4 depicts such a bar code used to identify a particular product and its manufacturer. The product number can be read by a scanner which is part of a *point of sale* (POS) terminal. The terminal, connected to a computer, reads the *universal product code* (UPC) and looks up the price in the computer's memory to compute the customer's bill. At the same time, it can update its inventory records to reflect the sale of the item. Another device at this point of sale will read your bank card so that the amount of your bill can be deducted from your bank account and credited to the merchant without your writing a check. This is an *electronic funds transfer* (EFT). You get documents reflecting the transactions, but the merchant and the bank have no documents to process.

Optical scanners may also be used to capture a digitized image of an entire document. This enables reference to be made to a source document, such as an airline ticket, without having to resort to a search of filing cabinets to retrieve it. This *image technology* enables the computer to store related documents, including pictures, diagrams, etc., for easy reference from an online terminal or another computer.

Capturing data at the point of transaction takes other forms involving special terminals. For example, fast food restaurants often employ a cash register with special keys representing the items sold. No product identification codes or prices need to be entered, it is only necessary to press the appropriate key and the computer takes care of the rest. An automated teller machine at a bank may use a *touch screen*. The transaction choices (deposit, withdrawal, etc.) are displayed on a screen and the customer touches the transaction he or she wants.

Figure A.4 A bar code which identifies a product (the code is named UPC—Universal Product Code)

A number of other forms of input device implement some means of choosing from a *menu,* or set of choices displayed on a screen. Sometimes these choices appear as *icons,* or pictures, representing the actions to be selected. A common input device is the *mouse,* which the user moves about on a table top to position a cursor on the display screen. When the cursor lines up with the menu choice or icon to be selected, a key on the mouse is pressed to input that choice to the computer.

It is also possible for some input devices to process handwritten characters. These may be input by an optical scanner from a paper document, or by means of a stylus writing on a special pad or *tablet* (see ph. A.1).

For a more complete review of the possibilities, see [9] or [6]. For more about data validation, see chapters 6 and 14. We will now evaluate some of the implications of the use of various input techniques.

Criteria for Selection of an Input Medium

The choice of an appropriate input medium is influenced by the characteristics of the application it is supposed to serve. Let us examine for a moment two extremely different applications: customer checkout in a supermarket compared to annual processing of statistics covering national production in the food industry. The supermarket cashier requires quick response time (the customer would not wait for a long time). High accuracy is necessary (charges must be precise). Control must be instantaneous (before the customer has left the cashier). Up-to-date information is vital (decisions on discount prices or price increases should immediately affect the system). The national statistics, on the other hand, are annual, hence response time is not a crucial factor. Accuracy is not that imperative. Source data from all over the country is recorded in a standard way and forwarded to a processing center. There is a voluminous amount of data.

Obviously an online data capture and verification technique would best fit the supermarket application, probably by means of POS terminals connected to a local computer and using a scanner for UPC labels. On the other hand, a traditional batch input, probably by keying in from source documents (questionnaires) to diskettes would be adequate for the statistics application.

In general, the following parameters guide the selection of an input medium:

1. *Reliability*—Degree of *accuracy* and *control* the user wishes to obtain
2. *Timeliness*—Speed of *response time* and degree of *data currency* desired by the user
3. *Volume*—Amount of data to be captured
4. *Scatter*—Geographical spread of data

Table A.1 specifies the characteristics of the supermarket and the statistics applications in light of the above parameters.

Once these parameters are specified, the decision maker reviews the potential alternatives and incorporates cost factors into the analysis. If an adequate solution does not emerge, then either expectation levels regarding those parameters must be lowered or the cost constraints should be relaxed.

Table A.1 Input Characteristics of Two Sample Applications

	Supermarket Cashier Application	National Statistics Application
Reliability		
Accuracy	Extremely vital	Not that important
Control	Extremely important	Moderately important
Timeliness		
Response time	Instantaneous	Can take weeks or months
Data currency	Up-to-date	Up to the last budgetary year
Volume	Relatively small (per cashier per day)	Very large
Scatter	Concentrated	Extremely scattered

Data Processing

Once the data has been captured and read into the computer, it is in the computer's memory, where it is manipulated and processed by computer programs. At this stage, users and managers are concerned with some characteristics of both the hardware and the software. We will discuss both aspects of the processing capabilities of computers.

The Central Processing Unit

The heart of a computer is the *central processing unit* (CPU) (see fig. A.5). It comprises three units: a control unit that monitors all the computer's operations; an arithmetic logic unit that performs arithmetic computations and logical operations (e.g., comparisons of data items); and an internal memory (storage) in which data and programs are stored. The CPU communicates with *peripheral devices* (input, output, and auxiliary storage units) to send them data from its memory or to receive data from them. In the case of small computers this communication takes place over a connecting link called an *input/output* (I/O) *bus*. Larger computers, needing greater capacity for simultaneous I/O operations, usually have something called *channels* for this purpose. More detail may be found in [9].

Bases for Choosing a CPU

CPUs range in price from a few hundred dollars to hundreds of thousands of dollars. The price will depend on the CPU's speed, the amount of memory, the number and variety of I/O devices it can utilize, and the degree to which it can carry out various operations simultaneously. All of these characteristics are tied very closely to the choices made about the software described in the next section.

The smallest (personal) computers are designed to do the work of one person at a time. Even a single user may make very heavy demands on the CPU in terms of the amount of processing or computation required, the quality of visual display it must support, or the amount of I/O activity it must manage. Thus, different uses will require different "sizes" of CPU. The larger, more powerful personal computers have come to be called *workstations*. Many of these workstations can also serve more than one user, and execute more than one program at a time.

Figure A.5 A schematic diagram of CPU, channels, and peripherals

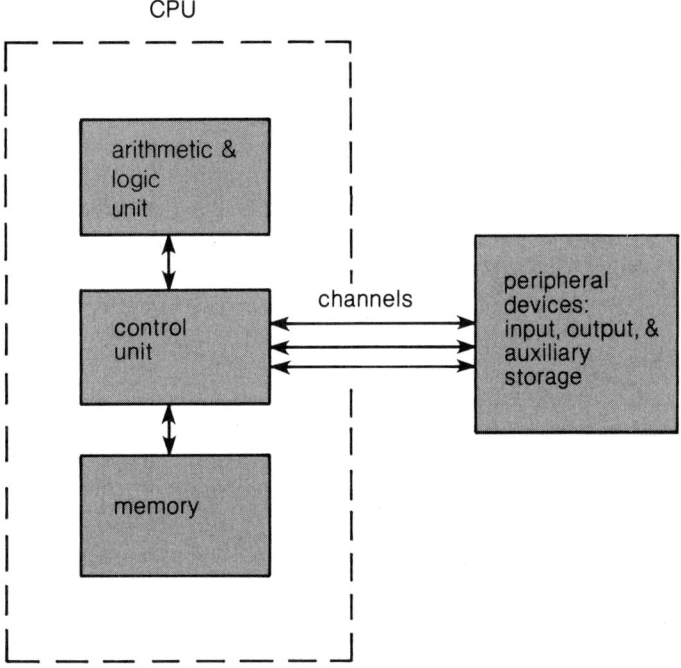

A *mainframe computer* is generally one which is intended to serve many users simultaneously, frequently by running many different programs concurrently. Mainframe computers usually have much greater I/O capability, and the use of a mainframe computer may be dictated simply by the need for a very large auxiliary storage that is able to support a number of simultaneous accesses to its contents. Mainframe computers are available in a wide range of capabilities and prices.

Prior to the widespread use of personal computers, computers that were smaller and more limited than the current mainframe computers were introduced. These came to be known as *minicomputers,* because of their smaller physical size and their smaller capabilities. In the context of current terminology, we can simply think of these as small mainframe computers. Some computers are also described as *mid-range,* simply indicating that they are somewhere between small and large.

The choice of computer also dictates to some extent the range of choices of I/O devices. A particular device may only be compatible with a specific I/O interface specification. Mainframe computers tend to provide more limited choices in terms of possible vendors of compatible devices. With personal computers the choices are broader, but the type of bus used by the CPU will determine what those choices are.

So, for a single user to do word processing, for example, the smallest and least expensive personal computer may do nicely. An airline reservation system handling transactions from hundreds of locations throughout the globe, needing rapid response, and maintaining thousands of records about flights and passengers, may require the very largest mainframe CPU that can be acquired.

The uses that a computer is put to (its applications) determine how much work it has to do (its workload). *Workload* is a measure of both quantity and speed. Thus, for a transaction processing system, the workload is measured by the number of transactions that must be processed per unit of time. Estimating the number of computer operations, or instructions, required per transaction gives us the number of instructions that the CPU must be capable of executing in that same unit of time.

A computer's ability to do work (its capacity) has traditionally been expressed in terms of the number of instructions it can execute per unit of time, typically in *millions of instructions per second* (MIPS). Thus, if a CPU can deliver the number of MIPS required by the TPS, it would be a satisfactory choice. Unfortunately this is a little too simplistic, but this is the general idea behind various strategies, such as *benchmarks,* employed to determine what size CPU is required to do the job presented by the information system.

Many of the more recent CPUs introduced have what is known as a *reduced instruction set computer* (RISC) design. It is claimed that this design, because of its simplicity, leads to faster and more efficient CPUs. However, since the instruction set is the machine language of the computer, and virtually all programming is done in a higher level language, whether the CPU is a RISC one or not has no real effect on the information system for which it is used. The choice of a CPU will be based on the results it can deliver as part of a system, not upon its particular design.

Software

The term *software* broadly applies to all the programs that execute on the CPU in order to process data. Software can be divided into several categories, and each one must be considered by the user in selecting the appropriate hardware/software combination(s) for an information system. We will describe these categories and discuss some of the matters that must be taken into account in making choices. First we define some basic terminology. A *program* is any set of instructions to a computer that causes it to carry out some task. A *software package* is a collection of (one or more) related, cooperating programs to do all the tasks related to some data processing function. A *system* is a collection of any related, cooperating elements, thus there are both hardware and software systems. The terms software system and software package are often used interchangeably.

1. *Operating system*—This is what gives a computer its basic capabilities to control its peripheral devices and to run other programs. The operating system will sometimes be obtained from the hardware (CPU) vendor, sometimes from another source. Some operating systems only run on a particular manufacturer's computers (e.g., the VMS operating system for Digital Equipment Corporation computers, or the MVS for some IBM computers). Other operating systems (Unix, MS-DOS, OS/2, Windows NT) can be used with the computers from a variety of manufacturers. Since the operating system determines to some extent what other programs it is possible to use, this underlying software platform is an important

consideration. The operating system maintains the files of data kept by the computer (this will be discussed further in a later section of this appendix), so it is important to consider the file system provided and what data base management software is supported.

It is also important to consider the human interface provided by the operating system. This interface is the way in which the user is able to instruct the operating system, select which programs to run or which files to use, and monitor the computer's activity. The operating system should either provide an easy-to-use means of communication or be compatible with a separate software package that does. Since we are talking about human interaction with the computer, human preferences will enter into this choice.

2. *Utility programs*—Much of what has to be done on a computer is very common, standard, and routine—such as making a copy of a file, sorting the contents of a file, etc. A set of these utility programs is usually provided as a part of—or a companion to—the operating system, while more extensive utility programs (such as a word processing program), must be obtained and paid for separately.

3. *Programming languages*—Each particular type of CPU has its own particular set of operations, or *instructions* that its hardware can carry out. This is known as its *machine language* and consists simply of binary numbers, the ones and zeros that computers store internally. Programs written in *assembler language* are very close to this machine language, so they can only be run on a particular type of hardware. Most programs are written in some *higher level language* (COBOL, Pascal, C), so named because the languages are independent of a particular kind of hardware. Programs written in these languages are *compiled* (i.e., translated to machine language) to run on a specific kind of CPU, therefore are compatible with any computer for which a compiler is available.

Some of these languages (COBOL, FORTRAN, PL/I, BASIC) have been used since the earliest days of computers; others (Pascal, C, Ada) are somewhat more recent. Not every language is necessarily available for use with every operating system, but generally, this is not a problem. Most of the languages currently in use can be compiled under most of the operating systems currently in use.

4. *Application generators*—Programs written in one of the higher level languages still have to spell out, step by step, every operation that must be performed in order to process the input data to achieve a desired result. Application generators are programs that allow the user to specify the desired result in a more general way, and the generator produces a program that will accomplish that. Thus, these allow the user to express his or her needs at an even higher level than the higher level languages. Consequently, some of these software tools (Focus, Natural, Ramis) have been called "*Fourth Generation Language*" (4GL) software on the assumption that the first three generations were represented by machine language, assembler language, and the higher level languages, respectively. These fourth-generation software

tools generally are based on a data base management system. (The use of a DBMS will be discussed later in this appendix). They make inquiries about the data very easy to construct without having to write a program. At best, they extend the ability to make such inquiries to non-specialists. At least, they substantially improve the productivity of a 4GL specialist (as compared to a COBOL programmer). Since a particular fourth-generation software tool may be tied to a specific operating system, these choices must be coordinated.

5. *Application packages*—These are software systems offered by vendors. An application package may be very general (a word processing utility could also be termed a general purpose application package); or it may be very specialized (inventory control for a veterinary hospital). Obviously, the prices range from a few dollars to thousands of dollars depending on the extent of the application covered and the potential market for the package. One benefit of the high volume with which software is produced for personal computers has been the number, variety, and quality of application packages available.

In considering the acquisition of a package, it must be determined just how closely it fits the needs of the organization. For example, an accounting package may be closely aligned with the organization's accounting practices—or it may not. The extent to which the package has to be adapted to fit the organization, or the organization has to adapt to fit the package, could be a significant issue (and a significant cost). Again, a specific package may be written to run with a particular operating system, so this needs to be considered.

6. *Data base management software*—These software products are widely used in a variety of ways. Used independently, they could be classified as application packages; however, they are usually used in conjunction with other programs. A later section of this appendix will look at DBMS software in more detail.

7. *Telecommunications software*—Larger computers may communicate with terminal devices that serve as both input (keyboard) and output (display) units, while both small and large computers are linked for various kinds of communication lines to form networks of cooperating systems. Communication with terminals is usually provided by the operating system. Other forms of networking generally require special software. This will be discussed later in this appendix.

8. *User-written programs*—The above categories of software are all ones in which the software is obtained from a vendor of one kind or another. This category consists of the programs that the user organization writes "from scratch" by using programming languages (i.e., COBOL, Pascal, or C), or with the aid of a 4GL application generator. The benefit of writing these *customized* programs is exactly that matter of customization: they can be made to do exactly what is desired for the organization. The cost is that it requires people to write these programs, and to maintain them. In many cases there is no alternative, and in other cases it is the most cost-effective approach.

Figure A.6 A typical update path producing human-understandable and machine-readable outputs

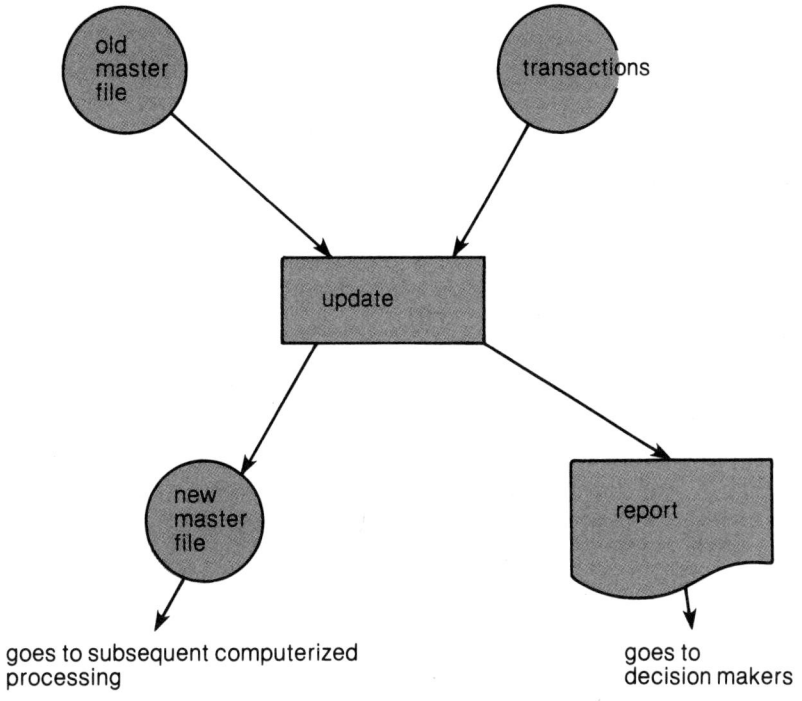

Output

The processing done by computer can result in two types of output: human-understandable output for decision making or other actions, and machine-readable output for further processing. For example, when you run an update program for customer accounts in a bank, you would like to produce an overdraft report so that someone in management can decide whether to honor the checks that caused the overdrafts. You would also like to have all customer balances recorded in a magnetic disk file so you can run the same update program after the close of the next business day. These specifications are characteristic of almost any update program (particularly under batch processing). Figure A.6 illustrates a typical update operation in a batch processing environment.

There are other possibilities. For example, consider a program that does billing for an electric power utility. The program will update the customer's record with the current meter reading and produce a bill. A report may be printed listing those customers who have not paid their previous bills so that management can take action, similar to the overdraft report above. The bill, however, has two kinds of output: human-understandable so the customer knows how much to pay; and machine-readable so the returned portion of the bill serves as an input document. (Actually the machine-readable portion is also human-understandable since it is in OCR characters.) The updated customer record needs to be recorded on a disk file so it can be processed again when the payment is made, and again the next month to produce another bill, similar to the updated bank customer record.

Output that "leaves" the computer is usually referred to as output, whether it is human-understandable, machine readable, or both. Output that is only machine readable and that is retained by the computer for further processing is called *auxiliary storage*. We will first look at the choices for output media. A more detailed discussion of auxiliary storage will follow in the next section.

Output Equipment

In the preceding discussion we refrained from using the term ''human-readable output'' because computer output can also be heard (e.g., an audio response of your bank balance); or it can be seen (but not read) as in a graphic display (e.g., a picture of an automobile part). In both cases the human user does not read textual output yet he or she can understand it. As common as these forms of output are becoming, much output is still of the more persistent, printed variety. Let us now review some of the possibilities for printing.

1. *Line printer*—These printers are normally used to print out voluminous reports or large numbers of bills or checks in a batch mode. Line printers operate at speeds ranging from 300 to 3000 lines per minute. Printing is done by pressing cast images of the characters against an inked ribbon, thus they are limited to printing a particular character set and type font. The paper used must be of the *continuous form,* fan-folded variety. Line printers are relatively expensive and therefore likely to be used with a mainframe computer or a special computer in a network that operates as a *print server.* Because they print at some centralized location, their output needs to be physically distributed to wherever it is required to go.

2. *Character-at-a-time printers*—Much less expensive printers are the character-at-a-time printers, usually of the dot matrix variety. These are commonly used with the personal computers or workstations. The *dot matrix printer* (illustrated in fig. A.7) uses an array of small pins to form the characters. In a graphics mode, the individual pins can be controlled to print dots to form pictures or other type fonts. These printers commonly print at 200 characters per second or more, but if a higher quality print (or graphics) is desired they print more slowly at perhaps 40 characters per second. Usually these printers can use either continuous form paper or be fed single sheets one at a time. Such printers are available for under two hundred dollars. Because they are inexpensive, they can be used wherever printed output is required.

3. *Ink jet printers*—Unlike the two previous kinds of printers that print by pressing a ribbon against the paper (*impact printers*), the *ink jet printers* are *non-impact* printers. They form characters much like the dot matrix printers, but instead of pressing pins against a ribbon, they print by ''squirting'' ink through a matrix of holes. These printers are also relatively inexpensive.

Figure A.7 A dot-matrix printer

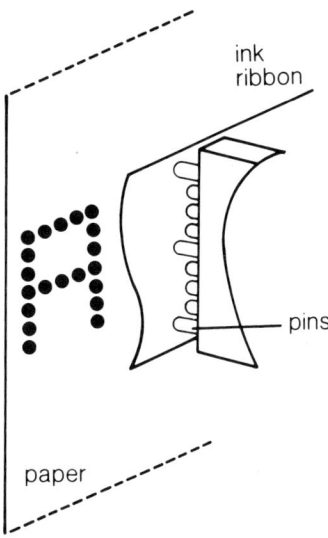

4. *Laser printers*— These are also non-impact printers. They function much like photocopiers, but instead of reproducing a picture of a document, the image is formed by a laser under computer control and printed on single sheets fed from a supply tray. Like the dot matrix printers, printed characters or pictures are composed of dots. With the laser printer, the number of dots per inch is higher, thus improving the print quality. The cost of a laser printer is related to its speed. Slower models (several pages per minute) are inexpensive enough (under $1,000) to be used with a personal computer or workstation. Higher speed and color printing models are expensive enough (up to or above $100,000) that, like line printers, they would be used with a mainframe computer or print server.

Any of the printer types may be used with blank paper or with *pre-printed forms*. Pre-printed forms reduce the amount of output that the printer must actually print and may contribute to a more attractive document; however, they are less flexible and require changing paper in the printer, control of forms stock, etc. Consequently, this approach is most attractive for high volume batch jobs such as billing or check writing. Note that checks usually must be printed on a special paper and have MICR encoding. For most printing needs, laser printers eliminate the need for pre-printed forms.

Displays
Since there is an enormous variety of displays on the market, we will only describe the basic choices. After all, when it comes to displays, seeing them is more helpful than reading about them.

We distinguish first between monochrome and color *visual display terminals* (VDT). *Monochrome displays* use only one color, so for screen variation they must produce shades of that color (i.e., shades of gray or green). *Color displays* are capable of displaying millions of different colors, although less expensive ones are limited to eight. Displays come in different physical sizes and with different levels of resolution. Resolution refers to the sharpness and clarity of the images formed. Large sizes, high resolution, and lots of colors are usually only required where high quality graphics are important to the application; i.e., where they are an aid to human understanding.

Output to a display may be used where no hard copy is required. For example, exhibiting the current status of arriving and departing flights at an airline counter requires only a display device that can be updated frequently. Output to a display is also useful where a dialogue with the computer is required—i.e., the user receives the output and must react to it by keying in a response (input). Such an I/O device, or terminal, requires both a display and a keyboard. For more information on output devices, see [6] or [9].

Auxiliary Storage and Files

As mentioned in the previous section, computers produce two types of output, one for human use and another for computer use. Most of the latter type concerns files; i.e., data to be stored for future use. This requires that data be transcribed from the computer's memory to some storage medium, usually a magnetic disk, from which it can later be read back into the computer's memory. These magnetic disks (or other devices) are called *auxiliary storage.*

Before discussing the kinds of auxiliary storage, we first want to introduce some major terms related to *file organization.* Knowledge of the terms will facilitate understanding of later material.

Terms in File Organization

We will start by presenting five common terms related to data and files. As you will see, the sequence of definitions goes bottom-up, from the most elementary to more comprehensive entities.

1. *Character*—An elementary component of data that signifies any symbol used in a language—e.g., a letter (A,B,C, etc.), a digit (0,1,2, etc.), and special symbols (?, !, #, etc.).

2. *Field (data item)*—A string of characters describing an attribute of an item—e.g., student name, customer balance, marital status, date.

3. *Record*—A group of fields describing an item—e.g., student record, inventory record, criminal record, bank account record.

4. *File (data set)*—A group of records pertaining to a certain subject—e.g., accounts receivable file, personnel file, savings deposit file, product file.

5. *Data base*—A group of files pertaining to a certain organizational unit—e.g., accounting data base, production data base.

Note that the last definition is unlimited in scope. It may define an accounting data base to contain all the bookkeeping files, but it can also include an entire business' data base, which may itself be a portion of the corporate data base, and so on.

Note also that the term ''data base'' is conceptual (similar to that discussed in ch. 5), while the practical realization of it may range from a set of traditional files up to the most modern data base management system (DBMS).

In addition to these general terms, we define several more specific terms:

1. *Key field (identifier)*—A field by which one may identify a record; e.g., Social Security number, bank account number, customer number. Normally file records are sorted by the order of their key fields.

2. *Master file*—A file containing all the records pertaining to a subject, one record per each key field; master files normally depict the status of their subject records as of a certain time—e.g., an inventory master file would contain all inventory items, one record per item, and depict the inventory status of the items as of a certain time. Master files are permanent and are periodically updated.

3. *Transaction file*—A file containing the recordings of physical transactions pertaining to a certain subject—e.g., all debit and credit entries of customers of a bank during a business day. Note that in a transaction file two or more records may have the same key field, for instance, when the same customer makes two or more transactions the same business day. Transaction files are temporary and are used to update master files.

4. *Historical files*—Previous versions (old generations) of master or transaction files. These are normally kept for backup purposes, for trend analysis and statistics, and for audit and control purposes (see ch. 14 on audit trail).

To conclude this definition section, we define two operations involving files:

1. *Retrieval*—The act of fetching a desired record from a file—e.g., locate the transcript of student #123.

2. *Update*—The act of modifying a master file by new transactions accumulated in a transaction file.

The major goal of a data processing application is, of course, to provide the most appropriate retrieval, whereas update is just a means to accomplish that. In other words, we do not update files if we do not foresee any retrieval request issued in the future.

Equipped with all these definitions, we can get back now to auxiliary storage devices and file organization techniques.

Magnetic Storage

Magnetic storage takes various forms but usually involves some metal or plastic coated with a magnetizable material on which data can be magnetically recorded. One form is magnetic tape, similar to that used in a tape player or VCR. The problem with this is that the computer has to start at the beginning and wind the tape from reel to reel in order to reach some particular data. To get back to the beginning, the computer must

Figure A.8 Schematic illustration of a disk pack: (a) a disk pack; (b) a disk pack and access arms—a side view; (c) a disk platter and an access arm—a top view

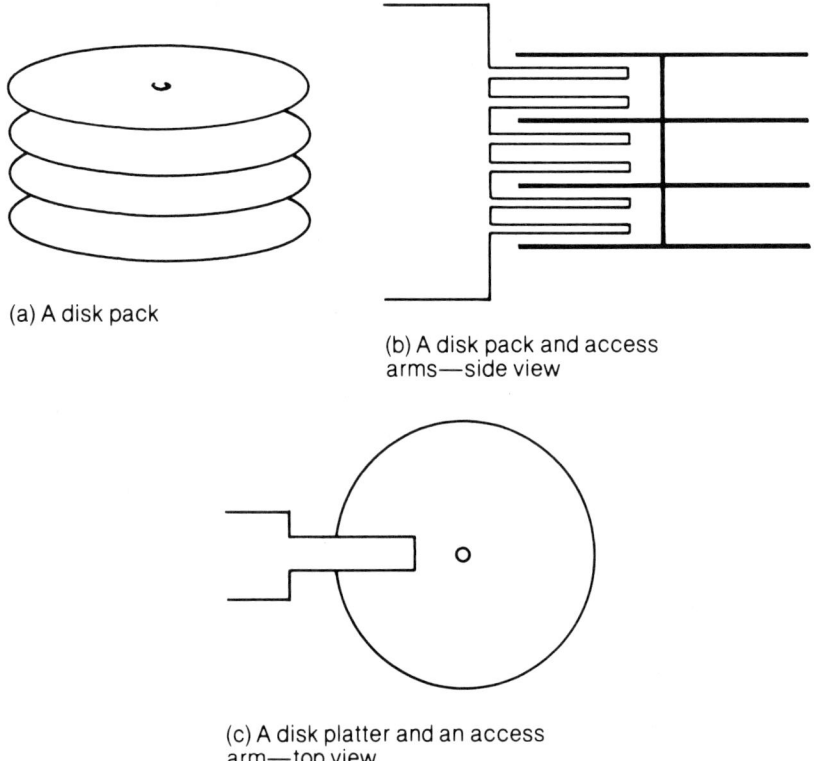

(a) A disk pack

(b) A disk pack and access arms—side view

(c) A disk platter and an access arm—top view

rewind the tape. As a result, this is most useful for data that is unlikely to be used often (archival storage), because it is just a copy being stored as a precautionary measure.

Direct Access Devices

A *direct access device* enables a computer to access a record located anywhere in a file without having to read in all the preceding records of that file. Direct access devices are usually *magnetic disks*. There are a wide variety of different models, but in all cases there is a disk (one or more) on which the data is recorded, and a *disk drive* that makes the disk turn (it must be moving in order to read or write data). Disks may be rigid and unremovable (a "hard" drive with one or more disks); rigid and removable (usually multiple disks in a *disk pack*); or flexible and removable *diskettes* (*floppy disks*).

Figure A.8a shows a schematic illustration of a multiple disk arrangement, such as a disk pack. It consists of several round disks (*platters*) that rotate around a spindle. The disk drive rotates the disks (commonly at 3,600 revolutions per minute).

A read-write *head* is positioned over the surface of the disk (usually one on each surface) and can be moved to any of a number of concentric circles (*tracks*) on which data is recorded. A group of access arms moves all the heads at the same time, like inserting a comb into the pack (see figs. A.8b and c). The drive moves the arms to be positioned over the desired track, activates the head corresponding to the desired surface, and waits for the rotating motion to bring the desired record to the read-write head (this wait cannot exceed the time for one revolution of the disk). While this may seem like a lengthy process, during the time it has taken you to read this paragraph a computer could complete hundreds of operations like that.

An inexpensive hard drive for a personal computer in 1992 might hold 40 million characters of data. Larger disk units for personal computers and workstations frequently store hundreds of millions of characters. Large *direct access storage devices* (DASDs) for mainframe computers can store hundreds of billions of characters. Floppy disks, on the other hand, usually store only one or two million characters, most commonly on a disk three and one-half inches in diameter. These are principally used where it is desirable to be able to write the files on one computer and then transfer the disk to another computer to be read. Floppy disk drives generally rotate less rapidly and transfer the data at a lower speed. (See [6] for a more detailed description of magnetic storage of all kinds).

The magnetic disk enables direct accessing to records because it is a three-dimensional storage device. Each record is marked with a three-attribute address: the distance of the track from the beginning of the pack (how far in the access arms must move); the surface (which head is activated); and the distance of the desired record from the beginning of the track (this is artificially marked since the track is, after all, round). Being a three-dimensional unit the disk pack enables the computer to skip over undesired records and get to a desired one, or at least get fairly close to it. How does the computer know the exact location of a desired record? That depends on the techniques used for file organization. These are discussed next.

Sequential Files

A possible, though not efficient, way to store records is simply to write them down without any order or reference to a key. This means that update and retrieval will consume a lot of time because each desired record has to be searched ad hoc. A better way is to sort the records by a key field in ascending or descending order; sorted files are labeled *sequential files.*

When a master file is sequentially organized, in order to retrieve or update records we must first sort the retrieval requests or the updating transactions in the same order as the master file; thereafter we can run the retrieval or update program. In this way the master file is read only once during each run of the program. Figure A.9 illustrates an update run of sequential files.

Figure A.9 demonstrates the two major deficiencies of a sequential update: (1) The transaction file must undergo a sorting process, which might be very time consuming, before being processed by the update program; and (2) all the records are copied from the old to the new master file, even those not changed.

Figure A.9 Update of a sequential file (the numbers in the boxes represent record key-fields)

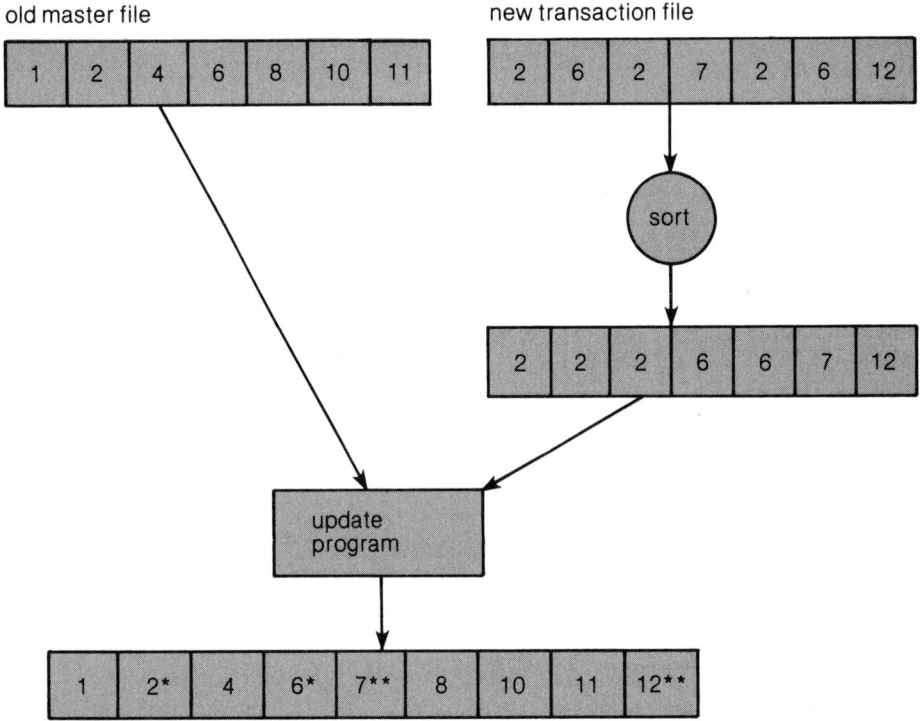

old master file

| 1 | 2 | 4 | 6 | 8 | 10 | 11 |

new transaction file

| 2 | 6 | 2 | 7 | 2 | 6 | 12 |

sort

| 2 | 2 | 2 | 6 | 6 | 7 | 12 |

update program

| 1 | 2* | 4 | 6* | 7** | 8 | 10 | 11 | 12** |

*updated records
**new records

Sequential files were prevalent for many years. Even today they are useful in many cases, so we should not undervalue this technique. However, the technique is basically primitive. In analogy, suppose that whenever you enter the branch of your bank to perform a certain transaction the teller has to locate your balance by scanning all the customer accounts from the lowest account number forward until he or she encounters your account. Or suppose that whenever you seek a book in the library you have to start searching from the northwest corner of the library and look for the book by scanning shelf after shelf. You wouldn't like it.

In principle, the sequential technique is similar to these analogies, but the computer works faster.

Table A.2 A Sample File Index

Key Range	Track Number
1–8	1
9–21	2
22–38	3
39–71	4

Direct Access Files

When we attach direct access devices to a computer, we can use them to store sequential files and gain the advantages of fast speed and large capacity that characterize those devices. However, this ignores the major advantage of such devices—the capability of directly accessing records. We make use of this capability by applying different file organization techniques.

The several feasible techniques can be classified in the following categories:

1. *Indexed files*—Suppose you sort your master file ascendingly by a certain key and then load the file on a disk pack (like a sequential file). While loading, the program writes down the range of key values of the records that have managed to get into each track or group of tracks. Upon completion of the loading, you will have an index telling you the track limits within which you can find each of the records. Table A.2 illustrates such an index.

   Obviously such an index does not indicate the exact location of each record, but it certainly narrows the domain of the search. In practice, indexes can be much more involved than the example in table A.2. For large files we can develop a hierarchy of indexes, each subordinate index narrowing the search range indicated by a superior one.

   The technique is similar to the way we look for a word in a dictionary, or for a telephone number in a telephone directory. We start from a general knowledge of the location of a group of words or surnames beginning with a certain letter of the alphabet, and we continue to narrow our search until we get to the page where the desired data is supposedly written.

2. *Direct (random) files*—Normally each record of a master file possesses a unique key—namely, a key field that distinguishes the record from any other record in the file (e.g., bank account number, Social Security number). Also, each location on the disk—each ''slot'' which may potentially contain a record—has a unique physical address. If we can find a mathematical formula (a transformation) that associates keys with addresses, then a computer program can use the formula whenever it has to write out or retrieve a record. This will provide the program with a physical disk address for any given key, so the location of the record can be directly accessed. Files organized by this technique are called direct (or random) files. Access in such cases is efficient and relatively quick. However, a transformation formula is not always devisable.

Table A.3 A Personnel File

Employee Number	Profession	Education	Rank
1	engineer	B.Sc.	12
2	engineer	M.B.A.	13
3	secretary	B.A.	9
4	secretary	high school	7
5	programmer	M.B.A.	12
6	system designer	M.B.A.	13
7	programmer	high school	9
8	programmer	B.Sc.	12
9	system designer	B.A.	13

3. *Inverted files*—Suppose you have a personnel file where each record contains various attributes of an employee, as exhibited in table A.3. Each row in the table represents a record of an employee. The file is sequentially organized.

   The same information can be organized by isolating each attribute and assigning to it all the employees having a similar value of the attribute. This is shown in table A.4.

   The data presented in table A.4 is exactly equivalent to that presented in table A.3, but the arrangement is different. This arrangement is labeled "inverted file." For certain queries—e.g., "list all the engineers employed in the firm"—it would be easier to use an inverted file. For other queries—e.g., "list all the information about employee number 6"—one of the previous organization techniques would be more convenient to use.

   In practice, whenever inverted files are used, they are commonly partially inverted—some of the attributes appear in tables, and the rest are collated in regular records. Clearly, this technique is feasible only when direct access devices are available.

4. *List-structured files*—In list-structured files, records are related by pointers that specify the sequence by which records can be retrieved or processed. Consequently there is no similarity between the physical location of a record and its relation to other records. When a record is read into memory, a pointer field embedded in the record directs the program to a subsequent record. Each record may contain several pointers, each associated with a different logical sequence. For instance, in the records presented in table A.3, one pointer will indicate a record with a subsequent employee number while another pointer may indicate the next engineer (or any other profession) in the personnel file. This means the file can be processed under various applications characterized by different information requirements without having to be reorganized.

Table A.4 An Inverted File

Profession Table

Profession	Employee Numbers		
engineer	1	2	
programmer	5	7	8
secretary	3	4	
system designer	6	9	

Education Table

Education	Employee Numbers		
B.A.	3	9	
B.Sc.	1	8	
high school	4	7	
M.B.A.	2	5	6

Rank Table

Rank	Employee Numbers		
7	4		
8			
9	3	7	
10			
11			
12	1	5	8
13	2	6	9

Some Concluding Remarks

The topic of file organization is very broad and involves a lot of technicalities. Selecting a file organization technique is usually a nontrivial problem, involving aspects of cost, efficiency, timing, and the like. (An extensive treatment of file organization can be found in [5]).

The contemporary trend in file organization is to install a *data base management system* (DBMS), which is a ready-made software package that monitors and integrates all the organizational data. A DBMS commonly uses some of the techniques we have mentioned; however, the user and the application programmer do not have to be aware of that because they communicate with the DBMS as an interface. It is the data base specialist (see ch. 12) who should master the technical details. The next section discusses DBMS from the viewpoint of the users.

Data Base Management Systems

In chapter 5 we first mentioned the notion *data base*. It referred to the collection of all the data pertaining to an organization or a unit in an organization. We said that data is usually generated through transaction processing systems, but once the data is captured, any echelon along the organizational hierarchy may use it, provided that information requirements have been well defined and appropriate programs have been implemented. This would imply that the same data can be used by different sets of programs; hence we distinguish between the data base—a set of data—and the applications—a set of programs. In a DSS this set of programs is the *model base.*

The term *data base* may refer to any collection of data that might serve an organizational unit, be it a manual archive or a group of files traditionally organized. However, the idea of a large corporate data base that can be flexibly shared by several applications or model bases has been realized by means of software packages specially devised to perform such tasks. These packages, called *data base management systems* (DBMSs), are the major concern of this section. We will explain their impact on the use of information systems by management and departmental users without getting into unnecessary technical details. For a technical description of DBMSs, we recommend any one of the following texts: Awad [2], Date [4], or Stamper[11].

DBMS Principles

At the beginning of the computer era computerized information systems were mostly utilized to relieve organizations of the oppressive burden of voluminous manual activities characterizing transaction-processing operations. Therefore, business computers were mostly used in transaction-processing applications. Only later, during the sixties, did it become apparent that data collected by several ''discrete'' systems must be integrated if an organization wished information systems to become useful for managerial decision making.

For instance, suppose the management of a manufacturing firm considers establishing an additional production plant. The factors to be considered relate to sales distribution, marketing costs, production costs, procurement costs, transportation facilities and costs, employee skills and salaries, and the like. The required information must be compiled from various data sources, each source handled by a different information system that takes care of routine transaction processing. If those systems have not been coordinated from the beginning, then data integration might be very costly or even impossible.

Problems of that kind have raised the need to develop software for data base handling. A great push to this trend was given by the *Conference on Data Systems Languages (CODASYL).* This group, who had previously succeeded in developing universal standards for the COBOL programming language, established a committee that started to publicize its ideas on data base handling at the beginning of the seventies. The essence of those ideas is outlined in the following sections.

Major Requirements of Data Base Software
An ideal DBMS should adhere to the following principles:

1. *Data independence*—The data base should be flexible enough to serve a
number of different applications, each approaching the data in a different
fashion through different search strategies. In other words, application
programs must not be affected by the technique by which the files are

organized (as opposed to the examples in the previous discussion on file organization techniques, where the logic of an update program, for instance, was highly influenced by the file structure). Ideally, any change in the data base structure should not impose changes on application programs. In fact, users and application programmers do not have to be aware of the physical layout of files.

The data base system should also refrain from data redundancy. This will avoid the need for multiple updates of similar data scattered among various files, hence it will reduce the likelihood of inconsistent data and increase the reliability of the output.

2. *Program independence*—The data base system should accommodate programs written in various programming languages. This would allow application programmers to select a programming language that best fits the application requirements regardless of the specific data base software and data structure in use.

3. *System independence*—The data base system should not depend on the operating system of the host computer. In other words, the data base software should be compatible with different versions of operating systems and utility software.

4. *Hardware independence*—The data base system should be compatible with different hardware configurations, even if they are manufactured by different vendors. Ideally, a data base system should run on any type of hardware that satisfies minimum configuration constraints without having to undergo a significant conversion process.

These principles are somewhat idealistic. In reality, DBMSs available in the market do not exactly adhere to all of these principles due to technical difficulties or commercial considerations. For instance, a DBMS produced by an independent software house is most likely to meet the requirements stemming from the third and fourth principles because the software firm wants to make the DBMS compatible with a wide spectrum of computers and thus enlarge the potential market for the product. The principles, at least, are now widely accepted as guidelines by which a DBMS can be evaluated.

Schema and Subschema

A DBMS that complies with all or most of the above requirements is normally a very complex piece of software containing a lot of tables and fine programming routines. Development and maintenance of a DBMS require a high degree of competence and expertise (see ch. 12 on the various professions related to information systems). Nonetheless, to understand what a DBMS is supposed to do is not difficult.

The DBMS is, in principle, an interface between two entities: users and data (see fig. A.10). The users, as represented by application programs, wish to retrieve some data required for decision making. The data is located on auxiliary storage in a fashion that looks very peculiar and awesome to an outsider. Neither the user nor the application programmer is interested in the physical structure of the data; all they desire is

Figure A.10 The DBMS as an interface between users and data

users

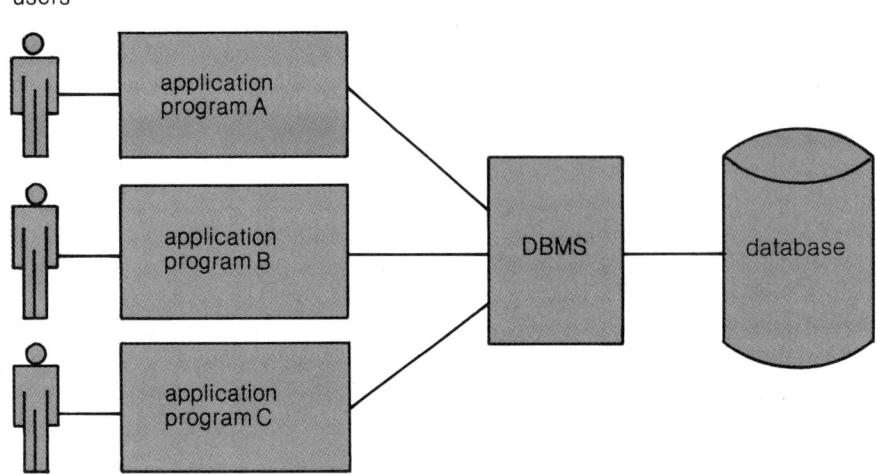

to get an effective retrieval instrument. The DBMS is that instrument. It translates the application program's demands into technical attributes that help get the right data and hand it over to the user. Obviously the DBMS must know how to build, maintain, and update the data base.

The interfacing role is carried out by means of tables, pointers, and programs. Two types of tables are imperative: *schema* and *subschema.*

The schema is a complete description of the data base structure as it is physically laid on the storage devices. It specifies in detail the format and the characteristics of each data item; it delineates relationships between various items; it restricts access to privileged items; in short, it is the "oracle" of the data base. Obviously the schema is an extensive table loaded with many technical details. The responsibility for it rests with the data base specialists.

The common user and application programmer would not get in touch with the schema. They normally need to access a relatively small portion of the data base, and the logic of the access (the search strategy) is not necessarily congruent with the phys- ical setting of the data. Therefore, upon submitting their specific requirements, they will receive from the data base specialist a subschema—a table depicting only the portion of the data base that is relevant to their needs. The depiction in the subschema is presented from the point of view of the application, regardless of the real physical structure of the data base. The relationship between a schema and subschema is illus- trated in figure A.11.

In analogy, suppose you have to pass through a dark labyrinth (the schema). Someone sets lights along the path that you have to take (the subschema) while all other paths remain dark. This should not bother you if you are assured of getting to

Figure A.11 The schema-subschema relationship

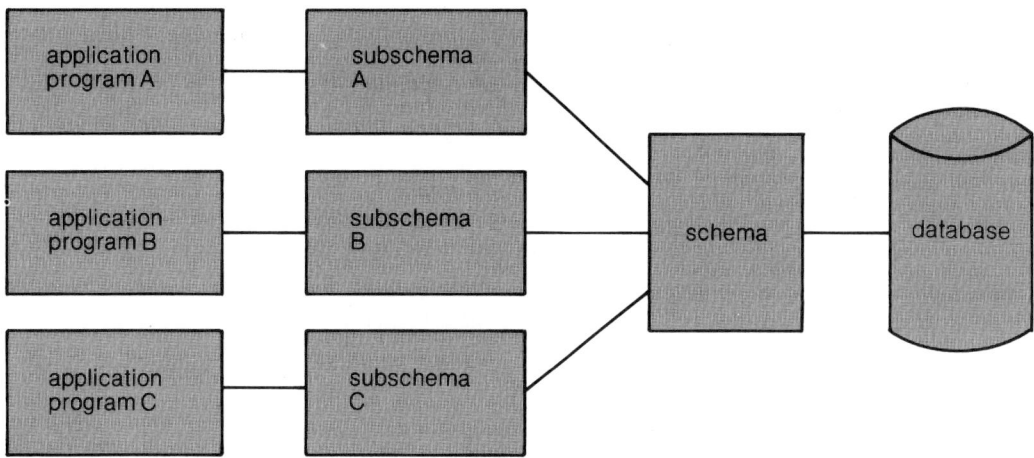

the desired destination. For the labyrinth supervisor (the data base specialist), this is all right, so long as there is a feasible path to the specified destination. Otherwise, the labyrinth is inadequately designed for your purposes and some corrective measures have to be taken by the supervisor, in accordance with your needs (i.e., redesigning the physical structure).

In conclusion, it is imperative that the user view of the data be presented to the *data base administrator* (DBA). This view reflects the information requirements of the user rather than the user opinion of how the data should be organized. The DBA and his or her team would tailor the physical structure to fit the user needs and provide the application programs with the proper subschemas. The next section presents possible user views of a data base from the eyes of a user.

User Views of a Data Base

There is an old story about a group of blind men who try to describe an elephant in their midst. Since each blind man is located at a different part of the elephant's body, their perceptions are all different, and the resulting descriptions are conflicting in the extreme.

The story is usually told to emphasize the disadvantages of not using the systems approach. However, suppose each blind man is interested in a different aspect of the elephantine system. Then why should any of them bother with other people's findings or with the elephant as a whole? Similarly, it is possible that various departmental users with assorted information requirements will view the same data base from different angles. We will now highlight some basic traits of data and then discuss some common approaches to data bases.

Figure A.12 Student's past performance record

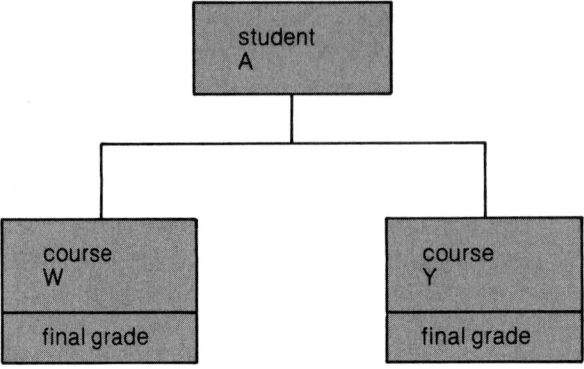

Data Relationship

Suppose we wish to describe data pertaining to a certain school. We can roughly divide the data into the following groups:

1. *Student information*—A list of all the students. A typical student record will contain (we exclude financial information on tuition fees and payments) personal details: name, identification number, address, date of birth, etc.; past performance: course numbers and final grades; present enrollment: course and section numbers.

2. *Course information*—A list of all the courses offered by the school. A typical course record will contain course title and number; prerequisite/corequisite courses (indicated by course numbers); number of sections currently offered; lecture times for each section; limits on class size (number of students per section); number of credit units (i.e., the proportional weight of the course in the calculation of a final graduation grade).

3. *Teacher information*—A list of all the teachers. A typical teacher record will contain personal details: name, address, telephone number, etc.; courses that can be taught (indicated by course numbers); courses and sections currently taught (indicated by course and section numbers).

The data items of the school are related one to another. For instance, when we examine a student's past performance, we see that the student may have taken a number of courses since he or she enrolled in the school. This is portrayed by figure A.12. The list of courses (and final grades) taken by an individual student maintains a one-to-many relationship, since many courses may relate to a single student record. This is labeled *1:N relationship,* and it leads to a hierarchical structure where one data item in a level is related to N data items in the next level. A similar structure can be devised for a family record, where several dependents relate to the head of the family; or to an assembly record, where several parts relate to the whole assembly.

Figure A.13 Teachers-courses relationship

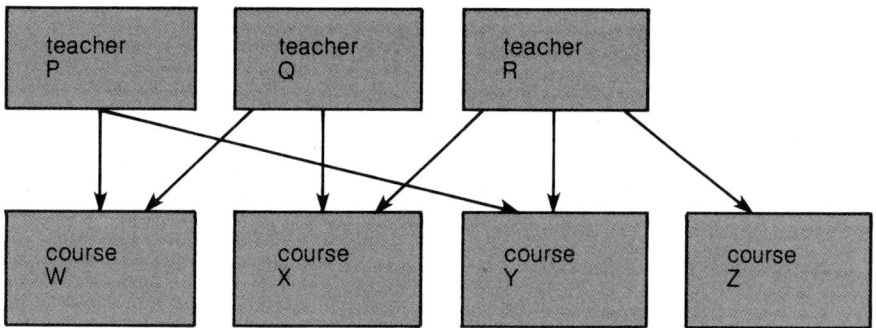

When we examine the relationships between courses and teachers' qualifications, we view a different structure: various courses can be taught by several teachers, as illustrated in figure A.13.

The arrows in figure A.13 indicate courses that can be taught by certain teachers, based on their qualifications, background, and preferences. Since each teacher has a different repertoire of courses he or she is qualified to teach, the relationship turns out to be of a many-to-many type: an *M:N relationship.* A similar structure can be devised for a production process in which different assemblies contain some identical parts.

Note that a *1:1* relationship is also possible, for instance, between a husband record and a wife record (in a nonpolygamous society). However, the one-to-one relationship is too simple; it is rarely applicable to any real case of data presentation.

The data relationships as previously described have nothing to do with the physical structure of the data files. They merely reflect the way users may view the data. Nevertheless, if a certain relationship typifies users' view of a data set, it might be a good idea to adjust the physical structure of the data to best fit the most frequent user requirements. This may result in a significant improvement in the efficiency of the DBMS. The next sections, therefore, briefly discuss some prevailing approaches to data structure (see Date [4]).

The Hierarchical Approach
The *hierarchical approach* (often called the *tree structure*) is particularly suitable to data characterized by 1:N relationships. Each data item generates a group of subordinate items, which may generate lower levels of subordinates, and so forth. Figure A.14 portrays a student record developing to a tree structure.

If we take the right side of figure A.14 (the list of courses currently taken by the student) and invert it, we get the student lists for all the courses currently held in the school. This is described in figure A.15, and it should remind you of the previous discussion on inverted files.

Figures A.14 and A.15 depict two different views of basically the same data (or part of it). Both conform to the hierarchical approach; however, the physical structure of the data does not have to comply with either arrangement unless it is proven to be

Figure A.14 A student record in a tree structure

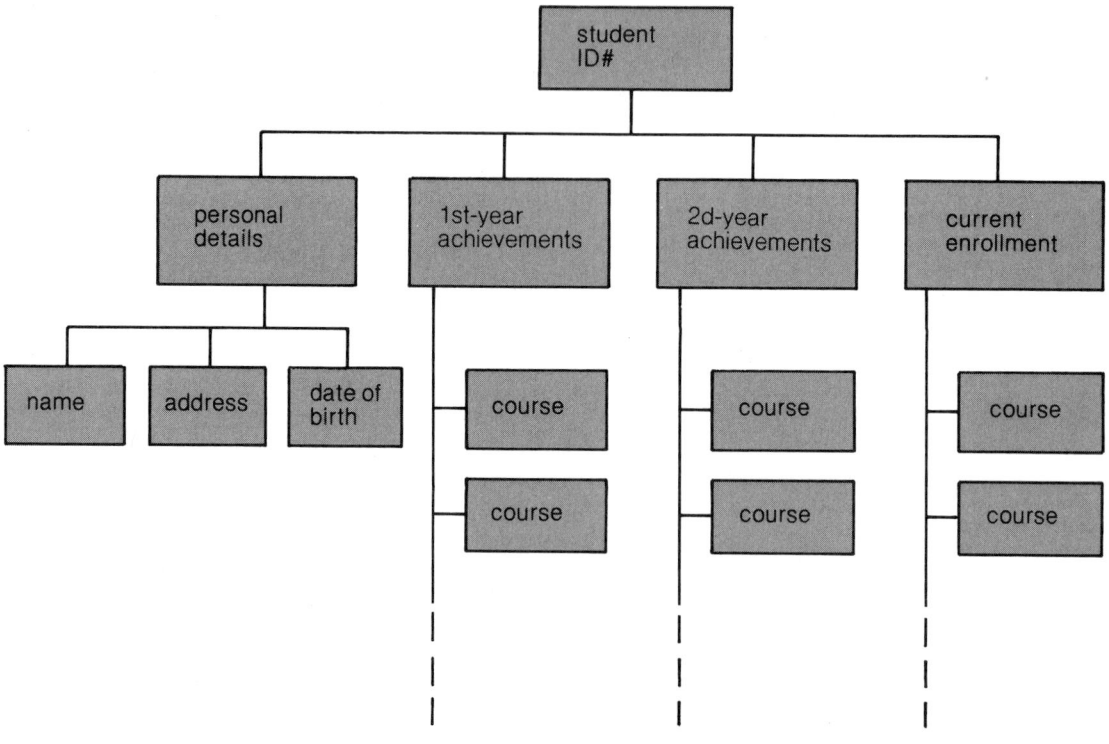

Figure A.15 A class list in a tree structure

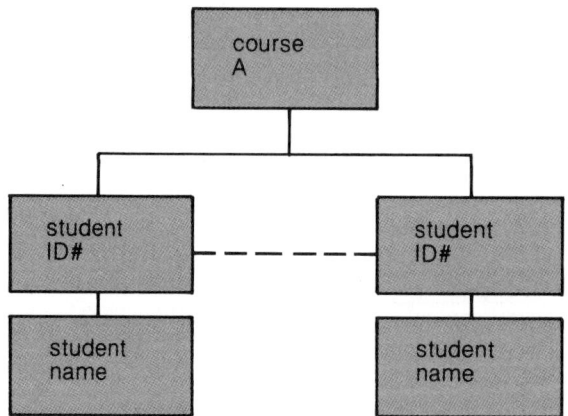

Figure A.16 Network presentation of a school data base

students   courses   teachers

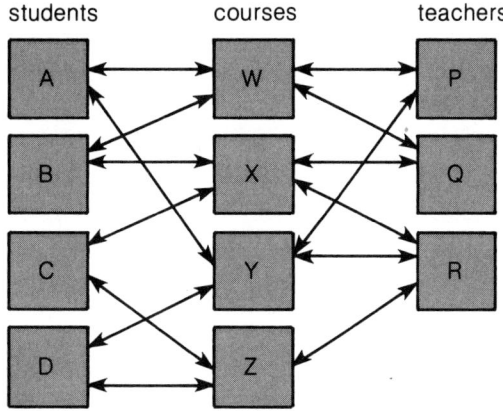

the most efficient structure. In other words, if the structure in figure A.14 typifies the most common access strategy to the data, it would be wise to tailor the physical layout of the data according to that structure. Otherwise another structure may be physically implemented. In any case, the data is not stored redundantly, hence switchovers from one logical structure to another (e.g., from fig. A.14 to fig. A.15) are possible due to pointers, tables, and supporting software rather than because of reorganization or duplication of data.

The tree structure is a relatively simple approach. It is mainly used in applications where 1:N relationships dominate—such as applications dealing with persons or families; e.g., personnel, Social Security, or student files.

The Network Approach

When M:N relationships are more apparent than 1:N, a *network approach* may better resemble the users' view of the data base. The network approach delineates the data base as a graph where nodes represent data entities and links represent relationships. Figure A.16 illustrates the network approach as applied to the school data base.

The boxes in figure A.16 represent records; the arrows represent actual relationships between records. Hence you can easily obtain the list of all courses taken by student A, or the class list of course Z, or the teaching qualifications of professor Q.

The network approach is characteristic of applications based on M:N relationships, such as allocation of machines to various job orders, production and inventory control of assemblies consisting of multiple, nonunique parts, and the like.

The Relational Approach

The *relational approach* is more basic than the preceding approaches. It views the data as a set of tables on which a variety of operations can be performed. If you select the appropriate operation, you get results similar to those that can be obtained from tree or network structures, but eventually you achieve better flexibility in data manipulation. This can be demonstrated with the school data base.

Table A.5   A Relational Approach to a School Data Base

Student Number	Student Name	Course Currently Taken
S1	A	W
S1	A	Y
S2	B	W
S2	B	X
S3	C	X
S3	C	Z
S4	D	Y
S4	D	Z

a) Student table

Teacher Name	Course Name	Status
P	W	teach
P	Y	teach
Q	W	qualified
Q	X	teach
R	X	qualified
R	Y	qualified
R	Z	teach

b) Teacher table

Table A.5 expresses the same data presented in figure A.16 but by means of two tables. Each row of table A.5a represents one course taken by a certain student; each row of table A.5b represents one course taught or one that can be taught by a certain teacher. Note that the rows in each table must be of a fixed length, hence some data is redundant.

Having these tables, we can obtain any information available by the tree or network approach. For example, list all the courses taken by student A; list all the students enrolled in course Z. In addition, we can perform some operations derived from set algebra, such as extracting data derived from various intersections of the tables. For example, list the names of all the students currently taught by teacher P; list the names of all the teachers currently teaching student B.

You can imagine that the larger the set of tables, the greater the variety of retrieval requests. This approach leads to greater flexibility in data retrieval, although there is some cost in data redundancy, and it may require more computer time to locate the data. For a simple description of this approach, see the first few pages of [4].

Object-Oriented Approach

Actually, this isn't really one approach because the term encompasses quite a number of different methods. This approach derives from the use of object-oriented programming languages, and has the same goal of allowing the user not to be concerned about details of data representation and structure. Instead of thinking in terms of records, fields, and characters, the user should be able to think in terms of the *objects* they represent (such as an automobile part or an organizational department). Objects belong to a *class*, and for each class certain *methods* are defined. The approach is primarily aimed at providing a more abstract way of dealing with the definition of data and the operations that can be performed on it. Since there is no specific theory behind this, a number of different ways of implementing it are being used, including extensions of the relational approach to incorporate these ideas.

Other Approaches

Still other approaches are employed as a means of representing data and its relationships. Semantic modeling systems, knowledge-based systems, functional systems, and others have been proposed and implemented in a search for better models for the management of data. For a brief discussion of some of these and a more extensive treatment of object-oriented technology, as well as a complete coverage of the relational approach, see [4].

DBMS Evaluation

The different approaches to data structures have led to development of a large variety of software packages (DBMS) dealing with data base organization, update, and data retrieval. These are offered by computer manufacturers as well as by software vendors who provide, in some instances, products that span a number of different hardware systems. For a summary table of commercially available products, see [1].

Structured Query Language

As is evidenced by the list of available products listed in [1], the most prevalent approach in current use is the relational approach. There are a number of reasons for this, not the least of which is the simplicity of its underlying model, which views all data as existing in tables. This is a very familiar notion for the user to accept, and it leads to easier implementation in a DBMS.

Contributing to the popularity of the approach and to the proliferation of *relational DBMS,* is the *structured query language* (SQL). Developed originally for use with IBM's relational data base software, it has become a standard language for defining data bases, entering and maintaining the data in the data base, and making inquiries against that data. The language was designed to be easy to use by those without knowledge of programming techniques. It deals with the conceptual view of the data as tables, so that the user can define what the *columns* of the table are to be, enter data to make up the *rows* of the table, delete or change rows, and extract data from a table or group of tables. Thus SQL has the desired characteristics of a fourth-generation language (4GL) in providing a simple user language for manipulating a data base. SQL can also be embedded in other *host languages* for more extensive and complex processing of the data base.

Since SQL has become a standard, most relational DBMS software utilizes it, again as evidenced by the product list [1]. This provides a basis for compatibility among products of different vendors, providing much of the impetus for the growth of the *client-server network* architectures that have become commonplace (see ch. 11).

Choice of Approach

The wide popularity and availability of relational DBMS software does not mean that other possibilities should be dismissed. The primary question is the adequacy of the DBMS for the applications of the organization. In other words, there is not a priority preference for a tree, a network, or a relational structure. A structure that may best fit a certain class of applications may be inefficient for another class. The characteristics of the majority of applications for a given organization should guide us in selecting the most appropriate approach. An organization having data that involves mostly personal records and family relationships may prefer the tree structure; a production company may prefer the network structure; and a design firm might prefer an object-oriented DBMS.

After all, each principal structure can be customized to comply with a different view of the data base. A network can be simplified to present tree structures because a tree is nothing but a simple network. A tree structure can be augmented to be network structure by adding secondary indexes and logical pointers to the tree segments. A relational structure can handle either network or hierarchical views. The majority of applicational requirements should dictate selection of the principal approach; applications of a different nature can always be accommodated by adjusting the schema.

Other Criteria

There are many more evaluation criteria related to the technical features of the DBMS. Some are listed here:

1. Data directory or catalog—Does the DBMS provide the user with a convenient directory (and dictionary) of the data items?

2. Redefinition—How flexible is the DBMS with regard to redefinition of files or tables and changes in file organization techniques (recall the data and program independence principles)?

3. Validation—Does the DBMS verify data validity and reject data that does not conform to initial specifications?

4. Security—Does the DBMS provide means to restrict the access to certain data (see discussion on security in ch. 14)? If so, what is the extent of the restriction? Does it encompass individual fields within records, complete records, or whole files? (The more flexible, the better.)

5. Ease of installation

6. Efforts invested in converting existing files to the new data base

7. Training—How much training will be needed for programmers?

8. Concurrent access—Is it possible for several programs to simultaneously access the same files? If so, does the DBMS prevent erroneous updates that might occur when several programs wish to modify the same record at the same time?

9. Update handling—Does the DBMS automatically modify data relationships whenever a certain data item is added, changed, or deleted?

10. Transaction processing—Does the DBMS keep track of online transactions for control purposes (see discussion in ch. 14)?

11. Retrieval—How flexible is the DBMS when it has to retrieve data, particularly when the search strategy does not conform to the initial structure of the data?

12. Programming languages—Which programming languages can be hosted by the DBMS?

13. Maintenance—What aids are available for the data base specialist to facilitate the DBMS maintenance?

14. Compatibility—Is the DBMS compatible with other computer models and other software?

15. Expansibility—Will the DBMS be efficient if it has to cope with larger volumes of data?

16. Performance—How efficient is the DBMS (response time, memory occupancy, disk space occupancy)? How is efficiency affected by the number of users and/or programs requesting the DBMS services at the same time?

Most of these questions call for an expert. However, it is very important for the manager and the user to understand the possible implications of this criteria for the applications they intend to install.

Telecommunications

The two principal building blocks that facilitate development and use of MIS are *DBMS* and *telecommunications* (teleprocessing). The former makes data integration possible; the latter brings information closer to the end users, who constitute nodes in a tele-communication network.

The notion of telecommunications implies that some geographical distance exists between the computer site and the users' locations and that data is electronically trans-mitted between them. Remote applications may be executed between two floors in the same building, between two offices in the same city, between two offices on the same continent, or between two places on opposite sides of the globe. A clearer way to define telecommunications is by examining the technical means associated with that technology.

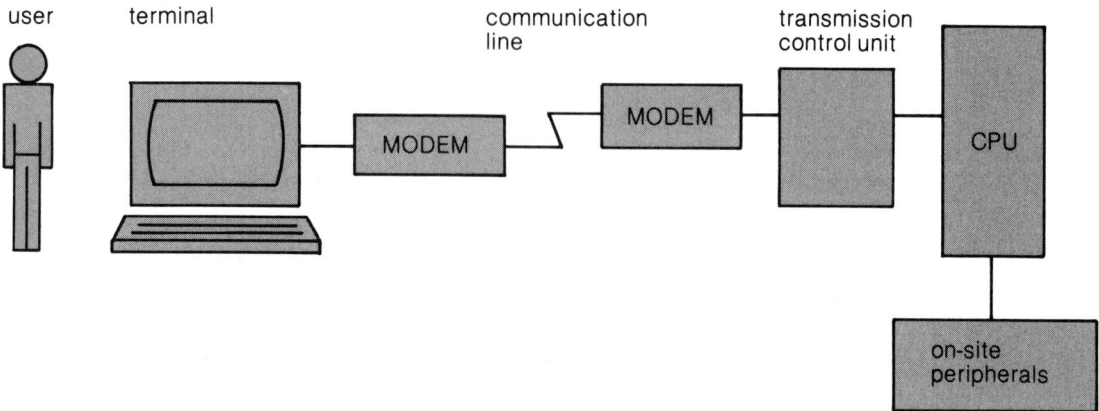

A network may consist of a single computer and one or more remote terminals, or it may consist of several computers and satellite terminals. The first type is labeled *terminal network;* the second type, *computer network.* We will now discuss these types of networks. Bear in mind that we are mainly interested in their implications for users and management rather than their technical characteristics.

Terminal Networks

A terminal network for telecommunications is usually composed of a single central computer and a number (which may be small or large) of terminals. Each terminal may be individually connected to the central computer, or several terminals may be clustered and connected to the computer via an intermediate device. The intermediate device may be a (small) computer, but it is not independent and is normally not so powerful as the principal computer.

We will first describe a very simple network configuration and then elaborate on possible expansions and uses.

The Basic Components of a Terminal Network
Suppose you and your friend are located in two remote places and wish to converse. How would you do it without arranging a face-to-face meeting? Simply by using telephones.

Similarly, suppose a computer is placed somewhere and a user is located somewhere else. How could they converse without physically moving one of them to the other's location? Simply via a telephone line augmented with some special gadgets. Figure A.17 illustrates the most simple configuration of a terminal network.

A user stands at the left side of figure A.17, next to a terminal or a microcomputer that serves as a terminal. The terminal is a piece of data processing equipment; therefore it handles data in a way that is not compatible with the range of electronic frequencies used on a telephone line. The transformation of electronic frequencies from data processing mode to telephone mode and vice versa is handled by a special device called a *modem*—made from the words "modulation" and "demodulation."

A regular telephone line connects the modem to the computer site, where another modem translates the telephone frequencies back to computer electrical pulses (and vice versa, depending on the direction of the transmission). The modem at the computer site is attached to a transmission control unit, which is a special peripheral device responsible for remote communications. (In certain cases the modem can be directly attached to the central processing unit—CPU—however, this is not very common.)

The control unit, controlled by the CPU, is a part of the normal configuration of a computer, which must also employ direct access devices. The computer software must be capable of treating remote processing in addition to local batch operations.

This description delineates a very simple network. In reality, terminal networks may be more complex and sophisticated. This depends, of course, on the traits of the various components of the network. We will now outline some common uses of terminal networks.

Interactive Processing

Unlike batch processing, *interactive processing* allows the user to conduct a dialogue with the computer while the program is running in memory. For this purpose, an interactive terminal must consist of a keyboard and an output means—a screen (the common terms are VDU, visual display unit; VDT, cathode ray *visual display terminal;* or CRT, *cathode ray tube*).

The central computer, however, employs software specially devised for interactive processing. In particular, this software handles *time-sharing* operations. The concept of time-sharing is essential to interactive processing. Since several interactive users may subscribe to the same computer at the same time, and since each user may wish to activate a different program, it is almost impossible to let each program stay in memory for the entire elapsed time the user is operating a terminal. Such an arrangement would require a huge volume of internal memory, whose utilization would be very low because a computer-person dialogue normally proceeds at a very slow pace. Instead, several programs share the same slice of memory by taking advantage of the fact that users react slowly to messages displayed on the terminals. While users are thinking and keying in, programs are interchanged between the internal memory and direct access devices.

Most often, users do not notice that a time-sharing mechanism maneuvers their programs while they are connected. However, excessive work loads might overwhelm the capacity of a computer, which, in return, reacts by exhibiting a longer response time. If this turns into a chronic ailment, then some corrective measures should be taken, such as rescheduling certain batch jobs, restricting the use of terminals by certain users during certain hours of the day, and upgrading or replacing equipment.

The interactive mode is commonly used in a large variety of applications. For programming activities, interactive terminals are very useful to key in source programs and then to debug and change them if necessary.

For jobs under execution, the interactive mode can be used for almost any activity along the data processing cycle (see fig. A.1):

Input data can be directly keyed in a computer, which verifies data validity on the spot.

Files can be instantaneously updated when a relevant transaction occurs.

Programs can be accessed during execution—in order to modify parameters, provide new data, redirect the flow of a program through various routines, check for intermediate results, etc.

Output can be displayed on terminals in order to trigger an immediate reaction.

Queries can be placed and responded to on the spot.

Customers can receive receipts or documents immediately after completing a transaction.

Interactive processing is frequently associated with the concept of *real-time* processing. This association is only partly justified, depending on how "real time" is defined. A narrow definition of real time is that files are updated and output is instantly available after a relevant transaction has occurred. Under this definition, interactive equipment is essential.

However, real time can be defined in a broader sense: files are updated and output is available before the user must make a pertinent decision. Under that definition, the paramount factor is the elapsed time of the decision-making process: how long the user can afford to wait from the time a relevant event has occurred until the time he or she is supposed to react. If the waiting time is very short, then interactive mode is imperative; otherwise it is not vital.

Finally, for managerial information systems such as DSS (decision support system; see chs. 5 and 6) the interactive mode is essential. Systems of this kind do not replace human decision making but, rather, support it. They are based on continuous interaction between the user and the pertinent programs, where the user feeds the program some data, observes the results, modifies some parameters, reacts to the new results, and so on. The user must be provided with a handy terminal and direct access capacity to his or her model base and data base.

Some Concluding Remarks

The network illustrated in figure A.17 is a simplified version of the most elementary kind of structure. In reality, most terminal networks are much more complex. They consist of many communication lines connected to a large variety of terminals. Very often terminals are clustered together and attached to a central computer via concentrators, minicomputers, and other means. This allows installation of, for instance, several visual display terminals together with printing facilities (e.g., a hard-copy terminal or a line printer), so the user may opt to direct some outputs to print while most of the dialogue is handled on the screens. In many cases a terminal network combines remote batch and interactive facilities. In fact, there is almost no limit to the number of variations that can be devised through a network.

Figure A.18 Sample topologies of computer networks

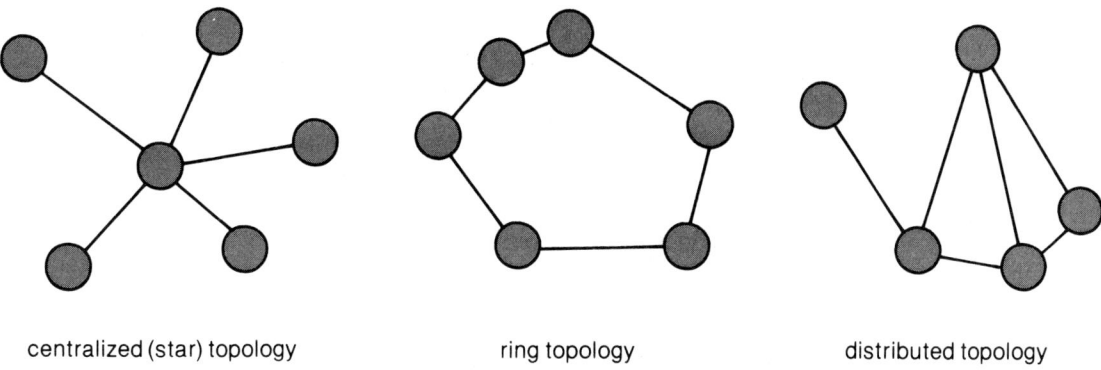

centralized (star) topology   ring topology   distributed topology

The technicalities related to terminal networks are numerous, covering topics such as transmission codes, transmission modes, equipment specifications, line discipline, and software requirements. (See [10] for technical details.)

We now turn our attention to a more comprehensive type of network that involves computers and terminals together.

Computer Networks

Unlike *terminal networks,* in which one computer provides the processing for a number of terminals, a *computer network* is composed of multiple computers. Such networks may take a wide variety of forms in terms of the relationships of these computers. It is also possible for any one of the computers in the computer network to have its own terminal network. Each computer in the network is considered a network *node.* If the computer has terminals, it is a *host* to those terminals.

There is no limit to the geographical spread of a computer network; it may be campuswide, citywide, nationwide, or global. Communication may be by either physical lines or radio transmission. The *topology* of a network can be centralized (star), a ring, or any combination of the possible connections (*links*) between computers. Some examples of these topologies are illustrated in figure A.18. Note that the star topology is more vulnerable to line failure because alternative routes between the star center and another computer node do not exist.

Networks may even tie together computers from different manufacturers. When the network involves different computer hardware and operating systems, then the network connection is usually made through an intermediate device (actually itself a small special purpose computer). Otherwise, connection to the network is much like connecting to a peripheral I/O device. On any particular network, all the computers must exchange data in a standard way and this is called the *network protocol.*

The technical details behind all of this are quite extensive. For more information see [10] or [12]. For more of a management perspective, see [7] and [8].

Computer Network Uses

There are a number of reasons for an organization to network some or all of its computers, or to connect to the computers of other organizations. The Internet (see ch. 15) is one example of an existing public network connecting a large number of independent organizations. It provides the ability to easily exchange data and programs with other organizations on the network, and a terminal user at one location can communicate with a terminal user at another location by electronic mail.

It is also possible that a user at one computer might run a program at another computer. For example, a business organization might require infrequent use of a certain mathematical programming package. Rather than acquire the software (and perhaps different hardware) they can transmit their data to a location that has the package and run the program there. The results would be transmitted back to them (and the business would be charged, of course). There are a large number of such networks that an organization might join, depending on its common interests with other organizations already on the network.

Within an organization, networks are established so that different computers within the organization may communicate. Some of the reasons would be exactly like those discussed above: exchange of data, programs, hardware and software capabilities. Within a computer network, users potentially have immediate access to hardware, software, and data anywhere within the network.

Wide Area vs. Local Area Networks

Both the terminal network described earlier, and public networks like Internet are *wide area networks* (WAN). In a wide area network the network connections leave the organization's own property and must use the facilities of a local or long-distance telephone company, or another communications carrier. *Local area networks* (LAN), on the other hand, are those in which the connections cover a short distance: within a building, a campus, or a compound. In fact, a terminal network can exist within such a local area. In this case, the *modems* are not required; the terminals are directly connected to the computer's transmission control unit. However, the term LAN is usually reserved to apply to local computer networks.

A consideration in WAN is whether the network will be continuously in place, using *leased line* connections, or established only on demand, using switched (dial up) lines. *Dial up lines* are usually less expensive, but they require fifteen to thirty seconds setup time for dialing to establish the connection between the initiator and the destination of the call. The preferred method will depend on the amount of data to be transferred and the frequency with which it will occur.

Since the LAN connections do not leave the property, it is not necessary to use telephone lines or other communications services. The computers could be connected in these ways, but it would either be more expensive, slower, or both. The LAN can be connected by the organization's own coaxial or fiber optics cable. Either permits very high transmission rates, and the connections are always in place.

Local Area Networks

For the last decade or more, we have faced a growing trend to fill workplaces with more and more computers and computer-based machines. These include personal computers and workstations, CAD/CAM systems, computer controlled manufacturing tools, printers, and facsimile machines. Connecting these devices into a common network makes possible the integration of data processing and office operations (see ch. 6), information systems and manufacturing systems (see ch. 15), electronic mail, and online data entry and retrieval using a central data base. Many observations indicate that about 80 percent of the communications in a typical organization take place within local environments, i.e., within the same office building, or among adjacent or nearby buildings.

A great impetus to the development of LAN technology came from the desire to connect a number of personal computers so they could share an expensive resource, such as a printer or a large disk storage unit. Instead of each computer having its own, lightly used printer, one computer in the network is equipped with a printer and each station on the network sends data to be printed to that computer. The computer with the printer becomes the network's *print server*. When one computer is equipped to act as a *file server*, it maintains files, or a data base, that the other stations on the network can share. This is more economical in terms of disk storage expense; but more significantly, it allows centralized control over the data and an assured consistency that would not be obtained if each computer maintained its own copy. Such a network can logically be substituted for the terminal network discussed earlier.

One result of the widespread use of LANs in these *server networks* has been the development of a large amount of software to support computer use in such an environment. Thus, the local area network of personal computers or workstations has become a common component of information systems in organizations of all sizes.

Criteria for Making Network Choices

Decisions as to whether to network or not, and decisions about the type of network to choose (terminals, computers, or both; LAN or WAN), depend on the organization and its IS needs. If an organization is to establish a network, it must examine a number of characteristics, such as the following:

1. *Network reliability, availability,* and *maintainability*—What is the expected accuracy of transmission and the probability of failure? What is required to restore service if a failure occurs? What fallback alternatives are there (i.e., backup connections provided by the topology, redundant data or computing resources if a node is not reachable)?

2. *Compatibility*—Can equipment of different manufacturers be accommodated? Can software from different vendors be used? Is the network able to communicate with other networks?

3. *Flexibility* and *extendibility*—How easily can computers or terminals be added to or removed from the network? How easily can communication lines or services be added, deleted, or changed?

4. *Simplicity*—Is the network simple to configure and easy to use? Are all the network technicalities transparent to the end user?

5. *Capacity*—How large a volume of transmitted data can be accommodated on each link? How much total volume can the network handle simultaneously?

6. *Response time*—Can each transmission from a computer to a terminal or to another computer be completed without causing an unacceptable delay for the receiving user?

7. *Security*—What means are provided to secure privileged data while it is transmitted? Can unauthorized users be denied access to the network, to individual nodes, to databases, or to files?

8. *Cost*—As a factor, cost speaks for itself. Cost considerations must include the computers, terminals, communication lines and interfaces, and the software. It should also take into account the effects of rapidly changing technology in all of the network components. Not the least consideration is that of the personnel required to support the network infrastructure.

Practical Conclusions for Information System Design and Use

The following is a list of practical conclusions for information system design and use.

1. Most business systems that process monetary data must have some written source documents at the starting point of a data processing cycle. Information systems that are devised for instantaneous control (e.g., traffic control, manufacturing process control), or that record the transaction as it occurs (e.g., automated teller machines, point of sale terminals), are able to exist with input that is not supported by written source documents. Nevertheless, paperless systems are unrealistic for many facets of business activity, and must be carefully considered by system designers.

2. Computerized systems provide two types of output: human understandable for human decision making, and computer-readable for further computerized processing. Once data has been converted to computer-readable form, the system designer must be very reluctant to delete it from the system. Reentering the data and re-verifying it would be time consuming and costly, so if the designer is not sure about further use of the data, it should be stored until it is certain that it is no longer needed.

3. Whenever possible, data input should be done under computer control so that validation and input can take place simultaneously.

4. When all or most of the data is known ahead of time, as with utility bills or checks, keying of that data can by avoided by preprinting or encoding the data in magnetic ink, OCR characters, or a bar code.

5. Both impact printers and laser printers are available in small, inexpensive versions or in large, high speed models. Printers can be chosen depending on the amount of printing to be done and the quality of printed output required.

6. Output that requires quick response or has an ad hoc nature and doesn't require hard copy can be directed to visual display terminals.

7. Memory size can be a limiting factor for programs in small computers. Although it is not usually a limiting factor with large computers, large programs still have a cost. They are more difficult to design, debug, and maintain, and there is additional overhead in their execution.

8. When selecting a computer, operating systems and capatible software may be more important factors than hardware. Both aspects should be thoroughly examined before making any acquisition decision.

9. Sequential files are frequently less efficient than direct access or indexed files. They are normally used only for small files or for backup purposes.

10. Any information system based on online interaction with a file requires that the file be organized in a way other than sequential.

11. When a file is large relative to the number of update transactions or queries directed to that file, a sequential organization of the file would be less efficient than any technique that provides direct accessing to the records.

12. In theory, the physical structure of a data base and the user view of the data (the logical view) do not have to be congruent. In practice, some similarity between those two might significantly improve the efficiency of computerized applications using the data base. Furthermore, if the user view and the physical structure are extremely disparate, some user requirements might be infeasible to fulfill. Therefore, it is imperative that users clearly present their requirements to the data base administrator (DBA).

13. A hierarchical (tree) structure of a data base usually conforms to applications related to individuals—e.g., personnel data, student data, insurance data, etc. A network structure data base usually suits applications where numerous resources and facilities take part in a number of activities—e.g., production control, distribution systems, allocation problems. In spite of these prejudices, each structure can be customized to look like the other one at the expense of possible reduction in efficiency.

14. A relational structure of a data base is ''the structure for all seasons''; namely, it can simulate hierarchical and network structures and provide more flexibility than any of those. Because of this and because of the simplicity of the table approach, it has become the most widely used structure.

15. The primary concern of a DBMS user is the DBMS adequacy to the specific applications of the organization. Beyond that there are many technical aspects of efficiency, reliability, data security, data verification, and the like that should be examined, preferably by an expert.

16. A DBMS is not a ''deus ex machina'' that resolves any informational problem an organization might have. It facilitates implementation of an information system by easing access to and integration of data. It cannot make up for poor management.

17. Networks are vulnerable to intrusion. Appropriate measures of prevention and detection must be devised in order to counter such attempts.

18. Interactive facilities improve the effectiveness of DSS.

19. An organization that has deployed computers in various places can facilitate data integration and IS development and use by connecting the scattered computers via a computer network (LAN or WAN).

20. An interorganizational computer network may provide the following benefits: access to remote data bases, access to external software, access to faster hardware, balancing computer workloads, backup arrangements, and rapid transfer of data.

21. Local area networks may be used simply to integrate computers that are needed for a variety of applications, or to apply a number of small computers to an information system, rather than using one large computer.

Summary

The principal theme of this appendix is information processing technology. The purpose of this coverage is to illustrate to the reader the ways in which the concepts and ideas presented in the other chapters can be implemented. The available tools—hardware and software—offer increasing flexibility to management in approaching the development and enhancement of information processing systems of any size for any type of organization. We start with a general review of information processing, emphasizing the ways in which the technology can be adapted to any particular situation. Later we focus on two particularly important aspects of the technology that provide much of the flexibility that is stressed: data base management systems and networks.

The appendix starts with a review of information processing technology, following the data processing cycle from input to output through processing and auxiliary storage.

Input devices and the input process are described. Some data is captured at the time of transaction, such as through a POS terminal. Some data must be taken from source documents and converted to machine readable form by keying it in through a keyboard. Some data may already be in machine-readable form, being preprinted in MICR, OCR characters, or a bar code.

If data is entered under computer control, either through a terminal or through a PC, validation can take place at that time; otherwise, it may have to be done as a separate operation.

Input media and devices are selected for the application they will serve. Selection criteria may include reliability, timeliness, volume of data, scatter of input sources, and cost.

The processing phase in the data processing cycle is performed by the CPU, which communicates with the peripheral devices which provide input, output, and auxiliary storage. CPUs are available in sizes that range from small personal computers to large mainframe systems. Choices are made depending on the speed or computing power the application requires, the amount of memory and auxiliary storage it needs, the number and variety of I/O devices it can support, and the number of users or programs that it must accommodate simultaneously. Computing power is frequently measured in MIPS or some similar *benchmark* statistic.

Great emphasis is put on the software and its interaction with the hardware, since the choice of one affects the choice of the other. Points to be considered include: the operating system to be used; utility programs provided; the repertoire of programming languages available; and what various vendors may offer in the way of application generators, application packages, DBMS, and telecommunications software.

The output phase of the data processing cycle is classified as having two categories: human-understandable output and machine-readable output. Human-understandable output includes a variety of visual display devices as well as a wide range of printers. The machine-readable forms include OCR and removable magnetic media, especially diskettes. Output devices are chosen based on their speed, the volume of output to be handled, the need for user response or the need for hard copy, and the possibility of the output being returned as an input document.

Output that is retained for further processing by the computer resides in auxiliary storage. Storage media enable various file organization techniques. The discussion defines some basic file organization terms: character, field (data item), record, file (data set), data base, key field (identifier), master file, transaction file, retrieval, and update. It explains how update and retrieval are carried out on sequential files.

The most common direct access device is the magnetic disk. It enables direct accessing by means of a three-dimensional address associated with each location on the disk. The common techniques for organizing files on a direct access device are indexed files, direct (random) files, inverted files, and list-structured files. Each of those techniques may be advantageous for a different kind of application. The application programmer must be aware of the specific technique chosen in order to tailor the programs to comply with the file organization technique. This is not true when the program communicates with a DBMS.

A DBMS is the realization of the abstract concept of a data base, namely, the consolidation of data gathered by discrete applications. A DBMS is implemented by tables, pointers, and programs that interface between user applications and the centralized data base.

A DBMS should adhere to the following principles: data independence (application programs should not be affected by physical data structure); program independence (various programming languages can communicate with the DBMS); and system independence (the DBMS should be compatible with various computer models). Commercially available DBMS packages do not always comply with all the principles, but usually with most of them.

A DBMS interfaces between the application programs and the physical data base by means of various tables, particularly the schema and the subschema. The schema is the overall description of the data base as it is physically stored on the direct access devices. A subschema describes portions of the data base that pertain to a certain application. Several programs communicate with the same schema through different subschemas.

A subschema represents the relationships the user perceives with regard to various data entities. The common relationships are: 1:N (one data entity is associated with several subordinate entities, each of which may also have several subordinate, and so on); M:N (several data entities are associated with several others). These conceptual relationships underlie various approaches to DBMS structuring. The primary ones are hierarchical, network, and relational approaches.

The hierarchical (tree) structure presents a data record by means of a tree. Data can be approached through the various branches of the tree in a top-down fashion. However, the logical structure (i.e., the user view) does not have to conform to the physical structure of the data. Alternative structures are obtainable if secondary indexes and appropriate pointers are inserted into the data base. The tree structure has been commonly used for personnel files.

The network structure presents the data base as a network where data items are the network nodes and relationships are the network links. This approach has been used where data items have multiple relationships, such as in a resource allocation problem in a production shop.

The relational approach presents the data base as a group of tables that may be related to each other through common attributes. Data manipulation is achieved through various operations that can be performed on the tables. Most of the operations derive from set algebra. The relational approach incorporates the major traits of the tree and network approaches, at the expense of data redundancy and somewhat lower efficiency.

Many DBMS are commercially available. The primary criterion by which to evaluate them is adequacy to the user's applications. Many technical facets should also be examined, such as data security, update handling, retrieval efficiency, ease of maintenance, and performance.

Telecommunications may involve a terminal network, a computer network, or both. The network may be either a WAN or a LAN, or a combination.

A terminal network consists of a central computer and satellite terminals connected to the computer via cables or by telephone lines and modems. Each terminal can be individually connected to the computer, or several terminals can be clustered at the end of a line. Terminals are generally used for interactive processing, i.e., in situations where a "conversation" is carried on between the user and the computer. Usually a keyboard is used for input, and a display device for output. Many types of applications take advantage of this arrangement, e.g., data input, online file inquiry and update, or heuristic decision making.

Computer networks connect several computers, each of which might be of a different type and might even belong to a different owner. If a computer network exists within a particular building or on private property (LAN), the connections may be made by a cable and are usually capable of a very high data transfer rate. A network which leaves the property (WAN) must use the services of a communications services company. If the network connections are by telephone lines, modems are required.

A local area network is often used as a means of connecting a number of personal computers or workstations in order that they can share hardware, software, or data. A wide area computer network can be useful to an organization that has deployed several computers in different places, since it can integrate data gathered at the various computer sites. Several different organizations can connect to a computer network in order to take advantage of resources possessed by other members of the network. Such resources may include unique data bases or exclusive software. A network member might wish to use another computer for backup purposes, to divert a work load at peak hours, or just to save time in data transfer or complex computations. A major use of computer networks is, of course, for electronic mail and access to public data bases.

Key Concepts

application generator
application package
auxiliary storage
bar code
batch processing
benchmarks
cathode ray tube (CRT)
central processing unit (CPU)
channel
character
CODASYL
data: capture, conversion, currency, scatter, validation, volume
data base
data base administrator (DBA)
data base management system (DBMS)
data independence
data processing (DP)
data processing cycle
data relationship: 1:1, 1:N, M:N
direct access storage device (DASD)
disk
diskette
display
dot-matrix printer
electronic funds transfer (EFT)
field
file: direct, historical, indexed, inverted, list-structured, master, random, sequential, transaction
fourth-generation language (4GL)
fourth-generation software
hardware independence
hierarchical approach
ink jet printer
input
input device
input/output bus
interactive processing
key field (identifier)
laser printer
local area network (LAN)
magnetic disks
magnetic ink character recognition (MICR)
magnetic storage
memory

millions of instructions per second (MIPS)
modem
network: computer, terminal
network approach
object-oriented approach
offline
online
operating system
optical character recognition (OCR)
output
output device
peripheral device
personal computer (PC)
point of sale (POS)
processing
program independence
programming languages: assembler, higher level, machine
real time processing
record
reduced instruction set computers (RISC)
relational approach
reliability
response time
retrieval
schema
sequential files
source document
storing
structured query language (SQL)
subschema
system independence
telecommunications
teleprocessing
terminal
timeliness
topology
transaction: physical, recorded
tree structure
UPC code
update
utility programs
visual display terminal (VDT)
wide area network (WAN)
workstations

References

1. "A DBMS For Every User." *Datamation* 38, no. 16 (August 1, 1992): 84–89.
2. Awad, E. M., and M. H. Gotterer. *Database Management.* Danvers, MA: Boyd & Fraser, 1992.
3. Blissmer, R. H. *Introducing Computers: Concepts, Systems, and Applications.* New York: John Wiley & Sons, 1991.
4. Date, C. J. *An Introduction to Database Systems Volume I,* 5th ed. Reading, MA: Addison-Wesley, 1990.
5. Folk, M. J. and B. Zoellick. *File Structures.* 2d ed. Reading, MA: Addison-Wesley, 1992.
6. McKeown, P. G. *Living With Computers.* 3d ed. San Diego: Harcourt Brace Jovanovich, 1991.
7. Martin, J. and K. K. Chapman. *Local Area Networks: Architectures and Implementations.* Englewood Cliffs, NJ: Prentice-Hall, 1989.
8. Martin, J. *Telecommunications and the Computer.* 3d ed. Englewood Cliffs, NJ: Prentice-Hall, 1990.
9. Parker, C. S. *Understanding Computers and Data Processing: Today and Tomorrow.* 3d ed. Chicago: Dryden Press, 1990.
10. Stallings, W. *Business Data Communications.* New York: Macmillan, 1990.
11. Stamper, D. and W. Price. *Database Design & Management: An Applied Approach.* New York: Mitchell McGraw-Hill, 1990.
12. Tanenbaum, A. S. *Computer Networks.* 2d ed. Englewood Cliffs, NJ: Prentice-Hall, 1989.

Questions

1. Describe the different methods of data conversion and input.
2. What hardware considerations should be examined before buying a computer?
3. What is the difference between a programming language, an operating system, and an application package?
4. There are two types of output—that which is human understandable and that which is computer-readable. Explain the distinction and give examples of each.
5. What is meant by "auxiliary storage"?
6. What are some differences between personal computers and mainframe computers?
7. For each of the following, what would be the key field (identifier)?
   a. personnel record
   b. library catalog
   c. insurance system
   d. bank customer file
   e. airline reservation system
8. Compare a sequential file to a direct access file.
9. Explain what is meant by a DBMS.
10. What criteria should be evaluated in comparing DBMSs?
11. What purpose does a modem serve?
12. What is the difference between batch processing and interactive processing?

13. What are some objectives of a network?
14. What are the major differences between a WAN and a LAN?
15. What are some considerations in acquiring or designing a network?

Problems

1. Create a table comparing the type of input medium used by an automated teller machine conducting a transaction, by a bank teller waiting on a customer, and by a bank manager needing decision support.
2. An insurance company is setting up an information system. What files might make up their data base? Select one such file and describe the records it might include and the possible fields within these records.
3. The following is a university student file in nonsequential order. Place the file in sequential order by identification number and create an inverted file by student name, major, minor, and grade point average where grades are grouped (e.g., 3.51–4.00, 3.01–3.50, 2.51–3.00).

Student	I.D. #	Major	Minor	Grade Point
James Smith	068325	Chemistry	Biology	3.82
Donna Lisper	123468	Physics	Mathematics	3.68
Janet London	356411	Chemistry	Mathematics	3.00
David Irwin	411368	Mathematics	Statistics	3.20
Linda Ellind	412361	Physics	Mathematics	3.11
Lyle Waite	036218	Mathematics	Physics	3.40
Ron Dovinger	216455	Chemistry	Biology	2.89
Allen Lipid	313362	Physics	Statistics	2.94
Anna Resoner	161839	Mathematics	Physics	3.59
Maryann Roe	568344	Statistics	Mathematics	2.46

4. Select a DBMS approach and sketch a structure for a data base application where a company has headquarters and many branches. The headquarters and branches are each composed of divisions, and the divisions are composed of departments. Many of these divisions are involved in sales, manufacture, and research and development of their individual product(s). The headquarters takes care of public relations and overall marketing.

Appendix B   United Movers Limited: A Case Study

United Movers Ltd. (UML) is a Canadian company that provides moving services to families who move from one location to another. UML is a mover only; it does not provide storage facilities and its services are limited to the province of Alberta.

Alberta is one of the largest Canadian provinces. Among the provinces only Quebec, Ontario, and British Columbia surpass it in area. Alberta occupies 255,285 sq. miles and its population in 1979 was about 1,700,000 people. Edmonton, the capital city, and Calgary are Alberta's largest cities. Within its borders, Alberta has the northernmost permanent agricultural settlement in Canada. Except for a tiny northeast corner that is part of the Rocky Canadian Shield, almost all the province is prairie. In recent years oil, natural gas, and coal—half of Canada's minable reserves—have added tremendously to its wealth. (Calgary is the headquarters for some five hundred firms connected with the oil industry.) Alberta is well served by highways. Some 3,700 miles are paved and there are, in addition, 42,000 miles of all-weather gravel roads and 4,000 additional miles of secondary roads. Calgary hosted the Winter Olympics in 1988.

UML was formed out of a merger of four independent local firms in 1973. After the formation, UML kept its independent character and since then, it operates in four separate branches located in Calgary, Edmonton, Lethbridge, and Red Deer (exhibits B.1 and B.2).

Due to the independent operating character of UML, the four branches do not have truck maintenance facilities. Each branch has its own gas supplies. UML also has a contract with a local gas company for UML's truck fuel needs during assignments. Maintenance and repair services are provided by local service stations and so far UML is pleased and its management intends to continue the maintenance of the trucks under the same policy.

The merger of four companies was accomplished in order to gain the following advantages:

1. *Efficient usage of trucks*—A truck that has been assigned to travel from point A to point B might be assigned on the next day to a route from B to A or nearby.
2. *Efficient utilization of personnel*—A loading crew does not have to join the truck for long-range routes and the unloading would be done by a local crew.

UML owns forty-nine trucks of various sizes, with the following breakdown of branches: the branch in Calgary operates fourteen trucks; the branch in Edmonton, fifteen trucks; the branch in Lethbridge, ten trucks; the branch in Red Deer, ten trucks.

ALBERTA

Peace River

Valleyview

Grande-Prairie

Whitecourt

EDMONTON

Hinton

Red Deer

Banff

CALGARY

Brooks

Medicine Hat

Lethbridge

Scale:

| 0 | 50 | 100 | 200 | miles |
| 0 | 80 | 160 | 320 | kilometers |

Figure B.2   Alberta distance chart

	Banff	Brooks	Calgary	Edmonton	Grande-Prairie	Hinton	Lethbridge	Medicine Hat	Peace River	Red Deer	Valleyview	Whitecourt
Banff	—	313 / 194	130 / 81	422 / 262	831 / 516	361 / 224	345 / 214	421 / 262	858 / 533	270 / 168	720 / 447	550 / 342
Brooks	313 / 194	—	186 / 116	424 / 263	884 / 549	670 / 416	161 / 100	112 / 70	911 / 566	302 / 188	773 / 480	603 / 375
Calgary	130 / 81	186 / 116	—	297 / 185	748 / 465	487 / 303	217 / 135	294 / 183	775 / 482	145 / 90	637 / 396	467 / 290
Edmonton	422 / 262	424 / 263	297 / 185	—	460 / 286	287 / 178	514 / 319	532 / 331	487 / 303	150 / 93	349 / 217	179 / 111
Grande-Prairie	831 / 516	884 / 549	748 / 465	460 / 286	—	469 / 291	965 / 600	992 / 616	200 / 124	600 / 373	111 / 69	281 / 17
Hinton	361 / 224	670 / 416	487 / 303	287 / 178	469 / 291	—	702 / 436	778 / 483	496 / 308	398 / 247	358 / 222	188 / 117
Lethbridge	345 / 214	161 / 100	217 / 135	514 / 319	965 / 600	702 / 436	—	167 / 104	992 / 616	362 / 225	854 / 531	684 / 425
Medicine Hat	421 / 262	112 / 70	294 / 183	532 / 331	992 / 616	778 / 483	167 / 104	—	1019 / 633	410 / 255	858 / 534	711 / 442
Peace River	858 / 533	911 / 566	775 / 482	487 / 303	200 / 124	496 / 308	992 / 616	1019 / 633	—	628 / 390	138 / 86	308 / 191
Red Deer	270 / 168	302 / 188	145 / 90	150 / 93	600 / 373	398 / 247	362 / 225	410 / 255	628 / 390	—	490 / 304	320 / 199
Valleyview	720 / 447	773 / 480	637 / 396	349 / 217	111 / 69	358 / 222	854 / 531	858 / 534	138 / 86	490 / 304	—	170 / 106
Whitecourt	550 / 342	603 / 375	467 / 290	179 / 111	281 / 175	188 / 117	684 / 425	711 / 442	308 / 191	320 / 199	170 / 106	—

Note: Top number is in kilometers; bottom in miles.

UML employs about ninety-six monthly paid employees. Each branch employs as many drivers as trucks. The drivers are paid a fixed salary plus a percentage on the mileage/hours they drive every month. UML's policy is to keep drivers satisfied by allocating approximately the same mileage/hours to each driver per month. The breakdown of monthly paid employees to branches is as follows: the branch in Calgary employs thirty-four persons; the branch in Edmonton, twenty-seven persons; the branch in Lethbridge, seventeen persons; the branch in Red Deer, eighteen persons.

Other employees are hired according to demand and paid according to actual working hours. Extra pay is given for out-of-town, overnight, and holiday and weekend assignments. The average number of employees required per loading or unloading an average household is three (including the driver), but for larger assignments, more employees may be required.

In the middle of the 1970s UML was the first mover in Alberta to equip many of its trucks with hydraulic tail lifts attached to the rear end of the trucks. Thus, heavy items were easier to lift, minimizing the possibility of damages during the loading/ unloading procedures.

In the late 1980s UML had a very good reputation in Alberta as a ''fast, safe service'' and as a reliable company with the minimum number of insurance damage claims among all its competitors.

The initiation of a moving job is normally handled in the following way. A potential customer phones in to any of the local branches and asks for information on prices and terms of agreement. If the customer is willing to have a quote assessment, the branch sends an evaluator to visit the customer's home. The evaluator has a preprinted form on which he or she marks amounts and types of furniture and appliances to be moved, and assesses volumes of clothes, kitchenware, and other items that should be packed. The evaluator also designates dates, addresses, floor and apartment number, and other pertinent information. Based on his/her best judgment, the evaluator is authorized to quote a price for the job. If the customer accepts the offer, the customer and the evaluator sign the form, which then becomes a contract. One copy is left with the customer and the other three copies are taken to the office. Operational data is added to the forms (e.g., truck size, special equipment, etc.); one copy is retained in the office and the other two are forwarded to the supervisor who schedules the job. On the day of the assignment, the driver takes the two copies and, upon completion of the move, the customer is asked to sign one copy, which is taken back to the office. The other copy is left with the customer.

UML is charging its customers on the basis of weight × mileage for out-of-town deliveries and volume for intracity jobs. Special charges are levied against the customers for (1) any extraordinary expenses, such as moving a piano, a big aquarium, or keeping a crew out of town overnight; and (2) packing and unpacking of clothes, kitchenware, and/or other big or small, fragile items. A customer may not claim for goods damaged in transit unless the packing and unpacking was done by UML personnel.

UML's preferred method of payment is COD; otherwise, a deposit must be paid before the move and the clients (customers) are invoiced later. Due to the individual operating character of UML's branches, each branch generates invoices and collects its own accounts receivable, reporting periodically to the head office. However, payroll checks are issued by the head office and they are written on each branch's current account.

The success of UML was due to the individual operating policy that the company had adopted, thus enabling the four branches to be very flexible in dealing with seasonal effects and fluctuations in demand for its services. Also, the hiring of casual and hourly employees by the branches on an "as needed" basis helped UML to keep wage expenses to a low level.

In the 1980s UML was doing well, despite the slow economic growth of Alberta. But because of the increasing size of the company, the president, Mr. Smith, was facing the following problems:

1. The allocation of trucks was not always efficient: there were many cases in which trucks returned empty from assignments. Sometimes large trucks were assigned to a small-size move; then, due to the unavailability of a large-size truck, two trucks had to be assigned to one large-size move, resulting in an almost doubling of the cost of the move.
2. The allocation of loading crews was inefficient. There were many cases in which loading crews were sent with the truck to unpack at a distant location where local workers were available.
3. There was no proper cooperation among the four branches. Orders were rejected sometimes in one branch because of overdemand while trucks stood idle in another branch.
4. Payments to hourly employees and commissions to branch managers were not paid on time because the head office in Calgary was not informed regularly. Furthermore, a branch could have liquidity problems (it had to take a short-term loan from the bank) while there were positive balances in other branches' bank accounts.
5. Branch reports and other necessary documents were not sent on time to the head office. As a result, the head office was not updated on branches' operations or needs. Information on truck fleet renewal needs and maintenance problems was not readily available to the head office.
6. Mr. Smith believes that information problems have increased the operational costs of UML, and that if they aren't resolved, UML will suffer losses in the near future. He does not believe that these problems have already affected the quality of UML services, but he is afraid that sooner or later customers will become aware of them, thus hurting the company's reputation.

UML—Assignments

Comments: Case study assignments by their very nature are broader than the material covered by a specific chapter. Albeit, we have tried to construct a sequence of assignments that will be congruent with the flow of material in the text. Thus, each of the assignments is marked with a chapter number. This number indicates the "lower limit" chapter below which it is not recommended to prepare the assignment. However, for some of the assignments, a delay of the submission date to a later stage will probably lead to more comprehensive reports. These assignments are marked with an asterisk (*).

Assignment 1 (Chapter 4): The Systems Approach

1. Regarding UML as a system, determine:
   a. the environment
   b. the goals and purposes
   c. inputs, processes, outputs
   d. subsystems and components
2. Who are the bodies that constitute the system trinity in UML?

Assignment 2 (Chapter 5): Information in Organizations

Regarding a single branch of UML—not the head office—as a system, describe its structure and analyze it in terms of Blumenthal's model. Any assumptions can be used as long as they are written explicitly at the beginning of your solution.

*Assignment 3 (Chapter 5): Information Flows

For the current operations, prepare a flowchart that traces the information flows in UML (excluding procurement and accounts payable). To the extent possible, indicate the timing of these flows. Show decisions that must be made and the information used in making the decisions. (You can use any assumption that you find necessary, as long as it is explicitly written at the beginning of your work.) Enclose with the flowchart a narrative description.

*Assignment 4 (Chapter 6): Transaction-Processing System

Briefly describe the structure of a computerized transaction-processing system for UML customer orders and for crew and truck dispatching. Include:

1. Main inputs and outputs
2. Main files
3. Main programs
4. Hardware requirements

(Report should not exceed eight pages.)

*Assignment 5 (Chapter 6): Characteristics and Requirements of MIS

1. What should be the upper-level management information requirements regarding a UML customer order system?
2. Describe briefly the characteristics of a management information system (MIS) based on the transaction-processing system you have analyzed in assignment 4.

*Assignment 6 (Chapter 8): Organizational Master Plan

Assume that UML management wishes to gradually computerize the company, starting from a customer orders system and a truck and crew dispatching system, continuing with bookkeeping and accounting functions, and ending with other operational functions. This should be done in parallel with the development of MIS and DSS for headquarters and for branch managements. Write a summary of a master plan for UML. Concentrate on application and personnel development plans rather than on hardware aspects. Do not discuss costs.

Assignment 7 (Chapter 10): System Design

For the customer order system you have analyzed in assignment 4, design in detail:

1. a customer order form that is filled out by the evaluator
2. an input screen for keying in a customer order
3. a printed-out customer invoice

Comment: If you have access to an appropriate software package, you can build prototypes of the above (particularly items 2 and 3) and submit the printouts of the prototypes.

Assignment 8 (Chapter 10): DSS Design

Design a DSS for VP Operations to control the past utilization of trucks and to improve efficiency in the future.
Comment: If you can access a spreadsheet program (e.g., LOTUS 1-2-3®), build a prototype on the spreadsheet and submit the printouts or the diskettes.

Assignment 9 (Chapter 11): Distributed Systems

1. Suggest a distribution policy for UML.
2. Analyze a few alternatives for centralizing or distributing the customer order system you have suggested in assignment 4.

Comment: For this assignment, it is recommended that you adopt a spectra table and draw distribution profiles.

Assignment 10 (Chapter 12): Organizing the IS Function

How should UML organize its information system activities? Prepare a proposal in which you discuss alternatives and make recommendations.

Assignment 11 (Chapter 14): Information System Controls

Discuss risks and propose appropriate control measures for the customer order system you have analyzed for UML in assignment 4.

Figure B.3 *a.* Balance sheet of UML as of December 31, 1989 (Add 000) *b.* Consolidated income statement for 1988

(a) Balance sheet of UML as of December 31, 1989 (Add 000)

Assets		Liabilities	
Current		Current	
Cash & short-term		Bank indebtedness	$ 320
investments	$ 1,400	Acc. payable and	
Acc. receivable			
(net)	300	Advance services	220
Gas supplies	150	Salaries payable	210
Cardboard supplies	190		
Prepaid expenses	120	Repairs payable	170
Fixed		Long-term debt	
Buildings (net)	$ 1,400	Long term liabilities	$ 2,750
Land (net)	2,600	Mortgage payable	1,100
Trucks (net)	4,200		
Equipment (net)	210		
		Stockholders' equity	
		Common stocks	$ 3,000
		Capital surplus	1,000
		Retained earnings	1,500
	$10,570		$10,570

(b) Consolidated Income Statement for 1988

Operating revenue	$18,000,000
Interest and other rev.	150,000
Total revenues	$18,150,000
Less:	
Expenses:	
Cost of services	$12,690,000
Administrative expenses	200,000
Depreciation other than trucks	560,000
Maintenance and obsolescence	700,000
Interest on short- and long-term liabilities	210,000
Advertising expenses	170,000
Net before tax	3,720,000
Provision for income taxes	1,674,000
Net income	$ 2,046,000

Figure B.4 UML organizational structure

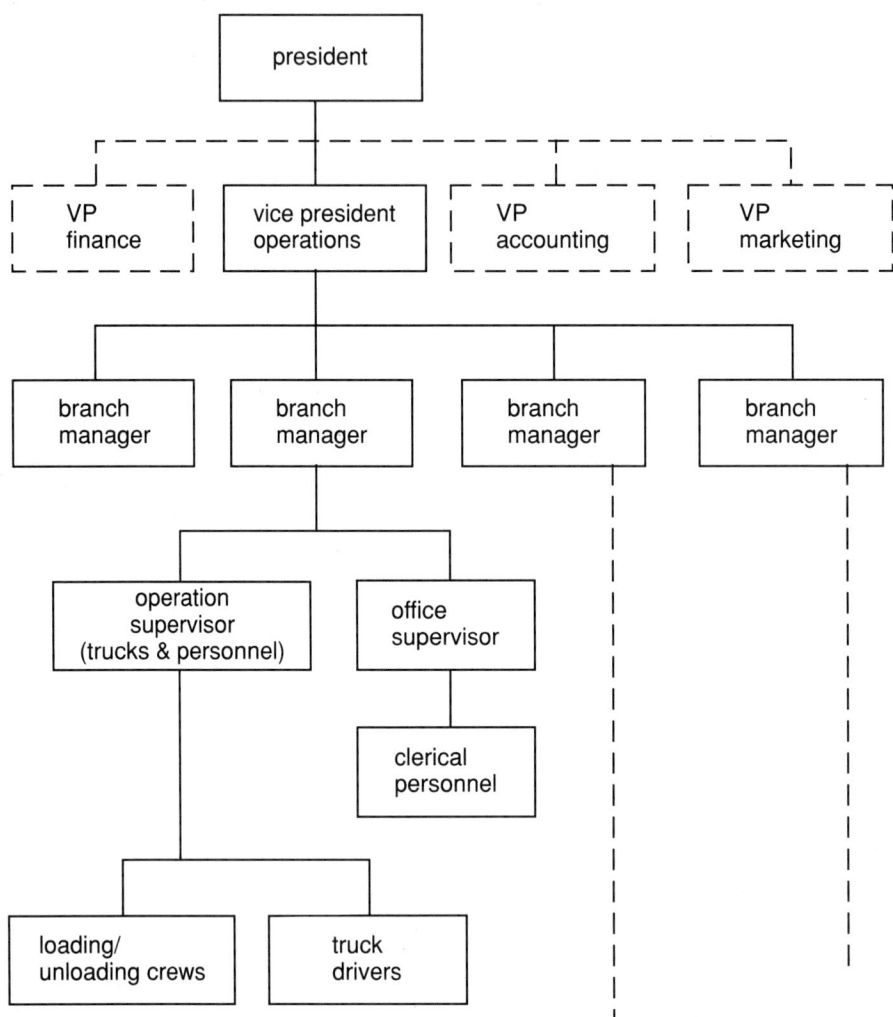

Figure B.5 Structure of a single branch of UML

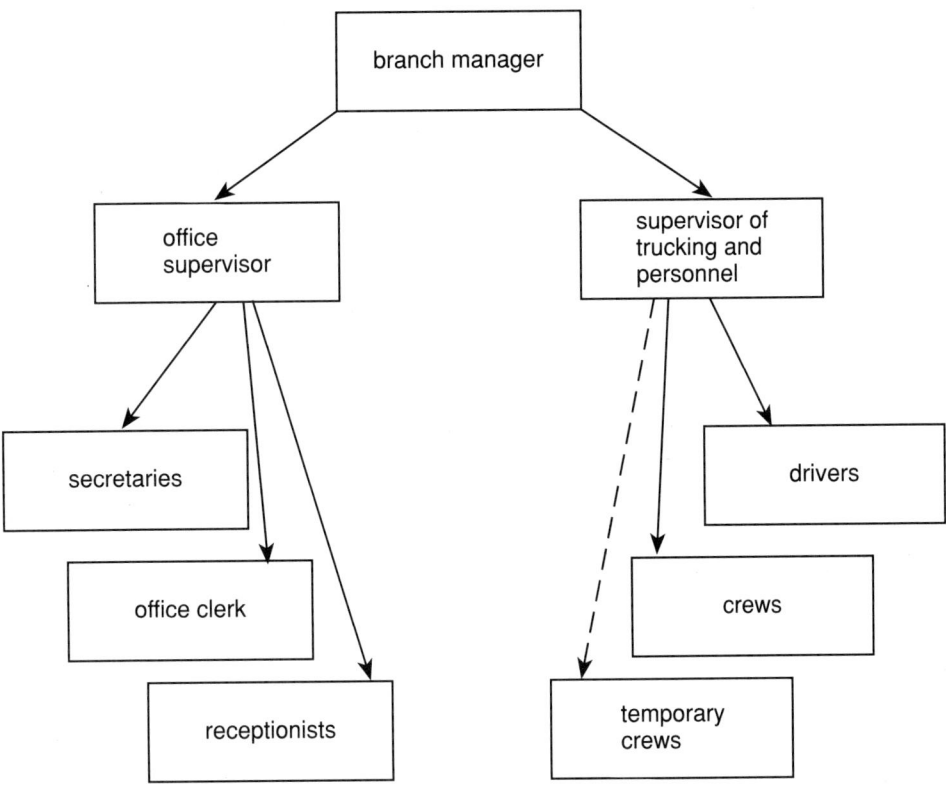

The total number of permanent employees at a branch depends on its size and the number of trucks.

On the average it is assumed:

(a) Eight to ten office permanent employees (excluding drivers and crews) at each branch.

(b) A ratio 1 to 3 of permanent employees to loading/unloading crews.

Index

Authentication, 517, 586
Authorization, 517, 537
Auxiliary storage, 614, 616–623
Awad, E. M., 412

B

Backup plan, 537
Balance sheet, 394
Bank of America, 227–235
Bar code, 605, 606
BASIC, 611
Batching, 517
Batch processing, 157, 158, 558
Bayes theorem, 50
Behavior, and information systems, 13–34
Benbasat, I., 25
Benchmarks, 610
Benefits, 68–70, 477–478
Bias, in cognitive process, 20–22, 31
Binding policy, 490
Black box, 89, 510, 532
Blumenthal, S. C., 123
Borovits, I., 471, 482, 486, 487
Bottom-up approach, 251–252, 253–254
Boundaries
    distribution, 382
    system, 87, 88
Broadcasting, 188
BT Industries, 546–547
Buchanan, J. R., 301, 376
Budget, 282, 338
Built-in control, 509, 513–516
Bulletin board, 583
Bus, 608

C

C (programming language), 611
CAD (computer-aided design), 559, 573
Calendars, electronic, 189
CallPath, 565
CAM (computer-aided manufacturing), 573
Career paths, 413, 414. *See also* Information system
    professionals; Professions
Carlson, E. D., 170, 310
CASE (computer-aided software engineering) tools, 316,
    358, 527, 556–558, 561
Cathode ray tube (CRT), 637
CD-ROM technology, 192–193, 554
Centralized information systems, 370, 372–373
Central processing unit (CPU), 23, 608–610

Change
    data, 339
    management of, 29–30
    parameter, 339
    procedure, 340
    requests for, 290, 351–352
    resistance to, 28–29, 32
Change plan, 283
Channel, 608, 609
Channel capacity, 60
Chapman, D. P., 22
Character, 616
Character-at-a-time printers, 614
Charter (mission), 205, 210, 238
Chauffeur, 183–184
Chemicals Research, Inc. (CRI), 505–506
Chief information officer (CIO), 206, 401, 467–469
Choice stage of decision making, 39–40, 42–43
Chunking, 17–18, 31
Churchman, C. W., 94–97, 99
CIM (computer integrated manufacturing), 571–574
CIO (chief information officer), 206, 401, 467–469
Ciphering, 514, 523, 537
Client. *See* User(s)
Client-server architectures, 368–369, 634
Closed-loop system, 102, 103
Closed system, 100
Clusters of subsystems, 91, 93
COBOL, 611, 624
CODASYL (Conference on Data Systems Languages), 624
Coding, and entropy, 57–59
Cognitive demons, 17, 18
Cognitive process, 14–24
    attention in, 14–15
    biases in, 20–22, 31
    identification in, 15–17
    information systems and, 22–24
    long-term memory in, 14, 19–20
    short-term memory in, 14, 17–18
Cognitive psychology, 5
Cognitive style, 25–26
Color displays, 616
Committees
    information system, 245, 293, 335
    steering, 296–297, 337
    user role in, 463–464
Communications
    in information system development, 268
    technological advances in, 577–578
Communications security, 514, 537
Communications specialist, 408
Communication theory, 5
Compatibility, 340–341

Hardware
    acquisition of, 479–483
    for decision support systems, 179
    environment and, 514
    information center consulting services on, 438
    trends in, 553–555
    utilization of, 472
Hardware control, 513–515
Hardware coordinator, 407
Hardware independence, 625
Hash total, 517
Head, 619
Header, 516
Hedberg, B., 53
Heitger, L. E., 487
Help screens, 527
Heuristic decisions, 45
Heuristic individuals, 25
Hierarchical approach, 629–631
Hierarchical structure of organization, 89–90, 116–119,
    122, 129, 431
Higher level languages, 611
Hill, N. C., 533
Historical files, 617
Holistic approach, 16
Hooper, J. W., 315
Horizontal dimensions of life cycle, 302–304
Horizontal ordering, 65
Horton, W. K., 527
Host languages, 634
Huber, G. P., 26
Human information processing, 14–26
Human/machine system, 101
Human-made systems, 99, 101
Hyatt Hotel Corporation, 369, 371, 372

I

IC. *See* Information center
Icons, 581, 606
Identification
    in cognitive process, 15–17
    of users, 586
Identifier, 617
Ideological training, 343
Igbaria, M., 471
Image demons, 17, 18
Image processing, 189, 190, 581
Image technology, 605
Immediate access analysis, 357
Implementation phase of life cycle, 263, 276, 288–289,
    342–350, 430, 464–465
Implementation team, 297–298, 342
Implementors, 274

Income statement, 394
Incremental enhancement, 314
Indexed files, 621
Indirect costing, 487
Industrial dynamics model of organization, 120–123, 129
Inference engine, 570
Information
    data vs., 153
    defined, 2
    external, 41
    internal, 41
    management, 131–133
    models of, 114–131
    operational, 131–133
    organizational. *See* Organization(s); Organizational
        information systems
    quantity of, 55–60
    value of, 47–60
Information advisor, 410
Information analysis, 277, 280–283, 430
Information analyst, 274, 279, 410–411
Information center (IC), 437–441
    broadening scope of, 439–440
    control function of, 439
    examples of, 440–441
    functions of, 438–439
    organizational location of, 440
Information economics, 5, 491
Information flow, 284
Information overload, 20, 24
Information processing technology. *See* Technological
    advances; Technology
Information requirements analysis, 333
Information security officer, 536, 537
Information services unit, 427–428
Information structure, 49, 51
Information system (IS), 2, 3
    activity list for, 377, 381
    attributes of, 61–68, 129, 131, 169–170
    behavior and, 13–34
    benefits of, 68–70, 477–478
    centralized, 370, 372–373
    cognitive process and, 22–24
    cognitive style and, 25–26
    decentralized, 370, 372, 373
    decision making and, 40–43, 44, 45–46
    design of. *See* Design
    development strategy for, 248–254
    evaluation practices of, 60–70
    factors in success of, 6–7, 336–342
    fields contributing to study of, 4–7
    function of, 467–473
    global, 578–581

of organizational information systems, 134–135, 147–197

of system, 89–94, 301

tree, 629–631

Structured Analysis and Design Technique (SADT), 358

Structured decisions, 43–47, 133–134

Structured decisions systems (SDS), 134, 135–137, 148, 150, 165–167

Structured English, 357

Structured Query Language (SQL), 556, 633–634

Structured systems analysis and design, 357

Structured walk-through, 275, 358

Stylus writing, 606

Subjective value of information, 48, 54–55

Suboptimization, 78

Subschema, 624–627

Subsystems

    clusters of, 91, 93

    components vs., 87

    defined, 78

    interactions among, 90–94

    interrelations of, 87, 89

Superordinates, 20

Suspense file, 164, 165

Synergism, 78

Synnott, W. R., 213

System(s)

    abstract, 99–100

    boundaries of, 87, 88

    characteristics of, 86–89

    classification of, 99–106

    compatibility of, 340–341

    components of, 87

    constraints on, 89

    control of, 102–106

    conventional, 306

    decision maker and, 96, 97–99

    defined, 2, 610

    design of, 277, 280, 283–286, 430, 464

    development of. *See* Information system development

    efficiency of, 24, 85, 341

    environment of, 87, 88, 96

    expandability of, 341

    flexibility of, 339–340

    goals of, 85

    interface with related systems, 340

    inter-organizational, 369

    knowledge-based, 570

    necessary conditions for, 94–97

    open, 100, 555

    personal, 306–307

    purposes of, 85

    scope of, 85–89

    small, 306–307

    structure of, 89–94, 301

    subsystem interrelations in, 87, 89

    technology of, 79–80

    teleological, 94–95

    user and, 95, 97–99

Systematic individuals, 25, 26

System designer, 96–99, 274, 283, 285–286, 411

System independence, 625

System-oriented professions, 408–412

System programmer, 406

Systems analysis, 5, 357

Systems approach, 77–108

    background of, 77–78

    defined, 78

    example of, 83–85

    for information system design, 80–85

    for problem solving, 80–85

    reasons for adopting, 78–80

    stages of, 80

System security, 535–538

System software, 174, 483

System testing, 286, 348–350

T

Tablet, 606, 607

Tabular display, 162

Tangible benefits, 69–70, 477–478

Taylor, R. N., 25

Team decision making, 40

Technical design, 280, 283

Technical feasibility, 280, 328

Technical services unit, 428

Technical support, 415

Technical support plan, 247

Technological advances, 550–596

    application trends and, 558–560

    artificial intelligence, 5, 568–577

    in communications, 576–577

    computer integrated manufacturing and, 571–574

    computer-related crime and, 590–593

    expert systems, 569–571

    fifth-generation computer systems, 574–581

    hardware trends and, 553–555

    information system management and, 561–563

    in networks, 577–578

    organizational and social implications of, 581–593

    in personal computing, 582–584

    personnel trends and, 560–561

    privacy and, 587–590

    remote work and, 565–567

    security and, 584–587